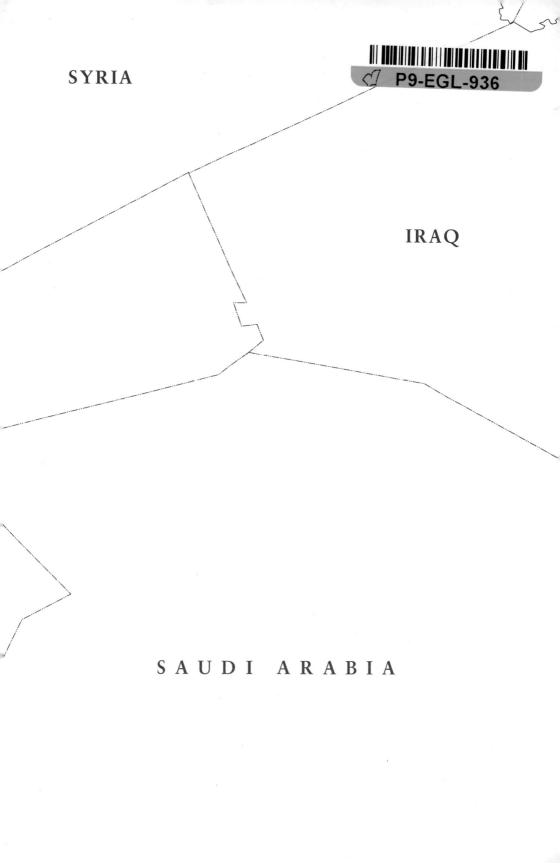

SYRIA

IRAQ

SAUDI ARABIA

THE HIGH COST
OF PEACE

YOSSEF BODANSKY

THE HIGH COST
OF PEACE

How Washington's
Middle East Policy
Left America
Vulnerable
to Terrorism

FORUM

An Imprint of Prima Publishing

Published by Prima Publishing, Roseville, California. Member of the Crown Publishing Group, a division of Random House, Inc., New York.

FORUM and colophon are trademarks of Random House, Inc. PRIMA PUBLISHING and colophon are trademarks of Random House, Inc., registered with the United States Patent and Trademark Office.

The opinions expressed in this book are solely those of the author and do not necessarily reflect the views of the members of the Congressional Task Force on Terrorism and Unconventional Warfare, the U.S. Congress, or any other branch of the U.S. government.

Library of Congress Cataloging-in-Publication Data
Bodansky, Yossef.
 The high cost of peace : how Washington's Middle East policy left America vulnerable to terrorism. / Yossef Bodansky.
  p.   cm.
 Includes bibliographical references and index.
 ISBN 0-7615-3579-9
 1. Middle East—Foreign relations—United States. 2. United States—Foreign relations—Middle East. 3. United States—Foreign relations—1989–.
4. United States—Foreign relations—1989–. 5. Arab-Israeli conflict. I. Title.
DS63.2.U5 B6 2002
327.56073—dc21   2002025768

02 03 04 05 06 QQ 10 9 8 7 6 5 4 3 2 1
Printed in the United States of America

First Edition

Visit us online at www.primapublishing.com

*In memory of the innocent children—victims of the vanity
of some unscrupulous leaders; of the virulence and the lust
for power of other leaders; and of the "civilized world"
that legitimized and hailed the actions of these leaders.*

Contents

Acknowledgments

THE HIGH COST OF PEACE could not have been written without the help of numerous people over many years. First and foremost are those anonymous individuals who contributed their knowledge and who provided the unique source material upon which this book is based. The nature and extent of their contribution is elaborated on in the "Note on Sources and Methods" in the back of the book. Suffice it to say that this book could not have been written without them. Special gratitude for the warm hospitality of many of these individuals.

As I embarked on this undertaking, I discovered just how blessed I've been with good friends whose help made this book possible. Unfortunately, two of my most important friends, who inspired me and provided immeasurable help throughout, cannot be recognized by name.

My "Best Friend"—a worthy scion of his family—opened my eyes in our lengthy all-night parleys to the complexities of his home country and the Arab World as a whole. Although my Best Friend is a cut far above the average younger generation of leaders, he remains a source of hope that with young, dedicated, and sophisticated leaders like him at the helm, the Arab World will be able to reverse its decline and assume a deserving place in a modern and freer world. Special thanks to my Best Friend's mother and family for their warm and generous hospitality.

No words can do justice to the contribution of "the Doctor." In lengthy and inspiring conversations, he elucidated the intricacies of Arab power structures, dynamics, decision-making processes, and the importance of personal relations among leaders and ruling elites. The Doctor gave me a whole new perspective of this complex, fascinating, and at times forbidden world. The depth of his knowledge and the breath of his vision are awe-inspiring. I'm humbled and proud to be considered his friend. One wishes the Doctor would soon attain the leadership position he rightfully deserves—for the Middle East will then be a better place.

Of those who can be recognized by name, special thanks go to the members of the U.S. House of Representatives—the Hon. Jim Saxton, the

Hon. Eric Cantor, the Hon. Duncan Hunter, the Hon. Tom DeLay, and the Hon. Don Sherwood, as well as the retired Hon. Helen Delich Bentley and the retired Hon. Bill McCollum—for their unyielding help and support, and for their friendship.

Vaughn S. Forrest, a soul mate and a great friend for more than two decades, implored me to write this book, and then was a pillar of support as I struggled with the research and typing.

Gregory R. Copley, president of International Strategic Studies Association, editor of *Defense & Foreign Affairs: Strategic Policy,* and primarily a friend for more than fifteen years, shared his vast knowledge. Always ready to lend an ear to my doubts, his sound judgment of strategic affairs helped me a lot. Special thanks to Pamela von Gruber.

Professor Murray Kahl was there with me and for me throughout the chaotic phase of writing. He helped by reading and commenting on early drafts, locating data on the Internet, "holding my hand" as my computers kept crashing, and just being a good friend.

Nagi Najjar, Executive Director of the Lebanon Foundation for Peace, provided extensive and unyielding support in more than one way. Warm thanks for his friendship and companionship as we traveled on so many occasions and to so many places while I was researching and writing this book.

Other dear friends rallied as well. The indefatigable "Jacques" did what only he can. Steve Rodan was most generous with his vast knowledge and deep understanding of Middle East security affairs. Yigal Carmon helped with his vast knowledge and deep understanding of the Arab world. Similarly, Guido Olimpio shared a lot of material from his unique sources. Dr. Assad Homayoun shared his unique insight and knowledge of Iran. Rosanne Klass kept my files bursting with clippings. And, last but not least, Shmuel Avyatar provided the unique and inspiring intellectual spark, as well as his insights about the situation in and around Israel.

Daniel Bial, my agent, took care of business as I kept typing. Steven Martin and Ben Domnitz, then of the Forum imprint of Prima Publishing, committed to this book in the aftermath of a rather stormy debate about Israel and the Middle East. David Richardson, who took over Forum, and the project team at Prima—Shawn Vreeland, Linda Bridges, Joan Pendleton, and many others—have done a tremendous job under the adverse conditions of "crazy" material, time pressure, and me as the author. Random House's Bill Adams completed the legal review with both verve and patience. Thanks to all for their contributions to the book's success.

    Last but not least thanks to my mother, Siona, for helping with French sources and for the flow of clippings from Israel, and thanks to my wife, Lena, for translating and helping with the Russian sources. As well, hugs and kisses to Lena and Masha for enduring my hectic typing and the loud jazz playing into the wee small hours and for their love. Special pats for Max—for being there.

A Note on Terms and Spelling

ANY BOOK DEALING with the Muslim world is bound to be full of strange names and terms. This one is no different. Moreover, there are several codes of transliteration for both Arabic and Persian—from the academically precise to what is commonly used in the media. To make the book as reader-friendly as possible, I opted to use the popular spelling of names as they appear in most newspapers and magazines. For example, although the proper transliteration of the name would be *Ussamah bin Ladin,* I go along with the commonly used *Osama bin Laden.* Similarly, instead of the proper *Umar Abd-al-Rahman,* I use the familiar *Omar Abdul Rahman,* and instead of *Tsaddam Hussayn, Saddam Hussein.*

Whenever possible I translated terms, albeit losing precision, and left in the original language only commonly known terms such as *jihad* or organizational names such as *al-Jamaah al-Islamiyah.* For non-translated terms I also used the common transliterations—for example, *jihad* rather than *gihad.* This should help the reader to relate the story told here to unfolding world events.

Significant Abbreviations and Organizations

ACC	Arab Co-operation Council
DFLP	Democratic Front for the Liberation of Palestine
Fatah (al-Fatah)	acronym for the Palestinian National Liberation Movement
FIALP	Front of the Islamic Army for the Liberation of Palestine (established by Iraq)
HAMAS	acronym for the Islamic Resistance Movement
HizbAllah	"Party of God" in Arabic (sponsored and controlled by Iran)
IDF	Israel Defense Forces
PA	Palestinian Authority
PLO	Palestinian Liberation Organization
Pasdaran	Persian for the Islamic Revolutionary Guard Corps (sometimes referred to as IRGC)
PFLP	Popular Front for the Liberation of Palestine
SAVAMA	Internal intelligence organization for Islamic Republic of Iran

1

The Seeds of the Conflict (1948–1988)

The Establishment of Israel; the Evolving Arab Challenge

ENTERING THE 21ST CENTURY, Israel finds itself in a unique situation. On the one hand, it is on the verge of economic growth and expansion that will take it from being a dependent nation, constantly in need of foreign assistance, to being a powerhouse in the world. On the other hand, it finds itself mired in a war with the Palestinians that is detrimental to every aspect of the country's life. Despite more than half a century of struggle and sacrifices, Israel faces existential threats similar to those faced in 1947–48; indeed the danger today is worse, because the Israeli population is now vulnerable to outright annihilation by weapons of mass destruction—a threat that did not exist even during the darkest days of the War of Independence. Moreover, for the first time since the late 1940s, Arab forces operate at the heart of the Jewish population.

How Israel was brought into this unprecedented predicament is a sad story. For the first forty years of Israel's existence as a modern nation-state, its leaders, however much they disagreed on other matters, were united in placing their country's security first. Starting at the end of 1988, however, some of those leaders were seduced by the United States into accepting a "peace process" that had other priorities. The elder George Bush and his advisers saw Israeli-Arab enmity as a destabilizing influence in world politics; the Clinton administration added to this concern a messianic zeal for peacemaking, combined with Bill Clinton's personal desire to divert attention from investigations into his personal activities.

Under increasing pressure from the United States, Jerusalem started to forgo taking care of Israel's essential security needs, instead making unilateral

1

concessions to an increasingly hostile Arab world. For while the Western world focused on the "peace process," the entire Muslim world has been undergoing comprehensive radicalization. At the same time, the Arab world's elites adopted a sociopolitical culture of chauvinistic militant Arabism, which they attempt to use as a shield against both the militant Islamism of their own people and the American hegemony in their midst. Seeking to rally their people behind their regimes, Arab leaders have repeatedly made ample use of the lowest common denominator among the region's masses: hatred toward the "taboo" that the Jews and Israel are.

———

ONE OF THE IRONIES in the Arab-Israeli dispute over "Palestine" is the oft-neglected fact that there *is* no Palestine in the Muslim or Arab tradition. Neither *Filastin* (Palestine) nor *al-Quds* (Jerusalem) is mentioned in the Koran. During more than a millennium when Muslims (both Arabs and Ottoman Turks) ruled the Middle East—from about 633 to 1917, with the exception of the century of the Crusaders' reign (1099 to 1187)—there was never a separate entity encompassing the general area of today's Israel/Palestine. The entire Fertile Crescent west of Mesopotamia was a single sociopolitical entity, and all the bureaucratic and administrative subdivisions of the area that is currently covered by Israel, Jordan, Syria, and Lebanon were lateral—west to east—with today's Israel and the territories routinely divided between two or three of these lateral strips.

Starting in the late 19th century, the Westernized Arab elite increasingly focused on the concept of a *Bilad al-Sham*—in modern terms, the Land of Greater Syria—as an Arab entity covering the western part of the Fertile Crescent. However, even that entity was alien to the vast majority of Arabs living within it. Lawrence of Arabia, the great proponent of Arab nationalism, grimly acknowledged this reality. In March 1917, Lawrence sent a dispatch to the British authorities about the political future of the region. "The words Syria and Syrian are foreign terms. Unless he had learned English or French, the inhabitant of these parts has no words to describe all this country," Lawrence wrote. "*Sham* is Arabic for the town of Damascus. An Aleppine always calls himself an Aleppine, a Beyrouti a Beyrouti, and so down to the smallest villages. This verbal poverty indicates a political condition. There is no national feeling."

The identity crisis still afflicting the Arab world has its roots in almost a thousand years of sociopolitical trials and tribulations. Toward the end of the first millennium, as the Arab empire began to crumble, control over the Muslim world gradually shifted to the Persian and Turkic empires, the true world powers of their days. This process continued until 1798, the date of

Napoleon's arrival in Egypt and the beginning of the modern Western sub-jugation of the Muslim world. There followed the Russian wars with Turkey and the conquest of Central Asia in the 19th century by Russia, culminating in the collapse of the Turkish Empire and its occupation by Britain during the First World War. With this, the imperialist powers artificially redrew the map of the Middle East. The Muslim world, particularly the Hub of Islam—the vast area between Central Asia and Central Africa, and between the Atlantic coast and the Indus river valley where Islam constitutes the preeminent and predominant power shaping all aspects of both individuals' life and communities' social order—has yet to emerge from this traumatic experience.

Historically, Muslims have identified themselves in two frames of reference: In current Western terminology, these are the supranational and the subnational. Significantly, both frameworks of self-identification differ from the primary framework used in the modern Western world, the nation-state. The supranational identity is the self-identification of all Muslims with a single entity—the *Ummah*, or Muslim Nation. The rise of political awareness in the Muslim world led to the emergence of subidentities represented by pan-Turkism and pan-Arabism, but these are still supranational. The subnational identity is the network of blood relationships—clans, tribes, extended families—that has dominated the everyday life of Muslims throughout their history. Thus, when the Western powers carved up the Muslim world into new statelike entities in the 20th century, these entities had nothing to do with the character and aspirations of the indigenous population. Furthermore, new ruling elites—be they royal families propped up by the Western colonial powers or Communist elites propped up by the Soviets—were imposed upon the population.

Thus, a separate Palestine—as well as a separate Syria, Lebanon, Jordan, Saudi Arabia, and Iraq—is the creation of the British and French governments. At the height of the First World War, these European powers decided to break up the Ottoman Empire—the last Muslim caliphate—for grand strategic considerations such as reducing the power of both Germany and Russia. In the aftermath of the war and of the Russian Revolution, Western European domination of the Middle East through the League of Nations mandate system became a strategic imperative.

At first, the region's intellectuals attempted to come up with justifications for the legitimacy of their new states' ruling elites. They envisioned the acceptance of statehood as the primary expression of modernity and progress among Arabs and Muslims. Indeed, virtually all political events in the Middle East over the last several decades, from the Islamic Revolution to the endless series of military coups and ensuing dictatorships, are, in the words of Elie Kedourie, a leading scholar of the Middle East, "the outcome, thus far, of one hundred and fifty years of tormented endeavor to discard the old ways, which have ceased to satisfy, and to replace them with something modern, eye-catching, and attractive. The torment does not seem likely to end soon."

The Arab elites now recognize their failure to establish institutions of responsible governance. As Palestinian journalist Said K. Aburish expressed it in *A Brutal Friendship: The West and the Arab Elite,* "There are no legitimate regimes in the Arab Middle East. The House of Saud, King Hussein of Jordan, Presidents Hosni Mubarak of Egypt, Saddam Hussein of Iraq, Hafez al-Assad of Syria, Yasser Arafat of the Palestinian Authority and the remaining minor Arab heads of state run various types of dictatorships. They depend on phoney claims to legitimacy while representing small special interest groups—minorities whose members owe their allegiance to them rather than the state as the representative and guardian of the interests of the people. The result is religious, tribal, army-based or hybrid ruling cliques and leaders who have one thing in common: they are opposed to the desire of the majority of the Arab people to have or develop legitimate governments."

Hence, the decision to establish "Arab states"—even if ruled by "Arab kings"—created a grassroots backlash. Under the relative freedom of British and French rule, the political awareness of intellectuals in the Near East had burst into the open. Most vibrant were the ideologies calling for the revival of a unified Arab entity, whether it was to be governed by Islamist theocracy or Westernized nationalism or Soviet communism. The German observer Hans Kohn noted the prevalence of this trend as early as 1930. "Beneath the cleavages and differentiation brought about in the Hither East by the War and the Peace, beneath the restless variety, the complex problems, the internal tensions and conflicts, there is no mistaking the historical tendencies and streams of consciousness driving steadily towards unity. This convergence of forces is not new, it is the revival of a past still living and acting in men's minds, in customs and songs, in turns of speech, and in the everyday products of a civilization," he wrote in *Nationalism and Imperialism in the Hither East.*

After the Second World War, leaders of various nation-states sought legitimization in pan-Arab terminology and ideologies, such as Ba'athism and Nasserism. Although none of them proved capable of realizing their aspirations, they continued to cling to their pan-Arab credentials. Consequently, as Tamara Sonn explained in *Between Qur'an and Crown: The Challenge of Political Legitimacy in the Arab World,* "the continued failure of the Arab leaders has spawned yet another reaction. The pan-Arab ideal was a counterfeit criterion of political success, predisposed to breed failure. It imposed a standard of political legitimacy unsuitable for the means required to achieve it. It called for geopolitically limited states to work with geopolitically unlimited leadership. The competition among regional leaders for that position was bound to breed instability. And the more those leaders failed, the more their peoples suffered."

As the modern world order proved disappointing to the Arab-Muslim masses—primarily because of its failure to deliver the promised prosperity and freedom from national dictatorships—there emerged another popular backlash, this time demanding a return to the roots of traditional Islam. This movement was supported by the rise of militant Islamism, spearheaded by the Muslim Brotherhood, which, since its founding in 1928, has become the core organization of Sunni Islamists. The Muslim masses have thus been drawn into the world of confessional politics—that is, contemporary politics based on the tenets of the historic Islamic sociopolitical and military actions of the first four caliphs who succeeded Prophet Muhammad and uses religious jurisprudence as the sole foundation for decision-making and policy formulation. They aspire to return to Islam in its genuine and original meaning—an all-encompassing way of life covering the spheres that Westerners divide between church and state. They demand that their rulers also return to their Islamic roots. But since these roots reject modern notions of statehood, the return to Islam essentially challenges the legitimacy and authority of the various ruling elites.

Enter a new generation of Arab-educated elites willing to be pragmatic in search of the basis for the comprehensive unity the Muslim Arab world needs if it is to survive. Haseeb Khair el-Din, the chairman of the Centre for Arab Unity Studies in Beirut, explores this theme in his monumental 1991 study *The Future of the Arab Nation: Challenges and Options*: "The country states that undermined the foundations of the Arab regional order are now faced with a threat to their survival, and their first option is therefore to attempt to close the breaches that are threatening their existence, in the yet unfulfilled hope of ensuring their future, which is at risk unless they modify some of their patterns of conduct." In its quest to survive and flourish in the emerging modern world, the new Arab elite sees any form of partial unity as an important step on the road toward Arab/Muslim unity; such would be a staunch coalition of nation-states to realize a common objective—for example, the destruction of Israel.

The rise of "Palestinian nationalism" and "Palestinian identity" has been an integral part of this all-Arab sociopolitical dynamic. In the absence of a traditional Arab or Muslim "Palestine," only militancy, Arabism, and Islamism have emerged as viable frameworks for Palestinian self-definition beyond the loyalties to family, clan, and tribe. Even the rebellions against the British Mandate authorities and the early Zionist endeavor were all in the name of Arabism and Islam, not Palestinian nationalism.

These are not matters of abstract theory; they have played a critical role in the alliances and rivalries among the region's leaders. The late Lebanese Druze leader Kamal Joumblatt described in *I Speak for Lebanon* an encounter he had with the late Syrian President Hafez al-Assad. The Syrians, Joumblatt recalled, "refuse to forget the days before the carve-up of 1919, when the Lebanese, the Palestinians, the Jordanians and the Syrians formed a single people, the people of historic Syria [that is, Bilad al-Sham], covering the area from the Taurus Mountains to Sinai and from the Iraqi steppes to the sea. Indeed, President Assad confirmed this quite unambiguously to Yasser Arafat not so long ago (around April 1976): 'You do not represent Palestine as much as we do. Never forget this one point; there is no such thing as the Palestinian people, there is no Palestinian entity, there is only Syria! You are an integral part of the Syrian people, Palestine is an integral part of Syria. Therefore, it is we, the Syrian authorities, who are the true representatives of the Palestinian people.'" "On this occasion, at least," Joumblatt concluded, "the 'Lion of Greater Syria' put his viewpoint frankly enough." Assad considered war with Israel to be a critical component in his quest for Greater Syria. His objective was "to put the Golan in the middle of Syria and not on its borders," he declared on February 27, 1986. "Israel's continued presence on the Golan will only increase our hatred for that historical enemy and augment our determination to fight it through to the end."

Ultimately, while parts of the Westernized Arab elite, including aspirants for power and leadership, may genuinely believe in a Palestinian identity or nationalism—Western concepts for which there are no indigenous terms in Arabic—they cannot base their political fortunes on these tenets. To gain popular legitimacy and support they, including Yassir Arafat, must go back to indigenous concepts and beliefs: namely, pan-Arabism and Islamism, which do not recognize the validity of "Palestine" or any other "Arab state," for that matter, including Syria.

———

THE ARAB-ISRAELI CONFLICT over the Land of Israel, or Palestine, is thus a lengthy, multifaceted dynamic involving the whole of the Muslim and Arab worlds. The megatrends affecting the most basic relations between the West and Islamdom, such as Islam's reaction to modernity and the spread of Western socioeconomic influence, must be taken into consideration when studying the ongoing interactions—that is, warfare, terrorism, and politics—between Israel and the Palestinians. At the core of the conflict, irrespective of the political and ideological formulations at any given time, is the clash between Islam and the West's forward post in the Hub of Islam. In current Islamist terms, it is the confrontation between Islam and "the illegitimate offspring of the Great Satan" over the control of Palestine and the holy mosques of Jerusalem. In other words, in contrast to the prevailing myths espoused in the Western media, it is less that the Arabs and Islamists hate the United States for supporting Israel than that they hate Israel because it furthers, by its very existence, the interests of the hated U.S.-led West. The failure of the West—particularly Washington and, at some crucial points, also Jerusalem—to recognize this fact is the basis of the current disaster.

The Arab reaction to the establishment of Israel in 1948 illustrates the overall Muslim approach. For the Arabs, Israel's triumph in the War of Independence amounted to more than just the humiliation of military defeat. Given the grave political and strategic ramifications of the establishment of a non-Muslim entity—and particularly a *Jewish* entity—on any part of the great Arab land, the founding of Israel is considered a *Nakba*: a calamity, a holocaust. In *The Cauldron: The Middle East Behind the Headlines*, the Iranian journalist Amir Taheri defined the significance to the Arab world of the mere existence of Israel:

> Israel was Jewish, democratic, largely western, socialistic and independent—reasons for which it could not but be disliked and feared by almost all the elites in its neighboring countries. More importantly, Israel humiliated the Arabs by its very existence. It stood out as a symbol of Arab divisions and weakness, a living testimony to the fact that all Arab nations had fallen by the roadside in the forward march of history. A rational reaction would have been to devote all energies to removing the causes of which the emergence of Israel in the midst of the Arab world was, at least in part, nothing but an effect. But the Arab reaction was emotional. Israel was seen as the cause of all the ills that afflicted the Arabs. Arab propaganda of both right and left developed the idea that the destruction of Israel would, as if by magic, solve all of the problems faced by Arab societies. Since it is apparently more human to unite against something rather than for something, Israel gradually became the major, if not the only, unifying factor in Arab politics.

Thus, for the Arab establishment, the Nakba and its ramifications have remained a living and perpetually unfolding reality. As Israel continued to exist, its destruction—the overturning of the Nakba—was becoming a matter of ever greater urgency.

Realpolitik also shaped events in the Arab world in the early- to mid-1950s. Most important was the struggle between Egypt's Gamal Abd-al-Nasser and Iraq's Nuri Said for hegemony over the region. The first crucial round in this struggle involved the effort by the United States and Britain to establish a regional defense organization—the Baghdad Pact—as part of the anti-Soviet system of alliances they were constructing around the world in the early 1950s. In response to the United States' backing of Said, the Soviet Union bolstered the position of Nasser and "progressive" circles throughout the Arab world. This duel between the superpowers kindled a political dispute between Iraq and Egypt over the guiding ideology of the Arab world; through this dispute, the essence of Arabism and Arabness was defined. Even though these political disputes had nothing to do with Israel or the Jews, the Israel factor was repeatedly used as a vehicle for legitimization—particularly at the grassroots level—as well as for the delegitimization of hostile Arab regimes.

Nasser was first to make cynical use of the Israel question. In order to strengthen its claim to legitimacy, his new revolutionary government portrayed itself as the guardian of the Palestinian cause and increased its sponsorship of Palestinian terrorism and insurgency against Israel. In the aftermath of the 1956 Sinai War, his and other "progressive" Arab regimes intensified their sponsorship of the nascent revolutionary Palestinian movement. The main outcome of this effort was the establishment of the Palestine Liberation Organization (PLO), with its declared objective of destroying Israel. This took place in the summer of 1964—that is, *before* the Six-Day War of June 1967. Yassir Arafat, leader of the new organization, was the most prominent of the Palestinian radical activists who had been living in exile since 1948, disguising their identities under *noms de guerre* that they continued to use long after they became public figures (Arafat's is Abu-Ammar).

Arafat's primary constituents in establishing the PLO were not the Palestinians living in the West Bank and the Gaza Strip, but rather the refugees of 1948. The original Palestinian Covenant, adopted in 1964, even dissociated the PLO from the West Bank and Gaza because they were then under Arab control. The first article of the covenant defined the Palestinian cause in all-Arab terms: "Palestine is part of the Arab World and the Palestinian people are part of the Arab Nation, and their struggle is part of its struggle." The main purpose of the PLO, according to the covenant, was the destruction of Israel by force of arms, and the Palestinians invited the assistance of the whole Arab world in achieving this goal. "The liberation of Palestine, from an Arab viewpoint, is a national duty," the covenant declared. "Accordingly the Arab Nation must mobilize all its military, human, moral, and spiritual capabilities to participate actively with the Palestinian people in the liberation of Palestine. It must, particularly in the phase of the armed Palestinian revolution, offer and furnish the Palestinian people with all possible help and material and human support."

The Palestinian movement was transformed by the Arab defeat in the Six-Day War. The new Palestinian Covenant, adopted in 1968, retained the definition of the Palestinian cause as an integral part of an all-Arab endeavor.

"Palestine is the homeland of the Arab Palestinian people; it is an indivisible part of the Arab homeland, and the Palestinian people are an integral part of the Arab Nation," read the first article. The new covenant continued to urge the destruction of Israel, but it now also laid claim to the parts of British Mandate Palestine occupied by Israel in 1967. "Palestine, with the boundaries it had during the British Mandate, is an indivisible territorial unit," read the new covenant. "Armed struggle is the only way to liberate Palestine. This is the overall strategy, not merely a tactical phase. The Palestinian Arab people assert their absolute determination and firm resolution to continue their armed struggle and to work for an armed popular revolution for the liberation of their country and their return to it. They also assert their right to normal life in Palestine and to exercise their right to self-determination and sovereignty over it." The PLO emphasized that there can be no compromise over the very existence of Israel. "The partition of Palestine in 1947 and the establishment of the state of Israel are entirely illegal, regardless of the passage of time," the covenant decreed. Arafat, despite his later involvement in the "peace process," has never—not even for a single minute—swerved from this position, which he stated most clearly in a 1972 interview with Oriana Fallaci: "Peace for us means the destruction of Israel and nothing else."

Meanwhile, the Soviet Union's growing involvement in the Middle East during the early 1970s led to its increased support for, and exploitation of, the Palestinian revolutionary movement. To further their joint aims, Moscow advised the PLO to develop a political image that would gain support from Western elites. Taking Moscow's advice, Arafat sent a high-level PLO delegation headed by Salah Khalaf—also known as Abu-Iyad—on a milestone visit to Hanoi. The Palestinians had lengthy discussions with a Politburo team led by General Vo Nguyen Giap, in which the Vietnamese told their Palestinian guests about their success in manipulating the Western media, to the point that they had a direct impact on the United States' ability to wage war against North Vietnam and the Vietcong.

In his book *Palestinian Without a Motherland*, Abu-Iyad related how he brought up the question of why the Palestinian armed struggle was considered terrorism whereas the Vietnamese struggle was lauded and supported throughout the West. His hosts attributed this phenomenon to the different ways the two liberation movements had packaged their goals. The Vietnamese team agreed to sit with the PLO delegation and help them develop a program that would appear flexible and moderate. Especially in dealing with the United States, the Vietnamese explained, one must "sacrifice the unimportant if only in order to preserve the essential." They emphasized that while the PLO must remain committed to its ultimate objective—namely, "the establishment of a unified democratic state in the entire Palestine"—in the near term it would be politically advantageous to accept transient phases and even interim solutions. The Vietnamese suggested that accepting "the division of the land between two independent states," without making it clear that this was only an interim phase, would neutralize the PLO's opponents in the West.

The Vietnamese team in Hanoi introduced the Palestinians to such issues as dealing with the U.S. media and with liberal political circles and institutions, and they provided insight on the power of the Jewish community. Disinformation and psychological-warfare experts assisted the Palestinians in formulating a "moderate political program" accepting the establishment of a "small Palestine" in the territories. Hanoi also promised to help the PLO persuade pro–North Vietnamese organizations in the West to accept the PLO's transient solutions by using "moderate, even vague" terminology to make these solutions appear nonthreatening to Israel. Abu-Iyad wrote that the PLO adopted the Vietnamese recommendations and began implementing them immediately.

The result was the Phases Program/Phased Plan, adopted as the resolution of the Twelfth Palestinian National Council in Cairo on June 19, 1974. The Phases Program/Phased Plan calls for the establishment of a Palestinian state on any part of the disputed territory that becomes available, whether through war or through a negotiated process, starting with the fledgling negotiations with Israel in the aftermath of the 1973 Yom Kippur War. In adopting this policy, the PLO leadership stressed that accepting any part of Palestine was legitimate as long as the entity established there would serve as the basis for the liberation of the rest of the country—that is, the ultimate destruction of Israel. The Phases Program/Phased Plan also served as a pacifier for the population of the territories that felt neglected by a PLO leadership dominated by 1948 refugees. In an interview with Arafat's biographer Alan Hart, Hani al-Hassan, a senior PLO official and a close confidant of Arafat, underscored this aspect: "Our Palestinian people on the occupied West Bank and in Gaza were desperate, and many of them were demanding a political programme which would give the Israelis every possible incentive to withdraw in exchange for peace. So Arafat had to tell them, 'I hear you.'" Meanwhile, the fact that the PLO did prioritize its objectives has since served to authenticate the myth that the PLO leadership was interested only in the territories and no longer sought the destruction of Israel within its 1949 boundaries (the boundaries codified in the cease-fire accords between Israel and its Arab neighbors at the end of the War of Independence).

Before adopting the Phases Program/Phased Plan, the PLO leadership had already made several quiet inquiries as to its appeal in the West. Most critical was the advance presentation of the concept to Washington at the urging of Egyptian President Anwar al-Sadat. Having successfully manipulated the Americans into getting him the Sinai interim agreements with Israel, Sadat told Arafat that he too could get more by persuading the United States to press Israel into concessions than through confrontation. In March 1974, a PLO delegation led by Khalid al-Hassan presented the concept of a Palestinian "mini-state" in a secret meeting with General Vernon A. Walters, then deputy director of the CIA and President Nixon's emissary. The PLO representatives returned from this meeting convinced that the United States would support their approach. Moreover, Sadat's dealings with Kissinger would prove instrumental in clearing the way for Arafat to make his historic speech at the United Nations on November 13, 1974. This event was a turning point in the legitimization of the Palestinian revolutionary movement and particularly of Arafat as its undisputed leader.

The Phases Program/Phased Plan has endured through all the ensuing years of negotiations and agreements with Israel. Even after the Oslo accords and with the PLO moving toward the establishment of an autonomous entity, if not quite a mini-state, in the territories, Arafat continues to reiterate its validity and relevance. The Oslo agreement "will be a basis for an independent Palestinian state in accordance with the Palestine National Council resolution issued in 1974," Arafat told Radio Monte Carlo on September 1, 1993. "The PNC resolution issued in 1974 calls for the establishment of a national authority on any part of Palestinian soil from which Israel withdraws or which is liberated." Arafat goes further, insisting that the Palestinian Authority was compelled to accept the mini-state in the territories as an interim stage because of the adverse conditions prevailing in the Middle East. He stressed this point in a November 1994 letter to the heads of the rejectionist front then based in Syria, Jordan, and Lebanon: "In order to obtain the goal of returning to Palestine, all of us sometimes have to grit our teeth. But it is forbidden that this harm the continued struggle against the Zionist enemy. Cooperation and understanding between the PLO and the rejectionist organizations is what will lead to the speedy retreat of Israel from the occupied territories in the first stage, until the establishment of a Palestinian state with its capital in Jerusalem. Only a state like that can then continue the struggle to remove the enemy from all Palestinian lands."

————

WHILE ARAFAT and his coterie were willing to proceed slowly in implementing the Phases Program/Phased Plan as long as there was Western legitimization and an unchecked flow of cash, their policies have been increasingly challenged by the young, impatient leadership rising in the territories, which has drawn on immense support from the increasingly radical

Muslim world. Arafat's greatest dilemma—especially since the original Intifadah, in 1987—has been how to reconcile the declared pursuit of the Phases Program/Phased Plan with the Islamists' demand for the unconditional destruction of Israel—the more so because Arafat himself ultimately supports that demand.

The original Intifadah brought home to Arafat and his Tunisia-based coterie the true strength and popular influence of the Islamists resident in the territories. When the Islamists launched the Intifadah in December of 1987, the secular-radical followers of the indigenous rejectionist organizations quickly fell into line behind them. Arafat and his PLO were taken by surprise, and not until several weeks later did they realize the importance of the phenomenon and become part of the action. Arafat's subsequent claims to have led this grassroots outburst are utterly groundless.

Even before the Islamists' dominant role in the Intifadah became clear, Arafat's loyal lieutenant Khalil al-Wazir—also known as Abu-Jihad—had been toying with the idea of integrating the Islamists into the PLO. A closet Muslim Brother, Abu-Jihad had long been mesmerized by the zeal and militancy of the Sunni Islamists and particularly the Palestinian "Afghans"—Arabs who had fought alongside the *mujahideen* in Afghanistan. As the war in Afghanistan was winding down, he sought to transform the struggle for Palestine into the "next Afghanistan"—a focus of all-Islamist militancy and solidarity. Not least, the myth of the Afghan mujahideen's triumph over the mighty Soviet Union could be used to suggest the possibility that the Palestinians would triumph in their own "Afghanistan." Abu-Jihad became obsessed with the idea of Islamicizing the Fatah (Arafat's own organization within the PLO); he even established a Fatah-affiliated branch of the Islamic Jihad in order to better integrate the PLO into the rising trend.

He also repeatedly tried to consolidate a unified Palestinian military command that would reflect the emerging power structure in Arab society. He wanted to bring the various groups under a single umbrella organization—a new-style PLO—that would reflect their diversity but ensure Arafat's overall leadership. In the spring of 1988, Abu-Jihad seemed very close to achieving his goal. In the first week of April, he chaired the first major gathering of all Palestinian organizations and sponsoring states in Tripoli, Libya, to draw up a common strategy for the escalation of the Intifadah. It had taken the personal influence of Abu-Jihad to bring all these diverse organizations together and convince them to seriously consider a unified strategy. Hence, his assassination by Israeli special forces on April 16, 1988, killed this fledgling alliance as well.

In contrast to Abu-Jihad, Arafat adopted a mistrustful attitude, at times bordering on hostility, toward the Islamists, whose members outshone the Fatah in the territories and whose leaders would not recognize his supreme leadership. Indeed, encouraged by the growing popular support demonstrated during the Intifadah, the Islamist leaders, particularly those of HAMAS, themselves yearned to take on leadership of the entire Palestinian struggle against Israel. However, they knew they could not completely wrest power from Arafat's hands. This dilemma was expressed in the HAMAS Covenant's dual approach toward the PLO.

HAMAS's formative period ended on August 18, 1988, when the organization consolidated its ideological profile in this covenant. By then, HAMAS was already well established as the leading force of the Intifadah in the Gaza Strip and was rapidly becoming the leading force in the West Bank. In its covenant, it claimed leadership over the Palestinian struggle as an integral component of the Muslim Brotherhood's global Islamist jihad. "From the point of view of the Islamic Resistance Movement, nationalism is a part of religious belief," the covenant said. "There is no greater and [more] profound nationalism than a situation where the enemy occupies Muslim land. Then the *jihad* becomes an obligatory duty for every Muslim man and woman." The covenant identified the PLO as "the closest organization" to the Muslim Brotherhood but emphasized HAMAS's profound disagreement with the "idea of a secular state" adopted by the PLO: "The secular idea completely contradicts the religious thought."

Meanwhile, HAMAS was urging that all the forces participating in the Intifadah unite under the banner of Islam. A manifesto published in *Al-Islam wa Filastin* on August 1, 1988, essentially adopted Abu-Jihad's vision. In this manifesto, HAMAS declared that "Palestine became the main concern of most Islamic, Palestinian forces and many Islamic forces in the world. A formula for the unity of Islamic, Palestinian forces must now be found as a condition for the establishment of the Islamic plan in Palestine."

That fall, the PLO struck back, publicly taking issue with HAMAS's covenant and emphasizing the PLO's own Islamic legitimacy. In an article in *Al-Watan* on November 1, Fahmi Huwaydi elucidated the PLO's position. "Despite expressions of appreciation and the complimentary tone used in the covenant to describe the relationship with the PLO," Huwaydi wrote, "HAMAS's position appeared to clash with the PLO's. HAMAS appeared to be condemning the PLO's appeal to establish a secular state as well as its attitude toward the idea of an international conference." In fact, Huwaydi explained, the main differences were over priorities. The PLO "truly wishes for an Islamic Palestine, but more importantly, wishes for a liberated Palestine." Although appreciating the Islamist struggle, the PLO "opposes fragmenting the resistance or dividing its ranks in the name of any Islamic action." "The liberation of Palestine under any banner," Huwaydi continued, "even a non-Islamic banner, is 1,000 times better than keeping Palestine under Israeli occupation. . . . This is not a question of involving or not involving Islam, but it is a question which has to do with how Islam is to be placed in its proper context so it can play an effective role in serving the nation's supreme interests."

In effect, the PLO was accusing HAMAS of attempting to assume the leadership of the Intifadah as a result of Abu-Jihad's assassination. The PLO, Huwaydi correctly noted, "associated HAMAS's announcement with the vacuum left by the death of Abu-Jihad, who had been schooled in the principles of the Muslim Brotherhood." For "he was the man who had planned and worked out the cooperation between Muslims and others in the Intifadah. His departure had stirred the ambitions of those who wanted to claim the positions of leadership for themselves."

The most profound difference between HAMAS and the PLO concerned the explicit declaration of the Palestinian commitment to the total destruction of Israel. The incremental approach that the PLO had learned from the Vietnamese and set out in the Phases Program/Phased Plan did not appeal to HAMAS's leader, Sheikh Ahmad Yassin. He agreed that a "Palestinian state must be established on any inch of Palestine we liberate," but always with the explicit acknowledgment that this did not involve "relinquishing the rest of our rights." Stressing that "the final liberation" was a common objective for all Palestinians, Yassin anticipated an "Islamicized PLO" and hinted that "an Islamic takeover of the PLO is not that farfetched."

Little wonder, then, that the PLO was anxious to claim a part in the grassroots Islamist revival. In early 1989, Arafat's cronies spread rumors that the Unified National Leadership, of which Arafat's Fatah is a leading member, had reached an agreement with HAMAS on cooperation and coordination of activities. In a major survey on the internal politics of the Intifadah, published by the PLO's *Filastin al-Thawarah* on July 23, 1989, HAMAS was identified as a religious movement "working for the establishment of a state based on the canonical laws of Islam in all of Palestine." While not disavowing its own interim phase of a Palestinian state in the territories, the PLO endorsed the HAMAS Covenant, which it quoted as committing the Islamists to "working so that the flag of Palestine can be flown over every part of Palestine."

In reality, the covenant said that HAMAS "is working for the flying of the Banner of Allah over every bit of the land of Palestine." Furthermore, believing that two states could not coexist in Palestine, Sheikh Yassin had rejected out of hand the possibility of ceasing the jihad until "a Palestinian-Muslim state" with "the *sharia* as the law of the state" should be established over all of Palestine, "from the [Mediterranean] sea to the [Jordan] river."

Consequently, throughout the ensuing Israeli-Palestinian negotiations and fighting, Arafat has been far more concerned with sustaining his Islamist credentials than with any other aspect of Palestinian policy. He has made sure the PLO did not adopt any policy that might conflict with Islamist tenets. He has played the role of an international statesman, collecting funds and honors along the way, but he has always been careful to demonstrate to the Islamists that, in the process, he was instigating greater pressure on Israel. The "peace process" of the 1990s would only aggravate the inner-Palestinian dynamics, which, in the end, both were dominated by Arafat and dominated his policies.

———

THROUGHOUT THE 1980S, as these dynamics were taking shape, the United States government was largely preoccupied with the climax of the Cold War and, to a lesser extent, with an economy increasingly dependent on imported energy. Consequently, Washington did not spend much time thinking about the aspirations of the developing world. The case of the Arabs and Muslims was especially problematic because they saw themselves in that decade as freeing their destiny from the shackles of Westernization imposed during the course of the Cold War. However, just as the Cold War was winding down, the Arab/Muslim world had to cope with an even more intrusive U.S. penetration—a result of the spread of information technology and the emerging global economy.

This was exacerbated by the firm belief in Washington that the Arabs wanted to be "like us" and therefore could, and should, be coached into following U.S. policies. When these policies started collapsing, Israel was there to be pressured into saving them. This logic would be at the core of the political adventure called the "peace process."

2

The Iraq Factor (1988—1990)

Saddam's War Against Israel and the West; the First Seduction of Israel

THE MIDDLE EAST entered a new phase when the war between Iran and Iraq, which had been going on since September 1980, finally ended in the middle of July 1988. Tehran had essentially been confronting the rest of the world alone, as the West, choosing what it believed to be the lesser of two evils—a secular socialist despotism, as opposed to a radical theocracy that had declared war on the "Great Satan"—had steadfastly supported the Iraqi aggressor. Finally, overwhelmed by Iraqi offensives (which included the use of chemical weapons), blocked by U.S. naval involvement in the Persian Gulf, and having lost somewhere between 100,000 and 300,000 soldiers, Iran's leaders accepted a United Nations cease-fire. Ayatollah Khomeini—who had earlier said that the war could not end until Iraq's secular Ba'athist regime had been overthrown—announced that accepting the end of the war was like "drink[ing] this chalice of poison," but Iran had no other choice.

While Tehran mourned, Baghdad's streets were filled with people singing and dancing in praise of Saddam Hussein. For Saddam himself, however, this moment was not the end of a debilitating war but rather the beginning of the true jihad—the holy war for the destruction of Israel. Iraq, Saddam declared, was now "the vanguard of the Arab world," having "stood alone" for the last eight years (never mind the help his country had received from, among others, the United States, Saudi Arabia, and Kuwait) "against an international plot to undermine the Iraqi revolution." This plot, he said, had been hatched by the Zionists and implemented by the Iranians. "World Zionism" had even succeeded in co-opting Islam—"the Arabs' religion"—as a cover for its conspiracies. Now it was time for the Zionists to be confronted and defeated.

The presence of Yassir Arafat at Saddam's side clearly demonstrated that this was not an empty threat. In the first months of 1988, Arafat had been desperately trying not only to gain control over the predominantly Islamist Intifadah but also to contain the eruption of armed clashes among rival Palestinian factions in Lebanese refugee camps. The indigenous Intifadah had suddenly threatened to marginalize organizations, like Arafat's, that were resisting Israel from a safe distance.

By the summer of 1988, Baghdad was the PLO's primary source of assistance and its potential salvation. A few months earlier, Saddam had promised that he would commit fifty-four army divisions to the struggle for Palestine the moment the war with Iran ended. At that time, Baghdad was already contributing $40 million a year to the Intifadah; and in July, even though Iraq was worn out by the Iran war and near bankruptcy, it sent another $50 million.

Arafat arrived in Baghdad in July and was at Saddam's side throughout the victory celebrations. Speaking in Baghdad later that month, Arafat repeated Saddam's main themes. "Now that the Iraq-Iran war is proceeding on the first steps toward its termination," he said, "we and all sincere men in our Arab and Islamic nation hope that a new stage will be initiated during which Muslim blood will be saved and efforts mobilized to confront the rancorous Zionists and their defeatist agents, who have exploited the Iraq-Iran war for more than eight years." Arafat stressed that Israel had always been the primary foe of both Iraq and the Palestinians. "This enemy, which is hostile to Arabism and Islam in general and to Palestinian rights in particular, has based all its calculations on the assumption that the war will continue forever and that it will continue to single-handedly deal with the Palestinian revolution and people. The blessed heroic Intifadah has taken place to foil the calculations of the enemies and the agents, and Iraq's resounding victories have been scored to deal them one blow after another."

Arafat's visit was more than just a symbolic gesture of support for Saddam. Together, the two men began to shift the attention of the Arab world to the Arab-Israeli confrontation, which had been neglected during the Iran-Iraq War. In late July, Saddam convinced King Hussein of Jordan to formally renounce his claims to the West Bank, clearing the way for Arafat to declare Palestinian independence, which he did in Algeria on November 15. This in turn set the stage for formal requests by Arafat for military help from Iraq and other Arab states "to liberate Palestine"—that is, to wage war against Israel.

———

IN THE FALL of 1988, reality hit Baghdad. Postwar Iraq was left with a huge army—about a million and a half men—and no civilian economy to speak of. The bloated military-industrial infrastructure, including the still-expanding programs for ballistic missiles and weapons of mass destruction, consumed virtually the entire technically skilled workforce. The oil industry, in disarray owing to neglect, provided only negligible revenues to offset the huge costs. On top of everything else, Iraq had accumulated a huge national debt; and, once the war ended, Kuwait and Saudi Arabia began discreet inquiries about repayment—in cash or by permitting Kuwait to pump oil from fields in border areas (actually, Kuwait had started doing so unilaterally within days after the cease-fire). Saddam considered these demands—and Iraq's economic predicament itself—a personal affront. In his mind, he, as victor in the war against Iran, should have been held in adulation as the supreme leader of all Arabs and not confronted with "petty problems" such as repayment of his country's debt. His new jihad, he concluded, would again get all the Arabs behind him—both politically and financially—as they had been during the 1980s.

For Saddam Hussein, 1989 was a major turning point, bringing the end of old ideologies and opening the door to the new, Saddam-dominated era. The end of the old era was symbolized by the deaths in June both of Saddam's arch-nemesis, Ayatollah Khomeini, and of his source of ideological legitimacy, Michel Aflaq, the founder of the Ba'ath Party (also called the Arab Socialist Renaissance Party). Moreover, Saddam interpreted the Soviets' withdrawal from Afghanistan and curtailment of activities in the Middle East as the beginning of the end of communism as a major force in the region. Hence the three ideologies that had dominated the Middle East for more than a decade—Khomeinism, Ba'athism, and communism—would do so no longer.

Saddam was thus in a position to usher in his own ideology, a new Iraqi "patriotism" based on a revival of the Babylonian empire with a militant Islamic character. Saddam had laid the groundwork for this development by amalgamating militant Islamism and Ba'athism, even insisting that Aflaq had secretly converted to Islam shortly before his death (a claim without any factual foundation). This alleged conversion legitimized Saddam's use of Islamist terminology to justify his imperial ambitions to the increasingly Islamist population of Iraq and the Arab world as a whole. Saddam began portraying himself as a modern-day Saladin—the Iraqi-born leader who defeated the Crusaders in the 12th century and unified a regional Arab empire. Saddam stressed that he, like Saladin, was born in Takrit (but ignored the fact that Saladin was a Kurd). Ultimately, however, the revival of the notion of Iraq as a distinct entity destined for glory and empire relied almost entirely on the pre-Islamic traditions of Babylon. The new Babylonianism reached an absurd level in September 1989, when Saddam crowned himself as Nebuchadnezzar II in a huge ceremony on the ruins of Babylon.

Meanwhile, Saddam had proclaimed his goal of establishing a pan-Arab political entity that would become a third superpower, on a level with the United States and the Soviet Union. Thus was he able to bridge the contradiction between his desire to be the leader of the Arab world and his quest for Iraqi empire-building. "I struggle for the realization of Arab unity," he declared, "and if necessary through the use of force, because I am determined to consolidate a single Arab 'country.'" He added that because he had a historical mandate to realize the pan-Arab destiny, Iraq had the right to exploit the assets of the entire Arab world.

This message was extremely popular with the Arab street, because Saddam presented himself as both the supreme leader and the redeemer of the downtrodden masses. "I see myself permitted to take money from the rich for my millions of poor children who are walking in torn coats and worn-out shoes," he said. "Two strata emerged in the Arab world as a result of the oil revenues: rich and poor. The personal income for a Kuwaiti is 50 times that of an Egyptian, and I ask, Why?"

However, appealing to the Arab street was not enough; he also needed the recognition and support of his fellow Arab leaders. He achieved this through a political masterstroke: the co-opting of Egyptian President Hosni Mubarak.

———

ALTHOUGH EGYPT had provided extensive military and economic assistance to the "Arab cause" (meaning Iraq, as opposed to non-Arab Iran) during the Iran Iraq War, Egypt was still, a decade after the Camp David accords, ostracized by the rest of the Arab world for having made peace with Israel. Mubarak yearned to break out of this isolation. Hence, although Egypt was bound by a peace treaty with Israel, Mubarak was willing to join the Iraqi-led jihad in return for Saddam's rehabilitating Egypt and especially his own person. Meanwhile, Saddam knew that Mubarak's involvement in his policies would reduce the apprehensions of the United States and Western Europe.

To dramatize his initiative, Saddam arrived in Egypt unannounced. In November 1988, a low-level delegation from the Iraqi Ministry of Culture was expected in Cairo. Faruk Hosni, the Egyptian Minister of Arts—the most junior member of Mubarak's cabinet—was dispatched to the airport to welcome them. To Hosni's astonishment, a smiling Saddam Hussein stepped out of the aircraft, followed by his most senior defense and intelligence officials. Saddam brushed aside apologies for the low-level reception but said it was urgent that he see Mubarak "now." A couple of hours later, leading Saddam out of their first private meeting, Mubarak was overheard to say, "I thought that they were joking when they said you were here. I had to leave my guest to lunch by himself."

Theatrics aside, Saddam's visit was a major success, for Mubarak instructed Egypt's defense and intelligence leadership to discuss follow-up steps with their Iraqi counterparts. To make the Egyptian-Iraqi alliance palatable both to the rest of the Arab world and to the U.S.-led West, the essence of the new pact—a military alliance preparing to confront Israel— was downplayed; and a wider, ostensibly economically oriented, alliance was announced. Saddam prevailed upon Jordan's King Hussein and North Yemen's President Saleh Ali, both dependent on Iraq, to join the alliance. He also insisted that Arafat be made a fifth, though secret, member.

The new Arab Co-operation Council (ACC) debuted in Baghdad in February 1989. Saddam had been correct in predicting that the West would interpret the presence of Mubarak and King Hussein as proof that the Council aimed at nothing more than becoming a regional Common Market. Subsequently, when the ACC failed to implement any of the advertised economic steps, Western officials reasoned that it was merely an attempt to enhance Saddam Hussein's prestige.

At the same time, Saddam launched a charm offensive at Saudi Arabia and Kuwait. In February, he urged Kuwait's Crown Prince Saad to visit Baghdad and agreed to provide Kuwait daily with hundreds of millions of gallons of water, of both drinking and agricultural quality. In March, during a visit to Baghdad by King Fahd of Saudi Arabia, Saddam suddenly insisted that the two leaders sign a nonaggression and noninterference pact. The startled Saudis argued that since there were no problems between their countries, such a pact would be meaningless. When Saddam continued to press, King Fahd went home to Riyadh for consultations. In late March he returned to Baghdad and signed the treaty. Meanwhile, to keep Washington sleeping, Baghdad endorsed Cairo's declared opposition to any anti-Israel military bloc.

In May, Saddam followed up on his masterstroke, arriving at the Arab League's Heads of State Conference in Casablanca in the company of Mubarak and insisting on Egypt's readmission as a full member. Iraq also gave large grants to governments and private entities throughout the Arab world in order to strengthen the image of Saddam as the new protector of all Arabs.

Meanwhile, Iraq expanded its military cooperation with Jordan. On the surface, there was nothing new in this, for Jordan had been Iraq's closest ally during the war with Iran. A Jordanian Army brigade had fought at the front, and Aqaba was the primary port for Iraq's importation of military and technical equipment. Despite this intimate access to the Iraqi military system, Amman grossly underestimated the speed of Iraq's recovery. When the Jordanians agreed in early 1989 to embark on joint war preparations, they were confident it would be several years before Iraq was capable of meeting its end of the deal. Instead, Iraq insisted on implementing specific military programs against Israel from Jordanian territory as early as mid-1989. The close cooperation between Iraqi intelligence and the most restless Palestinian terrorist elements within Jordan helped convince Amman that such cooperation was in Jordan's best interest.

In July, Iraqi fighters and reconnaissance planes were deployed to Jordanian air bases and started flying along the Israeli border for identification of potential targets. Intensive joint training and doctrinal development began in the fall. Iraq donated Chieftain tanks and other equipment captured from Iran in order to establish a new Jordanian armored division. Iraq also funded the entire undertaking, putting up the money for salaries, ammunition, and the construction of a new garrison.

The two countries' close military cooperation intensified in mid-February 1990, when they established a joint Mirage–F-1 squadron. They also decided on combined units for the new Mirage 2000 aircraft just ordered by both countries from France and paid for by Baghdad. (Ultimately, France refused to supply these aircraft because of Iraq's invasion of Kuwait that summer.) Amman permitted the deployment of Iraqi radar stations in Jordan and agreed on the integration of an upgraded Jordanian early-warning system into an Iraqi-dominated comprehensive C³I system (Command, Control, Communications, and Intelligence). Iraq also funded and supplied a new Iraqi-Jordanian Brigade. To an alarmed Jordanian senior officer, these developments represented the "Iraqization" of the Jordanian Legion.

King Hussein paid a high price for this Iraqi largesse: He had to agree to the buildup of the Palestinian terrorist infrastructure in Jordan. This process reversed the situation that had been in effect since "Black September" 1970, when he had the choice of turning his country over to the terrorists or expelling them through a massive use of military force, and he chose the latter. Now, Amman very quickly became the capital of the Intifadah, as the bulk of the organized Palestinian violence against Israel was directed from the PLO's new forward headquarters there. Moreover, Amman became the most important center for the Sunni Islamist organizations, most of them going under the banner of the Islamic Jihad, which were extremely active throughout the Middle East. For example, it was at its Amman center that the Beit al-Muqaddas faction of Islamic Jihad, under Sheikh Asaad Bayud Tamimi, prepared for its February 4, 1990, attack on an Israeli tourist bus near Ismailia, Egypt.

———

SADDAM HUSSEIN was unwittingly aided in his efforts by the fledgling administration of the elder George Bush. After the November 1988 elections, the Bush transition team, alarmed by the escalating Intifadah, asked President Reagan's secretary of state, George Shultz, to permit the revival of formal contacts between the United States and the PLO. These contacts, based on the idea that Arafat was the sole legitimate embodiment of the Palestinian cause, were the beginning of the "peace process." Essentially, Secretary Shultz and the Reagan administration took hold of this political hot potato, recognizing the PLO so that their successors could launch their foreign policy without major crises. In early 1989, in order to further smooth the launching of this policy, the new Bush administration asked Scandinavian and other Western European governments known to have good relations with Arafat to facilitate informal contacts for him with Israel or, if that was not possible, with individual members of the Israeli peace camp.

Washington was not alone in worrying about rising tensions and spreading violence in the Middle East. Despite Amman's increasingly close ties with Baghdad, in early 1989 the Israeli and Jordanian governments secretly agreed to work together to empower traditional forces in the territories through municipal and rural-council elections—frameworks where the traditional families and clans would have an advantage, at the expense of the PLO and HAMAS. If successful, such elections would have brought to power in the territories legitimate elements willing to negotiate peaceful coexistence with both Jerusalem and Amman and capable of implementing any agreements that were reached.

However, instead of supporting the peacemaking efforts of the two countries most directly affected by the Palestinian issue—both of which were staunchly pro-United States—the new Bush administration chose to accept the arguments put forward by Mubarak and by Western Arabists to the effect that Arafat's coterie within the PLO was central to any deal over Palestine. In fact, Arafat's forces were irrelevant on the ground; but by late April, the United States and Egypt were pushing Israel to meet with PLO-controlled Palestinian leaders in Cairo to discuss their inclusion in the upcoming elections. The aim was to empower the PLO at the expense of the traditional elements—exactly what Israel and Jordan had sought to avoid.

In early May, Jordan's Crown Prince Hassan (King Hussein's brother) sent a formal letter to Dennis Ross, special adviser to Secretary of State James Baker, criticizing the American policy. The letter was ignored. A few weeks later, in a major policy address to AIPAC (the American Israel Public Affairs Committee) in Washington, D.C., Secretary Baker stated that Israel should give up "the unrealistic vision of a greater Israel" and instead "reach out to the Palestinians as neighbors who deserve political rights." In the following days, Baker and other senior administration officials left no doubt that when they said "Palestinian," they meant the PLO.

Thus, with Prince Hassan's letter insultingly rebuffed, and with Jerusalem coerced into agreeing to meet with pro-PLO Palestinian representatives, Amman concluded that Washington *wanted* Saddam's and Mubarak's agenda to prevail. Ever the survivor, King Hussein stopped resisting his ACC allies. That summer, with guarantees from Cairo and Baghdad that the PLO would not conspire against him, he permitted Arafat's return to Jordan.

Even so, Amman watched with alarm as negotiations intensified between the United States and the PLO—particularly the so-called informal channel between Mohamed Rabie, a Palestinian American professor of economics very close to Arafat, and William B. Quandt, a former National Security Council staffer and one of Washington's leading Arabists. These contacts led to the Baker Plan, which called for Egyptian oversight of Israeli negotiations with a PLO-approved delegation. The combination of the United States' shifting the Palestinian issue to the Egyptian sphere of influence and its recognizing Arafat as the sole representative of the Palestinians put King Hussein in an untenable position. The Palestinian leadership in Jordan was pressuring him to follow suit. Given that the majority of Jordan's population is indigenous Palestinian, such a move would have delegitimized the very existence of the Hashemite Kingdom of Jordan. The only way Hussein could avoid a challenge to his throne was by giving the Palestinians what they wanted most—access to the Israeli border.

By early 1990, many terrorist organizations—some associated with Arafat's Fatah, others from the radical Islamist side—had opened headquarters in Amman under Iraqi sponsorship and were running recruitment and training programs in Palestinian refugee camps throughout Jordan. Among the most active groups were the PLO's Intelligence and Security Apparatus under Abdel Latief Abu Hijlah (better known as Abu-Tariq); the PLO's Special Operations Group under Colonel Hawari; Force 17, made up of Arafat's own bodyguards; the Organization of May 15 under Muhammad Amri (Abu-Ibrahim); the Organization of the Survivors of Hammah, a Syrian Muslim Brotherhood organization; HAMAS; and the Palestine Liberation Front of Muhammad Zaidan Abbas (Abu-al-Abbas), then operating under Arafat's direct control. As well, the Democratic Front for the Liberation of Palestine (DFLP) established a forward headquarters in Amman, and the Popular Front for the Liberation of Palestine (PFLP) established a base to support the operations of its Red Eagle units. The Jordanian security forces tacitly accepted the presence of Iraqi intelligence officers in the ranks of the various Palestinian groups.

Besides the radicalization of Palestinian Jordanian youth, Amman had to deal with conflict—up to and including armed clashes—between Palestinian nationalist and Islamist groups. In the wake of Secretary Baker's statement that the PLO was no longer involved in terrorism, Amman-based PLO commanders reorganized their operations, often by assuming the identity of organizations associated with the Islamic Jihad. Still, the Islamist factions remained active as well. On March 30, 1990, for example, the Islamic Jihad launched several 107-mm rockets from Jordan into the Israeli-held Jordan Valley. At first, Amman claimed that groups coming from Syria carried out the attacks; however, Islamist sources themselves insisted that their bases were in Jordan. Significantly, these operations enjoyed active support from Islamist elements within the Jordanian security services. Finally, in order to divert extreme Islamists and militant Palestinians away from activities against his regime, King Hussein instructed his security forces to assist them in their jihad operations against Israel

―――――

WHILE THIS ESCALATION in Palestinian terrorism was going on, profound strategic developments were taking place throughout the Middle East. In the winter of 1989–90, prominent Egyptians started talking about the coming war with Israel. For example, Osama al-Baaz, a confidant of President Mubarak, declared that a regional war was inevitable unless Israel agreed to all the PLO's demands. The well-connected journalist Mohamed Heikal was even more explicit. "A war between Israel and the Arabs will happen soon," he wrote. "There should be no doubt about it." Heikal predicted that the demands Israel would make upon Jordan in the upcoming U.S.-imposed peace negotiations would be so outrageous that the entire Arab world would repudiate them, whereupon a war for the restoration of Arab honor would erupt.

The PLO was extremely active in fanning the flames of war. On February 17, Arafat's confidant Hani al-Hassan demanded the revival of the Eastern Front—made up of Syria, Iraq, and Jordan—to confront the growing Israeli threat to the Arab world. Meeting with Saddam Hussein in Baghdad, Arafat himself predicted that Syria, then feuding with both Iraq and Jordan, would rejoin the Eastern Front and contribute to a decisive confrontation with Israel.

The concurrent shifts in Jordan's foreign and defense policies reflected the severity of the looming crisis. King Hussein had been enjoying the benefits of a de facto peace with Israel, including generous U.S. aid. However, once he became convinced that U.S. policy had shifted in favor of Arafat, Mubarak, and Saddam, he abandoned his relations with Israel and joined the camp tilting toward the war option. In late February, hosting an ACC summit in Amman, King Hussein publicly wore his Legion's red *kaffiyeh*—a highly significant militarist symbol in the Arab world. At the summit, he transferred the baton of Arab leadership from Egypt to Iraq when he called Saddam Hussein the "big brother" of the Arab world.

Militancy dominated the summit's deliberations. Mubarak's faint call for Israeli-Palestinian reconciliation was drowned out by the warlike statements of the other participants, especially Saddam, who declared that the Arabs already possessed the military might required "to destroy Israel and defeat the US." King Hussein vowed Jordan's unyielding commitment to the all-Arab cause. At Amman and in several subsequent meetings, Saddam stressed that 1990 provided a unique window of opportunity. He felt that the combination of the Soviet withdrawal from daily supervision of Arab affairs and the new pro-Arab attitude of the American government should enable the Arabs to get away with a decisive onslaught on Israel. Meanwhile, the "Arab Stone"—that is, the Intifadah—had already wrought enough attrition to put Israel on the defensive. Therefore, the timely application of stronger measures would turn the "stone" into a killing instrument, thus achieving "the final solution" of the Palestinian problem.

King Hussein was also pursuing rapprochement with Syria's Hafez al-Assad, who was receptive to the idea of military unity. In early March, Assad declared that the Arabs "must unify and march on the liberation way—the *jihad* way." Echoing Saddam, Assad stressed that the Arab commitment must be staunch because "the struggle with Zionism" would be "long and protracted" before the inevitable decisive victory was won.

On March 4, King Hussein traveled to Baghdad to discuss Jordanian-Iraqi military cooperation. The King noted that Riyadh had been arguing in Washington that the ACC's military buildup amounted to the encirclement of Saudi Arabia, and he warned that the United States might intervene in order to protect both Israel and Saudi Arabia. Saddam ridiculed the notion of a U.S. threat. Soon afterward he began demanding, both through formal diplomatic channels and in public speeches, that the United States withdraw its forces from the Persian Gulf and the Arab states. His deputy foreign minister, Tariq Aziz, argued that the United States was an active participant in the Zionist war against the Arabs and that the U.S. Navy's presence in the Persian Gulf was a key part of this war. The Iraqi media took up this campaign; as one editorial put it, "the U.S. has begun damaging the interests of the Arab Nation by threatening their national security, rights, and interests." Baghdad used Washington's concerns about Iraq's buildup of ballistic missiles and weapons of mass destruction to exacerbate anti-American feelings throughout the Arab world. At the same time, Iraqi officials expressed their irritation with the Gulf states for not evicting the Americans from their midst.

In the last week of March 1990, during high-level military meetings in Baghdad conducted by the PLO, senior Palestinian and Iraqi officials decided to transform the PLO's forces into a war-fighting Palestine Liberation Army (PLA). In a meeting with Saddam, Arafat said the PLO would be an integral part of an Iraqi-led war against Israel. "We will enter Jerusalem victoriously and raise our flag on its walls," Arafat declared. "We will fight you [Israel] with stones, rifles, and al-Abid [Iraq's strategic surface-to-surface missile]." Saddam replied, "You are not alone. We have always said that once the war [with Iran] is over, our efforts will be directed toward Palestine."

However, since Saddam regarded terrorism not as a tactic but as a "strategic weapon," he was not willing to leave it under Arafat's control. Iraqi intelligence, from its observation of the terrorist infrastructure in Jordan, recognized the dominant role of the Islamists. Hence, in early March, Baghdad established a new Islamist organization, the Front of the Islamic Army for the Liberation of Palestine (FIALP), as its own instrument in the coming terrorist war.

The first communiqué of the FIALP's General Command clearly defined its internationalist character: "The Front also calls upon all members of Islamic parties in the East and the West, from Palestine to Afghanistan and from Morocco to Lebanon, to join the military wing of the Front of the Islamic Army, which is the first auxiliary force for the blessed Palestinian Intifadah, the Islamic HAMAS movement, and the Islamic Unification Movement, and of the Egyptian, Jordanian, Syrian, and Lebanese armies standing along the entire front line with the enemy for the liberation of Palestine, which, the great and brilliant leader Saddam Hussein said, is before our eyes and we will strive to liberate. We hope to find a personality like Saddam Hussein among our ranks. Victory shall be ours, InshAllah, with the assistance of Allah and our Arab brothers."

In a statement issued on March 25, the FIALP declared that "Any aggression against any Muslim country is considered an aggression on all Muslims, and the perpetrators will regret their actions." The U.S. presence in the Persian Gulf was now defined as the primary objective: "The Islamic Army for the Liberation of Palestine warns that it will blow up 173 American companies operating in the Arab Gulf region and assassinate important American personalities, including American ambassadors." The United Kingdom was also an important objective: "We will shut up the government of the United Kingdom by any suitable means if England does not halt its campaign against Iraq."

Saddam kept fanning the flames. On April 2, he claimed that Iraq had "double-combined chemical [weapons]" in operational status. These weapons, he added, "existed during . . . the last year of the war [but Iraq] did not use [them] against the Iranians." These weapons, based on the latest Soviet technologies, are essentially a mixture of two types of chemical or toxic agents released simultaneously in order to overwhelm any protective systems the enemy might have. Iraq had used earlier versions of these weapons in Kurdistan in the 1980s; however, between 1984 and 1988, the Iraqis had shifted the mixture from mycotoxins ("Yellow Rain"), mustard gas, and non-persistent nerve agents to cyanogen, mustard gas, and nerve agents, raising the toxicity significantly.

Little wonder that Saddam presented the availability of these weapons as a sufficient counter to Israel's nuclear arsenal. Iraq was not pursuing nuclear weapons, he insisted. "Why should we need an atomic bomb? . . . Don't they know that we have double-combined chemical weapons to cause fire to devour half of Israel if Israel, which has atomic bombs, dared attack Iraq?" Moreover, he discussed Iraq's use of chemical weapons in response to Israeli aggression in the context of a declaration that Israel's very existence constitutes aggression against the Arab world.

A close examination of the official text of this speech reveals two fine points that would dominate Iraqi strategy in the coming years. First, Saddam explicitly stated that any attack on Iraq by any Western nation would prompt an Iraqi attack on Israel: "Any missile that would fall on Iraqi territory will be countered with flames that will eat half of Israel." This policy would be implemented in the Gulf War in early 1991. Second was the conditional clause concerning the unleashing of a chemical attack on Israel. In this cautious phrasing, Saddam signaled that he was frightened of Israel's nuclear arsenal and long-range delivery systems and by Jerusalem's resolve to use them. During the Gulf War, the latter point would prevail in Saddam's decision making.

Meanwhile, Cairo was growing apprehensive about Saddam's threats. On April 8, Mubarak traveled to Baghdad in order to gauge Saddam's intentions. Saddam stressed the centrality of his commitment to all-Arab security despite the financial burden. "For Iraq to maintain its national security, it requires, for instance, 50 infantry and armored divisions in the ground forces alone. But if Iraq were part of overall pan-Arab security, it perhaps would need only 20 divisions, and the cost of the 30 other divisions could be used for economic development and for upgrading the standard of living of the Iraqi people. From this perspective, it does not hurt Iraq to earmark the cost of 5 of these 30 divisions for strengthening the national security of other fraternal Arab countries." Despite this bravado, Saddam in turn was apprehensive about Mubarak's refusal to commit Egypt to the war against Israel and annoyed by Mubarak's failure to intercede with the Persian Gulf states and the United States to persuade them to forgive part of Iraq's debt and provide generous financial assistance.

So Saddam decided to teach Mubarak a lesson. Over the next few weeks, hundreds of thousands of Egyptian guest workers in Iraq were suddenly told that their visas and work permits had expired, and the security authorities told Iraqi employers that they did not have to give them their back pay. For Egypt, the economic implications were dire, because Egypt's foreign-currency reserves had depended heavily on the money these workers sent home. Over the same period, more than a thousand Egyptians working in Iraq were kidnapped or arrested by Iraqi intelligence, and most of them were tortured and executed. By late April, Egypt was flooded with unemployed former guest workers and with the coffins of those who had been brutally killed. Mubarak got the message.

———

SADDAM DARED be so bold in confronting Mubarak because he was convinced that Washington was now on his side, to the point of protecting Iraq against Israel. The first indication to this effect had come on April 5, when Prince Bandar bin Sultan, the Saudi Ambassador to Washington and a confidant of President Bush, arrived in Iraq on a secret mission. Prince Bandar brought assurances from President Bush and Prime Minister Margaret Thatcher, as well as from his own King Fahd, that neither the United States nor Israel had any intention of preemptively attacking Iraq. In a secret meeting at the Sarsank resort in northern Iraq, Saddam assured Bandar that Iraq did not intend to attack Israel if Israel did not attack Iraq. "The imperialist-Zionist forces," he said, "keep pushing this theory that I have designs over my neighbors. I don't have designs over my neighbors." Saddam added, "It's important that we don't allow the imperialist-Zionist rumor mill . . . to get between us."

Soon afterward, King Fahd called President Bush and requested reciprocity. Consequently, Washington elicited a promise from Jerusalem that Israel would not launch any weapon against Iraq unless it was attacked first. The Israeli guarantee, as conveyed by President Bush to King Fahd and Prince Bandar, and by them to Saddam Hussein, amounted to Israel's unilaterally renouncing its preemptive strike option in order to stay in the good graces of the Bush administration. In retrospect, Jerusalem's concession set a dangerous precedent.

Then, on April 12, a bipartisan delegation of U.S. senators visited Baghdad. Saddam complained bitterly to his guests about the American media's critical coverage of Iraq's human-rights record and of its weapons programs and suggested that the reporting reflected the Bush administration's hostility. Senator Alan Simpson (R-WY) quickly distanced the administration from the media. "There's no problem between you and the American government or the American people," Simpson said. "Your only problem is with our press, who are arrogant and hard to please." Saddam persisted, noting that he had been attacked by the government's own overseas radio network, Voice of America (VOA). Senator Robert Dole (R-KS) assured Saddam that the media attacks "[did] not come from President Bush." He added that the VOA broadcast was conducted by "a person who was not authorized to speak in the name of the government, a commentator of the Voice of America . . . [who has since] been removed."

The senators discussed with Saddam Iraq's plans to purchase grain and other agricultural products from the United States and specifically from the states they represented. The conversation was friendly, and Saddam's threats against Israel were virtually ignored. When it was mentioned that Congress might impose sanctions on Iraq because of its weapons programs, Senator Dole replied, "Let me point out to you that twelve hours ago President Bush told me that he and his government were hoping to improve relations with Iraq. I can even assure you that President Bush will oppose sanctions. He could even veto any such decision, unless any provocative act should occur." U.S. Ambassador April Glaspie, who was present throughout the meeting, concluded by endorsing Senator Dole's statement: "As American Ambassador, I can assure you, Mr. President, that this is indeed the policy of the United States government."

Nonetheless, Saddam worried about attacking Israel with his flanks and rear exposed not only to Iran but also to the pro-U.S. Gulf states. The latter were increasingly hostile to him because of Iraq's defaulting on its huge war debt; in contrast, the radicalization of Iraq's policies might be conducive to a rapprochement with Iran. Therefore, Saddam sent a personal letter to Iranian President Ali Akbar Hashemi-Rafsanjani, offering concessions in order to start the process of reconciling "the unfortunate conflict between the two sisterly Muslim nations." The initial Iranian response was positive. Tehran warned, though, that if the Iraqi-led Eastern Front attacked Israel, the United States would surely strike Iraq from bases in the Persian Gulf. Hence, the Iranians suggested, Iraq should join with Iran in driving the United States out of the Persian Gulf region before taking on Israel.

Israeli intelligence learned about this exchange almost immediately. On April 15, the U.S. Ambassador to Israel, William A. Brown, hosted an Easter lunch in Jerusalem for the Israeli political and security leadership. When the conversation turned to Saddam's recent threats, Major General Ehud Barak, deputy chief of the General Staff, declared, "Saddam Hussein is trying to fool the world. His plan is not to attack Israel. You should look south from Iraq. That is where he is really looking." Asked to clarify his statement, Barak said that he was referring to Kuwait and the United Arab Emirates (UAE). When Brown reported this exchange to Washington, he was met with disdain. The Israelis were taking Saddam's bellicose rhetoric too seriously, senior officials opined, and were looking for an opportunity to draw in the United States. Considering that Israel had destroyed the Iraqi nuclear reactor back in 1981, they added, it was only understandable that Saddam would fear new Israeli raids on the "alleged chemical weapons factories." Furthermore, since Iraq was such a good customer for American agricultural and industrial products, there was nothing harmful in tolerating Saddam's wish to assert himself as the leader of the Arab world. The Bush administration urged Jerusalem to stop worrying about Saddam and demonstrate more flexibility in the fledgling contacts with PLO-affiliated Palestinian leaders.

Ten days later President Bush sent Saddam greetings for the end of Ramadan, stressing that "ties between the United States and Iraq would contribute to the peace and stability of the Middle East." The next day, John Kelly, Assistant Secretary of State for Near Eastern Affairs, testified in Congress against sanctions: "This administration continues to oppose the imposition of sanctions, which would penalize American exporters and worsen our balance-of-payments deficit. Furthermore, I fail to see how sanctions could increase the possibility of our exercising a moderating influence on the actions of Iraq." Adel Darwish, the noted Egyptian-born British Middle East expert, later stressed the importance of these encounters to the formulation of Baghdad's strategy: "This episode gave Saddam the impression that Washington was supporting him as the guardian of their interests in the Gulf. He interpreted it as a green light to continue forcing his policies on his neighbors so long as American interests seemed better served under his guardianship." Saddam was now certain he could manipulate the friendly and naive Bush Administration.

———

IN LATE MAY, twenty-one Arab monarchs and other heads of state, as well as dozens of senior officials and staff, gathered in Baghdad for an all-Arab summit. The summit's undeclared but commonly accepted objective was to crown Saddam as the supreme leader of the Arab world—a position no one had held since Nasser's heyday in the 1960s. The only major leader missing was Syria's Assad, who had told Mubarak that he did not believe Saddam was sincere in his declared intention of helping the Palestinians. Hence, Assad told Mubarak, he declined to endorse Saddam. This snub did not spoil what was billed as a major Arab extravaganza.

The Iraqi hospitality was exceptionally lavish, and every effort was made to create an aura of unity. However, all the hoopla could not disguise the significance of two most unusual occurrences.

First, Libya's Muammar Qadhafi demanded a special gathering of all the heads of state, with no aides or stand-in officials allowed. Once the doors were closed, Qadhafi delivered an alarming and perceptive speech. Time was running out for the Arab world, he proclaimed. The Arab political system was on the verge of collapse because of the popular groundswell of Islamist radicalism. Furthermore, the new wave of radicalism was all-Islamic and thus undercut the region's Arab identity. "We all must, virtually today," Qadhafi warned, "establish a joint alliance to stand strong and steadfast against the radical-extremist Islamic groups that are seeking to take over the entire Middle East. They multiply with the speed of lightning. We are likely to wake up one morning to face the masses raising slogans to the effect that 'Islam is the solution to all our economic and social woes,' and demanding that we, the present rulers, vacate the arena." This speech insightfully described the state of the Arab masses even before they suffered the shock of the Gulf crisis.

Saddam took Qadhafi's forebodings seriously. At the same time, he knew that Iraq had no alternative but to attempt to exploit the militant Islamists; their networks were indispensable to launching terrorist operations at the heart of the West. Hence, after hearing Qadhafi's speech, Saddam determined to deliver a major victory that would cause the Islamists to fear him to the point where they would support his all-Arab—as distinct from all-Muslim—jihad.

Saddam had the full support of Arafat and the Palestinian delegates. Away from the microphones, they expressed total disdain for the Americans' notion of a "peace process" with Israel. The only way, they declared, at once to resolve the Arab-Israeli conflict and to contain the rise of the radical Islamist forces such as HAMAS was for "the real Arab forces"—namely, the Iraqi-led ACC—to coerce Israel into "concessions" under the threat of superior military might. It was therefore the obligation of the entire Arab world, the Palestinians argued, to facilitate Iraq's efforts to achieve strategic parity with Israel and specifically to acquire nuclear and other weapons of mass destruction. The Palestinians also addressed the other sensitive subject before the summit: Iraq's financial plight. "We believe that when Iraq builds itself up economically and militarily, it will create the material base for a balanced settlement of the Middle East crisis," a PLO representative said. "That's the main reason Iraq is threatened. Syria talked about gaining a strategic balance, but it's Iraq that did it. The main force of Israel is the atomic bomb, and one has to remember that the strategic balance between the superpowers finally led to détente."

The second irregular event during the summit was Saddam Hussein's own demand for a closed-door meeting, this one with President Mubarak, King Fahd, and several of the Gulf leaders. Saddam delivered a passionate and eloquent speech about the economic plight Iraq had fallen into while serving the all-Arab cause. "You are virtually waging an economic war against my country," he stated. Saddam also repeated a point he had made in his dramatic opening speech, hinting that Iraq had strategic alternatives— namely, the possible rapprochement with Iran. He acknowledged his recent exchange of letters with Hashemi-Rafsanjani, "which we hope will lead to direct and deep dialogue that would result in comprehensive peace."

Instead of meekly accepting Saddam's leadership, the Gulf leaders went on the verbal attack. Ignoring pleas from Mubarak and others to stop, the Emir of Kuwait taunted a quiet but seething Saddam, insisting that Kuwait would determine its own production rates, not only in border zones but also in areas claimed by Iraq. King Fahd was not far behind in his criticism of Saddam, although he was more considerate in his manner; essentially, he demonstrated compassion for Iraq's plight but put Saudi Arabia's interests first.

Ultimately, the Gulf leaders were so fixated on their oil and money issues that they completely missed Saddam's real objective. Yes, Iraq was in a dire economic state. However, Saddam's true goal was to be recognized as master by his vassals. In demanding financial assistance, he was in fact asking for an expression of subservience. Hence, for Saddam, the refusal to meet his demands was unpardonable.

———

SENIOR ARAB OFFICIALS described Saddam as being astounded by the show of defiance put up by the Gulf leaders. However, being pragmatic, he realized he had to modify his master plan. His reformulated strategy addressed all the challenges he was facing in a single coherent approach. He resolved first to consolidate his position as the leader of the Arab world through shock and intimidation and especially the humiliation of the United States—the patron of both the Gulf states and Israel. However, Iraq would *not* touch Saudi Arabia: Since the House of al-Saud was the Guardian of the Holy Shrines, doing so would have undercut Saddam's Islamic legitimacy. Once he made a bold move, Saddam reasoned, the entire Arab and Muslim world would be united behind him and America would be banished from the region. Then he would be in an excellent position to take on Israel. After such feats, his radical Arabism would be unchallenged.

Meanwhile, having agitated the Arab world with the ACC's active preparations for a major crisis, Saddam needed a strategic diversion to keep anyone from noticing that he had shifted his priorities from immediately confronting Israel to first confronting Kuwait and the United States. The possible need for such a diversion had long been on Saddam's mind. Hence, the Iraqi and Libyan intelligence services had begun preparing a few elite Palestinian squads drawn from Arafat's most loyal cadres and closely supervised by Arafat's confidant Abu-al-Abbas. At the time of the Baghdad summit, these terrorists had been undergoing intensive training in Libya for over half a year. Virtually the moment the summit concluded, Saddam and Qadhafi unleashed one of the teams.

On May 30, a squad of Palestine Liberation Front terrorists, under the command of Abu-al-Abbas, landed on the Nitzanim coast, on the southern shore of Israel. They were engaged on the beach by Israeli security forces and destroyed in a brief battle. Israeli investigators learned that this squad was part of a larger terrorist force that had disembarked on small attack boats from a Libyan mother ship (however, some of the men had drowned on their way to the shore). The terrorists' plan was to strike at the U.S. Embassy in Tel Aviv and at nearby beachfront hotels, killing as many civilians as possible. Such an attack would have preoccupied Israel and the United States, diverting their attention to Libya in the two crucial months preceding Iraq's invasion of Kuwait. Moreover, it would have contributed to the radicalization of the Arab street.

In early June, Washington received intelligence information from Israel and other allies, including some Arab states, indicating that Arafat himself had launched the May 30 operation. These data fit with what was known about the long-term relationship between Arafat and Abu-al-Abbas, whose cooperation began with the 1985 seizure of the *Achille Lauro* cruise ship and the killing of a wheelchair-bound American passenger by a Palestinian squad directly answering to Abu-al-Abbas. Moreover, Arafat was spending most of his time in Iraq— Abu-al-Abbas's chief sponsor—and was openly discussing the possibility of transferring the PLO's political headquarters from Tunis to Baghdad. Given the strength of both the direct intelligence and the supporting evidence, even the most staunch Arabists acknowledged that, at the very least, Arafat must have known about the attack in advance and done nothing to stop it.

Consequently, as anticipated in Baghdad, Washington immersed itself in a heated debate over what to do about Arafat and the U.S.-PLO dialogue. Arafat himself would not go beyond a general statement "condemning attacks against civilians in principle"; he would not repudiate Abu-al-Abbas. However, other Palestinian leaders who had dealt with the United States— most notably Salah Khalaf (Abu-Iyad)—sought informal contacts with sympathetic American interlocutors. Their argument was that the United States must sustain the dialogue in order to balance Saddam's growing influence over Arafat. Abu-Iyad told William Quandt that the May 30 attack "had been an Iraqi operation" designed "to put an end to the PLO's policy of moderation" and support for negotiations. "Saddam had something in mind," Abu-Iyad warned Quandt, "something big."

Even if one takes Abu-Iyad's argument about Iraq's responsibility for the May 30 attack at face value, it is amazing how the crisis was handled in

Washington. The discussion focused almost entirely on the likely effects on the Palestinian-Israeli peace process. The question of why Saddam should want to sponsor a terrorist attack on Americans in Tel Aviv was not considered.

Ultimately, the May 30 attack was a great success for Saddam and Arafat, even though the terrorist force was destroyed and, in the end, the Bush administration cut formal contacts with Arafat. Handling the crisis had consumed Washington's attention at a time when all eyes and ears should have been focused on Iraq and the Persian Gulf. When Washington finally turned back to Saddam Hussein, the die had already been cast.

――――――

ALTHOUGH SADDAM shared Qadhafi's reservations about the Islamists, he realized that the most committed terrorists were motivated not by nationalist aspirations but by Islamist zeal. He would have to burnish his own Islamic credentials if he were going to get these terrorists to fight and die for him. Sheikh Tamimi had provided an opening in mid-April, when he declared that "Iraqi president Saddam Hussein has the opportunity now to become a second Saladin in Palestinian history if his threat to use chemical weapons against Israel is true." Between mid-June and late July, Sheikh Tamimi traveled all over the Middle East urging both leaders and masses to join the impending jihad. "My task is instigation—instigating the *Ummah* to *jihad* for the liberation of all of Palestine," he told a London-based Islamist newspaper. Tamimi's priorities were reflected in the call by the Beit al-Muqaddas faction of the Islamic Jihad for first "confronting the US, striking against US interests," because the US was "the deadliest enemy of our people," and only then for "escalating the [Palestinian] Intifadah."

While preparing to use the Palestinian terrorists, however, Saddam remained wary. Back in March, he and Arafat had agreed to move PLO units from Algeria, Jordan, Sudan, and Yemen to training bases in Iraq for integration into the PLA. Now, in early summer, Saddam decided instead to transfer some of these fighters to isolated camps in the Libyan desert, where they could undergo thorough indoctrination prior to their deployment to Iraq. In any case, transforming the Palestinian recruits into reliable and capable fighters or terrorists would take a lot of time, and Saddam was running out of time. If Iraq were to launch terrorist attacks throughout the West and reach the heart of Israel, it needed to be able to use existing resources. Accordingly, Iraqi and PLO intelligence, in close cooperation with the East Germans, reexamined their operational options in Western Europe. They soon discovered that virtually all the local terrorist support systems were firmly in the hands of Syria and Iran. On the eve of the crisis, Baghdad realized that close cooperation with those two states was necessary for any terrorist operations in the West to succeed. This alone was enough to impel Saddam to follow up on his letter to Hashemi-Rafsanjani.

———

IN SHARP CONTRAST to the publicly emotional, messianic rhetoric characteristic of the Islamic Republic of Iran, the inner circles of government there had always been most prudent and pragmatic when it came to issues of national security. The Iranians approached the Iraqi initiative with great caution. Any setback to the United States and its allies in the Persian Gulf would serve the Iranian national interest, and the mullahs were certainly committed to the destruction of Israel and the establishment of an Islamist state in its stead. But the Iranians could not ignore the bitter legacy of their war with Iraq. Thus their reaction would be based on close examination of every detail of Baghdad's proposed plan and on maintaining Iranian control over the international terrorist system.

In late May and early June, Tehran had convened a major conference of Islamist terrorist leaders—mainly HizbAllah and Palestinian commanders—to discuss improvements in coordination and operational methods. A few central leaders, including Sheikh Tamimi, stayed in Tehran for further discussions. In a key strategy meeting with Ayatollah Ali Khamenei—Ayatollah Khomeini's successor as supreme religious leader of Iran—they defined "the struggles of the Islamic Republic of Iran against global arrogance, especially the Great Satan, the United States, and its illegitimate child, Israel, as a strategic posture." They reiterated that "waging a *jihad* and moving along the path of Allah are the foundational elements of the Islamic revolution." In practical terms, they committed their respective organizations to opening anti-Israeli fronts from both Lebanon and Jordan once the Iraqis launched their war in the Persian Gulf; this would provoke Israel into counterattacking and thus force the rest of the Arab world to side with Iraq.

These discussions served as the framework for subsequent negotiations between Tehran and Baghdad. Iran was not willing to become directly involved in the Gulf conflict, but it agreed to provide Iraq with access to the international terrorist network—particularly the infrastructure in Western Europe and the United States that had caught Saddam's eye. In June, Barzan al-Takriti, Saddam Hussein's half brother and Iraq's ambassador to Switzerland, was designated the Iraqi senior commander of terrorist networks in the West. He personally negotiated with Cyrus Naseri, an Iranian intelligence official serving as Hashemi-Rafsanjani's special representative, the modalities for coordinating terrorist operations in Europe.

The success of these negotiations convinced Saddam he could "teach [Kuwait] a lesson" with impunity. According to Sad al-Bazzaz—who would later defect, but who at that time was director of the Iraqi News Agency, general manager of Iraq's radio and television stations, and editor-in-chief of the government newspaper *Al-Jumhuriyah*—"the military option was not brought up for discussion until 28 June 1990," when Saddam summoned six confidants and raised the possibility of using military force against Kuwait. The military objectives discussed at that first meeting were limited to the disputed Rumaila oil fields along the Iraqi–Kuwaiti border and two islands overlooking the access to Umm-Qasr, Iraq's only port on the Persian Gulf. Saddam did not outline any specific force size, nor was a target date discussed. None of Saddam's six associates got the impression that he was considering imminent action.

Meanwhile, the more involved Iraqi intelligence became with the international terrorist network, the more it learned about the pervasive influence of radical Islamism in virtually all the radical organizations. This had far-reaching strategic ramifications. In order to expand popular support for his coming Great War, Saddam was even willing to call for a Shiite-dominated all-Islamic jihad aimed at the eviction of the Great Satan from the Middle East, the destruction of Israel, and the establishment of a Khomeini-style ecumenical Islamic rule over the Holy Shrines in Jerusalem, Mecca, and Medina. Having floated these ideas in Tehran through clandestine visits by emissaries such as the ever helpful Sheikh Tamimi, Baghdad concluded that such a grand design would be irresistible to both Tehran and Damascus. Indeed, strategic arrangements based on these principles were reached between Baghdad and Tehran, leading to a formal pact signed on July 28.

The fruits of this pact were seen most quickly in Lebanon, where Tehran was in control of the HizbAllah and most of the Palestinian terrorist forces. In June and July, hundreds of Iranian Revolutionary Guard special forces arrived in Lebanon and prepared to operate under HizbAllah's umbrella once the crisis erupted. In mid-July, Tehran arranged to transfer the most militant elements of the anti-Saddam Iraqi Shiite force, the Hizb al-Dawah al-Iqlimi, to HizbAllah bases in Lebanon so that they could take part in the jihad while not threatening Baghdad. HizbAllah commanders announced new operations against the United States and its allies.

As tension grew in late July, Iranian ambassadors and chargés d'affaires were evacuated from key posts worldwide, ostensibly called to Tehran for a special seminar with Iran's supreme leaders. In a sense, there *was* a seminar, at which the diplomats were told that Tehran was anticipating a worldwide escalation of "the export of the revolution" and were given instructions on how to "accomplish the heavy duty of defending the Islamic Revolution against the aggression of its hostile enemies." The diplomats heard that "If the Islamic Republic is to preserve its offensive policy toward the ringleaders of infidelity and oppression, as the leader Ayatollah Ali Khamenei has said, implementation of such a policy would be possible only through revolutionary and competent forces who are nonchalant towards worldly pomps and seriously devoted to the principles of the Islamic Revolution."

Western European governments were well aware of the gathering storm. The French government went further than any other. Having been forewarned about Iraq's plans, Paris moved unilaterally to remove a major "cause" for Iranian-supported terrorism on French soil. On July 27, France suddenly pardoned five senior terrorists whose release had long been demanded by Tehran and immediately flew them home. Tehran publicly interpreted the release as a "humanitarian and positive gesture" aimed at improving relations. Washington entirely missed this event.

———

WHILE SADDAM'S DISCUSSIONS with Iran were going on, he was conducting equally sensitive discussions with Mubarak. Back in early July, Mubarak had claimed that the Egyptian Armed Forces were not yet ready for war with Israel. Therefore, he said, the anti-Israel part of Saddam's grand design would have to be postponed. Instead, Mubarak offered to help in "blinding" both the United States and the Gulf states so that Iraq could attain maximum surprise and effectiveness in the Persian Gulf. These discussions seem to have been the final element in convincing Saddam to postpone the liberation of Jerusalem and concentrate instead on consolidating Iraq's supremacy in the Persian Gulf by swallowing Kuwait.

The rest of the Arab world—not to mention Israel and the West—was oblivious to Saddam's change of plans. On the night of July 10–11, King Fahd spoke by phone with the Emir of Qatar, Sheikh Khalifa. Fahd warned that the Iraqis were propelling the entire region into a needless and potentially disastrous war with Israel. He argued that Saddam must be stopped and also that Arafat must be coerced into accepting a political solution covering the West Bank and Gaza before the crisis engulfed the entire region. The King urged the Emir to follow the Saudi approach in upcoming discussions with the Iraqis—namely, to be polite but not agree to any of their demands. Neither King Fahd nor Sheikh Khalifa knew that Iraqi intelligence was recording everything they said. Saddam interpreted their conversation as further proof of the conspiracy hatched against him by the Gulf rulers in concert with the United States.

Saddam first hinted publicly at his change of plans in his speech on Revolution Day, July 17. He complained about the duplicity of the other oil producers and noted that "we have warned them." Iraq, he declared, would "stand up to those who have come with a poisoned dagger and thrust it into our backs. Iraq is not going to accept this."

Saddam's timing was chosen very carefully. A meeting of the Arab League had opened in Tunis the day before, and Arafat had attacked the Gulf states for betraying the Palestinian cause in language suggesting knowledge of the intercepted phone conversation. On July 17, even as Saddam was delivering his speech in Baghdad, his deputy foreign minister, Tariq Aziz, approached Chadli Klibi, the secretary-general of the Arab League, and handed him a special memorandum from Saddam for distribution to all states. The memorandum characterized various economic and military steps undertaken by the Gulf states as parts of a "Zionist plot against the Arab Nation" and swore that Iraq would not permit such a conspiracy to succeed. Klibi told Aziz the memorandum amounted to an ultimatum; Aziz did not respond. Klibi immediately showed the memorandum to the Kuwaiti ambassador, who was shocked but nevertheless refused to take it seriously.

The next day, Iraq began deploying forces near the Saudi and Kuwaiti borders. On July 20, an alarmed King Fahd called Saddam, only to be assured of Saddam's determination to resolve all outstanding disputes "in a brotherly way." Meanwhile, Tariq Aziz and King Hussein arrived in Alexandria for consultations with Hosni Mubarak. By now, Mubarak was living up to his word to Saddam that he would take charge of keeping Washington in the dark. In conversations with the Bush administration, he insisted that Saddam remained committed to peace but wanted more influence and due honor and that this was the point of his muscle flexing. When President Bush contemplated a show of force in the Persian Gulf led by the carrier *Independence*, Mubarak succeeded in dissuading him.

———

IT WAS DURING these crucial days that the "peace process" became the cornerstone of the United States' regional policy. Essentially, the Bush administration decided that the best way to placate Arab governments regarding any subject was to deliver a weaker Israel, and the most expedient way to do that was by seducing Jerusalem into unilateral concessions in the name of the elusive peace process. It did not take long for Arab governments to grasp the tenets of the American policy, and there quickly began a cycle wherein the Arabs would hint at their interest in the peace process in order to lead Washington into seducing and coercing Jerusalem into further self-defeating concessions.

It was also during these days that the first serious instance of Israel's seduction occurred. By July, Israel could no longer ignore the evidence of Saddam's designs. Apart from his threats against the Gulf states, there was accumulating intelligence on the buildup in Jordan of both Palestinian terrorist and Iraqi aerial forces and on Iraq's progress in developing ballistic missiles and weapons of mass destruction. Israeli intelligence learned that Iraq had undertaken a crash program to finish nuclear warheads, and the aerial units stationed in Jordan were carrying out reconnaissance flights covering sensitive areas of Israel within the range of Iraq's new ballistic missiles. In retrospect, it is clear that the Iraqi preparations, particularly in the nuclear field, were far more advanced than either Jerusalem or Washington estimated at the time. The real extent of the Iraqi capabilities would emerge only during the U.N. inspections following the Gulf War, supplemented by the reports of defectors (notably Khidhir Hamza, Saddam's "bomb-maker"). Nonetheless, what was known about Iraq's activities in the summer of 1990 was alarming enough.

On July 18, Israeli intelligence confirmed that Iraq had crossed the nuclear threshold—in other words, it could produce a nuclear weapon without any external input. Alarmed by this knowledge, Prime Minister Yitzhak Shamir—a hard-liner where Israel's security was concerned—dispatched Defense Minister Moshe Arens to Washington, along with the chief of Mossad and the chief of Military Intelligence, to brief the Bush administration. The delegation met with a high-level American team led by Secretary of Defense Dick Cheney. The Americans listened attentively but asked hardly any questions. When the Israelis had finished, Secretary Cheney indicated only that the administration would give the matter consideration.

Others in the administration reacted very differently. Some senior officials contacted Israeli and American Jewish leaders—ostensibly privately and unofficially—with a warning: Israel should stay out of the Iraqi issue. The United States' industrial and agricultural exports to Iraq were far too important to be threatened by Israeli "paranoia." Moreover, Jerusalem and its supporters were unaware of the "overall framework of relations" between Washington and Baghdad and were therefore not taking into consideration "other elements" of the administration's policy. When Jerusalem continued to insist that there was an imminent threat, U.S. officials briefed their Israeli counterparts on the latest information received from Mubarak about Saddam's commitment to joining the peace process. The administration demanded that Israel not do anything that might endanger Saddam's new moderation. The Shamir government went along with Washington's requests, partly because Jerusalem wanted to believe there was a negotiated way out of the debilitating Intifadah. Ultimately, Jerusalem was seduced into forgoing measures to address real threats to the security of Israel.

ON JULY 24, Mubarak arrived in Baghdad for a last-minute deception game. According to what Saddam later said to restore Mubarak's reputation, Saddam assured Mubarak that Iraq would not attack Kuwait so long as negotiations were taking place and then asked Mubarak not to divulge this point so that he wouldn't undercut Saddam's ability to apply pressure. Mubarak immediately left for Kuwait, where, according to the official Kuwaiti record of the conversation, he assured the emir that Saddam had told him personally that "he will not send troops and that he has no intention of attacking Kuwait." Mubarak omitted the conditional nature of Saddam's promise. Later that day, Mubarak also called Bush and Thatcher and repeated the same message.

The next day, Saddam tested the effectiveness of Mubarak's move when he met with Ambassador Glaspie. Saddam delivered a lengthy statement outlining Iraq's grievances. In a conciliatory tone, the Ambassador replied that the United States has "no opinion on Arab-Arab conflicts, like your border disagreement with Kuwait." On July 29, Arafat met the emir of Kuwait and delivered another warning from Saddam. The emir refused even to address the matter. He also refused to meet with Iraqi Vice President Izzat Ibrahim al-Duri and instructed the crown prince, whom he sent in his stead, to be hostile and uncompromising. Relying on Mubarak's report, the emir was sure he could safely call Saddam's bluff.

In the early evening of August 1, Saddam convened the leading members of the Revolutionary Command Council to hear Izzat's report of his encounter with Crown Prince Saad. As Sad al-Bazzaz later reported, once Izzat finished, Saddam announced that Iraq should annex the whole of Kuwait by force the very next day. All those in attendance endorsed this announcement enthusiastically. Lacking proper contingency plans or even up-to-date maps, Iraqi commanders were instructed to make contact with PLO activists in Kuwait, who would lead them to their objectives. When Iraqi tanks rolled across the border the next day, to the utter surprise of the United States and the Gulf states, Saddam and his allies had demonstrated that they could use promises and assurances to manipulate the United States, even at the highest levels of government and concerning the most vital issues. For the Arab world, this may have been the most important legacy of the Gulf crisis.

3

The Gulf Crisis (1990–1991)

"Infidels" on the Sacred Soil of Arabia; the Last Hurrah of the Old Regional Order

HAD THE SANDS of the northeastern coastline of the Arabian Peninsula not been soaked with oil, the Iraqi-Kuwaiti conflict would have been largely ignored in the West. For the region's people, the Arab and Islamic essence of the Iraqi offensive would have been clear, and Iraq's desperate effort to reverse the progress of history appreciated. But that was not to be. Seizing what it saw as the moral high ground and proclaiming the territorial integrity of Kuwait, the U.S.-led West rushed to protect its access to cheap oil with no thought of the potential consequences for its allies in the region. The Bush administration neither comprehended nor cared about the Islamic concerns of much of the Middle East. Consequently, even though the U.S.-dominated coalition devastated Iraq's military machine and nearly destroyed its socioeconomic infrastructure, the United States suffered a strategic defeat of historical significance. In the process, the United States seduced and coerced Israel—its staunchest ally in this turbulent region—into taking some of the defeat upon itself. Both Israel and the United States are still paying for Washington's self-inflicted fiasco.

———

THE GULF CRISIS, culminating in the Gulf War, was far more complex than the well-known buildup of the Western military coalition and the subsequent eviction of Iraq from Kuwait. For the West, the conflict was really over Saddam Hussein—the implications of one man's having control of more than 20 percent of Persian Gulf oil. The West went to war for a pragmatic reason, not a principled one, particularly given that Iraq's historical

41

claim to the territory of Kuwait is valid. Hence, no one in the Muslim world—whether a supporter or an enemy of Iraq—has ever accepted the declaration that the U.S.-led coalition was assembled primarily to protect a small country against an aggressor.

In the Arab portion of the Muslim world, the most profound issue concerned which trend would dominate the future—Islamism or Arabism. If Saddam were to tip the balance in favor of Arabism, he had to demonstrate his prowess as an all-Arab leader. The "reunification" of Kuwait with the "Iraqi motherland" was a natural choice for this demonstration, because the Arab world generally accepted Iraq's claim on Kuwait as valid and felt disdain toward the arrogant and self-indulgent House of al-Sabah. However, Iraq clearly occupied Kuwait in pursuit of its own interests as well as Arab interests. Therefore, although the occupation persuasively demonstrated Iraq's sheer might, it did not validate Saddam's claim to all-Arab leadership the way dealing with the Palestinian-Israeli issue would have. Essentially, the long-term acceptability of Saddam's move against Kuwait would be determined by the way Iraq addressed the Palestinian question.

Moscow, if not the United States, understood the significance of the Muslim factor in the Gulf crisis. Deputy Foreign Minister Yevgeny Primakov, the KGB's veteran Middle East expert, noted that Iraq was popularly admired in the Arab world as the single most important state assisting the Palestinian struggle. For the Arab masses, therefore, the occupation of Kuwait could be seen as an acceptable price for the just solution of the Palestinian problem. Indeed, Saddam's defiance of the United States and Israel was extremely important in Arab eyes. Washington neglected these considerations, Primakov pointed out, in building its anti-Saddam coalition. The Bush administration deluded itself into believing that it had the genuine support of the Arab-Muslim countries. In fact, it was fear of the United States, combined with the lure of bounties, that brought these countries into the coalition. And only the repressive character of their regimes kept popular outbursts of support for Iraq and the Palestinians to a minimum. The enmity toward the United States that pervaded the Arab world, Primakov observed, not only would not weaken over time, but would also get stronger and increasingly Islamist, since Islamism was the only popular trend encouraging confrontation with the United States.

If Washington, Riyadh, and Kuwait City were slow to recognize Saddam's intentions, Saddam was equally slow to perceive the United States' initial hesitant movements as a threat. His primary objective remained pacifying Tehran.

The Iranians responded positively to Saddam's initiative, notifying him that they had decided not to exploit the crisis to Iraq's detriment. This enabled the Iraqis to use units from the Basra area in the invasion of Kuwait.

Hashemi-Rafsanjani even ordered the Iranian army to limit its routine activities in order to avoid moves that might be interpreted as a threat to Iraq. Saddam, encouraged by the Iranian position, made a major conciliatory offer on August 15, recognizing Iran's sovereignty over the disputed Shatt al-Arab and agreeing to withdraw from the 722 square miles of border territory claimed by Iran. These concessions amounted to handing over to Tehran the strategic victory in the Iran-Iraq War.

Baghdad had correctly read Tehran's strategic priorities. While vehemently opposed to the Iraqi annexation of Kuwait, Tehran considered the deployment of U.S. forces to be a far greater threat to the region. By handing Iran the victory in the eight-year war between the two nations, Baghdad in effect permitted Tehran to postpone addressing the Kuwaiti problem until after the American and "apostate" Muslim forces had been dealt with.

On September 12, Khamenei confirmed the Iraqi assessment of Iran's priorities when he declared that "Muslim nations will not allow America to set up its security and defense system in the region." He defined the confrontation with the United States in Islamist terms: "The struggle against American aggression, greed, plans, and policies in the Persian Gulf will be counted as *jihad*, and anybody who is killed on that path is a martyr." This decree had a tremendous impact on the region's Shiites, including not only Iraq's large Shiite contingent (more than 60 percent of the country's total population) but also the al-Hassa Shiite community in Saudi Arabia and the Shiite majority (or near majority) in most of the Gulf states. Alarmingly, Khamenei invoked the specter of Shiite terrorism as practiced in Beirut by the HizbAllah: "It's surprising how the Americans don't take lessons. They saw how vulnerable their presence can be. Have they forgotten how a bunch of pious Muslim youth . . . swept them away and evicted them from Lebanon?" At the same time, Khamenei was careful not to endorse Iraq's moves, reiterating instead Iran's desire for "cooperation with Persian Gulf countries" against all aggressors and stating that reaching a solution to the Kuwait crisis was "the duty of regional countries" and not the United States.

IN FACT, as of early August 1990, the "regional countries" were neither psychologically nor militarily capable of meeting the Iraqi threat. When King Fahd was informed of the Iraqi invasion, he could not believe his ears; he personally checked first with the Saudi Embassy in Kuwait and then with Saddam Hussein himself. It was several hours before Saddam was willing to speak with him; when they did speak, Saddam sought to calm the king. He stressed that Riyadh should know there was no threat to Saudi Arabia in view of the treaty he himself had insisted that Fahd sign.

Riyadh did not buy Baghdad's assurances. King Fahd later recalled that he and his advisers "concluded that what is after Kuwait is with certainty the Eastern Region of the Kingdom of Saudi Arabia. If not, why this great force? Why this surprise?" Even so, there was a lingering ambivalence among the Saudi elite. As General Prince Khaled bin Sultan put it: "Despite our quarrel with its leader, Iraq was a brotherly country whom we had helped in its war against Iran, and whose regional role we valued as a counterweight to both Iran and Israel." Feeling personally betrayed by Saddam, the House of al-Saud revisited recent contacts in search of warning signs they had ignored. Prince Khaled now observed that back in February "Iraq was pressing to give [the ACC] a military dimension, which made it look even more like a hostile encirclement of Saudi Arabia." His brother Prince Bandar found new meaning in his meeting with Saddam in early April; Bandar now believed that in seeking assurances against U.S. and Israeli attacks, Saddam was attempting to secure his western flank.

Given the magnitude of the Iraqi force already deployed in Kuwait, the Saudi military knew they would need outside help to block an Iraqi offensive if, as they feared, their country was Iraq's ultimate objective. However, because of the Holy Shrines on the Arabian Peninsula, the deployment of foreign forces is forbidden by Islamic legal tradition. As Mohamed Heikal analyzed the Saudis' dilemma, "The king's role as Servant of the Two Holy Shrines would be meaningless if Saudi Arabia needed protection by a Christian country. Inviting foreigners to trespass on holy territory could rekindle the Islamic revolution, turning its full force against the Saud family, a prospect little better than bowing to Iraqi sovereignty." Therefore, while King Fahd did ask the United States, via Prince Bandar, for help with air power and for additional military equipment, he initially decided against having foreign ground troops based in Saudi Arabia.

However, the Bush administration determined that major U.S. forces would be required, either to persuade Saddam to withdraw or, should the need arise, to push the Iraqi forces out of Kuwait. Therefore, Washington began pressuring Fahd—first via Bandar and subsequently through a high-level delegation to Riyadh—to accept a major deployment of U.S. ground forces. Arriving in Riyadh on August 6, the Americans, led by Cheney, brought with them the latest intelligence—including satellite imagery—about the Iraqi deployment. Although, as the American officials conceded, the United States had no firm intelligence that Saddam had aggressive designs on Saudi Arabia, the overall character of the Iraqi deployment made it imperative to resolve the crisis quickly. The Saudi sensitivities were briefly addressed. "After the danger is over, our forces will go home," Cheney assured the Saudis. "I would hope so," Crown Prince Abdallah bin Abdul Aziz dryly responded. Bandar, who was translating for both sides, did not repeat Abdallah's comment for the Americans. At the end of a long discussion, Fahd agreed in principle to the deployment of U.S. forces provided there was also a large deployment of Arab and Muslim armies.

Even so, the issue was far from being resolved. The Saudis knew that the presence of "infidels" on the sacred soil of Arabia would be traumatic for the entire Muslim world. Therefore, King Fahd sought endorsement from Saudi Arabia's highest religious and judicial authorities, the *ulema*. Initially, he encountered stiff opposition. "All the senior *ulema* were categorically against the idea," a court official told Saudi researcher Nawaf Obaid. Consequently, the king went back to consult with the Saudi high command about the Iraqi threat. Army Commander General Saleh al-Mahya pointed to the "pitiful lack of uniformed men" available for the defense of Saudi Arabia, and Air Force Commander General Ahmad Behery noted that, on its own, the Saudi air defense would be "futile." The king brought this information to the *ulema*, along with Cheney's promise that U.S. troops would not stay in the Kingdom "a minute longer than they were needed." "It was only after long discussions with the King," a Saudi senior official later told Obaid, "that Grand Mufti Sheikh Abdel-Aziz Bin Baz reluctantly gave his endorsement to the idea." However, it took a meeting of 350 *ulema* in Mecca for the king to eventually get permission for a temporary U.S. military presence—conditional upon strict enforcement of Wahhabi laws and expanded authority for the *mutaween*, Saudi Arabia's religious police. Even so, the king's pressuring the *ulema* led to a profound rift between him and some of his country's leading families, including the bin Ladens.

While the Bush administration's decision to commit U.S. military forces for the defeat of Iraq was fully justified, given the tremendous stakes for America's own vital interests, the operation was undermined by profound ignorance of the Arab-Muslim world. For example, Riyadh insisted on sustaining a complex "parallel command" arrangement between General Norman Schwarzkopf and Prince Khaled, who was now formally designated the Joint Forces Commander. For the Saudis, Prince Khaled was the defender of the honor and rights of the Muslim forces. His primary mission, in his own words, was "making sure our all-powerful American ally did not swallow us up." The Americans never understood the dynamics of this. For them, Prince Khaled was, in the words of General Schwarzkopf, the guy with "the authority to write checks."

More broadly, Obaid concluded, "US analysts have underestimated, overlooked, or misunderstood the nature, strength, and goals of the Wahhabi movement in Saudi Arabia, as well as the extent to which the secular leaders are beholden to this group." This ignorance—inexplicable in view of the lengthy presence of so many Americans in Saudi Arabia—resulted in the United States' committing cardinal errors in implementing essentially correct policies. Above all, much grief could have been avoided had the United States addressed the *supreme arbiter* issue.

The supreme arbiter is a political concept that has enabled Muslims to cope with the realities of the modern world. The supreme arbiter is a foreign power capable, through its sheer superior might, of compelling Muslims to take a particular action. Between the First World War and the early 1960s, France and Britain were considered supreme arbiters; consequently, Arab leaders could openly cooperate with them and benefit from the presence of French and British forces on their soil, without losing face. In 1990, in order to secure both the oil fields and the long-term stability of the conservative Arab regimes, the United States could, and should, have assumed this role.

After all, Iraq had struck a chord throughout the Muslim and Arab worlds. Given the brewing Islamist passions in the region, it was virtually impossible for any major Arab leader—and particularly the Guardian of the Holy Shrines—to confront the popular notion of anti-Western jihad. However, Islam recognizes limitations of power and inability to realize intentions. With honor at stake, even the conservative Arab states had to resist overtly cooperating with the Americans. Nonetheless, these same states would have eagerly acquiesced to American pressure applied in the right way. Rather than being forced to say publicly, "Thank you, President Bush, for helping us," the conservative Arab leaders should have been allowed to express indignation in public while saying, in the privacy of their own sanctuaries, "Thank you, Allah, for imposing President Bush upon us."

Had Washington thus made itself the new supreme arbiter of the Persian Gulf, there could have been a fierce and decisive military action against Saddam. There would have been no incentive for half-measures, trip-wires, or signals, none of which have any meaning in the Middle East. Not understanding this, however, Washington first offended the Arabs and then attempted to placate them by pressuring Israel into taking, or not taking, certain actions. This was not only shortsighted but also counterproductive: Since the Arabs are convinced that the United States is under Jewish control, they were certain that hidden agendas determined the United States' toughness with Israel.

DESPITE SYRIA'S CLOSE RELATIONS with Iran and active sponsorship of anti-American terrorism, the Saudis kept insisting on Syrian participation in the anti-Saddam coalition. This insistence was motivated primarily by ideological considerations: Syria was the other major country, besides Iraq, that adhered to the Ba'ath doctrine of revolutionary pan-Arabism; having Syria in the coalition would undercut Saddam's claim that he was fulfilling that doctrine. Riyadh also wanted Damascus to maintain open links to Tehran in order to defuse fears that once Iraq was defeated the coalition would turn on Iran.

From the very beginning, President Assad made sure he was not confused with the rest of the pro-American coalition. In late September, he made a rare trip to Tehran and, significantly, paid his respects at the tomb of Ayatollah Khomeini before beginning the substantive part of his visit. In the discussions between Assad and Hashemi-Rafsanjani, the deployment of Syrian forces to Saudi Arabia and the United Arab Emirates was described as an integral part of the Syrian-Iranian effort to constrain the United States. Iranian officials noted that "Syria believes that by sending a few military units to Saudi Arabia to confront the Iraqi incursion, it is possible to prevent the expansion of the U.S.-led Western influence in the region." Toward the end of Assad's visit, Hashemi-Rafsanjani elucidated their joint position. "We are certain that the American and Western military presence is not for saving Kuwait," he declared. "They have come to serve more important objectives, among them the problems Israel faces. We should not allow foreign forces and those hegemonist powers, who are all geared up to tighten their grip on vital oil resources in the Persian Gulf, the Red Sea, and other sensitive points of the world, to remain in the region." For as long as American forces remained in the Persian Gulf, they were preventing the Arabs and Iran from enforcing just and legitimate solutions to all the other problems in the region—particularly those involving Lebanon and Palestine. Hence, Assad stressed, Syria's participation in the coalition was aimed not at confronting Iraq but at removing the justification for the American presence.

———

BY EARLY OCTOBER, Saddam was convinced the Gulf crisis had reached a deadlock. Primakov—who had known Saddam since 1969 and who, on October 5, became the first non-Arab official to have a meaningful discussion with him since the crisis began—had the same impression. Primakov asked Saddam outright if he did not consider himself trapped in a Masada complex, a reference to the Jewish fighters besieged in the Masada fort in A.D. 73, who ultimately committed suicide rather than surrender to the Romans. He got "an affirmative nod" in response. Primakov warned that the coalition was committed to evicting Iraq from Kuwait, by horrendous warfare if necessary. Only a unilateral withdrawal could still save Iraq. "In case of a confrontation," Saddam replied, "I will make use of all the means at my disposal and expand the flare-up to other states, particularly Israel. [And] if I have no other alternative, and I have to choose between going down on my knees surrendering and between struggle, I will choose the second option." Saddam then stressed the centrality of the Palestinian issue to his strategy: "Since I'm a practical man, I believe that there is a way to bring about the withdrawal of [Iraqi] forces under certain conditions. But I will be able to do so only if the withdrawal from Kuwait will be tightly tied to the solution of all other regional problems." Saddam added that on August 15 he had surrendered "all the fruits of the eight years of war with Iran" in order to be able to focus on the current crisis; now the Iraqi people would not tolerate his surrendering both Kuwait and the Palestinian cause.

Since Washington's uncompromising stand left Saddam no way out of the Kuwaiti quagmire, it became imperative for him to shift the focus onto Palestine. What he needed was a spark to fire up passions throughout the Arab world. And Yassir Arafat provided that spark in the form of the al-Aqsa riots in Jerusalem.

Al-Aqsa Mosque is one of two mosques located on the Temple Mount (it is known to Muslims as the Haram as-Sharif, or Noble Sanctuary; the other mosque is the famous Dome of the Rock). On October 5, the Deputy Mufti of Jerusalem, Sheikh Muhammad Jamal, delivered an inflammatory Friday sermon, choosing as his theme the unfolding of a Jewish conspiracy to destroy the mosques on the Haram as-Sharif and rebuild the Jewish Temple in their place. (This was in fact the agenda of a miniscule Jewish organization called the Temple Mount Faithful. However, a week earlier this group had been forbidden by a court order to enter the Mount, and Israeli police made sure that the order was not violated.) Sheikh Muhammad urged his thousands of Arab listeners to attend a special prayer and sermon at al-Aqsa Mosque on October 8, which was a Jewish holiday (part of the festival of Succoth), but an ordinary working day for Muslims.

Following Sheikh Muhammad's sermon, stones, rocks, glass bottles, and iron rods were stockpiled on the Mount above the Western Wall (Wailing Wall). On October 8, several thousand Palestinians gathered at al-Aqsa Mosque. It did not take long for the crowd, excited by the preachers, to start showering the Jewish worshipers at the Wailing Wall 50 or 60 feet below with the amassed debris. They also attacked and burned the local police station. The Israeli security forces reacted with full force, and some 20 Arabs were killed and over 150 wounded before the riot was contained.

The presence of Faisal Husseini, Yassir Arafat's most senior representative in the territories, clearly pointed to the political significance of the riots and to Arafat's approval. Evidence of the advance coordination that had gone into the operation is suggested by the fact that the editorial on the riots that would appear in the next day's issue of Iraq's official newspaper, *Al-Thawra,* was provided to the Associated Press in Baghdad on October 8, almost immediately after the riots erupted.

Although the excuse for this irregular gathering of thousands of Palestinians on a working day was the Jewish conspiracy against their mosques, the themes of the incitement sermons were Muslim and pan-Arab. After the riots, the first reaction by Arab spokesmen was anti-American. Holding a blood-stained cloth atop the Haram as-Sharif, Sheikh Muhammad blamed the United States for the casualties because it was "giving the Israelis bullets." In Baghdad, *Al-Thawra* called the riots "a massacre that has been made possible with American aid and support to Israel" and predicted that the Arab reaction "will turn into a massive wave of indignation, which will take the pan-Arab struggle a step toward the liberation of Jerusalem and all other holy places and claim the Arab homeland from treachery and occupation."

Once it had gained the sympathetic attention of the Arab street by hammering at the al-Aqsa riots, Baghdad turned to rationalizing its Kuwait policy in Islamic terms. Baghdad challenged the validity of nation-states in the Arab world by identifying nationalism with the U.S. defense of Israel. "The racist massacre in al-Aqsa Mosque," Baghdad argued, "reveals that national legality has always been an instrument by the United States to impose its hegemony and not to be used in defense of people who fight racism and fascism." Baghdad stressed that retaliation must be decisive and all-encompassing: Iraq would soon lead the Arabs to "the liberation of Jerusalem and all other Holy Places"—that is, also Mecca and Medina. Similarly, *Al-Thawra* predicted the demise of Arab leaders who sided with the United States, because indignation over the Palestinian deaths "will sweep them away, even if they issue verbal condemnations of the crime."

On October 9, Saddam himself formally linked his war effort against the United States with the al-Aqsa riots. Iraq had developed a ballistic missile, Saddam announced, that was capable of striking both Israeli targets and U.S. forces deep inside Saudi Arabia. The new missile was named al-Hijara al-Sijjil—the Mighty Stone, in honor of the symbol of the Intifadah. "Al-Hijara became capable of reaching targets that are hundreds of kilometers from where it is launched," Saddam said, alluding to both the new ballistic missile and the Intifadah. "The faithful Palestinians faced up to you [Israel]," he declared, "with stones which no power on Earth can withhold from those who wish to use them. They are the Stones of the new missile, which the Iraqis have invented with the help of Almighty God and which can be launched from somewhere in the land of Iraq to reach the targets of evil when the day of reckoning comes." He repeated his demand for the withdrawal of all foreign forces from Arab lands. "There is no way out for you [Israelis] except to leave the land of Palestine and the sanctities of the Arabs, just as there is no way out for the armies of America and its allies except to leave the holy land of the Arabs and Muslims," Saddam warned. "There is room only for this; otherwise you will get what you will get."

Just as the news of the al-Aqsa riots reached Washington, the Bush administration was studying the reports of Primakov's discussions in Baghdad. However, in seeking guidance on the events in Jerusalem, Washington disregarded Primakov's findings, instead latching on to the rhetoric of Arab leaders. Cairo TV, for example, interrupted its regular programming to broadcast a statement by President Mubarak in which he described the riots as a spark that would envelop the region in flame and warned that the Israeli retaliation could lead to "grave consequences in the present critical circumstances." It did not matter to Washington, or perhaps it was not noticed, that the main reason Mubarak and other Arab leaders uttered such warnings was to placate enraged street mobs at home. And so the Bush administration echoed this rhetoric in its communications with the Israeli government. On October 15, Secretary Baker sent a letter to his Israeli counterpart, Foreign Minister David Levy, warning that "Israel, and not Iraq, will be the focus of world attention" unless Jerusalem accepted responsibility for the riots.

Whereas there should have been a clear separation between Iraq's naked aggression against Kuwait and close to a century of Jewish-Arab struggle over the future of Eretz-Yisrael/Palestine—and whereas the legitimate all-Muslim leaders, the House of al-Saud, were inclined to accept this separation—the Bush administration stepped into Saddam's trap and combined the two issues, thus legitimizing the core argument made by Saddam and Arafat. A decade later, American policy has yet to extricate itself from this trap. Furthermore, in terms of Arab understandings of honor, the leader of the world's greatest superpower had lowered himself to discuss issues at the level of the Arab world's pariah—a development incomprehensible to America's friends and foes alike.

———

THE AMERICAN REACTION to the al-Aqsa riots was neither unique nor intentionally anti-Israel. Washington kept making short-term compromises—some very painful—in order to feed the Moloch of a broad coalition united against Saddam. The next victims on the altar of the Gulf crisis would be the Christian Maronites of Lebanon.

Because Syria's participation in the coalition was of great importance to both the Saudis and the Egyptians, Washington remained unfazed by the statements of both Major General Ali Habibi, the commander of the Syrian forces in the Gulf, and Major General Muhammad Ali Bilal, his Egyptian counterpart, that their respective forces in Saudi Arabia "[would] not participate in any offensive." Within Syria itself there was a growing public clamor to join Iraq against the U.S.-led coalition. "The majority of the ordinary Syrians are sympathetic to Iraq," acknowledged an Iraqi opposition leader then in Damascus. "There is no acceptance of Syria and the US working together [against Saddam]." In early October, Washington rewarded Syria for remaining in the coalition by agreeing to the brutal Syrian occupation of Beirut.

On October 13, at 7:05 A.M. Beirut time, Syrian Su-22 fighter-bombers attacked the presidential palace and the Defense Ministry in East Beirut. Soon afterward, artillery manned by Syrians and opposition Lebanese opened a massive barrage on the government's strategic positions and the surrounding residential areas, inflicting heavy casualties on the predominantly Christian local population. Lebanon's president, General Michel Aoun, correctly concluded that the United States must have given the Syrians the green light to launch their air and artillery strikes; among other clues, the ever present Israeli Air Force was missing from the skies of Lebanon that morning. Realizing that Lebanon's struggle to free itself from Syrian occupation had been decided by Washington in favor of Damascus, Aoun left his bunker and headed for the French Embassy, where Ambassador René Ala was waiting for him with authorization for political asylum.

Meanwhile, Syrian special forces and their Lebanese allies—Elie Hobeika's predominantly Christian militia—started moving into East Beirut. By 10 A.M. it was all over. The commander of the Syrian advance unit, Captain Riad, contacted his chief, Brigadier Ali, to announce that he was in General Aoun's office, sitting at his desk. Nobody in Damascus had expected the Lebanese forces to collapse so quickly; the main Syrian armored and tank units had no instructions to move in before 3 P.M. In the meantime, the Syrian special forces and Hobeika's fighters roamed through the presidential palace complex, looting and pillaging. A few Lebanese units continued to resist, but they were overcome by massive artillery and rocket fire.

From the very beginning of the Gulf crisis, President Assad had invariably conditioned his participation in the coalition on Syria's being allowed to secure its hold over Lebanon. Washington had readily acquiesced, but the Shamir government had at first refused to abandon Israel's long-time Maronite allies. Cracks appeared in the Israeli resolve as a direct result of U.S. pressure over the al-Aqsa riots. Jerusalem could not endure Washington's coercion on all issues and promised not to interfere with the Syrian occupation of Beirut. It is noteworthy that the Syrian actions Israel was coerced into tolerating violated understandings that had been mediated and guaranteed by the United States in the mid-1980s.

The United States gained nothing from permitting the Syrian occupation. Syria's government-controlled media continued to herald the growing popular sentiment against the American presence in the Middle East. In early November, Radio Damascus reported that the Syrian government had reiterated its opposition to war with Iraq and urged that instead "there should be a pan-Arab

confrontation of that Zionist entity and its supporters [the United States]."
In Saudi Arabia, Syrian senior officers continued to declare that their forces
would not participate in any offensive operation against Iraq.

These sentiments were not limited to Damascus. In Cairo, several senior
officers told Mubarak privately that Egypt should support Saddam Hussein
against the United States. They warned that after the inevitable U.S. defeat,
Mubarak would be left as the pariah of a unified Arab world led by Saddam—
if, in fact, he was not assassinated like his predecessor, Anwar al-Sadat.

———

YEVGENY PRIMAKOV arrived in Washington on October 18, but the Bush
administration was still not prepared to listen to him. The main problem was
the administration's inability or unwillingness to honestly define the United
States' posture vis-à-vis the Muslim world. The administration was pursuing
America's legitimate interests—preventing Iraq from gaining control over too
large a segment of the region's oil resources—but it would not say so. Instead, it insisted that the United States was in the Persian Gulf to help its
Arab friends, Saudi Arabia and Kuwait. In late October, this charade exploded in Washington's face.

The leading Arab governments—including Riyadh, Cairo, and Damascus—
came up with a compromise with Baghdad that would have given Saddam
"an honorable way out of Kuwait." This all-Arab initiative was endorsed and
furthered by Moscow. Traveling to Damascus, Cairo, Riyadh, Baghdad, and
Tayif (where the Kuwaiti government in exile was located), Primakov obtained the Arab leaders' agreement to convene an informal summit that
would have led to Iraq's withdrawal from Kuwait but left Iraq in control of
major oil fields near the Kuwaiti-Iraqi border. Politically, this plan would
have undercut the U.S. posture in the region and would also have left Iraq in
control of more oil fields than Washington was willing to permit. Hence,
Washington scuttled it by putting irresistible pressure on the Saudi and
Kuwaiti leaders. For the Arabs, American intervention in their attempts to
prevent war constituted concrete proof that Washington was fighting for its
own control over the region's oil at their expense.

———

AT THIS POINT, there was a flare-up of Islamist militancy throughout the
Arab world, with Iraq skillfully feeding the flames. The indefatigable Sheikh
Tamimi led an Islamist campaign for the legitimization of Saddam, explain-
ing in a series of sermons that the Gulf crisis was only one manifestation of
a profound confrontation between Islam and the infidel West. "The West and
Israel . . . do not come to Saudi Arabia for the oil," Tamimi said. "The oil

reaches them from the Gulf states, and even Iraq did not declare that it would deny oil to the West. Thus, the West arrived in the region in order to prevent unity and the publicized spread of independent decision, so that Iraq remains subservient to the Western-Jewish influence. For this reason, we support Iraq, which is a legitimate obligation, and everyone who respects himself cannot accept a different position." He added that the Intifadah in the territories would continue until "the liberation armies arrive from Iraq to liberate Palestine."

Sheikh Tamimi then traveled to Baghdad and met with both political and religious leaders. When he returned to Jordan in mid-November, he proclaimed that "For the first and only time in this century, one of our Arab leaders is steadfastly standing up to and confronts the enemies of the Arabs—the Americans and the Israelis. . . . Saddam Hussein is the leader of [Islam's] triumph. He is the real Salah ad-Din [Saladin]." Sheikh Tamimi certified that Saddam's return to Islam was genuine and decreed that the Islamist community should give him its all-out support in his jihad. To demonstrate his own commitment, Sheikh Tamimi put the forces of the Islamic Jihad under Iraqi command.

The next step was challenging the legitimacy of the House of al-Saud as the custodians of the Holy Shrines. The negative themes—that the Saudis had permitted foreign forces on Arabian soil—had been hammered with great effectiveness ever since mid-August. Now the Iraqis added a positive theme: that the swallowing up of Kuwait was the first step in building a new all-Islamic empire. The theme was gradually refined into Islamist endorsement of the Iraqi commitment to resurrecting a single caliphate replacing the several Arab states.

The primary source of Islamist agitation within Saudi Arabia was Iraqi-supported Holy Mecca Radio. In short editorials sandwiched between popular Arab music, this clandestine, yet highly effective station, urged "the peoples of Hijaz and Najd"—Saudi Arabia's two main Sunni population groupings—to launch an Islamist uprising against the "al-Saud apostates" and the infidel forces contaminating the Holy Lands of Arabia. That autumn, these broadcasts were supplemented by tape cassettes and printed pamphlets taking the positions elucidated by the Saudi ulema in August one step further. By inviting the United States to send forces to Saudi Arabia, the Islamists argued, the House of al-Saud had *already* forfeited its right to guard Islam's Holy Shrines. The cassettes and pamphlets also contained instructions for building cells within Islamist communities and spreading the message. The mere exchanges of these forbidden items contributed to the creation of communal identity and commitment to the Islamist cause.

Even more important was the emergence of Islamist revolutionary agitation within the very centers of Islamic theology. An appeal to Saudi Arabia's

Western-educated youth was spearheaded by the intellectual elites of the Hijaz—that is, the academic communities in Mecca, Medina, and Jeddah. In the fall of 1990, these intellectuals combined their unchallengeable command of Islamic theology and comprehensive knowledge of world affairs into a unique bridge between the Western world and Islam.

The most effective member of this group was Safar al-Hawali, the dean of Islamic Studies at the Umm al-Qura University in Mecca. He argued that the essence of the Gulf crisis was "not the world against Iraq" but rather "the West against Islam." He used a combination of Islamic tenets and authoritative U.S. sources to prove the existence of a long-standing Western conspiracy to occupy the Arabian Peninsula and crush Islam. He also cited Islamic decrees stretching over a millennium to demonstrate that Muslims were never permitted to join with non-Muslims in battle, let alone when the intended war was against fellow Muslims. "If Iraq has occupied Kuwait," al-Hawali stated, "then America has occupied Saudi Arabia. The real enemy is not Iraq. It is the West." By this logic, there was no reprieve for the House of al-Saud, for it had facilitated the occupation of Saudi Arabia by U.S. forces and was now willing to join these infidel forces in attacking Muslim Iraq. This message, from al-Hawali and other Islamist intellectuals and preachers, was spread via cassettes all over Saudi Arabia. The Islamist arguments were cited in routine discussions with growing frequency—a clear reflection of their reach and popularity.

The United States was oblivious to these developments, but it couldn't help noticing the stream of defections from the Saudi and other Arab armed forces for Islamist reasons. Most remarkable was the mid-November defection of a Saudi F-15 pilot to Sudan. The U.S.-educated and -trained pilot explained that he had decided to defect because of "the Saudi regime's concessions of military command of foreign forces to the United States" and "the presence of American forces there." (High-level Saudi intelligence officers bearing a generous ransom visited Khartoum and brought the F-15 back.)

At the same time, Saudi Arabia was awash with pamphlets and cassettes aimed at the uneducated masses. These were crude and inflammatory, full of stories about the American forces committing murders, robberies, and rapes and engaging in generally indecent behavior. These pamphlets and cassettes stressed the intentional defamation of the Holy Lands of Islam by Westerners' wearing of Stars of David and crosses. As proof of the collapse of Islamic morality, they pointed to the "protest drive" by a few Western-educated Saudi women opposed to the ban on women driving. They warned of the coming punishment by Allah and urged the believers to throw out the infidels before it was too late. These pamphlets and cassettes were extremely popular—in the ranks of Saudi and other Arab military and support units as well as elsewhere.

THE COMBINED EFFECT of the Islamist propaganda and the hardened American policy was at once to embolden Saddam and to push him into a corner. He resolved that since the United States would block any negotiated settlement, Iraq should seize the military initiative. In early November, Baghdad officially announced that both Israel and Saudi Arabia would be attacked in retaliation for any use of force by the United States. "If war breaks out," Baghdad warned, "our counterattack will be destructive and will not be limited to the securing of our country's sovereignty. We shall expand the war and strike the aggressors and the dens of evil everywhere." Arafat quoted Saddam as vowing that "Iraq will aim its first missile against Israel and will use chemical and biological weapons if war breaks out in the Persian Gulf." President Bush's November 7 decision to dispatch more American troops to the region did not dampen Iraq's bellicosity. On the contrary, personnel changes in the Iraqi high command—specifically, the promotion of senior officers who had distinguished themselves in the great offensives of the Iran-Iraq War—reinforced the threat of an imminent offensive war.

The Iraqi military received a major boost, both professionally and in terms of morale, when the Egyptian General Saad al-Din al-Shazli visited Baghdad in mid-November. As the chief of staff during the Yom Kippur War, General Shazli had led the Egyptian Armed Forces in crossing the Suez Canal, breaching the Bar-Lev Line, and bringing the first major counteroffensive of the Israel Defense Force (IDF) to a halt. In Baghdad, General Shazli declared that he had come to help "the high combat capabilities of Iraq for defeating the Zionist-imperialist aggression," and he gave Iraqi senior officers valuable advice on confronting high-quality armored forces and coordinating large-scale offensive operations. The fact that Shazli is also a leader of the Sunni Islamist trend, and a firm believer that the salvation of the Arab world lies in Islamist revivalism and jihad, helped Saddam in his quest for Islamist legitimization.

As of late November, many signs indicated that Saddam was preparing for a major offensive around Christmas. The intelligence data included up-to-date material from a few high-level Iraqi defectors, particularly a general who had been in command of a brigade in Kuwait. According to these defectors, the Iraqi General Staff had recently concluded that a first strike from the United States would be extremely costly in lives and matériel and had therefore urged Saddam to attack preemptively. Iraq mobilized a quarter of a million reservists as the first step in converting the Iraqi presence in the Kuwaiti theater to an offensive posture. Meanwhile, the missile units in western and southern Iraq received their first targeting data against Saudi Arabia, and several armored, artillery, and air-defense units were deployed forward in the "offensive clusters" stipulated by Soviet military doctrine. Concurrently, emissaries from Baghdad were delivering instructions to Palestinian terrorist cells in Jordan, the territories, and Western Europe; and Jordanian military units began deploying to forward offensive dispositions very close to the Israeli border.

These developments caused a sharpening of the warnings by President Bush and Secretary Baker that the U.S.-led coalition would collapse the moment there was even a semblance of Israeli involvement in the war. Israel's ostracism was demonstrated vividly when both Baker and Bush avoided not only Israel, but even contacts with Israeli officials, during their comprehensive tours of the Middle East.

Jerusalem was all the more startled when, on his own initiative, U.S. Ambassador Bill Brown notified Defense Minister Moshe Arens that Iraq had just test-launched three ballistic missiles in an east-west trajectory, essentially demonstrating its ability to launch such missiles against Israel. Washington did not officially inform Israel of these tests even after U.S. officials leaked the story to Reuters. When Jerusalem finally requested the latest information about Iraqi missile activities, the Bush administration conditioned its response on ironclad guarantees that Israel would not operate against the launchers. In the end, even though Jerusalem provided such guarantees, Washington delivered nothing.

This grave situation prompted Prime Minister Shamir to visit Washington in early December. President Bush made every effort to make the visit successful, although he also sought to ensure that Israel would not deviate from the low profile and passive role allotted it by the White House. In private meetings with Shamir, Bush stressed the necessity of defeating Iraq through a coalition dominated by Arab states and warned that any Israeli move might provide these states with a "legitimate excuse" for withdrawing from the coalition—never mind that they had supposedly joined the coalition not to please the United States but to defend their own national interests against a common Iraqi threat. At the same time, Bush insisted that the war against Iraq would not come at the expense of the American security commitment to Israel. When the question of an Iraqi missile attack came up, Shamir promised that Israel would not launch a preemptive strike, although he insisted on retaining the right to retaliate if attacked.

As Christmas drew near, there were signs that Saddam had changed his mind about launching a preemptive strike against coalition forces. The first indication came in a statement he made to Spanish journalists: "Tel Aviv will be Iraq's first target if war breaks out in the Persian Gulf." The next day, senior Iraqi defense officials talked about the coming war in the context of responding to a coalition attack. Baghdad also stepped up its emphasis on the religious character of the war. "In this confrontation, there have been those who betrayed Jesus Christ and who betrayed the principles and values of Islam, one luring and leading the other," Saddam said in his New Year's Address. "May God curse them all." Religious Affairs Minister Abdullah Fadil declared that "Every Muslim will be a missile to be thrown against the enemy once he launches his armed aggression against Iraq."

On January 6—Iraq's Army Day—Saddam delivered a major speech in which he stated that Iraq's true battlefield was in Palestine. "What a great honor that you are united this time under the banner of the Mother of Battles," Saddam told his troops. "You are now prepared for a single historic battle after the return of the branch [Kuwait] to the trunk [Iraq]." The Mother of Battles "aims at liberating Palestine and the Golan Heights under the banner 'God is Great!'" Fighting together, the Iraqi Army and "the heroes of stones" had already "transformed the possibility of ousting the invaders into a tangible and visible reality."

Significantly, Yassir Arafat was in Baghdad for the Army Day celebrations. He delivered a bellicose speech to a rally of Palestinians who had volunteered to fight on Iraq's side, proclaiming that "If the US and its allies want to fight Iraq over Kuwait, then I say, 'Welcome, welcome, welcome to war.' Iraq and Palestine represent a common will. We will be together side by side, and after the great battle, God willing, we will pray together in Jerusalem."

The transformation of Saddam into a jihadist—a would-be martyr willing to sacrifice everything for the Palestinian-Islamist cause—was completed on January 11, when the Third Popular Islamic Conference convened in Baghdad. Some 500 Islamist scholars arrived from all over the world to demonstrate solidarity with Iraq. Saddam delivered an eloquent speech in which he marginalized the Kuwait issue. "If the Americans want this problem resolved, they must put Palestine first," he declared. "In fact, with or without settlement of the Gulf crisis, Palestine and Jerusalem must be liberated." His speech was interrupted by applause and vows to follow him in a jihad aimed at "defeating the infidels" all over the world.

Not surprisingly, the Bush administration failed to notice any of this as it readied itself for the last diplomatic confrontation between James Baker and Tariq Aziz in Geneva and, subsequently, the launching of the air war.

————

ON JANUARY 17, after the first cycle of U.S. air and missile strikes, Radio Baghdad returned to the air around 5:30 A.M. Baghdad time. At 7:15, Saddam addressed his people in a firm and defiant voice. He declared that the "fateful duel with the infidels" had begun and vowed that "the entire Arab Nation would fight to the end." He announced his intention of setting the world on fire, starting with Palestine, Lebanon, and the Golan Heights. He ended his speech with several traditional Islamic war cries deriving from the battles against the Crusaders.

Around noon, Saddam delivered another scorching speech. Last night, he said, "the treacherous forces and the Satan Bush" unleashed the long-predicted "mother of all battles." Saddam then vowed in the name of Islam to escalate the struggle between Islamic truth and Western evil. "Because the Iraqis are all sons of the Prophet, faithful and brave, they all bravely confront the enemies," he declared. Iraq's anticipated success would begin with the overthrow of "the Satan in the White House" and be followed by the demise of the Arab regimes supporting the coalition; the war would ultimately lead to "the eradication of criminal Tel Aviv." Consequently, "the Arab man will be liberated everywhere," and tranquility and peace will reach those who conducted the jihad and strove for victory.

And still the Bush administration could not bring itself to accept the centrality of the Palestinian issue to the Arab position. While American officials praised Jerusalem for its "restraint," the beginning of the air campaign against Baghdad confirmed Israel's fears. Within hours, eight Iraqi SCUDs had slammed into Israel—five in the Tel Aviv area and three in Haifa. That night, Saddam Hussein sent a written order to General Hazim Abd-al-Razzaq al-Ayyubi, commander of the Iraqi surface-to-surface missile corps, ordering him to commence operations: "Begin, with God's blessing, striking targets inside the criminal Zionist entity with the heaviest fire possible. . . . The strikes must be carried out with 'ordinary' conventional ammunition for missiles. The firing must continue until further notice."

The next day, January 18, the supreme leadership of the PLO sent a detailed letter to Fatah's most senior overseas activists. The letter aimed to give those activists confidence to pursue their instructions despite the general public impression of stunning successes in the U.S. air campaign against Iraq. Both the style and the air of authority in the letter indicate that Arafat wrote it himself. A copy was obtained by Israeli intelligence and immediately shared with the Bush administration. This was the first authoritative document Washington had seen outlining Iraq's war strategy.

According to the letter, the essence of this strategy was "to absorb the first strike" while concentrating on preparations for a decisive confrontation on the ground. "So far, the Iraqi air power has not joined the struggle because it remains sheltered underground," the letter explained. "As far as Iraq is concerned, the decisive phase has not yet begun, for the adjoining ground war is the heart of the struggle." Special attention was paid to Iraq's ballistic missiles: "As far as the Iraqi missiles are concerned, they are hidden and will not be activated until the decisive struggle, because otherwise they will be exposed to the danger of destruction. There is no danger that Iraq is losing its ability to operate the missiles available to it, because while most of the fixed launchers are dummy launchers, Iraq still has mobile launchers available and ready for action." The letter concluded with a statement of the PLO's own objectives in the war: "The Palestinian Liberation Organization, that warned from the very beginning that the situation in the Middle East would deteriorate as long as the Palestinian problem was not solved, emphasizes that a separate solution of the Gulf crisis, without a solution of the Palestinian problem, would not lead to peace and stability. . . . The PLO's offer to find a solution to all the region's problems was meant to achieve worldwide stability and peace. On the other hand, the American regime, uncertain as to its international legitimacy, chose war. . . ."

By this time, King Hussein had realized that an inevitable outcome of the promised Iraqi jihad for Jerusalem would be the swallowing up of Jordan by Arafat and Saddam. This awakening led him to resume secret contacts between Amman and Jerusalem, and on January 5, Prime Minister Shamir and King Hussein secretly met in London and reached an agreement on jointly tackling the coming war. The king pledged to prevent Iraqi use of Jordanian airspace (except by ballistic missiles, which he could do nothing about) and territory against Israel in return for an Israeli pledge not to initiate an anti-Jordanian campaign in case of an Iraqi-Palestinian offensive. Shamir also asked the king to deliver a clear warning to Saddam that any use of weapons of mass destruction would elicit "special retaliation." The two leaders commiserated with each other about the Bush administration's insensitivity to the region's undercurrents.

Israel's fears about weapons of mass destruction were entirely justified, as the then chief of Iraqi military intelligence, General Wafiq Samarrai, acknowledged after his defection: "Some of the SCUD missiles were loaded with chemical warheads. They were kept hidden throughout the war." Alluding to the threat delivered via King Hussein, he explained that "We didn't use them because the other side had a deterrent force."

Altogether, the Iraqis launched between thirty-nine and forty-three SCUDs (actually, modified al-Hussein missiles) in a total of seventeen attacks. These attacks spanned thirty-nine days (from January 18 to February 25) out of the forty-three days of the Gulf War (January 17 to February 28). Seven of the attacks resulted in casualties.

———

SADDAM HAD MADE the ballistic missile a status symbol, a measure of his regional importance. The turning point in the missile war came when Riyadh decided that Iraq's launching of ballistic missiles was indeed an expression of strategic importance and no longer just the action of a pariah state. With the war being characterized as a U.S.-dominated air campaign, the Saudi King and his defense minister, his brother Prince Sultan (Prince Bandar's father), decided that it was imperative for their country to demonstrate its own strategic capabilities.

Saudi Arabia's ballistic missiles came from China. In the mid-1980s, the Pakistanis had undertaken a persistent diplomatic effort to push Saudi Arabia and the People's Republic of China (PRC) into closer cooperation. A major development took place in 1988, when representatives of the PRC, meeting with Prince Bandar in Islamabad, agreed to sell Saudi Arabia various sophisticated items, including DF-3A (CSS-2) ballistic missiles and HY-2 (Silkworm) missiles. The Saudis were impressed by the performance and discretion of the Chinese advisers. These contacts culminated in the decision to establish diplomatic relations between Riyadh and Beijing in July 1990.

When King Fahd and Prince Sultan personally decided that it was imperative for Saudi Arabia to have strategic capabilities, they called on Beijing. On January 9, thirty-five Chinese military experts arrived in Riyadh to activate the DF-3As and prepare them for launch. After the first four Iraqi SCUDs fell near Riyadh on the night of January 20–21, the king decreed that Saudi Arabia must retaliate in kind. Soon afterward, the Chinese teams launched three DF-3As with HE warheads toward Iraqi oil refineries. The Saudis originally wanted to launch unconventional warheads but were discouraged from doing so; thus, little or no damage was done, but the Royal honor was restored.

For Jerusalem, the Saudi exercise meant trouble ahead. Israeli intelligence knew about the Saudis' plans, and once the retaliatory launch took place, they feared escalation of the Iraqis' missile offensive. Most alarming was the possibility that if Iraqi intelligence learned of the Saudi desire to use unconventional warheads, Saddam might decide to retaliate as if such warheads had really been used. Moreover, Jerusalem had doubts about Amman's ability to enforce the January 5 agreement, for Iraqi missile launchers and supply vehicles were now being sheltered in Jordan during the daytime and deployed to launch positions in western Iraq after nightfall. Hence, Jerusalem decided that it was necessary to tackle the Iraqi missile threat directly by deploying a large number of special forces, along with appropriate air cover, into western Iraq to hunt down the Iraqi launchers.

However, in order to minimize conflict with the January 5 agreement, Moshe Arens called Dick Cheney and asked for the United States to arrange for an aerial corridor over Saudi Arabia that would enable the Israeli Air Force to reach western Iraq without violating Jordanian airspace. Cheney would not commit to arranging for the air corridor, but indicated that the United States would not stand in Israel's way. "If you operate there, we will simply leave the area west of 42 degrees longitude," he told Arens. Arens interpreted the comment as an indication that Cheney "had reconciled himself to an Israeli operation against the launching sites." Jerusalem's relief did not last long. That same day, Bush transmitted a message to Shamir via Deputy Secretary of State Lawrence Eagleburger urging, perhaps even warning, Jerusalem not to strike Iraq and promising that the coalition would make every effort to seek and destroy the Iraqi launchers. (Jerusalem would learn long after the war that the administration had decided that if Israel attacked after all, U.S. forces would vacate the area in accordance with the Cheney-Arens understanding. Jerusalem was not notified at the time, however, lest this decision give it an "incentive" to intervene.) "Keeping Israel out of the war" had become the mantra of Western politicians, even though the key Arab coalition members made no such demand. Toward the middle of the war, when the coalition victory was certain, some Arab leaders—even Syrian Foreign Minister Faruk al-Shara—reassured foreign diplomats of their ability to tolerate Israeli action.

Following President Bush's promise, the coalition allocated virtually the entire British Special Air Services to "SCUD hunting." This proved to be an exercise in futility. Despite the heroic efforts of the men in uniform, not a single launcher was hit, let alone destroyed, and not a single launch was prevented. "We heard that the commander of the enemy coalition declared that the U.S. Air Force destroyed all our mobile launchers," General al-Ayyubi wrote in his wartime diary. "What launchers could they be talking about? Even the decoy launchers were not touched. Not a single launcher, equipment, or missile from al-Hussein Force was hit throughout the battle." Simply put, the coalition had no clue how or where to search for the Iraqi missiles.

Furthermore, the coalition's effort in western Iraq largely ignored the ten-division-strong al-Quds Corps, earmarked for the war with Israel. The Corps—not touched during the war in the Kuwaiti theater—included 1,500 pieces of artillery (out of Iraq's total of 4,500), 2,000 tanks (out of 6,000), 200 combat aircraft (out of 705), and 50 ballistic-missile launchers (out of 60 to 100). In late January, intelligence from Palestinian and Jordanian sources revealed that Baghdad had decided to divert additional forces westward rather than risk losing them to coalition bombing. In discreet contacts with Jerusalem, Amman acknowledged that the Iraqi force buildup might reach a point where Israel would have no option but to attack despite the January 5 agreement. Still, American pressure on Jerusalem—including threats to withdraw U.S. Patriot batteries deployed to defend Israel—persisted.

Toward the end of the war, the Iraqis launched two SCUDs against Dimona, where Israel's nuclear reactor is located. General al-Ayyubi wrote that "The rocket attack was meant to avenge the Zionist strike at the Iraqi Tammuz Nuclear Reactor [in 1981] and the children of the Intifadah and the children who were killed in the bombing of al-Amiriyah Shelter [in Baghdad] by the murderous aggressors." In fact, the two SCUDs landed harmlessly in the desert. Their warheads proved to be made of concrete and metal; Israeli intelligence officials assumed they were "a primitive model of a biological warhead," where the concrete was "used to protect the bugs inside." Another interpretation was that the Iraqis hoped that the heavy concrete blocks would crack the dome of the reactor on impact, thus releasing radioactive pollution into the air. Either way, that strike—launched on February 25—was clearly designed to draw Israel into direct involvement in the fighting. By now, however, with the war on the verge of conclusion, Shamir assured Bush that Israel would not retaliate unless something uniquely horrible happened.

ALTHOUGH THE BARRAGES of ballistic missiles failed to provoke Israel into joining the war, they had a tremendous impact on the Arab world and, consequently, on Saddam's handling of the closing days of the war. In northeastern Saudi Arabia, near the Kuwaiti border, Egyptian soldiers cried "Allah-hu-Akbar!" and shot into the air enthusiastically when the radio reported the first missile attacks on "the Zionist entity." It took their officers some time to calm them down and remind them that they were at war against the same Iraq. The Palestinians also reacted enthusiastically; throughout the territories people were dancing on the roofs, waiting to see the fiery trails of the SCUDs plummeting toward the Israeli coastal plain. Ultimately, because of his steadfast commitment to Arafat, Saddam remained a legitimate leader in the eyes of the Arab world.

Against this background Primakov visited Baghdad from February 11 to 13 to warn Saddam of the impending ground war and discuss ways to save his country. On February 13, Primakov publicly endorsed Iraq's claims of indiscriminate and intentional allied bombing of civilians. Then, upon returning to Moscow, Primakov reported that his negotiations "offered a glimmer of hope" for an Iraqi withdrawal. This report was designed to stall the coalition's ground offensive, buying Saddam time to position himself as the leader who could best further the all-Arab Islamist cause. The seemingly futile missile launches against Israel were in fact powerful symbolic gestures in this effort.

Saddam started this campaign with a Revolutionary Command Council communiqué on February 15 presenting the Gulf War in pan-Arab terms and declaring victory. Baghdad went to war, the communiqué explained, in order to demolish a U.S.-Israeli conspiracy to prevent Arabs from taking "the natural place they deserve in the world because of their glorious history and great contribution to human civilization." Thus, Iraq had been subjected to intensive bombing solely because of its commitment to the all-Arab cause. But heavy though the destruction had been, "Iraq triumphed in this confrontation. It triumphed because it remained solid, courageous, faithful, dignified, and strong-willed. It triumphed because it upheld the spiritual principles and values emanating from its true religion and rich heritage."

The next day, Radio Baghdad broadcast another communiqué declaring that the Gulf War confirmed Saddam's "historic-divine" posture: "It is not strange for the enemies to begin admitting, and for friends to start asserting, that the leader Saddam Hussein is a pan-Arab hero and one of the Arab nation's historic and exceptional heroes." By initiating the crisis and waging the ensuing war, Saddam was attempting to undo the whole history of injustice perpetrated upon the entire Arab nation by the West since the collapse of the Ottoman Empire. He had thus proved himself as "an Arab hero and a model of the true Islamic leader."

On February 22, Saddam acknowledged that pursuing the war would lead to heavy casualties. He stated that the effects of the allied bombings "dwarf[ed]" the destruction of Mesopotamia by Hulegu, Genghis Khan's grandson. He then stressed that just as Iraq had recovered from the Mongol onslaught, it would recover from the current devastation. He expressed no remorse for the suffering of his people, presenting it instead as a fair price for realizing the historical destiny of the Arab world.

ON FEBRUARY 24, the coalition's ground forces launched a major offensive, devastating the Iraqi Army, liberating a burning Kuwait, and occupying a sizable chunk of southern Iraq. In less than four days, Baghdad sued for a cease-fire on the basis of President Bush's conditions.

The ground offensive was launched even though Saddam had again reiterated his willingness to withdraw from Kuwait, this time with the Soviet Union guaranteeing implementation. Whether Saddam was trying yet another ploy or was serious this time—as Primakov insists—is largely irrelevant. Of crucial importance for the real outcome of the war was the flow of Iraqi refugees and deserters back to the population centers, bringing with them tales of the carnage and devastation at the front. CNN and other electronic media throughout the Arab world also broadcast vivid images of destruction. These scenes of horror highlighted the Islamist claim of American insensitivity, manifested in senseless destruction of the innocent as well as the guilty.

When, in March, the Shiites and Kurds of Iraq rose up against Saddam, having been encouraged to do so by President Bush, they were abandoned by the West and endured ruthless suppression by Saddam's army. One reason the United States failed to come to their aid is that the Saudi rulers urgently explained that their own Shiite community would rise up against them if their Iraqi cousins triumphed against Baghdad. A Shiite uprising would have destroyed Saudi Arabia's stability and territorial integrity—negating one of the principal reasons for America's intervention in the Persian Gulf.

Thus, while the Western-led coalition had triumphed militarily, the Islamists had their proof that Saddam was right after all: The Muslim world cannot deal with the United States. However, given Saddam's own sins against the Shiites, he and his ilk—the advocates of revolutionary Arabism—were also deemed unworthy as rulers of Muslims. The Arab street turned to radical Islam—the driving force behind political Islamism—as the sole viable solution to the plight of a shocked and devastated Arab world.

———

ONCE AGAIN, Washington was oblivious, even as America's arrogant behavior was helping to strengthen the Islamist cause. U.S. troops were making no move to withdraw from the sacred Arabian soil, despite the much-heralded original commitments. U.S. media aggravated the situation. For example, American TV news showed the whole world American soldiers in Saudi Arabia eating bacon—in Muslim eyes, a sacrilege. This both alienated America's closest Muslim allies and tarnished their leaders' Islamic credentials. As Ayatollah Khamenei summed it up, "The Americans have cheated themselves in this war. Everybody hates them now."

The United States was also pushing the Saudis and the Gulf states to pay billions of dollars to defray the costs of the war and to commit to huge weapons deals with American companies—this despite Saudi Arabia's own economic difficulties and its need to engage in domestic economic development in order to alleviate the building grassroots pressure from the Islamists. Across the Red Sea, Mubarak too was facing mounting problems—ranging from a growing Islamist opposition that conducted a wave of terrorist activities during the Gulf crisis to a worsening of Egypt's endemic economic woes.

The Bush administration determined that the optimal way to deal with all these problems—and to prove that the Gulf War was not anti-Arab, the prevalent sentiment by now throughout the Muslim world—was by reviving the Arab-Israeli "peace process." In early March, in the course of his victory speech to a joint session of Congress, President Bush declared that the time was ripe to move with "vigor and determination" toward closing "the gap between Israel and the Arab states and between Israelis and Palestinians" by eliciting major territorial concessions from Israel. "A comprehensive peace must be grounded in UN Security Council Resolutions 242 and 338 and the principle of territory for peace. This principle must be elaborated to provide for Israel's security and recognition, and at the same time for legitimate Palestinian rights. Anything else," Bush declared, "would fail the twin tests of fairness and security."

This initiative did not gain the support Washington expected from its Arab coalition allies. While all sides declared their commitment to the American "peace initiative," the Arabs would not commit to reconciliation with Israel and insisted on yet more unilateral concessions by Jerusalem. When Shamir refused to commit to such concessions, Bush went on the attack. In early September, he asked Congress for a 120-day postponement in dealing with Israel's request for American loan guarantees so that Israel could borrow commercially, but at favorable rates, $10 billion urgently needed to settle the flow of refugees from the Soviet Union and Ethiopia.

On September 12, about a thousand American Jews came to Capitol Hill to urge their representatives to approve the loan guarantees. A visibly angry George Bush called a press conference in which he accused Israel's supporters of endangering his Middle East policy. Pounding his fist on the lectern, the President declared that "A debate [on the Israeli request] now could well destroy our ability to bring one or more of the parties to the peace table. . . . We are up against some powerful political forces," he continued, ". . . very strong and effective groups that go up to the Hill. . . . We've only got one lonely little guy down here, [but] I am going to fight for what I believe." The President suggested he was putting his own political future on the line in order to do what was right for America: "The question isn't whether it's good 1992 politics. What's important here is that we give this [peace] process a chance. And I don't care if I only get one vote. . . . I believe the American people will be with me."

Bush then reinterpreted the U.S.-Israeli dynamics during the Gulf War. It was not that Israel had had to endure Iraqi missile attacks without retaliating in order to enable the United States to sustain a fragile Arab coalition protecting U.S. and European national interests. Instead, according to Bush, the United States had cajoled its Arab allies into confronting Iraq in order to save Israel. "Just months ago," Bush argued, "American men and women in uniform risked their lives to defend Israelis in the face of Iraqi SCUD missiles, and indeed Desert Storm, while winning a war against aggression, also achieved the defeat of Israel's most dangerous adversary." On top of everything else, Bush continued, the United States now had to subsidize an ungrateful Israel: During the current fiscal year, "despite our own economic worries," the United States had given Israel more than $4 billion in aid, which meant "nearly one thousand dollars for each Israeli man, woman, and child." In return, Bush was essentially saying, Israel had a duty to do what it could to enhance the United States' position in an increasingly hostile Muslim world.

————

EVENTUALLY ISRAEL went along and entered the "peace process," with great trepidation and some hopes. On the one hand, the declared positions of the Bush administration did not bode well. On the other hand, Jerusalem hoped that the new American hegemony could be used to break the Arab taboo vis-à-vis Israel and open the door for meaningful contacts.

The first venue was a comprehensive Middle East peace conference, co-sponsored by the United States and the (by now tottering) Soviet Union, to be convened in Madrid in October. Once the United States agreed to a joint Jordanian-Palestinian delegation at Madrid, Israel sought to use the conference as a mechanism for reviving real negotiations with the indigenous local leadership in the territories, which it had begun in cooperation with Amman in 1989. Jerusalem believed that with Arafat and the PLO delegitimized because of their support for Saddam, the United States would finally agree to alternative representation of the Palestinians. The Jordanians, for so long victims of PLO conspiracies, echoed the Israeli request. Saudi Arabia and Kuwait also signaled their hostility to the PLO. Still, the Bush administration insisted that the Palestinians would be represented by delegates affiliated with Arafat and the PLO.

In retrospect, the great spectacle of the Madrid conference amounted to the last hurrah of the old regional order that Bush had ostensibly saved in the Gulf War—the preeminence of Arabism in the Middle East. By mid-1991, this regional order was already gone. Thus, although the West and the pro-Western Arab governments won the battle over Kuwait, they in fact suffered a tremendous strategic defeat. Buoyed by Saddam's defiance, anti-American Islamism had become the dominant trend in the Muslim world, with unprecedented levels of grassroots support. However, it was Iran, rather than the beleaguered Iraq, that emerged out of the crisis as the driving force of the new Middle East. Although Iran's real struggle was against the Pax Americana, its primary and inescapable means was the ever popular quest for war against Israel.

4

The World War That Almost Was (1990–1993)

Tehran's Call to Arms and the Creation of the Islamic Bloc

WHILE IRAN EMERGED from the Gulf War resurgent, the Arab Middle East was in a state of communal shock. Not only had Saddam Hussein failed to achieve the long-overdue revival of Islamic glory, but the crisis he had instigated had also compelled the other Arab regimes to acknowledge their dependence on the hated United States. Ordinary Arabs were left wavering between resignation toward Western supremacy and a desire to relieve, through a wave of avenging terrorism, the burning shame left by the deployment of half a million "Crusader troops" on the sacred Arabian Peninsula.

In political terms, the Gulf crisis had brought to the fore the dichotomy between the world order imposed by the Western powers after the First World War (political ideologies derived from Judeo-Christian values and applied in the context of nation-states) and the grassroots longing for a return to a single Islamic Nation. Even the most pro-Western officials considered the defeat of Iraq to be the beginning of the real war—a war, as Egyptian diplomat Tahseen Bashir put it, "between moderates and extremists for the control of the Arab world." Bashir predicted further problems: "Unless there is new democracy and a new covenant between rich and poor, there will be a vacuum, and it will be filled by the next Saddam Hussein." The disputes he foresaw were not between nations but within nations. All the Arab governments were, and still are, dictatorial regimes ruling their subjects by force of arms, economic dominance, or both. Gradually, the deprived and oppressed Arab masses had started to see salvation in the fold of extremist Islam. By the early 1990s, no Arab leader, regardless of the might of his instruments of oppression, could hold on to power without taking this into consideration.

IN THE EARLY PHASES of the Gulf crisis, Tehran, Damascus, and their protégés saw a golden opportunity to direct the building rage among the Arab masses toward the establishment of "a new Muslim world order" under their hegemony. In an interview with the Iranian newspaper *Kayhan International* on December 22, 1990, HizbAllah leader Hussein al-Mussawi set forth the Islamists' aspirations: "We hope that the Islamic Republic [of Iran] with the cooperation of Syria and Muslims in Lebanon and Palestine, as well as all Muslims throughout the world, will be able to establish an Islamic world order. This can prevent the U.S. from imposing its power and order on Muslims. In this regard we hope that all Muslims cooperate with Iran, because Imam Khomeini's path is still continuing. This path is being continued by the leader of the Islamic Revolution, Ayatollah Khamenei. We hope the Muslims will be able to stand up against their enemies."

In early 1991, as the U.S.-led coalition was still fighting Iraq, the Syrians and the Iranians were preparing for the new, post-crisis Middle East. They envisioned nothing less than the consolidation, under their own Shiite-Allawite leadership, of an anti-American Islamic Bloc stretching from Lebanon to Pakistan. They would strive to justify their claim to leadership by orchestrating the onslaught on Israel that Saddam and Arafat had failed to deliver.

While still supporting Saddam's audacious political moves, Moscow began assisting the rise of this fledgling Syrian-Iranian bloc. In early February—even as Syrian military units were deployed in Saudi Arabia as part of the U.S.-led coalition—General Mustafa Tlass, the Syrian defense minister, visited Moscow and met with the senior members of the Soviet high command. Syria would receive huge sums of hard currency from the Gulf states for its participation in the coalition, and Tlass planned a massive weapons-acquisition program. The Soviets were most encouraging. They promised the Syrians new ballistic missiles capable of breaching the Patriot batteries the United States had provided Israel; they also promised the latest aircraft and aerial munitions, including smart bombs. While in Moscow, General Tlass gave the Soviet high command a detailed assessment of the Western weapon systems deployed in Saudi Arabia.

Meanwhile, Tehran took advantage of the world's preoccupation with Iraq to reorganize its own armed forces so that it could be a major postwar player. In essence, the Islamic Revolutionary Guards Corps (IRGC) were integrated with the regular armed forces, which were based on the Shah's old forces. The integration would begin at the command level and in logistics support, with the goal being to make the IRGC the dominant element in Iran's new military system. On February 18, 1991, Khamenei duly promoted twenty-eight senior IRGC commanders to the rank of brigadier or major general and placed them in posts previously reserved for Army personnel.

The IRGC's dominance in the reorganized armed forces formalized the new strategic posture Iran had been developing for a decade. The expertise behind Iran's military ascent was Soviet, as were Iran's primary weapon systems—including T-72 tanks, MiG-29 fighter aircraft, and SA-6 surface-to-air missiles. During the Iran-Iraq War, all these new weapons had been absorbed by IRGC units, while the army attempted to preserve its Western weapon systems and methods. Now Tehran announced its intention of acquiring additional high-performance combat aircraft, tanks, heavy artillery, armored fighting vehicles, and a comprehensive air-defense system from the Soviet Union. The Commander of the newly integrated navy, former Revolutionary Guards Minister Ali Shamkhani, stated that he expected to be acquiring submarines, new aircraft, and anti-ship missiles "from both Eastern and Western countries."

This military buildup was taking place in the context of high-level political exchanges between Damascus and Tehran on the details of their new strategic posture. They were also considering what to do about Iraq—an inescapable issue, since Iraq separates the two countries geographically.

Once the Gulf War ended, they moved quickly, with Syrian President Hafez al-Assad and Iranian Vice President Hassan Habibi formalizing the alliance on March 7 in a two-hour meeting in Damascus. Also present in Damascus were representatives of seventeen factions of the Iraqi opposition, including Shiites, Kurds, Communists, and nationalists. Senior Syrian and Iranian delegations met with these opposition leaders to help them form a single coalition to "coordinate and begin action immediately." According to an Iraqi opposition source, Saudi officials also attended one of these meetings, seeking and receiving Syrian and Iranian guarantees that there would be no "new Khomeini" in Iraq. The source clarified the Iranian assurances, explaining that Habibi's meeting with both secular and religious Iraqi opposition figures "proves that Iran has no intentions of establishing an Islamic republic in Iraq . . . that it respects the will and freedom of the Iraqi people to choose a successor for Saddam."

On March 8, Hashemi-Rafsanjani delivered the key Friday sermon in Tehran, warning Baghdad against any attempt to crush the Shiite popular uprising in southern Iraq. "If the Baathists do not listen to the voice of the people," he declared, "it will be their last mistake." However, he added, "If the Baathists surrender to the will of the people, we in Iran are ready for cooperation." Also on March 8, Syrian Vice President Abdul-Halim Khaddam delivered a speech in Damascus, in which he ridiculed Saddam for waging war on his own people using planes he had not dared to use against the coalition:

"We wondered why the Iraqi warplanes were banned from defending the Iraqi airspace and were sent outside Iraq during the war. . . . They are now bombarding Iraq and the Iraqis." Khaddam concluded by mocking Saddam's boasts: "And where is the mother of all battles now? Where is the great duel? This tyrant, who turned into a meek, peaceful lamb and stopped the fighting and made all those concessions . . . has once again turned into a tyrant to achieve the mother of all battles . . . in Iraq and against the Iraqi people."

Many Iranians were eager to assist the Shiite revolt in Iraq, especially as Saddam's Republican Guard began devastating the Shiite holy shrines in Najaf and Qarbala. The crisis peaked in mid-March, when the Grand Ayatollah Abul-Qassim al-Khoi—one of the most senior Shiite religious leaders in the world—issued a *fatwa* against Saddam. The fatwa decreed that anyone killed fighting Baghdad's troops was a martyr and thus assured a place in heaven. The fatwa also declared Saddam and his henchmen to be apostates, which meant that a Muslim was permitted to shed their blood. There can be no greater denunciation in Islam and no stronger call for an all-out rebellion. Baghdad reacted with fury, intensifying the assault on Najaf. However, Tehran prudently did nothing except issue protests.

On March 21, Grand Ayatollah Khoi, his son Mohammad Taqi, and a number of close associates were arrested in Najaf and taken to Baghdad. Khoi was shown on television meeting with Saddam and expressing his support for the violent suppression of the revolt. According to the Iraqi News Agency, Khoi declared that it was Allah's will that "enabled President Saddam Hussein to stamp out the sedition." From Tehran, Ayatollah Khamenei reacted swiftly: "The mercenary regime of Iraq has forcibly taken the Grand Ayatollah Abul-Qassim al-Khoi . . . and shamed him." Khamenei ordered a thorough investigation by Iranian intelligence and vowed retribution against the guilty parties.

Thus Iran laid the groundwork for direct intervention on behalf of the Iraqi Shiites. Large Iranian forces—about twenty divisions—began moving toward the Iraqi border. Tehran also deployed some 20,000 to 30,000 non-Iranian Shiite troops, mainly recruited from among Iraqi POWs and refugees. However, while the troops prepared, Tehran agonized. Several senior clerics were convened in Qom—the bastion of Iranian and Shiite commitment to pan-Islamist responsibility—and, after lengthy discussions, announced "Iran's support for the uprising of the Iraqi Muslim nation." By March 27, Iraqi forces, using tanks, helicopters, and heavy artillery, had recaptured every major city in southern Iraq. And still Iran did not intervene. In the end, Tehran decided it would rather have a stable—albeit ruthless and anti-Shiite—government in Baghdad than chaos and fratricidal violence.

Tehran quietly notified Saddam that Iran was prepared to help sustain his regime if Iraq would join the Iranian-Syrian axis.

———

IRAQ WAS at that time the only missing link in the Islamic Bloc stretching from Lebanon to Pakistan. Lebanon itself was under Syrian occupation in every respect short of a formal declaration. Jordan, too, was part of the bloc: Having committed his country to supporting Iraq, King Hussein had alienated the Saudi royal family and thus had no alternative but to slide under Syrian hegemony. To the east, Tehran had negotiated a myriad of strategic agreements with Pakistan—including Iranian subsidies for some of Pakistan's strategic-weapon programs and joint Iranian-Pakistani support for the Afghan mujahideen who had been fighting the pro-Soviet regime in Kabul. Now, a high-level Iranian delegation led by the speaker of the Majlis (National Assembly), Mehdi Karrubi, visited Islamabad to finalize agreements on military and defense policy, economic and technological cooperation, and foreign policy. Tehran went out of its way to praise the "Islamicness" of the Pakistani government, which was facing a growing Islamist challenge in the wake of the Gulf crisis.

The leaders of Saudi Arabia, Kuwait, and the other Gulf sheikhdoms and emirates were content to see Iran and Syria consolidate their axis as the key to containing and stabilizing Iraq and thus preventing a Khomeini-type popular Islamist revolt among their own oppressed Shiite populations. As had been the case for more than a generation, Riyadh and Kuwait remained convinced that they could buy stability by paying off Damascus and Tehran with money and strategic appeasement. That the new regional bloc sought to establish its Islamic legitimacy by reviving the confrontation with Israel bothered no one. After all, the lowest common denominator holding the Arab world together was the commitment to the destruction of Israel.

———

SYRIA'S DE FACTO annexation of Lebanon—which, as a Lebanese intellectual put it, was "only slightly more subtle than the takeover by Iraq of Kuwait"—had badly undercut whatever morality the Bush administration could claim at the beginning of its intervention in the Persian Gulf. The annexation, he continued, "was viewed as the West's reward to Syria for its role in the Gulf War alliance." Moreover, in completing its move, Damascus had crossed several "red lines" agreed upon with the United States and Israel. From this, Middle Eastern leaders learned that given the right political climate, Washington would look the other way.

When, during one of his many trips to the region, Secretary Baker announced the upcoming Madrid conference, all the Arab governments agreed to participate, not because they had suddenly decided to make peace with Israel, but because of overwhelming considerations in their bilateral relations with the United States. The Arab leaders were desperately trying to maneuver between near-term objectives vis-à-vis Washington and the building threat of an Islamic revolution among their people. Nassir Nashashibi, a Palestinian and one of the most sophisticated elder statesmen of the Arab world, explicated this dilemma: "Can Assad afford a peace arrangement with Israel? In my estimation—yes, in the near term, and no with a capital N in the further future. What do I mean? Peace between Israel and Syria, if attained, will be able to hold only for a brief period. I am willing to bet that the peace with Egypt will not be able to hold beyond the next five to ten years. The warning lights are already blinking: There is no real normalization. There are foci of objection and resistance. Peace will end in the wake of a massive uprising of the reactionaries that will incite the masses to pour into the streets, burn public buildings, empty the weapon storage-sites."

Even Khaled Maeena, the editor of the Saudi government's *Arab News*, acknowledged the emerging Islamist threat, although he added that "right now the pot is bubbling, not [yet] boiling."

———

MEANWHILE, the Palestinian movement, tarnished by Arafat's cooperation with Saddam during the Gulf War, needed rehabilitation if it were going to help further the Iranian-Syrian strategy. Hafez al-Assad provided the driving force behind this maneuver. Having been identified as a prominent sponsor of international terrorism and determined to establish a new moderate image, he set out to take over the PLO. The idea was to leave Arafat as a figurehead so that future terrorist operations would be attributed to him and not to Assad. Arafat went along with the plan, if only because, besieged by the rivalries within the PLO, he feared that the alternative was a purge. In May 1991, Faruk Kaddoumi visited Damascus on Arafat's behalf to negotiate the conditions under which Assad would tolerate Arafat's continued "leadership" of the PLO.

The Assad-Arafat arrangement soon took effect. In mid-June, Hakam Balawi, the head of Arafat's office in Tunis, chaired a meeting there of senior commanders of Fatah, the Fatah Revolutionary Council, and other Palestinian terrorist organizations. "On Arafat's personal orders," explained the newspaper *Sawt al-Kuwayt al-Duwali*, "they decided that the return to terrorism and violence was unavoidable in order to draw the world's attention to the PLO again."

Soon afterward, George Habbash of the Popular Front for the Liberation of Palestine, an Assad loyalist who had maintained close relations with Iraq during the Gulf crisis, held meetings with Saddam in Baghdad to discuss the emerging course of the terrorist struggle. These negotiations culminated in a secret agreement between Saddam and Arafat to transfer some 10,000 PLO fighters to Iraq to bolster a special force formed by Iraqi intelligence, which included commandos of the Iraqi Republican Guard as well as Palestinian, Yemeni, Sudanese, Jordanian, and other Arab terrorists. This special force was intended to protect Saddam and his family in case of an all-out popular revolt.

In early July, the PLO escalated its terrorist warnings. Muhammad Milhim of the PLO Executive Committee issued a statement in which he warned "the United States and the European countries" that unless a comprehensive solution to the Palestinian problem was found, "the next year would be a black one." He emphasized that in "giving peace a final chance," the PLO was insisting on world recognition as the full and sole representative of the Palestinian people. If these conditions were not met immediately, "a new action strategy [would] be adopted based on the military option for as long as the Zionist enemy continues to occupy our land."

On July 3, near the IDF's Mount Hermon stronghold, a squad belonging to the Democratic Front for the Liberation of Palestine ambushed a group of Israeli soldiers, killing one. This DFLP ambush had special significance because the perpetrators came from, and withdrew to, Syria in a path that passed through several Syrian military dispositions. The DFLP could not have conducted this operation without direct support from the Syrian armed forces. Damascus thus delivered a clear message that an escalation of terrorism was possible and that the key to such an escalation was in Assad's hands.

———

DURING THE SPRING and early summer of 1991, as the Soviet Union was wobbling toward its demise, the anti-U.S. strategic mantle passed to an informal grouping of rogue states—the People's Republic of China, the Democratic People's Republic of Korea (North Korea), the Islamic Republic of Pakistan, and the Islamic Republic of Iran. All aspirant powers, they were alarmed by the demonstration of American military might, resolve, and technological expertise in the war against Iraq. However, with time, these regimes jointly reached more realistic conclusions about the lessons of the Gulf War.

1. Since the United States will not tolerate regional powers that are not its puppets, there is no alternative to military confrontation—whether conventional or in the form of terrorism, subversion, and other unconventional modes of warfare.

2. It is possible—as demonstrated in a thorough survey by Chinese, North Korean, and Iranian experts of the damage sustained by Iraq—to fortify and conceal vital installations against attacks by the latest American non-nuclear weapons.

3. The United States would not have intervened to save Kuwait from a nuclear Iraq. As one source put it, "Had Saddam had nuclear weapons, Kuwaiti kids would still be singing his praises." Hence, all aspirant powers needed to acquire nuclear weapons to deter American intervention.

Since the summer of 1991, these three tenets have dominated the grand strategy of the rogue states.

———

FOR IRAN, the new strategic posture did not come as a sudden reaction to the Gulf crisis. By October 1989, the Institute of Strategic Studies, under Hojjat-ol-Islam Mussavi-Khoiniha, had been ordered to assess Iran's strategic requirements and formulate a long-term strategy. The results were presented at a major secret conference in May 1991. A leading researcher, Mohammad Behzadi Nia, emphasized the gravity of the U.S. threat in the wake of the Gulf crisis: "The new world order prescribed by President Bush is based on the ultimate imperialist influence of the U.S.A. on the potentially rich in natural resources regions of the world such as the Middle East. In the next decade, our country would be faced with the increasing presence of Western and especially U.S. elements in this region. This presence would be a direct threat to the stability of the Islamic Republic. . . . Our country does not have the necessary technical potential and industrial resources to counter this threat. The Islamic Republic must have a guarantee for its survival, and the most effective guarantee in this regard would be obtaining nuclear capability."

In the concluding session of the conference, Mussavi-Khoiniha delivered an overview of Iran's future strategy, pointing out that the American threat would continue to increase because Iran was emerging as "the only center of national liberation movements" committed to the anti-U.S. struggle. "This unique position, especially after the end of Communism, must be guaranteed. And I am sure that nuclear capability would make this need a practical fact."

Thus, in the summer of 1991, Tehran embarked on what Hashemi-Rafsanjani described as "ambitious and aggressive" plans for "the modernization, diversification, and nuclearization" of Iran's armed forces. Even as the Gulf War raged, Iran had carried out a major revamping of its armed forces and begun a serious weapons-acquisition program. It had also begun the large-scale production of SCUDs and their derivatives based on upgraded technology received from North Korea and the PRC. By early February 1991, Iran's center for missile development at Isfahan had begun producing what Tehran called "long-range missiles with high destructive power"; in mid-May, Iran tested two locally produced SCUD-Cs. Meanwhile, Syria spent on weapons all the "thank you" funds it received from the Gulf states for its role in the alliance. Syria also received the bulk of the war booty—including tanks, artillery, and combat vehicles—captured from Iraq.

Pakistan shared Iran's mistrust of "the new world order" advocated by President Bush. "The new world order does not allow any country in the Third World except the American surrogates to possess nuclear weapons," noted the well-connected commentator Ahmad Aziz-ud-Din Ahmad. Fully aware that no single country could confront the United States on its own, Islamabad stressed the growing importance of cooperation with like-minded powers, acknowledging that "the People's Republic of China and North Korea have been . . . supplying Iran, Pakistan, and other Muslim countries with medium-range missiles and nuclear technology for peaceful purposes."

Iran's quest for nuclear weapons took a major leap forward during a visit to Tehran by China's premier, Li Peng, from July 7 to 9. Li came to Iran to sign a series of military and economic agreements with Hashemi-Rafsanjani, worth a total of about $5 billion a year. Li also held lengthy discussions with Khamenei, Hashemi-Rafsanjani, and others of the Iranian elite. During these discussions, Khamenei enunciated the premises of the Tehran-Damascus axis: "What America calls the new world order is harmful to nations and advantageous to America's absolute hegemony. Therefore, Third World countries, particularly those in sensitive areas, should establish more contacts with each other." Li concurred, defining his visit as "a turning point" in the PRC's strategic posture.

Pakistan had been urging Iran to rely on the PRC as its primary source for military-nuclear technologies. This suited Iranian nuclear experts, who had encountered those technologies while working in Pakistan and had a high regard for them. Islamabad had also urged Beijing to respond favorably to Iranian requests. The Chinese had agreed in principle but conditioned their final decision on a thorough firsthand inspection of conditions in Iran. Accordingly, Li went to Isfahan, where he talked with the senior Chinese experts already assisting with Iran's missile program about their working conditions, their assessment of the Iranians' technological capabilities, and the overall security of the projects. He also inspected a PRC-made reactor optimized for the enrichment of uranium. Li was presumably satisfied with what he saw, because the PRC agreed to provide Iran with the expertise and technology required to complete its reactor.

After Li departed, the IRGC Commander, Major General Mohsen Rezai, left almost immediately for a high-level visit to Pakistan, where he met with the president, the prime minister, and the entire high command "to review issues in the area of defense and ways of consolidating unity between the two countries." The Iranian delegation also inspected a number of Pakistani military-industrial plants and new weapons manufactured with Chinese assistance. Tehran and Islamabad both presented the visit as a strategic milestone, with Pakistani officials stating that "making progress in the nuclear area and selling nuclear technology to Iran can be the greatest honor in the Islamic world."

The cooperation among Iran, Pakistan, and China accelerated throughout the summer; and in the late fall, in an interview with the Pakistani journalist Mushahid Hussain, General Rezai publicly described the "strategic relationship" between the IRGC and the Pakistani defense establishment as the core of a wider Islamic Bloc. "If there is unity among Iran, Pakistan, and Afghanistan," Rezai explained, "this will strengthen Muslim solidarity and enable the peoples of Soviet Central Asia and Kashmir to join in. China would also welcome such a development."

Meanwhile, the demise of the Soviet Union had become official in September, and with it the end of the Cold War. As a result of this development, Islamists became the United States' chief foe. In October, speaking at an international conference on ways to confront the Pax Americana, Ahmad Khomeini, the Ayatollah's son, emphasized the uncompromising character of the coming struggle. "After the fall of Marxism, Islam replaced it, and as long as Islam exists, U.S. hostility exists, and as long as U.S. hostility exists, the struggle exists." Rezai, in his interview with Mushahid Hussain, put a defiant twist on this theme: "Unlike Communism, Islamic fundamentalism has no . . . military might, [but] America is still scared of it."

———

EVEN BEFORE THE final Soviet breakup, and while Tehran was beginning its talks with Beijing, Iranian intelligence operatives were scouring Soviet Central Asia for weapons, technologies, and nuclear material, in search of a shortcut to operational nuclear capabilities. In summer 1991, one of these operatives was offered access to nuclear weapons in Kazakhstan. Tehran dispatched a delegation of senior officials, including U.S.-educated physicists, who returned convinced that the offer was genuine. In early September, the Iranian delegation returned to Kazakhstan to renew negotiations. Their Kazakh interlocutor told them he was speaking for a group of about twenty-five security, scientific, and government officials who were willing to obtain the "atomic bombs" for Iran. The weapons would come in separate pieces from different sites throughout Central Asia, but the group would assemble these pieces into operational weapons. At the same time, the Iranians and

their allies initiated a comprehensive effort to acquire delivery capabilities—
both ballistic missiles and strike aircraft.

These developments boosted Tehran's confidence in its ability to implement its grand strategic design. As Hashemi-Rafsanjani would put it later in
the year, it had fallen to Iran to acquire nuclear weapons for the entire region, if only because the Arabs had proved incapable of doing so. Such
weapons would be the key to a rejuvenated and vibrant Islamic unity. With
them, Hashemi-Rafsanjani concluded, it would be possible to eliminate the
Western presence in the Middle East and liberate Jerusalem. The Syrian
chief of staff, General Hikmat al-Shihabi, echoed this theme during a visit
to Tehran to discuss the two countries' defense policy. Shihabi stressed that
Syria was going to the peace conference in Madrid not to make peace with
Israel, but rather "to ensure the rights of the Palestinians and return of all
occupied territories."

In December, the Kazakh deal came to fruition, and Iran made its first
purchase of nuclear weapons. The deal included two 40-kiloton warheads for
a SCUD-type surface-to-surface ballistic missile; one aerial bomb of the type
carried by a MiG-27; and one 152-mm nuclear artillery shell. These weapons
reached initial operational status in late January 1992 and full operational
status a few months later.

The moment Tehran was certain about the weapons' availability, the coordination of a "nuclear umbrella" for Syria was begun, in order to give it
"strategic parity" with Israel. Iranian Vice President Sayyid Attaollah Mohajerani led a high-level delegation on a brief visit to Damascus on December
24–25. By then, the first round of post-Madrid talks between Israel and its
neighbors had taken place in Washington, and Assad was convinced that the
gap between Syria and Israel was irreconcilable, that only war could break
the deadlock. In mid-January 1992, Damascus announced Assad's decision
that "Syria will not go to the multilateral talks [to be held in Moscow at the
end of the month] because Israel is resisting peace and refusing to withdraw
from the occupied Arab territories." Damascus also objected to regional
arms control talks, because the West had begun by expressing "concerns over
nuclear defiance by the Islamic countries," instead of first compelling Israel
to "remove nuclear weapons and all weapons of mass destruction."

Thanks to Mohajerani's assurances of a nuclear umbrella, Damascus
was able to develop a coherent plan for its war with Israel, which it anticipated would break out sometime between June and September. Damascus's
plan was based on deterring a preemptive strike by the Israeli Air Force and
on hindering any deep aerial strikes by Israel through a series of deep strikes
of its own with SS-21 and M-9 ballistic missiles (Syria specifically acknowledged possessing these two missiles in its contingency plans even though

Damascus publicly denied ever obtaining the PRC-made M-9). Syrian pilots were duly dispatched for advanced training in Iran.

Meanwhile, Tehran modified its declaratory policy at the highest levels to fit its new strategic posture. In a Friday sermon on February 7, Khamenei argued that the United States posed a bigger threat to the world than nuclear proliferation. "Limit the arrogant power of the United States in the world," Khamenei declared, "and the nuclear threat will automatically be curbed." Khamenei refined his argument in a speech delivered to Air Force officers the next day. He claimed that the United States was using reports that Tehran was seeking nuclear arms as a pretext for dominating the Persian Gulf. "Whatever weapons Iran has," he countered, "they are not considered the slightest threat to the countries of the Persian Gulf. They are for the defense of high Islamic and human values. . . . We have never wanted, and do not want, to be the gendarme of the region," he continued. "Nor will we allow any power either regional or from outside—especially the United States, which is trying to play the gendarme—to assume that role."

On February 10, Hashemi-Rafsanjani elaborated on these themes in an authoritative address to foreign diplomats. "We consider armaments necessary for defense requirements," he said. "We are seeking nuclear technology for peaceful purposes, and believe this is the right of all countries which have the means." As for President Bush's proclamation of a new world order, "We believe no one should overstep his rights. We cannot accept that any country in the world should have the right to be superior to others or tell them what to do." In just a few months, Iran and its allies had taken giant steps toward fulfilling the grand strategy formulated in the aftermath of the Gulf War.

––––––

THE SYRIAN-IRANIAN confrontation with the West had two main components: the anticipated war against Israel and a terrorist offensive to deliver the jihad into the heart of the West. In early February, Iran convened an international terrorist conference involving eighty senior participants from twenty organizations. The conference was held under the guise of a commemoration of the Ten Days of Dawn (the victory of the Iranian Islamic Revolution). An indication of its importance was that Ahmad Khomeini personally led the participants to his father's tomb.

In the course of the conference, the terrorist leaders met with senior officials of the Iranian intelligence and security services and officers of the IRGC, as well as with representatives of various Islamic propaganda organizations. Together they formulated a doctrine and a strategy for the jihad. Among other things, Tehran asked the terrorists to refrain temporarily from attacking Western objectives in order not to attract attention to the Iranian-sponsored buildup until they were ready to strike out decisively. The commanders agreed to do nothing without first notifying Tehran.

One of the conference participants, Sheikh Sayyid Abbas al-Mussawi, the secretary-general of the HizbAllah, was to have a unique position in the anticipated strike against Israel that summer. His task was to lead the HizbAllah in creating a provocation that would draw Israel into a major escalation in Lebanon—so that the planned Syrian and Iranian ballistic-missile barrage against Israeli civilian and strategic objectives could be presented as retaliation for Israeli aggression. Mussawi was also in charge of preparing the HizbAllah's special-operations command for a terrorist offensive in Western Europe and possibly the United States.

Returning from the Tehran conference, Mussawi accordingly began to incite his followers. On February 14, he delivered a Friday sermon in Beirut, extolling the virtues of martyrdom. "Our greatest appeal to Allah is: God bless us with martyrdom and honor us with it," he told the gathered HizbAllah fighters. "We will carry on, we will sacrifice souls, children, and everything. We will divorce life with all its beauty and glory for your eyes, our leader, Imam Khomeini."

On February 16, Mussawi traveled to Jibshit, the village that housed HizbAllah headquarters for southern Lebanon, to consult with the local commanders and to inform them about their role in the coming clash with Israel. He then delivered a fiery speech to the HizbAllah fighters and the Iranian Pasdaran (troops of the IRGC) who were assisting them. He denounced the post-Madrid peace talks as yet another expression of the United States' "mad" drive for power over the Muslim world. "America wants to control the fountains of water, exactly like it controlled the oil fountains. America wants to dominate everything," he declared. However, "we shall shoulder our responsibilities and uphold the banner of jihad and confrontation until this state [Israel] falls, come what may, because our nobility and dignity are above all else." The excited crowd replied with shouts of "Death to America!" and "Death to Israel!" As Mussawi's convoy left Jibshit, it was ambushed by Israeli helicopter gunships. Mussawi was killed, along with his wife, child, and several bodyguards.

The sudden killing of Sayyid Abbas al-Mussawi at such a crucial point in the preparations for war had far-reaching repercussions. Since the early 1980s, Syria, Iran, and the HizbAllah had communicated primarily by word of mouth and, to a lesser extent, through handwritten, hand-delivered messages. The role of the trusted go-between was essential to the smooth running of such a complex operation as international terrorism. Sheikh Mussawi was one of the top emissaries of and for the HizbAllah. He was among the very few not only privy to the deliberations in Tehran and Damascus, but also entrusted with overseeing the key terrorist commanders' preparations and reporting back to the two capitals. To be sure, he was not the only high-level messenger, but he was the most important Lebanese Shiite in this role. HizbAllah existed in a world of clan and family loyalties, and its leaders entrusted much to Sheikh Mussawi that could not be shared with outsiders. When he was killed, his synthesis of this material was forever lost.

Ultimately, Tehran and Damascus were able to restore secure communications with the HizbAllah in Lebanon. However, they were hampered by their fear of intelligence leaks, and it took time for the new messengers to commit to memory all the intricacies of the operations they would be overseeing. In retrospect, Mussawi's assassination was the first major setback for Damascus and Tehran in their preparations for a major regional war.

———

MEANWHILE, Iran had already launched an audacious initiative to integrate Iraq into its strategic axis. Back in late December 1991, Saddam Hussein, through his half brother Barzan al-Takriti, had sent Hafez al-Assad a message proposing cooperation against "common enemies." Saddam praised Assad's strong position in the negotiations with Israel and his commitment to a strategy of confrontation. Soon afterward, the Iraqi trade minister met with the Syrian economy and foreign trade minister to discuss ways of evading the U.N. sanctions. Cross-border commercial activity began cautiously that same month, with Iraq exporting petrochemicals to Syria, while Syria reciprocated with consumer goods, mainly clothes and processed food. As early as the spring of 1992, goods from Syria and Lebanon were quite evident in Iraqi markets. At the same time, Iraq resumed military procurement from the PRC and North Korea, to be delivered via Iran. Sophisticated weapon systems, such as F-7 fighters and anti-shipping cruise missiles, topped the Iraqi list.

In April, high-level delegations met secretly near the Iran-Iraq border. Iraq's delegation was led by Qusay Saddam Hussein, Saddam's younger son and the chief of Iraq's security organ, and Sadun Hammadi, Iraq's economic czar; Iran's was led by Mahmud Bahramani Rafsanjani, Hashemi-Rafsanjani's brother and a senior intelligence official. The two sides agreed on a joint strategy in the Persian Gulf and the Near East as a whole, a joint oil export and pricing policy, and a campaign to attract European companies to wider economic involvement in the region in violation of the U.N. sanctions. The essence of the agreement was that in return for Iraq's recognizing Iran's strategic leadership, Iran would break the embargo—albeit clandestinely, so as not to tarnish Hashemi-Rafsanjani's image as a "moderate." Tehran also agreed to facilitate the buildup of the Iraqi military by providing false end-user certificates and permitting the flow of weapons across the border.

Over the next two months there were two major and several minor follow-up meetings. Even then, not all matters were resolved, primarily because of the extent of the Iranian demands. Of lasting importance, however, was the fact that Qusay Saddam Hussein and Hussein Bahramani, Hashemi-Rafsanjani's son and secret emissary, hit it off on the personal level. They enjoyed each other's company and looked forward to working together in the future.

By late May, the strategic treaty between Iran and Iraq was completed in principle, although it was not formally signed owing to lingering doubts in Tehran about the prudence of legitimizing Saddam. Iraq would remain the least trusted member of Iran's axis. Yet its mere location between Iran and Syria made it a crucial element in Tehran's grand design.

———

AT THE SAME TIME, Iran conducted two major combined-arms exercises, aimed at examining the ability of its reorganized ground forces to confront an army of the quality of the Israel Defense Force.

The first exercise, called Beit al-Muqaddas (the Temple in Jerusalem), was launched on May 22 and involved three armored and mechanized divisions, four infantry brigades, and support and special forces of the IRGC. The Iranian forces were to breach fortified positions of the enemy and then develop a swift, deep offensive into the enemy's rear with extensive fire support from artillery and combat aircraft. The importance of the exercise was underscored by the fact that its commanders were Hassan Firoz-Abadi, chief of staff of the Armed Forces, and Mohsen Rezai, commander in chief of the IRGC.

The second exercise, called Tabuk-5, was launched on May 27. Although it was essentially a massive offensive, of particular importance was the role of the special forces. On the eve of the main offensive, paratroopers of the Shiraz 55th Airborne Brigade jumped deep behind enemy lines. The main forces then advanced to link up with the positions seized by the paratroopers. As the main forces continued their advance, their surge was expedited by helicopter transfers of special forces throughout the rear of the enemy and the seizure of strategic objectives. Some of the offensive operations took place under conditions of chemical warfare. Major General Ali Shahbazi, chief of the Joint Staff of the Armed Forces and a rapidly rising expert on power projection, was in command of Tabuk-5. Both exercises were pronounced successful.

Tehran's confidence in its growing military capabilities was clear in its strong reaction to the June 21 warning by the commander of the Israeli Air Force about the danger of Iran's nuclear threat. In its official response, Tehran declared that "occupied Palestine [that is, Israel] can be considered a base for world arrogance inside the oil-rich Islamic world." Israel is "merely the progeny of world arrogance in the region, and implements the policies dictated to it by the United States." The commander of the Iranian Air Force added his own response to the Israeli threats: "Iran's Air Force is in a state of complete readiness to defend against any aggression, and Israel knows that it will pay a heavy price for any adventurism against Iran."

———

BY EARLY JULY, the strategic axis from the Mediterranean to the Indus was a reality, and Tehran urged the Gulf states to accept its leadership in order to effect the eviction of the United States from the Near East. Tehran pointed out that the Gulf crisis and the collapse of the Soviet Union "tilted the regional balance" against the Arab and Muslim world; however, newly acquired military capabilities permitted the restoration of the earlier strategic posture. The commitment to destroying Israel, Tehran concluded, could very well serve as the glue of an Islamic Bloc, uniting otherwise reluctant members.

Another factor, of which Tehran was well aware, was the upcoming U.S. elections. Ever since 1980, Tehran had been fascinated by the U.S. election process and the extent to which it rendered Washington incapable of making painful decisions and reacting swiftly. "All the buzzing about an imminent attack against the defiant Iraqi leadership and the posturing of a war-eager America cannot but be connected with the declining popularity in the polls of George Bush," Tehran argued. "Another American-led military intervention in the Middle East looms inevitable. Not only is U.S. prestige at stake but, with the fast approach of autumn, a besieged George Bush is desperate for a foreign policy victory to erase his image as 'whimperingly unable to respond' and assure a second White House tenure."

Khamenei followed this up in a sermon on July 29, in which he indicated that Tehran accepted Saddam's assertion that not he but the United States was responsible for the Iran-Iraq War. Khamenei explained that "during eight years of imposed war the enemy was openly fighting us. In appearance it was Iraq, but behind Iraq was the United States, NATO, and all the reactionaries." Therefore, Iraq was now a legitimate partner in confronting the evil West. "Today, in the world of Islam, we . . . have no right to make a mistake recognizing the enemy."

In early August, the Higher Syrian-Iranian Joint Committee met to formulate policies on regional issues. Assad emphasized that the two countries had identical strategic positions, especially concerning Israel. However, he poured cold water on the Iranian enthusiasm for war as originally scheduled, between June and September. He opined that it would be advantageous for Iran and Syria to reduce the United States' ability to intervene in such a war by opening a second strategic front simultaneously. He urged that they invite Pyongyang, then contemplating its own war for the unification of the Korean peninsula, to coordinate with them in order to stretch U.S. retaliatory capabilities. Iran reluctantly agreed to postpone the attack until the eve of the U.S. elections, by which time North Korea would be ready for war.

On August 23, Khamenei chaired a pivotal session of the entire Iranian leadership, including Hashemi-Rafsanjani, devoted to devising methods to ensure that "global arrogance will be cut down to size." "No doubt," Khamenei declared, "in the confrontation between Islam and global arrogance, the latter will be brought down to its knees, because Islam relies on the innate nature of human beings. . . . As long as we adhere to Islam and Islamic principles neither America nor other powers could harm our nation." The leadership resolved to cooperate with Syria and North Korea in preparing for the autumn conflagration.

———

IN THE MEANTIME, the crisis mood intensified. On September 14, Tehran again blamed the Gulf states for instigating a war on behalf of the United States and urged them to join the Islamic Bloc. "Islamic and Arab countries should not allow themselves to become puppets in the hands of the criminal United States and its agents in the region," Tehran admonished, "and should not act as Washington's instruments of power in imposing a cold war against Islam." On September 16, Hashemi-Rafsanjani convened an extraordinary two-day meeting at which the Iranian leadership and the IRGC high command thoroughly studied the Corps' readiness for war. Khamenei told the commanders that their commitment to the Islamic Revolution might soon be put to the ultimate test and that Tehran had great confidence in them. The newly elected Majlis speaker, Ali Akbar Natiq-Nuri, urged the commanders to increase their militancy: "Employ all your means to fight for your cause, and thus mobilize all their strength and power to confront the conspiracies of Islam's enemies." Ahmad Khomeini praised the officers' role "in confronting threats against Iran by its enemies" and stated, "We will never yield to America's filthy designs and demands." At the conclusion of the gathering, the IRGC officers reaffirmed their commitment to safeguarding the gains of the revolution. "It is incumbent upon us to prepare ourselves with all might . . . so as to confront the numerous conspiracies of the world arrogance, led by the criminal U.S.," read the officers' communiqué.

On September 22, there was a major demonstration of strength in the middle of Tehran—a flyby of thirty-five combat aircraft, including latest models purchased from Russia and China, as well as old U.S.-made combat aircraft from the Shah's Air Force, and several types of helicopters. As well, motorized anti-chemical-warfare units, heavy artillery, anti-aircraft units, and various types of bombs and missiles were paraded along Tehran's main streets.

On October 3, Hashemi-Rafsanjani chaired a meeting of the Supreme National Security Council to study "suspicious political movements" in the Persian Gulf. By this time, the Iranians had built up their missile sites on Abu-Mussa Island and along the littoral of the Straits of Hormuz, and the flow of new weapons from Russia and China was in full swing. Tehran realized that the tense standoff in the Persian Gulf could not continue much longer. One of the adversaries would inevitably try to break the deadlock, and Tehran was determined not to lose the initiative.

On October 10, Khamenei made an inspection tour of the special facilities of the Air Force's Eighth Shahid Babai Base in Isfahan, where Iran's aerial nuclear bomb was stored. Iran intended to use this bomb in a kamikaze-style attack against a U.S. Navy carrier in the Persian Gulf. Iran had several North Korean–trained pilots willing to undertake the mission, all of them with extensive operational experience, qualified on the latest Soviet aircraft.

Iran's two nuclear warheads were fitted to their ballistic missiles at Isfahan, although the warheads themselves were usually stored in Lavizan, in the Tehran area. Khamenei also visited these facilities and discussed the shift of emphasis from indigenous development of missiles to massive purchases abroad. He emphasized the long-range importance of developing and producing strategic weapons in Iran; however, he explained, under certain emergency conditions foreign weapons could be acquired "with our pride intact."

While in Isfahan, Khamenei received briefings on the accelerated conditioning of damaged aircraft and spoke with the Air Force officers about the coming challenges. "We have never been a warmonger, and we are not one today," Khamenei told them. "While being against war, and not wanting to engage in any kind of war, we should be ready to defend ourselves, and we should always maintain readiness. Today, thanks to your bravery and courage at various fronts, no one can think of being aggressive against us. Today, everyone understands that the Iranian nation and the Iranian Armed Forces are not to be mocked." Khamenei returned to Tehran confident of Iran's capabilities for confronting the United States in the Persian Gulf.

———

AFTER ALL THIS buildup, the war preparations suddenly fizzled out. There was a crisis in Pyongyang. North Korea's anticipation of war had caused a slowdown in the transfer of power from the ailing Kim Il-Song to his son Kim Jong-Il. Kim Il-Song was determined to remain in power long enough to "personally lead" the attempt to reunify the Korean peninsula by force; hence, various steps had been taken to slow Kim Jong-Il's rise to power. Most notably, he had been originally designated to lead North Korea's delegation to the summit meeting of the Non-Aligned Movement (NAM) in Jakarta in early September. The summit was to serve as his formal introduction as the Supreme Leader of North Korea, and several meetings with other leaders had been arranged for him. However, he was replaced at the last minute.

Hashemi-Rafsanjani did attend the NAM summit, and on his way back home he and his entourage visited Pyongyang to discuss the final coordination of the strategic surge against the United States. While Pyongyang remained officially committed to going to war on the eve of the U.S. elections, some of the Iranians came away with the impression that confidence was lacking at the highest level. The Iranians' reading of the situation was that Kim Il-Song was too old to lead, but that neither he nor anybody else really trusted Kim Jong-Il to take the country through a crisis that would amount to a world war.

In fact, the lack of confidence in Pyongyang resulted from the reluctance of the Army's high command to go through with the planned military adventure. This reluctance—combined with a desire for modernization on the part of younger officers who were Soviet-educated and had been influenced by Gorbachev's *perestroika*—had led eighteen officers to begin contemplating the advisability of a coup. Their plans included storming the presidential palace and killing both Kim Il-Song and Kim Jong-Il.

The plot was betrayed to the security police, and all eighteen were seized and promptly executed. According to a defector—a junior officer who claimed to have firsthand knowledge of the coup attempt—the plotters had echoed widespread sentiments in the armed forces. There is no evidence that they ever reached the point of even discussing their plans with a wider circle of fellow officers. Nevertheless, since the consolidation of Kim Jong-Il's power depended on the support of the military, it was imperative for Pyongyang to reassert its hold over the high command before any major action was taken, and so the trilateral grand design was derailed.

———

EVEN THEN, military preparations did not cease in Iran and Syria. Although the modernization of elite Syrian front-line units, especially 1st Corps divisions on the Golan front, had been largely completed in June, the Syrians used the extra time to upgrade the training of their troops. They also continued to deliver to the HizbAllah forces on the Israeli border weapons that they and the Iranians had purchased in Ukraine—especially SAGGER anti-tank missiles, new sophisticated mines, and 107-mm rockets—and they continued training these forces to engage Israeli armored columns.

Most significant was the behavior of the Iraqi Army. The original war plan had called for its mobilization and forward movement under the cover of major military exercises. In late October, Baghdad decided to go ahead with these exercises despite the cancelation of the war. Iraq's rejuvenated military capabilities were demonstrated on October 30 in a combined-arms offensive under the command of Defense Minister Ali Hassan al-Majeed. "The exercise was accomplished in an accurate and excellent manner," Baghdad reported, "showing optimum cooperation between different army corps." Damascus was most gratified to have confirmation of Iraq's military capabilities, since Iraq constituted Syria's strategic rear.

Meanwhile, the Iranians remained convinced that the U.S.-imposed peace process—still winding its way through the various post-Madrid talks—would soon collapse in a violent eruption, in which they were determined to get involved. To be better prepared, Tehran appealed to the PRC to accelerate the supply of weapons Hashemi-Rafsanjani had requested while in Beijing in September. Most important was the Chinese agreement to supply 100 to 150 additional combat aircraft, as well as several ships and submarines, which would enable Iran to project power well into the Indian Ocean and the Arabian Sea. Tehran had also asked Pyongyang to expedite the shipment of additional SSMs, to be divided equally between Iran and Syria. By the end of 1992, Iran's operational stockpile would consist of 200 Silkworms and more than 800 SCUDs. The size of these weapon deals and the accelerated rates of supply alarmed the Gulf states to the point of raising the issue with Tehran. On October 19, Tehran admitted that it was purchasing weapons from Moscow and Beijing and declared that it was determined to continue doing so.

Toward this end, Chinese Defense Minister Qin Jiwei arrived in Tehran on October 27 with a large, high-level military delegation. He met with Hashemi-Rafsanjani and with Major General Shahbazi, but even more important were the talks the Chinese delegation held with the logistics experts of the Iranian armed forces on weapon supplies and the construction of strategic industries. In retrospect, Qin Jiwei's visit planted the seeds of the Trans-Asian Axis, to be consolidated in the mid-1990s.

While all this was going on, Tehran was not neglecting its nuclear arsenal. In the fall of 1992, Iran signed a new deal with officials in Kazakhstan for the purchase of four 50-kiloton nuclear warheads, upgraded and adapted to fit on the SSMs purchased from North Korea. In a telephone conversation recorded in December 1992 between Tabatabai Kia, an Iranian diplomat in Geneva who handles money transfers for Iranian intelligence, and Abdul Rahmani, a senior Iranian diplomat operating in Central Asia, Kia wanted to confirm that "the guys who wanted to buy a few warheads . . . completed their task in the best manner possible." Rahmani confirmed that four war-heads had indeed been purchased but added that their delivery was post-poned due to "a technical problem"—ensuring clandestine transport. The warheads were eventually shipped to North Korea, where they were opti-mized for the soon-to-be-delivered Nodong-1 SSMs.

———

BY THIS TIME, Americans had gone to the polls and rejected the Bush ad-ministration—anathema throughout the Middle East because of its triumph in the Gulf War. Tehran was very curious about the incoming Clinton ad-ministration. Despite Bill Clinton's pro-Israel statements during the cam-paign, Tehran and the Arabs found several grounds for encouragement. Most important were the relations of the Clinton team with the Bosnian Muslims in Sarajevo and the calls of candidate Clinton for major interven-tion on their behalf against the Serbs. The Iranians, intimately involved with the Bosnian Muslim leadership, realized that something was going on behind the campaign rhetoric. In fact, their closer study of Bill Clinton's earlier po-sitions on specific issues and of Hillary Rodham Clinton's past as a radical leftist, including involvement in PLO-related "humanitarian" causes, rein-forced this impression. Ultimately, Iranian experts concluded, Bill Clinton, having run on domestic economic and social issues, would be susceptible to the lure of cheap oil and growing markets; hence there might be a chance for negotiations with America after all.

Hashemi-Rafsanjani moved quickly. Ibrahim Yazdi—who as foreign min-ister had taken part in the 1980–81 negotiations with Warren Christopher over the American Embassy hostages held in Tehran—traveled to the United States in early December. Officially, Yazdi was visiting relatives in California; however, he immediately contacted former Carter administration officials, who put him in touch with high-ranking members of the Clinton transition team. Reportedly, Yazdi even met with Christopher, who was co-chairing the transition team. Yazdi urged the Americans to improve economic and politi-cal relations with Tehran in order to preserve the "moderate" and "pragma-tist" regime of Hashemi-Rafsanjani. Although Yazdi claimed to be representing former prime minister Mehdi Bazargan, this initiative could not have taken place without the personal approval of Hashemi-Rafsanjani. Nonetheless, the new administration eventually rejected the Iranian request that money paid by the Shah for weapons be returned to Iran.

Tehran had warned Washington indirectly, via Arab intermediaries, of an impending "war between the CIA and the Iranian SAVAMA [Iranian In-telligence Service]" if its overtures were rejected. When the Clinton team did reject them, it was imperative to demonstrate the SAVAMA's ability to strike.

The morning of January 25, 1993—a mere five days after President Clinton was sworn into office—a man carrying an AK-47 assault rifle calmly walked along a line of cars stopped at a traffic light near the entrance to CIA head-quarters in Langley, Virginia, and methodically shot several Agency employ-ees, killing two and wounding three more. The killer was soon identified as Mir Amail Kansi, a twenty-eight-year-old Pakistani and one of Iran's "Afghans"—a network of foreigners who had fought with the mujahideen in Afghanistan. Although official Washington was reluctant to understand Tehran's message, virtually all the Arab governments did.

The good feedback from the Kansi operation emboldened Tehran to strike even more audaciously. On the morning of February 26, an Iranian-sponsored Islamist terrorist cell in the New York–New Jersey area detonated a huge car bomb in the underground parking lot of the World Trade Center. While the damage was moderate, the echoes of the operation reverberated throughout the Middle East. Again, the Arab rulers got the message: Just as we struck at the heart of America, we can also strike at your own centers of power.

5

Pipe Dreams and Deceptions (1992–1994)

Israel's De Facto Recognition of the PLO; the Clinton Administration's Double Game

DURING THE WINTER of 1992–93, Yassir Arafat was increasingly distraught over the way the peace process was playing out. He repeatedly told confidants that "we went to Madrid against our will and under despicable conditions" and that "we entered the [Washington] negotiations under most complex Arab and international circumstances, and under despicable conditions aimed to deprive the Palestinians of their rightful participation" in determining the future of the Middle East. Arafat was "petrified"—in the words of a confidant—by the high profile of the leading members of the Palestinian delegation to Washington: Faisal Husseini, the son of a legendary Arab commander who died in the 1948 fighting over Jerusalem; Haidar Abd al-Shafi, a veteran leftist leader from Gaza who was very close to the Islamist rejectionist organizations; and Hannan Ashrawi, an eloquent Anglican professor from Ramallah. Arafat feared that, because of his own decisive role in several anti-American terrorist operations (especially the cold-blooded assassination of two American diplomats in Khartoum in 1973), the Americans and the Israelis would prefer to strike a deal with the indigenous leaders from the territories and that, because of these leaders' popularity with the Palestinian people, this gambit would succeed.

The continued radicalization of the Palestinian population and the rise of HAMAS as the dominant force in the territories increased Arafat's anxiety. He realized that al-Shafi could easily make a deal with HAMAS's Sheikh Yassin. If they then accepted partial Israeli withdrawal and self-empowerment under U.S. auspices, Arafat would become irrelevant. It was therefore imperative for him to make deals with the Islamists, while at the same time taking steps to divide and rule the indigenous leadership.

Arafat also resolved to endear himself to the incoming Clinton administration in order to ensure that he remained the undisputed "Mr. Palestine" in Washington's eyes. Clinton was only too willing to go along. The prospect of Arafat's legitimization, however, greatly alarmed King Hussein, for so long a victim of Palestinian subversion and violence. At first, the king warned Jerusalem not to succumb to the temptations of a deal with the PLO and to concentrate instead on making another attempt to strike a deal with the traditional Palestinian leadership in the territories. Later, convinced that Washington was pushing Jerusalem into dealing with the PLO, King Hussein wrote to President Clinton, committing Jordan to making peace with Israel and urging U.S. involvement in "genuine" Israeli-Palestinian negotiations. The White House chose to ignore the king's advice. Thus, as Jerusalem was gradually waking up, Washington was becoming more deeply committed to Yassir Arafat.

EVEN BEFORE the Tehran-Damascus-Baghdad axis had solidified, and while Washington, Jerusalem, and Riyadh were still assimilating the strategic significance of the Iranians' acquisition of nuclear weapons, Israel had reached out to the PLO through a secret channel in Oslo. It was a daring, if not desperate, effort to drastically change the strategic dynamics of the Middle East before it was too late.

The "serious" and "parallel" discussions in Oslo that would come to dominate the peace process were set in motion as early as the spring of 1992, when the politically well connected Norwegian academic Treje Larsen met Yossi Beilin, an Israeli Labor Party politician and a confidant of Shimon Peres. Larsen suggested that even though the Washington negotiations between Israel and its neighbors were still going on, Israel should open a series of meaningful contacts with the Palestinians' real leadership—Arafat's coterie.

At this time Peres had just lost the Labor Party leadership to his longtime rival, the somewhat less dovish Yitzhak Rabin, as the party prepared for national elections. On June 23, Labor, with Rabin at the helm, edged out the incumbent Likud, led by Yitzhak Shamir; and in July Rabin set about forming a new government. Based on a coalition between the Labor Party and the leftist-liberal Meretz Party, it was the most dovish government in Israel's history. Rabin named Peres foreign minister; and Beilin, now Peres's deputy, hinted about his contacts with Larsen and got the nod to proceed. However, Peres did not disclose any of this to Rabin, who, aware of the Bush administration's objections to Arafat because of his support for Saddam, had forbidden direct contacts with Arafat's entourage. Once Bill Clinton defeated George Bush, however, Jerusalem no longer felt constrained, and on December 1, the Knesset began deliberating the repeal of the ban on contacts with the PLO. The new law would be approved on January 9, 1993.

Jerusalem also consulted Hosni Mubarak on the question of helping to shift Palestinian leadership to the local families and traditional power centers in the territories at the expense of Arafat. Mubarak asked for concrete ideas, and in mid-November Peres delivered the outlines of the "Gaza-Jericho first" proposal, according to which those areas would serve as the foundations of a Palestinian entity that would expand with time. Simultaneously, in a speech in Tel Aviv, Rabin warned Arafat that the resolution of the Palestinian problem would not necessarily include him. Rabin observed that "he who stands at the head of the PLO fears, maybe justifiably from his personal perspective, that if [interim self-rule] is created, . . . such a body will become the source of Palestinian identity, and then what will the organization sitting in Tunis do?" However, unbeknownst to the Israeli government, Mubarak saw in the "Gaza-Jericho first" proposal the opening Arafat was seeking to divert Washington's support to him. With the help of Tahir Shaash, a leading legal expert, Mubarak convinced senior PLO official Mahmoud Abbas (also known as Abu-Mazen) to respond positively to the Peres initiative as the only way for Arafat not only to get to Washington, but also to do so at the expense of the indigenous Palestinian leadership.

Mubarak then arranged for Faisal Husseini, the official head of the delegation negotiating in Washington, and Abu-Mazen to travel together to Saudi Arabia and the Gulf states to rebuild the support for the PLO that had deteriorated because of Arafat's embrace of Saddam. The trip culminated in Riyadh, where Abu-Mazen delivered a speech apologizing to the Saudis for the PLO's position during the Gulf War. At the same time, Arafat himself—working to secure his real power base—had traveled to Baghdad to demonstrate his continuing support for that same Saddam Hussein, who reciprocated by awarding him the "Mother of All Battles" order; both leaders delivered speeches emphasizing Iraq's support for the Intifadah. The Saudis got the message and canceled their plans for financial assistance to the indigenous Palestinian institutions in the territories. Consequently, these institutions remained completely dependent on funds from the PLO, virtually ending the possibility that the grassroots leadership could supplant Arafat.

———

ALTHOUGH THIS MANEUVER succeeded, Arafat was still facing a growing challenge from the Islamists in the territories. The outpouring of popular support for HAMAS following its assassination of an Israeli border policeman in mid-December 1992 and the subsequent Israeli banishment of 415 Islamist leaders to southern Lebanon convinced Arafat that he must come to terms with the Islamists. If he failed to do so, he would lose credibility with the people of the territories at the very time his political machinations in the West were beginning to show results. Therefore, Arafat appealed to Sudan's spiritual leader, Hassan al-Turabi, and the HizbAllah leadership in Lebanon for help in organizing a meeting with the HAMAS leadership.

Turabi agreed to sponsor such a meeting in early January 1993. On the eve of this Khartoum summit, Arafat used every possible means to stress his commitment to the armed struggle and the pursuit of Koranic principles. Significantly, he justified his involvement in the peace process by comparing it with the Prophet Muhammad's Treaty of Hudaibiya, signed with the Jewish tribe of Quraysh in A.D. 628. In that treaty, the Prophet, under duress, promised his enemies peace for ten years. However, he violated the treaty two years later, ostensibly in reaction to a provocation, but in reality as soon as his armies were ready; he then conquered Mecca and slaughtered all the Quraysh. "Negotiations with the enemy are no less vicious than any military operation carried out by our mujahideen and revolutionaries," Arafat declared. "We have not closed any of our options, which include jihad."

The Khartoum summit turned out to be a major humiliation for Arafat. The transcript, as published in the Lebanese newspaper *Al-Safir* on February 2, 1993, shows a nervous Arafat apprehensive about HAMAS's intent and ability to establish an alternative leadership in the territories. Arafat pleaded that by setting itself up as a rival to the PLO, HAMAS was playing into the hands of the United States. The key HAMAS leaders would have none of this. Mussa Abu-Marzuq, based in Tehran, and Ibrahim Ghawshah, based in Jordan, relentlessly attacked Arafat as being power-hungry; Marzuq explicitly accused him of embezzling the funds donated to the Palestinians by the Gulf states. Both Marzuq and Ghawshah accused the PLO of betraying the jihad for a dubious international recognition. When Marzuq pressured Arafat about the disastrous implications of the peace process for the Palestinian jihad, Arafat snapped, "You don't understand politics. I did not go to the [peace] talks of my own will." HAMAS flatly rejected Arafat's conciliatory offer that it join the PLO as its second most important constituent organization—after Arafat's own Fatah.

At the end of the summit, the PLO agreed "to step up the armed struggle against Israel" in cooperation with the Islamists and the rejectionists, and Ghawshah noted that the PLO agreed with the Islamists that all the territory of Palestine is a *waqf*—land that belongs to the Muslim Ummah and therefore cannot be ceded to non-Muslims. As Turabi summarized it, all the participants agreed that the objective was to gain control of all of Palestine "from the sea to the river" and that no territorial compromise was legitimate. In his last meeting with Turabi, Arafat reaffirmed his conviction that "the prospect for peace in the Middle East was zero" in view of Israel's overall positions.

Despite the summit's conciliatory closing, Arafat and the PLO were clearly at risk of being made irrelevant by the rising Islamist trend. At this point, Arafat authorized Ahmed Qurai (also called Abu-Alaa), a lieutenant of Abu-Mazen, to meet in London with Yair Hirschfeld, a dovish Israeli academic close to Beilin, to explore the possibilities of the "secret channel" that had been suggested the previous spring. A first round of substantive negotiations took place in Sarpsborg, Norway, in late January, with Israel represented by Hirschfeld and Ron Pundak, another academic. Beilin had approved this meeting on his own and notified Peres only after its conclusion; Peres apprised Rabin sometime later. In the second round, in mid-February, the two sides began drafting a Declaration of Principles (DoP)—an interim agreement creating a framework for a relationship between Israel and the PLO. Peres met with Warren Christopher, now the secretary of state, a few days later but did not tell him about the secret channel. The Norwegians broke the news to Christopher in late February, without informing Israel, and got Washington's endorsement.

Hence, just when Arafat might have sunk into complete oblivion, the Rabin government saved him through the Oslo process. Meanwhile, to ensure his continued acceptance by the Islamists, Arafat kept the HAMAS leadership, particularly the headquarters in Amman, up to date on the progress of negotiations—both the overt talks in Washington and the Oslo secret channel. Moreover, he expressed his support for the wave of Islamist terrorism unleashed in February and March, telling Ghawshah that the resumption of the jihad had pressed Israel into making further concessions in the Oslo negotiations.

Arafat's method worked. The Israeli academics continued to come back for further rounds of secret negotiations in Norway, regardless of the terrorism at home. The talks were conducted with zeal and enthusiasm, and the final draft of the DoP was agreed upon in mid-March. The DoP was a general document in which many key issues were glossed over, vague phraseology was rampant, and implementation was left to the parties' bona fides. The possibility that the Palestinians might be cheating never crossed the Israelis' mind. In fact, at that very time, Arafat and the Palestinian elite were already discussing their breakout from the agreement and indeed from the entire peace process.

During all of this, third parties were continually interceding with Jerusalem on behalf of the Palestinians, dangling the possibility of Palestinian flexibility in return for additional Israeli concessions. In mid-April,

Mubarak showed the visiting Rabin a document indicating that Arafat was receptive to accepting the "Gaza-Jericho first" principle. That this document was a recycling of the one worked on by Peres and Mubarak back in November, with a few additional Palestinian demands tacked on, seemed to go unnoticed by the Rabin government, which eagerly adopted it as affirming the viability of the Oslo process. Mubarak also visited Washington and got the White House to commit to pressuring Israel to demonstrate more flexibility.

In early May, buoyed by the results of the just-completed fourth round of the Oslo talks, Peres implored a skeptical Rabin to upgrade the secret channel to official status. In effect, this upgrade meant that Israel recognized the PLO as a legitimate political entity and Arafat as the leader of the Palestinians. Israel undertook this profound step unilaterally, without any reciprocal concession from the PLO.

Peres named another confidant—Uri Savir, the director general of the Foreign Ministry—as Israel's representative to the now official negotiations. Subsequently, Rabin authorized the drafting of a formally binding DoP based on the earlier drafts.

The next couple of months saw the Israeli-Palestinian negotiations degenerate into a Middle Eastern political bazaar. In early July, just when the Israelis were confident they had reached agreements on virtually all the major points, the Palestinians introduced a whole new set of demands as well as a negotiating style that could be characterized only as hostile brinkmanship. Arafat, knowing that Israel could not afford to let the Oslo process collapse, simply raised the price. Moreover, Israel had just conducted a series of military strikes against the HizbAllah in southern Lebanon, code-named Operation Accountability, and was receiving considerable international criticism. A clandestine exchange of letters between Rabin and Arafat, as well as Savir's "personal" assurances of the ultimate formal recognition of the PLO by Israel, finally persuaded Arafat in mid-August to authorize his negotiators to move forward.

———

AS THE VARIOUS Israeli-PLO negotiation channels were showing some progress, Arafat began justifying his actions to his supporters in both the Arab world and Western Europe. His position was intriguing. Even to Western European senior officials who had applied tremendous pressure on Israel to recognize the PLO, Arafat insisted he was a reluctant participant. It was Israel's economic strength and military superiority, he maintained, that had compelled him to come to the negotiating table, rather than any genuine desire for reconciliation, let alone recognition of Israel's right to exist. In his book *Secret Channels*, Mohamed Heikal corroborates Arafat's account.

Under circumstances of debilitating economic pressure, Heikal writes, "the PLO settled, in the Oslo 'principles' of August 1993, on a deal far worse than the Camp David accords it had denounced in 1978. The Oslo agreement astonished only those who had failed to notice how much the PLO's old determination had faded." This insistence that negotiations had taken place under duress was to serve Arafat's real objective: legitimizing from the very beginning a future breakout from the negotiated settlement.

The PLO participated in the peace process primarily because Arafat was desperate to guarantee his own political survival. He was convinced, and not without reason, that because of the Oslo process both Israel and the United States would work to keep him in power. At the same time, he was convinced that an opportunity had emerged to destroy Israel via the Iran-Iraq-Syria axis, with the militant Islamists (not the PLO's own forces) providing inspiration through a relentless and martyrdom-filled jihad. For while the Western world was celebrating the dawn of peace in the Middle East, the Muslim world was absorbing the myth that was the legacy of Afghanistan: that if armed jihad can defeat a superpower such as the Soviet Union, it can do the same to a small country like Israel. The escalating armed struggle by Islamists against the U.S.-led U.N. forces in Somalia confirmed this myth. Furthermore, the return of thousands of "Arab-Afghans"—Arabs who had fought alongside the mujahideen in Afghanistan—to their homes throughout the Middle East both spread the myth and made these highly trained fighters available for local insurrections. The challenge for Arafat was to harness the militant Islamists and have the Arab world see them as part of his PLO.

Arafat knew that, as a result of Oslo, Rabin and Peres would give him tremendous freedom of action. Uri Savir unwittingly clarified this point in the final session of the Oslo negotiations on August 20. Mahmoud Abbas himself makes the point in his book *Through Secret Channels,* citing the minutes of that meeting. Yoel Singer, the Israeli legal expert, asked that the PLO leadership in Tunis issue a proclamation that the Intifadah was over. Abbas's lieutenant Qurai refused, explaining that "this is not possible. The Intifadah continues because its causes continue, and unless there is tangible progress on the ground it will go on." Savir tried to soften the point. Stating that Israel now considered the PLO "the representative of the Palestinian people," he urged it "to shoulder responsibility" and "channel the people's energies toward peace." However, he immediately let the PLO off the hook by conceding that the Israeli government was not expecting a complete cessation of terrorism. "We are aware that HAMAS is there and we do not expect the PLO to control everything," Savir told Qurai.

BY EARLY AUGUST, the Palestinian delegates to the Washington talks—the genuine representatives of the Palestinian population in the territories—were increasingly disillusioned with Arafat's maneuvers. Finally, they refused to hand over to Christopher Arafat's reply to some queries from Washington. When an exasperated Arafat learned of this, he called Faisal Husseini and pleaded with him: "In the name of your martyred father, Abdul Qadir, in the name of the martyrs who have sacrificed their souls, please, don't shame me. Submit the document we've prepared to Christopher." Husseini cursed but obeyed. "We [the delegation] were the appetizers. The PLO is the main course," noted Saeb Erekat, who would soon become a key Arafat aide. Nevertheless, Arafat did not forget the incident or forgive Husseini. He resolved to ensure that his own coterie would be in total control of whatever piece of territory the PLO eventually obtained from Israel. The PLO had already obtained an ironclad guarantee from Israel that it would be formally recognized as the sole legitimate leadership of the Palestinian people. Israel had thus committed itself to imposing the PLO on the Palestinians in the territories—something the PLO had failed to achieve on its own through two decades of terrorism and politicking.

Peres arrived in Stockholm on August 18, ostensibly for an official visit, but in reality for a clandestine signing of the Oslo agreement. On August 20–21, in the middle of the night, Peres and several Norwegian officials oversaw the initialing of the Oslo agreement by Savir and Abu-Alaa, who then sipped champagne, a beverage forbidden to Muslims. The violation was entirely characteristic of this political process, which was ostensibly on behalf of a predominantly Muslim, and increasingly Islamist, population.

Peres and Norwegian Foreign Minister Johan Holst immediately traveled to Washington to bring the news to Warren Christopher and Dennis Ross, whom President Clinton had just named special coordinator for Middle East peace talks. Having examined the initialed document, Ross warned that Israel was pumping life into the dying PLO just as a sophisticated indigenous leadership was rising up in the territories. Peres snapped that Israel knew its own interests best and said the main problem would be presenting the agreement to both the Israeli public and the Palestinians. He suggested staging a signing event in Washington so that the agreement would look like an American initiative and thus be more palatable to the Israeli public.

For the Clinton White House, besieged by the attacks on its health care proposal and the hostile reception of the North American Free Trade Agreement (NAFTA) initiative, the Israeli request was a most welcome diversion. "Miracles do happen," Clinton remarked to an aide. The White House ceremony was duly scheduled for September 13, and the administration began trumpeting the President's latest foreign policy achievement, which dominated the Sunday talk shows. That the agreement was far from secure and that the United States had had very little to do with negotiating it did not matter to a White House enjoying a sudden flow of good media attention.

On September 13, Peres and Mahmoud Abbas signed the formal Declaration of Principles on the South Lawn of the White House in a ceremony presided over by Clinton, Rabin, Arafat, Christopher, and Russian Foreign Minister Andrei Kozyrev. President Clinton repeated the "miracles" theme, this time in reference to the sudden change of heart on both sides from violence to peacemaking. In his *Secret Channels*, Heikal captured the scene: "The contrast between Rabin's dark suit and dour manner and Arafat's tieless military uniform, black and white kaffieyeh and irrepressible grin could not have been greater. Rabin looked like a mourner at a funeral, Arafat an actor collecting his Oscar at a Hollywood ceremony. And yet when they made their speeches Rabin was inspirational and Arafat downbeat. There seemed to be no connection between body language and the spoken word." Clinton, meanwhile, received a sizable boost in the polls. For the politically savvy President, it was a powerful lesson that any progress in the Middle East peace process would be most popular with the public.

––––––

THE ACTUAL IMPLEMENTATION of the DoP proved challenging, given its imprecise nature and the PLO's refusal to abandon its anti-Israeli stand. There followed lengthy negotiations in which Arafat shifted between theatrics and genuine nervous breakdown. Even repeated interventions by Mubarak—determined to secure his reputation, in Washington's eyes, as the indispensable chaperon of Arafat—were largely futile. Nevertheless, Peres arrived in Cairo in early February 1994 to finalize a major agreement codifying the exact dimensions of the "Gaza" and "Jericho" that Arafat was to get. On February 9, in the middle of the signing ceremony, Arafat tried to cheat his way out of the agreement by only pretending to sign the map of Jericho. Peres caught him, and Mubarak forced him to sign. Whether Mubarak only scolded Arafat, as the formal version goes, or actually cursed him, as eyewitnesses insist, Arafat was not amused. Despite this omen, Israel committed to handing Gaza and Jericho over to the PLO authorities in the spring.

After further negotiations on a variety of details, Arafat and Peres met again in Cairo. On April 29, under the aegis of Christopher and Mubarak, they achieved a "breakthrough." Essentially, Peres succumbed to pressure from his three interlocutors and accepted Christopher's urging that Israel take "risks for peace." This entailed giving up many of Israel's sacrosanct security issues related to fighting Islamist terrorism so that Israel and the PLO could finally sign a "peace agreement."

The agreement signed on May 4, 1994, granted the PLO a five-year interim period of self-rule in the Gaza Strip and the Jericho area. The agreement created a new governing entity, the Palestinian Authority (PA), but
stipulated that it would be entirely under PLO control. The PA's Jericho base
would gradually expand as Israel vacated additional territory in the West
Bank. Israel also agreed to the establishment of a well-armed Palestinian
"police force" of more than 10,000 men. The agreement temporarily postponed decisions on many key issues, including Palestinian statehood, the definition of international borders, Palestinian control over the rest of the West
Bank and Arab East Jerusalem, and the "right of return" to their ancestral
homes of up to 4 million Palestinian refugees. In late May, Israel began to
implement its part of the deal without any guarantee that agreement would
be reached on the key issues left untouched. Echoing the Clinton administration, the Israeli government kept calling these unilateral steps "risks for
peace." Rabin was dismissive of public apprehensions concerning the
weapons provided to the PA police. "Stop being afraid," he told the Israeli
people. "There is no danger that these guns will be used against us. The purpose of this ammunition for the Palestinian police is to be used in their vigilant fight against the HAMAS. They won't dream of using it against us, since
they know very well that if they use these guns against us once, at that moment the Oslo Accord will be annulled and the IDF will return to all the
places that have been given to them. The Oslo Accord, despite what the opposition claims, is not irrevocable."

———

MEANWHILE, the initial setbacks in the official Washington talks with the
Palestinians had led the Clinton administration to focus on "the Syrian
track." The administration's approach was a combination of political expediency and a long-standing perception in the State Department. This perception
was most passionately held by James Baker's confidant Edward Djerejian, a
former ambassador to Syria and future ambassador to Israel, and at the time
of these talks assistant secretary of state for Near Eastern affairs. Djerejian
was, and still is, convinced that Syria is the key to the region and that the
United States' regional posture would be secured by an Israeli peace with
Syria. The Clinton White House was not interested in the details. It was interested only in the continuation of *any* Middle Eastern "peace process."

The love-hate relations between Rabin and Peres played right into Clinton's hands. Their rivalry had irrupted into the peace process two years earlier, during what proved to be the last year of the Bush administration. At
that time, when Peres latched on to the Palestinian issue, Rabin grabbed the
Syrian dossier, determined to outperform his partner and rival. Although he

had run on a security-oriented platform and had sworn never to withdraw from the Golan Heights, Rabin gradually raised the profile of the Syrian issue, going so far as to discuss the possibility of partial withdrawal from the sacrosanct Golan if that would bring about genuine peace with Syria.

Starting in the spring of 1992, Rabin endorsed several quasi-official initiatives to the Syrians, and Assad reciprocated. In these first back-channel contacts by journalists and academics under cover of international gatherings, the Israeli participants concluded that only a full withdrawal could break the Syrian deadlock. Jerusalem was apprised and did not say no. In August, Mubarak's adviser Osama al-Baaz arranged the first official meeting between Nimrod Novick, a special envoy from the Israeli Foreign Ministry, and Isa Darwish, the Syrian ambassador to Cairo. Novick immediately informed both the Egyptians and the Syrians that Israel was ready to withdraw from the Golan in exchange for a peace treaty. Yossi Beilin joined these meetings in early September, bringing assurances that Peres concurred in this position.

The cautious Assad could not reconcile Rabin's public statements with the assurances Damascus was getting in these meetings. In mid-September, Assad met Mubarak in Cairo to discuss the prospects of an agreement; on the basis of that meeting he decided to go ahead. Still, Israel and Syria remained far apart. For example, Damascus insisted on a speedy full withdrawal from the Golan but would not go beyond vague promises of eventual peace. Nonetheless, Rabin was encouraged by Syria's departure from its persistent refusal to even discuss a peace treaty and pushed for a summit with Assad, which, he was convinced, would provide a breakthrough leading to a peace treaty within a year.

Afraid that Rabin might steal the glory, Peres launched another channel of contacts in Paris, without Rabin's knowledge; when Rabin heard about this, he expressed his displeasure but was ignored. By mid-October, Peres's envoys—Novick and Beilin—had reached an understanding with their Syrian interlocutors based on an Israeli agreement in principle to withdraw from the entire Golan over five years. They agreed that Damascus would pledge (although not publicly) to restrain (not disarm) the HizbAllah in southern Lebanon. Significantly, Peres accepted the demand that the Israeli-Syrian treaty include a solution to the Palestinian issue, thus giving Assad standing, in Jerusalem's eyes, to address that vexed question.

Rabin counterattacked by soliciting greater U.S. involvement in the Syrian track to deprive Peres of the freedom to act. Although mired in the final phase of a bitter election campaign, the Bush administration obliged. However, the negotiations never progressed beyond a scenario based on a full Israeli withdrawal in return for a yet-to-be-defined peace.

———

THE DYNAMICS changed sharply in July of 1993, when violence escalated in southern Lebanon. Israeli artillery had routinely responded with heavy bombardment to HizbAllah rocket attacks into northern Israel. However, after the HizbAllah killed seven Israeli soldiers, Jerusalem responded with Operation Accountability. In this weeklong operation, the Israeli Air Force flew some 650 sorties, hitting 240 targets and killing 55 HizbAllah fighters. Tens of thousands of Lebanese fled their homes and villages.

The Clinton administration decided to capitalize on this incident to give the Syrian track high priority. On July 25, after exchanging numerous messages with Rabin and Assad, Christopher clinched a cease-fire agreement, including new "rules of behavior" in southern Lebanon. Beirut assented to the oral agreement. However, Christopher had arranged matters so that Damascus was the real guarantor of the HizbAllah's "good behavior," with Syria moving 35,000 troops into HizbAllah-controlled facilities. On that basis, Washington pressured Jerusalem to give Damascus "incentives" to rein in the HizbAllah, in the form of a rejuvenated peace process.

Within a week, Rabin had succumbed to the pressure from Clinton and Christopher. The turning point was Christopher's visit to the region. On August 3, he and Ross met in Jerusalem with Rabin and Itamar Rabinovich, Israel's ambassador to the United States, in order to ascertain Israel's position vis-à-vis Syria, particularly concerning the Golan Heights. The Israeli minutes kept by Rabin, as reproduced by Zeev Schiff in *Haaretz* on August 29, 1997, show a reluctant Rabin refusing to commit Israel to a future withdrawal. "I do not want to take the risk of giving an undertaking on the Golan Heights and then learning that al-Assad says he will implement his part only after the Palestinians agree," Rabin explained. When Christopher persisted in saying that he needed something tangible to work with, Rabin asked, "Let us assume that their demands are accepted. Is Syria prepared to sign a peace agreement with Israel on the assumption that its demands for a full withdrawal are met?" In response to a question from Christopher, Rabin listed the elements of Israel's perception of an acceptable agreement: withdrawal stretched over many years, comprehensive security arrangements, and U.S. participation in implementation. Rabin stressed that before any Israeli withdrawal, Jerusalem would have to conduct a referendum. He reiterated that these were his personal perceptions and that they should not leave the room—that is, not be shared with the Syrians.

Christopher and Ross saw Assad the next day, returned to Israel to update Rabin and ask for further clarifications, returned to Damascus with Rabin's response, and then continued back to Washington. During Christopher's return visit to Israel, Rabin understood from him that the American initiative had failed—that, in Christopher's words, "there was no breakthrough." A few days later, Rabinovich met with Ross to hear about the Americans' latest session in Damascus. "Particularly significant," Rabinovich later recalled, "was the fact that al-Assad did not agree to Rabin's demand that the agreement would be implemented in a manner that would give Israel, at an early stage, an 'overdose' of normalization for a restricted withdrawal. Al-Assad also did not agree to a relatively long implementation period." Nonetheless, Rabinovich was heartened by the Syrian use of the term "full peace," even though Assad steadfastly refused to divulge what he meant by "peace."

The Arab side gives a completely different picture of the Israeli position, on the basis of Assad's conversations with Christopher. In a series of articles in *Al-Hayah* in late November 1999, Patrick Seale, Hafez al-Assad's British confidant and biographer, provided an authoritative account of the Syrian side of the story based on access to Syrian records. "The Syrian track," Seale wrote, "did not see any movement until Rabin on 3 August 1993 asked then U.S. Secretary of State Warren Christopher to pass on an important message to the Syrian President which had the American diplomat touch down in Damascus the following day, 4 August. According to Syrian and American sources, al-Assad was informed that Israel was prepared to commit to a full withdrawal from the Golan Heights, provided its security concerns and its demands for normal ties with Damascus were met." As Seale recounts it, Assad put two questions to Christopher: "The first was, 'When Rabin speaks about withdrawal, does he mean full withdrawal to the positions which Israel held on 4 June 1967?' Christopher's answer was, 'I have a pledge for full withdrawal, but without the definition of a line.' The second question was, 'Does Israel claim any part of the territory, which it occupied on the Syrian front in June 1967?' The U.S. official's answer was, 'Not to my knowledge.'"

Obviously, there is a profound difference between the Israeli and Syrian versions of what Rabin said in that fateful meeting on August 3. Furthermore, there is no reason to doubt the veracity of either the contemporary Israeli record or the Syrian record. The discrepancy is evidently the result of an intentional misrepresentation of the Israeli position by Christopher. In order to keep the momentum of the peace process going, he took it upon himself to transform Rabin's hypothetical option into an explicit commitment, as well as to suppress all Rabin's caveats, particularly on the referendum issue. Jerusalem, of course, was not informed about what Christopher had done— thus sowing the seeds of profound misunderstandings between Damascus and Jerusalem.

On August 30, in the ongoing Washington talks, the Syrian representative, Muwaffaq Allaf, insisted on "a commitment to an Israeli withdrawal from the Golan Heights." The surprised Rabinovich later characterized

Allaf's position as a "misunderstanding or a misrepresentation of Christopher's mission earlier in August." As he recalled, "Rabin was very careful to emphasize to the secretary that he was engaging in a hypothetical exercise. . . ." It did not cross Rabinovich's mind that Allaf's insistence on a "commitment" accurately reflected what Christopher had conveyed to Assad.

President Clinton himself showed complete disdain for the Israeli security concerns. In an interview with Thomas Friedman of the *New York Times* on September 13, 1993, Clinton recounted in detail a phone conversation with Assad, in which he told Assad that Jerusalem's priority should be "making the Israeli people as comfortable as they can be with this"—namely, the withdrawal from the Golan. Clinton urged Assad to capitalize on the building momentum of the Oslo process. "I personally believe that it [the momentum] is a lot more important than the details of this piece of land on the Golan Heights or anything else," Clinton told Assad.

The Syrian record of the Clinton-Assad phone conversation, as conveyed by Seale, reveals an even greater cynicism on Clinton's part than he displayed to Friedman. "Clinton told al-Assad on the phone that Rabin needed the Syrian leader's help. Rabin, added Clinton, wanted to make progress on the Syrian track but he now lacked the necessary political muscle to make that happen. If the Oslo agreement had won strong support and if al-Assad silenced the enemies of peace, meaning the Damascus-based rejectionist Palestinian groups, Rabin would return to talking with Syria in pursuit of a comprehensive settlement and Syrian interests would be taken into consideration. Thus, as Clinton appeared to suggest, it was in Syria's interest to back the Oslo accord. Al-Assad did not fall for that but he did not want to hurt Clinton's feelings and so he let his ambassador show up at the signing ceremony for the Oslo accords at the White House lawn." Rabinovich, not knowing of that phone conversation, saw the fact that the Syrian ambassador shook hands with Rabin and Peres on the White House lawn as a source of great optimism.

If Seale's account is accurate, it starkly demonstrates just how out of touch with reality the Clinton administration was. Washington did not comprehend the centrality of Assad's commitment to Bilad al-Sham—the historic Greater Syria. In an article in *Al-Safir* on February 1, 2000, Heikal reflected on the profound implications of the Oslo accords. "The Oslo agreement came as a shock to President Hafiz al-Assad: The center of the cause (Palestine) was taken out of its wider context (historical Bilad al-Sham). This happened through a sudden attack," Heikal explained, "without his prior knowledge. And this sudden attack (Oslo) came at a moment when he thought he was close (it was said by 80 percent) to a solution with Israel that he wanted to be comprehensive of Syria's commitments within the frame-

work of historical Bilad al-Sham." Hence, not only had the Clinton administration unilaterally deprived Assad of his historical responsibility for the fate
of the entire Bilad al-Sham (which, after all, had been recognized by Peres in
the fall of 1992), but President Clinton also now wanted him to publicly
demonstrate support for the Oslo accords with Arafat.

For Assad, this was adding insult to injury. Damascus could not imagine
that the Clinton administration had never even heard of Bilad al-Sham, let
alone considered it in formulating its policy for the Middle East. It didn't
help that the PLO had leaked the fact that Syria was also negotiating with Israel, so that Arafat's acceptance of the Oslo accords would not appear to be
unique. An infuriated Assad ordered all talks with the Israelis suspended. A
few weeks later, however, he permitted the resumption of the academic channel in Oslo. In October, the Syrians and Israelis formulated a draft proposal
defining the general principles for a full withdrawal in return for peace and
normalization. At this point, both Cairo and Damascus were convinced that
Jerusalem had committed to a full withdrawal from the Golan Heights, despite numerous public denials by Israeli leaders. At the same time, apprehensive about what he saw as a U.S.–Israeli conspiracy to cut Syria out of the
Palestinian issue, Assad refused to permit his representatives to clarify the
Syrian perception of peace.

In early November, with the negotiations stalled, Peres sought King Hussein's support and got a commitment in principle to an Israeli-Jordanian
warm peace. Jerusalem and Washington sought to use this commitment to
pressure Syria. However, once the king publicly stated that Jordan would not
make a separate peace until there was "a meaningful breakthrough" on the
Syrian track, Damascus saw no reason to rush. Meanwhile, U.S. pressure on
Jerusalem to maintain "momentum" increased when Rabin visited the White
House in mid-November. Clinton started from the premise that Israel had already committed to a full withdrawal. "The Syrians expect a reaffirmation of
the commitments," Clinton told Rabin. A shaken Rabin made a futile effort
to persuade Clinton that no commitment had been made. "We call it a deposit," he explained in reference to his August 3 conversation with Christopher, adding that his was a hypothetical assertion that could be withdrawn.
Clinton would have none of this.

What Clinton was seeking was something dramatic for a summit between him and Assad scheduled for January 16, 1994, in Geneva. At this
summit, Clinton assured Assad of a complete Israeli withdrawal in return for
some form of "normalization" and "confidence-building measures," which
Assad adamantly refused. Clinton's offers of generous foreign aid, along
with the removal of Syria from the list of countries actively engaged in terrorism and drug-trafficking, did not move Assad, who was only willing to

state that Syria had "adopted the strategic option of peace" and that he was ready to establish "normal peaceful relations" with Israel in return for full withdrawal to the lines of June 4, 1967. He would not elaborate on Syria's perception of peace or on why he would not agree to normalization of relations. Returning to Washington, Clinton lied to Jerusalem, insisting that Assad had accepted "normalization" as part of the "comprehensive peace" that would follow "complete withdrawal."

On January 21, Damascus was traumatized by the sudden death of Assad's eldest son and intended heir, Basil, in what was officially called a "traffic accident." In reality, Basil was assassinated as the result of a power struggle in the uppermost circles of the regime—most likely over the control of revenues from the drug and weapons trade. A couple of days later, a stony-faced Hafez al-Assad stood by the grave of his son, with whom were buried his greatest hopes for an enduring legacy. "I won't let them see just how much they hurt me," he told a confidant. Damascus froze institutionally and moved to extremist positions.

Once again, Clinton would not accept this. Later that month King Hussein, then receiving treatment for lymphatic cancer at the Mayo Clinic, was called in by the White House and urged to intercede with Assad and to assist in pressuring Jerusalem. Hussein's efforts eventually took him to Damascus for a very informative meeting with Assad. The Syrians told the king they would not stand in the way of a separate Israeli-Jordanian peace, but they insisted there would be no progress on the Israeli-Syrian track. Assad hinted that if he did not get what he wanted by the middle of the year, "all options" were open for him, which Hussein took—quite correctly—to mean anything from a flare-up in southern Lebanon to a full war with Israel. Syrian officials also intimated that the Iranians—now with Chinese backing—were encouraging Assad to go to war in yet another American election year. Hussein returned to Washington to report his failure. Undaunted, the administration put on a public smile and set to work on the next phase of pressuring Israel.

There began a relentless campaign, direct and indirect, in public and in private, to convince Rabin that Assad had crossed his Rubicon in the January summit in Geneva and that now Rabin must reciprocate. Clinton portrayed Syria as the key to the Middle East and suggested that by resisting the administration's policy Israel was sabotaging the entire regional posture of the United States. In a mid-May speech National Security Advisor Anthony Lake elaborated on this view. "Syria plays a critical role in the wider sweep of regional peace," Lake explained. "Syria has used its influence both for ill, as when it rejected Sadat's peace with Israel, and for good, as when Damascus joined the Gulf War against Saddam Hussein and, most importantly, when it entered into direct bilateral negotiations with Israel." Lake argued that the

Geneva summit put Syria firmly in the good guys' camp: "Thus, when President Assad took the significant step of announcing in Geneva with President Clinton that Syria had made, in his words, a 'strategic choice for peace' with Israel, his nation's erstwhile extremist allies quickly grew very nervous. Palestinian rejectionist leaders, fearful that they would lose their bases in Lebanon and Syria, went off to Libya in search of new havens. HizbAllah leaders argued how best to pursue an extremist agenda in an era of Israeli-Lebanese peace. Iranian officials hurriedly visited Damascus but apparently left empty-handed, and when they got home, the Iranian clergy began criticizing the leadership for failing to prevent the emerging isolation of their nation."

Not only was there no factual foundation for Lake's assertions, but, in addition, even if they had been correct, they said nothing about the nature of the "peace" and "security" Israel would get in return for its complete withdrawal.

Nonetheless, for the Clinton administration this reading of recent events justified intensifying the pressure on Israel, culminating in a meeting between Rabin and Christopher on June 18. Jerusalem considered this conversation to be the most important on the issue of the June 4, 1967, lines. According to the Israeli minutes, as reproduced by Schiff, Christopher pressed Rabin: "It is vital for me to be able to say that if he [Assad] responds (positively) to your terms, I will be able to tell him things clearly at the end of the line. But that is not an undertaking to him. . . . " Rabin responded by stating what the United States could tell Assad on how far Israel was willing to go. "You can tell him that he has every reason to believe that that [full withdrawal] will be the outcome. But the Israelis will not spell it out before all our needs are met. You will be able to say that is your understanding, but he will not be able to receive it if he does not fulfill our demands." Christopher replied, "It is in my pocket! It is not on the table!" Jerusalem and Washington would both come to refer to Rabin's position as the "Pocket File." Jerusalem concluded from this exchange that the Americans would tell Assad that "it was their impression that Israel would agree to discuss the 4 June lines with a positive disposition if its demands were met."

Instead, Christopher assured Assad in mid-July that he had gotten a commitment from Rabin for an Israeli withdrawal to the June 4 line. Seale is very explicit about Assad's reading of these developments. "Christopher was not able to offer the clarification demanded by al-Assad in August 1993. It was not until he carried out another shuttle between Jerusalem and Damascus during the period 19–22 July 1994 that the U.S. secretary announced that Rabin pledged full withdrawal to the 4 June 1967 lines on the condition of meeting his demands within a peace deal, and the promise, as usual, that this pledge would remain secret to protect Rabin from his Israeli critics. A few days later, on 25 July, Clinton talked with al-Assad on the telephone and the two leaders agreed that the clarification represented a major accomplishment for the recent Christopher shuttle." For Damascus, Seale concluded, "it was clear that President Clinton and Secretary Christopher regarded the pledge as real and so they communicated it to President al-Assad."

Arab officials now acknowledge that Christopher violated Rabin's trust. A senior Lebanese official recently recounted Beirut's reading of the dynamics, adding some interesting details. "In May 1994, Christopher informed Rabin that al-Assad wanted an explicit official commitment from the Israeli Government that it was ready to withdraw to the 4 June 1967 line. He told him that al-Assad would suspend the negotiations with the Jewish state if he did not receive such a commitment. On 18 June 1994, Rabin agreed to the Syrian request. He informed the U.S. secretary of state that Israel would withdraw from the Golan to the 4 June 1967 line. This meant that it would withdraw from the al-Hammah village and the area around Lake Galilee. Rabin told Christopher: 'We will not announce our position officially until the Syrian leadership accepts our demands.' The U.S. secretary of state responded: 'Rest assured that your commitment is in my pocket and not on the negotiating table.'"

Thus, in July 1994, fearing that Assad would break off negotiations if he did not get Rabin's explicit commitment, Christopher gave it to him despite his promise to Rabin that the option would be kept in his pocket. Moreover, the Clinton administration did not disclose to Jerusalem the commitment made to Assad. Consequently, the ensuing negotiations were completely skewed because the Syrians *knew* the extent of the ultimate Israeli concessions and used that as a starting position.

Although the U.S.–Syrian exchanges continued until early August, they did not seem to be getting anywhere, and the administration, still looking for a breakthrough before the midterm congressional elections, resumed concentration on the PLO. It also kept a separate deal with King Hussein on the back burner in case some last-minute campaign hoopla was needed. By this time, Iranian First Vice President Hassan Habibi had traveled to Beijing, committing not only Tehran but also Damascus to the Trans-Asian Axis, and making nonsense of Anthony Lake's rosy depiction of the world scene.

———

BY EARLY 1993, Beijing had concluded that "the conflict of strategic interests between China and the United States . . . is now surfacing steadily," because Washington "absolutely cannot tolerate the rise of a powerful adversary in East Asia." The implications of Beijing's conclusions were laid out in a June 1993 textbook issued by the high command of the People's Liberation Army called *Can the Chinese Army Win the Next War?* This book presented eight scenarios by which Beijing could defend its vital interests while avoiding a direct military confrontation with the United States. It identified the optimal points of engagement as being at the extreme fringes of the new Trans-Asian Axis, where allies of Beijing—North Korea and Iran-Syria, respectively—were willing to confront the United States and its regional allies on their own.

These views meshed with Tehran's anticipation of an impending confrontation with the United States. In late September 1993, IRGC Commander Rezai pointed out that the most credible threat to Iran was a limited strike by the United States against key installations designed to reverse the strategic correlation of forces without engaging Iran in a full-scale war. Rezai warned, however, that the Americans would not be able to control the scope of such a war: If Washington "enter[ed] this military vortex, it [would] sustain irredeemable losses." Moreover, since the routine deployments of U.S. forces in the Near East could be "used for military purposes [against Iran] within moments," they should be considered legitimate targets. In late February 1994, Tehran began emphasizing its potential role in the Trans-Asian Axis. Apart from the global struggle with the United States, Tehran could offer its services in furtherance of Beijing's drive to acquire large quantities of oil from the Persian Gulf states.

Pakistan was wholeheartedly enthusiastic about the Iran-led Islamic Bloc and the wider Trans-Asian Axis. Islamabad stressed that "if there can be a new alliance or bloc, then it should include Pakistan, Iran, Afghanistan, the Islamic countries of Central Asia, and Turkey. That will be a natural alliance. . . . If China can be included in the present alliance, then there is no reason why U.S. hegemony in the world could not be resisted." Pakistan saw itself as the lynchpin linking the PRC and the Muslim world. "The history of cooperation and friendship between Pakistan and China is enviable," Islamabad explained. "No one will object to China's inclusion in the alliance of Muslim countries as China has not been seen to carry out aggression against any neighboring country, nor has it claimed the territory of its neighbors." Tehran differed only in seeing itself as assuming the leading role vis-à-vis the PRC. As Tehran put it, "the PRC sees it in the perspective of Iran and Pakistan, but Iran is more important." However, Iran recognized that much of the transfer of Chinese military technologies, primarily in such sensitive areas as nuclear weapons, would still have to be conducted via Pakistan.

The consolidation of the Trans-Asian Axis was completed in the summer of 1994 with the visit to Beijing by Habibi and twenty-six other senior Iranian officials, including the elite of Iran's economic and industrial establishment. Both Tehran and Beijing explicitly stated that the visit was "at the official invitation of the Chinese Premier," Li Peng, who had made the Trans-Asian Axis the cornerstone of the PRC's global strategy.

While Habibi was in Beijing, Tehran made public his vision of the future of Asia, specifically stating that these subjects were being clarified with the PRC at that very moment:

> With the forging of new political alliances on the international level and the changes in international balances, strategic unions are vital and mandatory for all Asian countries that do not want to be in the orbits of the U.S., European, or even Japanese pole, or be relegated to being marginal appendages. In fact, the era the United States envisions, where it will be the only power center in the world, has not yet taken shape. Close and consistent cooperation among the bigger independent countries, such as the Islamic Republic of Iran, the PRC, Kazakhstan, and even Pakistan, can be viewed in this context. High technology, unique manpower, limitless energy resources, and the enviable economic growth of these countries can all be molded into a firm and reliable "fourth pole" in Asia with the advent of the 21st century. Time is passing by swiftly; this opportunity should not be lost.

In view of the mutual praise exchanged by Habibi and virtually all the leaders of the PRC, Habibi's account should be considered as accurately representing the strategic vision of both Iran and China. Thus, amidst the fracturing of the post–Cold War world, a new strategic bloc was emerging, an alliance stretching from North Africa all the way to Northeast Asia. This expanded Trans-Asian Axis derived its might from the radicalization of the Muslim world, and its growing use of international terrorism and subversion as instruments of statecraft compounded the threat to the West.

This grand strategic dynamic must be borne in mind as the background against which the Arab–Israeli peace process was taking place.

––––––

THROUGHOUT THIS PERIOD, Yassir Arafat had to juggle two contradictory objectives: He had to satisfy the militant Islamists by facilitating terrorism, and he had to placate the United States and Israel so that they would continue to deliver the money and concessions he needed to survive. Since there was no way he could have taken on the Islamists even if he had wanted to, he had to convince Jerusalem that his reluctance to fight terrorism was in Israel's own interest. "I would suggest not making Arafat look like an Israeli agent, like an Uncle Tom serving his masters," chief PLO negotiator Nabil Shaath opined in November 1994, because "the effect on us is devastating."

Arafat ensured that his true sentiments were clear irrespective of all his juggling. He and his coterie never wavered from, or even denied their commitment to, their ultimate objective: the destruction of Israel. On the contrary, there was a growing Islamicization of Arafat's speeches—clearly expressed in his frequent citations from the Koran and his use of Islamic symbolism. This change of style reflected his increasing awareness of the Islamicization of Palestinian society, particularly the youth—the core of his power base.

In May 1994, on the eve of his planned return from Tunis to "Palestine," Arafat took the opportunity of an invitation to speak at a mosque in Johannesburg, South Africa, to state his goals. In this address, Arafat maintained that he was forced into the peace process by the economic conditions in the territories following the Gulf War. But that was a temporary accommodation, he stressed, and in fact the Cairo agreement he had just signed with Israel was "the first step and nothing more than that" on the road to Jerusalem. "The jihad will continue," Arafat declared. "Jerusalem is not only of the Palestinian people, but of the entire Islamic nation. . . . After this [Cairo] agreement, our main battle is not to get the maximum out of them [Israel] here and there. The main battle is over Jerusalem, the third most sacred site of the Muslims." He urged his audience to join the Palestinian struggle. "You must come to fight, to begin the jihad to liberate Jerusalem, your first shrine." As for the agreements signed with Israel, "I regard this agreement as no more than the agreement signed between our prophet Muhammad and the Quraysh in Mecca," Arafat stated, using the same comparison that he had used a year earlier, on the eve of the Khartoum summit. "As the Prophet Muhammad accepted it [the Treaty of Hudaibiya], . . . we now accept the peace agreement [with Israel], but in order to continue on the way to Jerusalem." Arafat told his listeners that the PLO needed them "as Muslims and as mujahideen," and he concluded by chanting: "Until victory, until Jerusalem, until Jerusalem, until Jerusalem."

The Johannesburg speech, along with other, similar pronouncements, left no doubt that as far as Arafat and his circle were concerned, no reconciliation with Israel—not even the acceptance of the very existence of Israel—was possible. Given this enduring taboo in the Arab world and the growing militancy of the Arab masses, Arafat realized that there was no option but an explosion. He was now determined to be in the lead.

———

THE BUILDUP of militant Islamist networks continued unabated throughout the spring of 1994, not only in the territories but also in Jordan. In fact, the Jordanian headquarters, training bases, and support facilities of both HAMAS and Islamic Jihad became crucial to sustaining anti-Israeli operations, given the successes of the Israeli security services in breaking local networks within the territories. Jordan-based headquarters even began issuing communiqués claiming responsibility for terrorist operations inside Israel. In mid-April, despite his close personal relations with King Hussein, Rabin issued a warning that unless Amman cracked down on the terrorist organizations on its soil, Israel would insist that Jordan be declared a terrorism-sponsoring state. Attempting to take back the initiative, Warren Christopher sent Amman a formal warning that "the HAMAS declarations would lead to Jordan's inclusion on the list of countries sponsoring terrorism." Alarmed, Hussein tried to assure Israel of his commitment to fighting Islamist terrorism once the time was ripe. The Rabin government, however, remained concerned, because it perceived the Jordan-based Islamist infrastructure as the greatest potential threat to the ability of its "partner in peace," Arafat, to consolidate his rule over Gaza-Jericho.

Arafat, for his part, was in no rush to return to "Palestine." His coterie continued to push back the date for his return with the flimsiest excuses. The real reason for Arafat's reluctance was fear for his life. He had learned that Israeli intelligence had obtained a recording of his Johannesburg speech; and he confided to his Force 17 commanders that—now knowing his real intentions—the Israelis would certainly assassinate him at the first opportunity.

In fact, Arafat had nothing to fear. Eager to preserve the aura of the peace process, the Rabin government simply closed its ears when presented with the Johannesburg recording. Instead, the Israeli security services launched Operation Blazing Desert, the largest such operation in Israel's history, to protect Arafat from assassination by Islamist radicals—or indeed by his own Fatah activists, who were accusing him of "selling out to the Israelis." On July 1, Arafat finally returned to Gaza for a three-day visit. At Mubarak's urging, the Israeli authorities went out of their way to accord him VIP treatment. In his speech in Gaza, Arafat underscored two points: (1) that the challenge ahead was rebuilding a Palestine destroyed by "the evil [Israeli] occupation" and (2) that "the jihad" would continue until Sheikh Yassin and other HAMAS terrorists currently in Israeli jails were released. (In fact, many of these Islamists were in jail for conspiring against Arafat and the PLO.) Not once did Arafat mention making peace with Israel or even a desire for Palestinian-Israeli coexistence.

Nevertheless, a few days later, the Rabin government accepted the Palestinian recommendation that Egypt and Jordan be formally invited to a joint conference on Palestinian refugees. This conference led to the creation of several quadrilateral committees to discuss unresolved issues from the Gaza-Jericho accord (such as arrangements for border crossings and for safe corridors between the Gaza Strip and Jericho) and the transfer of civilian responsibilities to the PLO in the rest of the territories. The next day, the conference announced Israel's intention of accelerating the extension of self-rule at new talks in Cairo in which the three Arab entities and Israel would jointly decide the thorniest issues. However, despite the Rabin government's penchant for unilateral concessions, the talks went nowhere, because the PLO made demands that even its Arab friends considered outrageous.

At this point, the Clinton administration, worried by the prospect of crisis, started using Mubarak to float ideas about the next phase of the peace process. This alarmed both Rabin and King Hussein, who met secretly near the Dead Sea and resolved that the Israeli-Jordanian relationship must be brought into the open in order to counterbalance the American tilt. To expedite the move, Jerusalem accepted Jordanian demands on virtually all outstanding bilateral issues—from disputed territory in the Arava Desert to water rights. A few days later, Christopher met Peres and Jordanian Premier Abdel Salam al-Majali in Washington. The Clinton administration was advised of the Israeli-Jordanian decision and was asked to give its blessing. On July 25, President Clinton presided in the White House over the signing of the Washington agreement by Rabin and King Hussein.

For Arafat, this was a warning sign that he might, after all, be expendable and that Washington might yet rejuvenate the pre–peace process Jordanian-Israeli solution for the territories, using the local leading families as the power base. Arafat immediately urged the Egyptians to revive communication channels with both Israel and the United States. The administration was most receptive, and when Christopher next visited the region, he took the occasion to give Arafat "a chance" to prove his commitment to fighting the Islamists. Consequently, Rabin met Arafat near Gaza on August 10. Arafat did nothing but complain—demanding, among other things, that Israel release Sheikh Yassin and transfer huge amounts of money to Arafat's own bank accounts in Tel Aviv and Western Europe. Rabin responded by threatening Arafat with the suspension of the entire Oslo process unless the PA started seriously fighting terrorism.

Pushed to the wall, Arafat agreed. In the next few days, his forces arrested forty-five HAMAS activists with great fanfare—including shootouts in front of TV cameras. However, only twelve of the forty-five were actually indicted. They were swiftly convicted and sentenced to long terms in jail, but a week later, while Israel's attention was focused elsewhere, they were quietly released.

With his leadership of the PA now acknowledged anew by Jerusalem, Arafat again chose to underscore his commitment to the Islamist cause. It was not lost on him that some of the PLO military units most loyal to him had turned Islamist. And so, in Palestinian forums, he stressed that the PA intentionally was not living up to the commitments it had made in agreements with Israel. The PLO had never renounced the articles in the Palestinian Covenant explicitly calling for the destruction of Israel; now Arafat told the Fatah leadership in Tunis, "I shall never change even a single article in the

Palestinian Covenant." The PA used the term "The State of Palestine"—instead of "The Palestinian National Authority"—in signing international agreements, such as an agreement with UNESCO. And there was a near total disregard of small details such as illegal activities of the Palestinian police and secret services, not only in the territories but also in Israel itself.

Because Arafat's support for the Islamists was motivated by both ideology and his quest for personal survival, neither the Islamists nor the PA authorities took seriously his threats of a crackdown on terrorism. Nobody confused the occasional arrest of a few Islamists and the destruction of their property with a thorough dismantling of the Islamist infrastructure—something that the PA not only could not do but also did not want to do. Several of Arafat's senior commanders supervising the PLO's campaign against HAMAS repeatedly declared their total support for HAMAS. In September, at the height of the pressure on Arafat to crack down on the terrorists, Jibril Rajub, his chief of internal security, asserted that the PLO and HAMAS had "blood ties and a single fate." Rajub rejected any notion of his forces fighting Islamist terrorism or even helping to prevent terrorism inside Israel. "We are not an insurance company," he said. "We are not responsible for the security of the Israelis, but for the security of the Palestinians." The PA security organs dealt with the Islamists only when they were implicated in conspiracies against Arafat.

As for Arafat himself, in early October, at the height of the HAMAS wave of terrorism within Israel, he wrote a letter to Sheikh Yassin and to al-Ahdi Hunim, a leading Islamist terrorist, both of whom were in jail in Israel. "My brother Sheikh Yassin, and my brother the sacred Sheikh al-Ahdi Hunim," he wrote, "I admire your participation in the struggle for the liberation of Palestine. It is because of you that Palestine is free. We've proven with the blood of our martyrs that the Palestinian people is 'the strong number' in the Middle East." Israeli intelligence intercepted Arafat's letter and brought it to the government's attention, but, as with the Johannesburg speech, no action was taken.

Arafat also affirmed that his participation in the peace process did not deviate from the PLO's 1974 Phases Program/Phased Plan—namely, that any segment of Palestine vacated by Israel should be taken and used as a springboard for the ultimate destruction of Israel. In a mid-November speech in Gaza, Arafat specifically applied this strategy to the establishment of the Palestinian Authority in the Gaza Strip. "The first step in the struggle against the Israeli enemy has been implemented," Arafat told a cheering crowd. "In 1974 we made a decision to establish our national authority on any liberated land."

Meanwhile, HAMAS's spectacular terrorism at the heart of Israel continued to escalate, with the most active networks operating with impunity from Arafat's own fiefdom in Gaza. Even the awarding of the Nobel Peace

Prize jointly to Rabin, Peres, and Arafat did not change the situation. Instead of taking on HAMAS and the Islamic Jihad, Arafat insisted that Mossad was trying to assassinate him and that the wave of terrorism was part of an Israeli conspiracy against the nascent Palestinian entity. However, there was a telling example of what Arafat's forces could do when they wanted to. On November 18, an Islamist mob of about 2,000 started rioting in Gaza. The moment they started denouncing Arafat, two carloads of security forces arrived and opened fire with assault rifles, killing 14 outright and wounding some 150. The shocked mob turned back and started ransacking stores in Gaza's main square while shouting anti-Jewish slurs. The PA security forces ceased fire and stood by.

———

WHILE ISRAELI-PLO RELATIONS were deteriorating, Israeli-Jordanian relations were surging. The moment King Hussein decided to bring his relations with Israel into the open, it was only a question of time before the few outstanding territorial and water issues were resolved. The bulk of the negotiations were conducted directly between the prime minister's office in Jerusalem and the king's palace in Amman, though the United States was kept informed of the progress.

In October 1994, with the Republicans led by Newt Gingrich describing the upcoming congressional elections as a referendum on President Clinton's domestic policy, it became imperative for the administration to divert the public's attention, and so the White House exerted pressure on Israel and Jordan to have "a Presidential event" before the elections. Hence, Rabin, King Hussein, and a host of VIPs from all over the world gathered at the Arava border crossing on October 26 for the signing of a peace agreement, with President Clinton overseeing the procedure. In fact, this was a purely symbolic event, because the documents were not yet complete. The real signing of properly ratified, legally obligatory agreements did not take place until November 10. By then, the White House, bruised by the Republicans' winning the House of Representatives for the first time since 1952, was not interested.

For Arafat and for Hafez al-Assad, however, the Clinton administration's ability to manipulate Israel and Jordan into the Arava event served as proof that Washington could deliver Israel when it wanted to. Therefore, its failure to do so on their behalf confirmed their fervent belief that Washington, whatever it said, was engaged in a conspiracy against them. As for the Clinton White House, the new environment in Washington would greatly affect how it did business, not least in the Middle East.

6

"Like the Wings of a Bird" (1994–1996)

Rapprochement Between Arafat and HAMAS; Dynasty Building in Tehran, Damascus, and Baghdad

ONCE THE WHITE HOUSE began to recover from the shock of the elections, President Clinton ordered an all-out effort to shape his own political posture for the presidential election of 1996. The White House recognized that the 1994 votes were less pro-Gingrich or pro-Republican than anti-Clinton, both because the electorate distrusted his domestic policies (especially the health care plan) and because personal scandals surrounded him. Changing the public's perception of the Clinton presidency, virtually at all costs, became a necessity. And so, within this context, the administration decided to exploit foreign policy as an instrument for furthering its domestic political agenda. This dynamic was aggravated by the Clinton White House's inherent loathing of the military and profound misunderstanding of how force is used as a political instrument. Consequently, starting in November of 1994, U.S. foreign policy would be largely determined by the average American voter's sense of being "better off," which, extensive opinion polls showed, meant being able to pursue a comfortable everyday life. Hence, two subjects came to dominate U.S. foreign policy: cheap oil and cheap consumer goods.

The quest for cheap consumer goods, from TVs and watches to shirts and toys, made it imperative to avoid a crisis with Beijing. However, since the administration had been loudly advocating human rights, democratization, nonproliferation, and other policies the PRC showed no inclination toward pursuing, Washington needed to be able to justify Beijing's actions. The administration's tactic was to use China's very noncompliance on the nuclear-proliferation issue as the key to avoiding confrontation with Capitol Hill over other issues: It was so important to deal with the proliferation question, the administration argued, that the United States had to ignore all lesser matters, such as the trade deficit. This logic, in turn, drove the PRC to continue, and indeed expand, its nuclear proliferation in order to divert Washington's attention from other aspects of its evolving posture in East Asia.

The quest for cheap oil, meanwhile, meant that Muslim interests would dominate U.S. policy in any area where Muslims were confronting non-Muslims. Hence, Bosnia had to become a Muslim state, come hell or high water, and the administration would bomb the civilian infrastructure of Yugoslavia for the sake of the Kosovo Albanians. Islamist revivalism was tolerated throughout the Hub of Islam, even when it endangered moderate governments traditionally friendly to the United States and strained relations with such close allies as France. The Clinton administration risked the alienation of Russia to a Cold War level in favoring the Chechens, and it impeded the emergence of genuinely independent post-Soviet countries in Central Asia and the Caucasus. Even the power of the American Jewish establishment did not suffice to prevent growing pressure on Israel to abandon the positions of its democratically elected government in favor of the political fortunes of President Clinton.

––––––

THE FIRST DYNAMIC in the Middle East where the new zeal of the Clinton administration manifested itself was the Syrian track. In the winter of 1994–95, the administration pushed to extremes the already tenuous Israeli-Syrian contacts.

Back in late July, the administration had established the "ambassadors' channel" in Washington between Israel's Itamar Rabinovich and Syria's Walid Mualem. Essentially, this channel was a series of informal meetings at Dennis Ross's home, also attended by National Security Council member Martin Indyk. Rabinovich viewed these discussions mainly as the basis of further mediation by the Americans. As he later wrote, he and Mualem "would explore and establish the limits of our position," and then the Americans would work with Rabin and Assad to try to impel them "to make new decisions and to move closer to the still nonexistent line of compromise." Rabinovich and the Americans were optimistic about the prospects of these contacts because of Mualem's growing informality—expressed, for example, in his preference for conversing on Ross's porch so that he could smoke freely. Still, Mualem would not deviate an iota from Assad's uncompromising position. Rabinovich reluctantly became "doubtful that our Syrian interlocutors had thought seriously and concretely about a 'warm peace' with Israel."

By the early fall, meanwhile, Israeli military intelligence had become extremely apprehensive about Syria's long-term objectives. In a mid-September article in *Yediot Aharonot*, military correspondent Ron Ben-Yishai wrote that sustaining the peace process was actually serving the Syrian military effort, because "no less than al-Assad wants to achieve an offensive capability, he wants to make sure that the IDF does not one day go beyond the cease-fire line on the Golan Heights and find itself in the suburbs of Damascus." Hence, Assad's sudden support for the peace process could also be explained by his desire to obtain a U.S. guarantee that there would be no Israeli preemptive strike before Syria was ready for an offensive war. Indeed, Ben-Yishai noted, several senior Israeli defense officials were convinced the Syrian policy was actually "a strategic deception," and they were worried that "al-Assad want[ed] to achieve through the negotiations a period of tranquility to permit his Army to complete what it lack[ed] in the air and in air defenses, and to absorb the quantitative and qualitative jump taken by his ground forces."

Not everyone in Jerusalem shared this perception, however. Rabin and Ehud Barak—who by now was Chief of the General Staff—were convinced that a frank discussion of the security issues among professionals would untangle the complexities and convince Assad that Israel had no aggressive designs. In fact, there was no foundation for this conviction. Ardent peacemakers were puzzled when Israeli-Syrian negotiations came to yet another futile climax in the fall of 1994. "I can't read very clearly the Syrian map," Yossi Beilin conceded. "It's difficult for me to understand why al-Assad didn't seize the opportunity if you [Israel] are ready to uproot and dismantle settlements, if you are ready to speak about sovereignty of the Golan. I missed something in the thought of the other side."

As of September, the Syrians remained immovable. Even so, Warren Christopher shuttled to the region once again and got "major concessions" from Assad—namely, that Foreign Minister al-Shara would travel to Washington with several senior officers (under a special waiver, needed because of Syria's sponsorship of terrorism and the drug trade); once there he would give interviews to Israeli media, and the officers would be permitted to meet with their Israeli counterparts. Christopher tried to elicit additional concessions from Jerusalem to reciprocate for what he termed "Assad's goodwill," but he was rebuffed by Rabin, who nevertheless reiterated Israel's willingness to withdraw from part of the Golan in the context of a peace agreement. Meanwhile, visiting London, al-Shara publicly answered a question from an Israeli correspondent.

Washington saw these developments as sufficient to warrant President Clinton's visiting Damascus. Clinton's visit was preceded by intense preparations, in which the White House and Assad's office worked out the language Assad would use in a joint press conference with Clinton so that the United States could justify removing Syria from the terrorism list. However, when an American correspondent raised the issue, Assad resorted to his old hard-line wording.

Washington and Jerusalem debated whether Assad's change of wording was intentional or the product of a "genuine misunderstanding," and they both concluded not that the Syrian position remained rigid, but that the Western media were the wrong instrument for Syrian public diplomacy. In fact, as Seale tells it, during the meeting with Clinton, Assad "proposed what he considered basic principles for the security arrangements," but Clinton deemed them unacceptably vague. Therefore, Assad saw no reason to go along with the wording Clinton was expecting him to use in public.

At the same time, Damascus did not want to stop the administration from working hard to deliver Israeli concessions. Therefore, Assad authorized security contacts in Washington, while ensuring that nothing tangible could result. He achieved this by naming Major General Hikmat al-Shihabi, his Chief of General Staff, as his representative. Although faithful to Assad, Shihabi was a Sunni Muslim and had therefore never been a member of the Allawite inner circle. Furthermore, his son, a physician, was (and still is) living in Los Angeles with his family; many in Damascus considered Shihabi "Washington's man" and a CIA spy. Thus, despite his stellar military record, Shihabi had little power. He could be expected to deliver Assad's message faithfully, but he would have no authority to make decisions, let alone to compromise.

In November, Barak—who would be Shihabi's opposite number in the official Chiefs of Staff meetings—came to Washington along with Rabin's military aide, Danny Yatom, for a series of preparatory meetings. In these meetings with Rabinovich and Mualem, supervised by Ross and Indyk, Barak presented the professional position of the IDF that the permanent border should be 8 to 10 miles east of the Jordan River and that Israeli withdrawal should occur over a span of at least five years. The IDF also expected extensive demilitarization in Syria, to reduce the risk of a sudden war. Mualem reiterated Assad's demand for a withdrawal to the June 4 line (as defined by Syria) as a nonnegotiable precondition. As well, Mualem declared, Syria would not accept any conditions on the size, composition, or deployment of its armed forces.

Rabin arrived in Washington on November 19 and was immediately subjected to intense pressure to provide "something for Assad"—that is, concessions Christopher could take to Damascus on his next shuttle trip in order to show "progress." After a bitter session at the White House, Rabin agreed to a reduction in the withdrawal time. However, he was talking about partial withdrawal *on* the Golan. When Christopher went to Damascus in early December, he presented Rabin's concession as a reduction in the time for a complete Israeli withdrawal *from* the Golan. The administration did not apprise Rabin of its misrepresentation of his position.

In mid-December, Shihabi arrived in Washington for the Chiefs of Staff meetings, at which he told the Israeli contingent—Rabinovich, Barak, Yatom, and the chief of Military Intelligence, Major General Uri Sagi—that he was sent by Assad to deliver a message to further peace. He then presented Syria's long-standing position on security arrangements and withdrawal requirements and did not deviate from it by an iota. Barak responded by emphasizing the importance of flexibility, reconciliation, and mutual security. Shihabi listened attentively and then reiterated Assad's position. Other than restating Assad's commitment to peace, Shihabi refused to address normalization, security arrangements, or confidence-building measures. All of these, he repeatedly stated, would be addressed after the Israeli withdrawal was complete.

At the concluding meeting in the Oval Office, chaired by Clinton himself, the president spoke in generalities and would not touch details. Both the Syrians and the Israelis came away with the impression that Clinton did not care what it would take to make his wishes come true. Still, the Israelis were encouraged by the fact that SANA—the official Syrian news agency—actually reported that there had been a meeting in Washington between the Syrian and Israeli ambassadors.

Even as the Washington meetings were reaching a climax, Hosni Mubarak was hosting a summit in Alexandria at which he discussed with Hafez al-Assad and King Fahd the urgent need to confront Israel militarily as an instrument for reviving and consolidating Arab unity. Mubarak and Fahd supported Syria's position that the peace process was detrimental to Arab interests and must be reversed. Senior Syrian officials stressed that "Israel has exploited the weakness and fragmentation of Arab ranks to impose separate agreements and to divert the peace process from its objectives and bases. Israel has indeed been able to penetrate the Arab ranks and promote a series of falsehoods, such as that it seeks peace and that it achieved peace with the Palestinians while the Arab territories remain under occupation." A senior Saudi official summarized Assad's position: "Syria is unhappy with the normalization process between Israel and several Arab countries at a time when there is no progress in the Israeli-Syrian and Israeli-Lebanese negotiations. Syria believes that this Israeli-Arab normalization considerably weakens the position of Syria in the negotiations with Israel."

The final communiqué of the Alexandria summit, as read by Egyptian Information Minister Safwat al-Sharif, left no doubt about the new policy. The communiqué stated that the three leaders "affirmed their call for Israel's withdrawal from all of the Golan to the 4 June 1967 line and from southern Lebanon and the occupied Palestinian territories, including Arab Jerusalem." In addition, "they also affirmed their support for the Palestinian people's efforts to exercise their legitimate right to self-determination. The three states called on the international community, especially the co-sponsors of the peace process, to work diligently to remove the obstacles created by the Is-raeli side to the peace process. In this context, the three leaders affirmed their demand for the establishment of a zone free of weapons of mass destruction in the Middle East, above all nuclear weapons."

While Syria's official media hailed the summit as, in the words of an edi-torial in *Al-Thawrah*, "a turning point in joint Arab action and in addressing the issues from a position of strength," Jerusalem was shocked by the sum-mit's resolutions. Israeli officials, in the words of *Haaretz*'s dovish analyst Gay Bekhor, considered the summit "the fiercest diplomatic collision of the last two years between the concept of a 'new Middle East,' promulgated by Israel among others, and the old Arab world order."

Emboldened by the support Assad's hard line received in Alexandria, Damascus concluded that the Chiefs of Staff meetings had "failed to make progress" and that a new policy should be adopted. In order not to be con-sidered responsible for the collapse of the peace process, however, Assad de-cided to ask Clinton to obtain assurances that he was certain Jerusalem could not agree to. On January 20, 1995, Assad sent Clinton a formal letter containing, in Seale's words, "what Syria considered aims and principles which should govern the security arrangements. . . . Above all, [al-Assad] was concerned that Israel should not use its security needs as an excuse to violate the 4 June line."

The administration did not reject Assad's outrageous demands out of hand. Instead, the White House encouraged Rabinovich to resume meeting with Mualem. Their meetings failed, predictably, to deliver any progress, and on March 18 Rabinovich was summoned to the State Department, where Christopher told him that his "time and his patience were running out"; un-less Israel delivered an incentive for Assad to sustain negotiations, Christo-pher said, Clinton would call the peace process off. This ultimatum started a cycle of hectic deliberations in Jerusalem on just how far Israel could go. The possibility that, given Assad's position, the entire Syrian track was an exer-cise in futility was not even contemplated.

———

FOR ARAFAT, President Clinton's presence at the initialing of the Israeli-Jordanian agreement in October 1994, as well as his facilitating of the Israeli-Syrian meetings in December, was a major omen. Arafat knew that both Jerusalem and Amman wanted Jordan to be responsible for the Pales-tinians, and he interpreted Clinton's presence at Arava as proof of U.S. com-plicity in the conspiracy against him.

Arafat also worried that Israel was calling his bluff. On December 13, Colonel David Yahav, Israel's assistant chief military judge advocate for international law, issued a harsh report on the Palestinian Authority's compliance with agreements with Israel. Yahav listed systematic violations of the most fundamental points and suggested that the whole question of cooperation and coordination with the PA should be reexamined. Although the Rabin government suppressed Yahav's report, Arafat didn't believe that Jerusalem's tolerance would last. Hence, he spent the winter of 1994–95 building bridges to the Islamists and consolidating his own power structure.

Once firmly in control of Gaza, Arafat had immediately established the infrastructure of a police state based on a myriad of overlapping internal-security organs. Personal loyalty to Arafat determined the key personnel and command echelons of these forces. Most important were the Preventive Security Service, under Jibril Rajub and Muhammad Dahlan, with more than 2,000 men; the General Intelligence Service, under Amin al-Hindi, with 1,000; and the Military Intelligence Service, under Arafat's brother, Musa, with 500 to 600. In addition, the PLO maintained the Palestinian National Security Forces, the Palestinian Police Force, Force 17 (Arafat's own Praetorian Guard), and a host of smaller intelligence and security detachments. By early 1995, the PLO had well over 15,000 "policemen" in the Gaza Strip alone, although the agreement with Israel permitted only 9,000.

Ultimately, Arafat could not afford to confront terrorism even if he had wanted to, because the Palestinian security establishment was riddled with Islamists. The entire high command of Arafat's security organs had blood relations—in most cases, brothers or first cousins—within the high command of the terrorist organizations. If ordered to go beyond make-believe suppression of the Islamists, they were likely to rebel or, at the very least, defect en masse. And so, for example, while by the PLO's own estimates, there were over 26,000 "unregistered" weapons (weapons not permitted under the interim agreement with Israel) in the Gaza Strip alone, by the spring of 1995, in all their anti-terrorism operations, the authorities had confiscated a total of 11 weapons.

In reality, Islamists were predominant among the younger generation. For example, Colonel Munir Makdah, a former protégé of Arafat and the chief of his Fatah forces in Lebanon, had reorganized those forces as the Companies of the Black 13 September Organization, named in reaction to the signing of the Oslo accords on September 13, 1993. Makdah did not conceal his commitment to the destruction of Israel. "We will not lay down our weapons until complete liberation," he stated. "Sooner or later we will throw the Zionists into the sea." On April 15, 1995, Makdah inspected the Ein Hilweh camp in southern Lebanon, where seventy suicide-terrorists were completing their training course. This new martyrdom commando force, under the authority of the Palestinian Islamic Jihad's military wing, the Fighting Islamic Forces, was being prepared for spectacular operations in both southern Lebanon and Israel. It joined the HizbAllah-Pasdaran reinforcements that Iran had allocated to southern Lebanon two years earlier, as well as a host of Syrian-controlled Palestinian units.

Even as the PLO realized that it could not buck HAMAS and survive, so the HAMAS leadership recognized the need to cooperate with the PA to secure the freedom of action it required. HAMAS's Sheikh Mahmoud Zahar defined the relationship between the PLO and HAMAS: "Like the wings of a bird, they must work together."

Still, the threat of an Islamist uprising against the Palestinian Authority was always there. In mid-April, HAMAS formally put Arafat on notice: "In making the decision to confiscate weapons, the Palestinian authorities are playing with fire. The outcome of this policy will be to take us into a new phase . . . [and] nobody knows its boundaries and its outcome." However, Israel was still the primary objective: "Rabin, don't be glad about the numerous arrests of our sacred brothers. The Palestinian Authority crossed the red lines, and our response will be against the Israelis—and at the heart of Israel." The Islamists put Arafat to another test on April 20, with a communiqué issued in Gaza and signed by the Islamic Front for the Salvation of Palestine. Its language was internationalist Islamist: it urged the Front's "holy fighters in Egypt, Algeria, France, Britain, and the United States to strike against Zionist interests and Jewish symbols worldwide, especially in America." The signature on this communiqué was not the name of a real organization but rather an "identifier." By using the term "Islamic Front," the authors were stressing their affiliation with Hassan al-Turabi's National Islamic Front and other elements of the internationalist Islamist trend—a trend Arafat was desperate to ally himself with. Moreover, by emphasizing that the struggle would include strikes in the United States, the communiqué sought to make too close a relationship with the Clinton administration impossible for Arafat.

Arafat himself, in a series of public speeches, left no doubt where he was going. For example, on June 19 he declared, "We shall continue with this hard and long jihad, on the road of martyrdom, on the road of sacrifices, . . . the road of the fallen, the road of victory, the road of glory, not only for our Palestinian people, but for our Arab Islamic Nation as well." Arafat urged his listeners not to forget about the old Arab cities in pre-1967 Israel and to wage the jihad until the whole of Palestine was liberated. Not once did Israel's "partner for peace" mention peace and compromise.

———

THE GRIM REALITY finally began to sink in with the PA leadership that public support for Arafat and the "solution" he represented was evaporating. Arafat's return to Gaza with promises of international aid had brought widespread expectations of economic miracles, but conditions had only worsened, mainly because of the corruption of his regime. Arafat's cronies and the security system consumed the bulk of the foreign aid donated to the PLO for humanitarian assistance and development projects. The extent of the misuse of foreign funds was widely known, and the Islamists offered strong criticism. Yet Arafat, fearing a conspiracy against himself, could not afford to discontinue the flow of funds to his security people. Therefore, he needed tension with Israel—especially the periodic closure of the Gaza Strip, preventing Gazans from working in Israel—so that he could blame Israel for the economic collapse. Even so, an opinion poll conducted in May concluded that a plurality of Palestinians would prefer an Islamic state. "Forty percent believe the Islamic system of government is best," according to the survey's summary, "while representative democracy comes in second at 26.2 percent."

Arafat himself was visibly feeling the strain. In March 1995, for example, he told a visiting American delegation that senior Israeli security officials had ordered a recent series of suicide bombings in order to harm him and derail the peace process. According to one participant, Arafat was shaking with rage during the entire meeting: "We saw a man isolated, at least partially, from reality and driven by paranoia." Arafat had markedly raised the number of armed guards around him, and he never moved without his "emergency button"—an electronic buzzer that activated an elaborate security system. According to one of those present at a meeting between Israeli and Palestinian officials, when Arafat was momentarily separated from his emergency button, he went crazy.

———

BY JUNE 1995, the Gaza Strip had become—in the words of the clearsighted chief of research of Israeli's Military Intelligence, Brigadier General Yaakov Ami-Dror—"a terror academy for all HAMAS and Islamic Jihad. PLO and HAMAS don't discuss an end to anti-Israel terrorism; they negotiate cessation of terrorism from Gaza." Israeli intelligence experts warned that the only way to prevent a marked escalation of Islamist terrorism in Israel was for the IDF to reenter the Gaza Strip, putting an end to the peace process.

The Palestinian leadership was also calling for an end to the peace process. Arafat had fired the first shot in a speech in Gaza, announcing that "the self-rule agreement signed with Israel" was a "failure." Most significant was Arafat's explanation of the reason for this failure: These agreements were intended to create an atmosphere of coexistence between Palestinians and Jews. This could not be tolerated, because "Israel remains the Palestinians' major enemy, not only now, but also in the future." These sentiments were echoed in a series of statements and leaflets distributed throughout the territories by Arafat's own Fatah movement, as well as by the Islamists.

Even then, the Clinton administration would not let go. Rather than admit failure, the White House intensified pressure on Israel to "look at the big picture" and take "leaps of faith." Despite all the evidence of Arafat's real intent, Clinton's message was effective because it was exactly what Peres wanted to hear.

At the same time, Washington sought help in shepherding Arafat. Enter Hosni Mubarak, Washington's self-declared Arab best friend. Mubarak was maneuvering to have Washington empower him as its regional cop at the expense of an Israel emaciated by the ongoing struggle. Enthroned in such a power post, Mubarak would be able to influence the conservative Arab oil states to invest lavishly in sustaining his regime. Consequently, Cairo pressured Washington to continue coercing Israel into self-defeating concessions in the name of peace.

Meanwhile, Mubarak had received a sudden wake-up call in the form of an Islamist attempt on his life while he was visiting Addis Ababa. By the fall, he had concluded that it was counterproductive to confront the Islamists. Instead, he embarked on a devious strategy of making deals with them while attempting to beat them at their own game—inciting anti-Israel jihad. His first step was facilitating a series of PLO-HAMAS negotiations in Cairo, which the White House, mesmerized by its own efforts in the region, chose to ignore. The dovish government of Israel, unwilling to challenge the Clinton worldview, went along with the charade.

———

WHILE ALL EYES were on Israel and the territories, a trend with long-term implications emerged within the Tehran-Damascus-Baghdad Axis. By mid-1995, Ali Akbar Hashemi-Rafsanjani, Saddam Hussein, and Hafez al-Assad were increasingly preoccupied with the future of their own families and regimes. In a society dominated by blood loyalty, as the Muslim world is, no aspiration can be more important than preserving one's family's position. Hashemi-Rafsanjani was virtually obsessed with his sons' accumulating fortunes to sustain the family for generations to come, while both Saddam and Assad were convinced that only their chosen sons could be worthy heirs to their revolutionary legacy. All three believed that the alliance among their countries would materially improve their chances of carrying out their plans. Their sons and designated heirs shared their conviction that their hold on power and riches would depend on their joint maneuvering against external and internal enemies. Indeed, the "sons of" were the real driving force behind the consolidation of a tighter regional alliance.

Hussein Bahramani and Qusay Saddam Hussein had hit it off on the personal level during the negotiations in the spring of 1992. Over the next two years, Qusay's elder brother, Uday, gradually became the dominant player in negotiations with Iran and a close and trusted friend of Bahramani. The two became partners in a wide variety of companies and front organizations all over the world committed to the subversion of international sanctions against Iraq—for example, by exporting Iraqi oil and smuggling in weapons and other strategic goods via Iran. They not only made fortunes from the overhead, but also became deeply convinced that their future lay in close cooperation.

These relations matured in a secret visit by Uday to Tehran at the invitation of his business partner—a visit encouraged by Saddam. Accompanying Uday were the chief of Iraqi intelligence, a senior military official, and several members of Saddam's own special security force. Bahramani was with Uday at all times during the visit. The two men co-chaired a series of meetings with senior officials of both their countries to discuss regional and bilateral security issues. After the Iraqi ideas were studied at the highest levels in Tehran, Uday met with Hashemi-Rafsanjani himself and with the high commands of the Pasdaran and of the Iranian intelligence service, VEVAK. After a thorough questioning, the Iranians became convinced that Uday's father was sincere in seeking closer relations, and Hashemi-Rafsanjani ordered the expansion of the secret negotiations. It was the first strategic breakthrough of the younger generation.

Soon afterward, Tehran succeeded in midwiving a rapprochement between Damascus and Baghdad. It was not a simple matter, because of the bitter rivalry between Saddam Hussein and Hafez al-Assad over the leadership of the Ba'ath Party. The key to the new relationship was a Syrian-Iraqi deal, finalized in early December 1995, redrawing their common border. The new border gave Syria sovereignty over the very productive Safiyah-39 oil field, which Iraq handed over with all its pumps and pipes in working order. The rapprochement stepped up cross-border trade, especially in agricultural products and artisanry—traditionally very profitable for both sides—and Damascus now considered Baghdad a full partner in future strategic gambits.

———

MEANWHILE, the Clinton administration had been busily following up on Christopher's March 18 ultimatum to Rabinovich. Once again, the Rabin government ignored the regional dynamics and Israel's own red lines, agreeing to yet another push on the Syrian track. With Israel's cooperation assured, Washington invited Damascus to accelerate the negotiations. In early May 1995, Faruk al-Shara visited the White House and delivered Assad's "expectations."

On the basis of Syria's demands and Israel's continued flexibility, the administration put together a document titled "The Aims and Principles of the Security Arrangement." Rabin arrived in Washington in late May and, as expected, approved the language of this document. However, fearing that virtually the entire Israeli public would reject outright the concessions and withdrawals he had already committed to, Rabin asked that the document be treated as a "non-paper" and kept in great secrecy. Ross explained that it "was not meant to be a formal agreement" but "was designed to create a baseline, or provide a framework for the ensuing discussions." Nevertheless, the Clinton administration would consider Rabin's acceptance of the document as a formal commitment binding on future Israeli governments. Furthermore, on June 6, Clinton wrote Assad a letter, hand-delivered by Ross, which, according to Seale, said, "As I told you in Damascus, and as I assure your foreign minister, I have in my pocket a pledge by Prime Minister Rabin on full withdrawal to the 4 June 1967 [line]." Clinton did, however, emphasize the sensitivity of this message, saying that "it would not be proper to talk about it publicly."

Indeed, Rabin had every reason to conceal the extent of his flexibility. He had agreed to restrict security arrangements on the Golan Heights to the areas adjacent to the border, and he had accepted the Syrian demand for "some compensation in another sphere" wherever there was no geographical parity in the security arrangements. The principles also reiterated the "sovereignty and territorial integrity" of both parties—the euphemism for Syria's rejection of any supervision over its deployment of armed forces.

Still, in late June, Vice President Abdul-Halim Khaddam pointed not to Israel's concessions but to the remaining differences. "We cannot say that an agreement has been reached on certain points of significance," he said. "Any security arrangements that are at the expense of either party cannot eventually lead to the establishment of a balanced peace." Khaddam added that there would be "no normalization because Israel wants swift change," and there would be "no reduction in size of the Syrian Armed Forces for as long as Israel maintained its nuclear capabilities." Syria was convinced that it had leverage over the Rabin government because of the Israeli elections planned for 1996. As Syrian Information Minister Muhammad Salman put it, "Rabin needs the Syrian vote in the elections so that he can return to power."

With Israel committed to a full withdrawal in return for vague promises of a yet-to-be-defined peace, the Clinton administration arranged the second round of Chiefs of Staff talks. In preparation, Brigadier General Tzvi Stauber of the IDF Planning Branch prepared an analysis of the Israeli-Syrian document in which he explained that one of the security-arrangement principles "would seem" to justify the Syrian claim that the "zero line"—the line on both sides of which the security arrangements were to be implemented—is either the international border or the June 4 line. Still, to maintain the charade that Israel had not committed to a full withdrawal, Rabin publicly instructed Israel's new chief of staff, General Amnon Shahak, to argue that the IDF must remain on the western edge of the Golan Heights even during peace.

On June 27, Christopher chaired the meeting of the Chiefs of Staff and their delegations in Washington. The Israeli presentation, made by Stauber, was conciliatory and stressed Israel's need for early-warning capabilities. Shihabi rejected the Israeli position outright because Stauber's plan did not include an irrevocable commitment to withdrawal to the June 4 line, sought to leave warning stations of some sort on the Golan, and interfered with the size and deployment of the Syrian armed forces. Shahak sought to prevent the collapse of the talks by agreeing with Shihabi that the air- and space-based system would provide "sufficient" early warning, but to no avail.

Two subsequent meetings failed to deliver any progress. Nevertheless, the Americans were upbeat because of the Israeli flexibility. Ross identified fifteen points of agreement that he would later use as the basis for talks at the Wye River Plantation in Maryland. Rabinovich echoed Ross's line, telling an interviewer, "My impression is positive, although the discussions exposed the gaps and basic differences that still exist in the Syrian and Israeli approaches to the issue."

Ultimately, a subject not discussed in Washington—the Syrian-Iranian sponsorship of the HizbAllah in southern Lebanon—doomed any immediate resumption of the talks. The moment the chiefs of staff ended their meeting, Damascus resumed facilitating the HizbAllah attacks on the IDF and the South Lebanon Army (SLA). Pressed, the White House opined that Damascus would not attempt to curb the fighting until it was convinced that Israel had agreed to all its demands on the Golan Heights. Jerusalem started working on "a political solution," which would entail persuading the Syrians to agree to incorporate the Lebanese quagmire into the Golan deal.

By now, however, Israel was immersed in a major political scandal. Likud leader Binyamin Netanyahu had leaked the full text of the Stauber document, and the public was enraged by the concessions Rabin had committed to. With the polls turning against the Labor Party, Rabin notified Washington he had decided to freeze the Syrian track until after the elections.

SETTING THE PATTERN for the remainder of Bill Clinton's tenure in office, the White House took the stalling of one track as a signal to jump to the other track. The summer of 1995 saw numerous cycles of shuttle diplomacy on the Palestinian track by Christopher, Ross, and lesser officials, leading to a marathon of late-night meetings between Peres and Arafat. The administration's efforts at this point concentrated on making the PA an "irreversible" entity. The White House's mantra—repeated to the U.S. Congress as well as to Israel—was "The more you give them, the more they'll have to lose." This mantra dominated the peacemakers' perverted logic—perverted because it stood in stark contradiction to the supposed purpose of the actions Israel was expected to take: If the PA was to be made "irreversible," why should Arafat fear that he would "lose" it? The fact that the PA made its intentions vis-à-vis Israel abundantly clear was simply suppressed and ignored.

A striking example is the lack of reaction in both Washington and Jerusalem to Arafat's bellicose speech of August 6, 1995. The timing was significant, because at just this point the administration was pushing Israel and the PA into a round of intense negotiations in Taba, Egypt, on an agreement intended to renew "the spirit of Oslo"—the agreement that came to be known as Oslo B or Oslo II.

This speech was one of Arafat's most explicit statements in public (as opposed to addresses at closed events, like the one in Johannesburg in 1994). Arafat went out of his way to incite his hearers into a frenzy, and they responded by repeatedly interrupting him with shouts of "Soul and blood we shall give for your sake, Abu-Ammar!"

Arafat opened by declaring that the diplomatic process was a continuation of the armed struggle. He hailed "the blood of the martyrs of the Palestinian people, who did not stop for one moment from the noble sacrifice of their blood, their soul, their money, and their potential to defend this land." As for the Oslo agreement, "If any one of you have any objection to the Oslo accord—well, I have a thousand objections. But my brothers, I would like to remind you of something. The Prophet when he signed the Hudaibiya accord . . . Umar ibn al Kattib called the agreement 'the despised agreement' and asked, 'How can we accept such a humiliation of our religion?' But, my brothers, it is all the same with the Palestinian people."

The Palestinian struggle had had its ups and downs: "There were days when they said, 'There is no Palestinian people. The Palestinian people is finished.' And here is the Palestinian people. They remain on this land, to fight on this land and around this land as it is said, 'And they shall stand on the front line until the Day of Judgment.'" Arafat stressed repeatedly that the essence of the Palestinian struggle was the armed jihad: "The longest revolution in the modern era is the Palestinian revolution. The longest revolution, the longest Intifadah, seven blessed years. . . . I am saying this because we are in the midst of negotiations now. However, if the Israelis think that we have no alternatives [to negotiations]—by Allah, [I swear] that they are wrong.

The Palestinian people are prepared to sacrifice their last boy and their last girl in order to wave the Palestinian flag . . ." Before Arafat could finish the sentence, the audience erupted, shouting, "Soul and blood we shall give for your sake, Abu-Ammar, so that the Palestinian flag will wave over the walls of Jerusalem, its mosques and its churches!"

Arafat repeatedly cited the Koran about the inevitability of the Muslims' return to Jerusalem: "And they will enter the Mosque [of al-Aqsa] as they entered it the first time!" Then he joined the crowd in shouting several times: "Allah will not break his promise! God willing, we shall all pray and sit in Jerusalem as we do now!"

The crowd went wild, with Arafat shouting above them: "And I say Jerusalem.

"And I say Jerusalem, whether someone likes it or not.

"Jerusalem the capital of the State of Palestine, whether someone likes it or not.

"And whoever doesn't like it, let him drink from the sea of Gaza!"

For anyone who was paying attention, Arafat's August 6 performance gave a remarkable window on his approach toward peace with Israel.

―――――

THE MOOD of the rest of the PA leadership matched Arafat's own, in stark contrast to the optimism about "peace" shown by the Clinton administration and the Israeli Left. In early September, Muhammad Dahlan, the chief of the PA's Preventive Security Service in Gaza—and, as such, the man in charge of the PA's struggle against Islamist terrorism—explicitly stated the PA's position regarding the extradition of wanted terrorists to Israel. The issue came up in response to a question about the PA's search for Yahya Ayash, or "the Engineer," HAMAS's chief bomb-maker. "We reached a decision," Dahlan stated, "and it was made at our highest possible level—of course on the basis of Arafat's opinion—that we will not extradite to Israel members of our people, including wanted [members] of HAMAS. We are not willing that in our history books it will be written that we surrendered Palestinians to Israel." Dahlan acknowledged that this policy was in violation of signed agreements. "Even if there is a clause in the Agreement, and Yoel Singer of [Israel's] foreign ministry can specifically point to it, we will not extradite members of our people to Israel."

Such statements reflected Arafat's conviction—and that of the Fatah leadership—that the peace process was finished, for neither Jerusalem nor Washington could have been expected to tolerate the overt quest for the destruction of Israel by its "peace partners." In mid-September, the Fatah leadership in Tunis concluded that "the Oslo agreement has reached a dead end after two years of arduous negotiations" and that "if an agreement is reached during the current negotiations, the concessions imposed on the Palestinian side would only add to the injustice." On September 23, a PLO member with Islamist sympathies briefed Arab officials and Muslim leaders in Athens on the Oslo B negotiations, using inside information provided by a Jerusalem-based land surveyor who had taken part in the negotiations. The briefer called the proposed agreement "dismal" and "scandalous" and warned of dire consequences if it were accepted: "Arafat practically succumbed to Israeli dictates and accepted limited Palestinian control in civilian fields and only within the confines of certain towns, villages and hamlets. . . . Meticulous security checks, including searches, personal frisking, and long delays, as well as the erection of numerous Israeli and PA roadblocks and checkpoints, will suffocate economic activities in the West Bank."

The U.S. Congress, too, was less than enthusiastic and voted restrictions on the distribution of U.S. aid, criticizing Palestinian violations of past agreements. The PA reacted with fury to the Senate's decision to put conditions on the spending of the American taxpayers' money. On September 23, the PA's Ministry of Information issued a special communiqué, which was mentioned, but not quoted in full, by Palestinian Radio and, the next day, in a small item buried on page 7 of the newspaper *Al-Quds*. The reason for the low-key treatment of such an important communiqué was its harsh and uncompromising language.

The PA called the Senate decision "a vagrant intrusion in internal Palestinian matters." It asserted that "Congress allows itself to act in a racist manner towards the Palestinian people by denying it the simplest right to civil institutions. . . . It would be more suitable for the members of the American Congress to know well that the Palestinian institutions and rights are not for sale or exchange for all the funds in the entire American Treasury. . . . According to all criteria, this is a clear relinquishment of the supposed U.S. role as a neutral sponsor."

———

AMAZINGLY, none of this bellicosity derailed the Oslo B negotiations, and on September 25, on the eve of the Jewish New Year and after a seventy-hour marathon of negotiations in Taba, Peres and Arafat initialed a landmark agreement aimed at consolidating the peace process and providing for the expansion of Palestinian self-rule throughout the West Bank. Rabin and Arafat would sign the final agreement in the White House on September 28.

The Taba agreement was a complete Israeli capitulation, on matters ranging from the size and timetable of IDF withdrawals from the territories to toleration of Palestinian violations of previous agreements. Nonetheless,

Peres was upbeat, insisting that most of the difficult issues had been resolved. Israeli negotiator Uri Savir denied any American pressure and hailed "the mutual understanding that the time has come to conclude this agreement." The one remaining sticking point was the Palestinian demand for the prompt release of thousands of prisoners held by Israel—particularly HAMAS and Islamic Jihad terrorists convicted of killing Israelis. "We are not going to sign before we resolve the issue of the prisoners," stated Palestinian Justice Minister Freih Abu-Medein. Israel again capitulated.

For the Clinton White House, this was an indication that Israel could be made to compromise on the Golan Heights as well. Even before Oslo B was signed, Christopher made the connection: "I've always thought that progress on one track tends to incentivize parties on another track, and I hope that'll be the effect here." He acknowledged, however, that negotiations would extend into the following year and might require another round of shuttle diplomacy.

The Oslo B accords that Rabin and Peres committed to signing envisioned a swift and massive withdrawal from the West Bank with virtually no security guarantees, to be followed by elections that would turn the PA into a statelike entity. By the end of 1995, the IDF would have withdrawn from six West Bank cities, and a few months later, from the bulk of Hebron. Whereas previous agreements required the PLO, as a precondition to holding elections, to eliminate all sections of the Palestinian Covenant calling for the destruction of Israel, the Taba agreement gave the PLO until two months after the elections. The PA committed to conducting "a wide-ranging operation to confiscate all illegal weapons immediately after the extension of self-rule," but only "within the framework of the agreement" and not as an integral part of Oslo B. Even the dovish General Avraham Tamir, among the architects of the 1979 Camp David accords with Egypt, sharply attacked the Taba agreement. "They're signing an agreement without security," Tamir said.

With Rabin and Peres already on their way to Washington, the PA engaged in a piece of last-minute brinkmanship. PA officials stressed that, as Arafat's aide Saeb Erekat put it, "At this moment we have not yet finalized dates for the [Israeli] redeployment, and that's a major hanging issue in the whole agreement." The PA was insisting on setting an early date for the Israeli withdrawals as a condition for Arafat's signing. "It's really very serious," Erekat said. "Every effort is being exercised now." By the time Arafat arrived in Washington, Israel had agreed to complete the withdrawal by the end of the year and to include the target dates in the agreement.

To ensure the continuation of Israeli flexibility, Clinton brought Mubarak, King Hussein, and Russian Foreign Minister Kozyrev to Washington to sign the agreement as formal witnesses and guarantors. Signaling the administration's next objective, representatives of the Lebanese and Syrian governments were also present. Clinton called Oslo B "a milestone on the path toward reconciliation" between Israel and the Palestinians. "The time is approaching when there will be safety in Israel's house and when the Palestinian people will write their own destiny," he said. "Israeli mothers and fathers need no longer worry that their sons will have to patrol the streets of Nablus."

Rabin, for his part, said that "the partners in peace" should unite against "the evil angels of death by terrorism" and prevent hatred from filling the Middle East. "We have matured in the two years since we first shook hands here. Today we are more sober. We are gladdened by the potential for reconciliation but are also wary of the dangers that lurk on every side." Speaking directly to Arafat, Rabin added, "Do not let the land flowing with milk and honey become a land flowing with blood and tears. We are not alone here on this soil, in this land. And so we are sharing this good earth today with the Palestinian people—in order to choose life. We are not retreating. We are not leaving. We are yielding—and we are doing so for the sake of peace."

And then they signed. On October 10, Israel began its West Bank pullback and released hundreds of Palestinian prisoners.

There was a public outcry in Israel once the details of the agreement became known. Instead of attempting to calm the public's anxieties, Rabin exhibited defiance and disdain. "I will lead," he stated. Politicians from all other parties started calling for early elections as a referendum on the Labor Party's peace policy. The peace camp resisted vehemently, accusing their opponents of incitement. That the General Security Service (GSS) engaged in active provocations, ostensibly in order to flush out extreme right-wing militants, did not help the national mood.

The right-wing extremist who assassinated Yitzhak Rabin on November 5, 1995, was not only known to the GSS but also an active participant in some of its anti-right-wing provocations. This relationship, on top of some still unexplained circumstances surrounding the shooting, led to the spread of conspiracy theories accusing Peres. After this, the first major political assassination in modern Israel's history, the country went into a period of profound soul-searching.

The Clinton administration, terrified by the assassination and its potential aftermath, organized a huge show of world leaders for the Jerusalem funeral. In Washington, cynics opined that Clinton wanted "to make sure that Rabin's funeral did not become that of his policies as well." Indeed, Clinton promised Peres to do everything he could to ensure the continuance of the peace process.

Shimon Peres officially became prime minister on November 22, 1995, when the Knesset ratified his new government. He took the defense portfolio for himself—thus solidifying his control over dealings with the PLO. He would ensure the timely completion of all the IDF withdrawals except the one from Hebron. But it would take several weeks before Israel recovered sufficiently to resume tackling the peace process.

———

WHILE THE WHITE HOUSE was shepherding Israel and the PLO toward the Oslo B agreement, Arafat was preoccupied with far more important negotiations—the ones in Cairo between the PLO and HAMAS. The fact that Israel, at Taba, was being coerced into taking additional risks in the name of peace at the very same time the Palestinians were discussing the modalities of waging jihad against Israel, gives some indication of the sincerity of the Clinton White House, for although it had chosen not to take notice of the Cairo negotiations, it knew they were going on.

The record of the Cairo talks clearly shows that the PLO accepted the majority of HAMAS's demands. Two key provisions, as they appear in the September 20 draft of the PLO-HAMAS agreement, still dominate the relationship between the two organizations. Paragraph 3 expresses respect for "the commitments of the Palestinian Liberation Organization ensuing from the agreements signed with the Israeli government which require the cessation of all military operations in, or launched from, the areas under the Palestinian National Authority." However, the PLO and HAMAS interpreted this as applying only to operations launched from Area A, the area under full PA control. Paragraph 12, meanwhile, forbids the PA to take preventive security measures, lest these undermine "confidence [and] cooperation" between the Palestinian Authority and HAMAS.

In early October, as the Cairo negotiations were reaching an advanced stage, a five-man HAMAS delegation traveled from Gaza and Amman to Khartoum to consult with Sheikh Turabi and the HAMAS international leadership. The main question was, Could Arafat be trusted? The delegation brought with it a message from Arafat, as well a letter from Sheikh Yassin to the HAMAS leadership abroad expressing support for reconciliation between HAMAS and the PA. The Palestinian HAMAS leadership, particularly the Gaza-based branch, had become convinced that it was imperative to reach national reconciliation, albeit without sacrificing the continuity of the jihad against Israel. Khartoum duly gave its permission for the local HAMAS leaders to continue seeking an "accord of national unity" recognizing "the right to resist occupation"—that is, to continue armed struggle and terrorism. However, any agreement reached in Cairo would have to be closely inspected in Khartoum prior to ratification by HAMAS.

Iranian intelligence was also intimately involved in the negotiations, even telephoning leading PA security officials and HAMAS leaders to get firsthand assurances. In one of these conversations, Jibril Rajub—chief of the Preventive Security Service in the West Bank—assured the Iranians that the HAMAS cadres "are nationalist elements, and I don't expect them to carry out actions that are detrimental to Palestinian national interests." A senior commander of the Izz al-Din al-Qassim Brigades—the elite terrorist arm of HAMAS—in Gaza assured Tehran that their commitment was only "not to do anything that would disrupt the Israeli pullout from Palestinian population centers in the West Bank." Sheikh Jamal Salim, a HAMAS member from Gaza, also alluded to an agreement on temporary measures, explaining that the HAMAS made "some short-term concessions in order not to lose substantial long-term rewards."

In mid-October, when the accords still had not been signed, a desperate Arafat accused the international leadership of HAMAS of blocking understandings already reached in Gaza. "The members and leadership of HAMAS in Gaza want to reach an accord, but the HAMAS leadership outside the area has put up obstacles," Tayeb Abdel Rahim, the PA secretary-general, told the Egyptian paper *Al-Ahram*. However, he added, "I don't think that the internal leadership will allow the external leadership to continue to stall."

Discussions within the HAMAS leadership and with HAMAS's key sponsoring states—Sudan, Iran, and Syria—continued for almost a month. The PA also consulted several other Palestinian terrorist organizations and the Egyptian government. In the aftermath of the Rabin assassination, however, both HAMAS and the PA felt a sense of urgency, and in mid-December, senior officials met in Cairo and reached an "understanding" on the extent of cooperation in the anticipated resumption of terrorism against Israel. HAMAS reiterated its commitment not to act against Israel or Israelis from territories under the PA's direct control until the completion of the IDF's redeployment and the elections for the Palestinian National Council. In return, the PA promised not to interfere with the Islamists' command, control, and communications or with their flow of funds. Most important was the institutionalization of constant contacts, including operational coordination, between the Islamists' headquarters in Gaza and their supreme headquarters in Damascus and Tehran.

On December 22, Salim al-Zaanun—the acting chairman of the Palestine National Council (PNC)—briefed Arab journalists on the agreement. "This should be understood by all. We are not the defenders of the Israeli entity. We consider it sufficient to obligate HAMAS not to embarrass the PA, which is responsible for security in the areas it has received, and from which it will not allow actions," Zaanun declared. "If Israel wants to spare itself HAMAS attacks, it had better hurry and withdraw from the rest of the territories."

HAMAS's chief negotiator, the Amman-based senior commander Khalid Mashal, was also present and stressed the Islamists' commitment to the continuation of terrorism as an integral component of a joint anti-Israeli jihad with the PLO. "HAMAS views its action as support for the Palestinian negotiators [with Israel] and the Palestinian Authority," he stated.

Zaanun elaborated on the PA's understanding of the agreement in a December 25 interview with the Jerusalem *Al-Manar*. The key issue, he said, was preventing an immediate escalation in terrorism in order to deprive Israel of an excuse to delay the forthcoming pullout. That did not mean, he hastened to add, that either the PA or HAMAS had permanently rejected terrorism: "The laying down of weapons by HAMAS was not discussed in Cairo." He conceded, however, that the concord between HAMAS and the PA was not complete: HAMAS had refused to legitimize Arafat's supreme leadership by participating in the elections to the Palestinian National Council. Arafat had had no choice but to swallow the indignity.

The main difference between the HAMAS-PA agreement and the various agreements between the PA and Israel was that this one reflected the reality on the ground, not the self-delusions of politicians. In courting the "soldiers" of the Intifadah, the PA was aiming to deal with the young leadership that had grown up inside the territories. Through intimate contact with Israel, these young men were both aware of the extent of freedom in Israel (far exceeding anything in the Arab states) and radicalized by Islamism as the only ideology capable of stopping the spread of Western ideas and values into the Arab world. Incapable of challenging this trend, Arafat and his lieutenants put themselves under Islamist guidance, if not outright control.

IN DECEMBER 1995, Peres and his team, desperate to revive some movement in order to strengthen the peace camp's chances in the coming elections, turned again to the Syrian track. Ross embarked on another round of shuttle diplomacy, carrying with him to Damascus Peres's assurances that he not only would abide by Rabin's guarantees of a full withdrawal but also would not stress the "nature of peace" if negotiations were renewed. Even so, it took a visit by Christopher to persuade Assad to agree to the resumption of direct talks. At that, Assad insisted that Peres first commit to addressing all the issues raised in the Chiefs of Staff talks—particularly the question of strategic parity and stability. Peres agreed. He then went even further. "Give me peace and we will give up the atom," he declared. "That's the whole story. If we achieve regional peace, I think we can make the Middle East free of any nuclear threat."

Trilateral negotiations—with a U.S. delegation led by Ross acting as an equal partner—opened in late December at the Wye River Plantation. Savir, who had done the most to establish the talks' modalities, took over the Israeli delegation from Rabinovich. "Peres said he needed us to conclude a framework agreement before the elections," recalled Yoel Singer, the delegation's legal adviser. Aware of this, the Americans were sure they could squeeze the Israelis. Indeed, the Syrians insisted on an American presence in virtually all sessions so that pressure could brought to bear whenever the Israelis attempted to stand their ground. One of the Syrians' first major achievements was persuading Israel and the United States to change the definition of the ultimate objective of the talks from "normalization of relations" to having "ordinary peaceful relations"—in essence, nonviolent coexistence. When the Syrians demanded that Ross take the entire "Aims and Principles" non-paper as the legal basis for the Wye negotiations, Ross complied, and the Israelis went along. The Syrians resisted economic ties, pointing to the disparity between the Syrian and Israeli economies, and American offers of lavish foreign aid to narrow the gap did not change the Syrian position. The first round of Wye ended inconclusively in early January 1996.

After some more shuttling by Christopher, the second round of Wye talks was held in late January, and the last round in late February. Ross considered the Wye process a great success and opined that more was achieved in its last week than in the preceding four years. Mualem believed the delegations had completed 75 percent of the work needed for an agreement.

By now, however, virtually everyone in Israeli public life was questioning the advisability of rushing to an agreement on the eve of crucial elections. Even Ehud Barak, the new foreign minister and self-declared heir to Rabin, publicly expressed his doubts. The Syrians replied by facilitating a marked escalation of HizbAllah attacks on southern Lebanon and northern Israel, despite Christopher's assurances to Peres that Assad had promised to restrain the HizbAllah as the Wye negotiations progressed. In mid-February, Peres declared his decision to go for elections in May. This decision brought the Wye process to a near halt.

The Syrians accordingly decided to wait till after the elections to chart their course for the next period. In addition, the Syrians knew that Tehran had resolved to unleash a new wave of Islamist terrorism in Israel. In late February, Iranian Vice President Habibi arrived in Damascus on one of his periodic visits for strategic coordination. Habibi and Syrian Vice President Khaddam concluded that the U.S.-Israeli peace process was aimed at breaking the Syrian-Iranian strategic bloc. "Under these circumstances," Iranian officials explained, "coordination between Iran and Syria, while strengthening their position vis-à-vis common enemies, will also fortify Syria's stance in the face of pressures brought on it to make it give way to the concessions that the Zionist regime wants." In early March, the rising wave of Syrian- and Iranian-sponsored terrorism in Israel precluded any notion of peace negotiations, and the Wye format collapsed.

———

THIS WAVE OF TERRORISM set the tone for 1996, which would be a year when military preparations increased and the parties once again almost went to war. While the power posture of Syria and Iran dominated regional dynamics, the Palestinian Authority used the combination of Oslo B and its agreements with HAMAS to consolidate its own military capabilities. Israel, still mourning Rabin, failed even to realize that these dynamics were afoot.

7

Violence on the Road to Peace (1996–1997)

Clinton Versus Netanyahu; the Widening "Circle of Confrontation"

FOR YASSIR ARAFAT, 1996 started with a clear vision of where the Palestinian movement was heading. On January 30, he outlined his plan in a closed-door speech to forty Arab diplomats in the Spiegal Salon at the Grand Hotel in Stockholm. His remarks were titled "The Impending Collapse of Israel." "We will take over everything, including all of Jerusalem," he stated repeatedly.

Arafat's plan, which aimed at nothing less than causing the Jews to abandon Israel, had two main components: terrorism and a dramatic increase in the Palestinian population. "Within five years we will have six to seven million Arabs living on the West Bank and in Jerusalem. All Palestinian Arabs will be welcomed back by us," he declared. "You understand that we plan to eliminate the State of Israel and establish a purely Palestinian State. We will make life unbearable for Jews by psychological warfare and population explosion; Jews will not want to live among us Arabs!"

Islamism dominated both components of Arafat's plan. As the Intifadah and the post-Oslo wave of terrorism had shown, only the Islamists had the zeal to persevere in martyrdom terrorism; the Islamists, therefore, not the Palestinian Authority, would spearhead Arafat's campaign. As for his declared intention of more than quadrupling the Arab population of the territories, it had long been established that the concentration of Arabs in economically deprived areas breeds Islamism. Hence, the squeezing of four to six million additional Arabs into the PA-controlled territory would transform virtually the entire population into radical Islamists ready to burst into action against Israel with no thought for their own safety.

Arafat could not have adopted this plan if he were not already committed to an Islamist solution to the Israel problem. Indeed, his peroration in Stockholm echoed the Muslim Brotherhood's uncompromising tenets. "I have no use for Jews," he exclaimed; "they are and remain Jews! We now need all the help we can get from you in our battle for a united Palestine under total Arab-Muslim domination!"

This was completely in line with his reaction, back at the beginning of the month, to the assassination of Yahya Ayash ("the Engineer"). As HAMAS's chief bomb-maker, Ayash had been responsible for the death and wounding of hundreds of Israelis in the previous year's wave of terrorism. Israeli intelligence finally tracked him down in Gaza and booby-trapped his cell phone; he was killed when he answered it on January 5. Arafat personally visited the Ayash family to express his condolences and led a massive funeral procession. He eulogized Ayash as a martyr for a noble cause and bitterly criticized Israel for assassinating him. Arafat also met with the HAMAS leadership in Gaza to express his solidarity with their jihad. HAMAS leader Mahmoud Zahar reciprocated. "As you say in all your speeches, Mr. President, we all yearn to become martyrs," he told a satisfied Arafat—the Arafat of the PLO-HAMAS agreement, not the "fighter of HAMAS terrorism" that Clinton and Peres were pretending he was.

———

THE CLINTON ADMINISTRATION and the Peres government started 1996 as if the HAMAS-PLO rapprochement had never happened. On January 10, even as Warren Christopher was pushing the Israelis along the Syrian track, he launched yet another round of shuttle diplomacy on the Palestinian track. This led to Peres's meeting with Arafat on January 24 to work out modalities for implementing Oslo B as well as for the PA's fighting terrorism. On February 7, after complex negotiations, Christopher secured yet another commitment from Arafat to amend the Palestinian Covenant. Peres hailed this commitment as a major step clearing the way for the next phase of Israeli-Palestinian talks.

When Peres then called for elections in May, Mubarak and Arafat were convinced they could pressure him into additional unilateral concessions. They reasoned that since the Israeli public considered the elections to be a referendum on the peace process, the government would be desperate to demonstrate progress, no matter the cost. Peres's recent behavior seemed to confirm this analysis. In early February, citing pressure from HAMAS, Arafat had demanded that Israel return the bodies of martyr-terrorists to the PA for Islamic burial. Senior security officials urged Peres to refuse because returning the remains would encourage the recruitment of more prospective martyr-terrorists, but he overruled them. Then, on February 11, he requested members of his government not to discuss the PLO's failure to honor its pledge to amend the Palestinian Covenant because such pressure would "embarrass the Palestinian Authority and enable charges of 'cooperation with Israel' to be leveled at it." So, in accordance with Arafat's and Mubarak's reading of these events, the PA decided on a dramatic move.

Arafat had been aware all along that HAMAS was planning to avenge Ayash's assassination. In fact, negotiations on how HAMAS could do so without implicating the PA were already going on between the chief of the PA's Preventive Security Service in Gaza, Muhammad Dahlan, and Muhammad Deif, the chief of the Izz al-Din al-Qassim Brigades. Dahlan and Deif were old friends, having operated together against Israel in Gaza and shared time in Israeli jails. Some of their meetings took place at the headquarters of the Preventive Security Service in Gaza—meaning that Arafat's claim that his security forces were unable to locate Deif at Israel's repeated requests was outrageous. Now, in late February, when Arafat decided to jolt Israel, he approved the launching of a series of martyrdom operations provided they could be attributed to HAMAS. Whether Arafat himself said anything explicit to a HAMAS leader, or whether he left it to Dahlan, is immaterial. Arafat set the timing of the strikes and approved of the carnage that would follow.

On the morning of February 25, the first HAMAS martyr struck on a crowded bus in Jerusalem. A half hour later, another terrorist dressed as an IDF soldier blew himself up at the Ashkelon junction. Between them they killed a total of twenty-four Jews and wounded over eighty. The initial reaction of the Israeli government met Arafat's expectations. "The Palestinian Authority must outlaw those who act illegally," Peres declared, thus in effect exonerating Arafat and the PA. "We will not halt the peace process," Peres went on; "we will continue with it. At the same time, we will take all appropriate means in order to strike at terrorists everywhere, both before and after they commit their criminal acts."

On the morning of March 3, another martyr blew himself up on a bus in the center of Jerusalem, killing eighteen and wounding a dozen. The next day, the Purim holiday, a terrorist waited patiently at a crosswalk in Tel Aviv until there were enough people around him. When he finally detonated his bomb, 13 people were killed and 115 injured, many of them children, teenagers, and mothers celebrating the holiday.

On March 10, in the face of clear evidence that the PA had extensive and advance knowledge of this series of martyrdom bombings, the Israeli government leaked to *Haaretz* its own version of the PA-HAMAS negotiations. According to this account, senior members of Arafat's intelligence services had attempted, with Arafat's knowledge and approval, to convince HAMAS to postpone the bombings until after the Israeli elections. Even if this version of events had been true, Arafat would have had advance knowledge of the impending carnage and yet had not warned his "partner in peace." *Haaretz*'s sources further conceded that negotiations between HAMAS and the PA continued even after the first round of bombings and that no senior member of Izz al-Din al-Qassim was arrested by the PA.

Nevertheless, the next day, Peres praised Arafat for undertaking measures against Islamist terrorism. He pointed out that Islamist religious leaders were being detained, mosques were being searched, and hundreds of HAMAS officials had been arrested. That none of these was a member of the elite arms of HAMAS or the Islamic Jihad seemed irrelevant to Peres.

Furthermore, the Islamist leadership maneuvered Arafat into demonstrating his own ongoing contacts with Islamist terrorists. Immediately after the bomb exploded in Tel Aviv, Arafat delivered a message from HAMAS to Peres, via an Arab member of the Knesset, Abd-al-Wahab Darawshe. In the message, HAMAS offered to cease its bombing campaign if Israel called off its manhunt against HAMAS. Arafat handed this message, along with a personal letter from himself, to Darawshe. Less than an hour after Darawshe passed these documents along to Peres, the leaders of the Izz al-Din al-Qassim Brigades faxed from Gaza the entire text of their offer on their own letterhead. This timing left no doubt that Arafat, or at the very least someone extremely close to him, coordinated the phrasing of the offer to Peres with the highest levels of the terrorist leadership in Gaza.

Indeed, the PA was sliding into active participation in the armed struggle against Israel. Even the PA's leading negotiator with Israel, the "moderate" Nabil Shaath, warned, during a speech in Nablus, of dire consequences if Israel did not acquiesce to the Palestinian demands. "If the negotiations reach a dead end," Shaath declared, "we shall go back to the [armed] struggle and strife, as we did for 40 years. . . . If and when Israel says, 'That's it, we won't talk about Jerusalem, we won't return refugees, we won't dismantle settlements, and we won't retreat from borders,' then all the acts of violence will return. Except that this time we'll have 30,000 armed Palestinian soldiers who will operate in areas in which we have unprecedented elements of freedom." Similarly, Marwan Barghouti, the Gaza-based Secretary of Fatah, confirmed that PA "soldiers" had already received orders to open fire on IDF forces if they tried to operate against Palestinian terrorists in areas claimed by the PA. He also bragged that the PA had significantly larger quantities of weapons than allowed by the agreements with Israel.

The Peres government's reactions to these developments had much more to do with the priorities of the White House than with Middle East realities. Clinton knew that the peace process itself, rather than Peres, was up for reelection in May. Given the extent of the administration's involvement in the peace process—and particularly given Clinton's need for Jewish support in his own reelection campaign later in the year—Clinton resolved to do whatever he had to do in order to ensure that Peres won and that Jerusalem continued accepting the administration's vision of the peace process.

At first, the White House exerted tremendous pressure on Israel to absorb the terrorism—in the administration's lingo, to demonstrate "maturity" and "restraint." When the Israeli public became extremely irate after the first martyr-bombings, the administration organized the Sharm-el-Sheikh summit on fighting terrorism—a major show attended by Clinton, Russian President Boris Yeltsin, and most of the Western world's leaders. The summit was designed to demonstrate international support for Peres, who, in turn, hailed Arafat as a "partner" in the fight against terrorism.

The practical outcome of the Sharm-el-Sheikh summit was best summarized by Brigadier General (Ret.) Yigal Pressler, Peres's special adviser on fighting terrorism. On the surface, Pressler observed, the summit was a major success. All the heads of state demonstrated solidarity with the Israeli victims of terrorism in a very moving event and then issued firm declarations of their intent to confront Islamist terrorism. "At the conclusion of this meeting, the leaders stood in one line linking their arms together in the air, thereby symbolizing their unity in the struggle against terrorism," Pressler wrote. However, he continued, "In effect, this gesture symbolizes, as is often the case when arms are raised, the surrender to terrorism! There was no practical result in the wake of this gathering, and the main conclusion that one can draw is that gatherings, as important as they are, cannot take the place of unified action in the fight against terrorism." This lack of unified action was irrelevant, however, to the Clinton administration, which got what it wanted: a politically powerful signal of world leaders' support for Peres.

In the eyes of the Arab world, meanwhile, the wave of martyrdom bombings signaled a turning point in the Islamists' quest for dominance over the struggle for Palestine, even though Arafat remained at the titular helm. Leading Islamist scholars had endorsed the HAMAS and Islamic Jihad operations, which thus became precedents to be emulated. Hence, the real challenge facing Israel was, and still is, not the specific agreements it might have with any of its Arab neighbors, but the rise of militant Islamism throughout the Arab world. The question of recognized borders, or the extent of Israeli withdrawal toward the 1967 lines, is irrelevant considering that the ultimate objective was, and still remains, the eradication of a non-Muslim entity from Arab land. Irrespective of what Arafat intended when he approved the spate of Islamist bombings at the heart of Israel, their most significant impact was on the Arab and Muslim worlds. Rejuvenated, leaders and masses alike demanded a return to the uncompromising jihad. An emboldened Arafat was only too eager to comply.

———

UNLIKE THE CLINTON administration and the Peres government, Arafat and the Palestinian Islamists were acting in accordance with the strategic trends prevailing in the Muslim and Arab worlds. Most important were the maneuvers of Iran and its allies. Back in mid-December 1995, Tehran had delineated its regional outlook in the Sixth International Seminar on the Persian Gulf. Addressing that conference, senior Iranian officials explained that since the strategic circumstances in the region had changed, there was no longer any need for the sanctions against Iraq. Declaring that the primary threat to the region was the United States' efforts at "strengthening hegemony," they emphasized the importance of European efforts to counterbalance the United States and also stressed the strategic significance of the PRC-led Trans-Asian Axis. For the first time, Iraq participated, semi-officially, at the conference. An Iraqi representative discussed the urgent imperative of establishing an Iranian-led "strategic alliance, or at least tactical cooperation, to foil the conspiracies of the United States and Israel in the region."

In practical terms, Tehran demonstrated its growing influence by facilitating a major escalation in HizbAllah's operations in southern Lebanon. In January 1996, Washington and Jerusalem were openly discussing the imminent beginning of Israeli-Lebanese negotiations, in the context of a reported Syrian crackdown on HizbAllah activities in Lebanon. To give credence to the reports of Syrian efforts to restrain the HizbAllah, Tehran conducted a disinformation operation—arranging an alternative route for transporting weapons to the HizbAllah, as if the normal supply routes via Damascus were no longer available. For this operation to succeed, the Iranian shipment had to be captured and publicly displayed by a third party. So, on January 25, Iran supposedly attempted to deliver military supplies to the HizbAllah through Turkey. The attempt "failed," and Ankara publicly rebuked Tehran. Western sources duly suggested that this indicated the success of U.S. pressure on Syria.

Once this point had been made, the escalation of hostilities in southern Lebanon resumed. This resumption included the firing of long-range Katyusha rockets into northern Israel, which led Israel to launch Operation Grapes of Wrath, a two-week operation in which the Israeli Air Force flew some 1,800 sorties and attacked 500 targets. However, in embarking on the escalation that led to this retaliation, the HizbAllah and its Syrian and Iranian patrons were much better prepared than they had been for Operation Accountability three years earlier. After fifteen days, the Israeli strikes had killed only some twenty HizbAllah fighters, and Katyushas were still being launched into northern Israel. The operation was brought to an end when Israeli artillery, firing at a HizbAllah position, accidentally hit a shelter inside a U.N. compound in Qana, killing over a hundred civilians.

The implications of this cycle of violence were profound. Tehran had demonstrated to friends and foes alike that it could easily cause a flare-up in the region through its proxies. Damascus needed no additional reminder. Indeed, the Syrian forces in Lebanon tightened their grip on the government, demanding that actions be taken to reduce the "Israeli influence." Beirut complied, moving swiftly to silence any potential opposition.

At the same time, relations between Syria and Iraq continued to improve, to the point where Assad and Saddam met secretly in northeastern Syria. At this summit, the two leaders agreed to prepare for the anticipated collapse of the peace process and the ensuing war. They also spoke of their respective efforts to ensure that their sons would succeed them.

Indeed, it was the joint effort of their sons that had brought Assad and Saddam together. Uday Hussein's friend and business partner, Hussein Bahramani, also had very good business relations with the estranged sons of Rifaat al-Assad (Hafez al-Assad's brother), who were still operating in Damascus. They arranged for meetings between Iraqi emissaries and confidants of their cousin Bashar al-Assad, who had risen in power politics following the untimely death of his brother Basil.

There was a sense of urgency in Uday's efforts to consolidate his power base because of mounting tension with his brother Qusay over the eventual succession process. One area of dispute was the anticipated role of Barzan al-Takriti, Saddam's half brother. Qusay considered Barzan's participation in any future government a necessity in terms of restoring relations with Western Europe, which he saw as the key to Iraq's economic recovery. Uday, on the other hand, considered his uncle Barzan an obstacle to his own rise to power, and he was determined to demonstrate that there could be economic recovery without Western help. He pointed to the success of his joint ventures with Bahramani and argued that the expansion of such activities to Syria could drastically improve Iraq's economy. Indeed, during 1996 Syrian-Iraqi relations continued to improve; the movement of goods and people across the border increased markedly, and both governments approved the reopening of direct telephone links.

Meanwhile, Hafez al-Assad was convinced, to a great extent on the basis of intelligence he received from Tehran and numerous Arab capitals, that he must acquire additional protection against a "U.S.-Israeli conspiracy" to destroy his regime in the name of counterterrorism. In mid-June, Iran and Syria signed a new agreement on military cooperation. A key provision called for Syrian units to conduct joint maneuvers with Iranian units in northern Iran. These Iranian units would then form the core of an expeditionary force committed to fighting Israel on the Syrian front. For such an Iranian expeditionary force to reach Syria, however, it would have to travel through Iraq, which was one reason why Bashar had concluded that only very close coordination with Iraq could assure the Assads' staying in power. Bashar also knew that his father was deeply worried about the growing instability in Iraq and the possibility of the country's being partitioned among the Kurds in the north, the Shiites in the south, and the Sunnis in the center. Such a recognition of separate identities could quickly spread throughout the Middle East, fracturing Syria and virtually all other Arab states. Bashar was convinced that his father was so determined to prevent this that he would be willing to put aside his old rivalry with Saddam.

With his father's health deteriorating, Bashar decided to launch an audacious initiative, inviting Uday for a secret visit to Damascus—patterned on the dramatic visit Uday had made to Tehran. Trusted emissaries of the two younger men shuttled among Damascus, Baghdad, and a host of European meeting places to work out a draft of "a unionist project" for Syria and Iraq, which they would eventually invite all the region's victims of U.S. economic imperialism—primarily Libya, Sudan, and Iran—to join. The draft discussed by the emissaries of Uday and Bashar stressed that Saddam would retain his personal stature, most likely being designated secretary-general of the Arab Socialist Ba'ath Party.

Baghdad sought to prevent an international crisis in reaction to these maneuvers by floating a rumor that Barzan al-Takriti would soon succeed Saddam. Given Barzan's close relations with the Western Europeans, the idea was well received; in fact, in conversation with senior Arab officials, some senior Western European officials raised the question of supporting Barzan's ascent to power. In the context of these contacts, the Europeans related their perception of the situation in Iraq. "The expatriate Iraqi opposition," as one of them put it, "is fragmented along ethnic and ideological lines, and its constituents have nothing in common except for the willingness to depose Saddam. In the final analysis, all the expatriate opposition leaders have admitted that the only hope lies in a move from within the Iraqi military that would 'invite' them to take over after a coup topples the incumbent regime in Baghdad." The Europeans were most alarmed about the U.S. reliance on the Kurds as the springboard for destabilizing Baghdad, especially since this approach was vehemently opposed by the Arab governments.

Meanwhile, Saddam was redividing responsibilities between his sons. In mid-August, he removed Uday from his post of commander of the Fidayeen Unit—the 40,000-strong elite force responsible for the security of the regime's top personnel—and replaced him with Qusay, who now controlled all eight of Baghdad's intelligence and internal-security services. Saddam's objective was to give Uday, for foreign consumption, a good clean image as a young leader preoccupied with commercial issues and rapprochement with the outside world, while Qusay would be seen as the ruthless guardian of internal security.

Ultimately, Hafez al-Assad, Saddam Hussein, and Ali Akbar Hashemi-Rafsanjani knew that for their new regional posture to stand a chance of being palatable to Western European and conservative Arab governments, it had to symbolize a new era and new beginnings. And what can be more symbolic of rejuvenation than handing over the mantle to the younger generation? To be sure, neither Saddam nor Assad was about to step down the next day, and confidants of Hashemi-Rafsanjani were quietly examining the possibility of extending his term beyond the limits set by the Iranian constitution. But the introduction of the younger generation into the uppermost levels of power had begun. In terms of the peace process, it meant reiterating the commitment to war against Israel as the instrument of making the sons the standard-bearers for the Arab-Muslim world.

———

MILITARY MOVES indicating active preparations for war had begun soon after the Assad-Saddam summit, when Iran began readying the expeditionary forces it had promised Syria and Iraq. In late May, Iran conducted its largest military exercise ever, code-named Velayat. The essence of Velayat was a multiple-corps deep offensive following an advance exactly as long as the distance between Iran and Israel. The objective of Velayat was to confirm Iran's ability to send a strategically effective expeditionary force to contribute to a regional war against high-quality armies. The initial exercise, at which the entire Iranian top leadership and high command were present, revealed deficiencies in a key special-forces unit. These were corrected, and the improvements were demonstrated in a follow-up exercise in late October.

The Velayat maneuvers, involving more than 200,000 troops, were held in an area between Tehran and Qom covering approximately 2,000 square miles, with the key offensive clashes taking place in an area of about 500 square miles in the desert of Kushk-e Nosrat, close to Qom. The decisive part of Velayat was divided into two stages.

First, beginning on the evening of May 23, the Iranians carried out an overnight assault on enemy positions. The attack started at dusk, when a special squad of parachutists landed behind enemy lines and conducted a series of raids, destroying command positions and ammunition depots. They also prepared and secured a landing zone for the main paratroop force. After the paratroopers landed at night, two infantry armies advanced to infiltrate the enemy's positions and prepare for operations behind the lines.

Then, in the early morning hours of May 24, fighter-bombers and helicopter gunships, as well as the heavy artillery units of the ground forces, began a concentrated offensive on the enemy's positions. Immediately afterward, tank and mechanized units stormed in from all points to take on their assigned targets. Their persistent advance deep into enemy territory was supported by fire from the air, artillery, missile launchers, and heavy weapons.

At the end of that week, Iran's spiritual leader and commander in chief, Ayatollah Khamenei, met with the senior officers for a special Friday prayer. In his sermon, he stressed the significance of the Velayat exercise and, in case there had been any doubt, specified its intended target. "The armed forces of the Islamic Republic of Iran," he told the officers, "only pose a threat to the aggressor and anyone who plans to attack this country, this nation, and this system [of government]. Today, . . . the threat to the region's security comes from the regime occupying Jerusalem. This regime threatens the territorial integrity of its neighbors and other countries of the region. The supporters of the Zionist regime will be blamed for any acts of aggression, invasion, and any move of this regime against its neighboring countries in the holy land of Palestine."

———

AS MAY 29—the date set for the Israeli elections—approached, the Clinton administration intensified its direct involvement in Israel's domestic affairs. The administration provided the Israeli peace camp with political advice and access to expertise, and it encouraged major Jewish contributors to the Democratic Party to support Peres. The Sharm el-Skeikh summit was only the first in a series of events organized by the White House to enhance Peres's position. Then, in early March, Clinton sent much-publicized letters to various Arab leaders urging them to crack down on Islamist terrorist activities in their countries. In mid-March, the White House announced a special grant to Israel of $100 million to help fight terrorism (although the strings attached to this grant made it largely irrelevant).

Unlike some of the politicians, the Israeli people recognized the elections as a referendum on "peace"-and-terrorism versus security. Ultimately, the majority of Israel's Jews chose to end terrorism, whatever that might do to the peace process, and voted for Binyamin Netanyahu's Likud. (Israeli-Arab voters made the opposite choice, narrowing Netanyahu's majority considerably.) Having made the triumph of Peres such a personal issue, Clinton saw ˙ personal affront in this outcome. Therefore, he decided to attempt to bring

Netanyahu down as soon as possible, in the meantime exerting whatever pressure was necessary to coerce him into sustaining the peace process.

Although flattery and statements of friendship were exchanged between Jerusalem and Washington in early June, Arab and Iranian leaders sensed the enmity and decided to capitalize on it. Once again, Tehran was pleased to observe, a window of opportunity coincided with an American election year.

———

WITH IRAN'S ABILITY to contribute significantly to the military effort against Israel proven in the Velayat exercise, Damascus and Tehran started formulating a joint war strategy. In mid-August, Iraq was brought into a trilateral "joint command" specifically aimed at preparing for "a major war against Israel." A key component of this joint command was the coordination of the three countries' ballistic-missile plans.

In late August, Syria began force movements in Lebanon and near the Golan that quickly changed the strategic posture in the region. In the first phase of these movements, mechanized units were deployed from Bhamdun and Dahr al-Baydar in central Lebanon to positions very close to the Israeli-held security zone. These Syrian forces were deployed in such a way that any Israeli retaliation would kill Syrian soldiers, thus creating an excuse for escalation. In addition, two regiments of the 14th Special Forces/Commando Division were deployed from the Bekaa Valley to forward positions overlooking Israel's key early-warning station on Mount Hermon.

In the second phase, completed in mid-September, units of the 10th Mechanized Division were deployed along the Beirut-Damascus Highway all the way to the Bekaa, replacing the units that had redeployed to the south. The third regiment of the 14th Special Forces/Commando Division was deployed from Beirut to forward positions in southeastern Lebanon, overlooking Mount Hermon from the west. This deployment was intended to permit Syria to strike Israel's key early-warning station on a moment's notice, thus harming, if not paralyzing, Israel's ability to detect a major surprise attack. By late September, the Syrian forces, deployed behind a thin layer of Lebanese Army units, were in a position to instigate a provocation of strategic dimensions.

At this juncture, an intelligence fiasco aggravated Israeli anxieties. Yehuda Gil, a veteran Mossad agent, retired since 1989, had cultivated a senior Syrian officer as a major source. At Mossad's urging, Gil had maintained sporadic contact with this source even after his retirement. However, he had begun embellishing on the Syrian's material and, at times, even adding data of his own in order to enhance the significance of his source and, consequently, his own standing.

Now, in the summer of 1996, Gil attributed to his Syrian source a warning that Syria was planning to launch a swift attack on the Golan Heights in the area of Mount Hermon. Assad, Gil explained, was convinced that Israel had no intention of living up to the commitments made by Rabin and Peres and therefore had decided to try the war option. According to Gil, however, the Syrian deployment was aimed only at grabbing a small piece of land. Gil also reported that Assad had not yet given the final order. In a subsequent report, Gil stated that the attack would probably start as soon as a large Syrian military exercise ended; however, if there were heavy rains, the attack might be postponed until spring.

Actually, Gil's reports were largely correct—the main exception being the statement that Assad had not decided to go to war. The Syrian deployments were indeed optimized for the type of operation Gil warned about. Hence, several senior IDF officers and government officials proposed that Netanyahu order the mobilization of reserves. However, subsequent studies of multiple-source material failed to confirm Gil's assessment, and the reserves were left unmobilized in order to avoid unnecessary escalation.

Nevertheless, Netanyahu decided to solicit Clinton's help in preventing the outbreak of war. On September 13, Netanyahu arrived in Washington for a working visit and briefed Clinton on the growing tension. Clinton immediately sent Dennis Ross to Damascus with a sharply worded message. Assad read the message carefully and asked Ross to immediately send a reply to Netanyahu via Washington. As the White House repeated the message to Netanyahu, Assad insisted on Israel's adherence to Rabin's "deposit" of August 1993 and "non-paper" of May 1995, which Syria interpreted as commitments to withdraw to the June 4 line. While reiterating Syria's desire to make peace, Assad warned that "all options would be open" if he did not get his kind of peace agreement.

In addition to talking to Ross, Assad had sent Ambassador Mualem to the State Department with a written message: "Syria does not intend to go to war with Israel. Our army movements are made for defensive purposes and out of caution. We do not want to be surprised. We learned our lesson in 1982 in Lebanon, and we are no longer taking chances." On September 16, Christopher summoned Israel's Ambassador Eliyahu Ben-Elissar and told him that Damascus's response was that "its military moves are defensive in nature," but that "if no progress is made in the peace process and the negotiations remain frozen, Assad would feel free to use every option and act." Ben-Elissar immediately relayed the American message to Jerusalem, which took it at face value, for nobody imagined the Americans would make a deliberate misstatement on such a crucial matter.

Meanwhile, Israel and Syria were also maintaining secret communications through former ambassador Edward Djerejian and George Nader, a Lebanese American who publishes a paper on Middle East affairs and is friends with Dore Gold, at that time a senior adviser to Netanyahu. A few days after Jerusalem received the Syrian reply, Nader had a conversation with senior officials in Damascus, who wondered why Netanyahu's response to Assad's message had been so negative. When Nader told the Syrians the content of the message as relayed by the Americans, the Syrians were incredulous. "They have fooled the Israelis," one official said. "The Americans are playing a double game." Nader hurried to Jerusalem with an authoritative text of the Syrian response.

A few days later, Damascus asked Washington for an explanation. "Why should you care?" a senior U.S. official told Mualem. "This is for your own good. It would not hurt Netanyahu to worry a little."

Mualem could not hide his anger. "This is a sensitive situation," he replied. "We are not negotiating. I cannot understand how you allow yourselves to do such things."

Israel would subsequently learn that, in consultation with Ross and with Clinton's knowledge, Christopher had altered the Syrian message. The Clinton administration "did not appreciate" Netanyahu's "excessive self-confidence" and therefore had decided "to make him sweat a little." So, instead of transmitting accurately the Syrians' calming message, Christopher added the crucial sentence, "Syria reserves every option to itself."

One possible reason for this desire to scare Israel was the fact that the Netanyahu government had called the Clinton administration to account about its treating Rabin's "deposit" and "non-paper" as legally binding. When the Netanyahu government first learned of these documents, it conducted a thorough study of the issue and determined that Rabin had never intended to commit Israel to anything. The Americans were informed accordingly. When the administration procrastinated, Dore Gold traveled to Washington armed with documents proving Jerusalem's point. Consequently, on September 18, Gold and Ross formulated a personal and confidential letter from Christopher to Netanyahu declaring the "non-paper" null and void under international law. Netanyahu considered this letter one of the most important documents Israel had received from the United States concerning the Syrian track.

While these diplomatic maneuverings were going on, tension continued to mount, largely because of continued Syrian military movements. The immediate crisis peaked on October 12, when, at 4 A.M., the Israeli Air Force scrambled fighters to encounter a suspicious movement of Syrian helicopters in the Hermon area. Upon spotting the Israeli fighters, the helicopters retreated deeper into Syrian territory. Although there was no engagement, Netanyahu feared that war might break out at any moment.

A few days later, Ross returned to Jerusalem with intelligence warnings that Syria was considering a military move in the near term. This information corroborated the IDF's conclusion that Syria was preparing to launch an offensive on the Golan Heights. Meanwhile, alarmed by the tension, Moscow sent Primakov—who by now had replaced Kozyrev as foreign minister—to see Assad. Soon afterward, Moscow transmitted to Jerusalem Syria's assurances that it "had no plans to attack Israel."

Ultimately, the entire episode was a strategic deception initiated by Damascus. Assad knew that Israeli and U.S. intelligence must have accumulated enough data about the Syrian force movements to lead Israel to consider a preemptive strike. The calming messages delivered through numerous channels were intended to avert such a strike. To what extent Primakov was a willing or a duped emissary is yet to be determined.

Through all of this, the Syrians were trying to make sense of Christopher's tampering with Assad's message. Damascus concluded, and senior officials in Tehran concurred, that Washington *wanted* Israel to attack Syria. Since it was clear, their reasoning went, that the peace process could not deliver Syrian capitulation, Washington had resolved to punish Assad. Hence Syria's best response would be a quick land grab on the Golan. Then Damascus could issue an ultimatum: Unless the United States delivered Israel, the crisis would escalate into a regional war involving Iran and Iraq as well. As with past wars—especially the 1973 Yom Kippur War and the 1990 invasion of Kuwait—the Palestinians would provide the last-minute strategic diversion.

———

IN LATE SEPTEMBER, the PA entered into a major military agreement with Syria establishing the modalities under which the Palestinian "police" forces and other "armed elements"—that is, terrorist organizations—would cause a flare-up within Israel in case of an escalation in the north. As part of this agreement, Syria agreed to provide weapons and advanced training to PLO units in the refugee camps in southern Lebanon—units that had been disarmed under the Israeli-Lebanese agreements. The Syrians quickly followed up, distributing weapons ranging from small arms to Katyushas in the refugee camps. The forces of Munir Makdah were among the first to be equipped and trained through this program. Moreover, at the PA's request, the Syrians began intensive training of PLO anti-aircraft units. This was the first phase in a major Syrian-run effort to organize and train Palestinian units to better use the growing number of heavy weapons—anti-tank and anti-aircraft missiles, Katyushas, and the like—being smuggled into Gaza. The cadres trained in Lebanon would then infiltrate Gaza to take command of the local units.

The PA and the Syrians also agreed to infiltrate military and intelligence teams into PA-controlled areas, giving the teams Palestinian IDs and having them serve as military attachés training and advising the Palestinian police. In the fall, the Syrians started deploying these teams, comprising Syrian intelligence personnel and Palestinians from the ranks of the Popular Front for the Liberation of Palestine (PFLP), the Popular Front for the Liberation of Palestine - General Command (PFLP-GC), and the Palestinian Islamic Jihad. The Syrians established two intelligence networks, both enjoying the protection of the PLO security apparatus. The first was a counterintelligence network. The PA and Syria were in agreement that only a fresh team, employing ruthless means, could truly eradicate the remnants of the Israeli intelligence networks in the territories. The second network was made up of military intelligence and special-forces teams charged with identifying targets in the deep Israeli rear and detecting preparations for war. In case of war, these teams could conceivably conduct special operations inside Israel.

The PLO's own preparations for war were evident. In Gaza, Arafat ordered the speedy completion of his four-story-deep personal command bunker. All over Gaza the PLO was rapidly building a chain of command centers and storage sites for ammunition and weapons—all of them underground and well fortified. The PA's security services were accumulating stockpiles of anti-tank and anti-aircraft weapons forbidden by the Oslo accords. Moreover, the PA began transferring heavy weapons to HAMAS and other Islamist forces in case the need for deniability should arise.

In late September in the Old City of Jerusalem, the Israelis opened a second entrance to the Hasmonean Tunnel, an archaeological tunnel that runs right under the edge of the Temple Mount. Arafat capitalized on this event to unleash his forces. It was a well-planned operation, covering the entire area controlled by the PA. In Jerusalem, a mob on the Temple Mount threw stones down at the Jewish worshipers at the Western Wall. Later the same day, hundreds of Arabs crowded the Damascus Gate, and several incendiary bottle-bombs were thrown at the police. In Hebron, hundreds of Arabs demonstrated violently against the Jewish community. In Ramallah, some 2,000 Palestinians rioted, throwing stones at IDF soldiers; when the troops opened fire with rubber bullets, PA policemen and terrorists returned their fire from within a building under PA control. In the Gaza Strip, eight busloads of Arabs arrived at the Netzarim junction and began hurling bricks and stones at the IDF soldiers stationed there.

The fighting expanded markedly the next day, characterized by numerous exchanges of fire between IDF soldiers and Palestinian police. On the third day, mobs of Muslims resumed throwing stones near the Temple Mount, wounding both Israeli police and Jewish worshipers at the Western Wall. In Gaza, Palestinian police ordered high school students to participate in violent demonstrations in Gush Katif.

In all, fifteen Israelis were killed in this mini-Intifadah, whose primary objective was to involve the PA security forces in direct fighting with the IDF and so create adversarial relations. For Arafat, the crisis also served as a demonstration to both Israel and the Palestinians that the Islamists did not have a monopoly on the armed struggle. In retrospect, it was a test of whether Israel would retaliate for such a flagrant provocation or swallow and proceed with the Oslo process. Arafat could not but have been encouraged by the outcome.

———

THE MINI-INTIFADAH also served as a strategic diversion against both Jerusalem and Washington. The Clinton administration rallied immediately to the defense of the peace process, pressuring the Netanyahu government to make additional unilateral concessions in order to convince Arafat to call off the violence and resume negotiations. The White House stressed that it was essential for Clinton's reelection campaign to show progress in the negotiations and that "Israel's best friend in the White House" was "expecting" Jerusalem to deliver such an achievement. Washington simply ignored the indications of impending war on every front.

The Syrian Armed Forces' offensive exercises and related troop movements had continued through the fall, with numerous units ending up much closer to the Golan Heights than their permanent deployment areas and in a high state of readiness. Of special importance were the exercises involving SCUD missiles, including the launching of a SCUD-C under conditions of offensive war.

In mid-September, the Egyptian armed forces conducted their largest military exercise since the late 1970s. The ten-day Badr-96 exercise simulated a strategic deep offensive against Israel and included a large-scale call-up of reserves, a major amphibious landing on the Sinai coast, and a nighttime assault crossing of the Suez Canal. The defense minister, General Mohamed Tantawi, stated that Egypt conducted Badr-96 out of concern about Israel's unconventional military capabilities. In mid-October, senior officers of the Egyptian Army took a tour of the Sinai, including areas near the Israeli border, in violation of the peace agreement with Israel; it was a commanders' tour aimed at acquainting them with the peculiarities of a theater in which they might have to operate. At the same time, Cairo encouraged the resumption of calls for war at the political level. Brigadier General (Ret.) Mohammed Muawad Gad al-

Moula was permitted to establish a new political party committed to reviving "the 'victorious spirit' of the October 1973 War." "We have no choice but to adopt a platform for rebuilding a strong Egypt and preparing a new generation capable of fighting any attackers," al-Moula declared. "We have to prepare for a fresh confrontation with Israel." Cairo's belligerent rhetoric soon led to bilateral and multilateral discussions with Iran, Iraq, Syria, and Jordan. According to high-level Iranian sources, the initial phase of these consultations led to the adoption of "pan-Arab cooperation," making it possible "to impose a military blockade on Israel from the north, east, and south."

In the second half of October, Damascus began conducting "irregular movements" with its SCUD units, and Syrian troop movements started getting too close to the Golan Heights to be ignored as routine. Taken in the context of the latest Syrian exercises with SSMs (surface-to-surface missiles) and major armored forces, these activities amounted to crawling toward forward positions near the Golan. Following a briefing by Syrian officials, Lebanese sources reported that "The Syrians are capable of pre-empting Netanyahu's strike by initiating the attack."

Also in October, Iraqi military units, including armor, artillery, and missile units, began moving from central Iraq toward the Syrian border; and Iraq began a call-up of reservists and the activation of units that had been dormant since the Gulf War. The majority of the main roads leading toward the Syrian border were taken over by the Iraqi military and closed to civilian traffic. By this time Iran had begun delivering, via Syria, a whole range of vastly improved weapons to the HizbAllah and other terrorist forces based on the border with Israel. Among these weapon systems were the truck-mounted Fajr-3 240-mm rockets (which, with a range of around 26 miles, could hit major Israeli objectives from beyond the security zone), the highly lethal FAGOT anti-tank guided missiles (Soviet design), and 35-mm Oerlikon automatic guns (a Swiss weapon good against both helicopters and surface targets). In early November, second-tier states were brought into "the circle of confrontation." Most significant was the Syrian-Pakistani military agreement, which arranged for sending Pakistani officers and key equipment to Syria.

In late November, Damascus shared a comprehensive intelligence assessment with its Arab allies and a host of terrorist organizations. The Syrian briefing began by explaining that it was imperative to break the deadlock in the region before President Clinton—who by this time had won reelection—could resume his concentration on the peace process. The briefing emphasized the possibility that "the Israeli Army will launch an imminent large-scale military operation against the Syrian Forces stationed adjacent to the Golan, in addition to the Syrian Forces that were relocated in Lebanon."

Taken as a whole, however, the Syrian briefing left no doubt that Damascus was determined to pursue its own assertive war aims, not just repel a putative Israeli aggression.

How deeply Iran was committed to supporting the Syrian war effort was of crucial importance to Damascus. In fact, Tehran was taking its commitment very seriously. In the first week of December, Foreign Minister Ali Akbar Velayati was dispatched to Damascus for urgent high-level consultations. He arrived carrying an extremely important message from Hashemi-Rafsanjani to Assad and then conducted extensive discussions with Assad and other senior officials. Iranian sources highlighted the discussions in which Velayati "referred to foreign pressures and Zionist plots and underlined the need to strengthen cooperation between Iran and Syria." According to the sources, the Syrian president stressed that "this cooperation will help establishment of peace and tranquility in the whole region." Both Damascus and Tehran agreed that there was going to be a lot of violence on the road to regional peace and tranquility.

———

DURING THE FALL of 1996, numerous sources reported that the vast majority of both civilians and military leaders in most Arab states, as well as in Iran and Pakistan, believed that Israel was especially vulnerable, and that, at the very least, there was a unique opportunity to begin the process of its destruction. It would also be a historic opportunity for the Muslim world to repel the United States' intrusion in the Hub of Islam—even though all the key players continued to reassert their commitment to the Clinton administration's peace process. In late November, Nail Mukhaybar, one of the most authoritative Arab commentators on Middle East affairs, observed, "The question is no longer: Will the expected and planned war between Israel and Syria ever break out? It is rather: When will the war break out?"

By mid-December, Syrian and Iranian intelligence were becoming increasingly apprehensive about Israel's reading of the strategic situation. Syrian intelligence had acquired data that pointed to "secret movements" by Israeli forces on the Golan Heights and in southern Lebanon. Most alarming to Damascus was information acquired by electronic intelligence suggesting that "Israeli command posts were redeployed" for a possible war.

What Syrian intelligence had detected was actually a high-level command and headquarters exercise aimed at testing the major IDF units' ability to communicate and coordinate theaterwide operations. This was a static map exercise, and no actual units were moved. Significantly, however, in preparing for this exercise, the IDF was certain that Syrian intelligence would not detect it, and therefore Jerusalem decided not to inform the Syrians about it.

Meanwhile, units throughout Syria were put on wartime alert, and Damascus also sounded the alarm in Tehran. The ever prudent and professional Iranian intelligence service insisted on checking the Syrians' raw intelligence against their own data; the Iranian experts then concurred with the Syrians and recommended that their government begin preparing for intervention in accordance with the Syrian-Iranian agreement. Tehran took the precaution of approaching the uppermost circles of power in Riyadh through both official and emergency channels, informing them that Iran was determined to provide Syria with all possible help but assuring them that the anticipated massive troop movements were aimed solely at assisting Syria in its war with Israel and would not be aimed at the Arabian Peninsula. At the same time, Syrian intelligence summoned leaders of Islamist and Palestinian rejectionist organizations and instructed them to prepare for a wave of violence both in southern Lebanon and in the territories in order to harass Israel and hinder the IDF in carrying out its own war plans.

However, Damascus still remained very apprehensive about its ability either to withstand an Israeli preemptive strike or to preempt the anticipated Israeli attack. Hence the Syrians summoned the U.S. ambassador to the Foreign Ministry and presented their intelligence data about the "secret movements" of Israeli forces and the activation of the Israeli command posts. They demanded that Washington either stop Israel from launching the war or else support a Syrian preemptive strike; if Israel did attack, the Syrians told the ambassador, there would be massive retaliation and extremely heavy casualties throughout Israel. Similar messages were also sent via France and Germany. Assad then personally called President Mubarak, who, in turn, personally called Prime Minister Netanyahu and warned against attacking Syria. Using the good offices of all these intermediaries, Jerusalem went out of its way to convince the Syrians that their information was mistaken and Israel had no aggressive intentions.

Then, in late December, a bus exploded in the middle of Damascus. The real cause of the explosion was a crisis building between Jamil al-Assad—one of the president's brothers—and high-level Syrian military and intelligence officers. Never politically ambitious, Jamil and his sons were content to be responsible for the Syrian elite's drug exports and money laundering. By the summer of 1996, General Ali Duba, the chief of Syrian intelligence, had begun suspecting that Jamil was embezzling the profits. In early December, while Hafez al-Assad seemed weak and dependent on his cronies, Duba and his partners felt confident enough to take on Jamil. According to Jordanian sources, the bus bombing was designed by Syrian intelligence on orders from Ali Duba to kill several of Jamil's key people (as well as a host of innocent passengers). Jamil himself did not need the warning: He had already fled to

France, where some of his relatives and cronies joined him a couple of days after the bombing.

Although the bus bomb was actually part of the power struggle in Damascus, the Syrian leadership quickly attributed it to Israeli intelligence. Those at the very top knew the truth, but the bulk of the Syrian intelligence and military establishment was roused by the reports of Israeli responsibility for the carnage. The lie quickly took on a life of its own, and, in the first days of January 1997, the Syrian high command concluded that the bus bombing had been an Israeli provocation aimed at inciting Syria to launch a retaliatory strike. Such a move would in turn be used by Jerusalem to justify an Israeli military assault. The Syrian depiction of the Israeli strategic dynamics essentially mirrored Syria's own doctrine and contingency plans, and so Syria's senior officers found it especially believable.

Then, on the afternoon of January 3, the slide to crisis suddenly halted for no apparent reason. The Islamist terrorist leaders were called in by Syrian intelligence and ordered to stop their preparations. Succeeding weeks saw an overall slowdown in Syrian military activities. When major rainstorms hit the Middle East, forward units were pulled back to the shelter of their permanent bases, and thousands of reservists were released. The threat of war seemed to have subsided until the weather improved.

In fact, the real reason for the sudden change of plans was a deterioration in Assad's health that necessitated prostate surgery on January 7. Damascus could not conceivably risk war while the almighty commander-in-chief was incapacitated.

Even though war did not break out, the swift slide to the brink of war exposed the mood among the top echelons in Damascus and Tehran. The struggle within the Syrian military and political elites only increased the danger, since a major crisis was a proven instrument for consolidating power in Damascus. However, the peacemakers in Washington kept ignoring this reality.

———

IN EARLY JANUARY, using the channels opened during the just-resolved crisis as well as the good offices of the Saudi ambassador to the United States, Prince Bandar, the Clinton administration signaled Damascus that any peace initiative would be appreciated and rewarded. On January 26, after a few days of floating trial balloons, Syria clarified its position. Through an intermediary he knew would immediately brief both Washington and Jerusalem, Ambassador Mualem implied that, encouraged by recent messages from Israeli Foreign Minister David Levy, Damascus was seriously interested in resuming peace negotiations. However, Mualem made Syria's return to the peace process conditional on the United States' agreeing to perform the role of a dedicated and impartial mediator and specifically on a pilgrimage to Damascus by the new secretary of state, Madeleine Albright. Only after such a visit, Mualem explained, and after the Clinton administration guaranteed the implementation of the "non-paper" (even though Warren Christopher had clarified in writing that the "non-paper" was not binding on either Israel or Syria), would Damascus agree to resuming negotiations on the basis of U.N. Security Council Resolutions 242 and 338, as well as the host of "understandings" reached since the Madrid Conference.

The Clinton administration leaped on this Syrian initiative and began preparing for the revival of the Syrian-Israeli track. However, the administration did not know, or did not care about, the real reason for the Syrian about-face: namely, Hafez al-Assad's perception that Washington's involvement was critical if his son Bashar were to succeed him.

Assad's surgery had revealed cancer at an advanced stage. The promise made by Radio Damascus on January 8 that the President would return to his office "within a few days" was yet to be fulfilled. Moreover, high-level sources in Damascus insisted that the need for surgery had been known since early December, but the operation had been postponed until Assad had neutralized the main threats to his rule. Assad was also again seriously depressed, as he had been in the winter of 1983–84, when he was convinced he was going to die any day. His depression was only deepened by the absence of his late son and original designated heir, Basil. Indeed, he left his bed only once after his surgery—on January 21, the third anniversary of Basil's death, when he went to lay flowers on the grave.

The preparations of Bashar al-Assad to take on the mantle of leadership continued in earnest. Ever since Basil's death, Bashar, a physician, had immersed himself in military studies, and he had actively participated in negotiations with his Iraqi and Iranian counterparts. But those negotiations took place behind the scenes. Now, Arab observers in Damascus and Beirut noted, it had become imperative to bring him into the limelight and demonstrate publicly that he had attained the aura of a leader. Consequently, his father now designated him a special emissary, in his place, for highly sensitive missions such as discussions with the leadership of the HizbAllah, including its shrewd deputy secretary-general, Naim Qassim, on future operations in southern Lebanon.

Meanwhile, the bad blood between Assad and his brothers had intensified markedly. Official Damascus had always insisted that Basil's death was caused by a car accident. Now, in early January 1997, sources very close to Hafez al-Assad confirmed for the first time that Hafez's two brothers had assassinated Basil. This confirmation did not result from any new information, but rather reflected Hafez al-Assad's growing apprehensions. Incapable of relying on his brothers, and in doubt about his son's ability to hold on to power on his own, Assad was convinced that a masterfully generated crisis was needed to rally the Syrian military and intelligence elite behind him and Bashar. Only devotion cemented with blood would ensure their loyalty. On the other hand, Assad was afraid that a major external assault on the regime, especially if conducted by the United States, would lead rivals to betray him. He knew that his brothers had good relations with Paris, and he feared they might be able to cut a deal to resolve the power struggle.

The wily Assad concluded that the only way to break out of this grim scenario was to ensure Washington's commitment to the stability and survival of his regime. Hence, the moment he heard Clinton suggest that the emphasis in the peace process should be reoriented toward Syria, and with Jerusalem backtracking from Netanyahu's strong statements about the strategic importance of the Golan, Assad knew he had found his regime's salvation. All he had to do was suggest a renewed interest in the peace process and Washington would come running, with Jerusalem in tow. For as long as the peace process was back on track, there would not be an Israeli attack. This would give Assad the time and peace of mind he needed to complete the grooming of Bashar as well as to prepare for that politically cleansing war.

FROM THE VERY BEGINNING of the Oslo negotiations, Hebron had been a unique issue second only to Jerusalem. The Jewish community that had returned to Hebron after the Six-Day War—unlike the Jewish community in any other Arab city—had taken over historical Jewish property. As of the end of World War I, when the British Mandate authorities took over "Palestine," Hebron was one of only four cities there in which Jewish communities had existed continuously since Biblical times. Then in 1929, rioting Arab mobs slaughtered much of the Jewish community, and the British authorities forced the surviving Jews to evacuate. The revival of the Jewish community in Hebron after the Six-Day War was considered by the bulk of Israel's Jewish population a restitution of historical rights. Hence the notion of vacating Hebron would be traumatic for any Israeli government.

In the summer of 1996, soon after Netanyahu had consolidated his government, the White House decided to make Israel's withdrawal from Hebron the showpiece demonstrating Clinton's ability to force Jerusalem to go along with him. In August, Netanyahu organized a team chaired by former chief of staff Dan Shomron specifically to handle the Hebron issue. Shomron's team had to deal with pressure not only from Dennis Ross but also from Mubarak, whom the United States had recruited to make any progress in Israeli-Arab dynamics conditional on a major compromise on Hebron.

Then, toward the end of 1996, Israeli intelligence learned that Arafat was planning a new series of violent riots as a "spontaneous" protest against the continued Jewish presence in Hebron. In mid-December, Israel presented the Clinton administration with data that it could not ignore. Consequently, the United States put pressure on Arafat and Mubarak to bring the negotiations to a quick conclusion; the administration even resisted the Palestinians' last-minute attempt to force a renegotiation of agreed-upon articles. Israel succeeded in ensuring the continuance of a Jewish community in Hebron under the protection of the IDF despite the forthcoming withdrawal from the bulk of the city. Moreover, Israel gained a series of written guarantees from the United States regarding future phases of the peace process—particularly a guarantee that Israel would have sole responsibility for the size and timing of future interim withdrawals—and regarding the PA's implementation of a long list of previously signed agreements.

Shomron and Saeb Erekat signed the Hebron agreement on the night of January 14–15. It had almost immediate repercussions for Arafat. In pushing the Hebron negotiations through, he had promised his lieutenants results he could not deliver. He had created the impression that in return for his signing the agreement, the Americans and the Western Europeans would impose upon Israel unconditional implementation of a three-phase pullback from virtually the entire West Bank, the release of all Palestinian prisoners, the establishment of an extraterritorial safe passageway between Gaza and the West Bank, the opening of the Gaza airport to unsupervised international flights, and the transfer of international crossing points to the unilateral control of the PA. Arafat had also told his adherents that the Hebron agreement stipulated that Israel must transfer more than 85 percent of the West Bank to the PA's jurisdiction by mid-1998, or one year before the finalization of the permanent-status negotiations, whichever came first. When the United States endorsed Israel's rejection of these demands, Arafat had to confront growing alienation among his closest aides.

Meanwhile, the Islamists, not only in the territories but also throughout the Muslim world, believed that Arafat had surrendered to Israeli pressure in agreeing to let Jews remain in Hebron. They vowed to escalate their jihad for the salvation of Hebron, and organizations sponsored by Iran and Syria began activating terrorist cells inside the territories. Not without reason, Arafat now feared that leadership of the liberation jihad would once again shift to the Islamists. It became imperative for him and his coterie to regain control over the growing militancy in the territories by becoming its leaders and champions. At the same time, Arafat realized the Netanyahu government was not capitulating. On the contrary, Israel started building in Har Homa, a suburb of East Jerusalem—a clear demonstration of resolve. Hence

Arafat's lieutenants began a series of clandestine consultations with Islamist leaders in the territories and throughout the Arab world, in order to ascertain just how crucial they considered the return to armed struggle. The response was a resounding cry for violence.

On the night of March 9, Arafat and a few close aides met secretly with the heads of HAMAS, the Islamic Jihad, and other rejectionist organizations to discuss the resumption of terrorism within Israel. Arafat opened the meeting with a diatribe against Israel. In earlier meetings, Arafat had qualified his remarks with a disclaimer that he was not sanctioning terrorism—not so this time. All the participants agreed that it was imperative to shock Israel into major concessions, as well as to punish Jerusalem for its intransigence. As the discussion heated up, Arafat began uttering a sentence suggesting the use of force. He was interrupted by one of his aides, who advised him to be careful in what he said. A leader of one of the rejectionist groups noted that there was no need for Arafat to be explicit—those present understood him well. The other leaders nodded or murmured in agreement.

A few days later, the leaders of HAMAS and the Islamic Jihad met again with senior PA officials. In this meeting, the PA officials stated that Arafat would endorse and permit terrorist attacks within Israel. To demonstrate the PA's sincerity, Arafat ordered the release of all HAMAS and Islamic Jihad prisoners. Within days, their cadres were enjoying greater freedom of action than they had had before the wave of suicide bombings the previous spring. In Islamist mosques and gatherings in Gaza and throughout the West Bank, the youth talked openly about Arafat's "green light" to strike.

On March 21 a bomb exploded in the Apropos Cafe in Tel Aviv, killing three young women and injuring dozens. Before acting upon Arafat's green light, the HAMAS high command in the territories had communicated with the HAMAS command center in Damascus, seeking advice and permission to proceed. The HAMAS command center in turn consulted with both the Syrian and Iranian governments before giving its own green light. For Tehran, these consultations confirmed that Arafat was indeed ready to embrace the Islamists' commitment to a terrorist jihad as the sole method for dealing with Israel.

The following week, the PA conducted a major test in Hebron. This flare-up was distinctive because of the direct involvement of the Palestinian police. Initially, the security forces simply refrained from interfering with the rioters. However, by the time the riots ended in early April, PA police, intelligence, and security forces were in almost total control of events, to the point of actually directing clashes with Israeli security forces and settlers. As part of this effort, the PA paid youths the equivalent of $10 to $17 per day for taking part in riots and attacking Israeli soldiers. The PA had also deployed over

1,500 "policemen" in Hebron—instead of the 400 permitted by the recent agreement—and they were armed with forbidden weapons. By mid-April, Arafat's aides were convinced they could operate with near impunity, since the riots did not cause Israel to cancel the Hebron agreement. Meanwhile, the PA security forces had proved they could run major outbursts of "popular rage," even though the driving force was the Mosque.

These operations—starting with the bomb in the Tel Aviv café—were planned for a time when Arafat and his inner circle would be out of the country, at the Organization of Islamic Countries (OIC) summit in Pakistan. For Arafat, the Islamabad summit also offered an excellent opportunity to revive direct contacts with Tehran. He met with President Hashemi-Rafsanjani, while his aides held numerous discussions with their counterparts from Iran and other radical Muslim states.

Back home, Arafat's own Fatah was circulating a bulletin to its cadres analyzing the relationship with Israel and outlining the steps to be taken by the PLO and the PA. This bulletin stated that "Israeli Prime Minister Binyamin Netanyahu has declared war against the peace process and against the Palestinian people, and is using all weapons at his disposal in this war." However, the Palestinian weapons already confronting Israel were more than a match for the Israeli "killing, destruction, breaking pledges, and reneging on treaties." The bulletin criticized the United States for siding with Israel and concluded, "Netanyahu's bulldozers must stop, and so must the campaign of arrests, the closure [of the Gaza Strip crossings], the economic blockade, the settlements policy, and the judaization of Jerusalem. Only then can the dialogue and negotiations be with us, and only then will the U.S. mediator be in a position to be a genuine sponsor of the peace process."

The bellicose tone of this Fatah bulletin was most alarming to Israel in view of the concurrent increase in the smuggling of weapons into the PA-controlled areas and the beginning of the production of weapons and ammunition in Gaza. Most important were the numbers of Katyusha rockets and anti-tank and anti-aircraft missiles smuggled into the Gaza Strip. Using the trunks of their cars, Palestinian VIPs traveling on passes provided by Israel brought forbidden weapons from Gaza into the PA's urban enclaves in the West Bank. Ultimately, the flow of weapons smuggled into the Gaza Strip with the help of Egyptian Military Intelligence was of even greater significance strategically than militarily.

8

"A Contract Is a Contract, and a Vow Is a Vow" (1997)

Mubarak's Claim to Lead the Arab World; Arafat's Way of Fighting Terrorism

SEEING A VULNERABLE Israel and a strategically resurgent Syria, Hosni Mubarak set about reinforcing his position with the Arab war camp. He was well aware that if Cairo were to legitimize the abrogation of a peace treaty that had lasted almost two decades, it would have to make a strong case concerning its grievances against Israel. Cairo's most important audience would be the conservative Arab regimes, which not only supported Egypt financially and politically but, once hostilities broke out, would also be needed to intercede on Egypt's behalf with the United States and Western Europe. Therefore, the justification Mubarak chose illuminated his objectives in the impending crisis.

The Egyptian "cause" was set forth in a study, substantiated by a dossier of legal documents, on the valid boundary line between Israel and Egypt. The study, submitted to Mubarak around March 1997, reiterated the longstanding Egyptian claim to a sizable part of the Negev Desert—an area that fell within Israel's 1948 borders, most of which had even been allocated to the Jewish state by U.N. Resolution 181, passed in November 1947. Cairo coveted this area because it would provide on-land continuity between Egypt and the eastern portion of the Arab world—crucial to Egypt's claim to leadership.

The area in question is a narrow triangle whose northern tip is at Rafah on the Mediterranean coast—currently the border point between Egypt, Israel, and the PA's Gaza. The western side of the triangle runs along the present Egyptian-Israeli border—which has been fully recognized as an international border since the beginning of the last century and whose validity was reaffirmed in the peace treaty between Israel and Egypt signed at

Camp David in 1979. The eastern side of the triangle runs from Rafah to Awja (Nitzana in Hebrew), some 3 to 5 miles east of the border, and on to Birini, along the Israeli-Jordanian border. The base of the triangle is a 20-mile line from Birini to Umm al-Rashrash, the site of the old British post on the shores of the Gulf of Eilat (Aqaba). The triangle covers about 580 square miles—that is, one and a half times the area of the Golan Heights. The loss of this area would deprive Israel of access to the Gulf of Eilat and thence to the Red Sea. Inside it are the entire city of Eilat and the natural resources and chemical plants of the Western Negev.

Mubarak publicly revived the issue of on-land continuity on April 25, 1997, in a speech commemorating "the liberation of the Sinai." Addressing the command echelons of the 2nd and 3rd Armies—which crossed the Suez Canal in the Yom Kippur War—Mubarak stressed that the task of liberating Egyptian lands was yet to be completed. He declared that "Umm al-Rashrash is an Egyptian territory which we will not abandon," and he complained that Israel had ignored his demands, going back to 1982, for the return of the triangle. Given Israel's persistent refusal to even consider the Egyptian claims, Mubarak told his officers, Egypt should seek other means for the liberation of its sacred land.

Mubarak's claims were neither new nor frivolous. On the contrary, they revived public discussion of Egypt's own understanding of its manifest destiny. At the core of the problem is Cairo's conviction that the mere existence of Israel—or at the very least its hold over the bulk of the Negev—has prevented Egypt from becoming the undisputed leader of the Arab world. In other words, even in its 1949 boundaries, Israel prevents Egypt from realizing its historical mission.

The roots of this concept lie in the composition of the Arab world, which is divided into two parts: the Maghrib, the Arab West, which includes most of North Africa; and the Mashriq, the Arab East, which stretches from the Mediterranean to the border with Iran and includes all of Arabia proper. For historical and cultural reasons, Egypt, although located in North Africa, has always considered itself the leader of the Mashriq. Over the centuries, Egyptian rulers launched countless military campaigns into the territories of today's Israel, Jordan, and Syria in order to protect the on-land connection to the lands of the Mashriq.

Ever since Israel consolidated its control over the Negev in 1949, it has constituted a Jewish wedge between Egypt and the rest of the Mashriq. The repeated efforts by Egypt's President Gamal Abd-al-Nasser to establish Arab unity, including a short-lived formal union with Syria in the 1950s known as the United Arab Republic, failed, and Egyptian intellectuals attributed this failure to the lack of territorial continuity. "Part of the Arab World is in Asia and the other part in Africa," Mohamed Heikal wrote in 1975, "and Israel separates them. This is an impossible situation, both historically and geographically, for a Nation insisting that it is a Single Nation."

The demise of Iraq as a viable contender for Arab leadership following the Gulf War, and the demonstrated dependence of the Arabian Peninsula on Egyptian military aid, revived Cairo's quest for leadership and, hence, its commitment to the on-land connection. At first, Cairo concentrated its efforts on establishing an artery across Israel as an integral part of the Palestinian state expected to result from the U.S.-sponsored peace process. A March 1992 PLO document called "Suggested Guidelines for Comprehensive Development" highlighted the importance of such an artery. The document assumed that the territory provided to the Palestinian state would include as a minimum not only all of the territories, but also a corridor 3.12 miles wide and 28.12 miles long between Gaza and Hebron. The document demanded that Israel not only surrender sovereignty over this corridor—which is within the 1948 boundaries—but also remove the nine settlements existing within it.

When the Oslo accords and subsequent Israeli-PLO agreements failed to deliver the corridor, Mubarak resurrected Egyptian initiative to unilaterally establish territorial continuity. Military confrontation with Israel as an instrument for reviving and consolidating Arab unity had been the key subject of the December 1994 summit in Alexandria among Mubarak, Assad, and King Fahd. At that summit, the three leaders decided that there was no alternative to containing and ultimately destroying Israel.

The issue of Israel as a wedge preventing Arab unity was explicitly discussed in Cairo following the summit. An editorial in the government-owned paper *Al-Ahram al-Masai* warned that "Israel will continue its policy of instigating separation among the Arab States, and will continue to work in order to deepen the disagreements between them. Israel is trying to split the Arab World both politically and geographically by separating the Maghrib from the Mashriq." Since the United States had officially certified the current Egyptian-Israeli border in 1982, Cairo knew Washington would not endorse its claims. Hence, in spring 1997, Egypt's manifest destiny was in the war camp.

———

BY NOW, Arafat was laying the groundwork for the expanded jihad. The September 1996 military agreement between the PA and Syria had its first tangible results in the spring of 1997, as Syrian experts—some working in the joint intelligence headquarters in Gaza, others concealed in the ranks of the various Palestinian security organs in the West Bank—assisted their Palestinian counterparts.

In April and May, a select team of these Palestinian and Syrian experts completed a thorough study of the security situation in Israel, and particularly in the territories. The study argued that even though the spectacular terrorist strikes at the heart of Israel had had a great impact on official Jerusalem and the Israeli public as a whole, these operations also had some political drawbacks. As a rule, they involved only very small, secretive cells and thus had no mobilization value. Moreover, such strikes, particularly martyrdom strikes, were unambiguously associated with the militant Islamists, not the PLO. Thus, even though these operations remained crucial to pushing Jerusalem into capitulation, from the PA's point of view they were effective only in the context of a wider populist jihad—a new Intifadah.

However, the PA leadership acknowledged that for objective reasons there was no longer the potential for a major populist Intifadah. With the exception of a small segment of Hebron, the bulk of the Palestinian population no longer had regular contact with Jews (whether the IDF or settlers). Consequently, there were no longer points of friction where "spontaneous" clashes involving large crowds could be instigated. Moreover, as the PA security authorities had learned from a series of clashes organized in the Gaza Strip to test the Israeli reaction, it was very difficult to incite crowds to travel long distances to an obscure section of road and be ready to hold their ground when faced with massive retaliation by the IDF.

Instead, the Syrians recommended that the PA take as its model the popular war waged against the IDF in Lebanon between late 1982 and early 1985, principally by Palestinian and Shiite irregular units under the command of Syrian special forces and Iranian intelligence. It was the aggregate impact of those relentless and attrition-inflicting attacks, the Syrians claimed, that brought about the Israeli withdrawal to the security zone in southern Lebanon. For the territories, the Syrians suggested a similar campaign against means of transportation and general infrastructure—such as electricity and telephone lines, water and oil pipelines, and pumping stations. For these strikes to be effective, they would have to be conducted by professional special forces, which could operate from, and withdraw into, the PA-controlled Arab cities.

The idea was first to accomplish a profound disruption of the settlers' routine and sense of security. The IDF would then be compelled to deploy disproportionately large forces to protect the settlers and permit them to go about their business. This in turn would cause disruption in Israel and bring about a call from the peace camp to abandon the territories—much as had happened in Lebanon. Occasional spectacular terrorist strikes, including martyrdom operations, would reinforce the calls for major concessions and even for a unilateral withdrawal.

The Palestinians expected that the IDF would eventually start to avenge and attempt to prevent Palestinian strikes by closing in on, perhaps even entering, the major cities, instigating an all-out mobilization of the Palestinian population behind the PA. The Syrians cautioned, however, that the Israelis were also aware of this potentiality, and therefore the IDF would not enter the cities.

Even so, Arafat decided to go ahead with the plan. In early May, he gave the order for it to begin. He also ordered the escalation of other forms of armed struggle, including a brief campaign of terrorizing and killing Arab land dealers suspected of selling to Jews. Beyond the gruesome spectacle of the torture and summary execution of a few such dealers, the PA used this campaign to authoritatively reaffirm Arafat's denial of Israel's right to exist—by stressing that the law forbidding Arabs to sell land to Jews applied to Arab holders of Israeli citizenship and applied within the "Green Line" (the border established by the 1948–49 cease-fire agreements following Israel's War of Independence). That is, the PA was claiming legal authority over Israeli territory. PA Justice Minister Freih Abu-Medein made this point explicitly, warning land dealers "who have taken Israeli identity cards and think they have become Israeli citizens" not to suppose "that will buy them protection." Abu-Medein added that the reason for the ban on selling "Palestinian property" within the pre-1967 Israel was the PA's commitment to ensuring that, when they were able to return to their homes, the 1948 refugees and their legal heirs would retain ownership. Since "Palestinians own 90 percent of the land within the Green Line," it was imperative that the law protecting Palestinian lands apply to these properties as well.

Simultaneously, Arafat ordered the establishment of a new special force designed to wage the new type of war the study had recommended. Arafat himself tightly controlled this entity through a small number of highly trusted confidants: Amin al-Hindi, chief of the General Intelligence Service; Musa Arafat (Yassir's brother), chief of Military Intelligence; Faysal abu-Sharah, chief of Arafat's own Force 17; and Ghazi Jabali, chief of the PA Police Force. Jibril Rajub, chief of the powerful Preventive Security Service, would handle liaison with the Islamist terrorist organizations in the West Bank. The actual operations would be carried out in a deniable manner—as if by volunteers and renegades. The organization of the new force began in great secrecy in mid-May, and its core was deemed operational by early July.

This core comprised about 500 members of the Fatah's inner apparatus, the Tanzim, selected from the most loyal cadres of the PA police, security, and intelligence services. They were paid an extra $1,200 a month for being ready to strike out at a moment's notice. The PA made special efforts to ensure the clandestine nature of the new Tanzim special forces through a web of compartmentalized cells, activated directly by their commanders as required. This arrangement not only enhanced security but also ensured Arafat's control over each and every Tanzim action.

Of great significance was the background of the people making up the fighting core of the new Tanzim special forces. From the uppermost command layer answerable directly to Arafat down to the fighters themselves, the vast majority came from the elite within the territories. These young Fatah terrorists were strongly adversarial toward Arafat's "Tunisians" (the PLO leaders who had returned with Arafat from Tunisia and now constituted the core of the corrupt PA establishment). The territories' elite, who enjoyed genuine popular support in the cities of the Gaza Strip and the West Bank, had been hardened by fighting and imprisonment during the first Intifadah in the 1980s. In their long years of underground activities and jail terms, they had developed a comprehensive system of cooperation, communication, and intelligence sharing with local networks of HAMAS, the Islamic Jihad, and other rejectionist groups. All these characteristics made the new Tanzim special forces highly suitable for the planned operations against Israel.

Arafat also ordered the expansion of the military forces deployed to confront the IDF in case they advanced into any of the Arab cities under PA control. Storm units, which included martyr detachments, would use heavy weapons—rocket-propelled grenades (RPGs) and mortars, anti-tank missiles, and anti-aircraft missiles—as well as human bombs to bleed the IDF on live TV, leading public opinion in Israel to start demanding that the government succumb and withdraw.

In preparation, the PA established several underground (and illegal) production lines for weapons and ammunition, including a factory for bombs, mines, and grenades in Gaza; a factory for RPGs and light mortars in Ramallah; and a factory for ammunition and bombs in Nablus. The spring of 1997 also saw an increase in weapon smuggling, primarily into the Gaza Strip from Egypt via tunnels, and from Syria, Lebanon, and Egypt by fishing boats and small cargo vessels. However, the PA encountered problems transferring heavy weapons from Gaza to the West Bank because of greater Israeli supervision over VIP vehicles—to date the primary means of transferring such weapons. Hence, via the Iraqi Ambassador to Jordan, himself a senior intelligence officer and a close confidant of Saddam Hussein, Arafat also arranged for the allocation of weapons and ammunition from Iraqi arsenals and their transport through Jordan. The exposure in mid-1997 of one smuggling network gave indications of the quantities involved. When apprehended in Jordan, the network was preparing to ship across the Dead Sea, to a site near Jericho, a rubber boat loaded with shoulder-fired SAMs, anti-armor RPGs and their launchers, and numerous hand grenades, handguns, and machine guns. Jordanian security authorities confirmed that this operation was conducted on behalf of the PA. "The consignment was delivered to a Palestinian security officer named [Captain] Salih," a Jordanian security official reported. "The initial investigation points to the involvement of Colonel Jibril al-Rajub's Palestinian Preventive Security."

Concurrently, official PA media and the mosques began markedly intensifying a campaign to incite the masses. The Friday sermon delivered at al-Aqsa Mosque on July 11 by Sheikh Ikrama Sabri, the PA-appointed Mufti of Jerusalem and Palestine, was one of many sermons loaded with politics and hatred. "Oh Allah, destroy America, for she is ruled by Zionist Jews," Sheikh Sabri pleaded. He assured his listeners that the Arabs would soon inherit the Jewish settlements: "The homes the Jews are building will become Arab property, with Allah's help. Allah shall take revenge on behalf of his Prophet against the colonialist settlers who are sons of monkeys and pigs. Forgive us, Muhammad, for the acts of these sons of monkeys and pigs, who sought to harm your sanctuary." The identification of the Jews as sons of monkeys and pigs is based on the Koran (5:60); hence the violence Sabri called for was sanctified.

On July 19, thousands of HAMAS supporters marched in Hebron, burning Israeli flags and urging the resumption of terrorism. "Our grenades and bombs will burn those who insulted our Prophet," one of the banners declared. Naif Rajub, the regional HAMAS leader and Jibril Rajub's brother, warned that Israel was planning to destroy al-Aqsa Mosque in order to build a Jewish Temple (a frequent incitement theme) and urged the crowd to liberate Jerusalem by force of arms before this happened. Large numbers of PA police and security forces were present. They did not interfere, and some even participated in the incitement of the crowd, shouting such slogans as "Jews, Jews, the army of Muhammad will return!"

The Voice of Palestine, the official PA-controlled radio, began broadcasting in wartime mode, urging total mobilization for the struggle against "the Tel Aviv regime and its bloodthirsty occupation forces." Broadcasts emphasized that neither reconciliation nor even coexistence was possible between Jews and Muslims irrespective of who was in power in Jerusalem.

Senior PA officials openly echoed this propaganda. In mid-June, Colonel Jihad Massimi told the Jerusalem paper Al-Quds about an Israeli conspiracy to spread AIDS among the Arab youth—the fighters in the coming struggle—by sending in infected prostitutes. Israel was also accused of distributing in the West Bank chewing gum laced with drugs that increased the sex drive of young women, both to break up families through dishonor and to send girls into prostitution. In Jerusalem itself, activists operating under

Jibril Rajub distributed *Leaflet No. 1 of the Jerusalem National Command*, which had the same format as the leaflets issued by the National Leadership of the Intifadah during the late 1980s. *Leaflet No. 1* instructed its readers to "hit mobile and stationary targets of the Israeli occupation in East Jerusalem." The leaflet stressed the need to strike at the Israeli police, at municipal and national insurance and tax authorities, and at settlers. It also announced progress toward the establishment of "strike committees" patterned on the violent squads of the Intifadah.

And so, in the summer of 1997, the Palestinian leadership was creating among its constituency an atmosphere of impending war—not just the revival of the Intifadah, but also the eruption of a regional war in which the Arab states would rally to the defense of the Palestinians and the destruction of Israel.

———

AS THE MIDDLE EAST geared up for such a war—with Egypt, ostensibly a close ally of the United States, assuming a leading role, and the PA violating even the latest agreements signed with U.S. guarantees—the Clinton administration sought to step up the peace process, concentrating on the next phase of the Israeli withdrawal in the West Bank. Furthermore, President Clinton and his new secretary of state, Madeleine Albright, insisted on determining the magnitude of the Israeli withdrawal, repudiating the commitment made by Albright's predecessor, Warren Christopher, in mid-January.

There were bad omens from the very beginning of the second Clinton administration. In spring 1997, Albright was attempting to deal with the *Washington Post*'s "discovery" of her Jewish roots. In reality, she had already been fully aware of her Jewishness—as a result of childhood experiences in Belgrade (where her father served as a Czechoslovakian diplomat) and repeated efforts, starting in the 1980s, by relatives in Czechoslovakia and Israel to contact her. For whatever reasons, she had embraced denial. Now, in emotional reaction, she seemed determined to prove that she was impartial where Jewish interests were concerned. Furthermore, she was, and still is, an advocate of the school of social globalization—in other words, she is convinced that the international community has the right to impose social, political, and economic "solutions" on various peoples. Hence, she was committed to forcing "liberal" solutions on Israel's Jews (and also on the Serbs), to suit her view of where they should be—that is, cut down to proper size. Essentially, she became a zealot for Clinton's drive—at once ideological and cynically political—to bring the Israelis into line.

In early March, pursuant to its recent agreements with the Palestinians, the Netanyahu government decided on the magnitude of the next phased withdrawal—essentially an additional 2 percent of the West Bank, plus consolidation of the Palestinians' rule over 7.1 percent where they had had only a civil presence. The PA raised hell. When Jerusalem pointed to the Christopher letter, the PA repeated that it would not accept such "humiliation." With Arafat-sanctioned Islamist terrorism on the rise in Israel itself, however, Jerusalem was in no mood to compromise.

Throughout the spring, the Clinton administration continued its preoccupation with the next Israeli withdrawal as if the whole issue of Palestinian noncompliance did not exist. Cairo, drawn into the political process by the administration, urged not only accelerated withdrawal but also the cessation of Israeli construction in Har Homa as an inducement for the Palestinians to return to the negotiating table. Meanwhile, well-timed leaks from the White House and the state department left no doubt that the administration was adamant on obtaining at least 13 percent net withdrawal.

In June, Dennis Ross arrived in Jerusalem to take over the mediation. He tried to persuade Arafat to return to security cooperation as well as to tolerate some Israeli building in Har Homa, but to no avail. For the Israelis, Ross had a more comprehensive program, including the start of negotiations on a permanent-status agreement in parallel with the ongoing negotiations on interim arrangements, as well as a unilateral commitment not to create "new facts" in the territories—a euphemism for freezing activities in the settlements and in Jerusalem—and to stop denying Israeli citizenship to Arabs in East Jerusalem. Netanyahu replied that Israel could not accept such a set of demands while Arafat kept violating previous commitments.

Given Arafat's refusal to consider any meaningful participation, however, the peace process could be sustained only by extracting additional unilateral concessions from Israel. In July, Ross secretly traveled to Israel with an extremely strongly worded message from Clinton to Netanyahu. Clinton wrote that unless Jerusalem made new decisions the peace process would collapse, with detrimental consequences for Israel. He added that he expected Ross to bring back tangible results.

Ross also gave Netanyahu the U.S. proposal for a compromise, the key points of which were (1) the freezing of development in Har Homa until development of the nearby Arab neighborhood of Tsur Bakhr reached a comparable level, (2) a revival of Israeli-Palestinian security cooperation, (3) a cessation of all hostility (thus equating retaliation with provocation), (4) acceleration of negotiations on the permanent-status agreement, and (5) an end to the expropriation of land and to new construction except in the current fenced areas of settlements. Moreover, while the U.S. demands upon Israel were precise and action was expected immediately, the demands upon the PLO were vague and the timing was left intentionally undefined. Although Netanyahu strongly opposed the Clinton plan, he was in no position to reject it outright. Instead, he called for high-level discussions about "clarifications" and "amendments," to be led by Ross and Government Secretary Danny Naveh.

During the Naveh-Ross discussions, the administration rejected all demands that it force the Palestinians to comply with past agreements. Israel produced the latest intelligence about the involvement of Arafat and his inner circle in terrorism, but the Americans brushed it aside. Toward the end of July, the Israelis provided confirmation of Arafat's "green light" and of forthcoming HAMAS operations, but the information was once again ignored. In a late July meeting in Washington, an exasperated Ross told the Israelis that, barring major unilateral concessions, President Clinton was left with two options: either permit the peace process to collapse or come out publicly with his plan and blame Israel for its failure.

Subsequently, a meeting was arranged in Brussels between Arafat and Foreign Minister Levy. They agreed to relaunch the peace talks, which had been suspended since March. However, a few days later HAMAS committed a major terrorist strike at the Mahne Yehuda market in Jerusalem (details below). This finally provoked Albright to deliver a harsh speech demanding that Arafat comply with past agreements; at the same time, however, the White House privately warned Israel not to react with force against the Palestinians.

By now, public opinion in Israel was running high against a return to negotiations. Moreover, as Israel was learning the extent of its neighbors' war preparations, the defense establishment demanded from a sympathetic Netanyahu "time out" to reassess the country's security position.

———

THE FINAL DASH to the new Arab/Iranian strategic posture began in Tehran in early July with high-level consultations among the ambassadors of Syria and Palestine, a representative of Arafat, and the Iranian political and military leadership. Both ambassadors concurred with the Iranian conclusion that "armed struggle" was "the only way to liberate Jerusalem from the claws of usurping Zionists."

At follow-up discussions in Damascus, the Syrian and Iranian delegations agreed that the struggle necessitated consolidating a regional military alliance. However, Iran remained apprehensive about further rapprochement with Iraq, whereas Syria continued to consider Iraq an integral component of a viable regional alliance. Finally, Syria suggested that Egypt be brought in as a counterweight to Iraq. With Tehran's blessing, Damascus embarked on a series of secret discussions with Cairo, winning Mubarak's provisional approval. On

July 22, in a closed-door speech honoring graduates of the military and police academies, President Mubarak stated that Iran "has tried to establish military relations with Egypt." Although he added that "we do not rush into such decisions," he did not rule out such an alliance.

When Mubarak's speech was leaked a few days later, both Tehran and Cairo hotly denied the possibility of an alliance. However, on July 26, Tehran's key newspapers editorialized on "improvement in Tehran-Cairo relations to counter the Zionist expansionist policies," and Tehran's official media reported that "More than any time in the past, Egypt now knows the real nature of the Zionist regime." Tehran added that "if all the oppressed, with Iran in the front line, join hands, Zionists will become increasingly vulnerable."

Several Arab officials in Western Europe and the Gulf States, known to be close to Cairo, echoed these sentiments. These officials noted that they "would not be surprised" by the emergence of a regional military alliance including Egypt, Iran, Syria, and other Arab states. These officials anticipated "extensive Egyptian-Iranian-Arab military coordination even before normal diplomatic relations between Cairo and Tehran are restored." As before, the estimates of these highly placed, well-connected officials proved very accurate. Actually, their comments were not speculations but trial balloons floated to test the reactions of Washington—which completely ignored them—and the Arab world—which gave them a tacit but warm endorsement.

President Mubarak resolved to move fast. On July 29, he paid a sudden visit to Damascus, ostensibly to pursue "joint coordination between the two Arab states." As Palestinian officials would later tell the PA's primary organ, *Al-Hayah al-Jadidah*, the main achievement of the Damascus summit was Mubarak's obtaining from Assad "concise and clear answers" to all his questions concerning the Syrian-Iranian contingency plans. Mubarak was satisfied and affirmed that Egypt would join the alliance. Not the least of his motives was avoiding an Islamist eruption at home.

On his way back to Cairo, President Mubarak made an impromptu stop in Amman. King Hussein left a meeting with David Levy to go to the Amman airport to meet with Mubarak, who urged him to join the emerging regional order. Hussein declined, and Jordanian officials would later deny that the alliance had even been discussed.

At the same time, according to several high-level PA/PLO sources, Egyptian officials briefed Arafat about the progress toward a regionwide military alliance. According to those officials, Damascus had already initiated steps aimed at upgrading the Iranian-Syrian-Egyptian cooperation plan to the level of a comprehensive alliance with political, military, and economic dimensions.

The sense of urgency in Damascus became apparent on July 31, Armed Forces Day on the Syrian calendar. This is a sacred day for the Ba'ath elite, if only because the military was, and still is, the prime guarantor of their survival in power. However, on July 31, 1997, the keynote speech was delivered not by Hafez al-Assad, as was usual, but by the chief of staff, General Hikmat al-Shihabi.

Shihabi's very important speech anticipated a major war for the liberation of the Golan Heights. "Syria will not give up a grain of its soil," Shihabi proclaimed. "Our Armed Forces will fulfill their obligation, and will return the Golan to us unless this is attained through peaceful means." Shihabi was confident about Syria's prospects if war did break out. "Israel is afraid of the Syrian Army because it is aware of the heavy losses it can inflict in case of a conflict. The Army is ready to confront all of those who threaten the security of Syria and Arab security as a whole," he said, in a veiled reference to the regional factor.

The most important point in Shihabi's speech was his explanation of why he and not President Assad was delivering the main address: Assad was in Tehran on a surprise visit to discuss "the strategic relations" between Syria and Iran. According to Syrian officials, important developments necessitating Assad's visit had come up so suddenly that even the Iranian leadership learned of Assad's impending visit only a few hours before he and his entourage flew to Tehran in three aircraft.

The importance of Assad's visit was underscored by the sheer size of the Syrian delegation: some 300 senior officials, including most of the Syrian cabinet, as well as senior military officers and security and intelligence officials. The highlight of the visit—and the impetus for it in the first place—was Assad's news that Mubarak had agreed to join the alliance. The huge Syrian delegation then went to work, addressing with their Iranian counterparts the practical aspects of the forthcoming escalation and, possibly, war.

Iran's top leaders left no doubt about the theme of the summit. Israel "is an illegitimate entity . . . and its nature is against peace," Ayatollah Khamenei told President Assad in a meeting shown on Iranian TV. It was therefore imperative for the Arab states to "correct their stance toward [Israel] and the so-called Middle East peace process," which had already "proved to be fruitless and an illusion." Iran's outgoing president, Hashemi-Rafsanjani, was even more explicit in a statement carried by Syrian TV. "The circumstances of the region require a Syrian move," he told Assad. "We consider . . . [it] important to carry out an Arab-Iranian action that faces head-on the anti-Arab and anti-Muslim alliance headed by Israel and the United States."

Thus, by late July 1997, Iran and the Arab world believed that conditions throughout the Middle East were uniquely propitious for an onslaught against Israel. The Arabs perceived Israel as a country deeply divided—as demonstrated by the raging debate over the prospects of peace and the proper reaction to Arafat's terrorism—and also militarily weak—as evident from the Knesset's own findings about shortcomings in the IDF. In this context, Mubarak's visit to Damascus was a turning point. Cairo had now openly joined a military alliance actively involved in preparations for war against Israel. Even if such a war did not break out, Mubarak's involvement in such an alliance was, at least in spirit, a violation of the 1979 peace treaty with Israel.

Meanwhile, it had taken some time for the Arab world to fully grasp the significance of Mubarak's "triangle." Now, in early August, Cairo again raised the issue, this time in an article in *Al-Wasat*. The choice of venue for this release is important. *Al-Wasat* is a London-based weekly owned by Prince Khaled bin Sultan. Prince Khaled was the Joint Forces commander during the Gulf War; he is the son of Prince Sultan, Saudi Arabia's minister of defense, and the brother of Prince Bandar bin Sultan, Saudi Arabia's influential ambassador to Washington. Thus, the mere publication of Mubarak's grievances in *Al-Wasat* amounted to an endorsement of them by the uppermost echelons in Riyadh—including their most pro-U.S. elements.

———

BACK IN EARLY JUNE, Arafat had convened his closest aides and ordered the escalation of violence under the tight control of the PA security organs, particularly Jibril Rajub's Preventive Security Service. The primary objective of this escalation would again be to gauge the Israeli reaction to provocations. Hebron was selected as the main theater because of the settlers' presence there, and Tanzim activists immediately recruited a large number of youths, ordering them to escalate clashes and specifically to increase the use of firebombs. The Tanzim leaders explicitly stated that their actions were part of "an effort to set the territories on fire under orders from Arafat." Emboldened by the success of these initial operations, Arafat ordered a further escalation in early July. His new orders called for launching the Lebanon-style war earlier decided upon, as well as selected spectacular terrorist bombings in Jerusalem to be portrayed as local reactions to Har Homa.

The Jerusalem case was uniquely complex because it involved the bitter power struggle going on between Arafat and Faisal Husseini. The Saudi government and the Gulf Islamists were funding Husseini's effort to build illegal Arab neighborhoods in East Jerusalem and provide other services to the Arab population. Fearing loss of standing, Arafat had to regain control. He chose to do so by instigating violence, because of its mobilizing impact. In some of his discussions with the uppermost leadership of the Tanzim, Arafat told them that the time had come to "kill Jews."

When senior security officials asked on several occasions who would implement his wishes, Arafat would smile and say, "*Alladina amanu . . .*" This was a quintessential Arafat exercise in deniability. Literally, his answer means "Those who believe in Allah's Law." However, these are the opening words in one of the key verses in the Koran (4:76) codifying the Muslim way of warfare. The full sentence reads "*Alladina amanu yuqatiluna fi sabil Allah,*" which means, "Those who believe in Allah's Law fight to annihilate in the path of Allah." The rest of the verse urges believers to annihilate "the friends of Satan"—a term frequently used to describe Jews. There should be no doubt that Arafat's listeners knew exactly what he meant by uttering those two words.

One such exchange took place during Arafat's visit to Nablus in early July. He met with the leaders of the city, including Governor Mahmud Alloul and Chief of Police Jihad Massimi, and demanded "popular" demonstrations against the Israeli government's policies. The local leaders pointed out that riots would be difficult to organize in the absence of outright Israeli provocation inside Nablus. Arafat then observed that "a regime of limited actions against the Israelis" should be established in order to create an appropriate environment. He did not instruct that any specific operation be undertaken either by the Tanzim squad in the ranks of Massimi's PA Police Force or by the local HAMAS group it was cooperating with. He simply expressed his confidence that "Believers" will always succeed. He left it to his trusted confidant General Ghazi Jabali, the chief of the PA Police Force, to make the explicit and thus incriminating call to Massimi when the time was ripe.

In mid-July, three officers of the Palestinian police from Nablus were captured on their way to commit a terrorist strike near Har Brakha, a Jewish settlement. The three policemen were armed with Uzi submachine guns—which the PA police were not supposed to have. They also carried instructions from Massimi to ambush cars and "kill Jews." Furthermore, Israel had intercepted the orders sent to Massimi from Jabali in Gaza. Following the arrests, an assertive Massimi told Roni Shaked of *Yediot Aharonot*, "If there is a decision to return to armed struggle, all the mountains of Palestine will be full of fidayeen. There is desire among Fatah members to return to the [armed] struggle. Tens of members come to me every day, demanding to renew it, and I, just like other leaders, restrain them. If we hadn't stopped this trend, the situation would have been much worse."

At about the same time, the Nablus area saw the execution of a suspected land dealer, the activation of a sixteen-man HAMAS terrorist squad, and Massimi's dispatch of police officers on terrorist raids. These activities confirmed the close cooperation between the Nablus PA security forces and the local HAMAS forces. The PA was also known to be cooperating with HAMAS cells in Tulkarm, Ramallah, Hebron, and Bethlehem.

On July 15, an Israeli security forces roadblock picked up Colonel Munir Abushi, the deputy commander of the PA police in Tulkarm, who was traveling with a colleague to Nablus for consultations that would have included Massimi. Then, on the night of July 24–25, Israeli security forces captured Ghassan Mahmud Abd-al-Rahman Mahdawi, who had become the commander of the Islamic Jihad forces in Tulkarm after escaping from jail in Israel. Mahdawi enjoyed Abushi's protection and patronage, and his Islamic Jihad networks received extensive operational support from the Tulkarm PA police. The capture of both Abushi and Mahdawi resulted in the cancellation of several terrorist attacks that were to have been carried out jointly by detachments of the PA police and Mahdawi's Islamic Jihad networks.

A major bombing planned for Jerusalem in mid-July was averted only when a senior HAMAS operative accidentally blew himself up in Bethlehem while preparing the bomb. This led the PA security forces to "expose" his network's bomb factory in Beit Sakhur. Actually, the PA security forces had known about this HAMAS cell and its bomb factory at least since April, when the Israeli security forces had originally informed them about it. The factory, a two-story house, contained more than 60 pounds of high explosives, a supply of timers and watches, and some finished bombs already packed into plastic boxes ready for dispatch. The house also contained stores of IDF uniforms, wigs, beards, makeup, skullcaps, prayer shawls, and cellular phones. Needless to say, all the leaders of this HAMAS cell succeeded in eluding the PA police.

Senior Palestinian officials, who could no longer ignore the documented involvement of PA police officers and other security personnel in the riots and terrorism, intimated that the situation involved a spontaneous outburst of frustration and rage stemming from socioeconomic misery and Israel's refusal to abide by agreements. The Clinton administration leaped on these explanations and, once again, began urging Israel to demonstrate more "flexibility."

Alarmed by these developments, the Netanyahu government rushed to offer a fig leaf to its partner in peace. In a secret meeting on July 16, Ami Ayalon, the chief of Israel's General Security Service, warned Arafat of the support for terrorists among the PA police and security forces and opined that the terrorist activities must be part of a coup attempt against Arafat. Official Jerusalem promptly leaked the warning, delivered as a justification for continuing the peace process. For his part, a smug Arafat denied all rumors of conspiracies against him.

Arafat did order a series of perfunctory arrests and summary military trials. He also established a commission to unearth the truth about the situation in Nablus. According to Palestinian officials, the commission immediately ran into problems because Israel refused to provide pertinent intelligence. Nevertheless, as far as Washington and Jerusalem were concerned, the charade was complete, and the pursuit of the Oslo process could continue.

———

THE OUTBREAKS of violence during the summer of 1997 were but fledgling operations in a campaign designed to gain momentum in the fall. Arafat had promised his coterie a major Israeli unilateral withdrawal in September and had assured them that he had contingency plans for an all-out eruption if Israel did not deliver.

Even without the possible intervention of armed forces from neighboring Arab states, Arafat's plans for the fall were alarming. They included a horrific strike contrived to compel the IDF to invade Area A—the main Arab cities controlled by the PA—leading to carnage among Arab civilians (to be placed intentionally in harm's way and in front of TV cameras). Arafat calculated that the threat that this fighting would escalate into a regional war, with an ensuing oil embargo, would bring sufficient pressure from Western Europe, the United States, and the Israeli opposition to lead the Netanyahu government to succumb to his demands. This scenario was discussed during the summer with senior officials in Cairo, who endorsed Arafat's analysis and promised Egypt's all-out support.

Palestinian senior officials also discussed the scenario with their counterparts in Tehran and Damascus, who agreed up to a point but were convinced that once the IDF began to roll forward no international pressure would stop it. Therefore, the Muslim world would have to capitalize on Israel's initial preoccupation with the Palestinians and the political constraints imposed by the international reaction to deliver a major surprise attack. Such an attack, Damascus and Tehran argued, stood a chance of destroying Israel once and for all. The Palestinians did not reject this scenario, nor did they refuse the help that the Syrian and Iranian experts offered.

How serious these offers were can be gauged by HizbAllah's central role in the preparations for terrorist strikes. In early July, HizbAllah leaders called a high-level meeting in the Bekaa Valley with local terrorist leaders, including Mustafa al-Liddawi of HAMAS and Talal al-Naji of the PFLP-GC. The general secretary of the HizbAllah, Hassan Nasrallah, who chaired the meeting, told the participants that Tehran was upset with the unexplained delays in carrying out the agreed-upon spectacular terrorist operations. Nasrallah reminded the local leaders that HAMAS headquarters in Damascus and Tehran were supreme and that their instructions as to the timing of escalation were orders, not suggestions. This was a reminder to the HAMAS leaders that they must abide by their previous agreements irrespective of "green lights" from Arafat. However, the Nasrallah's main concern was the anticipated long-term escalation in the overall terrorism campaign. In order to enhance HAMAS's ability to carry out additional operations, al-Naji reported, the PFLP-GC had agreed to train HAMAS terrorists in two camps controlled by Syrian intelligence that were reserved for the most loyal terrorist elite. The three organizations also agreed to cooperate closely in sending terrorists into Israel from abroad so that they would be immune to Israeli penetration of local networks.

Following this meeting, the entire HizbAllah leadership traveled to Tehran and met with the top leaders there, who confirmed Iran's endorsement of their plans. Upon returning to Lebanon, Nasrallah summoned al-Liddawi to convey Tehran's instructions. It was imperative, Nasrallah emphasized, to rely on the headquarters in Damascus and Tehran in order not to implicate Arafat in the planning of terrorism. In mid-August, large shipments of weapons and ammunition began arriving at the PFLP-GC's camps in the Tusaya area, where the training of Palestinian cadres from Lebanese refugee camps was already in full swing.

———

IN HIS COURTING of the HAMAS leadership, Arafat even interceded with the U.S. government on behalf of Mussa Abu-Marzuq, incarcerated in the United States as a suspected terrorist while his extradition to Israel to stand trial for complicity in several HAMAS bombings was debated. Eventually, Israel gave up on extraditing Marzuq, fearing HAMAS retaliation, and King Hussein agreed to admit him to Jordan. The moment Marzuq arrived in Amman in early May, Arafat sent a confederate with a personal invitation to "return to his land and continue his contribution from inside Gaza."

Marzuq, politely declining for the time being, sent Arafat a message on his perception of future relations between the PA and the Islamists. Marzuq later repeated his opinion in his first major interview, printed in the June 1997 issue of the London-based *Filastin al-Muslimah*, a HAMAS organ. Marzuq stressed HAMAS's desire for closer cooperation with the PA and acknowledged that HAMAS should amend its modus operandi in accordance with the prevailing conditions in the territories. However, he warned, there could be no compromise over the ultimate goal: an Islamic state replacing Israel. "HAMAS," he said, "pursues a fixed unwavering policy with regard to the Palestinian people's framework, be it through its dealing with the organizations that oppose the Oslo accord, which the HAMAS Movement rejects, or with those that signed the accord." Marzuq insisted that "there ought not to be any violent clashes, internecine fighting, or conflicts" between Islamists and the PA. However, HAMAS would not shy away from such a confrontation if that was the only way to attain its objectives. "Should HAMAS pay such a price, so be it, because this price would be paid to serve the interests of the people and not the private interests of HAMAS itself."

By now, Arafat was speaking openly about the return to armed struggle in interviews with Saudi-owned periodicals read by the Arab elites. On July 24, the London-based *Al-Sharq al-Awsat* published an interview conducted by Arafat's crony, Salih Qallab. This Saudi-owned paper is a major outlet for the nationalist-Islamist elite and is very close to Crown Prince Abdallah. Thus, Arafat was able to lay out his vision for those leaders of the Arab world most likely to come to his aid in time of need.

Arafat declared that there would be no compromise from the Palestinian side despite the punishment endured during the current stalemate. "The Palestinians have endured sufferings for a whole century," he exclaimed. "The Palestinian people, who have been hardened by events and tribulations, will continue to be ready to make more sacrifices until they exact their full undiminished rights, and foremost among them their right to self-determination and their right to establish their own independent state with its capital in holy Jerusalem, which is the heart of the Palestinian people and without which there can be no full and lasting solution."

After Arafat described at great length the deadlock in the region, Qallab asked whether "there will be an explosion" in the absence of a breakthrough.

"Everyone, especially in Israel," Arafat responded, "should know that a lack of progress in the peace process on the Palestinian track would put the entire region at the mouth of a volcano. Leaving matters as they are would lead to general anarchy whose future dimensions nobody can predict."

"Do you mean that leaving the situation as it is would lead to war?" Qallab followed up.

"No," Arafat corrected, "it would lead to chaos. War is only a small part of chaos." As Arafat uses the term, "chaos" means the combination of a major war in the Middle East and worldwide international terrorism, primarily by Islamists. He warned Washington in particular of the possibility of international terrorism: "If the U.S. administration does not act quickly to get the peace process out of the bottleneck there will be an explosion; hundreds of secret extremist organizations will emerge in this region, and the entire world will suffer."

On the night of July 28, Arafat met with the senior commanders of the PA intelligence and security forces in Hebron and demanded that they prepare for "a long struggle against Israel." He also hailed the new era of the PA's co-operation with the Islamists. The still lingering question of just how specific Arafat really was in endorsing this cooperation is most important given the ensuing events.

On July 30, the Palestinians returned their jihad to Jerusalem, with the bombing at the Mahne Yehuda market. Two martyr-terrorists exploded the large bombs they were carrying shortly after 1 P.M., killing 14 and wounding well over 160. In fliers distributed in Jerusalem, HAMAS claimed responsibility, but the HAMAS leadership later categorically denied it. Initial evidence suggested that the two martyrs arrived from abroad (Arab sources insist they came from Colonel Makdah's Iran-trained suicide forces in the Ein-Hilweh camp in southern Lebanon) but then relied on the local infrastructure in Judea to procure the bombs and other support. In any case, their activities could not have taken place without the PA security authorities' knowledge. Subsequent investigation would identify the terrorists as locally based and confirm they had been dispatched by HAMAS only after receiving a green light from Arafat in person.

Even before the completion of the Israeli investigation, circumstances pointed to a direct role for Arafat. In mid-July, he was under increasing pressure to confront the corruption and mismanagement of the PA. The Palestine National Council even suggested that he sack his entire cabinet, because they were all immersed in corruption, which was starting to affect support from the United States and Western Europe. As a result, Arafat needed to come up with a diversion that would cause Washington, Western Europe, and even Jerusalem to embrace him as the lesser evil.

The bombs in Jerusalem, conveniently occurring on the same day as the PNC conference on corruption, served this purpose. The United States, Western Europe, and Israel immediately shifted emphasis from demanding that Arafat get his administration in order to demanding that he start fighting Islamist terrorism. Accusations that he and his coterie were complicit in terrorism were brushed under the rug in order not to embarrass the PA. And even though senior PA security officials, including Rajub, openly stated that the PA would not suppress the militant Islamists on Israel's behalf, toleration of Arafat as the "only viable choice" stuck.

———

ARAFAT'S NEW-FOUND ACCEPTANCE did not prevent him from intensifying his courtship of the very organizations he was supposed to be crushing as the core of his relations with Israel. On August 4, he traveled to Amman and had a lengthy private meeting with Marzuq. He also had an all-night session at the Iraqi Embassy, which included long phone conversations with

Saddam Hussein in Baghdad. According to Jordanian security officials, Saddam promised Arafat massive Iraqi assistance if the PLO in turn assisted Iraq in the destabilization of Jordan.

On August 6, in a speech delivered to a conference of Fatah senior officials, an emboldened Arafat called on the Palestinians to prepare for a "great battle." He vowed that the jihad would continue until the Palestinian flag was hoisted over Jerusalem. "The campaigns behind us," he said, "were relatively easy compared to the campaigns facing us. We are all living martyrs, ready at a moment's notice to express our loyalty to the message of the armed struggle we have started many years ago." He alluded to the PLO's 1974 adoption of the "Phases Program/Phased Plan" as a turning point in the Palestinian armed struggle: "The Palestinian Revolution was resurrected as of 1974 and it is drawing its might as the greatest revolution of the 20th century. The Lion Cubs [the Fatah youth] that carried the revolution [on their shoulders] now know they must unite [and as] a single body confront the enemy at this difficult hour."

During this speech, Arafat repeated several times a crucial slogan—"A contract is a contract, and a vow is a vow"—which the audience chanted with him. The use of this Islamist saying, usually associated with HAMAS, is most important in revealing Arafat's state of mind. A contract—such as the Prophet Muhammad's Treaty of Hudaibiya or Arafat's own agreements with Israel—is a transient agreement that a believer is not obliged to abide by once it has outlived its usefulness. A vow—such as the declaration of the entire land of Israel "from the sea to the river" as a sacred *waqf*—is an eternal religious obligation.

In mid-August, Arafat convened a Conference of National Dialogue to reach a consensus with the Islamists. With HAMAS still adamantly opposed to any recognition of Israel's right to exist, the mere participation of HAMAS leaders meant that Arafat had accepted their conditions. This conference would have three sessions—in Gaza, Ramallah, and Amman—as well as a session in Damascus not formally associated with the other three. Through this process, Arafat invited pressure from both the Islamists and his own Fatah cadres to escalate the armed struggle against Israel. This way he would be able to claim, and not without reason, that there was a public clamor for escalation.

The Damascus conference, convened on the eve of the three PLO-sponsored conferences, was designed to publicly raise issues Arafat was afraid to raise at his own events. Abu Muhammad Mustafa, the HAMAS representative in Damascus, was straightforward: "We demand Arafat admit to the failure of the Oslo Accords. He has two options: either declare a complete mobilization, renew the Intifadah, and join HAMAS and Islamic Jihad in their [armed] struggle against Israel, or resign and admit failure." Mustafa declared that HAMAS had given up on tolerating the gradual pursuit of the destruction of Israel through the political process: "We gave the peace process a chance after the Madrid Conference. But today it is clear that what was taken by force must be reclaimed by force." Khalid Mashal, the political leader of HAMAS, went further, saying that martyrdom was "the only instrument capable of blocking the settlements and the Judaization of the Holy Places. These actions constitute a source of hope for our people, and a hope of freedom for our thousands of prisoners." Mashal left no doubt that with such vital interests at stake, the martyrdom operations would continue.

The first Conference of National Dialogue convened a few days later in Gaza, with Arafat welcoming HAMAS leader Abdul Aziz Rantisi with a hug and kisses on both cheeks. When Rantisi addressed the gathering, he stated that "the resistance option in all its forms is the best option for regaining our rights from Israel." Nafiz Azzam, a senior leader of the Islamic Jihad, emphasized the need to solidify the Palestinian ranks in order to be able to conduct a worthy jihad.

The next day, Arafat traveled to Ramallah to chair a similar conference for West Bank leaders who could not come to Gaza. All the speakers reiterated the need to launch a joint armed struggle against Israel. The representative of the Islamic Jihad warned that if Israel continued to starve the Palestinians, "they will eat the flesh of those who starved them."

The final conference, in Amman, was somewhat diminished by the Jordanian security authorities' refusal to allow a large number of terrorist leaders to enter Jordan. Nevertheless, many were able to be present, including the PFLP's George Habbash, the DFLP's Nayif Hawatimah, and Abd-al-Majid Thneibat, the leader of the Muslim Brotherhood of Jordan. Arafat left no doubt where he stood. "There was an Intifadah for seven years," he declared. "Seven years. We can erase [the peace process] and do it all over again from the beginning."

A little-noticed incident that summer revealed how desperate Arafat was to instigate a regional war. In late July and early August, Syrian intelligence in Lebanon arrested over 100 Fatah operatives. These operatives were organized in clandestine cells, carried forged documents and large sums of money, and had major stores of weapons and explosives. The Syrians had learned that the primary mission of this Fatah force was to conduct sabotage, bombings, and murder inside Syria and Lebanon, in such a way as to implicate Israel as the perpetrator.

In deploying these terrorists to Lebanon and, ultimately, Syria, Arafat was preparing a fallback so that he could flare up the entire Middle East in the highly unlikely event that Damascus abandoned its active preparations for war and resumed negotiations with Israel. Considering the importance of Syrian cooperation to the overall military capabilities of the PA, Arafat's willingness to embark on such provocation illuminated the depth of his desperation and determination.

By late August, Arafat was also laying the groundwork for the escalation of anti-Israeli violence in the territories. The Netanyahu government, Arafat insisted, had unleashed special commando death squads to assassinate him and his closest aides. "We are taking these plots very seriously," he said, "and consider them a dangerous initiative."

For their part, not only did the PA security authorities openly refuse to suppress the militant Islamists on Israel's behalf, but they also actually hailed them as brethren in the joint struggle against Israel. Jibril Rajub, one of the most senior officials dealing with Israel on issues related to terrorism, told an interviewer for *Al-Wasat*, "They are our comrades in the struggle. I am one of those people who see HAMAS and the Palestinian Islamic [Jihad] movement as a part of the national liberation movement with an Islamic dimension. It is my duty and my task to maintain such relations. If the Israelis do not like that, well, that is their problem, not mine."

9

"Legacy" and Vindictiveness (1997–1998)

Clinton Seeks His Legacy as Peacemaker; Netanyahu Stands His Ground

FOR CLINTON, Albright, and National Security Advisor Sandy Berger, neither the spectacular bombings in Jerusalem nor the evidence of Arafat's direct responsibility for them offered a legitimate reason to suspend the peace process. On the contrary, the growing tension was all the more reason to speed it up. The three resented and mistrusted Netanyahu's steadfast insistence on addressing other issues crucial to Israel's security, such as Iran's massive strategic buildup and particularly its programs for weapons of mass destruction. They considered his preoccupation with regional dynamics in general to be an intentional diversion from sustaining the "momentum" on the Palestinian track. Consequently, fearing that they were losing control over the situation and believing that only Israeli concessions would prevent the collapse of the peace process, the administration orchestrated pressure campaigns on Jerusalem from numerous Arab leaders. On August 4—even as Arafat was in Amman, meeting with Marzuq—Mubarak implored Israel to return to the negotiating table before it was too late. Jordan's Crown Prince Hassan and Prime Minister Abdel Salam Majali traveled to Jerusalem for urgent talks with Netanyahu on August 6 and delivered a similar message.

Jerusalem finally succumbed to the pressure. On August 10, Dennis Ross arrived in Israel to organize a working session between Arafat and senior Israeli officials. However, the session quickly foundered over key security and anti-terrorism issues; the Netanyahu government attempted, at risk of annoying the Clinton administration, to get the message across to Arafat that a crackdown on terrorism was central to any further negotiations. When Arafat claimed he was doing all he could, Israel passed along the names of key terrorists and their exact whereabouts, demanding that the PA arrest them. Under U.S. pressure, the PA did so, but then swiftly released them, in Arafat's now-customary "revolving door" violation of his July 1997 agreement with the United States.

At the same time, Arafat authorized a major bombing in Jerusalem to generate a new crisis that would paralyze the peace process. On September 4, a three-man HAMAS martyrdom team blew themselves up on Ben Yehuda Street, causing heavy casualties. This operation was intentionally run via a local network in the Nablus area to conceal HAMAS's responsibility and the PLO's endorsement. In fact, the senior commanders involved had received authorization from their superiors in Tehran via the HAMAS forward headquarters in Damascus.

Albright was soon to pay her first visit to the region. On the eve of her arrival, Government Secretary Danny Naveh and Yitzhak Molcho, Netanyahu's lawyer and confidant, secretly met with Mubarak's envoy, Osama al-Baaz, to hear about his recent meeting with Arafat. According to al-Baaz, Arafat had warned the Egyptians that the Israelis were conducting various conspiracies under the guise of pressing for permanent-status negotiations. There was no terrorist infrastructure in the territories, Arafat had insisted, and hence he had no clue of what was demanded of him. The PA had arrested all the Islamists on "Netanyahu's list," not because they were guilty but in order to demonstrate sincerity.

On September 9 Albright arrived in Israel "to salvage the peace process." From the very beginning, her relationship with Netanyahu was characterized by tension and mistrust. Albright believed Netanyahu was stalling when he insisted that an "all-out commitment" by Arafat to seriously fight terrorism must precede steps by Israel to implement any further withdrawal. When Netanyahu stated that Israel was not an American puppet, Albright took it as a personal affront. The deterioration in their relationship became irreversible when she called for "time out" over the settlements and he criticized her in front of her aides for doing so; from his point of view, there were tacit understandings between him and Clinton on this issue, and Israel had abided by them scrupulously. Albright retaliated for his criticism by publicly insisting that an "interim agreement" was crucial to the peace process, whereas Netanyahu had been pressing to bypass the interim steps and advance directly to permanent-status talks.

Leaving Israel, Albright and Berger concluded that Jerusalem was "not serious" about participating in the peace process. Berger was convinced that Netanyahu responded only to raw pressure, and he and Albright resolved to treat Netanyahu "harshly."

The White House began increasing the pressure on Israel almost immediately, with its proposals for renewed negotiations. Although the administration's publicly presented proposals were evenhanded, additional demands were made on Jerusalem in private: most importantly, a demand that it maintain a time-out on settlement activities during the entire negotiation period. There would be no new settlements, only limited building would be permitted in the immediate vicinity of existing houses, Israel would cease demolishing illegal Arab construction, and there would be no expropriation of land—not even for common-good projects also serving the Palestinians, such as roads. Jerusalem succumbed to Clinton's pressure. Soon afterward, the administration—mainly Albright and Martin Indyk, who by now was the U.S. Ambassador to Israel—started firing a constant stream of complaints about each and every Israeli action in the settlements. Essentially, they made it clear that by "time out," they actually meant an indefinite total freeze. Netanyahu's attempts to present his government's position got nowhere.

Nevertheless, Netanyahu and Arafat met at the Erez checkpoint on October 8—their first meeting in several months. However, attempts to arrange follow-up meetings broke down over the PA's foot-dragging on its commitment to crack down on Islamist terrorism.

———

EVEN AS ARAFAT'S skill in maneuvering between the Islamists and Jerusalem was paying off, his physical condition was becoming a major political issue among his own people. The deterioration in his health was officially denied, but he was increasingly referred to not as the *Rais*—the president—but as the *Khetyar*—the old man.

In mid-September, during a conference of Arab foreign ministers in Cairo, Arafat collapsed suddenly in the middle of an argument with Hamad bin Jassim, the foreign minister of Qatar. By the time a doctor arrived, Arafat's lips had turned blue and his eyes had rolled back. Several Palestinian and Egyptian officials present were convinced that he would not survive, or that if he did, his ailments would affect his ability to function.

Egyptian officials attributed Arafat's health problems to lingering effects of injuries he had sustained during an April 1992 plane crash. He had also suffered a mild stroke after quarreling with President Mubarak and King Hussein in Cairo in May 1996, although Arab officials at the time insisted that he only had a "stomach disorder." Palestinian officials now acknowledged that he was suffering from several illnesses, including Parkinson's disease. TV footage in mid-September captured an Arafat whose hands were shaking too badly for him to cut a ribbon for a construction site in Gaza. Arafat himself, sixty-eight or sixty-nine at the time, confided to several members of his coterie that he did not believe he would reach his seventieth birthday.

The PLO/PA elite, knowing it would be crippled by Arafat's death, insisted that he was "not suffering from anything more than spells of strain and exhaustion" and that these were "normal" given "the worries on his shoulders and the many burdens which he carries." They attributed "the rumors" about his health to Israeli machinations aimed "to throw the Palestinian scene into confusion."

The lack of an obvious successor made things even worse, from the PA's point of view. Arafat's coterie had been afraid to name a successor while Arafat was still alive. Finally, however, in the wake of his collapse in Cairo, the leading members of his innermost circle held quasi-official discussions. They sought to establish a committee of successors in order to reduce the potential for factional fighting; those mentioned as contenders for membership in this committee were Mahmoud Abbas (Abu-Mazen), Arafat's deputy; Faisal Husseini, who by now was the PLO's leader in Jerusalem; Ahmed Qurai (Abu-Alaa), the speaker of the PA Parliament; and Faruk Kaddoumi, a radical PLO official close to Damascus who remained in exile in Tunis because of his opposition to the Oslo process.

However, several high-level Arab sources (mainly Palestinian, Egyptian, and Jordanian officials) ridiculed this list. Assuming that power remained in the hands of PLO-related leaders—far from a certainty, given the Islamists' rising power—the only viable contenders, these sources insisted, were Jibril Rajub and Muhammad Dahlan. Both were much younger than those on the quasi-official list; they had risen to power in the territories and enjoyed the trust of the Islamists; above all, they held the keys to the PA's internal-security machine and police/military forces. Moreover, since their power bases were in the West Bank and the Gaza Strip respectively, they might be induced to share power. Indeed, members of Arafat's coterie acknowledged that no successor or successors would be able to consolidate power unless Dahlan and Rajub supported them and arranged for Islamist acquiescence. The Arab sources could not see why either Rajub or Dahlan would agree to play second fiddle to an older leadership that would view them as a constant threat, when they could become the top leaders in their own right.

Arafat himself was not oblivious to these maneuvers and rumors. Rather than confront reality and arrange for his succession, however, he was increasingly determined to complete his jihad before he died.

————

ARAFAT'S PERSONAL EVOLUTION had a direct impact on the PA's relations with the Islamists, particularly HAMAS. Arafat was now assiduously defending HAMAS, privately, in discussions with the United States and

Israel, and publicly. Despite mounting evidence to the contrary, he continued to insist that the perpetrators of the martyrdom bombings in Jerusalem had come from abroad and enjoyed no support from the local Palestinians. All this time, he remained in direct communication with the Amman headquarters of HAMAS. In early September, after the bombings on Ben Yehuda Street, he again traveled to Amman for a meeting with Mussa Abu-Marzuq to coordinate their efforts. According to Arafat's apologists, Abu-Marzuq assured Arafat that HAMAS was not responsible for the Jerusalem bombings and that the martyr-bombers had come from abroad. This assertion was ostensibly corroborated by the publication in Amman of fairly accurate background intelligence distributed by Tehran-sponsored Islamists. In fact, Khalid Mashal—a leading figure in HAMAS whom Mossad would attempt to assassinate later that month—oversaw both the actual bombing operations in Jerusalem and the distribution of the cover story in Amman.

Arafat went along with the charade. Then, in late September, the identity of the martyr-bombers and their origin in a village near Nablus became known. Initially, Arafat's coterie stuck with the story that he had relied on the information provided by Abu-Marzuq. Subsequently, as evidence emerged that the PA security authorities had known about the perpetrators since 1996 but failed to arrest them, Tayeb Abdel Rahim, Arafat's secretary, rushed to take the blame, writing a letter of resignation in which he claimed he had erroneously informed Arafat that the Jerusalem bombers had come from abroad. Arafat turned down Rahim's resignation offer.

At the same time, PA-affiliated institutions were making every effort to outperform the Islamists in their own domain. For example, the PA encouraged virulent anti-Israeli, anti-Jewish, and anti-American propaganda through the mosques and mass media it controlled. Essentially, the PA was inciting the Palestinian street so that it would be impossible to come to an agreement with Israel on anything—including Israel's very existence. Thus, Arafat could, and did, argue in Washington that if the PA attempted to go further in implementing the accords he had signed, he, Arafat, would be toppled by an irate Palestinian public, and the entire peace process would collapse.

Most significant were the sermons delivered at al-Aqsa Mosque in Jerusalem by Mufti Ikrama Sabri, who had been named to that position by Arafat himself. In one such sermon in mid-September, the Mufti proclaimed, "America is the chief of the terrorists. Oh Allah, destroy America, her agents and her allies! Cast them into their own traps, and cover the White House with black!" Madeleine Albright's visit to Palestine, Sabri asserted, was designed "to support the Israeli position regarding deceitful security and fanatical settlements." This was but one component of a grand conspiracy against Islam. "The strategic covenant between Zionism and the Crusaders is a satanic alliance hostile to Islam and the Muslims. . . . Oh Allah," the Mufti concluded, "destroy America, her agents and allies! Allah, raise the flag of Islam over al-Aqsa mosque, Jerusalem and Palestine."

The HAMAS-affiliated mosques also participated in this incitement campaign. For example, after the IDF closed down the mosque in Dura—which doubled as a HAMAS center—the local imam, Sheikh Naif Rajub, gathered thousands in front of the mosque and declared its closure to be "the most evil form of terrorism." "Can you think of a form of terrorism more diabolical than preventing believers from praying at the house of Allah?" Sheikh Rajub asked. He stated that Israel was not fighting HAMAS, but was "waging war on Islam, on the mosques, and on our Prophet Muhammad." These and similar sermons put the PA's crackdown on the Islamists in perspective, especially given that Sheikh Rajub, a senior HAMAS activist, is the brother of Jibril Rajub, the man entrusted by Arafat with the crackdown on Islamist terrorism in the West Bank. Mahmoud Abbas, the secretary of the PLO Executive Committee, openly stated that the PA "will not wage a war to liquidate HAMAS or Islamic Jihad per se." For, he asserted, "According to the democratic outlook of the Palestinian community, HAMAS is a political movement. It operates in accordance with the provisions of the Palestinian law."

Working both sides of the street, sources close to Arafat claimed that some of the arrests of HAMAS supporters were conducted as an expression of Arafat's anger at being misinformed by HAMAS about the origin of the Jerusalem bombers, "and not because of orders from Israel or the USA." Concurrently, the *Palestine Times* of Jerusalem reported that a high-ranking PA official had intimated that the arrests were meant only to "mitigate the intensive pressure being exerted on us by the Israelis and the Americans." The official was most explicit: "We told our brothers that we didn't mean to hurt them . . . they didn't commit anything wrong after all . . . we just want to silence those SOBs for a while."

By late September, Arafat held that Israel was preparing for a war aimed at reoccupying the PA-held enclaves. He stressed that this Israeli threat was directed at all Palestinians—in other words, the Islamists and the PLO needed to cooperate in order to defeat Israel. In late September, he ordered a state of high alert for the entire PA security apparatus. Significantly, in forming their contingency plans, senior PA security officials held consultations with senior commanders of HAMAS and Islamic Jihad—the same master terrorists the PA had been unable to locate when it was a question of arresting them. In these discussions, the PA officials acknowledged that they had an arsenal of well over 30,000 small arms and machine guns, as well as sizable stockpiles of grenades, high explosives, Katyusha rockets, and anti-tank and anti-aircraft missiles.

The campaign for national unity extended beyond the protection of HAMAS and Islamic Jihad terrorists in the PA-controlled enclaves; the PA now encouraged the overt integration of Islamist terrorists into its own security forces. According to Ghazi Jabali, the commander of the Palestinian police, more than 150 members of rejectionist terrorist organizations—ranging from HAMAS to the PFLP—were serving in the ranks of the Palestinian police. Among them were at least 25 terrorists whose extradition for actual attacks against Israel had been formally requested by Israel's Ministry of Justice.

In late September, the PA special forces held an exercise in the Gaza Strip in which they resisted and defeated an effort by a simulated Israeli military force to abduct a Palestinian leader from a PA-held area. Concurrently, HAMAS was preparing for spectacular terrorist strikes in Israel's major cities during the Jewish High Holy Days. These plans were canceled only after Mossad attempted, and failed, to assassinate Khalid Mashal outside the HAMAS office in Amman, leading the intelligence services of the sponsoring states, Iran and Syria, to order a stand-down of operations inside Israel until counterintelligence issues had been resolved.

———

SECRET NEGOTIATIONS resumed in the fall among PA, U.S., and Israeli officials, even though the official PA media continually ridiculed the American efforts to revive the peace process. For example, following the Arafat-Netanyahu summit on October 8, the PA-controlled media flatly stated that negotiations could not continue so long as Netanyahu remained in power. The Jerusalem paper Al-Quds explicitly made any progress in the peace process conditional on a change of government. "Until such changes, which might produce an Israeli political leader who clearly states that settlement activity fundamentally contravenes peace," an Al-Quds editorial concluded, "crises will continue, opportunities will be lost, and the region will be exposed to violence and tension at the expense of the security, stability, and the real interests of the region's people."

By now, Sheikh Ahmad Yassin, the spiritual leader of HAMAS, dominated Palestinian political dynamics. Yassin had been released to Jordan from an Israeli jail on October 1, after Mossad's Amman debacle, and returned to Gaza a week later to a triumphant welcome. Neither the Islamists nor Arafat's coterie failed to recognize that King Hussein engineered Yassin's release and that Arafat had nothing to do but welcome Yassin and witness the outpouring of popular adulation. However, Sheikh Yassin was careful never to challenge Arafat's authority as a political leader or the PA's standing as the sole entity legitimately negotiating with Israel. Yassin personally reassured Arafat that "Any dialogue with the Israeli government must be carried out through the Palestinian Regime [i.e., the Palestinian Authority]. There never has been, and there will never be, any direct negotiations between HAMAS and Israel." Throughout his widespread media and public appearances, Sheikh Yassin emphasized HAMAS's role in supporting Arafat's hardening negotiating position. "The presence of HAMAS is a pressure card in the hands of the Palestinian Authority against Israel," Yassin explained. "What else does the Authority have? . . . HAMAS, as a pressure card, is not against the Authority, but with it. I pray to Allah they understand this."

Nor did other HAMAS leaders conceal their ultimate objectives. In an early October interview with Aaron Lerner of the Independent Media Review and Analysis (IMRA), Gaza HAMAS leader Abdul Aziz Rantisi stated that HAMAS would retaliate "in the same way that they [the Jews] dispossessed our people. They killed thousands of Palestinians in tens of massacres and they destroyed homes. So I think it is just to do with them as they did with us."

———

AS OF MID-OCTOBER, although Palestinian officials were insisting that the PA was continuing to crack down on Islamist terrorism, they were already anticipating the imminent release of the remaining HAMAS prisoners in PA jails. Senior PA security officials, notably Dahlan, stated that with Israel's release of Sheikh Yassin and other HAMAS prisoners, there was no justification for the PA's holding its own HAMAS prisoners. Dahlan also expected the imminent reopening of the sixteen HAMAS institutions in Gaza closed down by the PA, starting with the Islamic Mujamaa (a kind of charity for youth—that is, would-be terrorists). As the PA and Sheikh Yassin's representatives negotiated the modalities for the release of prisoners and the revival of overt HAMAS activities, Arafat made every effort to demonstrate that he, not Yassin, was the driving force behind these negotiations.

Meanwhile, the HAMAS leadership continued to raise the ante. They publicly insisted that the jihad must continue until the complete destruction of Israel. "Israel as the Jewish state must be wiped off the map," Sheikh Yassin told the Stockholm paper *Svenska Dagbladet*. "The suicide bombings will not stop in the present situation." Yassin added that the deals Arafat had made with Israel were unacceptable as ultimate objectives. "If someone had stolen $1 million from you, would you then be satisfied if the thief returned $100? That is Arafat's solution, but we are demanding that everything both above and below ground be returned to us."

Speaking to a local audience, Yassin was even more explicit. *Al-Quds* quoted his defense of martyrdom bombings. "Suicide means that a person is tired or has given up living," he explained, "and therefore he kills himself. This is forbidden by Islam. Those who give their lives for the defense of their land know where they are going. They are doing this to get close to Allah, and what you are talking about is self-sacrifice and not suicide. This will stop should Israel agree to a temporary ceasefire [*hunda*] in accordance with certain conditions." Given the PA's control over *Al-Quds*, Sheikh Yassin's call for war was made at the very least with the tacit approval of Arafat and the leadership of the Palestinian Authority.

Sheikh Yassin continued to hammer away at the need for jihad in public forums in Gaza, where his support among Fatah and PA cadres was openly demonstrated. One such address was delivered to between 3,500 and 5,000 people gathered at the Islamic University in Gaza. "We have made a covenant with Allah to be mujahideen unto death," he told the crowd. "We will remain united as a people and will stand against any enemy, no matter how strong he is. We will win in the end and will establish our independent state with Jerusalem as its capital."

Rantisi was even more explicit, urging the Gaza students to resume martyrdom bombings at the heart of Israel: "The day is close when our mujahideen will reach Jaffa, Haifa, and Tel Aviv." Rantisi ridiculed the U.S. threats against HAMAS. "I want to tell the U.S. secretary of state that we have a commitment to Allah to follow up on our jihad against the Zionist terrorism."

Leading Fatah and PA officials also increased their attacks on Israel, bringing their rhetoric to levels comparable to that of the HAMAS leaders. For example, Gheith Abu-Gheith, Arafat's adviser on clans, declared that Palestine, "which passed through many different stages of jihad since the 1910s, is a nation that knows how to take back and regain its rights." Palestine could be "a nation of peace, a nation of jihad, [or] a nation of martyrdom," depending on the circumstances.

Writing in the PA's daily *Al-Hayah al-Jadidah*, Fuad Abu-Hijla, a leading commentator, defended the enduring validity of the Palestinian Covenant. "Like myself, many in the Palestinian public still believe in the Covenant and see it as our nation's only source of authority in the current and upcoming stages of the conflict. . . . The Covenant—from 'A' to 'Z'—is a Palestinian document which battles the Zionists, rejects the turning of the Palestinian cause into a Pan-Arab and religious cause, rejects the use of Palestinian blood for non-Palestinian purposes, and stresses the national identity of this nation and its historic struggle, while clearly accenting Palestine's Arab and Islamic identity."

Moreover, *Al-Hayah al-Jadidah* reprinted a major paper that had originally run in Fatah's publication, *Our Position*. In this paper, Fatah gave up on the ability of the international community to impose on Israel an agreement acceptable to the Palestinians: "It is impossible to rely on international or Arab national circles as long as Netanyahu's claws of hatred dive into our Palestinian blood in search of oxygen-rich blood cells." Despite the PA's efforts, "our movement found in Netanyahu something it could not ignore, which is the dismemberment of the agreement by the fangs of hatred and the chewing of the peace by the teeth of the Talmud. Therefore, there was no escape from a heated clash that placed the national security forces in the trenches of defense of the Palestinian people and its liberty."

Through all of this, the ascent of the Palestinian Islamists and Arafat's accommodations with them formed part of the dynamics within the Arab world and had little or no connection with anything the Netanyahu government did or did not do. However, Netanyahu remained under relentless pressure from the Clinton White House to persevere with the peace process. Similar pressure came from the Israeli peace camp, which, in its insistence that there was no alternative to Arafat as a negotiating partner, did not recognize that there was nothing to talk about with Arafat. Even the most ardent post-Zionists on Israel's extreme Left did not wish for the destruction of Israel and its replacement with an Islamic state—and Arafat would settle for nothing less.

———

ON NOVEMBER 4, Israeli and Palestinian negotiators began yet another round of formal talks in the United States, even though most of the Palestinian team remained in Gaza as a symbol of Arafat's protest. Once the United States had guaranteed that it would supervise the PA's implementation of outstanding commitments, the Israeli cabinet authorized three senior ministers to draw up proposals for a permanent-status agreement, combined with an Israeli troop withdrawal. When the talks resumed in the second week of November, however, the Palestinians still refused to discuss their obligations until Israel rescinded its commitment to continue building settlements in the territories and also committed to a sizable withdrawal. The talks stalled.

Jerusalem hoped to overcome the impasse through low-key meetings between Netanyahu and Clinton. Netanyahu was going to be in Washington to address a major Jewish event, and he knew that Israeli prime ministers routinely met with the American president when they came to Washington. On this occasion, however, Clinton did not have time for such a meeting; high-level sources at the White House leaked that he was intentionally snubbing Netanyahu. Undaunted, Netanyahu attempted to arrange a meeting when he and Clinton were both in Los Angeles. Not only was Netanyahu again rebuffed, but the airport authorities also parked the two presidential aircraft side by side, and senior White House officials brought the media to see the embarrassing spectacle. These officials also gloated that they had made sure that no congressional or Jewish leader complained to Clinton over this public insult.

———

IN DECEMBER, Madeleine Albright scheduled three cycles of separate meetings in Europe with Netanyahu and Arafat. Albright began by reiterating the administration's insistence that the second Israeli withdrawal be not less than 13 percent of the West Bank's area, whereas the Israeli government was unwilling to cede more than 9 or 10 percent. There were also profound disagreements over what the PA was actually doing to fight Islamist terrorism and over the CIA's oversight of its activities.

Meanwhile, the Netanyahu government was running into a major political crisis. On January 4, 1998, Foreign Minister David Levy resigned from the government, and even from the Knesset, over the proportion of the budget earmarked for domestic and social expenditures. Levy's resignation reduced Netanyahu's parliamentary majority to a single vote. Netanyahu himself took over the Foreign Affairs portfolio.

Exploiting this political crisis, Ross arrived in Israel on January 6 to organize the long-anticipated second Israeli troop withdrawal. However, when he could not secure any kind of guarantee from Arafat regarding previous PA commitments on security-related issues, the Israeli government decided to postpone the withdrawal. The Palestinians countered with a resolution to stop cooperating with Israel until Israel unilaterally withdrew from a substantial part of the West Bank.

Despite the impasse, Clinton, Netanyahu, and Arafat decided to go ahead with the trilateral summit in Washington scheduled for mid-January. Once again, the Clinton administration's tactic was to increase the pressure on Jerusalem. Consequently, when Netanyahu arrived in Washington on January 20, Clinton presented him with a new proposal for further Israeli troop withdrawals. The administration also notified Mubarak and other Arab leaders that the United States was about to offer the Palestinians a plan for a phased withdrawal of Israeli troops provided Arafat came up with "acceptable language" reaffirming the PA's resolve to rein in Islamist terrorism. Arafat refused even this.

Ultimately, this visit turned out to be a milestone event, heralding a profound change in the character of the U.S. involvement in the peace process. This turnaround occurred *not* because anything had changed in the Middle East, but because of what was happening in Washington, D.C.

IN EARLY JANUARY 1998, President Clinton's attention was not on the Middle East. Independent Counsel Kenneth Starr—initially appointed to investigate the Whitewater charges against the Clintons—was closing in on the Monica Lewinsky story. On January 7, Lewinsky signed an affidavit in the

Paula Jones case falsely denying that she had had a romantic relationship with the president. On January 17, Clinton himself was summoned for a deposition and provided what, three years later, he would acknowledge was less than honest testimony. On January 20, 2001, as part of a last-minute deal with Robert Ray, the independent counsel who succeeded Starr, Clinton stated, "I tried to walk a fine line between acting lawfully and testifying falsely, but I now recognize that I did not fully accomplish that goal."

However, at the time, the President was convinced his cover-up would withstand scrutiny. Then, on January 18, the Internet's *Drudge Report* broke the story of the Linda Tripp tapes, which implicated Clinton in apparent perjury. Initially, the White House put on a brave face, pooh-poohing the *Drudge Report* while scurrying to get control over material evidence—such as the President's gifts to Ms. Lewinsky—before they were subpoenaed. Meanwhile, the Washington media machine was grinding away, and by January 20, as Netanyahu was meeting in the White House—literally, in the Lincoln Room—mainstream journalists finally realized that there was something big in the Drudge story.

Danny Naveh, who attended the meeting between Netanyahu and Clinton, recalled that the President appeared completely calm except for excursions to the bathroom every quarter of an hour or so. He concentrated on the Middle East as if that was the only issue on his mind. Slowly chewing on an unlit cigar, he asked what Jerusalem would require from Arafat in order to resume withdrawing from the West Bank. When Naveh outlined the series of security-related agreements already signed but still unimplemented, Sandy Berger interjected, "That will be very difficult." Berger demanded that Israel be "reasonable" in its demands on Arafat, and Clinton did not alter his expectations for Israeli concessions. The issue was not resolved by the time the meeting ended or, for that matter, by the time Netanyahu returned to Israel.

The next day, January 21, the White House was apprised that the Lewinsky story would be published in the mainstream media. On the morning of January 22, the crisis exploded on the front page of the *Washington Post*.

Bill Clinton had always been obsessed with his place in history. Now, with Monicagate erupting, his advisers were determined that he would leave the White House with a legacy as a peacemaker. Thus, despite the inconclusiveness of Netanyahu's visit, the White House issued a flood of statements promising the reinvigoration of the peace process.

A few days later, Arafat arrived in Washington expecting the administration to deliver significant unilateral concessions from Israel. Arafat openly demanded that Israel immediately turn over 60 percent more of the West Bank, in addition to the 27 percent it had already turned over, along with

Gaza. Coming out of a meeting with President Clinton in which he was told about the latest Israeli offers, Arafat said, "What he [Netanyahu] is offering us is peanuts and we cannot accept it."

The most telling aspect of Arafat's visit to Washington was the way he addressed the Palestinian Covenant issue. He brought with him a letter to President Clinton, a close examination of which shows that the PLO acknowledged that the covenant was not yet amended. The key paragraph read, "All of the provisions of the Covenant which are inconsistent with the PLO commitment to recognize Israel are no longer in effect. As a result, Articles 6 through 10, 15, 19 through 23, and 30, have been nullified. And the parts in Articles 1 through 5, 11 through 14, 16 through 18, 25 through 27, and 29, which are inconsistent with the above-mentioned commitments have also been nullified. These changes will be reflected in any official publication of the Charter." In other words, the changes were *not* reflected in any current document.

However, Arafat adamantly refused to convene the full 600-member Palestinian National Council (PNC)—the only body capable of amending the covenant, in accordance with the covenant's own provisions. Instead, Arafat offered Clinton a compromise: He would convene the PLO Executive Committee, whose twenty members were elected PNC delegates. "The PLO Executive Committee is the alternative to the PNC," PA negotiator Nabil Shaath explained. However, Shaath acknowledged that the PLO Executive Committee did not have the legal power to formally amend the covenant. Even State Department spokesman James Rubin could not call Arafat's document anything more than an "important step for completing the process of revising the covenant."

———

IN THE WEEKS before Arafat's trip to Washington, the Palestinian leadership, including Arafat himself, had been nothing if not forthright about their position on the points at issue. In early January, Arafat had reiterated that the peace process was taking place in accordance with the 1974 Phases Program/Phased Plan, which authorized the PLO to establish a Palestinian state on any area Israel withdrew from and then use this land as a springboard for the ultimate liberation of the entire Palestine—that is, the destruction of Israel. Other senior PA officials did not conceal that they shared this interpretation. For example, Abdel Azziz Shaheen, the PA minister of supplies, told *Al-Hayah al-Jadidah*, "The Oslo Accord was a preface for the Palestinian Authority, and the Palestinian Authority will be a preface for the Palestinian State, which, in turn, will be a preface for the liberation of the entire Palestinian Land."

Moreover, the PA continued to insist on the "right of return"—namely, the flooding of pre-1967 Israel with the refugees of 1948 and their descendants, as outlined by Arafat in his January 30, 1996, speech in Stockholm. The right of return had always been a sacred cause for Arafat, going back to the PLO's establishment three years *before* Israel's acquisition of the territories in the Six-Day War. Now as then, Arafat's basic constituency comes from the pre-1967 Israel, and for them no Palestinian state confined to the West Bank and Gaza constitutes a solution of the Palestinian problem.

Arafat confirmed this understanding in the midst of the preparations for the Washington summit. In the first week of January, he delivered a stirring speech in which he appealed to the residents of the refugee camps in Lebanon (all of whom are refugees of 1948 or their descendants) to support him in the common struggle. Discussing the coming talks in Washington, he stated, "We have now placed the refugee problem at the top of our list of priorities. We are one people and we will insist on all our rights, including the right of return."

On the eve of Arafat's departure, PNC Speaker Salim al-Zaanun said, "We will resort to all resistance methods if matters reach an impasse or if Netanyahu cancels the peace process and the Oslo agreement." Arafat himself also warned of a new Intifadah if the administration did not deliver what he wanted. "We are ready to sacrifice for Palestine with our souls and blood," he told a crowd of thousands in Gaza on January 18. "Did you forget the Intifadah? We had seven years of Intifadah, and we are ready to start anew. . . . Our people is a people of martyrs." To ensure the impact of his declaration, Arafat repeated: "I want to tell the people, far or near, that we are ready, that we are a nation of martyrs."

Nevertheless, the White House accorded Arafat all the honors due a head of state. The bulk of his discussions with President Clinton and other administration officials were on the extent of the Israeli withdrawal. Very little was said about the Palestinians' living up to their own signed obligations. There was a pro forma mention of the need to fight terrorism and extremism, but nobody entertained hopes for implementation. Arafat left Washington confident that there was no need for the PA to do anything concerning the various agreements with Israel.

During February, as the Monicagate crisis was escalating, so was the PLO's brashness—and, ostensibly by sheer coincidence, so was the new U.S.-Iraqi crisis, in which the Clinton administration was attempting to build support for the use of force in response to Saddam Hussein's persistent refusal to cooperate with U.N. monitors. Ultimately, the United States and the United Kingdom launched a series of air strikes against Iraq and then called off further strikes in the context of a flimsy U.N.-negotiated compromise that, again ostensibly by sheer coincidence, followed a relaxation in the President's legal woes.

———

BACK IN JANUARY, with the Iraq crisis mounting, Tehran sent clandestine messages to key Arab capitals urging closer cooperation. Baghdad reacted quickly, proposing the formation of a common front against the American efforts. Baghdad offered enticements to Tehran, including cutting support for the Iraq-based Iranian opposition terrorist group the Mujahideen ul-Khalq and reexamining Tehran's demand for some $100 billion in compensation for the Iran-Iraq War.

The moment Iran signaled interest in the Iraqi overture, Saddam dispatched Foreign Minister Muhammad Said al-Sahhaf as his personal secret emissary to Tehran. Baghdad, Sahhaf assured his hosts, was ready to commit itself formally to the new relationship with Tehran that Damascus had been working to arrange. Sahhaf convinced the Iranians that Baghdad was serious, and before he left Tehran he and Kamal Kharrazi, the Iranian foreign minister, signed a memorandum of understanding.

The key cooperation would be in security and intelligence matters, and soon after Sahhaf's visit, senior intelligence and security officials from the two countries began meeting secretly to discuss the practical aspects of their new alliance against the American military presence. On February 5, Qusay Saddam Hussein, in charge of the Iraqi intelligence system, and Rafia Daham al-Takriti, Iraq's chief of General Intelligence, traveled to al-Shalamja, on the Iraqi side of the Iran-Iraq border, to meet the Iranian intelligence minister, Qorban Ali Dari Najafabadi, and other senior Iranian officials. The two delegations reached agreement on several key issues, including joint sponsorship of terrorism all over the world. They also agreed to escalate any American attack on Iraq into a regional war against Israel—thus making it impossible for any Arab or Muslim country to cooperate with the United States against Iraq.

Ultimately, though, Hosni Mubarak effectively prevented his fellow Arabs from supporting the American use of force against Iraq. Cairo's position throughout the crisis was the result of Mubarak's reevaluation of the overall role of the United States in the Middle East. Believing the Clinton administration had made a deal with his own Islamist enemies, Mubarak resolved to strengthen his ties with the Islamists' key sponsors, Tehran and Khartoum. He had already concluded that by joining the Iranian-led strategic alliance and participating in any ensuing conflict with Israel, he could not only ensure that Egypt would continue to have a prominent role in the Arab and Muslim world but also secure his own political survival. A major step was the formalization, in early February, of the strategic cooperation between Iraq, Iran, Syria, and Egypt informally agreed to the previous July.

Rather than face up to the new reality in the Middle East, the Clinton White House decided to blame Israel for the failure of its Iraqi policy. Senior officials, and subsequently Clinton himself, stated that it was because of the stalemate on the Palestinian track that they had been unable to generate support among the Gulf States—and particularly permission to use bases—for their planned attacks on Iraq. Although Riyadh and all the other local regimes—both publicly and in confidence to Albright and other senior officials—based their opposition to the Americans' plans on their reading of the regional situation as a whole, the administration completely ignored this explanation.

———

ARAFAT COULD AFFORD to be increasingly audacious and defiant because he and his coterie had excellent inside information from the White House. An article in the London newspaper *Al-Sharq al-Awsat* by Bassam Abu-Sharif, an Arafat confidant, hinted at the nature of the PLO's inside track. The article was about the British-American consultations on Iraq and the linkage to the Palestinian-Israeli peace process.

Abu-Sharif identified the mid-March Camp David summit meeting between President Clinton and British Prime Minister Tony Blair as a milestone in the formulation of U.S. policy toward the Middle East. "The discussions focused then on a military strike against Iraq and the potential adverse effects of such a strike on U.S.-Arab and British-Arab relations," Abu-Sharif reported. He then stressed the authority of his sources: "According to what I have been told by a person who is very close to Hillary Clinton, the lady of the White House, who is heroically defending her husband, the matter was raised within the framework of the collapse of the peace process as a result of the intransigent Israeli position." According to Abu-Sharif, Bill Clinton complained to Tony Blair about "all the U.S. efforts that had been doomed to failure." Furthermore, "he also explained to him the reasons that caused the U.S. Administration to be unable to advance the peace process, most importantly the U.S. Congress's position supportive of Netanyahu due to the U.S. Presidency's weakness as a result of the campaign against President Clinton for moral reasons. President Clinton expressed a clear view to the effect that the cause of the deadlock lies in the Israeli Government's position of refusing to implement the signed agreements." As Abu-Sharif quoted Clinton, it was not the air attacks against Iraq but rather "the tension on the Palestinian scene" that had caused "the rift that afflicted U.S. and British relations with their Arab allies."

Abu-Sharif then analyzed the overall situation in Washington on the basis of the inside information provided by his source. "We recall here that the Clinton Administration's efforts were paralyzed after the campaigns staged by the extremist Christian right wing in the United States in cooperation and coordination with Netanyahu's team," Abu-Sharif explained, in terms reminiscent of Hillary Clinton's "vast right-wing conspiracy."

Significantly, Abu-Sharif acknowledged that, ultimately, the Israeli call for fighting terrorism was in agreement with the overall interest of the U.S.-led West. Hence, the primary challenge facing Arafat was to maneuver the PA politically into supporting the Clinton White House. "Difficult missions in the Middle East should be tackled delicately, sensitively, and credibly," Abu-Sharif warned his Arab readers; "otherwise Netanyahu's call for violence and counter-violence will be in line with the West's stand, which is biased and uses different standards and criteria when dealing with the resolutions of international legitimacy."

———

IN ACCORDANCE with these recommendations, Arafat conditionally accepted the American proposal for a second withdrawal of 13 percent. He added a PA commitment to entering accelerated negotiations toward a permanent-status agreement and vague phraseology concerning the PA's abiding by previously signed agreements. As expected, the White House leaped on this "flexibility" and "forthcomingness," and Clinton began relentless pressure on Netanyahu to reciprocate.

When Jerusalem refused to accept the U.S. demand for a 13 percent withdrawal, Albright warned Netanyahu repeatedly, both in person and in harshly worded messages, that the United States would deem Israel guilty if the peace process collapsed. Another point of contention was the Hebron agreement of January 15, 1997. Back then, the State Department had formally confirmed, in a "note for the record," that "further redeployment phases are issues for implementation by Israel rather than issues for negotiation with the Palestinians." Furthermore, the "letters of assurance" sent by then secretary of state Christopher to both the Israelis and the Palestinians referred to "Israeli responsibility" for determining the size and location of subsequent withdrawals. This pledge by the highest officials of the Clinton administration had convinced the Netanyahu government to withdraw from Hebron. Now, in the spring of 1998, the Clinton administration was brazenly ignoring its own guarantees.

In early April, the U.S. Senate rallied to Israel's aid. Led by Joseph Lieberman (D-CT) and Connie Mack (R-FL), eighty-one senators signed a letter to President Clinton warning him against "publicly presenting a peace proposal which is known to be unacceptable to Israel." The letter reiterated the Senate's opinion that "it would be a serious mistake for the United States to change from its traditional role as facilitator of the peace process to using public pressure against Israel." The senators stressed that while Israel had "kept the promises it made at Oslo, and today is prepared to withdraw from even more territory of the West Bank before final status negotiations, . . . the Palestinians have not provided Israel with adequate security and Chairman Arafat has refused to conclude negotiations for the remaining interim status issues, even though Israel's current offers move the Palestinian people significantly forward in their quest for self-governance." And, they added, "Chairman Arafat may hope that American frustration with the pace of the process will lead to an American decision to force even more from Israel. Instead, the United States should quietly urge the Palestinians to accept Israel's latest offer and move to final status negotiations." The senators reminded President Clinton of Christopher's letter of assurances and concluded, "American Middle East diplomacy . . . has always worked best when pursued quietly and in concert with Israel."

The administration reacted swiftly. Albright met with Natan Sharansky— the former Soviet refusenik, who was by this time Israel's minister of industry and trade and was in Washington on an official visit—and asked him why Israel had to "incite the Congress against the administration." Clinton himself was incensed by what senior officials termed the "Israeli muscle flexing" and resolved that Netanyahu had to go. For the second time the Clinton administration would intervene directly in an Israeli election, assisting the Labor Party and the peace camp generally in their quest to topple the Netanyahu government.

———

THROUGHOUT the first months of 1998, senior administration officials had been telling Congress that the vicious cycle of violence in the Middle East would stop only if Israel and the United States accepted an agreement more or less on Arafat's terms. Now it was Arafat himself who spoiled the administration's party. On April 18, he gave a lengthy and revealing interview to Egypt's Orbit TV.

As he had done many times before, he compared the agreements he had signed with Israel to the Treaty of Hudaibiya. "When the Prophet Muhammad made the Hudaibiya Agreement, he agreed to remove his title 'Messenger of Allah' from the agreement. Then, Omar bin Khatib and the others referred to this agreement as the 'inferior peace agreement.' Of course, I do not compare myself to the Prophet, but I do say that we must learn from his steps and those of Sallah al-Din. The peace agreement which we signed [with

Israel] is an 'inferior peace.'" With this allusion, Arafat refers to Saladin's reliance on the Hudaibiya precedent when he violated his cease-fire agreement with the Crusaders and launched the surprise attack that allowed him to capture Jerusalem in 1187. Arafat's listeners understood its relevance to Arafat's view of the validity of agreements with Israel.

Moreover, according to Arafat, the Palestinians' determination to resume the armed struggle did not depend on whether he, Arafat, was alive at the time: "This nation of giants has created 100,000 Arafats. We are a nation of giants which has been struggling with World Zionism for 101 years, and we are capable of beginning it all again. I say this not in the name of Arafat but in the name of the new generals." He concluded the interview by declaring, "I would also like to say that I envy the martyrs and I hope to become one of them, though it has been decreed thus far that I continue to live."

Although the Clinton administration heard frequently from both Israel and the U.S. Congress about these and comparable statements by Arafat and his coterie, it consistently ignored them.

10

"Partners in Peace" (1998–1999)

Resumption of Israeli-Palestinian Negotiations; Continuance of Palestinian Incitement

BY THE SPRING of 1998, with President Clinton besieged by the mounting Monicagate scandal and with Congress seriously looking at the possibility of impeachment, Arafat had every reason to be confident that the administration would do its utmost to deliver Israel. Then, on May 6, First Lady Hillary Rodham Clinton, speaking by satellite to young Arabs and Israelis, declared her support for the creation of an independent Palestinian state. "I think that it will be in the long-term interest of the Middle East for Palestine to be a state, to be a state that is responsible for its citizens' well-being," she said. "I think that is very important for the Palestinian people, but I also think it is very important for the broader goal of peace in the Middle East."

Although White House press secretary Mike McCurry was quick to note that these comments were a "view expressed personally by the First Lady [that] is not the view of the President" and that her comments were "not part of any kind of calculated strategy," subsequent events suggested otherwise. In fact, the cool, calculating, and politically suave Mrs. Clinton had floated a trial balloon, which Mr. Clinton seized a few hours later, in an address to the National Leadership Conference of the Arab American Institute (AAI). Discussing the peace process, the President first claimed that all he was "trying to do [was] to regain that momentum." However, a few moments later he elucidated his ultimate goal: "Keep in mind, what we are trying to do is to get the parties over a hurdle so they can get into these final-status talks so we can stay on the timetable established a few years ago by both the Palestinians and the Israelis to finish the whole thing by this month next year."

The President did not explain why it was so important to complete these complicated and protracted negotiations within a year. The answer lay in Arafat's stated objective: namely, to unilaterally declare the independence of the Palestinian State in May 1999. At midnight on April 29–30, 1998 (coinciding with where Israel's Independence Day fell on the Western calendar that year), Arafat called his coterie to a meeting at his Ramallah headquarters. "Next year in May, I will announce the independence of Palestine," he said, rising from his chair. "My decision is final. Next May there will be a declaration of independence." Arafat loyalists later explained that he interpreted the five-year interim period that began with the signing of the Cairo agreement in May 1994 as fixed and mandatory. In reality, the five-year point was a goal and never considered obligatory; the agreement required the fulfillment of numerous conditions by both sides before the permanent status of the Palestinian entity was determined in negotiations. Nevertheless, if one combined the statements made a few hours apart by Mrs. Clinton and the president, one was left with no doubt that the White House had adopted the Palestinian position.

In view of mounting congressional support for the Netanyahu government, Secretary of State Albright met with Arafat in London on May 18 and, according to the senior Palestinian negotiator, Saeb Erekat, told him that the Clinton administration was about to hold a "comprehensive evaluation" of the progress in the negotiations. Erekat had no doubt that the Clinton administration considered the Netanyahu government the cause of the current crisis, because "Albright did not ask President Arafat to make any change of any kind to his stand." A confident Arafat even announced that he planned to "snub" Speaker Gingrich and his congressional delegation by not showing up to a meeting scheduled for May 27 in the Middle East. Arafat was content to sit quietly and wait for the Clinton administration to deliver Israel.

———

THE NEW PHASE of American pressure on Netanyahu started during Vice President Al Gore's visit to Jerusalem in late April for Israel's Fiftieth Anniversary celebrations. Gore scolded Netanyahu for insisting that "a mere 2 percent [of the West Bank]" could have an effect on Israel's security. Instead, Gore explained, "the big picture" should top Israel's priority list. Netanyahu listened attentively but did not budge.

In early May, Albright met several times with Netanyahu and Arafat in an effort to press them into the framework of the administration's "compromise plan." When neither would agree, she started threatening Netanyahu, saying that unless he accepted her demands, she would have to recommend that the United States end its involvement in the negotiations. Then, she warned, the president would publicly announce the collapse of the peace process and blame Netanyahu and Israel for the "catastrophe." The next day, Naveh and Molcho told Ross that Netanyahu still believed there could be a constructive way for Israel to agree to the elusive 13 percent withdrawal. Clinton, Berger, and Albright were now convinced they knew where to apply pressure.

It took the personal initiative of a Jewish supporter of Clinton's to get the president and Netanyahu to talk on the phone about their outstanding differences. At the end of their conversation, in a classic Clinton acrobatic, the president came up with the idea of a 10 percent withdrawal coupled with the "allocation" of an additional 3 percent to a "natural reservation," so that the withdrawal would and would not be 13 percent depending on whose definition one used. Netanyahu concurred, and Ross and Molcho produced the appropriate phrasing, along with a vague, less-than-fig-leaf guarantee of Palestinian implementation of past commitments. Given Israel's internal political situation, Netanyahu requested, and Clinton promised, that the Israeli concessions would be kept in confidence.

Clinton, however, was still incensed over Netanyahu's audacity in relying on the intercession of a major contributor to whom the White House could not say no. Therefore, Clinton instructed Ambassador Indyk to leak to his protégé, Defense Minister Yitzhak Mordechai, that Netanyahu had actually agreed to a 13 percent withdrawal and not the 10 percent he was talking about in the security cabinet. This revelation led to a major crisis among Netanyahu's key ministers.

In mid-May, as Netanyahu prepared to return to Washington, Jerusalem was all too aware of the White House's goal. "The Americans have decided to finish us off," said a senior official close to the prime minister. "They have decided to do anything necessary to topple Bibi [Netanyahu] and bring Ehud Barak to power." Another senior Israeli official identified Albright as the driving force behind this effort. "Albright," he explained, "does not see anything wrong in principle with toppling a democratically elected government. She sees this as a legitimate 'weapon.'" An important component of the White House's campaign was "to instill the idea in Israeli minds that Netanyahu, personally, is an impediment to the close relations between the U.S. administration and Israel."

A few days before Netanyahu's arrival, Clinton delivered the keynote speech at the conference of the Association of Arab-American University Graduates, one of the more radical Arab American organizations. The conference was dedicated to the *Nakba* (the catastrophe that Israel's establishment was), and Clinton spoke under a banner proclaiming "50 Years of Usurpation." "We will win," Clinton told the crowd. That "We" was not lost on Gaza. The next day, the official PA newspaper, *Al-Hayah al-Jadidah*, carried an editorial titled "Who Rules the United States?!" hailing the collapse of "Jewish control" over America. "Mrs. Clinton's [May 6] statement was considered the beginning of U.S. pressure," the editorial stated, "not because of its substance, but because of its timing. . . . Furthermore, President Clinton's meeting with Arab graduates from U.S. universities was also considered a form of pressure that President Clinton put on Netanyahu."

Despite all these maneuvers, Netanyahu was startled to discover, upon arriving in Washington, that the understanding he had just reached with Clinton was no longer valid. The White House now insisted on a straightforward 13 percent withdrawal. In a lengthy and rancorous meeting with Albright, Netanyahu offered an 11 percent withdrawal, with the additional 2 percent in a third phase. Albright held out for 13 percent now, and another sizable withdrawal later. Moreover, other most senior officials repeatedly told Netanyahu that the administration would not accept the Israeli demand that the next withdrawal be contingent upon the Palestinians' fulfilling their Oslo obligations—particularly on such key issues as extraditing terrorists and reducing the size and armament of their police force. Netanyahu's protestations that the United States had specifically guaranteed these points in the Hebron agreement were deemed "outrageous insults" by unnamed senior American officials.

In contrast, Congress went out of its way to welcome Netanyahu. Benjamin A. Gilman (R-NY), chairman of the House International Relations Committee, said, "Mr. Prime Minister, you are not only among friends, you are among *mishpochah* [family, in Hebrew]." Senate Majority Leader Trent Lott (R-MS) said, "Only Israel can make the decision about what is necessary for them to be assured of their security. I hope the administration will . . . not show partiality toward the Palestinians." House Speaker Newt Gingrich (R-GA) blamed Arafat for "inciting people to emotionalism and violence" instead of living up to his commitments. This show of support for Netanyahu by congressional Republicans did nothing to endear him to the Clinton administration.

———

DURING THE SUMMER of 1998, Israeli-American negotiations—primarily between Ross and Molcho—became increasingly tense and hostile. The issues addressed at this stage were the size of the third-phase withdrawal, the possibility of a unilateral declaration of independence by Arafat the following May, the United States' expectations from a permanent-status agreement, and the possibility of the United States' assisting Israel in absorbing the costs of the eventual agreement, estimated at over a billion dollars. As well, Jerusalem demanded that the PA present to the U.S. a detailed plan for fighting terrorism, including modalities for CIA supervision; that the Palestinian Covenant be legally canceled or amended; and that some thirty terrorists accused of violence be extradited to Israel or, in cases where the victims also included American citizens, to the United States. The Clinton administration considered the Israelis' demands outrageous and so informed them.

While these negotiations were taking place, Arafat did not tone down his public hostility toward Israel. For example, in a late June interview with Qatar-based al-Jazeera television, he urged the Gulf Arabs to contribute funds for the struggle to secure the Islamic character of Jerusalem against "this Satan, the Satan of money, the Satan of influence, the Satan of discord, the Satan of the robbery which the government of Israel is attempting to commit." In early July, during celebrations of the Prophet Muhammad's birthday in the Gaza City Great Mosque, Arafat was formally recognized as an Islamic, and not merely a political, leader. During a sermon hailing his contribution to the anti-Israeli jihad, Sheikh Nimr Masri introduced two new quasi-official titles for Arafat: "The Faithful President" and "The Friend of the Prophet."

Meanwhile, the PA was intensifying its military buildup, with the specific objective of having a fighting force ready for the May 1999 declaration of independence. By now, the PA fielded a force of well over 30,000 troops, instead of the 18,600 permitted by accords with Israel. The smuggling of weapons—including heavy machine guns and anti-tank rockets and missiles—had intensified markedly. With this buildup the PA was doing something new—explicitly recruiting prominent HAMAS and Islamic Jihad terrorists into the ranks of the Palestinian security forces so that those forces would be representative of all the elements confronting Israel. Israeli intelligence provided the CIA with a list of twenty-one prominent terrorists serving in the Palestinian security forces, four of whom had been convicted by the PA itself for involvement in the 1996 suicide bombings. With Islamist terrorism on the rise again, Washington could not ignore the subject completely. Hence, under Ross's reluctant supervision, an Israeli team of terrorism and security experts started working with their CIA counterparts to resolve this issue. However, when senior Palestinian officials informed the CIA that they would not implement any of the arrangements the team devised, Ross did not push the matter further.

In early July, the PA instigated a crisis in Gaza as a demonstration of defiance. The crisis started when Palestinian Supply Minister Abdel Azziz Shaheen demanded that Israel permit a convoy of twenty-two Palestinian trucks to use a coastal road under Israeli control without any security inspection. The Israelis refused and blocked the convoy; soon afterward, previously deployed Palestinian police units set up roadblocks at major intersections throughout the Gaza Strip, blocking all traffic. After nightfall, the two sides dug trenches and took up positions facing each other, and the Palestinian troops aimed their weapons at the Israelis. Israeli commanders later described the Gaza standoff as the tensest incident since the mini-Intifadah of the fall of 1996. In the end, Israel succumbed to pressure from Ross and permitted the convoy's passage as a one-time gesture of goodwill. Arafat declared victory and vowed revenge for Israel's blocking the convoy at all. "We will not accept anyone harming the lives or jobs of our people in the Gaza Strip," he proclaimed.

———

FOR THE CLINTON ADMINISTRATION, these developments offered no justification for reducing the pressure on Netanyahu. On the contrary, Albright and Ross began phoning him almost daily. The CIA provided a secure phone, which a CIA officer brought to the prime minister's office whenever such a call was to be made. The essence of these conversations was an idea, formulated by Ross, for a phased implementation of the second withdrawal, with every phase conditional on the Palestinians' implementing some portion of their undertakings. The principle of the Ross plan was to get the mechanism going by having Israel immediately start to withdraw. Then, once the PA stopped implementing its part of the deal, the White House would pressure Israel to stay the course nevertheless.

In early July, Albright invited a Palestinian delegation to Washington to hear the Clinton administration's latest ideas. The Palestinians considered the initiative an exercise in futility. "The peace process is not only in a state of deadlock," said Hannan Ashrawi, one of the delegates. "We feel that it has been destroyed by Prime Minister Netanyahu." Nevertheless, Albright presented to them Ross's ideas about phased withdrawal, as well as the ideas developed by the Israelis and the CIA about security cooperation. The Palestinians rejected all of these out of hand.

Soon afterward, American, Russian, and Western European diplomats warned Arafat that it was becoming extremely difficult to get Israel to begin withdrawing given the lack of direct Israeli-Palestinian contacts. Having a summit with Netanyahu to break the deadlock, they advised, would give the Americans a justification for increasing the pressure on Jerusalem. Arafat balked at the idea, but eventually agreed to a series of meetings starting in late July. These talks led nowhere—not surprisingly, given the gap between the two sides' positions. Chief PLO negotiator Nabil Shaath told reporters that the talks would end in "two, three or four days . . . unless the Israelis come up with a miracle and declare their acceptance of the American initiative and are ready to withdraw."

To a great extent, however, the PA had no alternative but to attend this cycle of talks. On the eve of the first planned meeting between Mordechai and Mahmoud Abbas, a major bomb was supposed to go off in Jerusalem. A known second-tier HAMAS activist from Al-Amri refugee camp, in the PA-controlled area north of Ramallah, drove a Fiat Ducato van to Jaffa Road near Zion Square, in the heart of Jerusalem. He had a work permit and an ID card provided by the PA security authorities, as well as fake Israeli license plates. The van was loaded with gas canisters, some 160 gallons of flammable liquids, and dozens of pounds of nails in paper bags arranged around the central charge. It was pure luck that the van caught fire before the terrorist could successfully detonate it on this busy street. When Israeli negotiators raised the issue, the PA's Nabil Abu-Rudeineh blamed Israel for the bombing attempt. "This is a suspicious incident," he said. "You have to ask the Israelis. It sounds like an event fabricated to torpedo the current Israeli-Palestinian efforts."

Concurrently, the PA security forces in Nablus resumed their ambushes in the nearby Jewish settlements, one of which resulted in the death of two young Israelis. IDF investigators determined that it had been a thoroughly professional undertaking; the terrorist squad had posted lookouts to observe the settlers' patrols and laid its ambush at an ideal spot. As the head of the IDF's Central Command, Major General Moshe Yaalon, later noted, "The terrorists observed the settlers' activity, saw the [patrol] vehicle make a few trips around the settlement, and prepared the ambush meticulously."

Arafat himself set the tone for these activities. In a July 29 speech to the Organization of Islamic Countries' Jerusalem Committee in Morocco—a speech prominently carried by *Al-Hayah al-Jadidah*—Arafat asserted that "The Israeli policy of ethnic cleansing has taken on the ugliest of forms in recent months. We shall continue to act against the settlement onslaught . . . to save Holy Jerusalem from the Judaizing monster and the despised settlements." Arafat declared that the Israelis "are determined to destroy the Dome of the Rock and Al-Aqsa Mosque on the Temple Mount and to replace them by building Solomon's Temple." This was the beginning of a major confrontation, Arafat warned: "Israel has started the war over Jerusalem, but with Arab and Islamic assistance, this shall be our faithful jihad—to defend holy Jerusalem from the danger of Judaization and the Zionist plot."

———

TALK OF JIHAD was by no means confined to adults. Children's summer camps and related TV programs took as their overriding theme the unity of Palestine and the imperative of fighting the Israelis in order to liberate the land. "Where are you from?" the narrator on one TV program asked a little girl. "Beer Sheva," she answered. The narrator then explained that "Beer Sheva is one of the Palestinian cities which is now occupied." In fact, Beer Sheva has been part of Israel since 1948, and the six- or seven-year-old girl had lived all her life in Gaza, under Arafat's PA. Another children's program clarified this seeming contradiction by showing girls dancing and singing: "I love my country. My house is in Gaza but I come from Haifa." A frequently broadcast clip showed a girl in front of a map of the entire Palestine. "They [the Israelis] took everything; they burnt the forests and changed the names," she declared emotionally. "But it is still my country—my country, Palestine."

In the summer camps for boys organized by the PA's education department, the children were divided into groups named after Israeli cities—Haifa, Acre, Safed, Jaffa, Tiberias, Deir Yassin. They wore T-shirts showing a unified Palestine in which Israel did not exist. Young children were taught how to use assault rifles. Yelling "Commando!" and "Jihad!" they jumped through a ring of fire. The songs taught in these camps included "We'll Throw Them into the Sea," "Revolution Until Victory," and "My Children—in the Suicide Squads." The children's visits to Israel, many of them organized and subsidized by peace-camp organizations in Israel and the United States, were called in Arabic "visits to cities in occupied Palestine." At the end of one summer program in Gaza, there was a kite-flying event called "kites without borders." Each kite bore the name of a village that was destroyed in 1948.

The Children's Club TV show features a primary school classroom with posters of Mickey Mouse and Donald Duck on one wall and a smiling, fatherly Arafat on another. Several of the festively dressed 6–8-year-old children on one program announced their intention of becoming suicide bombers, to the applause of their teachers. "And when I shall wander into the entrance of Jerusalem," announced one girl, "I will turn into a suicide warrior." On another program, one boy explained what should be done with the Jews: "We will throw them into the sea. The day is near when we will settle our account with stones and bullets." Not a single utterance throughout these activities for children suggested coexistence, let alone peace, with a legitimate Israel.

———

AS THE U.S.-SPONSORED negotiations with the Palestinians were tottering, Netanyahu was pushing for a breakthrough with Syria outside the patronage of the Clinton administration. These new Israeli-Syrian contacts were the belated maturing of initiatives started back in the spring of 1997. At that time, the Lebanese American George Nader had told his Israeli friend Dore Gold that Damascus was interested in luring American investments to prevent the collapse of the Syrian economy and was prepared to reward a successful effort with political goodwill. Consequently, several American businessmen friendly with Israel, including New York investment manager and Republican activist Ron Lauder, traveled to Damascus to study the prospects for economic development. While nothing came of this visit in terms of investment, Lauder and others did establish direct contacts with the Syrian leadership.

Now, in the early summer of 1998, Netanyahu attempted to capitalize on Lauder's contacts and Nader's goodwill in order to establish direct communications with Assad. Netanyahu's objective was the formulation of a joint declaration of principles defining the essential points of a Syrian-Israeli peace treaty. Nader arranged the meetings with Assad, and Lauder used his private plane to shuttle between Jerusalem and Damascus via Cyprus, delivering messages; at the peak of these contacts, Lauder was shuttling twice daily. By late August, the Israeli-Syrian dialogue had reached such an advanced stage that Netanyahu sent with Lauder a draft of a "Treaty of Peace Between Israel and Syria." In this draft, Netanyahu expressed his willingness to consider withdrawal to a new borderline based on the 1923 international border (as distinct from the June 4, 1967, line), in return for comprehensive security arrangements, including retention of the Israeli early-warning facilities on the Golan.

Assad did not reject Netanyahu's ideas out of hand, and Lauder kept shuttling between Jerusalem and Damascus until late September. At that point, however, it turned out that the Syrians were interested only in acquiring a detailed map of the extent of the proposed Israeli withdrawal. Netanyahu refused to provide such a map, lest it be used against Israel as the Rabin "non-paper" and "deposit" had been. In any case, Assad had refused to commit Syria to any specific demilitarization or other confidence-building measures on Syrian territory. Consequently, the parties reached a deadlock and contacts soon afterward ceased. Jerusalem informed the Clinton White House about them only in mid-November, when American pressure to revive the Syrian track became relentless.

———

THROUGH ALL OF THIS, Netanyahu was fighting for his political survival. On the day before the summer recess, the Knesset voted 60–6 in favor of the first step toward dissolving and forcing new elections. Immediately, the still undeclared election campaign got underway with attacks on Netanyahu from the Left for not doing enough for peace and from the Right for making too many concessions to Arafat. These two opposed camps were united only in seeking to undermine Netanyahu. Once again, the Clinton administration took sides. For example, when former chief of staff Ehud Barak, who was now Israel's opposition leader, visited the United States, senior officials—including Berger and Albright—accorded him the treatment due a head of state and openly indicated that he was their candidate.

In late August, sensing Netanyahu's vulnerability, Arafat announced that he had canceled a meeting with Molcho because he was no longer interested in what he called "useless talks with Israel." Further undermining the Israeli government's authority, the U.S. Embassy encouraged talks between Arafat and opposition (Labor and Meretz Party) members of the Knesset, and Arafat told them that the Palestinians were "losing patience with the lack of progress in the peace negotiations."

Still determined not to be blamed for bringing down the peace process, Netanyahu officially abandoned Israel's long-standing demand—on the basis of Article 33 in the Palestinian Covenant itself—that the Palestinian National Council be convened to annul the clauses of the covenant calling for Israel's destruction. Netanyahu also formally declared his willingness to carry out the 13 percent withdrawal in the West Bank, and he even ignored a renewed spate of terrorism, including a bomb in Tel Aviv. Consequently, Ross announced his return to the region in order to salvage an agreement.

The Clinton administration's immediate goal was to have something ready to sign in Washington on September 13—the fifth anniversary of the signing of the Oslo accords. This plan hit a snag the moment Arafat realized what he would have to do in order to obtain the 13 percent withdrawal—that is, accept an agreement legitimizing Israel's right to exist. He wrote Clinton a letter raising doubts that Israel would carry out the 13 percent withdrawal and demanding a firm U.S. commitment to forcing Israel into an unconditional third withdrawal. The administration was very understanding about the PA's refusal to cooperate even after Netanyahu had been coerced into doing exactly what Arafat had demanded all along. "The Palestinians have withheld final approval," U.S. officials explained, "not because they have changed their mind, but because they believe this position is more strategic in case Israel decides to raise further demands."

In all of this, the White House was fixated on the Israeli withdrawal and the sustaining of "momentum." Senior U.S. officials traveling with Ross openly stated the administration's priorities, noting that the withdrawal issue had been "at the heart of U.S. diplomacy during the past year" and that its resolution would enable the parties "to focus on secondary issues" such as cooperating on security, fighting terrorism, and amending the covenant. They demonstrated complete lack of interest in the PA's hateful incitement against the Jews and Israel. The logical question—Can a population so incited, and an entity so inciting, be trusted as genuine "partners in peace"?—was never raised.

Once again, President Clinton had other concerns. With Independent Counsel Kenneth Starr closing in on him and impeachment hearings increasingly likely, a foreign policy "achievement" was a must. Moreover, the White House was convinced that any major progress in the peace process would improve the Democrats' chances in the 1998 congressional elections, commonly perceived as a launchpad for the 2000 presidential election. With the juicy details of his relationship with Monica Lewinsky prominently featured in the mainstream media, Clinton announced a summit at the Wye River Plantation in Maryland—Netanyahu and Arafat would themselves lead high-level delegations. Even though the Wye summit would convene on the eve of the congressional elections, Clinton stressed that he and his chief officials would personally lead the negotiations. He did not bother to mention that doing so would allow him to stay out of the media's limelight and minimize any negative impact on the elections.

————

PREPARATORY TALKS made clear how profound were the differences between the two sides despite the "agreement" on a 13 percent withdrawal. Israel provided the CIA's professional team with extensive material about the PA's cooperation with, and direct participation in, anti-Israel terrorism. Netanyahu set as a precondition for his coming to Wye a requirement that the United States come up with a well-defined plan for confronting terrorism that would include meaningful CIA supervision. Meanwhile, Arafat was trying to extort as much as possible in return for a promise that he would consider postponing the declaration of statehood scheduled for the following May; he would not hear anything about security cooperation.

At this point, fearing yet another stalemate, the administration hit upon the idea of pressuring Jerusalem to form a national-unity government, which would give Barak a prominent place in the government and, of course, in the Wye summit. Indyk and other senior officials went so far as to meet with Barak and other Labor Party leaders and urge them to join the government before Wye. The Americans argued that only Labor's participation would guarantee Israel the flexibility required to sustain the peace process. When the Netanyahu government learned about these contacts and raised the issue with the U.S. Embassy, the Americans claimed they were encouraging the formation of a national-unity government in order to protect Netanyahu against being toppled in a no-confidence vote as a result of the Right's defection. Barak told Netanyahu that he and his Labor colleagues would consider the American suggestion, but only if their participation would be crucial to "salvaging the peace process." Instead, Netanyahu appointed the uncompromising Ariel Sharon as foreign minister and took him, as well as the hawkish Sharansky, along to Wye.

On the eve of Wye, the Palestinians reminded Israel of the alternative to withdrawal. First came a series of violent riots in Hebron organized and carried out by the Fatah's own Tanzim squads. These operations soon escalated into attacks on Jewish targets with automatic fire—the first time the Tanzim squads had gone beyond leading violent demonstrations. Then, on October 19, the first day of the Wye summit, a HAMAS operative threw two hand grenades in a bus station in Beer Sheva during the morning rush hour, injuring at least sixty passengers. "What happened this morning is part of our continued resistance to the occupation of our land," Sheikh Yassin announced.

––––––

THE WYE SUMMIT was billed as the do-or-die milestone on the Palestinian track. The administration's idea was that if the Israeli and Palestinian delegations were essentially locked up together for ten days, they would start getting along on the personal level, building trust so that they would become more willing to make concessions. The Americans' supervision was carried out by an always-present high-level team—mainly Albright, Berger, Ross, and the new CIA Director, George Tenet—and Clinton himself was in Wye more often than not.

From the very beginning, Berger and Albright made their priorities clear. "What are you doing to our Arafat?" Albright asked the Israelis whenever Arafat went into one of his mood swings. Berger repeatedly threatened Netanyahu with Washington's declaring the collapse of the Wye initiative and blaming him. Eventually, the Israeli delegation resigned itself to the 13 percent second-phase withdrawal and an additional 2 percent in the third phase. The Israelis remained adamant, however, on securing in return a series of long-term tangible commitments on peaceful coexistence. Among the Israeli demands were the cancelation of the Palestinian Covenant and a public proclamation by Arafat that the PA no longer sought the destruction of Israel; the implementation of a CIA-supervised security plan, including the collection of illegal weapons (that is, the disarming of HAMAS, the Islamic Jihad, the Fatah, and the Tanzim); the building of an industrial park near Gaza to alleviate economic hardship while reducing the Palestinians' dependence on employment in Israel; and a commitment by Arafat to give up his unilateral declaration of independence on May 4, 1999. In addition, Netanyahu refused to release convicted terrorists "with blood on their hands."

Arafat and his delegation, for their part, aspired to gain for the PA as many aspects of recognition as a de facto state as possible, while taking as few tangible steps as possible concerning the security issues and the covenant.

Most intense were the negotiations over the covenant. Netanyahu wanted a legally binding process in which Arafat and the PA would irrevocably renounce the destruction of Israel. The Americans, who in effect negotiated for the Palestinians, held out for symbolic gestures that Arafat could live with. Eventually, the administration decided to hinge everything on Clinton's visit to Gaza and Jerusalem in December, during which he would personally oversee the cancelation of the covenant. (In fact, it would prove to be a non-cancelation, because the event did not follow the script in Article 33; but by that time everybody had a vested interest in not clarifying the issue: Clinton needed a media-grabbing event, Arafat wanted to be able to tell his people he had not canceled the covenant, and Netanyahu had to show a tangible achievement from the disastrous, one-sided Wye agreement.)

Two major issues not directly related to the Israeli-Palestinian dynamics had a major effect on Netanyahu's stance in the negotiations. The first was the Clinton administration's implicit threat not to provide Israel with an airlift and other emergency military assistance in case of a regional war, at a time when the IDF was still recovering from the crisis wrought by budgetary cuts and outright neglect under the Rabin-Peres government.

The other issue was the possible release of Jonathan Pollard, the convicted Israeli spy. Politically, the release of Pollard would have sweetened the pill of the Wye accords for Netanyahu's supporters from the Right. Throughout the negotiations, Clinton dangled this possibility in front of Netanyahu whenever the President wanted more Israeli concessions. On the summit's last day, at 4 A.M., Clinton changed his position and informed Netanyahu that Pollard would not be released after all, ostensibly because Tenet had threatened to resign if Pollard were released. Clinton subsequently insisted he had never suggested he would release Pollard. "Clinton can make everybody hear what he wants," a Jewish supporter of the president explained. However, by the time Netanyahu was told that Pollard would remain in jail, he had already committed to signing the Wye accords.

The closing days of the Wye summit were characterized by a series of mini-crises over Israel's "red lines." "You are holding here the President of the United States and wearing him out with your petty issues," Albright erupted at one point. What Netanyahu had done was refuse to give up on key security issues despite "creative" formulations by Clinton that would have absolved the CIA from responsibility for PA violations. Arafat conducted his usual last-minute brinkmanship, and Netanyahu engaged in some brinkmanship of his own, going so far as to order his delegation to pack their luggage before the summit was finished. Ultimately, Netanyahu succeeded in forcing the Americans and the Palestinians into some compromises on security issues—reinforcing the Clinton team's conviction that Netanyahu had to go. Whether he knew it or not, Netanyahu was sacrificing his political career on the altar of Israel's security.

By the time Netanyahu, Arafat, and Clinton signed the Wye accords on October 23, 1998, nobody had any serious illusions they would constitute the turning point in the quest for Middle East peace that all the participants referred to in their speeches. Clinton's approach was the most pragmatic: He was determined to engage Israel in a web of agreements so that there would be no way back for Jerusalem, irrespective of what might happen in the coming Israeli elections and notwithstanding the virtually inevitable eruption of Palestinian violence. As for the principals to the negotiations, Netanyahu needed a peacemaker's fig leaf in order to court the wary Israeli Center in the election campaign, and Arafat rejoiced in the forthcoming U.S. recognition at virtually no cost to the PA.

———

THE WYE ACCORDS, in which the PA committed once again to desisting from anti-Israeli incitement, did not curb the PA media or the PA-appointed preachers. On November 3, for example, PA-TV carried a religious program on the nature of Judaism. "There is no light nor teaching in their Torah today," viewers were told. "Their Torah today is just a collection of writings in which those people wrote lies about God, His prophets and His teachings . . . the Jews are the seed of Satan and the devils. . . . To their Prophets they attribute the greatest of crimes: murder, prostitution, and drunkenness. The Jews do not believe in God nor in the End of Days. . . . They invented it [the Torah] as a history book for the Jews, full of promises to Abraham, Isaac, and Jacob that they would be given the land of Palestine. . . . Their history is full of rebellion and humiliation—God protect us from humiliations! They have distorted the faith and exchanged the gift of God for heresy, rebellion, and prostitution."

An early November article in the PA-controlled *Al-Hayah al-Jadidah* picked up this theme: "Corruption is part of the nature of the Jews. So much so that it is only on rare occasions that one finds corruption in which Jews were not behind it. Their intense love of money and accumulating wealth is well known, and they do not care what method is used to achieve it." The Jews' "plotting mentality," furthermore, had given them a disproportionate influence over the United States. "It is interesting," the article concluded, "how those who are harmed by their curse continue to remain under their influence . . . among those who have been harmed in this manner are Bill Clinton, the president of the largest country in the world. . . . He began to carry out what World Zionism dictated to him out of fear that his proclivities would become revealed. Even though he is the head of the biggest country in the world, he understands that he is a servant of his desires, with which the plotters tripped him up." The obvious implication of this diatribe was that the Jews had coerced the United States into supporting an agreement unfavorable to Palestinian interests. Therefore, given the inherent duplicity of the Jews, it was impossible for the PA to adhere to such an agreement, despite the fact that Arafat had signed it.

Nevertheless, the Netanyahu government approved the Wye accords, and the Knesset ratified them. Consequently, the government ordered the IDF to conduct the first phase of the withdrawal, in effect raising the PA-controlled Area A from 3 percent to 10 percent of the territories and reducing the Israeli-controlled Area C from 73 percent to 71 percent (the rest being the jointly supervised Area B).

THE PAINFUL Israeli withdrawal—which neither Clinton nor Arafat had believed would take place—only served to highlight Jerusalem's vulnerability to American pressure. Hence, the PA was emboldened to start reneging on its latest commitments even before Clinton's visit to Gaza. In early December, the PA maintained that having a plan for confiscating weapons at some undetermined future time constituted implementation of its commitment to confiscate weapons—thus triggering the next Israeli withdrawal. The same logic applied to Arafat's signing a "presidential decree" on stopping anti-Jewish incitement in PA-controlled media and schools, rather than just stopping it. When the United States concurred with the Israeli insistence on "action" concerning weapons collection, Erekat came back with a progress report according to which "10 rifles, 2 grenades, 3 mines" had been confiscated from over a million Palestinians.

In late November, Arafat instructed Marwan Barghouti, the secretary of Fatah, to create a sense of urgency on the eve of Clinton's visit. On December 1, Barghouti convened a strategy session in Ramallah with the key leaders of the Fatah and the Tanzim. After deliberations that dragged on until midnight, they resolved to capitalize on the grassroots desire to secure the release of Palestinian prisoners in Israeli jails as the instrument for getting mobs rioting in the streets. The meeting worked out a detailed plan: The Tanzim would launch an ostensibly spontaneous "Intifadah for the prisoners," increasingly inflaming the Palestinian street, until the climax on December 14—the day of Clinton's visit to Gaza. After Arafat approved the plan, it was written up as a leaflet of the Fatah-controlled Palestinian Prisoner Club. The leaflet, headed "There can be no peace without the release of all the Palestinian and Arab prisoners from Israeli jails," was widely distributed throughout the territories. "Some 3,000 prisoners in jail have launched a hunger strike which will continue until their release," the leaflet stated. "We will not leave them alone in their struggle. . . . Our slogan is 'Freedom or Martyrdom.' The Palestinian Prisoner Club calls on all Palestinians to help the prisoners with their Intifadah for freedom. . . . We appeal to President Clinton to pressure Israel to release the prisoners. Their release is a fundamental condition for peace in the region."

The Tanzim duly began setting the Palestinian street ablaze with processions and violent demonstrations, with the demonstrators hurling stones and firebombs and setting flags on fire. Tanzim activists and the mobs they incited clashed with the IDF, leaving two Palestinians dead and some 200 injured. Then, on the eve of Clinton's arrival in Gaza, the "spontaneous" riots expanded to include public demonstrations against the Jewish settlements. Although these outbursts of hatred and violence were orchestrated by the Tanzim—part of Arafat's own Fatah Movement, which is the ruling party of the Palestinian Authority—nobody in Jerusalem or Washington openly questioned the viability of Arafat's recent commitments.

The Clinton administration's preference for engineering make-believe spectacles rather than tackling real challenges reached new heights on December 14, when Clinton himself presided over a meeting of the Palestinian National Council. Clinton's mere presence accorded the PA de facto recognition as a statelike entity. Clinton listened and applauded enthusiastically as Arafat rambled through a relatively mild speech asserting his right to declare independence—in violation of a Wye provision—and then called for a show of hands on annulling the Palestinian Covenant. Most of the delegates leaped to their feet, hands up high. Clinton again applauded. He then told the Palestinians, "What you have just done has nothing to do with the Israeli government—you were talking directly to the Israeli people." Back in Jerusalem, he told both the Israeli government and the media that the Palestinians had just annulled the Palestinian Covenant calling for Israel's destruction, thus opening a road to peace to be paved with additional Israeli concessions.

Not only was the Gaza spectacle a farce never intended to amend the covenant—for Article 33 stipulates the exact procedures to be followed for any amendment to be legal—but the PA-controlled media stressed that point repeatedly. Arafat himself was quick to deny that any changes had been made to the covenant. The official Voice of Palestine Radio announcement stated that "the PLO Central Council endorsed with an 81-vote majority President Arafat's letter to President Bill Clinton on amending [sometime in the future] some provisions of the Palestinian Charter." An official PA communiqué quoted Arafat's pronouncement that "amending the National Charter is none of Israel's business" and that "the Palestinians are carrying out what was . . . passed in the Palestinian committees and councils, and not on foreign orders."

Nevertheless, Jerusalem sought to put the best face on the Clinton visit. Israeli officials endorsed the United States' plan to resume the meetings of the working committees, which were expected to continue discussions on the release of prisoners and the next Israeli withdrawals. Clinton then pronounced the Middle East peace process "back on track" and said that Albright would soon return to the region to help sustain "the momentum."

Clinton's true sense of the dynamics of the Middle East was revealed when he publicly equated Palestinian terrorists and Israeli victims of terrorism. First, Clinton and Albright comforted several little girls whose fathers were among the terrorists "with blood on their hands" whom Israel would not release from jail. "Your father would be proud of you," Clinton told one girl. Clinton elaborated on the point at a meeting with Palestinian VIPs in Gaza. "I've had two profoundly emotional experiences in the last less than 24 hours. I was with Chairman Arafat, and four little children came to see me whose fathers are in Israeli prisons. Last night, I met some little children whose fathers had been killed in conflict with Palestinians, at the dinner that Prime Minister Netanyahu had for me. Those children brought tears to my eyes. We have to find a way for both sets of children to get their lives back and to go forward. . . . If I had met them in reverse order I would not have known which ones were Israeli and which Palestinian. If they had all been lined up in a row and I had seen their tears, I could not tell whose father was dead and whose father was in prison, or what the story of their lives were, making up the grief that they bore." The Israeli government was too shocked to react.

———

As President Clinton was shuttling between Jerusalem and Gaza, the House of Representatives was getting ready to vote on his impeachment. The real objective of the mid-December Middle East trip was to capture the imagination and support of the American people, particularly the politically effective Jewish community, and persuade them to exert pressure on Congress to permit the president to continue unhindered in his peacemaking endeavor.

This did not happen. Hence, returning to Washington, Clinton immediately turned to another popular cause: bombing Iraq for Saddam Hussein's failure to cooperate with U.N. weapon inspections. Between December 16 and 20—the week the full House was to debate the bill of impeachment—the United States and United Kingdom fired some 415 cruise missiles and dropped more than 600 bombs on Iraqi targets, causing negligible damage and only bolstering Saddam's resolve and his standing in the Arab world. "Operation Desert Fox," as the administration named it, was immediately redubbed "Operation Desert Starr" (after Kenneth Starr) by Washington cynics. In the short run, Clinton's ploy worked, for the House debate was postponed for a couple of days. In the long run it backfired. As the futility and arbitrary timing of the bombing campaign became clear, more and more officials openly talked about the *Wag the Dog* syndrome—a reference to a current movie in which a besieged White House stages a war in Albania in order to distract public attention from a president's failings. On December 19, the House of Representatives voted to impeach the president of the United States.

Meanwhile, despite the explicit Iraqi threats to strike at Israel, the administration pressured Netanyahu to refrain from retaliating under any circumstances. However, unlike the Bush administration in the 1990–91 Gulf crisis, the Clinton administration did not promise to come to Israel's aid in case the Iraqis did attack.

As for the Palestinians, less than a week after giving Clinton a thunderous welcome, the Palestinian Legislative Council (PLC) expressed its rejection of "the U.S.-UK attack on sisterly Iraq" and its "solidarity with and support for the fraternal Iraqi people, whose suffering increased under the recent attack." Arafat also instructed the Tanzim to resume the popular riots, which had been contained during Clinton's visit. This time the rioters bore English-language placards condemning the American and British strikes, and Tanzim operatives burned American, British, and Israeli flags. In Gaza, demonstrators burned the large American flags that had hung on the PLC building during Clinton's visit —in front of obliging American TV cameras.

As the bombing campaign in Iraq was ending, the riots were diverted into violent clashes with the IDF, in which several Palestinians were wounded. Through the new CIA-supervised security-coordination mechanism, Israel demanded that the PA prevent the riots from spilling over into Israeli-controlled areas. However, the administration refused to address the issue and instead urged Jerusalem to calm the situation by forbidding the IDF to clash with the rioters.

Meanwhile, in Damascus, the United States suffered the worst mob attack on one of its embassies since the invasion of the Tehran embassy in 1979. A mob of well over ten thousand demonstrated in the streets, shouting "Death to America!" Then a select thousand or so, all Ba'ath stalwarts, were permitted by the Syrian security forces to march through the upscale al-Rawdha neighborhood and storm the embassy and the ambassador's residence. With Syrian security forces looking on, the rioters used heavy stones to breach the embassy's outer defenses. Even though the Marine guards fired tear gas, the rioters succeeded in scaling the walls and tearing down the U.S. flag. They also smashed the windows of the ambassador's residence and destroyed his car, then broke into the residence itself and rampaged through the ground floor, smashing everything in sight. The ambassador's wife barely made it to the lockable "safe haven" room upstairs. Syrian Defense Minister Mustafa Tlass lauded the rioters; his statement was repeated in the official newspaper, *Tishrin*, with approving commentary. Foreign Minister Faruk al-Shara expressed regret but insisted the incident had been "spontaneous." In order not to harm the peace process, the State Department confined itself to a pro forma protest.

———

DURING BILL CLINTON'S visit to Jerusalem, he met with Barak and personally promised him all-out support in challenging Netanyahu. Therefore, when Netanyahu did offer to form a national-unity government, Barak refused. On December 24, 1998, the Knesset voted a second time to disband, making general elections necessary.

Although the Clinton team decided to avoid an outright endorsement of Barak, the Labor Party and its allies hired as campaign consultants three Americans who had been prominent in Clinton's 1992 election campaign: James Carville, Robert Shrum, and Stanley Greenberg. None of these high-level Democratic activists would have agreed to get involved in a foreign election campaign without the blessing of the Clinton White House. Indeed, Carville told the *New York Times* that he "regularly briefs the President on the progress of the Labor leader's campaign."

Almost daily, unnamed senior officials at the White House and State Department provided the Washington media with stories about Netanyahu's derelictions concerning the settlements, building in Jerusalem, even Israeli-Russian relations. Most effective was the blame assigned to Netanyahu for the evident failure of the Wye accords. At the core of this campaign was the fact that, as the *Jerusalem Post's* David Bar-Illan put it, "Netanyahu made the incredibly naive assumption that he could rely on unwritten understandings with America to bridge vague agreements." High-level Israeli sources explained that in the concluding phase of the Wye negotiations, Clinton, Netanyahu, and Arafat "solemnly agreed" that at each stage of the accords' implementation, the Palestinians would first honor their obligations and only then would Israel carry out the withdrawal associated with that stage. At Clinton's insistence, this agreement "was not put into writing to avoid embarrassing Arafat." Now, the White House exploited this vagueness against Netanyahu.

In March, the White House sent Ross to the Middle East to coerce Israel into another unilateral withdrawal to prevent the collapse of the peace process. If Netanyahu agreed, he would demonstrate his susceptibility to American pressure; if he refused, a major crisis between Jerusalem and Washington would ensue, thus warranting the administration's support for Barak. However, confronted with the evidence concerning the Palestinians' persistent violation of the Wye accords and other obligations and reminded about the trilateral undertaking at Wye, Ross conceded that Israel was right to refuse further withdrawals. He even told *Haaretz*'s David Makovsky off the record that "The Clinton administration has decided to accept the position of Israel that it need not implement the second pullback from the West Bank under the Wye agreement until the Palestinian Authority has adhered to all its obligations."

The administration erupted with fury. State Department spokesman Jamie Rubin, and soon afterward Albright herself, flatly contradicted Ross's findings and issued stern warnings to Israel. "On the Palestinian side," Albright said in a message to the American Jewish Committee, "we have seen serious efforts to prevent terrorist strikes, to renounce the Palestinian Covenant, and to avoid a unilateral declaration of statehood. On the Israeli side, implementation has stalled and, unfortunately, unilateral settlement activity has persisted. This is a source of real concern to us, because of its destructive impact on the ability to pursue peace." This pressure campaign continued unabated until the day of the Israeli elections.

The administration remained silent when, on April 28, in passing a resolution to postpone the declaration of independence, the Palestinian National Council affirmed that the boundaries of the eventual Palestinian State would be the November 1947 boundaries set out in U.N. Resolution 181. Indeed, the administration had assisted Arafat in arranging a meeting with U.N. Secretary-General Kofi Annan on March 21, in which Arafat received official confirmation that Resolution 181 was still valid. That maneuver and the entire preoccupation with boundaries other than those codified in the 1949 cease-fire accords between Israel and its Arab neighbors violated both the letter and the spirit of the entire Oslo process.

Even Palestinian officials associated with the peace camp and with Oslo had begun revisiting the issue of borders. In late December, the chairman of the Palestinian Legislative Council and chief Palestinian negotiator, Ahmed Qurai (Abu-Alaa), had explained to IMRA's Lerner the official PA position regarding Israel's future borders. Although all previous agreements had used Israel's pre-1967 borders as their point of reference, Abu-Alaa now maintained that the borders of the future independent Palestinian State would be the boundaries set in 1947. "The borders which were set by the U.N. partition plan resolution in 1947 were the relevant boundaries for U.N. Resolution 181, which is the basis of international recognition of the creation of the State of Israel," Abu-Alaa declared, dismissing as irrelevant any agreements signed by Arafat or, for that matter, himself.

Meanwhile, the Barak-led "One Israel" coalition and its American advisers were conducting a sleek U.S.-style campaign, showering the public with glitzy ads. Their activists also tore down the posters of the Likud and other opposition parties and disrupted their public gatherings. The Barak campaign was by Israeli standards an exceptionally expensive undertaking. Within a short time, the Labor Party—which was already burdened with a $25 million debt—managed to spend some $50 to $80 million on its anti-Netanyahu campaign—ten times what the Likud spent. The money was raised in outright violations of the strict Israeli laws on campaign financing. In early 2000, the state comptroller of Israel issued a damning report on the funding of the Barak campaign, determining that huge amounts of money, some from foreign donors, were funneled through bogus and intertwining foundations. The government fined "One Israel" an unprecedented $3.2 million and launched a still unfolding criminal investigation.

In fact, most of Barak's funding was collected in the United States through several prominent Clinton supporters, including Daniel Abraham, Lawrence Tisch, and Haim Saban. For example, in early 1999, Barak attended a fundraiser at Saban's Beverly Hills mansion, where he essentially delivered a campaign speech. The invitation was for "a Special Evening Honoring Ehud Barak, Chairman, Israel Labor Party," and the guests were instructed to "Make checks payable to the Shefa Fund." Saban matched his guests' donations, raising the total collected that evening alone to about $600,000. Saban's guests had no illusions as to what was going on. One of them, Danny Dimbort, the Israeli president of Nu Image productions in Los Angeles, acknowledged to *Yediot Aharonot* that he wrote the Shefa Fund a check for $10,000 at Saban's event in order "to help Barak win the election."

With such massive intervention on his opponent's side, Netanyahu and the Likud lost the elections on May 17, 1999. The Israeli public was apprehensive about alienating the clearly anti-Netanyahu United States and afraid of the horrific war the Americans predicted would break out if Netanyahu were permitted to ruin the peace process. A new era had dawned in the Clinton administration's Middle East policy.

11

A Toy Story (1999)

Barak's Capitulations; Arafat's Growing Confidence

THE KNESSET confirmed Ehud Barak's government on July 7 in the aftermath of convoluted coalition-building negotiations. It would be the most leftist/dovish government in Israel's history.

Even during the post-election/pre-confirmation period, Barak both directly and indirectly had an impact on the regional dynamics. Just like Rabin, whose self-appointed heir he was, he turned first to the Syrian track in order to alleviate the threat of a regional war. For a long time, the Clinton administration had been demanding the withdrawal of the South Lebanon Army (SLA) from the Jezzine enclave—a predominantly Christian area north of the Israeli-held security zone—as a sign of good faith toward Syria. Netanyahu had argued that such a move would amount to legitimizing Syria's hegemony over Lebanon; therefore, his government—with help from the U.S. Congress—had resisted the administration's pressure. Barak, however, was eager to prove himself in accord with the Clinton administration, and he was convinced that Israeli concessions over Lebanon would induce Syrian goodwill and reciprocity regarding security arrangements on the Golan Heights. Hence, during the election campaign, SLA Commander General Antoine Lahad was informed that if Barak came to power, Jezzine would be given up in order to jump-start negotiations with the Syrians on a Lebanon-first basis.

Bowing to the inevitable, and with Netanyahu still in power, Lahad worked out with the IDF withdrawal plans to be completed under favorable conditions. The withdrawal from Jezzine took place in late May, immediately after the Israeli elections. The triumphant HizbAllah forces that entered Jezzine initially behaved themselves, inflicting minimal retribution on the civilian population and on former SLA personnel who elected to stay behind. However, as soon as the Clinton administration lost interest in Lebanon, the judicial and extrajudicial persecution began.

Ultimately, the sacrifice of Jezzine bought no benefits from Damascus, because Clinton had other priorities set for Barak. In early July, hours after the confirmation of his government, Barak called Clinton, who invited him to come to Washington the following week. In the meantime, Clinton urged Barak to "renew the diplomatic momentum" on the Palestinian track. Clinton recommended that, as a "confidence-building gesture," Barak freeze all settlement construction and implement Arafat's understanding of the Wye accords. Barak explained his preference for delaying the implementation of certain sections of the interim accords until the final-status talks; and he also informed Clinton that he intended to meet with Mubarak, Arafat, and King Abdallah II of Jordan (who had acceded to the throne in January, upon the death of his father, King Hussein) before he came to Washington.

Meeting Mubarak in Alexandria, Barak learned that the Palestinian issue was top priority for him too. Mubarak was willing to grant Barak an "extension" of about two months to "learn the problems" associated with the Wye accords, but he stressed that he would make no gestures toward Barak until Israel completed its Wye withdrawals and froze all construction in the territories. Barak reiterated his determination to further the peace process on both the Palestinian and Syrian tracks. "I am determined to make peace, while protecting Israel's national interests," he told Mubarak.

Barak met Arafat at the Erez checkpoint. "Our primary objective today was to establish a basis of mutual trust, so crucial to the possibility of any future agreements," Barak said. "Both sides have suffered enough." His government would abide by all of Israel's international accords, he told Arafat; however, he believed there were better ways to reach a permanent agreement than by blindly following Wye, and he would like to work with Arafat to devise a framework based on Wye "but not prisoner to it." On the settlements, Barak came closer to the Arab demands than any previous Israeli prime minister. "We will not establish any new settlements, nor will we dismantle any at this stage," Barak said. "I am committed to a block of settlements. All of this will be dealt with in the final-status talks."

Arafat called Barak "a friend and partner" and agreed to give him six to eight weeks to formulate an outline for the continuation of negotiations. "I hereby reiterate my full commitment to work as a partner with Mr. Barak to achieve the peace of the brave, as I did with my partner, Mr. Rabin. A just, comprehensive, lasting peace must be achieved on all tracks, including the Syrian and Lebanese tracks," Arafat declared. "The Palestinian Authority will continue to carry out its responsibilities pertaining to the agreements it signed. We expect the Israeli government to implement all of its Wye River obligations. This includes the freeing of Palestinian prisoners; continued implementation of the Hebron agreement; construction of the Gaza port; and the opening of a 'safe passage' from Gaza to the West Bank. We will continue to express our lack of tolerance for violence and terror, whether the terror is committed by Israelis or Palestinians." Arafat then slapped Barak in the face by reiterating his demand that Israel discontinue all settlement activities and rejecting any notion of forgoing scheduled Wye withdrawals in favor of final-status negotiations.

————

ON THE EVE of Barak's arrival in Washington for his first state visit, President Clinton told a Democratic fund-raiser in Florida that he was "as excited as a young kid with a new toy." While Clinton feigned an apology for the "toy" remark, and Barak graciously brushed it off as a non-issue, in retrospect this comment, more than anything else that would be said during the two men's short but intense relationship, accurately characterized Clinton's attitude toward the eager-to-please Barak.

The administration had been working to create the impression that it respected Barak's ideas. For example, Ambassador Edward Walker, Indyk's successor, said, "We will be not a player, but a helper and facilitator," echoing Barak's stated preference for direct Israeli-Palestinian negotiations. When Barak arrived in Washington, Clinton gave him a warm welcome. However, in his public remarks before their first private meeting, Clinton made his expectations clear. "I am delighted to welcome Prime Minister Barak to Washington," Clinton said. "America will help as you move forward, as you put implementation of the Wye River Agreement back on course"—Wye, rather than the combined negotiations Barak had proposed to Arafat. Barak immediately changed his own course to conform to Clinton's statement. "We abide by an international agreement, Wye Agreement included. It had been signed by an Israeli freely elected government, by the Americans and by Chairman Arafat. We are committed to live up to it. But there is a need," he clarified, "to combine the implementation of Wye with the moving forward of the permanent status agreement. But only through an agreement with Arafat after mutual, open, frank and direct discussion." Then, remembering his coalition partners in Jerusalem, Barak reiterated his belief "in a strong block of settlements that will include most of the settlers in Judea-Samaria and the Gaza Strip."

Starting with this visit, Clinton accorded the just-elected Barak special treatment—including a weekend at Camp David—normally given only to veteran leaders and longtime friends. Clinton won Barak over through this kind of personal attention, rather than substantive discussions. In the process, Israel virtually lost its sovereignty—that is, its ability to make decisions affecting its own vital security interests.

———

DESPITE ALL THE OPTIMISM expressed by Barak, Clinton, and even Arafat, one lingering issue remained unresolved. A permanent fixture in all the formulations concerning the eventual final-status agreement was the requirement that the Palestinian Authority contain Islamist terrorism. And that, Arafat could not, and would not, do. On the contrary, just as the Israeli-Palestinian track was being rejuvenated, Arafat was concentrating on solidifying his agreements with HAMAS and its primary sponsor, Iran.

In early July, while Barak was shuttling from Alexandria to Gaza and getting ready to visit Clinton for the first time, Hussein Sheikh ol-Islam, the Iranian ambassador to Damascus and a staunch supporter of the HizbAllah, outlined Tehran's perception of the peace process. In principle, Sheikh ol-Islam explained, Tehran had no objection to a negotiated settlement between Israel and Syria, because it would expedite the return of the Golan Heights to Syria. However, the Arabs' and Muslims' ultimate objective—the destruction of Israel—would not change because of an Israeli withdrawal. Sheikh ol-Islam stressed that Tehran was aware of the prevailing circumstances in Damascus and would tailor its approach to the peace process accordingly. Tehran expected that the Israeli-Syrian negotiations would resume "soon" and that there would be "great achievements before the American President engages in the 2000 elections" because, the ambassador said, "Clinton will exercise pressure to reach a peace agreement." Sheikh ol-Islam added that Syria and Iran had resolved to expand their sponsorship of the HizbAllah, because "continuing the [HizbAllah] operations will pressure Israel to withdraw." And, he predicted, "the operations [would] continue after the resumption of the peace talks."

Shortly afterward, Arafat's Fatah movement echoed these sentiments in a major policy paper on the Palestinian approach to the negotiations. The Arabs must overcome "the difficulties which resulted from the pro-Israeli bias of the Oslo Agreement," the Fatah paper declared. "To prevent a total breakdown in the peace process, it is time to lay down new terms of reference for negotiation." Fatah flatly rejected Barak's proposal for combining the interim Wye-related negotiations with permanent-status talks. As far as Fatah was concerned, the Oslo-to-Wye process already required Israel to withdraw from virtually all the territories, including Jerusalem, and stipulated that permanent borders would be discussed beyond that. Furthermore, if the permanent-status negotiations were to attain "real peace and stability," the result would have to be a contiguous Palestinian state—a state that has "its borders with Egypt in Gaza in the South and with Jordan in the East"—rather than, as at present, a collection of isolated pockets.

Finally the Fatah paper emphasized that the permanent agreement must include the unconditional implementation of the right of return. "The historic peace agreements grew out of the need to put an end to all wars in the region and to establish a true and lasting peace. Such a peace, called first by Palestinians and now by Barak, echoing them, the 'peace of the brave,' must ensure the rights of Palestinians as set forth in international resolutions. These rights must include, among others, the Palestinians' right of return to the land from which they have been exiled. The term 'peace of the brave' implies that both parties to the peace should achieve historic rights based on principles fair to both."

Just as Barak was returning from Washington, Sheikh Yassin warned Arafat against any further sellouts to Israel. "Beware of normalization," Yassin urged, "and remember that those betting on Barak will have their hopes dashed. You want Palestine without using force, without jihad or martyrdom. You want a gift from Barak and the U.S., the ones that attacked Tunis and killed Abu-Jihad, attacked Lebanon and killed Abu-Yussuf al-Najar and his colleagues" (a reference to the April 1973 raid in which Arafat's closest aides in Black September were assassinated; the raid was led by Barak, who at that time commanded an elite special-forces unit). The Zionists understand "nothing except the language of force," and anyone who believed that it would be possible "to recover Palestine without this" was dreaming.

What was happening in the peace process, Yassin continued, was "a surrender that would never be accepted" by the Palestinians. "We consider Palestine to be Islamic from the [Jordan] River to the [Mediterranean] Sea," whereas what was being offered under the Oslo and Wye accords was a tiny Palestinian "state" dotted with Jewish settlements and crisscrossed by Israeli roads. "What I want," Sheikh Yassin concluded, "is not a meaningless and weak state shredded into bits by settlements but a victorious and sovereign one capable of waging jihad."

These were not idle words, for a new generation of HAMAS terrorists was already preparing for operations. Significantly, these terrorists were not known to Israeli or U.S. intelligence services; they came out of an exclusive IRGC training camp located not far from Tehran—a major complex also used to train Islamist fighters for and from the Balkans. The training program, directly supervised by Ayatollah Khamenei, included advanced bomb-making techniques for both martyrdom and remote-control bombing, network organization, counterintelligence and security measures, clandestine communications, and other skills required to make HAMAS a highly proficient organization rather than just a network of dedicated individuals. By early July 1999, graduates of this program were already running a web of clandestine cells in both Gaza and the West Bank. As pressure began building on Arafat to immerse himself in negotiations with Barak, Arafat notified Sheikh Yassin and other HAMAS leaders that once the talks stalled, he would give these HAMAS cells the green light to take on the Zionists.

Throughout this period, Arafat himself was talking with the Syrian-sponsored Palestinian terrorist organizations in order to bolster their support for Fatah. In early August, he met with a PFLP delegation, resulting in what PNC Speaker Salim al-Zaanun called "a major success." He also met with the DFLP leader, Nayif Hawatimah, who later reported Arafat's guarantee that the PA would not compromise on the right of return in the final-status talks.

———

IN LATE JULY, Barak and Arafat met at the Erez crossing to discuss the Israeli plan for combining implementation of the Wye accords with acceleration of the permanent-status talks. Barak noted that Clinton had endorsed his plan, and Arafat agreed to set up a joint panel that would issue recommendations within two weeks. Ultimately, however, Arafat knew there was no reason for the PA to accept the Israeli proposal, because Barak assured him that if the PA refused to accept any recommendations to change Wye, Israel would implement it as it stood.

The next day, senior Palestinian officials disclosed that Arafat was "very disappointed" by Barak's attitude and considered their summit meeting a "resounding failure." According to chief PLO negotiator Nabil Shaath, Barak would have to "stop talking and start acting" if he did not want the peace process to collapse. Shaath added that Barak could not legitimately oppose releasing Palestinian prisoners because he, too, "has blood on his hands."

Early August found the Clinton administration in a quandary over how to cope with Arafat's refusal to accept the generous deal it had brokered. The only option was to extract greater "flexibility" from Barak. Toward that end, Albright announced that she was postponing her forthcoming trip to the region until she could "see real progress on both the Syrian and Palestinian tracks." Although no party was directly blamed for the impasse, only Israel was negotiating on both tracks. Albright also notified Barak that she had no intention of mediating between him and Arafat: They should arrive at a resolution by themselves before she arrived. Since Arafat was not handed a comparable demand, Jerusalem had no doubt that Albright had placed the onus to deliver "results" on it. At the same time, however, U.S. officials concurred with Barak's position that "permanent-status talks are part of the Wye accords" and criticized Arafat for "placing obstacles" on the road to meaningful talks.

Barak understood what was expected of him, and the next day he named his personal envoy to Arafat—Brigadier General (Res.) Yitzhak Segev, a former military governor of the Gaza Strip who was known for his good relations with the local Palestinian elite and who was now running the Children of Abraham charity promoting Israeli-Palestinian peace. Segev met with Arafat to jump-start the stalled contacts between Saeb Erekat and Barak's attorney, Gilad Sher, on Wye's implementation and to assure Arafat of Barak's sincerity.

In Jerusalem, senior diplomatic sources stressed Barak's conviction that "a compromise will ultimately be found." They added their perception that "the Palestinians have not yet accustomed themselves to the new atmosphere and are turning every little thing into a drama in an effort to enlist Arab and international pressure against Israel." In fact, the PA had just declared a "crisis" in the talks, and Arafat turned down Barak's offer to discuss the impasse. Instead, Arafat delivered an emotional speech, urging Palestinians to "march to the walls of Jerusalem" so that "every child [could] wave a Palestinian flag on the Temple Mount." Alarmed, Barak assured Washington that if Arafat continued to reject his proposal, Israel would begin unilaterally implementing the next phase of the Wye withdrawals in September.

Barak was now focused on attaining what he termed "a pre-final-status agreement." Toward this end, Israel would unilaterally release prisoners and evacuate settlements. In return, Barak sought Arafat's agreement to a revised Wye withdrawal map and a joint declaration outlining the principles for final-status talks. Barak was convinced that the key to his success lay in Arafat's failing health—that is, Arafat would be amenable to compromises once he was assured that he would become the first president of a Palestinian State before his death.

In fact, Arafat's reaction was to send emissaries to both HAMAS and Fatah activists to convey word that he would appreciate some "pressure" on Israel and the Americans. Regarding the HAMAS leadership's desire to launch a new wave of martyr-bombers at the heart of Israel, Arafat, his emissary said, regarded the HAMAS martyrs as Palestine's "strategic weapons"—the way states regard their ballistic missiles. He would be ready to use them the moment Palestinian strategic interests were in danger; however, the emissary continued, that was not the case now. For the time being, HAMAS deferred to Arafat and confined itself to ambushes and other shootings in Samaria and the Hebron area. Meanwhile, the Fatah Hawks launched violent demonstrations at Netzarim junction, in Hebron, and at Joseph's Tomb in Nablus.

Arafat was fully aware of the political implications of his cooperation with HAMAS. "We gave Israel security during the elections, enabling Barak to be elected, and now you prefer the Syrians to us," a senior PA official complained to Ron Ben-Yishai of *Yediot Aharonot*. "The hint," as Ben-Yishai interpreted it, "was that only one mass terrorist attack would be enough for Israel to put the Palestinians back at the top of the agenda."

IN LATE AUGUST, Albright announced her intended arrival in the Middle East to oversee the signing of an agreement on implementation of the Wye accords. Since there had been no progress warranting Albright's optimism, this announcement forced the Israelis to accelerate negotiations. The pressure on Barak was further increased when Erekat announced that he would go to Washington to coordinate positions with Albright before her visit. To prevent the Palestinians from taking the lead, David Levy publicly predicted the completion of an agreement before Albright's arrival. A senior Israeli official even knew the agreement would be called "The Agreement for the Implementation of the Wye River Memorandum and the Resumption of Talks on the Permanent Status." A couple of days later, Erekat, who had stayed in Jerusalem at Barak's request, agreed with Sher upon a timetable for implementing the Wye accords, including fixed dates for two further sets of West Bank withdrawals. In principle, the PA agreed to stretch out the timetable stipulated in Wye in return for Israel's willingness to withdraw from a greater segment of territory during the first phase.

Arafat, meanwhile, had traveled to Egypt to consult with Mubarak, who assured him the Palestinians would get virtually everything they wanted if they signed an agreement while Albright was in the region. Consequently, Erekat sent Barak two "gap-bridging" proposals that, once accepted by Israel, would effectively conclude the negotiations. As a final sweetener, Barak offered to recognize a Palestinian state as early as January 2000, in exchange for a postponement of the formal negotiations on Jerusalem and the right of return until after the next Israeli elections and the final-status talks.

Still, with Albright already in the region, Arafat launched a last-minute war of nerves, putting the entire agreement in doubt, by renewing his demand for the release of 50 terrorists who had killed Jews. Israel had already agreed to release 350 terrorists who had "only" killed fellow Arabs or wounded Jews. The night of September 2–3, Albright met with Barak for over three hours. While officially the Clinton administration was "taking a back seat" in this round of negotiations, Albright implored Barak to take the extra step to come to an agreement before she left. Barak finally concurred and accepted a new clause "prohibiting either side from taking unilateral steps to alter the status of the West Bank and Gaza Strip in permanent status talks," which in the Palestinian interpretation endorsed by Albright was a euphemism for "prohibiting the Israelis from building new settlements on the West Bank." A gracious Arafat announced on the afternoon of Friday, September 3, that an agreement had been reached and that it would be signed the following evening in Sharm el-Sheikh.

––––––

A FEW HOURS after Arafat's announcement, the imam of al-Aqsa Mosque delivered a sermon about the ills afflicting the Muslim world and the means of overcoming them. "There is a dangerous disease," he said, "that was intensified inside the hearts of the Muslims today. The Muslim Ummah has lost herself because of this destructive disease. This disease is heedlessness. The Muslims today are heedless when it comes to applying the laws of Islam in their lives, or when it comes to living their life according to the rulings of Quran and Sunnah." The imam surveyed numerous manifestations of this disease—from the behavior of the secularized individual to communal patterns of behavior—and then zeroed in on the most threatening new development: "Finally, heedlessness comes when you take non-Muslims as friends and protectors along with the current rulers in the Muslim world today. It also comes when some of the Muslims negotiate with Jews over Islamic lands." Therefore, the Imam implied, before the Muslim masses can confront heedlessness, they must first rid themselves of the rulers who are pushing them into the fold of the West.

The day after the signing at Sharm el-Sheikh, two car bombs exploded in northern Israel, one in Tiberias and the other in Haifa. The Tiberias car bomb exploded prematurely, killing two terrorists and injuring four bystanders, one of them critically. The Haifa bomb also exploded ahead of time, killing the terrorist. The terrorists were identified as Israeli-Arabs aided by HAMAS elements from the PA's autonomous areas. Given Arafat's view of martyr-bombers as strategic weapons, the decision to carry out two simultaneous attacks aimed at inflicting heavy civilian casualties attests to strategic planning at the highest echelon of HAMAS. The discrepancy between the experienced engineers who had prepared the bombs and the inexperienced terrorists who blew themselves up suggested a well-planned but hastily implemented operation. Ultimately, despite its apparent failure, this operation served both the Islamists and Arafat: The Islamists had demonstrated their viability and defiance, while Arafat had "proof" that his efforts in "confronting terrorism" warranted Israel's and the United States' looking the other way on all his other violations of the accords he had signed.

The Sharm el-Sheikh Memorandum was presented as a refinement of, and renewal of commitment to, the 1998 Wye accords, the 1995 Interim Agreement (Oslo B), and all other agreements concluded since September 1993. Sher called the memorandum "a new way to fulfill earlier commitments." It stipulated an accelerated resumption of the permanent-status negotiations on the basis of U.N. Security Council Resolutions 242 and 338, and it set a target date of one year for the completion of the entire scope of negotiations. In addition, Israel committed to unilaterally opening a safe-passage road between Gaza and Hebron and permitting the Palestinians to build a full-scale seaport in Gaza.

However, the Sharm el-Sheikh Memorandum differed significantly from all previous Israel-PA agreements. The Memorandum stated only that both sides would "make every effort" to reach a final-status agreement. Further-more, it committed Israel to a series of specific withdrawals that would give the PA control of 41 to 42 percent of the West Bank, while delinking these Is-raeli withdrawals from Palestinian implementation of past and present com-mitments. To ensure that Israel would not raise the issue of Palestinian implementation as a reason to stop the withdrawals—Israel's only leverage over the PA—Albright attached to the memorandum a letter to Arafat af-firming the delinking. "It is our understanding," Albright wrote, "that the implementation of the outstanding [Israeli] commitments emanating from the Memorandum will proceed as agreed upon and scheduled regardless of developments in the negotiations related to Permanent Status issues." More-over, the memorandum cleared the way for the unilateral declaration of Palestinian independence by permitting Arafat to declare the independence of all the territory then under PA control if Israel and the PA failed to reach an agreement by the target date.

"I assert that we extend our hand once again to Mr. Barak, a new part-ner in the peace process," Arafat said publicly, "and we are ready for contin-uing cooperation to make the peace of the brave a reality." To his confidants, Arafat claimed that the memorandum committed the United States to sup-porting a unilateral declaration of Palestinian statehood within a year, and he emphasized that this and other U.S. commitments were the sole reason he had signed it.

At the end of the week, the Islamists put Arafat on notice that this was not good enough. In his Friday sermon, the Imam of al-Aqsa Mosque pro-claimed that Muslims must be ruled by an Islamic government. He then ar-gued that most of the commitments the PA had made over the course of the Oslo process were un-Islamic. In formulating his definition of corrupt and un-Islamic "rulers," the Imam clearly had Arafat in mind: "The corruption starts from the top, and the corruption is fought from the top. Look at the ef-fect when the rulers legislate a law that permits usury, or permits alcohol, and another law that permits the establishment of casinos, or when the rulers legislate a law that forbids carrying Islam and portrays sincere active Muslims as terrorists and fundamentalists. The rulers are responsible for subjugating the Muslim Ummah to the imperialist infidels."

In case anybody had missed the point, the Imam criticized the PA for committing even to coexistence with the hated Jews. "Now listen to one of the Oslo agreements the rulers here are trying to implement now," the Imam warned. "They are collaborating with the imperialist infidels to falsify history in order for the treason to become a heroism; they want the next generation to discard its Islamic identity. They want to efface the Islamic concepts that talk about the Jews in order for the next generation of Muslims to accept the existence of Israel as a fact and as an advantage. What kind of lowliness they are trying to implant in our next generation! Islam says about Jews that they are enemies. Islam says about the Jews: 'Fight them,' 'Kill them,' 'Drive them out.' Islam says about the Jews that they are infidels. But these corrupt rulers want us to say that the Jews are brothers in belief, that they are our cousins, that they are our neighbors, that they are our partners in the peace process."

The Imam then outlined the proper Islamist solution to the challenge that the PA and allied Arab governments constituted: the establishment of an Islamic caliphate. "I swear by Allah that the Islamic State is close and it will overthrow all their thrones. It will overthrow this alleged peace process. . . . Allah had promised us through Prophet Muhammad (peace be upon Him) that a guided Khilafah [caliphate] will be established. It will be established over the thrones of these corrupt agents to the imperialist infidels. It will liberate this Masjid [al-Aqsa Mosque], it will kill Jews, and it will open Rome [that is, overthrow the Vatican]. This means that the coming Islamic state will become a superpower!" Throughout the sermon, the crowd interjected, "God is Great!" "Slaughter the Jews!" and a host of other militant rallying cries.

Even though the PA had just committed to curbing incitement and even though the Imam was Arafat's own appointee, the PA did nothing to prevent this sermon from being delivered and subsequently broadcast throughout the PA area and the entire Muslim world. Jerusalem was immediately advised by the Clinton administration not to do anything about this outburst of hatred in order to "give Arafat time" to get his PA in order.

———

IN OCTOBER, Israel started implementing the Sharm el-Sheikh Memorandum as if everything were on track. The IDF started evacuating small Jewish outposts in the West Bank, and Israel opened the safe-passage road between Gaza and Hebron without imposing strict security measures. Two days later, a terrorist squad from Gaza attacked Jews near Hebron. The PA had done nothing to prevent the incident and made no attempt to investigate it, and the new arrangements in Hebron hampered the IDF's ability to investigate. Nevertheless, Israel did not block the road, and the IDF continued preparing for the major withdrawal scheduled for November 5. The incitement in the PA-controlled media continued unabated, and the PA cited "technical difficulties" as the reason why the Israeli-Palestinian incitement committee could not meet. Starting in mid-October, there was a rash of "escapes" from jail of terrorists whose long-term incarceration the CIA was supposed to monitor.

It was against this background that CIA Director George Tenet arrived in Israel in late October for discussions with Barak and Israel's intelligence chiefs on what Tenet called "methods of cooperation with Palestinian security services" in combatting regional terrorism. Tenet urged Israel to maintain a "realistic" approach toward Arafat's difficulties in furthering the peace process rather than insisting on a crackdown on Islamist terrorist organizations.

Little wonder that Barak was beginning to doubt the viability of the peace process. At the same time, he could not bring himself to confront the Clinton administration with the grim reality. Therefore, he started to float the idea of unilateral separation as Israel's most realistic objective. In a cabinet meeting on October 24, he stressed "the need for a physical separation between Israel and the Palestinians as a logical imperative—from a political, security, moral, and economic standpoint." He noted there was no need to sever all contact with the PA. "We are talking," Barak told his ministers, "about a separation that will create good neighborly relations, mutual respect and cooperation—and give expression to the interests of both sides." He added that the "long-term security interest of the State of Israel" would be served better by improving the PA's economy than by political dynamics such as a peace process.

Fatah in effect gave the PA's reply in a major policy document issued in late October. The document lamented the revival of the peace process under American supervision and noted that the primary challenge facing the Palestinians was disengaging from the constraints imposed upon them by the regime of international negotiations so that they could pursue their real objectives. Fatah declared that the Palestinians should not waver from their "call for One Palestine." One Palestine, in effect, "would not only mean people living in Gaza and the West Bank"; rather, "it would include all Palestinians, in the Diaspora and wherever the land of Palestine exists in the minds of Arabs and Muslims and of peace-loving peoples throughout the world." As before, Fatah emphasized sharing the burden with the Islamists: "Our own internal unity is vital to our effort: both those Palestinians who support the Oslo agreements and those who oppose them must shoulder their responsibilities. It is not useful at this point for any single party to turn its back on the negotiations now, on the grounds that it rejects the terms of reference of the negotiating process."

Having been presented with this document, the Clinton administration chose to ignore its implications for the advice Tenet had just dispensed to the

Israelis. Instead, the administration immediately rallied to sustain the peace process by arranging for a trilateral summit in Oslo in early November. First Barak and Arafat met in order to iron out lingering issues concerning the implementation of the Sharm el-Sheikh Memorandum, but their meeting led nowhere. The next evening Clinton joined them in an effort to reach common ground. Still, all they could agree to do was to meet again in early 2000 to finalize the framework agreement for the final status. Although the trilateral summit ended without substantial results, the administration hailed it as a great success. "We have infused new life into the process," President Clinton summed up

Once again HAMAS demurred. "Clinton, Arafat, and Barak met in Oslo," its communiqué said, "to liquidate what remains of the Palestinian rights by rescheduling the phases of the so-called 'final solution' [HAMAS actually used the term usually associated with the Jewish Holocaust], which will be implemented in several years' time. In the interim, the Zionist Enemy will certainly legitimize all facts created by the Oslo accords." HAMAS noted the circumstances of the Oslo summit and the needs of the key participants for personal achievements at the expense of the Palestinians. "This summit was . . . attended only by an American President who begs for peace in order to enter history, a Chairman of an Authority who begs for the survival of the Oslo accords, and a swindling, arrogant Zionist Prime Minister who imposes his conditions on the other two." Thus, according to HAMAS, Clinton and Barak were able to pressure Arafat once again into committing to "concerted efforts to suppress our people's right of jihad and resistance by hunting down our mujahedin. . . ." However, HAMAS vowed to continue its jihad, with or without the PA's support.

In fact, Arafat's Fatah was not far behind HAMAS. In an interview with IMRA's Aaron Lerner, Marwan Barghouti elucidated the Palestinian position on the right of return. Having the right to live in a Palestinian state was not enough, he explained. The refugees from Israel proper currently living in the West Bank or Gaza needed to be able to return to their hometowns or villages: "Even though these Palestinians can live in a Palestinian state where they are right now, they are still refugees." No permanent-status agreement that did not permit them to return to Israel would be acceptable. Asked whether the long-term implication would not be the establishment of one state between the Jordan and the Mediterranean, Barghouti replied, "This would be the best compromise. That there be one state. Then there would be no problem with the right of return. Israelis would live in every place and Palestinians live in any place. Why not."

———

A NOTEWORTHY INCIDENT in the fall of 1999 was the speech of Suha Arafat (Yassir's wife) welcoming Hillary Clinton to Ramallah. Mrs. Arafat claimed that the Palestinians had been and were the victims of horrendous Israeli aggression—for example, she stated, "Our people have been submitted to the daily and intensive use of poisonous/toxic gas by the Israeli forces, which has led to an increase in cancer cases among women and children." Mrs. Clinton sat motionless until Mrs. Arafat finished her speech, whereupon Mrs. Clinton embraced and kissed her.

Hillary Clinton would not talk to the press in Ramallah, but twelve hours later a statement was issued in her name—not condemning or even disputing Suha Arafat's assertions, but rather indulging in the same sort of moral equivalence her husband had expressed in Gaza the previous year. "What was said today in Ramallah," said the First Lady, "is an example of why the President at Oslo urged the parties to refrain from making inflammatory charges or engaging in excessive rhetoric and to deal with any issues at the negotiating table."

While the attention of Washington and Jerusalem focused on Mrs. Clinton's awkward response, the Palestinian media defended Suha Arafat while reiterating and expanding her accusations. *Al-Hayah al-Jadidah* explained that "the main motive for the White House's eagerness to condemn sister Suha's statement . . . lies in its wish to make New York Jews happy in order to get a few votes supporting Hillary Clinton's candidacy" for the U.S. Senate. "Israel has conducted a premeditated campaign against the Palestinians and their land," said a lengthy article in *Al-Manar*, which concluded that "Suha Arafat's statements represent what the people suffer from the hated Israeli colonialism." And that endured, said the article, even as the peace process was unfolding. Meanwhile, the 1999 Palestinian Prize for Culture was awarded to Muhammad Daoud Odeh—Abu Daoud the unrepentant terrorist chieftain who, among other operations, planned the 1972 massacre of the Israeli athletes in Munich. Abu-Daoud received the prize for his autobiography, which described the planning of the Munich attack as well as numerous other Black September operations.

Soon afterward Iran weighed in, through Abdullah Safieldin, the Tehran representative of HizbAllah. Safieldin gave an interview to the Tehran newspaper *Javan* that ran under the title "A Second Intifadah Bigger Than the First One Is on Its Way."

Safieldin warned that "the signing of an agreement between the Zionist regime and certain Arab countries" would not result in the cessation of Palestinian terrorism. "Be sure," he said, "that there is a second Intifadah on its way, and this will be bigger than the first one that happened a few years ago. It is true that the Zionist regime has gained some advantages from the horrible leader of the Palestinians [Arafat], with the full backing of America, but this is not the whole story." Palestinians should take heart from the HizbAllah's activities in Lebanon, which "caused the unbreakable epic of Zionism to collapse," and which "with its jihad and martyrdom . . . showed that Israel had no choice except to withdraw and retreat from the occupied lands." "And now," he continued, "there are even murmurs about the possibility of the total elimination and total purging of that 'cancerous lump.'" The current dynamics in the territories made imminent the eruption of popular rage: "Because the Palestinian nation is consumed with anger, sooner or later the security which the Zionists are seeking will be shattered and eliminated." Safieldin assured his audience that HizbAllah would rush to assist the Palestinian struggle, and he brushed aside the notion that the peace process would have any impact on this dynamic: "The issue of resisting the Zionists is not an issue for one group or organized movement, or even one government; this is an issue for all Arab nations and Islamic nations."

Undaunted, the Israelis and the Americans continued to seek creative ways of addressing the hardening Palestinian position. Ross traveled to the region and met with both Barak and Arafat in order to gauge the progress in the final-status talks. Barak reiterated Israel's willingness to withdraw from an additional 5 percent of the West Bank. Arafat reiterated his insistence that more populated areas and contiguous areas be handed over. An exasperated senior official in Barak's office concluded that the Palestinians would "try to do everything so as not to reach an agreement in February" because they weren't "ready for the compromises needed to move ahead."

The PA seemed determined to prove the point, launching a series of riots and clashes with the IDF throughout the West Bank, as well as a walk-out of Arab workers in Gaza. Typically, Fatah activists would organize hundreds of rock-throwing youths for these clashes, which often lasted several hours; the PA security forces would stand by, not intervening even when formally asked to do so by Israel.

On Friday, November 26, the preacher at al-Aqsa Mosque widened the focus, stressing that the struggle in Palestine was but one component of a global jihad. "You, Muslims here in Palestine, are part of the great Islamic cause," the preacher declared. "You are one example of the imperialist infidel attack on Muslims." This attack had started at the beginning of the 20th century when the Jews and the West conspired to destroy the Ottoman Empire so that the Jews could control Palestine as a springboard for the West's anti-Muslim onslaught. All subsequent U.N. resolutions, the preacher said, sought to legitimize a Jewish presence of one kind or another in Muslim Palestine. Therefore, the Muslims of Palestine had a holy mission: "The boundaries of your state are the Globe. Our mission is to convey Islam to all the people of the world. Let then rise who wants to work for the sake of Allah alone to win his paradise. Let him rise to realize the momentous cause for this Muslim Ummah."

The Palestinian cause, the preacher explained, was at the core of the global Islamist revival, because the Jewish quest for Palestine had been the prime instrument for destruction of the Muslim caliphate. "There is no other issue in the world that consumed so much time and efforts like the case of Palestine. There is no other issue in the world that contained so many fallacies like the case of Palestine. All the cases of the world were resolved except the case of Palestine. You all know that the struggle is initially between Islam and Infidels. This is a historical fact. You all know that the countries of al-Sham (includes Palestine, Lebanon, Syria, South of Iraq, and Jordan) are the main target of occupiers to colonize the Muslim world, like the Tatars, the Crusaders." This historical trend still continued: "The reality of the [present-day] struggle reveals the fact that our struggle is not only with the Jews but also with the states that had created Israel and they are still supporting the Jewish state. The imperialist states had created Israel to tear apart the Muslim lands, so that Israel becomes a dagger in the body of the Muslim Ummah. . . . So it's important for the infidels to have the Muslim Ummah busy with Israel to distract the Ummah from her main cause (i.e., re-establishing the Islamic Khilafah State)."

However, the current dire situation of Muslim Palestine should not cause the believers to despair, but rather should galvanize them for the struggle ahead. "Allah had promised us victory soon after we stick to his *Deen* [Divine Law]. . . . The Prophet Muhammad said, 'Allah vouched for al-Sham and its inhabitants.' So we, here in Palestine, will stay patient until the victory of Allah comes. We will not retreat, and we will not follow the traitors who had surrendered the lands to the occupiers. May Allah help the sincere workers to establish the Islamic Khilafah State," the preacher concluded, with a veiled criticism of Arafat and the peace process.

———

BY THE END of November, with the talks still stuck and with Ross and Albright due in the Middle East in early December, Barak was determined that Israel not be blamed for the impasse. Then on December 1, as the final-status committee was convening in Ramallah, Fatah organized some six thousand youths for a rally in support of the PA's hard stand. The next day, Barak instructed the Israeli negotiators to drop the long-standing demand that the PA collect all guns exceeding the quota set by the Oslo agreements. Barak now said that these guns did not represent a threat to Israel and that the Israeli demands were only a source of friction. In gratitude, PA media highlighted a speech delivered by Arafat less than a year earlier in which he stated that these guns would in fact be used against Israel: "The guns are ready to protect the right of Palestinians in eastern Jerusalem, as the capital of the future Palestinian state. Our guns are ready and we are ready to use them against whoever will try to prevent us from praying in Jerusalem." Nevertheless, Barak instructed that a new round of negotiations start, to include "discussions" on the location of follow-up withdrawals. Barak hoped this sign of flexibility would persuade Arafat to resume meaningful negotiations.

Instead, the Palestinian Authority's leadership was working hard to reach an understanding with the Islamist and rejectionist leadership, urging them not to take the PA's participation in the negotiations seriously. Tayeb Abdel Rahim, a senior Arafat aide, addressed a rally of over 1,500 PFLP activists and assured them that Arafat would approve a permanent accord with Israel only after "all" the Palestinian conditions had been met. These conditions included complete Israeli withdrawal and the evacuation of all Jewish settlements, as well as unrestricted permission for all Palestinian refugees to reclaim their property in Israel. "Israel also must agree to an independent Palestinian state," Abdel Rahim told the cheering crowd. "These are the four red lines which we have made clear to the Israeli delegation, and unless they are implemented there will be no successful conclusion to the negotiations."

When Ross arrived in Israel in early December in preparation for Albright's imminent arrival, the PA delegation immediately walked out of the negotiating session, accusing Israel of intransigence. In an interview with Palestinian journalists, senior PA negotiator Yasser Abed Rabbo explained that Israel would not accede to the Palestinian demand that all construction in the Jewish settlements cease immediately and unconditionally. To ensure a "conducive" environment for Albright's visit, the next day Barak stated that "the settlements are causing Israel great damage" and announced that his government would not issue any new building permits in the settlements. Yossi Beilin, who was now the minister of justice, observed that there was no point in further building in settlements "that would at any rate be transferred to the Palestinians." In those settlements that were not to be uprooted, Beilin added, "construction may continue unrestricted only after the consummation of a final-status deal." Abed Rabbo quickly rejected Barak's initiative, stressing that "nothing less than a total halt to all Jewish construction" would be acceptable.

By the time Albright arrived, the PA was noticeably slowing down the formal negotiations. With the Holy Month of Ramadan approaching, the Palestinian track all but froze in early December 1999.

———

IN FACT, although Albright met with Arafat while in the Middle East, neither she nor Clinton was focusing on the Palestinian track. In the aftermath of the Sharm el-Sheikh Memorandum, American analysts had told the administration that, rhetoric notwithstanding, the differences between Israel and the Palestinians were virtually irreconcilable. Hence, in urgent search of his "legacy," Clinton turned again to the Syrian track. (The fact that, in the meantime, the White House was urging Israel to make more concessions to the PA apparently did not worry the president.) Hence, when Albright arrived in the Middle East, she was carrying Clinton's recommendations for accelerating the Syrian track.

12

The Road to Damascus (1999–2000)

Switching to the Syrian Track; Lebanon Heats Up

THE SYRIAN TRACK had always been Barak's favorite. Having been involved in the Chiefs of Staff talks in the winter of 1994–95, he considered
himself an expert on Syria. During his election campaign, he had committed
to withdrawing the IDF from southern Lebanon within a year, in the context
of a larger settlement with Syria. Therefore, once Barak won the elections on
May 17, 1999, Assad decided to test the waters by dispatching Patrick Seale
to Israel. Barak met with Seale himself and ensured that Seale met with the
prospective senior officials earmarked for key positions in the Syrian-track
negotiations.

Seale was fairly optimistic as he returned to Damascus, for two reasons:
He interpreted Barak's reminiscences of his meetings with Shihabi as indica-
tive of Israel's willingness to pick up negotiations from the point where they
had broken down; and he took the public statements of Barak and other
dovish candidates during the campaign, preparing the public for "painful
compromises," as indicating that a decision to withdraw from the Golan
Heights had already been made. Barak sent Assad a message through Seale
saying that the two countries had missed an opportunity in the mid-1990s
through mutual misunderstandings and that this sorry state of affairs must
be rectified. Assad took note but remained noncommittal until the Americans made their position known.

Meanwhile, Damascus certainly did not want Israel to withdraw from
Lebanon before addressing border issues with Syria. As Syrian officials would
later tell the Lebanese newspaper *Al-Nahar,* "a one-sided Israeli retreat from
Lebanon will put the Golan issue into the deep freeze and is a most dangerous

move." And so, to put pressure on Israel, Assad oversaw a marked escalation in HizbAllah attacks, including heavy volleys of Katyusha rockets into Israeli cities and settlements in the northern Galilee. This flagrant violation of the understandings reached after the Grapes of Wrath operation of 1996 should have served as a stark warning to Jerusalem, especially since the HizbAllah's uppermost leadership made the purpose of the attacks explicit. "Had there not been a state in the region called Syria, led by His Excellency President Hafiz al-Assad, Lebanon would have remained a mere satellite to Israel," Hassan Nasrallah, the HizbAllah secretary-general, declared in early June. "It would be fair to state that the efforts exerted by Syria in Lebanon have achieved security and stability." In early July, Sheikh Naim Qassim, Hizballah's deputy secretary-general, told a gathering of religious and resistance officials that "the Israelis plan on using force to dictate their terms, and the 'peace' that they will impose will be a peace of force. . . . [E]nemy Prime Minister Barak has said that peace rests on force and the strength of the army." However, Qassim continued, "the resistance is the counter-force that will break Israeli power." Jerusalem did not take the HizbAllah's logic seriously and instead reiterated its commitment to withdraw from southern Lebanon within a year.

In mid-July, during his visit to Washington, Barak told Clinton he had a plan for reaching a comprehensive peace by October 2000—that is, while Clinton was still in office. Clinton reciprocated by sending Assad a letter urging him to take advantage of this unique opportunity. Even though Clinton's letter seemed to confirm Seale's impressions, Assad was still wary; and when Jerusalem did not immediately commit to withdrawing to the June 4, 1967, line, Assad wondered if Barak's initiative was not a trap.

To test the Israeli attitude, Assad instructed Rafik Jawjati, an adviser to the Foreign Ministry and former ambassador to Washington, to seek out Israeli officials while attending the Wilton Park conference hosted by the British Foreign Ministry from July 26 to 29. The Israeli delegation included Shmuel Limoneh, a senior official in the Defense Ministry who, while serving in Israeli Military Intelligence during the early 1990s, had produced an assessment that Syria was seeking to negotiate peace, which was ultimately adopted by the Rabin government. Jawjati and Limoneh developed good personal relations and conducted lengthy conversations during the conference. Jawjati's friendliness persuaded the Israelis that he was trying to convince them of Assad's real interest in resuming negotiations, albeit on his own terms. Back in Damascus, Jawjati reported that Barak was essentially ready to withdraw from the Golan but was apprehensive about the Israeli public's reaction.

Assad was now certain that Israel could be coerced into withdrawing to the June 4 line even without a warm peace. Therefore, Damascus began to press the point that if the United States was serious about its role as the world's leading superpower and the sponsor of the peace process, it must deliver Israeli compromises. "We need to hear from the Americans that Barak wants to withdraw to the line of June 4, 1967," Ambassador Mualem told the very prestigious *Middle East Insight*. Senior diplomats in Damascus were asked to convey the same message to Washington. "If the Israelis think that they could start serious talks about any proposal less than providing guarantees for a full withdrawal from the Golan, they deceive themselves," one of these diplomats told *Al-Quds al-Arabi*, adding that if Albright wanted to come to Damascus, "she'd better come with specific proposals; otherwise she will irritate President Assad."

Nevertheless, Barak remained confident: "Once I get into a room with Assad, I envisage no problems in reaching a deal . . . but we are still trying to get into the room," he said at a briefing. Barak also asked Finnish Foreign Minister Tarja Halonen, who was visiting the Middle East, to tell Assad and al-Shara that he was most interested in direct contacts. On August 6, 1999, Assad responded formally to these initiatives in a letter to President Clinton. While not ruling out the resumption of negotiations, Assad reiterated Syria's hard-line positions. The president was "disappointed," in the words of White House staffers. By that time, however, the administration had already committed itself to Assad's remaining in power, to the detriment of the long-term national-security interests of both Israel and the United States.

————

IN THE EARLY SUMMER of 1999, some forty Sunni officers interested in having good relations with the United States, Turkey, and Saudi Arabia sought to topple the Assad regime. Significantly, they were all relatives or supporters of Chief of Staff Hikmat al-Shihabi or of former chief of Military Intelligence Rifat al-Najjar. First, the conspirators made contact with a European-based faction of the Syrian Muslim Brotherhood—whose members were cooperating with both the CIA and Turkish intelligence in Bosnia, Kosovo, and Chechnya—and sought their opinion about the advisability of dealing with the United States. Encouraged by the Muslim Brothers, the officers sent a senior delegation, led by a major general, to the U.S. Embassy in Amman. The officers met with the U.S. military attaché and explained that they wished to overthrow the Assad regime in order to bring Syria into the modern world through democratization and economic development. They told the attaché that they were seeking U.S. understanding, perhaps even help. He replied that he would need to check with Washington and suggested they come back in a week.

The Syrian officers also discreetly approached the Turks and the Saudis but were advised that these countries' support was conditional on Washington's decision.

When the delegation returned to the U.S. Embassy a week later, the attaché asked for a full list of the coup's leadership and details of their plans so that Washington could determine the optimal form of assistance. Naively, the Syrians complied. Their plan was to strike the next time Assad was out of the country. A squadron of fighter planes would attack the presidential palace; and at the same time infantry units, along with two artillery battalions and an armored battalion, would seize the Army headquarters and arrest Defense Minister Mustafa Tlass and his deputies. Another infantry battalion would seize the radio building, so that a brigadier general could read "Communiqué Number One" announcing the coup to the nation. The Syrian delegation got the impression from the attaché that they had Washington's tacit support.

On July 23, King Hassan of Morocco died, and Assad announced that he would lead a large delegation to the state funeral. The Clinton administration hesitated but finally decided to save Assad. On the morning he intended to travel to Morocco, just as he was getting ready to leave the al-Muhajirin Palace for the airport, Sandy Berger called him and pleaded with him to wait for the U.S. ambassador, who was already on his way to the palace. The ambassador arrived about an hour later, handed Assad a large sealed envelope, and, per his instructions from Washington, asked for permission to leave. Assad called in Bashar, and together they opened the envelope. It contained the details of the planned coup and the names of the officers involved. There was enough documentation to convince Assad and a more skeptical Bashar of the veracity of the American warning. Assad immediately called the airport and ordered that Prime Minister Mahmud al-Zubi lead the Syrian delegation in his stead.

That day, Assad ordered a discreet but thorough purge of the Sunni military elite. The military units the plotters had planned on using were transferred to remote areas near the Turkish and Iraqi borders, and predominantly Allawite and Druze units were brought to Damascus. The Americans requested that Hikmat al-Shihabi be spared, and Assad agreed; he also decided to keep communications with the Clinton White House open.

This story has an ironic twist. Because Washington betrayed an intended coup that was supposed to be pro-American against a regime that was on the United States' own terrorism and drug-trafficking lists, the Islamists concluded that Assad was in the Americans' pocket and was prepared to strike a deal. "The outlines of a catastrophic cave-in to Israel are becoming clearer ever day," wrote the Islamist commentator M. S. Ahmed in the *Crescent International,* "and prospects of a separate peace treaty between Syria and the Zionist state become stronger. Islamic as well as secular groups opposed to a deal are being increasingly suppressed, and Arab leaders applaud the new opportunities for a 'comprehensive Middle East peace settlement' while secretly plotting to convene an Arab League summit to bless the expected giveaway of Palestine. U.S. and Arab leaders, as well as their media, are already in a celebratory mood, secure in the knowledge that Syria's president Hafez al-Assad is salivating to cut a deal on their terms, provided he recovers the Golan Heights, and that Yassir Arafat is the kind of man who would 'do business' on desperate terms once boxed into a corner." The Islamists were apprehensive about America's use of the struggle against "international terrorism" to undermine the entire Islamist movement. Ahmed identified Hosni Mubarak, himself a victim of Islamist subversion, as a champion of "peace" for that reason.

In fact, official Cairo was also alarmed by the prospects of an Israeli-Syrian deal. In mid-August, the well-connected journalist Lamis Andoni conveyed Cairo's perceptions in a piece in *Al-Ahram Weekly.* For the Clinton administration, Andoni explained, "An Israel-Syria peace agreement would have important regional benefits: a secure Israeli-Lebanese border; the end of the Arab-Israeli conflict; the isolation of those parties that continue to reject peace and reconciliation; and the easing of pressure against normalization of relations between the Arab world and Israel." Ultimately, this trend would lead to "a regional security order, led by Israel and probably Turkey, that would open markets and ensure American economic and political influence in the region." Such a development would come at the expense of Egypt's leadership posture.

———

IN THE AFTERMATH of the aborted coup, Assad was determined to prove—especially to the Iranians, whose continued support would be crucial to Bashar's succession—that he was not Washington's man. Therefore, he encouraged yet another marked escalation in HizbAllah operations against the IDF and the SLA. Assad's objective was not just the liberation of southern Lebanon but also the continuation of the jihad against Israel, as clearly expressed in the name of the HizbAllah operation: "The Road to Jerusalem."

The overall operation included attacks of various intensities. Emphasis was on ambush, roadside bombs, and missile attacks on IDF and SLA patrols and strongholds, with the primary intention being to inflict casualties. However, HizbAllah also periodically launched Katyusha barrages toward Israeli civilian targets as a reminder of the potential for escalation, and it conducted several audacious special operations, including the assassination by bomb of the Israeli commander of South Lebanon. Ultimately, the HizbAllah leadership was convinced, and not without reason, that the attrition would increase pressure on the Israeli government to withdraw on Syria's terms.

HizbAllah's initial success emboldened its state sponsors. Starting in July, flights from Iran to Damascus increased markedly, bringing heavy weapons, ammunition, and other matériel to Syrian warehouses, from which they would be sent on to HizbAllah. However, just in case Assad was tempted to sign a peace agreement, Khamenei instructed a high-level committee of Iranian intelligence and Pasdaran officers to devise worst-case contingency plans for sustaining HizbAllah as an underground operation under hostile conditions.

These developments were not unnoticed in Israel. Barak reacted, however, by directing the IDF to start working secretly on detailed plans for withdrawing from Lebanon even without an agreement with Syria and Lebanon. For political reasons—in order to encourage the United States and Syria to expedite negotiations—his office leaked this ostensibly secret decision. However, the possibility that Israel would capitulate without any negotiated settlement only emboldened the HizbAllah and its sponsors to strike harder.

Both Barak's optimism and the Arabs' apprehensions were premature. When Madeleine Albright visited Israel in September for the signing of the Sharm el-Sheikh Memorandum, Barak proposed a return to the Syrian negotiating table without preconditions. Albright, however, held to the administration's acceptance of Syria's position that Israel must first make certain commitments—particularly to full withdrawal from the Golan—before formal negotiations could resume. Barak could only express regret that Albright had not been able to come up with a starting-point formula during her visit to Damascus, but he remained confident that one could be found.

Syrian officials and media hastened to dash that confidence. The messages conveyed via Albright and other foreign officials "have been repeated so often by Barak that they no longer attract any attention, and their content rings so hollow that they're almost laughable," wrote Ameed Khouli, editor-in-chief of the official *Al-Thawrah*. "Ehud Barak is fooling himself if he thinks that Syria would be prepared to submit to blackmail to make it go back on its well-known position"—the position that Israel had to pull out of the Golan Heights completely as a precondition for a peace agreement.

Syrian media now highlighted Syria's sponsorship of the HizbAllah operations. In a mid-September interview with *Tishrin al-Usbui*, Sheikh Qassim told the interviewer, "We believe that Al-Assad's Syria is a real basic and strategic support for the resistance against Israeli occupation. Were it not for its political and general support, there would have been confusion in the Lebanese arena and the general balance of power in the region." Qassim stressed the political sacrifices Damascus was making in order to facilitate HizbAllah operations. "Syria comes under big pressure to stop its support for the Lebanese resistance, under the excuse that it is terrorism against the United States and Israel, and yet it stands up and affirms the Lebanese people's right to resist." Qassim dismissed the possibility that Syria would curtail HizbAllah operations in the context of a peace deal with Israel. "We actually believe that HizbAllah's relationship with Syria is not a temporary one linked to some incidence, condition, or the resistance. We believe that our relationship with Syria is a strategic one due to the existence of common causes and convictions. . . . [T]he United States and Israel . . . have tried repeatedly to influence this relationship by dealing with each side separately. Thank God, however, President Hafiz al-Assad's awareness and discerning political vision has helped a great deal in consolidating this relationship."

Still, Barak remained convinced that an agreement was at hand. He even briefed General Lahad, commander of the South Lebanon Army, that he was "making every effort to reach a peace agreement that would allow for an Israeli Defense Forces withdrawal from Lebanon." This was not only talk. Concurrently, the Israeli Ministry of Defense began infrastructure work in several outposts along the border between Israel and Lebanon, and the IDF installed numerous sophisticated electronic gadgets along the border.

Barak was certain he was in control of the political dynamics. He knew Assad was afraid that if the IDF unilaterally pulled out of Lebanon, that would make it less, not more, likely that Syria would gain a complete Israeli withdrawal from the Golan Heights. However, by committing to a withdrawal date a year away and in the context of an agreement, Barak believed he was enticing Assad into returning to the negotiating table so that he could present the Israeli withdrawal as his own achievement. Israeli military intelligence warned the government that Assad was actually preparing for the forward deployment of HizbAllah and Palestinian rejectionist forces the moment Israel withdrew, but Barak ignored the warnings, convinced that he could maneuver Assad to the table.

IN LATE SEPTEMBER, although the Clinton administration, following the Sharm el-Sheikh Memorandum, was still concentrating on the Palestinian track, Albright met Faruk al-Shara at the U.N. General Assembly in order to, in the words of a senior U.S. official, "continue to see whether there can be a formula established to restart the [Israel-Syria] negotiations." Albright would also, the official added, "try to ensure that if the talks are restarted that there will be an ability to move quickly through the myriad issues." Al-Shara was less optimistic. "The meeting with Secretary Albright was good and constructive," he said, but then he added: "I think the progress has not been achieved yet. There is no breakthrough." In an editorial on the meeting, the government-owned newspaper *Tishrin* urged all Arab states to unite and cease all efforts toward normalization with Israel until the Golan issue was resolved. Nevertheless, Albright concluded and Clinton concurred that if Israel would just withdraw, the Syrians would sign "something," and Clinton's legacy would be assured.

The next day, before meeting with Israel's David Levy, Albright told European colleagues that "Middle East stability is endangered by Israel's remaining in the Golan Heights." In her meeting with Levy, she emphasized that her contacts with Syria had entered "a critical phase" and warned that Israel's relations with the other Arab countries were becoming contingent upon progress on the Syrian track. Although Levy responded by cautioning against accepting a scenario in which "bilateral relations will become hostage to the Israel-Syria track," Barak rushed to offer a new basis for the renewal of talks. He announced his acceptance of "Rabin's position" in all matters relating to the Syrian track—leaving vague the understanding of what Rabin's position actually was. Even President Ezer Weizman, a staunch supporter of the peace process, urged prudence. "I'm beginning to think that we don't have to run after Assad so much," he said. "At some point, there's a limit. If he wants, he'll come, and if he doesn't want, he won't come."

To break the deadlock, Clinton invited al-Shara to the White House to discuss ways to expedite negotiations. That attempt failed, mainly because Clinton did not address the sole issue Hafez al-Assad cared about: the succession of Bashar. The White House thought Assad was mainly concerned about the risk level of formal negotiations and resentful of intimations by Albright that America was unwilling to recognize Syria's "special role" in Lebanon. Even when the succession issue came up, it was in the wrong context. The Americans were convinced that Assad wanted to complete a deal before handing over the reins so that Bashar would not have to justify the agreement against challengers in Damascus. Assad, however, had no interest in an agreement per se—he wanted American assistance in assuring Bashar's survival and well-being, including large-scale financial aid to enable him to buy off his enemies. And that factor was completely ignored.

WHILE BARAK made ever more frantic efforts to contact Assad, even opening a secret channel to Damascus using the French as intermediaries, Tehran continued to solidify its dominance over southern Lebanon. In early October, HizbAllah Secretary-General Nasrallah led a high-level HizbAllah delegation to Tehran for consultations with Iran's key leaders, including

Khamenei, Hashemi-Rafsanjani, Majlis Speaker Natiq-Nuri, and Hashemi-Rafsanjani's successor as president, Mohammad Khatami. Tehran promised the HizbAllah extensive help, including new types of rockets, mortars, and anti-tank missiles. The Iranians also discussed with their guests practical steps to unify the anti-Israeli efforts of the Palestinian and Lebanese groups operating in southern Lebanon, as well as to establish means for channeling Iranian support to the Palestinian terrorist groups, particularly HAMAS and the Islamic Jihad. Significantly, these discussions were also attended by Imad Mughniyah, who, besides being the chief of the HizbAllah's security apparatus—known as the Islamic Jihad Apparatus—was in charge of HizbAllah international operations and responsible for coordination with Osama bin Laden. Mughniyah's participation reflected the centrality of terrorism in Tehran's designs for the HizbAllah.

Tehran and the HizbAllah agreed to convene a major conference in February 2000 in order to formulate a long-term strategy concerning Israel, with emphasis on the liberation of Jerusalem. "Freedom of al-Quds [Jerusalem] is our common goal, and we should not let aliens hatch plots to sow discord among us," Khatami told Nasrallah. Khatami praised the HizbAllah as "a liberation movement" defending "the freedom, Islamic and Arabic dignity of the occupied land" but advised that it "should continue its activities with more patience in order to achieve its goals while preserving its unity and to make itself immune from possible harms."

Soon after Nasrallah's return to Lebanon, HizbAllah secretly formed a new suborganization called the Lebanese Brigades. Formally, the Brigades were a grassroots organization that had nothing to do with HizbAllah. Keeping the two groups separate meant that attacks on Israel and the SLA could continue even if Damascus demanded that the HizbAllah cease operations. Damascus was in on this ploy from the very beginning, permitting the shipment of Iranian Katyushas via Syria and encouraging the Syrian-based Palestinian rejectionist groups to form their own deniable subgroups.

Concurrently, to demonstrate that an Israeli-Syrian agreement would not relieve HizbAllah's pressure on Israel, Iran started an airlift directly into Beirut airport, landing at night and when there was cloud cover in order to elude Israeli surveillance. These flights—which came on top of the ongoing airlift to Damascus—delivered very large quantities of matériel, including new types of weapons; Sheikh Muhammad Fadlallah, the spiritual guide of the HizbAllah, even boasted that the HizbAllah had acquired an "unusual" weapon that had not been used as yet.

To encourage Damascus to maintain its uncompromising position, Tehran offered various foreign-aid programs, including a $200 million cement factory, ten grain silos worth a total of $180 million, and several electricity projects worth a total of $100 million. Iranian officials stressed that these and future projects were being provided as "part of the Iranian-Syrian strategic alliance." In addition, Iran increased its contribution to Syria's programs for developing ballistic missiles and weapons of mass destruction. Tehran announced that when Foreign Minister Kamal Kharrazi traveled to Damascus in early November for a conference commemorating the centenary of Khomeini's birth, he would bring with him the documentation related to these aid programs. Iran's ambassador to Damascus told Arab reporters that Kharrazi planned to meet both Hafez and Bashar al-Assad, as well as the leaders of the HizbAllah, Islamic Jihad, and the Palestinian rejectionist organizations.

Israeli intelligence duly noted these developments and repeatedly tried to warn the Barak government but was essentially ignored. As a senior security official put it, "The Prime Minister makes no use of the assessments of situations he gets [from IDF analysts] and adopts an optimistic approach although progress in the field is minor."

Undaunted, Barak informed the Americans in early October—and his office leaked this idea to the Israeli media soon afterward—that he did not rule out the possibility of a unilateral IDF withdrawal from Lebanon as early as January 2000 as an incentive for the Syrians to resume negotiations. Damascus reacted with fury. Syrian officials told *Al-Nahar* that "a unilateral Israeli withdrawal from Lebanon will put a lid on chances for peace between Israel and Syria." Egypt was quick to endorse the Syrian warning. According to senior officials quoted by the government newspaper *Al-Jumhuriyah,* Clinton had informed Mubarak that "Israel is preparing to launch an all-out war against Syria in case there is no progress on the two countries' negotiating track before April 2000." *Al-Jumhuriyah* declared that "it is imperative for the Arab countries . . . that are friends of the United States to emphasize that they will not be able to stand with their hands tied if any aggression is carried out against Syria." Still, Jerusalem and Washington continued to consider unilateral withdrawal from southern Lebanon to be the best means of eliciting cooperation from Damascus.

———

NOT ONLY IN Damascus but also in other Arab capitals and even in Paris—with which Damascus held extensive consultations—the Israeli preoccupation with security arrangements on the Golan and in southern Lebanon was seen as a dangerous deviation from the principle of land for peace. The Arab governments also saw danger in the Clinton administration's desperate desire to come up with "a deal." One senior Arab diplomat opined, "If the negotiations do not resume before the end of 2000, an explosion will be inevitable within weeks or months that you can count on your fingers. The present situation cannot continue as it is." The Arabs were convinced, he added, that administration policy was driven solely by the upcoming U.S. elections and the need for a "legacy." Clinton's attempt at "bridging differences" was actually aggravating the tension, especially given the recent example of Kosovo, where the Americans had unilaterally and unexpectedly resorted to violence when a political quagmire developed. The Arab diplomat expected that if Israeli-Syrian negotiations again collapsed, there would be "the pointing of all the fingers of accusation against Syria," with the administration saying "it has run out of patience and will not be upset if Damascus was taught a hard lesson."

For their part, Washington and Jerusalem refused to take seriously—even before French President Jacques Chirac told both Clinton and Barak that "Assad is even more ill than is commonly believed"—Assad's claims that he was in no hurry to strike a deal. Assad was determined, Jerusalem and Washington believed, to bequeath Bashar a peace agreement with Israel. According to this logic, Assad's procrastination would have to be confined to the approximately 250 days until the deadline for Israel's unilateral withdrawal from southern Lebanon.

Hafez al-Assad shattered these beliefs in early November when he sent Bashar to Paris for high-level talks as if he already held the Israeli portfolio. While Bashar's main business in Paris was a failed attempt to reach a compromise with his uncle Rifaat over the succession issue, the visit was also intended to send a message to the Americans. This signal was reinforced by official Paris, which insisted that with Bashar firmly in charge, Damascus was in no rush to conclude any deal before Hafez's death.

Moreover, Syria fully lived up to Iran's expectations concerning the two countries' strategic relations. Among other things, Damascus fulfilled its promise to organize an intellectual/political seminar commemorating the centenary of Ayatollah Khomeini's birth. In his address to this seminar, the Syrian Information Minister, Muhammad Salman, stressed the "strategic" essence of Syrian-Iranian relations and insisted that Damascus "will not abandon a single inch of our land"—a rejection of the call for a negotiated compromise. Key participants included the HizbAllah's Nasrallah, Ramadan Abdallah Shallah of the Palestinian Islamic Jihad, and representatives of other Palestinian rejectionist organizations. They all repeated the Iranian hard-line position rejecting any deal with Israel.

Despite all these explicit signals from Damascus, the White House insisted it was certain of Assad's real intentions and urged Barak to offer a string of unilateral concessions in advance of any negotiations. Barak responded by ordering the IDF to accelerate the plans for unilateral withdrawal from Lebanon, still scheduled in principle for July 2000. When the

General Staff expressed apprehensions, Barak answered with a convoluted theory showing why Assad would have no choice but to strike a meaningful deal along the principles of Lebanon First. As the officers remained doubtful, Barak insisted he had received inside information from Clinton indicating that this scenario would work.

Barak himself traveled to Paris on November 10 and asked the French to pass a message to the Syrians affirming his eagerness for serious negotiations. Barak's message stated that Israel was "on the verge of a historic opportunity to make the peace of the brave with Syria" and added that Assad was a "strong, responsible, and serious leader." Barak concluded, "I am convinced that we can achieve a peace agreement that would satisfy both Syrian interests and Israeli sensitivities." Bashar al-Assad reacted with disdain, stating that "a unilateral Israeli pullback from Lebanon is a time-bomb."

In order to appease Damascus, Barak now proposed through Washington that "the international border between Syria and Israel, adjusted for security considerations, [would serve] as the basis for negotiations between the two countries." At the same time, however, his office leaked that "There is no justification for the June 4 line. It entails an area which Syria seized in an act of aggression, and its control there puts Israel's water sources at risk." At this point, Bashar al-Assad summoned Hassan Nasrallah and HizbAllah senior commander Hossein Khalil to Damascus for sensitive consultations on the HizbAllah's role in case of an Israeli withdrawal. Bashar assured the HizbAllah leaders that in return for their cooperation, he would see to it that the HizbAllah would have "a prominent role" in the next Lebanese government.

Nasrallah in turn urged Damascus and Tehran to authorize escalation, which he was confident would bring about the "near collapse" of the IDF and the SLA, instead of considering a peace plan. "We are close to defeating the enemy's army in the south and the western Bekaa," Nasrallah said. "Therefore, we must not retreat or hesitate but press onward with vigor and strength. . . . We must preserve this accomplishment," he added, because "this situation has not been given to us free of charge. We have paid for it with thousands of martyrs, wounded, and prisoners from the mujahideen and the civilians."

In late November, IDF Intelligence stressed the determination of both Syria and Iran to prevent the delinking of the Lebanese and Syrian issues. A senior intelligence officer told the Knesset that "Syria will not allow Israel 'to have it all.'" For Damascus, he elaborated, "there cannot be a situation where Israel lives in peace and tranquility along the Lebanese border while continuing to hold onto the Golan Heights." At the same time, Damascus was reluctant to launch a general war against Israel and instead "will do everything to heat up the Lebanese arena." The officer noted that Iran and Syria were introducing into Lebanon weapon systems optimized for provoking a major Israeli reaction; most threatening were the Iranian-made rockets capable of hitting the Haifa area. Such an attack would compel Israel to retaliate, and "this might eventually lead to an escalation that will lead to a direct confrontation with Syria."

———

THE CLINTON ADMINISTRATION was not oblivious to Iranian and Syrian activities in support of HizbAllah. Indeed, the administration grew increasingly gloomy about the prospects of the peace process. Speaking at a farewell dinner given for him by Arab correspondents in Washington, Martin Indyk, about to return to Israel as ambassador for the second time, acknowledged that "the U.S. administration is pessimistic about the prospects of Israel resuming the peace talks with Syria soon." After a meeting with Dennis Ross, Israeli Ambassador to the United States Zalman Shoval sent a top-secret cable to Jerusalem—subsequently leaked to *Yediot Aharonot*—stressing the profound skepticism prevailing among senior American experts and officials. "President al-Assad is busy with domestic problems and power struggles in Syria's leadership," Ross had told Shoval. "We don't discern in him any sense of urgency with regard to the need for an agreement with Israel."

Suddenly, on the eve of Albright's December visit to the Middle East, Assad dangled a lure the Clinton administration was only too eager to swallow. Damascus used a top French official who was visiting Syria to deliver a message to both Washington and Jerusalem. The French official warned the Americans and the Israelis that since Assad was facing serious problems within the Ba'ath Party, Israel should not expect any concessions, including any softening of the conviction that Rabin did in fact commit Israel to a complete withdrawal from the Golan Heights. Nevertheless, the official stressed, Israel had better reach an agreement with Syria now because, once Assad was no longer in control, "it will take at least fifteen years to achieve any agreement with Israel." Alarmed, the administration asked Riyadh to intercede with Damascus in order to enable Albright to announce the revival of the Syrian track during her visit to the Middle East. The Saudi emissary assured Assad in the names of both Clinton and Albright that the future negotiations would inevitably lead to an Israeli withdrawal to the June 4 line as interpreted by Syria. He also conveyed Clinton's promise that the moment Assad committed to signing an agreement with Israel, the United States would provide the Syrian armed forces with the latest weaponry, of the same type supplied to Egypt.

Little wonder that when Albright arrived in Damascus a couple of days later, she was assured that Assad was "still interested" in renewing talks, provided all his demands were met. That evening, Albright noted that she was leaving Syria "feeling much more hopeful than I did when I arrived this afternoon." She then traveled to Israel, where, in lengthy meetings with Barak, she emphasized the first part of Assad's message and virtually ignored the second part. Barak assured her that the question of withdrawal to a June 4 line (but not necessarily the line demanded by Assad) would not constitute an obstacle to peace if Syria agreed to a formal peace treaty. Having agreed once again to follow the United States' "recommendations," Barak rushed to tell reporters that there had been developments in the contacts with Syria.

That night, Clinton announced in Washington that there would be talks between Barak and al-Shara aimed at reaching a permanent peace deal. Clinton said he had told both Assad and Barak that they "bear a heavy responsibility." Both sides "still need to make courageous decisions," he commented. "But today's step is a significant breakthrough, for it will allow them to deal with each other face to face, and that is the only way to get there." White House officials noted that the outstanding issues included borders, normalization of relations, security arrangements, the withdrawal from Lebanon, a timetable, and water. Israel, they added, having been prodded for months, had made significant concessions, allowing these talks to take place.

Barak accepted the Clinton administration's outline for the structure of the talks, but claimed he was still insisting on long-standing Israeli "red lines." Although he had been demanding a full peace treaty, he now was willing to settle for a declaration of principles at the Washington meeting in order to end the state of war between the two countries, with a full peace treaty to follow several months later. This approach was tailored after the final phase of the Israeli-Jordanian process in 1994, which was also timed to suit Clinton's election needs. Officials in Barak's office added that at the outset of the talks he would raise Israel's demands for security arrangements, including an early-warning system on Mount Hermon, the complete demilitarization of the Golan Heights, a significant reduction of Syrian forces between the Golan Heights and Damascus, and Syria's prevention of HizbAllah attacks against Israel. As well, Israel would insist on controlling its water sources, which meant denying Syria access to Lake Kinneret. However, the officials conceded, the agenda for the talks would be based on "the 60 points of normalization" outlined at the 1995–96 Wye Plantation meetings—which meant that Israel accepted the Syrian demand that the new talks would resume where the previous ones had broken down. The White House claimed—Israeli officials intimated—that Assad's ill health was the sole reason for his absence from the summit's opening session and that a true summit meeting between Assad and Barak somewhere in the Middle East was highly likely if the Washington negotiations made sufficient progress.

Barak's faith in Clinton's assurances continued even when Syrian officials went out of their way to contradict Clinton both privately and publicly.

For example, in an interview with the London *Al-Mustaqillah*, Mustafa Tlass stressed "the 'Rabin pledge' . . . regarding the complete withdrawal from the Golan." This pledge, he said, is "known to all U.S. and Israeli leaders," and "the Barak government's efforts to evade it means that it is not serious about achieving peace." Barak did not consider this and comparable statements sufficient cause to reevaluate the advisability of going ahead with the negotiations. When senior Israeli officials questioned this decision, Barak reiterated that Clinton had offered him personal assurances.

Assad, meanwhile, was convinced that simply by agreeing to the Washington negotiations, he had made a major concession to Clinton without receiving sufficient appreciation. Initially, Assad demanded a new "deposit" from Barak. Assad's idea, as conveyed through Albright, was for Barak to sign and hand to Clinton a new document—which would be kept secret until negotiations had ended—pledging to withdraw to the June 4 borders. Barak refused to sign anything in advance. Clinton then sent Assad a message stating that his own letter of June 6, 1995, in which he affirmed Rabin's original "deposit," was still valid as far as the United States was concerned. (Never mind that this statement contradicted formal clarifications to the Netanyahu government by Ross and Christopher.) Assad realized that Clinton's message was not an official U.S. commitment guaranteeing a full Israeli withdrawal. Nevertheless, convinced from his conversations with Albright that Clinton would ultimately "deliver" a full withdrawal, Assad agreed to send al-Shara to Washington. At the same time, however, he ordered escalation in southern Lebanon as a reminder of Syria's alternatives.

———

NOT ONLY was there a marked escalation of HizbAllah attacks on IDF and SLA forces, but the HizbAllah also flagrantly drew ammunition, supplies, and reinforcements from Bekaa Valley bases that were under Syrian supervision. Furthermore, on December 10, the Syrian media ignored the upcoming Washington talks, instead giving prominence to a HizbAllah manifesto on the organization's "Identity and Goals."

The "Identity and Goals" document authoritatively describes HizbAllah's doctrine and practices. "HizbAllah is an Islamic struggle movement," the document explains. "Its emergence is based on an ideological, social, political, and economical mixture in a special Lebanese, Arab, and Islamic context." Although HizbAllah was formed in response to the 1982 invasion of Lebanon by Israel, its character and ultimate objectives are all-Islamic. Its theological character was profoundly influenced by the Shiite Islamic Revolution in Iran. As early as the 1980s, as a result of the Iranian connection, HizbAllah's priorities shifted from the immediate goal of liberating southern

Lebanon from Israeli occupation to the long-term goal of realizing Khomeini's all-Islamic vision—the destruction of Israel. "The seed of resistance is also deep in the ideological beliefs of HizbAllah," the document stated, "a belief that found its way for expression against the Zionist occupation of Lebanon. And that is why we also find the call for the liberation of Jerusalem rooted deeply in the ideals of HizbAllah."

A couple of days later, HizbAllah demonstrated its character as a "struggle movement" by launching a heavy and wide-ranging series of attacks on the IDF and SLA—including roadside bomb attacks, close-quarter ambushes, and mortar and rocket barrages against Israeli and SLA patrols and outposts. Although Israel launched a dozen air strikes and numerous artillery barrages in retaliation, fighting continued well into the night. Senior HizbAllah officials were quick to stress that this was only the beginning of a major escalation. Sheikh Qassim ruled out any pressure from Syria in connection with the negotiations: "I do not believe that the Lebanese and Syrian officials are going to ask the [HizbAllah] to stop its operations, which are, at any rate, not connected with the Middle East negotiating process. Any halt of operations will only strengthen the Israeli position," he declared.

The Syrian media also took a hard line, repeating long-standing demands for an Israeli commitment on withdrawal as a precondition for any negotiations. Syrian officials argued that the mere resumption of negotiations amounted to Jerusalem's giving Damascus an advance commitment to a full withdrawal. "The problem was the land, the rights, and the necessity of having a total pullback to the June 4 borders. The talks are resumed on this objective basis," wrote Ameed Khouli, the director-general of *Al-Thawrah,* in a front-page editorial. "Syria would not have sacrificed eight years of heavy political work and complicated negotiations and achievements to restart the talks from the zero point."

Damascus even permitted the publication of an article critical of Syria's return to the peace process. The article, by Ali Aqleh Ursan, the chairman of the Syrian Arab Writers Association, first appeared in the relatively obscure journal of the Writers Association, *Al-Usbu al-Adabi* (*The Literary Magazine*). However, it was quickly picked up by mainstream Arab media—particularly the London-based *Al-Hayah,* which is considered the most important Arabic-language newspaper in the world—and won warm endorsement. Several senior officials from Syria and other Arab states asserted that Damascus had permitted Ursan to publish his article because he had put on paper what Assad believed but could not afford to say out loud for fear of retribution by the Clinton administration.

Ursan started by reiterating the official Syrian position that the mere resumption of talks presupposed that Israel accepted Syria's interpretation of the "Rabin Deposit." However, Ursan warned, the imprecise nature of the de facto concessions by "the Zionist entity" opened the door for American pressure on Syria to come up with unwarranted concessions on such issues as security arrangements and water rights. Any such pressure would be outrageous given the concessions Syria had already made by agreeing to come to Washington. "This will be the first time in history," Ursan explained, "that a Syrian Foreign Minister negotiates with a minister or Prime Minister of the occupying enemy."

The magnitude of Syria's concession in agreeing to bilateral talks, Ursan continued, had to be understood in the context of Syria's steadfast pan-Arab posture. The "Arab-Zionist conflict" is an "existential conflict," and the potential outcome of any negotiations should be assessed accordingly. *Any* peace agreement would serve the objectives of the Clinton administration (the legacy issue) and the "Zionist entity" (to have its right to exist recognized by the Arab world). Having withdrawn to the June 4 line, "the Zionist occupier would have gained borders, water, normalization, and a reputation for striving for peace." Damascus, on the other hand, would find itself the Arab power that had abandoned the struggle "for the removal of the Zionist occupier from Palestine." Thus, Ursan declared, the essence of the peace process imposed by the Clinton administration was an attempt to coerce Damascus into putting its particular interests ahead of the interests of the entire Arab world. But no power on earth—not even the United States—can deliver such an achievement. "The problem of Palestine will remain an existential conflict with the Zionist occupiers, until victory, the removal [of Israel], and the liberation [of Palestine], even if it takes a hundred years."

From the very beginning, the Syrian negotiating strategy was closer to Ursan's position than to the assurances Clinton had given Barak. The most important deviation from the agreed-upon format was the last-minute Syrian insistence that the entire process take place in Washington rather than in, or near, the Middle East. This change of venue made a Barak summit with Assad—as alluded to by the White House—impossible. As well, in order to ensure that the promises the United States had made to Assad would be implemented according to Damascus's interpretation, Syrian officials insisted on the "personal intervention" of Clinton and on a U.S. presence at all stages of the negotiations.

———

WHEN THE FORMAL negotiations opened with a brief ceremony in the White House Rose Garden, Clinton and Barak appeared enthusiastic, in contrast with the dour al-Shara, who refused to shake Barak's hand. Clinton said he was encouraged because all were "prepared to get down to business."

There would be obstacles along the way, he cautioned, but "for the first time in history, there is a chance for a comprehensive peace between Israel and Syria and indeed all its neighbors." Barak echoed Clinton's optimism, stating that Israel was determined to work with its "Syrian partners" and do everything "to bring about the dreams of children and mothers all around the region to see a better future for the Middle East at the entrance to the new millennium." Al-Shara, having conveyed Assad's greetings, argued that since "Israel provoked the 1967 Middle East war," Israel was responsible for reversing its consequences; "it goes without saying that peace for Syria means the return of all its occupied land." He also indicated that there would have to be an Israeli-Palestinian agreement before there could be a "just and lasting peace" in the Middle East.

As usual, ceremony and symbolism were far more important to the administration than substance. U.S. officials noted that Clinton was disappointed by al-Shara's "hostile speech" and his refusal to "talk or shake hands with Barak." The officials reported that Albright and others had "attempted for hours yesterday to convince al-Shara to shake hands, to no avail." However, neither Clinton nor Barak seemed worried that there was no breakthrough, or even progress, on substantive issues. The second day was devoted largely to working out an agenda for continuing the discussions in early January 2000 in a secluded setting. (Ultimately, both sides agreed on Shepherdstown, West Virginia.) Still, the Americans shared Barak's expectation that he could reach a "core agreement" with the Syrians during the January talks. In fact, a senior official in the prime minister's entourage claimed that Israel had achieved its primary goals in Washington: establishing personal ties between Barak and al-Shara and scheduling another round of talks. The official added that Barak's objective in the next round would be "to reach a declaration of principles which will include an article allowing Israel to withdraw from Lebanon."

DESPITE THE LACK of substance in the Washington talks and a sudden surge of HizbAllah operations in southern Lebanon, Barak began to prepare the Israeli public for an agreement with Syria. He argued that the spread of long-range ballistic missiles throughout the region "had made much of the Golan Heights' security value obsolete." He added that "the Golan's water resources are not crucial to Israel, and shouldn't interfere with the progress of the talks with the Syrians, because in four or five years, Israel will have been able to desalinate enough water for its needs. Until then, Israel can import water from Turkey." A total withdrawal from the Golan, Barak claimed, "would have a shock-wave effect on Assad, the Syrians, and the Arabs as a whole, transforming the Middle East from a conflict-ridden arena to an area of peace." Barak could not, however, provide any indication, other than Clinton's assurances, that the Syrians shared his vision.

Damascus moved quickly to dispel Clinton's and Barak's illusions. In an article in the *Jordan Times,* the well-connected Jordanian journalist Musa Keilani described the Syrian position on the basis of high-level contacts in Damascus. If Keilani meant his article to have an immediate impact on both Washington and Jerusalem, he chose his outlet well, for the *Jordan Times* is routinely read by all diplomats in the Middle East. Keilani quickly laid out the Syrian approach to *reaching* an agreement with Israel. "The Arab World," he wrote, "is expecting that Arab dignity and honour will be held supreme in any Syrian-Israeli agreement." Although al-Shara did not say so in Washington, Keilani declared, Syria was "ready to open its borders with Israel, exchange ambassadors, and launch trade ties" as part of an agreement. The mere presence of al-Shara in Washington was an affirmation of this point. However, Syria would not be pressed into implementing this commitment until after "the Golan is returned to Syria in its entirety." Keilani specified that the Syrian definition of the Golan included areas seized by the Syrian military during the 1950s, the economic infrastructure built by Israeli settlers since 1967, and access to the Sea of Galilee. The Israeli withdrawal, Keilani concluded, "should also include Al-Hammah spa and hot water springs region, the best Middle Eastern wine factories on the Golan, along with a littoral part on Lake Tiberias which has always been part of Syria." Israel's failure to commit in advance to handing these and comparable resources over to Syria would make any future negotiations futile.

Another warning voice was that of the British Arabist correspondent David Hirst. Although Assad "has long insisted that Syria really does want a final peace," Hirst observed, "he is afraid of peace" and "would still, when it came to the crunch, hesitate to accept it." The main challenge was not in the details of the deal offered by Clinton, but in the mere existence of a bilateral Israeli-Syrian deal, separate from a Palestinian deal. "For him," Hirst elucidated, "peace of the kind on offer amounts to the historic failure of a generation, a system, an ideology: so central has Palestine been to all that Ba'athism ever stood for."

Thus, for Assad, any peace agreement would amount to giving Israel an "existential boon" in return for abandonment of the Palestinian cause—which was central to the Ba'athist Bilad al-Sham doctrine. It would also potentially leave Syria in a strategically inferior posture, if the southern Lebanon issue was resolved but the entire peace deal was not completed in Assad's lifetime. And Bashar, Assad knew, could not be trusted to accomplish this undertaking soon after coming to power. Hence Assad must personally decide to sign or not to sign. "It is his choice, his alone, and one that may soon be upon him. No successor could make it," Hirst concluded.

Barak reacted by stating merely that the upcoming negotiations "would be extremely tough" and their outcome "uncertain." Senior Israeli officials still hoped to reach a compromise with Syria over many of the points of contention; they seemed completely unaware of the gravity of the challenge in Assad's eyes. Even the Research Division of the IDF's Military Intelligence claimed that "Israel and Syria have never been this close to achieving peace." However, in analyzing Assad's more conciliatory attitude, the IDF study did note that "Assad seeks to leave his son Bashar a more stable country in possession of the Golan Heights."

Consequently, in late December, the Clinton administration decided to invite Bashar to the White House. By doing so, administration officials reasoned, they could at once recognize Bashar's new stature and avoid the embarrassment of his father's avoiding a meeting with Barak. Arab diplomats were advised that the invitation to Bashar would be formally issued after the successful completion of the first round of the Shepherdstown talks. These diplomats were asked to float the idea in Damascus so that Assad would have an additional incentive to be forthcoming. The Syrian reply was that in principle both Hafez and Bashar al-Assad could meet Clinton but no Israelis, and that neither of the Assads would accept any invitation to Washington except for the signing of a peace agreement.

On the eve of the Shepherdstown talks, Damascus once again used obscure periodicals to state Assad's real position. On January 1, 2000, for example, *Al-Usbu al-Adabi* carried an article by Zbeir Sultan about the essence of peace with Israel on the basis of Egypt's experience. "The events following the notorious Camp David Accords," Sultan explained, "proved that the peace of the Zionists is merely one form of the war they conduct against Arabs and Muslims. It pursues the goals of the Zionist scheme in a new way, different from the traditional warfare of armies and weapons." Sultan repeated the now routine accusations that Israel was using its embassy and research centers in Cairo as centers of espionage and subversion aimed at destroying the fabric of Egyptian society. He cited the most virulent accusations as factually proven—among them "the spreading of AIDS in Egypt through pretty, HIV-positive Jewish girls who came from Israel in order to sell themselves to Egyptian youngsters seeking pleasure." He also referred to "Zionist gifts for children made of animal-shaped chewing gum" laced with chemicals that "cause sterility." "For university students," Sultan reported, "[the Zionists] dispensed chewing gum that arouses sexual lust. The Zionists have not missed a single dirty method to shake Egyptian society, even its religion and beliefs." Sultan included in the methods of the "Satanic war waged by Zionism" the spread of poisoned seed to destroy Egypt's agriculture and the downing of an EgyptAir plane. This record, Sultan concluded, should have convinced everyone that "Zionism hates the Arabs indiscriminately." Using normalization and the peace process, "the Zionists will attempt more and more to realize the biblical dream of establishing a Zionist Entity from the Euphrates to the Nile."

———

BARAK ARRIVED in Shepherdstown convinced that Clinton had already secured a "core agreement" for him. Indeed, he and Clinton were both so confident that they started planning the timing of the referendum on withdrawal from the Golan which Israeli law demanded: It would be held in mid-March, after Super Tuesday, so that Clinton would be free to campaign for Barak. Their enthusiasm was not dampened even when the American spin doctors decided that the opening ceremony would be brief and without speeches in order to avoid the sort of embarrassment al-Shara had caused in the Rose Garden. Instead, Clinton would make a brief statement, and there would be a tightly controlled photo-op.

Once the talks began, profound disagreements surfaced almost immediately. The Syrians insisted on resolving the border issue—that is, the exact line of the Israeli withdrawal—before addressing any other issue, whereas the Israelis wanted to discuss normalization and security first and then set the depth of Israel's withdrawal accordingly. By the first afternoon the talks had virtually stalled; plans for Clinton, Barak, and al-Shara to have dinner that evening were canceled because of the level of tension. Clinton arrived the next morning for a special trilateral meeting to "solve" the procedural dispute, essentially through Barak's accepting the Syrians' proposed sequence of topics. The participants also decided to limit the summit to one week rather than, as originally planned, continuing until a "core agreement" was reached. But even these concessions could not bridge the gaps, and, on the third morning, the American intermediaries requested an adjournment in order to ease the building tension. The daily press briefing by State Department officials offered a good indicator of the "spirit of Shepherdstown": Some Arab journalists complained when an Israeli journalist was seated at their table, saying that they risked being arrested when they returned to Damascus.

By now, the talks were completely stalled. Even a Clinton charm offensive could not break the deadlock. At that point, the administration came up with its own seven-page "Shepherdstown Document," drafted by Clinton, ostensibly as a summary of the areas of accord and discord and as the basis for an eventual "core agreement." However, it essentially incorporated the principles the Clinton administration had been pursuing all along.

On the last night of the summit, Clinton hosted a special dinner for the three delegations that quite accurately reflected his administration's awareness of, and sensitivity toward, the peculiarities of the Middle East. On the eve of the dinner, U.S. officials leaked that "Clinton was personally involved in the dinner arrangements" in a last-ditch effort "to extricate the delegation leaders from the pressure cooker of the [negotiations] and serve them up some good cooking in a different atmosphere." However, Clinton's menu included wine (forbidden to Muslims) and non-kosher food (forbidden to Jews; incidentally, the Jewish members of the U.S. delegation did not partake). Clinton led a lively conversation on all the issues on the agenda, and State Department officials later claimed that "the atmosphere was relatively warm and cordial" even though "the discussion was serious and thorough." The officials noted, quite seriously, that "despite the wine, Syria's Foreign Minister did not shake hands with Barak." On January 10, the parties returned to the Middle East.

———

IT DID NOT take long for the Shepherdstown Document to be leaked—first by al-Shara to his friend Ibrahim Hamidi, who wrote about it in *Al-Hayah*, and subsequently by Israeli government sources to Akiva Eldar of *Haaretz*. Essentially, in formulating this document, the Clinton administration had taken the Israeli "red lines" of last resort—as described to Clinton by Barak in great confidence—and used them as the Israeli starting point. In addition, the timetables for reaching, and ultimately implementing, a peace agreement were determined not by Israeli security considerations but by the White House's resolve to secure Bill Clinton's legacy and boost the presidential campaign of Al Gore and the senatorial campaign of Hillary Clinton.

Ultimately, the Syrians' positions, as reported and largely endorsed in the U.S. document, were virtually identical to the positions they had first introduced in the early 1990s. In contrast, the Israelis' positions not only had become more flexible but, when it came to the withdrawal from the Golan, also went far beyond the "red lines" formulated by the IDF (in, among other things, a series of studies done when Barak was Chief of Staff). Furthermore, Israel had agreed to the rebuilding of the Syrian armed forces with Western weapon systems, despite the bitter legacy of the comparable rebuilding of the Egyptian armed forces since the early 1980s. Essentially, Israel, with U.S. encouragement, had committed to a series of profound unilateral concessions solely in order to get the Syrians to return to the negotiating table. Moreover, Jerusalem had adopted certain positions on the basis of Clinton's promises concerning items such as weapon systems, early-warning technologies, and U.S.-dominated peacekeeping forces, as if Clinton would still be in office after January 2001 and as if Congress had not already expressed objections to these types of commitments. Barak seemed preoccupied only with getting permission from his government's legal advisors to use the Clinton spin team to prepare for the referendum on withdrawal from the Golan.

Meanwhile, to prove the assertion Barak had floated after the Washington summit in December—namely, that the strategic value of the Golan Heights had fallen in recent years—Jerusalem now leaked the results of a command-post exercise that had examined the IDF's ability to cope with a massive Syrian offensive in which the Israeli deployment on the Golan and the early warning stations on Mount Hermon could not prevent the initial seizure of territory by the Syrians. This leak was disingenuous because the government did not provide the results of what would have been the truly meaningful scenario—a Syrian attack following a total withdrawal from the Golan. Actually, the Barak government had forbidden the IDF to conduct simulations of such a scenario, after preparatory studies raised the specter of horrendous civilian casualties and the possibility of near-defeat—and that, even without the Syrian use of ballistic missiles and weapons of mass destruction.

Furthermore, these exercises did not take into consideration the ongoing Syrian military buildup—particularly the construction of a 2.5-mile-wide water reservoir in the Kuneitra area. This reservoir not only prevented large quantities of water from reaching Israel, but also constituted a formidable obstacle on the road to Damascus. Consequently, it strategically reduced Syria's risk of facing retaliation in case of a major war with Israel.

Just as the Shepherdstown talks were to resume in mid-January, Damascus formally notified Washington that the Syrian delegation would not return "until Israel agrees to retreat all the way up to the June 4, 1967, borders." After several days of skirmishing, in private and in public, among the three sides, Clinton called Assad and spoke for about an hour in an effort to break the impasse. Assad merely repeated that Faruk al-Shara would not return until Israel agreed to withdraw unconditionally. When Clinton's efforts to keep the talks going on the experts' level failed as well, the administration finally had to admit that the Syrian-Israeli talks were truly stalled.

Instead of taking this as a signal to pause for serious reflection on the whole peace process, Barak—in a move that would set the tone for the hectic year to come—took Clinton's advice and, in the words of a senior Israeli official, decided "to take advantage of the Syrian stubbornness to push forward on the Palestinian track." Clinton and Albright promised full support for Barak's renewed effort to reach an Israeli-Palestinian agreement on permanent-status principles by mid-February 2000.

13

Jumping from Track to Track (1999–2000)

Clinton and Barak Grow More and More Frantic; the Islamists Calmly Plot Their Future

BY THE WINTER of 1999–2000, the entire Arab and Muslim world was giving up on the Clinton administration's peace process. Friendly and hostile governments alike realized that there was no alternative to crisis and that they must be ready for war—which alone would break the administration's stifling embrace.

In the eyes of the Arab leaders, Clinton had managed to coerce Assad into sending al-Shara to Washington in December primarily because of the recent bombing of Yugoslavia—a campaign launched against a sovereign state that did not constitute a threat to the security of the United States but had dared to stand up to the Clinton administration. This was in addition to the ongoing sporadic bombing of Iraq. Damascus clearly had these campaigns in mind when it agreed to the resumption of the Washington negotiations. "I'd rather have Shara go to Washington than have American bombers come to Damascus," Assad told an Iranian emissary.

Cairo was not immune to the general sense of crisis. In the late 1990s, Egyptian officials had used such terms as "strategic dialogue" and "strategic alliance" to describe U.S.-Egyptian relations. Now the Egyptians could not get the Clinton administration to believe that their policy vis-à-vis Iraq, Libya, and Sudan did not necessarily clash with American national interests. And the White House's complete lack of sensitivity to the peculiarities of the Muslim world merely aggravated the situation. Outbursts of intense anti-American sentiments from both the Egyptian street and the intelligentsia were one result of the administration's failures, and Cairo knew that senior American diplomats were reporting these events back to the State Department.

Most critical to the development of the Arab world's hostile posture were the Iraqis' predictions of an impending crisis with the United States despite Egypt's intervention on their behalf. In late December, Baghdad launched the Iraqi Wolf operation, dismantling sensitive industrial and oil installations and removing special documents from the president's office and the Defense and Interior Ministries in anticipation of U.S. attacks.

In late December, Palestinian sources claimed that U.S. troops in Saudi Arabia, Turkey, and Kuwait had been put on "maximum alert" pending "a new barbaric U.S. attack on Iraq in the next three weeks." Washington, these sources noted, had "warned Arab states against any rapprochement moves toward Iraq that might curb the negative impact of the embargo." The United States additionally "warned Arab states against any serious endeavor to hold an Arab summit involving Baghdad." The sources did not rule out "Israel's involvement in the prospective offensive one way or the other," and they stressed the widespread opposition to the heavy-handed U.S. approach and especially to any involvement in military activities against "brotherly Iraq."

Tehran did not fail to proclaim what Arab leaders feared to say publicly. In his Friday sermon on December 31—International al-Quds (Jerusalem) Day—Iran's Supreme Leader, Ayatollah Khamenei, reiterated the conviction of Islamdom that the annihilation of "the Zionist regime" was the only way to end the sufferings of the Palestinian people and to solve the Middle East crisis as a whole. "From Islamic, humanitarian, economic, security, and political points of view, today the presence of Israel is a very big threat against the regional nations and states," Khamenei declared. "And there is only one solution to the Middle East problem, namely the annihilation and destruction of the Zionist state." Significantly, Khamenei identified the Palestinian "right of return" as an integral component of the Muslim world's drive for the annihilation of Israel: "The Palestinian refugees must return to their homeland. There are eight million refugees (inside and outside Palestine) who are the main owners of the Palestinian lands. . . . The owners of Palestine, that is the Palestinian Nation, (must) form a government which must decide whether to keep those who have migrated to Palestine from other countries." Khamenei's sermon and similar speeches by other Iranian leaders were given widespread and sympathetic coverage throughout the Arab world.

———

IN LATE 1999, the HAMAS leadership accepted the possibility of an independent state on a part of Palestine. Since the vast majority of Palestinians wanted such a state, the leadership explained, HAMAS was not going to stand in the way of this development—although the ultimate goal was still the complete liberation of Palestine. A key article in the December issue of the

HAMAS organ *Filastin al-Muslimah* clarified that this stance did not reflect a change in core doctrine, but rather an adaptation to meet prevailing conditions. Similarly, the article insisted that HAMAS leadership itself had decided to reduce the pace of terrorist operations based on the dynamics in the territories, not as a matter of inability to carry out operations or susceptibility to pressure from Arafat. The primary objective of the "Islamic Resistance" operations since 1997, the article explained, was to increase grassroots support among the Palestinians, rather than to intimidate the Israeli public or halt the peace process; the intensity of operations thus fluctuated in accordance with the needs of the Palestinian street. "The reconciliation," HAMAS observed, "is eating from the bread of history, while the caravan of resistance is moving onwards to the future."

This message was echoed by Abu Muhammad Mustafa, the HAMAS representative in Tehran, in a mid-December interview with the Tehran newspaper *Abrar*. Mustafa explained that the grassroots outreach of HAMAS served as a damper on Arafat's willingness to compromise. "The Zionists know full well that Arafat is ready to make concessions," Mustafa said, "and it is the presence of the Islamic groups that has prevented this to a certain extent. In any case, they know the Islamic groups can mobilize the people and bring them onto the scene against any concessions Arafat has given them. . . . The Zionists are well aware that as long as the people and the Islamic groups remain unconvinced, Arafat will not be able to achieve anything."

Mustafa emphasized the continuity in HAMAS's principled position despite the changes in regional politics: "The stance of HAMAS is the same as it was, and it has not altered in any way. . . . From the political vantage-point, we are opposed to the Oslo accord and its outcome. . . . We believe the land of Palestine is an Arab-Islamic land that belongs to Muslims and the Palestinians themselves. If Arafat relinquishes even an inch of Palestinian soil, he cannot be a representative of the people of Palestine." What might be changed, Mustafa explained, were the specific tactics. Ultimately, however, "with all the resources we have, we will continue our confrontation with the usurpers. Perhaps this resistance may undergo some change because of circumstances—that is, it might be weak at times, or become stronger at other times—but in any case, the consensus is the continuation of resistance."

Mustafa did not belittle the difficulties facing HAMAS in its routine operations. However, he attributed them mainly to the activities of the CIA and the Israeli security forces in the territories rather than to the PA's crackdown. In addition, Mustafa noted, to avoid unnecessary clashes with the PA and the hostile powers, HAMAS would no longer claim responsibility for operations; cells of the HAMAS military arm, he said, "were successful in the operations we did not announce, and similarly, operations continue to take place that are never mentioned by the Zionists themselves." Overall, "what is important is the determination and decision to continue the military operations, not its implementation."

———

MEANWHILE, THERE were ominous signs that the Arab world was preparing for a major war. Acceleration of Syria's strategic weapons programs was significant—especially the testing of a chemical warhead and the testing of an auxiliary system aimed at overwhelming Israel's fledgling Arrow ABM defense. Damascus had long denied having chemical weapons; now the Syrian air force conducted an undeniable test, dropping chemical warheads onto the desert floor to test their actual performance. The Syrians also test-fired in rudimentary surface-to-surface mode some older surface-to-air missiles they had converted using North Korean technology. The idea behind this conversion was to overwhelm the Israeli defenses with a massive first barrage so that SCUD-type ballistic missiles would face little or no defense.

By early 2000, Syria had also completed a major phase of its conventional buildup and acquired new capabilities optimized for stopping an Israeli counterattack on the Golan Heights. The most important components of this buildup were marked improvements in training, upgrades of primary weapon systems, and the introduction of new electronic-warfare and anti-tank systems. Israeli Military Intelligence concluded that Syria "has in some cases caught up [with] or even exceeded Israel in some areas of military prowess." Israel was most apprehensive about the new anti-tank capabilities, built around long-range KORNET anti-tank guided missiles, with which Syria could endanger Israeli armor offensives on the Golan by being able to strike Israeli tanks before their systems could detect the threat. Syria had also acquired electronic countermeasures to jam Israeli communications, radars, and other sophisticated systems. Ultimately, Israeli Military Intelligence concluded that Syria had vastly improved its ability to launch a limited offensive on the Golan as well as slow down and wear down an Israeli counterattack. While the IDF was still confident of its ability to defeat the Syrian military, the price in men, equipment, and time—a crucial political and economic commodity—would be higher than before.

Developments in Cairo had comparable significance. The Egyptian national security elite had conducted extensive studies of the Israeli military posture, with a view to developing a new strategy capable of defeating the IDF in a future war. A December 1999 article by Major General (Ret.) Musad Shishtawi Ahmad in the Cairo paper *Al-Difa* elucidated Cairo's understanding of Israel's security posture.

Israel, Shishtawi explained, relies on a "military creed" based on the Jewish "historic and religious" legacy. At the core of this "creed" is Israel's "firm conviction that it could not afford to lose one single war because that would mean its total annihilation." Israel is a small country surrounded by a huge Arab-Muslim world. "Hence, Israel has always sought to expand its strategic depth by waging wars and occupying Arab lands. It has also insisted on demilitarizing the lands it withdraws from and setting up early warning posts therein in order to have more time to carry out plans to mobilize the reserve forces, which constitute the main bulk of the Israeli Defense Force." As a result of the 1973 Yom Kippur War, Israel is fully aware that "the Arabs have richer human and material resources, which makes them more capable of fighting such lengthy wars [defensive wars] before making the transition from defense to offense." Consequently, Israel is now "focused on aborting the Arab attacks in the initial stage" through offensive military actions.

Shishtawi noted that the peace process—which he counted as beginning in the late 1970s, with the Camp David Accords—had not altered Israel's basic strategic tenets, for "the Israeli strategy seeks to achieve regional accomplishments to bolster the position of Israeli negotiators." Despite the peace treaties and the ongoing negotiations with its Arab neighbors, Israel was still "trying to secure the ability to fight for longer periods of time." Furthermore, "Israel has resumed its feverish arms race with the Arab parties to the conflict and launched a series of hostile military operations such as destroying the Iraqi nuclear reactor in 1981 and invading South Lebanon in 1982." The Israeli Air Force was the primary instrument of this strategy. It was therefore imperative for the Arab world to create a political-strategic posture in which the Israeli Air Force "can be isolated or neutralized" by "sophisticated air defense systems." The challenge was urgent, because Israel was already committed "to developing the capability to strike or launch counterattacks against two fronts simultaneously." Furthermore, "Israel will not be satisfied with its qualitative superiority. It will pay more attention to quantity as well because its military forces could suffer from a sudden collapse, particularly in view of the growing size of the Arab armies and the expected high casualty rates in any future war. The Israeli strategy may also focus on implementing gross deterrence, which may not be directed exclusively against the armed forces. It might seek to destroy the infrastructure and the vital economic targets of its enemies. It will also maintain its commitment to launching pre-emptive strikes as a viable option in any future traditional war." Given the essence of the Israeli "military creed," Shishtawi concluded, no peace process could be expected to reduce the lingering threat of Israel's aggressive strategy, and Egypt would have to act accordingly.

These and similar statements emanating from Cairo, combined with changes in force structure and deployment patterns of the Egyptian military forces, caught Jerusalem's attention. In early January 2000, the IDF conducted a large command exercise examining the potential impact of the new Egyptian capabilities, particularly in the case of a war between Syria and Israel. The IDF examined two scenarios: in the first, Egypt deployed forces into the Sinai only as a demonstration of displeasure with Israel; in the second, Egyptian forces actually joined the war. The IDF's conclusion was that, given the high-performance U.S.-made weapon systems the Egyptians now had, the use or threatened use of those forces would severely complicate the IDF's ability to sustain a war with Syria or Iraq.

All these developments were components of an overall reexamination by the Arab and Muslim ruling elites of where they were going. To a certain extent, these elites were influenced by the millennium craze in the West—widely perceived as part of the Great Conspiracy against Islamdom (the entire Muslim world was addicted to a conspiracy theory anticipating the West to stifle and destroy the Muslim world in order to prevent Islam's ascent in the 21st century). In a January article in *Al-Ahram Weekly*, Gamil Mattar, director of the Arab Center for Development and Futuristic Research, best described their state of mind.

While the threat to the Arab world had been mounting, Mattar stated, Arab leaders had proved incapable of confronting it except in raising emotions. Consequently, "Arab resentment of Britain, France, the Zionists, and the U.S., sparked in the early days of the [20th] century, did not subside as [that century] ended. In the throes of their rage," Mattar lamented, "the Arabs were incapable of examining their plight calmly and planning for their future. Despite their great wealth, the Arabs never ceased to indulge in mudslinging and smear campaigns as the world watched." Hence, almost without realizing what was happening, Arab governments found themselves ensnared in the U.S.-sponsored peace process.

The long-term ramifications of the peace process, Mattar argued, should be assessed in the context of Jewish expansionism and aggression. "The Israelis," he wrote, "see the 20th century as a predominantly Zionist century, and predict that the 21st century would be so as well. During the last century, Zionism developed into a bellicose theory. Moving slowly but surely, the Zionist settlers, and later the Israelis, engaged in blackmail campaigns to win a few more meters of Arab land that would accommodate more Jewish immigrants. These came first in small numbers, then in droves, one million emigrating from Russia alone. The Zionists dream of a land that stretches from the Nile to the Euphrates, of a population that includes all the Jews of the world, and of influence over all the major capitals in the region."

By contrast, Mattar declared, in agreeing to the peace process, the Arab world acknowledged its weakness, if not actual defeat at the hands of the Zionists and their Western patrons. "Whatever we assumed was the dominant character of the century, because of reason, ignorance, or fear, today we must admit to the world, and to ourselves above all, that the 20th century was the century of Zionism. Throughout the greater part of the century, Arab rejection of Israel remained absolute and categorical, yet weak. By 1999, all the Arab rulers—even those who had procrastinated until reactions from Damascus were forthcoming—had recognized Israel." This trend, Mattar maintained, could only bring about the further splitting of the Arab world and, consequently, further weakening and decline.

While some foresaw a dramatic, perhaps violent, breakout from the stifling-by-peace, Mattar was not optimistic. "Part of the conflict," he noted, "has been carried over to the new century, and the new page is smeared with past sins. The Arabs are suspicious of the future, and cannot trust that times to come will be more generous with them than the century that has passed. But they know full well that they have not changed in their hearts, and for that reason do not deserve a better future." Mattar warned that both Zionism and the Arab world were at a historical turning point. "The twentieth century witnessed the birth of Zionist revolution and of Arab nationalism. But as the century came to its end," he observed, "the destinies of Arabs and Zionists diverged. Zionism is still moving forward, intent on realizing its dream despite apparently insurmountable difficulties, while the Arabs are marching in place, resisting the sense of despair which is always a characteristic of middle age." Only a confrontation with Israel could provide the needed rejuvenation. "Those who genuinely seek a better future," Mattar urged both the Arab street and the opinion-forming elites, "should prevent Zionism from triumphing. Let them bring pressure to bear on their rulers and carry the struggle forward."

Mattar's analysis reflected the state of mind of a growing majority within the Arab and Muslim worlds. But neither the Clinton administration nor the Barak government took these developments into consideration when formulating their regional policy.

IN EARLY JANUARY, even before the Shepherdstown talks had definitively fallen apart, Barak reopened the negotiations with the Palestinian Authority that had virtually frozen in early December. Clinton, still desperately yearning for his "legacy," strongly encouraged the move. If the Syrian track did collapse, there would still be some hope for the Palestinian track.

To jump-start the negotiations, the administration urged Israel to unilaterally implement the next phase of withdrawals under the Sharm-el-Sheikh

Memorandum largely in accordance with Arafat's demands, to assist in consolidating full PA control over contiguous areas. In addition, Ross called Arafat with an invitation from Clinton to come to Washington in mid-January bringing draft proposals for the framework agreement, the signing of which was still scheduled for February.

Dutifully, Barak instructed the Israeli delegation in charge of implementing the Interim Agreement to be forthcoming and flexible. Little wonder that agreement on further Israeli withdrawal was quickly reached, with Israel committed to implementing it within two days. This withdrawal comprised 5.1 percent of the West Bank and covered some of the "improved" territory Arafat had long demanded. In the process, the IDF vacated six bases and some sections of road, including the main artery connecting Nablus and Jenin, that the Netanyahu government had considered crucial for sustaining Israel's security in Samaria, especially if the need to suppress a widespread Palestinian uprising should arise. Within a few months, the IDF regretted handing over the facilities.

Israel also agreed to release twenty-two Palestinian prisoners as a gesture for Ramadan. Still, a senior Palestinian official stressed that the PA had "compromised" in accepting the Israeli withdrawal and had done so only after being promised that the final stage of the West Bank withdrawal, scheduled for January 20, would be subject to agreement by both sides—yet another Israeli concession, giving away the hard-won guarantee by Christopher that Israel alone would determine the size and timing of withdrawals.

On the night of January 9–10, Oded Eran, the head of the Israeli delegation, met with Arafat for a late-night session. Eran assured Arafat of Barak's commitment to profound compromises in the forthcoming negotiations. Consequently, Arafat authorized the resumption of the final-status talks the next day. The Palestinians demanded that the next withdrawal be the first item on the agenda, and the Israelis complied. Within a few days, Israel had accepted the bulk of the Palestinian demands for the size and location of the January 20 withdrawal, which would bring the total of land under the PA's control to 43 percent—18.2 percent under full PA control (Area A) and 24.8 percent under joint authority of the PA and Israeli security forces (Area B).

However, at the last minute Arafat introduced additional demands—the most important being that the East Jerusalem suburb of Abu-Dis be turned over as part of Area A instead of Area B, as agreed upon. As well, the PA now claimed that the just-completed withdrawal covered only 4.7 percent—rather than 5.1 percent—and demanded additional territory in the forthcoming round. When Arafat rejected the Israeli proposal that the final decision on the contested areas be part of the framework agreement, Barak instructed that the withdrawal be delayed until his own return from Washington. Unfazed, Palestinian officials announced that Arafat would complain to Clinton that Barak was intentionally procrastinating.

Arab officials realized that the real motive behind Arafat's last-minute brinkmanship was to have a "crisis" to use as an excuse for his principled unwillingness, or inability, to reach a permanent agreement with Israel. Clinton's intention in inviting Arafat to Washington was to give the White House the opportunity to work with him on the framework agreement. Indeed, Nabil Shaath had expected Arafat to seek "American support for Palestinian just rights" on such key issues as "Jerusalem, settlements, refugees, borders and water." However, such discussions would have entailed Arafat's formal recognition of Israel's right to exist and the end of the Palestinian-Jewish conflict—something Arafat could not bring himself to undertake. Therefore, having a remaining unresolved issue, in the form of the January 20 withdrawal, gave Arafat something to discuss in Washington rather than the framework agreement.

Once again, Arafat used a Fatah communiqué to state what he could not say in his capacity as chairman of the PA. Fatah announced that a major crisis was unfolding because Israel would not "fulfill one of its obligations under the Sharm el-Sheikh Memo"—namely, the January 20 withdrawal. The delay was an issue of great significance, the communiqué explained: "This date [January 20] was taken into full consideration when the PNA agreed to reach a framework agreement in February of this year. By choosing this timing, the PNA aimed to show that there is no connection between the interim issues and the final status ones." For the PA, Israel's insistence on not discussing Arafat's demands outside the framework agreement negotiations was an attempt to combine the two tracks. The use of interim issues as a hostage with "the aim of gaining further concessions from the PNA" thus "endangers the peace process and threatens its credibility," Fatah declared.

Henceforth, the communiqué announced, the Palestinians would adopt the Syrian negotiating position: "The Israeli-Syrian negotiations consist of one phase. Israel cannot, therefore, blackmail the Syrians because it cannot use the interim issues as a hostage." In the negotiations with the PA, however, Israel was desperately attempting to break away from this principle: "By postponing the Israeli withdrawal which is due January 20, 2000, Barak wants to blackmail the Palestinian side on the third phase of Oslo II. At the end of this phase, Israel is supposed to withdraw its forces from all occupied territories with the exception of areas related to the final status issues: Jerusalem, borders, settlements and military installations." If the model of Israeli-Syrian negotiations were applied to the Palestinian track, Fatah argued, "Israel should withdraw its forces to the pre-1967 borders, which means: (1) Complete withdrawal from Jerusalem, (2) Complete withdrawal from all areas occupied in 1967 and the cessation of the settlement question, (3) Resolution of the issue of water on the basis of international law." The communiqué noted that the Syrian approach to "security arrangements" would require "finding a just resolution to the problem of Palestinian refugees," for "this reinforces U.N. Resolution 194 and stands against the conspiracy of settling Palestinian refugees where they live now." Only when these steps were fulfilled could a myriad of steps for economic cooperation and normalization of relations be implemented.

The communiqué concluded with an urgent appeal to the Arab world to pressure the United States to apply the principles of the Syrian track to the Palestinian track: "A united Arab stand based on international legality will elicit U.S. and international support in a way that influences the Israeli attitude. The billions of dollars that Israel has demanded in military assistance contradict the spirit of the peace process. Investment in peace should be preferred to investment in war. Revolution Until Victory!"

Arafat also sent Barak a reminder of the alternative to dealing with him, in the form of a bomb that exploded in a trash can in downtown Hadera, injuring twenty-two people. An unknown group called "The Forces of Umar al-Mukhtar" claimed responsibility for the Hadera attack. However, the explosives and fuse were identical to those used in a series of bombings in Netanya in November 1999. The next day, Israeli intelligence provided the government with solid proof that "the Palestinian Authority knew in advance of yesterday's terrorist bombing in Hadera but did nothing to stop it." In fact, the Hadera bomb had been planted by an Islamic Jihad cell operating out of a PA-controlled city in Samaria.

Even the Hadera bomb was not enough to make Barak pause and reexamine the viability of the negotiations. Instead, that night he hosted Arafat at his home in Kokhav Yair (in the coastal plains not far from the West Bank) for a meeting that lasted several hours. The two men discussed future withdrawals and failed to come to an agreement. Barak also told Arafat he was postponing the January 20 withdrawal by three weeks. Barak justified this move by the need to delay the target date for reaching the framework agreement, originally scheduled for February 15, by a similar amount of time. These delays did not constitute a violation of the Sharm el-Sheikh Memorandum, Barak pointed out, because postponements of up to three weeks were permitted. Arafat swallowed the announcement quietly and returned to Gaza fuming.

Barak pursued this approach because he believed he could coordinate Israel's position with Clinton prior to Arafat's visit to Washington and have Clinton persuade Arafat to be sensible. Barak expected that an intensive series of meetings spanning several weeks and involving Israel, the Clinton administration, and the PA would succeed in producing a framework agreement on permanent status. These meetings would start immediately after Arafat's return from the United States. Barak insisted that he and Arafat had agreed on this approach during their meeting in Kokhav Yair—an assertion Arafat hotly denied. However, Israeli officials noted that Barak, Arafat, and Clinton would soon be meeting at the World Economic Forum in Davos, Switzerland, and would have a chance there to resolve any outstanding differences.

———

IN WASHINGTON, Arafat insisted that he had agreed only to a two-week delay in the next Israeli withdrawal. He resented being asked by Clinton and Albright "to lower his expectations for the agreement" and to be ready for "hard and unavoidable compromises." He was also unhappy at being told by Clinton that February 13 should be considered "a target date" and not "a deadline," and that the administration now viewed the framework agreement as a mere "declaration of principles" rather than the "detailed draft of a future peace agreement" that Arafat insisted it should be. However, Clinton was interested in Arafat's proposal that an exchange of territory in the permanent-status agreement be compensation for the Israeli annexation of settlement blocks.

Despite the disappointments in Washington, the Palestinian leadership was highly encouraged by the overall results of Arafat's visit. "Most important is the support we get from the United States, in its role as a sponsor of the peace process," noted an internal memo of the Central Council of the Palestine Liberation Organization. "The U.S. president, in fact, is more than a partner in the process and has proved himself more trustworthy than some others, including the U.S. special envoy, Dennis Ross." According to the memo, Clinton had already recognized, and committed himself to supporting, "the rights of the Palestinian people [including] the right of return, the right to self-determination, and the right to establish the state of Palestine with Jerusalem as its capital." The memo specified the preconditions for further discussions: Israel's withdrawing completely from "Palestinian and other Arab territories occupied by force in 1967"; "ensuring that East Jerusalem is the capital city of the state of Palestine"; unconditionally and completely eradicating all settlements; "enabling Palestinian refugees to return to their lands" inside Israel proper; and guaranteeing that "Palestinian self-determination and the establishment of a Palestinian state with full sovereignty, including complete control over its resources, are matters not subject to negotiation"—which contradicted the long-standing U.S. and Israeli understanding that a future Palestinian state would be disarmed and subjected to external supervision. "By acting on the suggestions made in this paper, the Central Council will attain freedom and peace for the Palestinian people."

By now, Jerusalem was pleading for time. Eran estimated that a final agreement between Israel and the Palestinians could not be reached before September at the earliest. Given Arafat's stalling, Barak decided to avoid the Davos conference so that he would not be subjected to more pressure from Clinton. Instead, Barak issued a statement that he had "decided to accelerate talks with the Palestinians on several levels." Barak did talk with Clinton over the phone following Arafat's visit, but the conversation was inconclusive.

On January 31, Israeli and Palestinian negotiators started "marathon talks" to attempt to reach a framework agreement on permanent status by February 13. To accelerate the talks, Ross planned to arrive in Israel on February 2, and Barak announced a summit with Arafat on the next evening. At issue were the Israeli draft maps. Israel wanted to annex settlements situated on the "Green Line"; in return, Israel would evacuate the majority of settlements on the mountain plateau as well as the town of Kiryat Arba near Hebron. The Palestinians flatly rejected these maps, insisting on unconditional withdrawal to the pre-1967 borders.

For the sake of "goodwill," the Israeli government on February 2 approved a third and final interim withdrawal and empowered Barak to present the compromise to Arafat at their summit. In fact, the summit was acrimonious and ended in sharp disagreement over the withdrawal plans, particularly regarding the areas around Jerusalem claimed by the PA. Barak and Arafat agreed to revive the final-status negotiations as scheduled; however, they would not hold a joint press conference as they had planned.

Despite Ross's efforts over the next few days, the Palestinians adamantly refused to accept the withdrawal unless areas around Jerusalem were included. An emergency meeting between Eran and Erekat convened by Indyk at his home also ended without agreement. Erekat acknowledged that he would not make the slightest gesture except on Arafat's instructions, and Arafat refused to make decisions. Eventually, the PA notified Israel and the United States that it was suspending negotiations, although, at the urging of the White House, the PA agreed to continue "informal" talks.

———

ARAFAT IMMEDIATELY REACTED by unleashing another cycle of terrorism and highlighting his close relations with the Islamists. He first ordered the release from prison of HAMAS leader Abdul Aziz Rantisi, who had been jailed for publicly opposing peace with Israel. "My release came as a result of the contacts made by brothers in the movement and members of the Authority," Rantisi said. The next day, HAMAS went into action, preparing a powerful car bomb for an Israeli city; however, the two terrorists working on the car in the village of a-Dik made a mistake, and it blew up prematurely, killing them. In a mid-February interview with IMRA's Aaron Lerner, Rantisi stressed that the PA had given HAMAS a "green light for attacks" on Israel because "the Palestinian Authority is sure that the peace process will end in a big zero." Alluding to the resumption of terrorism in Israeli cities, Rantisi commented, "The orders of our religion are not to kill children, women, elderly, or civilians. But at the same time Islam gives the Muslims the green light to do with their enemies in the same way." And since Israel kept killing civilians and stifling the Palestinian nation, Rantisi argued, retaliation "is up to the [HAMAS] military wing."

Again, a Fatah communiqué elucidated Arafat's position. "In spite of assurances and flowery declarations, the Israeli government, by its refusal to implement the signed agreements and to carry out its commitments under the Oslo-Wye-Sharm interim accords, has resolutely plunged the whole peace process into a most dangerous crisis." The noble stand of the Palestinians offered a contrast: "The PLO, the PNA, and the Palestinian people as a whole, who have chosen Peace as a historical, strategic option, reject adamantly these attempts to empty the peace process of its substance and to impose a diktat on the Palestinian negotiators." In conclusion, the communiqué for the first time formally connected Israel's military activities in Lebanon and its negotiating positions on the Syrian track with progress on the Palestinian track. "Israeli state terrorism in Lebanon, and the criminal attacks on Lebanese civilian populations, besides causing a spectacular regression in the prospect of Israeli-Syrian and Israeli-Lebanese negotiations, will only reinforce the idea, among all the peoples of the region, that Peace with Israel is a lure, while convincing the Israeli people that violence remains the basis of Israel's relationship to the rest of the area." In other words, even if Barak met all or most of Arafat's demands, Arafat could point to events in Lebanon or Israeli policy toward Syria as his reason for maintaining the deadlock.

Undaunted, Barak assured his cabinet on February 13 that "We intend to reach an agreement with the Palestinians, based on the understanding that such a framework agreement will include or must include profound and painful flexibility from both sides." Arafat, who was visiting Morocco at the time, responded with fury: "Palestinian-Israeli negotiations are revolving in a vicious circle manufactured by the Israeli Government. This dangerous situation requires a universal stance that must tell the Israeli Government to take its hands off Jerusalem. Your support is essential . . . to free Jerusalem and Palestine from this cancerous Judaization." Stung by the criticism, Barak instructed his security aide, Danny Yatom, to make changes in the withdrawal maps and allow the PA to participate in determining the adjustments. Senior members of the Israeli defense establishment, including Amnon Shahak, a former IDF chief of staff and at this time the head of the ministerial map committee, were completely unaware of the policy change until they were asked by journalists for their reaction.

At this point, Arafat unleashed yet another wave of terrorism. Attacks on Jewish traffic and vandalism of Jewish properties throughout the West Bank were particularly significant—not because of the damage caused but because the attacks were carried out by members of the Palestinian Security Forces on Arafat's own instructions. In the Gaza Strip, Palestinian security personnel hurled Molotov cocktails at IDF posts and patrols. When Major General Yom Tov Samiyeh, the commanding officer of the IDF's Southern Command, met with senior PA officials and told them the IDF regarded these incidents with extreme gravity, they virtually laughed in his face.

Jerusalem, however, was already on the defensive. On Barak's instructions, the Israeli defense establishment prepared a new rough draft of a permanent-status map of the West Bank with only six settlement blocks remaining under Israeli sovereignty: Gush Etzion, Northern Samaria, Western Samaria, Western Binyamin, Eastern Binyamin, and the eastern Mount Hebron area. Moreover, some of these blocks would not be contiguous with the State of Israel. According to the map, twenty-three other settlements would be evacuated. When Ross returned to Israel, Barak indicated that he was also willing to offer the PA implementation of the northern safe passage route between Gaza and the West Bank and the transfer to the PA of the purchase tax that Israel was collecting from the Palestinians. Ross expressed his support, but his subsequent shuttles between Jerusalem, Gaza, and Cairo failed to gain Arafat's cooperation.

Arafat himself told an Italian interviewer, "Ehud Barak has disappointed me, even though he was elected to the position of prime minister because of me." In fact, Barak was "even worse than Netanyahu"; to express his contempt, Arafat referred to the two of them as "Barakiyahu." He also stressed the growing frustration of the Palestinian street, explaining that the prevalent sense that nothing had really changed since Barak took power was pushing "people" into grassroots violence. At the same time, the PA instructed its security and police forces to launch a policy of "increased friction" with their Israeli counterparts in all their joint activities. In one security-coordination meeting, the PA officials warned that if Israel arrested suspicious Palestinians at the Jordan River crossings (as codified by Israeli-Palestinian agreements), "it will lead to bloodshed." The PA officials also demanded first access to Palestinian suspects irrespective of existing agreements and practice. At various contact points, particularly Hebron, PA police did nothing to stop Arabs who were attacking Israeli civilians and policemen; at times they encouraged the culprits, and always they blocked the Israeli security forces from chasing them. After this matter was discussed in the Israeli Security Cabinet, Shlomo

Ben-Ami, the Internal Security Minister, instructed the Israeli police and other security forces to demonstrate "utmost restraint" in order "not to sour" the spirit of the negotiations.

By mid-February, Arafat was making the future of Jerusalem a major sticking point in the negotiations. Ismael Nawahda explained the basis for this intransigence in a sermon delivered in al-Aqsa Mosque, in which he emphasized the sacredness of Jerusalem to the entire Muslim world. "The Zionists must understand that Jerusalem was our first Qibla [the direction to which Muslims turn during prayer] and the third of the three holiest mosques [after Mecca and Medina]." Therefore, Nawahda told tens of thousands of worshipers, "al-Quds al-Sharif [Holy Jerusalem] was, is, and will always be the key to peace or war."

———

FAISAL HUSSEINI, who held the PA's Jerusalem portfolio, underscored the centrality of the Jerusalem issue. In early March, he announced that all future meetings between Palestinians and visiting foreign diplomats would take place in the Orient House or in other locations in Jerusalem to be determined by the PA. The Israeli Foreign Ministry protested that Husseini's statement was in "flagrant violation" of the PA's commitment not to establish offices in areas in which it did not have formal authority. Members of Arafat's inner circle quickly reacted with disdain, noting that Arafat had instructed the PA to cease acceding to Israeli demands concerning meetings at the Orient House, because of "Israel's unilateral measures in Jerusalem at Har Homa and Ras al-Amud." The future of Jerusalem, they declared, was at the core of the dispute between Israel and the PA, and no Israeli withdrawal offer would change that.

Had everything gone in accordance with Arafat's plans, at least one spectacular bombing would have taken place by then within Israel, turning everybody's attention to the carnage. Consequently, the focus of the Israeli-Palestinian negotiations would have shifted to the PA's efforts at fighting Islamist terrorism, and Jerusalem would have been ready to make additional concessions in terms of withdrawals and tolerance of previous violations. HAMAS Gaza had started logistical support activities in mid-February, renting a safe house in Taibe—an Arab township in Israel—and contracting with four Israeli Arabs to provide services ranging from transportation to food supplies. Meanwhile, HAMAS cells in Samaria had organized a six-man detachment and built two powerful suitcase bombs in preparation for simultaneous suicide bombings. In late February, the six men and their bombs were infiltrated into the Taibe safe house. The operational cooperation between HAMAS Gaza and the Samaria branches, as well as the use of Taibe—the hometown of Arafat's confidant Ahmad Tibi—testifies to the extremely high levels at which the operation was discussed and ultimately approved.

Israeli intelligence learned about the operation, and on the night of March 1–2, special forces surrounded the safe house. After a brief siege, the anti-terrorist forces killed four of the HAMAS terrorists and wounded and captured a fifth; the sixth escaped. The four Israeli Arabs who provided support services were also arrested. Intelligence data confirmed that the terrorists had intended to strike on March 2 or 3—perfect timing for Arafat's brinkmanship strategy. The Voice of Palestine Radio called the terrorists "holy martyrs" and harshly criticized the Israeli security forces. Ahmed Qurai (Abu-Alaa), speaker of the PA Parliament and one of the key negotiators with Israel, explained that the aborted HAMAS operation epitomized the growing despair in the territories because of Israeli intransigence. He warned that "if Israel does not turn over parts of the West Bank that Palestinians believe they are entitled to under the interim peace accord, they will send their own police to take control of the territory."

At this point, Ross returned to Israel to help revive the talks. On March 7, he met with Arafat and Barak in Israel to discuss some of the outstanding issues. The next day, they met again in Ramallah to discuss the outline for a new round of talks to be held in Washington. "We are on the verge of a breakthrough in the negotiations with the Palestinians," Barak told reporters.

On March 9, the three men traveled to Sharm el-Sheikh for a follow-up session with Mubarak. Ross and Barak's primary objective was to get Mubarak's help in convincing Arafat to accept the Americans' revised schedule—having the final-status principles signed in May and the completed agreement in September. Ultimately, however, Barak himself caved in under pressure from Mubarak and Ross and promised that Israel would consider transferring areas surrounding Jerusalem to full Palestinian control. Nevertheless, Barak claimed the summit "resulted in measurable progress."

Even as Mubarak was hosting these negotiations, an article in the government-owned *Al-Ahram* elucidated Cairo's position on a crucial question, the right of return. In this article, the commentator Salman Abu-Sitta explained that "contrary to the myths and misinformation campaigns propagated by the Israelis . . . the right of return is physically possible." He noted that the vast majority of Israelis live in cities: "This leaves 3 percent of Jews, the rural residents of the *kibbutzim* and *moshavim,* in control of the vast Palestinian land. . . . Thus we have here a tiny minority of 200,000 Jews obstructing the return of five million refugees." Abu-Sitta cited a recent poll conducted by the PA showing that 90.8 percent of respondents would refuse to accept a Palestinian state if the cost were forfeiting the "right of return."

Egyptian high officials handed out copies of Abu-Sitta's article and mentioned that it was endorsed by "the highest echelons" in Cairo—a euphemism for Mubarak.

————

IN MID-MARCH, the Israeli cabinet approved withdrawal maps for an additional 6.1 percent, as agreed with Arafat. The withdrawal included filling in an area between Jericho and the PA village of Ouja, until then connected only by a narrow strip of PA-controlled territory; the filling in would enable secure transportation of goods (including weapons) from Jordan via Jericho into the heart of Samaria. Israel also agreed to vacate several towns in the Jericho, Jenin, Bethlehem, and Hebron areas. By the time the withdrawal was completed in late March, the PA had full or partial control over 98 percent of the Palestinian population and approximately 40 percent of the territory of the West Bank.

Meanwhile, the new era of cooperation in fighting terrorism had hit a snag. Following the Taibe incident, Israel provided Jibril Rajub, head of the PA's Preventive Security Service, with information about a HAMAS safe house in southern Nablus. When Rajub's people "failed" to locate the house, Israel was asked to "lend" them a HAMAS prisoner so that he could point it out. After the HAMAS leadership in Nablus reached an agreement with the PA on vacating the house in question without any retribution, Rajub refused to return the prisoner to Israel because he could not bring himself to transfer a Palestinian to Israeli hands. Jerusalem swallowed the insult and did not disrupt the Washington talks on security cooperation.

Even so, the talks stalled as soon as the last withdrawal was completed. The PA negotiators cited instructions from Arafat to renege on agreed-upon positions on key components of the final-status principles. When Barak rejected demands for more concessions, Arafat accused the Israelis of "hardening their positions." Ross and other American officials failed to break the deadlock.

————

BY THIS TIME, Clinton was looking for something dramatic after a slow start to his last year in office, and Barak was eager to comply. Clinton ensured Barak's cooperation through frequent phone calls—private, intimate, and personally bonding calls as far as Barak was concerned. In a series of such calls in early 2000, Clinton told Barak that he had managed to arrange a summit meeting with Hafez al-Assad for late March, and he was sure that once he was face to face with Assad, he would be able to secure a peace deal for Israel. He intimated that "given the right conditions"—that is, the right kind of Israeli advance concessions—it might even be possible to transform the summit into a trilateral event, with Barak joining Clinton and Assad. Swept up in Clinton's egocentric overconfidence and flattered by his attention, Barak simply could not say no.

For his part, Hafez al-Assad was obsessed with his death and legacy, especially Bashar's ability to consolidate power as his successor. To his confidants, "Al-Assad seemed to be a man in a real race against time." He sought to impress on them the notion that "his accomplishments during his life entitle him to a grand funeral at his death"—a funeral "like that of [Gamal] Abd-al-Nassir." He viewed both the peace process and a possible war not as objectives in their own right but as instruments for promoting Bashar's ascent and survival. For Assad, no issue was beyond exploitation and manipulation as long as it furthered Bashar's interests. And he made no effort to conceal this attitude.

Meanwhile, Martin Indyk's return as ambassador to Israel, after a brief period back in Washington, had a profound impact on Barak. The two men had a close relationship, and Indyk used his own strong influence as an extension of Clinton's hold over Barak. During the period when Clinton was regularly phoning Barak, Indyk worked on persuading him that there was a good chance of a breakthrough if only Israel reassured Syria of its sincerity. On the weekend of January 28–29, the administration arranged a secret meeting between Shahak and a representative of Assad in Geneva. Officially, the discussions addressed various formulas relayed by Washington for resuming negotiations. However, the real challenge was how to assure Assad that any new negotiations would begin with Israel's acknowledged, though undeclared, commitment that it would fully withdraw from the Golan Heights in exchange for full relations with Syria. Assad's emissary acknowledged Damascus's awareness of the Israeli commitment, and Shahak returned convinced that Indyk was right and the chances for peace were good.

Completely missing from the Israeli calculations were the military buildup in southern Lebanon and the growing audacity of the HizbAllah. By early 2000, the Iranians had deployed several hundred Pasdaran officers to Beirut and the Bekaa, where they trained a small number of HizbAllah fighters for specific "quality actions" against the IDF and the SLA as part of Tehran's commitment to "drowning the peace process in blood." Operating in teams of two to four, and relying on comprehensive support from the front-line HizbAllah forces, these quality teams were responsible for intelligence collection and for special operations such as assassinations. They were also responsible for overseeing martyrdom operations in southern Lebanon, although the would-be martyrs were prepared by a different group in the Bekaa. Encouraged by the White House, Barak interpreted these developments as merely Syria's means of putting additional pressure on Israel for further compromises.

In late January, immediately following the Geneva meeting, Damascus decided to test Jerusalem's commitment to the peace process by instructing the HizbAllah to deliver major strikes. First, Colonel Akel Hashem, the commander of the SLA's western brigade and the designated successor to SLA Commander Antoine Lahad, was killed by a roadside bomb near his home when he went to meet with some tobacco dealers. An on-site operative detonated the bomb via remote control. The assassination—videotaped by the HizbAllah and broadcast on their TV station—was a serious blow to the SLA's morale. It was a major achievement for HizbAllah to have planted such a powerful bomb inside the security zone and also to have obtained up-to-the-minute intelligence as to when the tobacco merchants would arrive. The next day, HizbAllah launched a rocket attack on the IDF's Galgalit outpost on the eastern front of the security zone, killing three IDF soldiers.

At first, Barak vowed that Israel "will do everything to ensure that those who attacked Hashem get their due punishment." After the attack on Galgalit, he declared that "the Government of Israel will not accept the continuing activities of the HizbAllah and will act persistently to protect its citizens in the north and IDF and SLA soldiers. Our enemies are those that will pay the price." But then Clinton sent Barak a personal communication reminding him of the "understandings" of the Geneva meeting and pleading with him not to put revenge ahead of the peace process. Barak reversed himself completely. According to a government leak, Israel "would not avenge the HizbAllah attacks" because a sharp response would "lead to the collapse of the diplomatic negotiations with Syria."

Even in saying this, Barak did not conceal his awareness of the Syrian sponsorship of the HizbAllah. "There is no doubt in our mind that the Syrians can do more [to stop the HizbAllah]," he said. "However, we have no interest in a general escalation and we will not lose sight of the larger goal, which is a deal with Syria and an agreement with Lebanon that will allow a redeployment of the IDF to international borders." Having to choose between the advice of the Israeli high command to take "swift and harsh action" against the HizbAllah and the assurances of Clinton and Indyk that an agreement with Syria was within reach, the prime minister of Israel chose the latter. Barak argued that since contacts with the Syrians were "hanging by a thread," it was in Israel's interest to make sure that the U.S. initiative did not collapse. "One incident in South Lebanon and a harsh response on our part, and everything goes down the drain," he said, echoing Clinton's approach. To his confidants, he added that there was no reason to intensify Assad's "inferiority complex" through a military defeat when it was still possible to entice him into joining the Clinton-sponsored peace process.

14

"Lebanon Today—Palestine Tomorrow!" (2000)

The Failure of the Clinton-Assad Summit; the Betrayal of Lebanon

BARAK'S DECISION to go along with Clinton's assurances was all the more inexcusable in view of the annual national assessment that Israeli Military Intelligence submitted to him in the last week of January. This assessment concluded that even if an Israeli-Syrian peace treaty were signed, Syria would resist normalization efforts and remain Israel's primary military rival. According to the assessment, Damascus would prohibit its citizens from visiting Israel and would foil attempts at commercial trade and cultural and technical exchanges. Mossad concurred with this assessment. "We are talking about a peace that will be colder than that between Israel and Egypt," an official source told Steve Rodan, the chief editor of the Middle East News Line (MENL).

In early February, Israeli intelligence confirmed, and promptly reported to the prime minister, that Damascus had permitted Tehran to re-arm HizbAllah with emphasis on offensive capabilities. Significantly, Damascus had approved the additional weapon supplies in early January—just when Israeli and Syrian officials were meeting in Shepherdstown. Tehran had started an airlift to Damascus airport almost immediately, and now, in early February, the pace and magnitude of the weapon shipments were increasing. From Damascus, Syrian trucks transferred the weapons to warehouses throughout southern Lebanon. The new supplies had already enabled HizbAllah to increase its attacks against Israeli and South Lebanese troops and positions. Nonetheless, fearing an adverse impact on the peace process, Barak ordered the IDF to refrain from striking the warehouses or intercepting the Syrian trucks.

At first, Barak sought to stifle the criticism from the Israeli security and intelligence elite by visiting command headquarters in Metullah, in the northern Galilee, and explaining his policy to the local officers. Instead, he met with calls for action. "We have to return to the time when we were the pursuers, and they were the pursued," one officer told Barak. Confronted with pressure from both sides, Barak zigged and zagged. He finally approved a special operation: the assassination of Ibrahim Akil, the number-two HizbAllah commander in southern Lebanon. On February 5, an Apache gunship launched two missiles at Akil's car. However, hearing the helicopter's distinctive noise, Akil managed to jump out of the moving car before it exploded. HizbAllah immediately vowed revenge. "This will not go unanswered," its statement read. "The resistance will choose the place and proper means and will find a way to put an end to the Zionist excesses."

That afternoon, HizbAllah announced the beginning of artillery and mortar bombardment of the IDF's Karkom outpost in the western sector of the security zone. Civilians in the northern Galilee moved to shelters in case of Katyusha attacks. That night, in the midst of a violent rainstorm, a HizbAllah special team placed a roadside bomb near the Karkom outpost. It was detonated at noon as an IDF armored personnel carrier passed by, and a heavy barrage of artillery fire began immediately in order to impede the IDF's rescue efforts. One Israeli soldier was killed and seven were wounded, four of them seriously, in this engagement alone.

The next day, the Security Cabinet instructed the IDF to act. However, at Barak's insistence, the cabinet accepted the White House's urging that if Israel needed to retaliate, the targets be Lebanese infrastructure rather than— as demanded by the Israeli defense establishment—Syrian military installations directly supporting the HizbAllah operations. That night, the Israeli Air Force struck a HizbAllah arms depot, HizbAllah broadcasting stations, and three electricity transformer stations. A HizbAllah spokesman called the Israeli operation "an attack by cowards, that will only lead us to intensify our attacks on Israel." That afternoon, HizbAllah units resumed their attacks on IDF and SLA outposts.

In Jerusalem, senior officials in the prime minister's office pronounced the Air Force strike a success because of the message it sent to Damascus. "Damascus must decide whether it will continue to support HizbAllah and its violent war against Israel or renew negotiations, as Israel will not abide Syrian attempts to impose political pressure through violence," the officials declared. Indyk praised Barak's great restraint and commended his desire to leave open the possibility of continued talks with Syria. Both Jerusalem and Washington ignored the official statement by the Syrian government, saying that the Israeli air raids "have effectively torpedoed the Middle East peace process." The next day an Israeli soldier was killed by an anti-tank missile fired at the Dlaat outpost in the eastern sector of the security zone, and an SLA soldier was killed by a rocket fired at the Razlan outpost. In retaliation, the Israeli Air Force bombed HizbAllah radar bases in Tyre and two HizbAllah compounds in a village in the Bekaa. No Syrian objectives, including the forward weapon storage sites sustaining the HizbAllah's barrages, were hit.

An international scandal erupted when Israeli Foreign Minister David Levy, briefing foreign diplomats, warned, "If Katyusha rockets were to fall on northern Israeli communities, the earth of Lebanon would ignite. Vital interests of Lebanon would go up in flames and it will take many years to rehabilitate them." European diplomats in Beirut insisted that Israel had violated the understandings reached after the Grapes of Wrath operation four years earlier, while HizbAllah had abided by them. The diplomats added that "HizbAllah acted wisely in the way it limited its operations." In this atmosphere, HizbAllah could afford to be forthcoming. Sheikh Naim Qassim promised not to shell northern Israel "at this time," while reserving "the right to do so any time." However, even as the Grapes of Wrath Monitoring Committee—composed of Israeli, Syrian, Lebanese, U.S., and French representatives—was convening in Nakura, HizbAllah launched a heavy mortar attack on the IDF's Beaufort outpost.

The Clinton administration reacted predictably, urging restraint on all sides. "We are doing our best to get the peace process back on track," Clinton said. "It is clear that the bombing is a reaction to the deaths in two separate instances of Israeli soldiers. And what we need to do is to stop the violence and start the peace process again, and we're doing our best to get it started, and we're working very, very hard on it." Albright chimed in: "This is one of the things that happens as you begin to have some success in the peace process, that those who do not have a stake in it try to take action. We hope very much and are encouraging restraint." She reported that she had called al-Shara and "urged them [the Syrians] to do what they can to control the activities of the HizbAllah." Both Albright and the president completely ignored Syria's record of active support for HizbAllah operations.

In Damascus, the government-owned newspapers echoed the connection the Clinton administration had made between the situation in southern Lebanon and the peace process—although with a threatening twist. "The treacherous Israeli attack was aimed first and foremost against the peace process," said the editorial in *Al-Baath*, "and revealed the true face of Israeli Prime Minister Ehud Barak, who is dragging the region into a spiral of violence and tension." The Syrian media declared that it was completely unreasonable to ask HizbAllah to stop attacking Israeli and southern Lebanese targets. "It is impossible to accept it," an editorial in *Al-Thawra* stated, "because all the laws in the world recognize that people resist foreign occupation and take up arms to defend their motherland."

BY MID-FEBRUARY, HizbAllah shelling and retaliatory bombing by the Israeli Air Force had become a virtual routine, with almost daily fatalities among either the IDF or the SLA. Anticipating further escalation, the Security Cabinet authorized Barak, Levy, and Defense Minister Mordechai to decide proper retaliatory measures day by day. Simultaneously, Barak intensified his efforts to find a solution for the Lebanon problem that would permit a unilateral withdrawal. Toward this end, Israel enlisted the help of Germany and France: France was asked to persuade Beirut to go along with the Israeli plan for withdrawal from southern Lebanon, while Germany was asked to persuade Tehran to talk HizbAllah into some semblance of cooperation.

By now, the Lebanese apprehended that their country might once again become a pawn in the maneuverings among the United States, Syria, and Israel. Hence, on February 16, the Lebanese Foundation for Peace sponsored a Lebanon Awareness Day on Capitol Hill, bringing in numerous leaders from Lebanon and the diaspora, including Member of Parliament Dory Chamoun and Archbishop Paul Sayah of the Maronite Church. These leaders pleaded with Congress not to ignore the survival of Lebanon when pursuing the peace process but rather to help rid Lebanon of the Islamist and radical terrorists who, in the course of instigating clashes with Israel, were destroying their country. They stressed the horrendous effect the continuing Syrian occupation was having on Lebanon's delicate religious and demographic tapestry. Free of Syrian occupation, they maintained, a democratic Lebanon would be happy to live in genuine peace with all its neighbors.

The Lebanese emissaries struck a chord with Congress. Many members of both the House and the Senate, along with members of the U.S. defense and intelligence communities, had long feared that a unilateral Israeli withdrawal would merely empower HizbAllah and its sponsors, with a concomitant increase in international terrorism, drug trafficking, and other illegal activities sponsored by the Syrian government in and through Lebanon. Congress was especially worried about the ramifications of Israel's eagerness to leave Lebanon so long as the Clinton administration continued to renege on U.S. commitments and to ignore U.N. Security Council Resolution 520, calling for mutual withdrawal of Israeli and Syrian forces. Hence Congress started seeking alternatives to the Israeli plans for unilateral withdrawal. Particularly promising was the idea of empowering southern Lebanon as the basis of a Free Lebanon; this would entail applying American sanctions to push the Syrians out and encouraging Beirut to reach a warm peace with Israel through a series of economic incentives that would also open up Free Lebanon to Western economic relations.

Meanwhile, Damascus continued to raise the ante. Syrian officials assured their Lebanese counterparts that the real motive for the proposed Israeli withdrawal was a "Zionist plan" to impose on Syria a siege identical to the U.S.-led stifling of Iraq. The Syrian officials explained that withdrawing the IDF would allow Israel to strike the Syrian forces in Lebanon. Then, when Syria retaliated, Israel and the United States would consider Syria responsible, "calling for imposing sanctions on it" and as a consequence "putting some of its areas under air embargo." In their contacts with European diplomats, senior Syrian officials emphasized the need to obtain Israel's commitment to complete withdrawal from the Golan before the now inevitable unilateral withdrawal from Lebanon. Jerusalem announced that Clinton would convey such a commitment in person in his upcoming summit with Assad.

In late February, Jerusalem attempted to assure Damascus that its commitments concerning the Golan were still in effect. In a lengthy cabinet discussion, which was promptly leaked by Barak's senior aides, Barak noted that four of his predecessors "had agreed to a withdrawal to the June 4, 1967, border" in their negotiations with Syria. "Both the U.S. and Syria understand that this is our position, and I'm not planning to erase the past," Barak declared. He acknowledged that his and Assad's understandings of the June 4 line were slightly different, but he expressed his confidence that a compromise could be easily reached. In an effort to alleviate Assad's apprehensions, Barak offered to complete the Syrian-Israeli agreement before Israel withdrew from southern Lebanon.

On the night after Barak's address to the cabinet, a HizbAllah team planted a powerful roadside bomb in the village of Ein Kinya. The next morning, the bomb was detonated under an SLA jeep, killing five soldiers. HizbAllah then bombarded SLA and IDF outposts throughout the security zone. Several SLA and a few IDF soldiers were wounded. Israel reacted with the now customary shelling but omitted aerial bombing. The Israeli restraint stemmed from Barak's confidence that he was now on the verge of a "masterstroke" in playing the Syrians against HizbAllah.

———

IN MID-FEBRUARY, German efforts with Tehran had started to deliver results. Barak's statement to the cabinet convinced Tehran that Jerusalem had no intention of undermining the Syrian position. Hence, Tehran instructed HizbAllah to agree to indirect negotiations with Israel over the fate of southern Lebanon. The first round of negotiations took place in Berlin on March 1 and 2, with Germany, Israel, Iran, and HizbAllah all represented by senior intelligence officials and diplomats accustomed to clandestine negotiations. Having assured the Iranians and the Lebanese of Israel's sincerity, the Germans limited their role to that of impartial go-betweens.

The Iranians, seizing the initiative, focused the discussions on one key issue: Israel's behavior vis-à-vis Lebanon after a withdrawal. The Iranians sought and got guarantees that Israel would initiate no operations there. Tehran was also assured that Israel understood that any unwarranted operation would explode the entire region because both Iran and Syria would rally to the defense of Lebanon and HizbAllah. The Israeli delegation acquiesced to the continuing presence of Syrian and Iranian forces in Lebanon as stabilizing elements. The only contentious issue was the Israeli preference for extending the rule of the government of Lebanon all the way to the Israeli border and for introducing an international force dominated by U.S. and Western European elements. The Iranians objected, and both sides agreed to discuss the issue with their governments and meet again in a week's time.

The day before the resumption of the Berlin talks, Barak made Israel's commitment to a unilateral withdrawal formally irreversible. Without even being made to explain his reasons, he won unanimous support from the cabinet for his pledge to end Israel's military presence in southern Lebanon before July. The cabinet reaffirmed the government's preference for reaching an agreement with Syria that would facilitate the withdrawal but emphasized that Israel would withdraw its troops even in the absence of an agreement. Such key issues as the disarming of HizbAllah and the nullification of indictments of SLA personnel would be addressed in future Israeli-Lebanese negotiations rather than in the ongoing contacts with either Syria or Iran. The cabinet also did not rule out Lebanese demands for the resettling of Palestinian refugees in Israel—amounting to a partial Israeli acceptance of the "right of return."

The second round of the Berlin talks opened on March 7, with all sides represented by higher-level officials than before. Significantly, the Israeli delegation included a representative of Uri Lubrani, the Israeli Government's Coordinator of Activities in Southern Lebanon and a former ambassador to Iran. The Germans, expecting the talks to continue for several days, put their guests in specially rented villas. As before, the Germans shuttled between the delegations.

The Israeli officials relayed the sense of the cabinet that Israel was eager to withdraw to the international border as soon as possible and had no future ambitions in Lebanon. Israel asked nothing from HizbAllah and Iran except guarantees that the withdrawal would take place without any disruptions or threats of cross-border operations. The Israelis reiterated that Jerusalem did not care what happened in post-withdrawal Lebanon, so long as the border remained quiet.

The HizbAllah officials reacted harshly to the Israelis' opening proposal as conveyed by the Germans, insisting they could not and would not agree to any restraint on their ability to wage the jihad as they saw fit. The Iranians, rushing to calm them down, asked for and received Israeli clarifications that not having any interest in the situation in Lebanon indeed amounted to abandoning the demand for an international force to replace the IDF in southern Lebanon. HizbAllah then raised the issue of SLA personnel and was assured that Israel would disarm the SLA and ignore HizbAllah activities in southern Lebanon as long as its border was not threatened.

With Israel capitulating on every point, the senior Iranian delegate took aside his German counterpart—an intelligence official long involved in Iranian and Middle Eastern affairs—and asked for his personal assurances that there were no hidden agendas in these negotiations. The German assured the Iranian that Israel was desperate to get out of southern Lebanon and that Barak had ordered his representatives to reach an understanding at all costs. The next day, the Iranian in turn assured the German of Tehran's readiness to ensure peace, security, and stability along the border provided that Damascus agreed to the principles of this understanding. On March 10, the Germans notified the Israelis that they had a deal.

Back in Jerusalem, Barak did not disclose—even to the IDF high command—the commitments made by Israel in Berlin. He did not instruct the Israeli defense establishment to make any amendments to its preparations for the coming withdrawal, now code-named Operation Morning Twilight. On March 12, Barak met with the chief of staff, Lieutenant General Shaul Mofaz, and other leading generals to discuss their objections to unilateral withdrawal. The generals presented Barak with detailed intelligence about the determination of HizbAllah and the Palestinian rejectionist organizations to exploit any minor disagreement on the line of withdrawal as an excuse for escalating violence against Israel's northern communities. The IDF recommended that the SLA be reinforced and left in control of the security zone and that Israel provide continued ground and air support after the withdrawal. Barak listened attentively and promised that the IDF's recommendations would be presented to the cabinet later that day. He did not even hint that he had already committed Israel to doing exactly the opposite.

The next day, because of recently accumulated intelligence concerning the arrangements Tehran and Damascus had made to protect HizbAllah, Barak ordered the IDF on the offensive as if the Berlin agreement did not exist. The Pasdaran presence in Lebanon had escalated into an "independent stronghold" in the south. Two to three hundred Pasdaran officers and long-range missiles had been deployed. Meanwhile, two Syrian-controlled organizations, Ahmad Jibril's PFLP-GC and Colonel Abu Musa's branch of the PLO, had begun to supply HizbAllah with ammunition and long-range weapons just in case Syria attempted to hamper its operations as part of a future agreement. And so the Israeli Air Force hit these organizations' camps, destroying seven long-range cannons and four mobile Katyusha rocket launchers. Israel also bombed a few houses near the villages of Maifadoun and Nabatiyeh used as forward positions by Iranian intelligence. HizbAllah retaliated with a barrage of forty Katyusha rockets; Israel responded by bombing terrorist targets in Zabkin. Fighting continued for the next couple of days.

———

ISRAEL DID NOT REACT more sharply to the HizbAllah attacks because of the approaching Clinton-Assad summit. Clinton was upbeat about the summit's prospects. "I wouldn't waste Assad's time if there was nothing to talk about," he told the White House press corps. He alluded to a prediction by Mubarak that Israel and Syria were close to signing an agreement and said that only technical details remained to be ironed out. Syria publicly shared the optimism. "Bill Clinton will succeed within weeks in resuming peace negotiations between Syria, Lebanon and Israel," General Tlass opined. However, Damascus was also working to reduce expectations, especially regarding the Syrian commitment to normalization. An editorial in the official *Tishrin* reiterated that Barak "knows very well that not only are his demands impossible, but also that they are the farthest thing from the mind of the Syrian citizen."

Barak was most accommodating, even at the expense of Israel's national security. On the eve of the summit, he reaffirmed to Clinton that Israel would go along with the security arrangements recommended by Washington even though Major General Amos Malka, Israel's chief of Military Intelligence, had just returned from the United States with bad news about the early-warning systems being offered as a substitute for Israel's station on Mount Hermon. Malka briefed the cabinet that the proposed replacements were mere "paper solutions" that would require at least five years to complete. Nevertheless, Barak would not go back on his agreement for a speedy withdrawal from the Golan.

On the eve of the summit, Barak himself unwittingly underscored the absurdity of the entire process when he explained that the summit's ultimate objective was to determine once and for all Syria's position concerning a peace agreement. "Clinton," he said, "just like Israel, does not know where Assad stands."

By now, Clinton was deceiving both sides in order to get their support for his efforts. He assured Barak that the coveted peace agreement was within sight as a result of his coming up with creative formulas that fudged such contentious issues as access to the Kineret water. At the same time, he assured Assad that he had in hand far-reaching concessions from Barak, as well as U.S. guarantees for Bashar's survival. In reality, Clinton had nothing in hand other than his lust for legacy.

Assad arrived in Geneva on March 26 with great expectations for "an historic endeavor" that would go far beyond the mere revival of the peace process. On the basis of Washington's assurances, Damascus was certain that Clinton would be bringing the long-sought confirmation from Barak regarding the June 4 lines, as well as lower expectations on the part of Israel and the United States for normalization and warm peace. For Assad, the summit with Clinton was the threshold to a new era in Syrian-American relations. Indeed, he brought along a large delegation to see him in his hour of glory.

Clinton's opening gestures were reassuring, though purely symbolic. He met Assad in the corridor and approached him as a personal friend. He complimented Assad on his beret and told him he was looking well, though in fact Assad's health had taken a turn for the worse, and it showed. All this schmoozing was utterly foreign to the cool and aloof Assad, although he perceived it correctly as an expression of Clinton's trying to make friends. In terms of Middle Eastern body language, however, Clinton was broadcasting insecurity and an inferior starting position, which Assad was determined to exploit.

The long-term significance of this summit meeting lies in the impressions that Assad and the Syrian delegation formed about Clinton rather than in the precise text of the lengthy exchanges between the two leaders. The summit consisted of a five-hour dialogue broken into two sessions. The formal agenda, a senior Arab official reported, was nothing less than "a comprehensive discussion of the future of the region in all its aspects and post-peace prospects." The main problem, as before, lay in the two sides' profoundly different interpretations of this broad topic. Clinton was obsessed with achieving a here-and-now breakthrough in the peace process, while Assad cared only about the future—namely, the consolidation of Bashar's reign after his own death.

Assad dominated the first session of the summit, delivering a lengthy presentation about Syria and the Middle East. In this talk, which lasted almost two hours, he delved into the dangers emanating from any "Syrian concessions" regarding the June 4 line or normalization. He asserted that even a largely symbolic gesture would be interpreted as Syrian weakness and thus make any political settlement fragile. During the break, Clinton called Barak, urging him to adopt the Syrian perception of the future border and informing him that the next session would deal with the other aspects of the peace process, especially security arrangements and water. However, Assad dominated the second session as well, speaking for ninety minutes about the Arab constants in dealing with Israel, as well as the irreversibility of Lebanese-Syrian unity.

When Clinton finally had a chance to speak, he replied that he fully understood the Syrian position and had faithfully conveyed it to Barak during the break. However, he said, the extent of the Syrian demands meant a protracted effort would be needed before Barak's cabinet would accept them—that is, unless Assad made things easy for Barak. Clinton argued that given the turbulent situation in the Middle East, it was imperative to resume negotiations before a mistake led to a new wave of violence. The step Clinton had in mind was for Assad to receive Barak in Damascus. If he met Barak soon, Clinton told a stunned Assad, the United States would be most generous in contributing to Syria's stability and prosperity. When Assad prodded Clinton to elaborate on the future commitments he was referring to, he got nowhere beyond general assurances of lavish financial support. In that case, Assad told Clinton, they should concentrate on reviving the basic negotiations at lower levels; leaders' visits, he said, should wait until after a peace treaty was signed. Indeed, only after the Israeli withdrawal was completed could the Arab political taboo be erased—and even then, Assad opined, the historical enmity between Arabs and Jews could not be expected to vanish overnight. Perhaps the first visit of an Israeli leader should wait until at least two years after an agreement was signed.

Assad came out of the summit distraught, according to his confidant Patrick Seale. "Instead of the good news he was expecting to hear about the border, he felt disappointed when Clinton began to list Barak's maximum demands [for normalization]," Seale reported. "The summit did not recover after this regrettable start and became a total failure. . . . The Syrian President returned home in a sore mood feeling he was cheated." Assad was especially hurt by Clinton's misunderstanding of his approach to the peace issue. "I am not going to give Syrian territory and water to the one who usurped this territory and water," he told his aides on the flight back to Damascus, "because future generations will judge me for taking this decision. As for shaking hands with Barak, we consider this a humiliating action before we regain our rights in full. We have no desire to regain the Golan in this manner. At any rate, Hafez al-Assad is not Anwar al Sadat, and I have no ambition to become Yassir Arafat."

The explanations offered by American and Israeli officials as to why the Geneva summit failed demonstrated just how little they really understood Assad. The most prevalent explanation for the summit's collapse was Assad's refusal to accept Barak's demand for a narrow stretch of land around Kineret's northeastern shore that would have turned it into an Israeli lake. However, water was not a real issue, for, as Seale reported in *Al-Hayah* in early April, there was a "creative" solution at hand that Barak could have accepted. Similarly, only partially correct was an explanation suggested by highly placed Israeli sources that the summit collapsed when Clinton broke the news to Assad that Congress had refused to endorse the $15 billion aid package Clinton had originally promised. Clinton did raise the issue as a temporary hindrance, but Assad looked at it in the greater context of the viability of long-term U.S. commitments.

The real issue was that, whereas Assad had come to Geneva to discuss what for him were most profound historical issues—namely, establishing and consolidating his dynasty in Damascus—all he got in return for his willingness to engage in the peace process were Clinton's pleas for a signature on some document and a promise to make some symbolic gesture such as shaking Barak's hand sometime before Clinton left office. This stark contrast between the two views of the relevant time frame, reinforced by Clinton's obvious lack of interest in Bashar's survival, traumatized Assad. Significantly, during the summit, rumors persisted among Arab sources that Bashar had been brought clandestinely to Geneva, using false papers and a disguise, to be available for a possible introduction to Clinton as Assad's chosen heir. Despite repeated hints from Assad during their lengthy meeting, Clinton showed no inclination to seriously address the Bashar issue.

Alarmed and confused by Assad's hostile departure from Geneva, Clinton asked Barak to suspend any unilateral step that might anger or frighten Assad. Barak immediately agreed to freeze for three weeks all preparations for the withdrawal from Lebanon. However, in a speech delivered the day after Clinton's request, Barak acknowledged that "the Syrians are not ripe for peace at present." Therefore, he explained, Israel would eventually redeploy its forces from Lebanon to the international border "in a manner that will enable us to protect the northern residents and the IDF . . . as well as provide support to the South Lebanon Army that has served on our side for so many years." Soon afterward, he summoned Mofaz and instructed him that the IDF should begin preparing for the withdrawal, but he still did not tell Mofaz about the Berlin "understandings."

––––––

DAMASCUS'S ASSESSMENT of the Geneva summit and its view of the unilateral withdrawal from Lebanon were elucidated by Seale in an April article in *Al-Hayah*. "What is dangerous about this dispute is that it could make President Hafiz al-Assad and Israeli Prime Minister Ehud Barak lose a historic opportunity to achieve peace. For this opportunity might not recur for many years. But what is more dangerous is that the collapse of the peace process and Israel's unilateral withdrawal from Lebanon in July could drown the region in a new whirlpool of violence, and possibly even war." Several Arab officials were quick to assert that Israel would not be permitted to benefit strategically and militarily from a unilateral withdrawal from southern Lebanon. In fact, Lebanese Defense Minister Ghazi Zaayter explicitly threatened to ask Damascus to send Syrian forces all the way to the Israeli border. "Asking Syrian forces, legally deployed here, to accompany the Lebanese army to the evacuated areas would be one of the important possibilities in case of such an Israeli redeployment," Zaayter said. "And it would not be difficult for any normal person to understand that this would bring Tel Aviv within the range of Syrian missiles."

Meanwhile, the SLA Commander, General Antoine Lahad, said that his men were ready to hold the line: They would choose to "die on their own land" rather than live in Israel as refugees. The SLA had "paid a high price over the past twenty-three years," he reminded his listeners. "We've lost sixty-five soldiers and had hundreds more wounded." Now, they were prepared to stay and fight: "I've never feared for the SLA's future," he said. "After the withdrawal you'll see the SLA standing on its feet."

The Israeli defense establishment favored taking Lahad at his word. The high command urged Barak to concentrate on reaching an understanding with both Damascus and Beirut that would leave the SLA in place. "Any arrangement is better than nothing. The coming months will be more critical for southern Lebanon than the past ten years," said Brigadier General Benny Ganz, the commander of the IDF's liaison unit with the SLA. "Israel is obligated," he added, to consider the welfare of the SLA's men. In internal discussions with Barak, the General Staff continued to object to the withdrawal plan; one senior officer said the withdrawal was an "unprecedented gamble with citizens' lives." If the SLA proved unable to hold the security zone, HizbAllah would resume attacking northern Israeli towns at the first opportunity.

Syrian-sponsored organizations made it clear that withdrawing from one piece of Arab territory was not enough. Munir Makdah, the Palestinian Islamist commander and former friend of Yassir Arafat, declared that "Israel will not enjoy peaceful and quiet borders if it continues with its plans to withdraw. There will be no peace, no security, and no stability to the occupier [of Palestinian lands]." He ridiculed the notion that an international force could protect Israel's northern border and vowed that "the Resistance will continue even if all the armies on earth are massed on the frontier between Lebanon and the Zionist entity." These were not empty words. Arafat and the Palestinian Islamists had already started delivering large quantities of weapons and ammunition to their supporters in Lebanon's twelve Palestinian refugee camps.

By mid-April, HizbAllah had stepped up the frequency and intensity of Katyusha rocket launches against both military outposts in the security zone and Israeli communities in the northern Galilee. The IDF responded with aerial bombing of the villages from which the Katyushas were being fired and with audacious raids by special forces against HizbAllah units deep inside Lebanon. Thus began a cycle of violence in which successful Katyusha barrages led to heavier retaliation and more preemptive strikes, which prompted even heavier Katyusha barrages, and so on, with both sides sustaining a mounting number of casualties. In late April, HizbAllah sent a martyr-driven truck bomb into an SLA outpost, killing three SLA soldiers, including the outpost's commander. Nevertheless, Barak instructed the IDF to accelerate the dismantling of outposts.

As far as the IDF knew, however, Israel remained committed to sustaining the SLA in southern Lebanon. The IDF and SLA high commands were still looking at a two-month period—until early July—during which the SLA would be expanded, reinforced, and readied to assume responsibility for holding the security zone with only emergency artillery and air support from Israel. The SLA was assured of improved weapon systems and larger stockpiles of ammunition.

The SLA high command had no reason to suspect duplicity from Israel. Reinforcement of the SLA started immediately, with Israel supplying twenty to twenty-five long-range 160-mm self-propelled mortars installed on tank chassis as well as several 130-mm artillery pieces and large quantities of ammunition. SLA crews were being organized to train on, and pick up, additional tanks and other heavy weapons. Nabih Abu Rifai, the commander for the SLA's eastern sector, reported that his units "were expecting to receive further supplies of heavy weapons and ammunition in coming weeks." The SLA's morale was high, and its key units, as General Lahad had said, were eager to hold the line on their own.

Senior Israeli defense officials and senior SLA commanders discussed their plans and hopes with U.S. defense officials. As of late April, Lahad was optimistic and precise. "I need three things," he told an American interlocutor: "(1) I need Israel not to stop the money—keep the flow of money coming under the table so I can keep paying my soldiers. (2) I need logistics also so the SLA won't be short on ammunition. (3) I need the border not to be closed, because I don't have sophisticated hospitals in the South; in this instance all my wounded should be transported to northern Israel to be treated. When I have those three things, I can hold 200 years." Senior Israeli defense officials consulted by Lahad's American interlocutor had no problems with Lahad's requests and were confident Israel would do even more to sustain and support the SLA.

———

IN EARLY MAY, HizbAllah's Katyusha barrages became heavier and more accurate, causing more casualties and widespread damage. This offensive was possible only because of a massive supply of rockets from stockpiles held by the Syrian Army in Lebanon. Given the direct Syrian involvement, the IDF demanded, and got, permission to strike Syrian military installations inside Lebanon. However, hours before the bombing was to begin, Indyk contacted Barak and demanded that Israel not strike at Syrian objectives because their destruction might make it impossible to resurrect the Syrian-Israeli negotiations. Barak accepted the American demand and at the last minute overruled his own high command.

Soon afterward, Terje Larsen—who had launched the Oslo process eight years earlier and was now Kofi Annan's special coordinator for the Middle East peace process—arrived in Jerusalem after two days of talks in Beirut. He brought with him an offer for modalities of a withdrawal that would be acceptable to the Lebanese and Syrian governments: The key item was the dismantling of the SLA. Larsen assured his interlocutors that there should be no concern for the safety of Israelis living in the border zone; he had received "assurances," he said, from "Lebanese officials" that they had "guarantees" from HizbAllah that innocent border inhabitants and SLA family members would not be harmed. However, both Beirut and HizbAllah insisted that immediately following the Israeli withdrawal, the SLA commanders and troops be arrested and tried for "high treason"—punishable by death. Larsen declared, and Annan and Albright concurred, that that was the best deal Barak could hope for.

On the basis of Larsen's account, Jerusalem started preparing for an imminent withdrawal. Visiting local IDF units, Barak told a gathering of officers he was on the verge of making "a vital, strategic decision" concerning southern Lebanon: "The withdrawal from Lebanon is not merely an election promise. There are one thousand and one hundred graves in Israel; one thousand and one hundred families whose lives were ruined by the consequences of our presence in Lebanon." Barak also met with Lahad and assured him of Israel's "enduring commitment" to the SLA and determination to ensure the SLA troops' ability to defend their homes.

Meanwhile, the IDF began gradually pulling out from isolated outposts at the edges of the security zone, such as Taibeh in the center of the security zone and Rotem on the Mediterranean coast. At first, Israel refused to agree to disarming the SLA unless UNIFIL (the U.N. Interim Force in Lebanon) or some comparable international force guaranteed the safety of the local population. However, during negotiations with U.N. officials in New York on Barak's behalf, Uri Lubrani agreed to strip the SLA of its heavy weapons in return for vague promises about UNIFIL's advance toward the border. This was in profound contradiction to Jerusalem's public position (although in line with the Berlin understandings), and, once again, Barak neglected to inform his high command.

Barak did try to elicit help from Clinton and Albright in persuading Annan to improve the conditions of the Israeli pullback, but met with their refusal. Instead, the Clinton administration pressured him to concentrate on some promising "vibes" from Arafat—raising the prospects of an agreement with the Palestinians within a month or two, provided Israel no longer carried the "baggage" of Lebanon. At the same time, Germany and France were urging Israel to quickly implement the Berlin understandings. Using the good offices of Annan and Larsen, Lubrani updated these understandings into arrangements for handing over the Shiite area of the security zone to Shiite civilians, albeit protected and supported by the HizbAllah.

The deal, as it unfolded, reflected Lubrani's penchant for regarding the Shiites as the key to regional arrangements. His network of contacts and sources in southern Lebanon would dominate the implementation of the Berlin understandings. Final coordination on the ground was organized through a few Shiite senior SLA officers who had relatives—in some cases very close relatives—in the ranks of HizbAllah and other Islamist organizations. One of the most important of such emissaries was Colonel Ghazi Dhawi, the administrative commander of the SLA's eastern sector, who was close to Lahad. Dhawi's twenty-eight-year-old, ostensibly estranged son held a high-ranking field position in HizbAllah. Father and son had in fact maintained contact at all times, serving as each other's insurance policy against retribution. On the eve of the withdrawal, Colonel Dhawi decamped to Beirut, where he lives to this day. This was the sort of contact Lubrani relied on in order to ensure HizbAllah's "cooperation" in the Israeli charade.

Lubrani's original arrangements with the U.N. officials saw the handover of the Shiite sectors of the security zone as the first phase in a protracted process stretching over a couple of months—that is, until early July. However, in early May, HizbAllah and Iran, and consequently the United Nations and the United States, announced they would have none of it. They warned of regionwide escalation unless Israel withdrew immediately. Finally, Barak capitulated, agreeing to a swift pullout and the dismantling of the SLA.

Significantly, Barak authorized and oversaw all these negotiations and commitments not only without consulting the IDF's high command, but also without even informing them of the new patterns and schedules. That Mofaz had no idea the withdrawal would be accelerated is evident from his May 9, 2000, interview with *Maariv*. Mofaz ruled out an imminent pullout, given the IDF's wish "not to be dragged into an escalation led by HizbAllah . . . , certainly not before we have completed our preparations for the redeployment." Mofaz had no indication, either, that the Israeli government was planning to abandon the SLA. "The behavior of the SLA and the southern Lebanon population depends on their decisions, not on ours," he said. "It is hard to say today whether they will leave South Lebanon or not, and General Lahad explicitly expressed his and his people's wish to continue living as Lebanese citizens in an independent and free state." Thus, the Israeli defense establishment was actively pursuing what it believed to be the government's policy—namely, to prepare the SLA to hold southern Lebanon following Israel's July pullback. Several entities in Israel and overseas, including the U.S. Congress, were kept informed of the progress of these activities, with the Israeli and southern Lebanese officials involved convinced that they were implementing the policies of the Israeli government.

However, these contradictory policies could not continue running in parallel forever, and toward mid-May, there was a sudden alarm in Jerusalem. Barak's office learned that Lahad had been invited to brief the Likud leadership about the future of the SLA. Had Lahad been allowed to give this briefing, Likud might well have demanded that Barak keep the promises made to Lahad rather than go ahead with the sudden pullout he had just secretly committed to with Clinton. Therefore, Ronni Bondi, Barak's chief political adviser, ordered Lahad to cancel his meeting with Likud and come to an emergency meeting with Barak instead. At the time no explanation was given to Likud, but Barak's office leaked that Lahad had been sent to France for a two-week vacation.

In their meeting, Barak told Lahad that the evolving international situation would make it impossible for Israel to sustain an expanded security zone and an enlarged SLA following the IDF's pullout. At the same time, Barak stressed the Israelis' enduring commitment to the safety and well-being of their Maronite and Druze brethren; therefore, he explained, Israel would rather have the SLA's hard core sustain three predominantly Christian enclaves—Qleia, Rumaish, and Alma—as the strategic key to southern Lebanon. Israel, Barak assured Lahad, would continue to provide all-out civilian and military support to its Lebanese allies. Barak also intimated that should conducive conditions arise in the future, Jerusalem would support the expansion of the security zone in accordance with the original plans. As for the SLA officers and officials from the Shiite zone, as well as those who did not want to stay in the new emaciated security zone, they could always come to Israel or emigrate to France. In that connection, Barak suggested that Lahad should forthwith accompany Lubrani to Paris for negotiations with the French government.

Lahad asked, and was permitted, to have a brief meeting with his senior officers to inform them about these drastic changes. He outlined the new Israeli plan and assured his officers that this was the best short-term solution given the complexity of the international situation and the pressures on Israel. "Your primary mission," Lahad told his officers, "will be to seize and hold the isolated outposts the IDF will evacuate as interim steps pending the pullout still scheduled for early July."

In Paris, it did not take long for Lahad to realize that something was wrong. Scheduled meetings were repeatedly postponed, and senior officials he had routinely met in the past could not be located. When he decided to return home, Lubrani urged him to stay a little longer to participate in some "most important" meetings. In retrospect, it is clear that no such meetings had been scheduled. Instead, Lubrani was keeping Lahad isolated in Paris so that he would not be able to rally the SLA when Israel withdrew in accordance with the "understandings" he, Lubrani, had reached with Iran and HizbAllah. When the crisis started to unfold and Lahad was desperate to return to his people, El Al was unable to find a seat for him on any flight.

On May 19, Mofaz met with Barak and asked for a week's forewarning in order to complete preparations for an orderly handover of the security zone. Barak assured Mofaz that his concerns were irrelevant, for the diplomatic process would necessitate at least a month's stay for the IDF. "We have to get organized in terms of agreement with the other elements. . . . We have to deal with the SLA on several fronts. The aim is to obtain pardons. International aid has to be arranged for southern Lebanon. All these things require another few weeks. And the IDF, which has carried out its mission efficiently in the past two years, will know how to stand and strengthen the SLA," Barak told his chief of the General Staff just three days before the security zone collapsed.

———

MAY 21 started with a HizbAllah attack on IDF positions in the Har Dov area (known to the Arabs as the Shebaa Farms) on the slopes of Mount Hermon. This attack was a milestone, partly because it was the first attack in the area since April 1996, but more importantly because the HizbAllah communiqué talked about the Israeli withdrawal in terms of here and now, whereas, in terms of public knowledge, the pullout was not scheduled to take place for a month and a half. Thus, HizbAllah was signaling that it had foreknowledge of the accelerated Israeli withdrawal—that, contrary to the subsequent protestations of the Barak government, an Israeli-Iranian/HizbAllah deal had been kept secret not only from the SLA but also from the IDF.

Meanwhile, the IDF was preoccupied with the routine and mundane. On the morning of May 22, senior officers of the IDF's Northern Command conducted a table war game called "The Morning after the Evacuation" based on a summer pullout scenario. The exercise ended a little before 2 P.M., and the officers dispersed to their units and headquarters. Shortly thereafter, IDF lookouts in the Galgalit and Olesh outposts reported a large procession

of civilians, mostly women and children, coming down from two nearby Shiite villages, crossing the Litani River, and heading toward the security zone.
At about the same time, the SLA troops in the Taibeh outpost reported "puz-
zling events occurring" inside the Taibeh village. It transpired that a Shiite
crowd had gathered in the center of the village; they held communal prayers
and were addressed by the local imam, who instructed them to march on the
Taibeh outpost. As the procession began ascending toward the outpost, the
IDF's regional command consulted with Robin Abbud, the Shiite commander of the SLA's 70th Battalion, about the SLA's ability to hold the outpost. Abbud was convinced there was no problem, and the IDF's local liaison
officer concurred. However, that afternoon the local SLA garrison received
an order—the source of which is still unknown—to vacate the outpost without resistance. The men quickly complied.

Senior Israeli officers were baffled by these developments. Jerusalem did
not answer requests for consultations and instructions, even those addressed
to the highest levels. During the night, SLA and IDF officers redeployed the
SLA's 70th Battalion along a new blocking line intended to keep the Shiite
procession—which had now acquired an armed HizbAllah escort—away
from the Israeli border. The SLA units deployed quickly and manned ad hoc
barriers constructed by IDF combat engineers. Their main mission was to
block the procession's movement toward the village of Adaysah because such
an advance would establish access to the Fatma Gate.

That night, Abbud discussed with senior Israeli officers his apprehensions that there was "a deal between the HizbAllah and Israel" that neither
he nor they were privy to. The IDF officers ridiculed his worry, considering it
a justification for the loss of the Taibeh outpost. Meanwhile, Brigadier General Moshe Kaplinsky, the commander of the IDF's Galil Division, ordered
the immediate evacuation into Israel of all forces and equipment not essential for combat in the security zone. He also ordered the swift return to base
of a myriad of Israeli special-forces teams that had been roaming around
and laying ambushes throughout southern Lebanon.

As of the morning of May 23, the IDF was still convinced it was facing
a local incident. The IDF's Northern Command decided to continue with a
planned exercise on the Golan Heights attended by Mofaz and all the regional senior officers. However, they asked that the command post be constantly updated about the situation in the security zone. By now, a new
Shiite crowd had formed near the Irish UNIFIL battalion at the western exit
from the village of Shaqra, and, despite Israeli requests, the U.N. troops refused to disperse them. Helicopters hovering over the crowd and tank fire
into nearby hillsides failed to stop the march on the local SLA outpost. Suddenly, the majority of the SLA troops left their positions, while the SLA

company commander and a few soldiers drove the unit's jeep toward a HizbAllah advance party. By noon, the Shiite civilians and their HizbAllah escorts were closing in on Bint-Jubayl—thus severing the link between the western and eastern sectors of the security zone.

The chaos was aggravated by the seemingly intentional absence of key senior personnel. General Lahad was still in Paris—stranded and desperately trying to return home. Colonel Noam Ben-Tzvi, the chief IDF liaison officer with the SLA's Western Brigade, was in the Netherlands preparing for his next assignment as military attaché, though his replacement was not due to arrive for several days. Significantly, the local General Security Services (GSS) chief (known only as M.) responsible for SLA personnel issues was overseas on vacation.

As these events were unfolding, the Barak government reached a high point in its duplicity, issuing an explicit denial of an early withdrawal: "The Defense Minister's Media Adviser wishes to clarify that there is no order regarding an IDF pullout from Lebanon on June 1. The IDF is preparing to withdraw from Lebanon and will do so when conditions are ripe. Israel is working to carry out the withdrawal in the framework of United Nations Security Council Resolution 425 and will exhaust all chances of doing so. The SLA's presence in any given outpost does not obligate the IDF regarding any particular withdrawal date." Technically, it can be argued, this statement was not a lie: The communiqué denied rumors regarding a pullout the following week, whereas the pullout would actually begin that very day.

At midday, Mofaz consulted with the senior officers attending the exercise on the Golan Heights. They concluded that unless the IDF was authorized to go on the offensive, the worst-case contingency plans, calling for a twenty-four to forty-eight-hour pullout, should be activated. However, a small group of senior officers who had extensive experience in Lebanon insisted that the SLA could still be empowered to hold the line. The command group contacted Barak, asking for instructions and arguing that his decision to extend the presence in southern Lebanon was becoming more irrelevant by the minute. Still, Barak refused to authorize either the evacuation of outposts or a move to the offensive. When Mofaz pressed him for a decision, Barak promised to convene the cabinet that evening. Exasperated, Mofaz ordered the Galil Division to assume direct responsibility for the predominantly Shiite central zone in case the mob and its HizbAllah escorts attempted to break into Israel. He also ordered that the Israeli base in Bint-Jubayl be evacuated during the night.

Meanwhile, many SLA units were holding the line and functioning quite routinely. During the morning, IDF and SLA units exchanged fire with HizbAllah forces in several sectors of the security zone. That afternoon, Barak arrived at the northern border to assess the situation, just as the civilian population was being ordered into bomb shelters until further notice. Returning to Jerusalem, he convened an emergency meeting of the Security Cabinet, which authorized him to determine the date of the pullout and to give the IDF open-fire orders should the need arise. That night, the quick evacuation of the IDF's Liaison Unit from Bint-Jubayl, coupled with the news about the cabinet's decision, dealt the SLA's morale a death blow. The entire SLA Western Brigade disintegrated. SLA battalions in the eastern sector were also collapsing, as they learned that the IDF's local units were receiving "orders to get ready" for a hasty pullout.

The IDF high command was issued the order to begin the pullout at 8 P.M. on May 23. Formally, the order was to begin implementing the worst-case contingency plan, called "Internal Horizon." About 1,000 soldiers and 200 vehicles were involved in the withdrawal operation, which was nearly completed that night. In a few places, soldiers were suddenly told that they had five minutes to pack up their personal weapons, web gear, and vests. In one post, food and drink were left on the table; in another, panicky soldiers simply ran the four miles to the border. In the rush to get out before daylight, the IDF abandoned ammunition, communications equipment, clothing, personal gear, and more. In Hatzbaya, the IDF left sophisticated equipment intact, although the computers were either destroyed or evacuated. The last of the IDF soldiers crossed the border into Israel at 6:45 A.M. on May 24, 2000.

———

PUBLICLY, the IDF's high command expressed great satisfaction with a successful pullout. Meeting with the Israeli media on the morning of May 24, Mofaz urged the nation "to rally and unite around the IDF on this historic day." He emphasized that "the orderly retreat" had been accomplished under difficult conditions "without even a scratch to IDF troops," and he warned HizbAllah and other forces in Lebanon not to exploit the withdrawal to strike at northern Israel. "The planes are ready, the pilots are on the alert, and their abilities are well known," he said.

Privately, Mofaz and the rest of the high command were furious at Barak for compelling the IDF to undertake an operation they had regarded all along as a major error. They could not forgive Barak—himself a former chief of staff—for using his position as an elected leader to stifle any professional dissent, let alone for keeping them in the dark about his real plans, thus preventing them from preparing a realistic pullout scenario. The primary point of contention, however, was the fate of the SLA.

On the evening of May 23, shortly after the pullout began, Israeli senior officers notified their SLA counterparts that they would have to leave Lebanon immediately along with the IDF. This announcement came as a

shock, for the Maronite and Druze units were still planning to hold their enclaves as agreed between Barak and Lahad only a couple of weeks earlier.
Furthermore, the SLA units did not have time to destroy their facilities and
their heavy weapons before evacuating the security zone. The men had to
abandon these tasks in order to collect their families and personal belong-
ings. The confusion was aggravated when Israeli artillery started to destroy
SLA weapon-storage sites even before SLA and IDF troops had cleared the
sites; no casualties were incurred, but there were many close shaves. However,
the Air Force was able to destroy most of the forty SLA tanks and artillery
pieces in one site. Toward morning, the troops were ordered to cease efforts
to destroy heavy weapons and simply proceed toward the border; the Israeli
Air Force and artillery would finish destroying these weapons the next day,
they were told. Consequently, several sites—including a huge logistics farm
at the entrance to Fatma Gate, with large quantities of weapons and equipment intended for the post-withdrawal SLA—were left intact. But then, at
first light, Barak ordered that "no plane is to cross the border, no attack helicopter is to cross, instructions for opening fire are on hold." Israeli and
Lebanese troops watched as HizbAllah seized the abandoned equipment.

The morning of May 24 saw long lines of cars, packed with whatever
possessions their owners had been able to grab, jamming the few gates on the
Israeli border. Altogether, some 1,600 families of SLA personnel—totaling
over 6,600 people—were desperately trying to cross into Israel. Ultimately,
most would have to abandon their property and proceed on foot. People who
had fought shoulder to shoulder with Israel for twenty years, and were eager
to continue, were now impoverished refugees with only the clothes on their
backs. Near the Fatma Gate, an IDF senior officer acknowledged his baffle-
ment: "Whoever tells you that this is the scenario he expected is simply lying.
The worst thing that could happen happened—our old friends in Lebanon
stand squeezed together, empty handed and running for their lives. We were
not prepared for it."

Significantly, there was a sole exception amidst this devastation. Small
groups of Lebanese working for the GSS and for MI unit 504—all of them
protégés of Lubrani—had been forewarned about the decision to dismantle
the security zone. They arrived at the border ahead of time, their cars filled
with large suitcases and trunks. GSS teams were there to meet them and expedite their crossing into Israel.

By the afternoon of May 24, the security zone was no more, and IDF
forces were attempting to establish a line along the still unmarked international border. In many areas, vital security systems—from electronic fences
to secure roads to fortified positions—were far from complete. Subsequently,
the IDF would have to move to tactically inferior positions: The United Na-

tions had determined that Israel was infringing on Lebanese territory, and Barak ordered unconditional compliance with U.N. demands. However, Barak himself was basking in the glory of the successful withdrawal. With the vast majority of Israelis in shock over the perfidy of abandoning Lebanon and the shame of the IDF's fleeing under HizbAllah fire, Barak was sending self-congratulatory messages to such world leaders as Clinton, Annan, and Chirac, pointing to Israel's compliance with Security Council Resolution 425 and demanding international protection for Israel's northern border.

———

IN A REAL SENSE, however, Barak was no longer interested in the situation on Israel's northern border. For the last several weeks he had been concentrating increasingly on what Clinton intimated might be a dramatic breakthrough with Arafat. In his preoccupation with the Palestinian track, Barak completely failed to notice the profound implications of the Arab and Muslim world's initial reaction to the Israeli retreat. Iranian Foreign Minister Kamal Kharrazi immediately traveled to Lebanon to congratulate the Hizb-Allah leaders. He proclaimed that all Arabs must learn from HizbAllah's "reconquest" of southern Lebanon that "this is the way to liberate occupied Arab lands," and he promised Iran's unyielding support for the campaign for the liberation of Palestine. In Gaza, thousands celebrated in the streets, chanting: "Lebanon today—Palestine tomorrow!"

15

Self-Induced Blindness (2000)

Arafat Prepares for His War of Independence; Clinton and Barak Blindside Themselves

IF BARAK was oblivious to the implications of the Israeli withdrawal from Lebanon—not just the physical withdrawal of those few days in late May, but the entire political-military dynamics that began in early 2000—Arafat was not. In fact, those events changed Arafat's core attitude toward Israel, enticing him to reevaluate Israel's apparent invincibility. He and his colleagues examined the entire political process leading to the unilateral withdrawal—the seemingly devastating impact of the mounting attrition (even though, objectively, there were very few casualties and a fair rate of military success) on the morale and image of the IDF, the impact of the activist Left (especially the Four Mothers organization and its political champion, Yossi Beilin) on the Israeli political landscape, and the media's susceptibility to influence by the Left and willingness to "convey the message" rather than merely report the facts. Arafat and his coterie concluded that Israel's internal weaknesses were beyond the reach of any help Clinton might give Barak at an hour of need.

In early April, Arafat instructed his commanders and intelligence officials to prepare to reactivate a host of Palestinian military options—ranging from isolated clashes to a full-fledged terrorism campaign. By this time, he had resolved to go ahead with the declaration of full Palestinian independence. However, he argued that no legitimate state can be established on the basis of "handouts of oppressors and occupiers." A state must emerge through a war of independence that will provide its founding myths. With the Clinton administration already committed to bringing about Palestinian statehood, most likely in September—on the eve of the U.S. elections and, symbolically, on the fifth anniversary of the White House signing of Oslo B—a well-timed eruption of "spontaneous popular violence" would likely lead the administration to coerce Barak into granting the best possible conditions. At the same time, this eruption of violence would give Arafat his war of independence. Realizing this, Arafat made a dramatic change in his strategic-political objectives—from the need to wear Israel down in a campaign of terrorism to the need to actually defeat Israel—with a concomitant change in military requirements. Bristling with optimism, Arafat reminded confidants that the Palestinians had already won their first war against Israel using only stones.

However, having lived through the siege of Beirut in 1982, Arafat understood the real power of the IDF, and he was not eager to repeat the experience. Therefore, rather than have the Palestinians try to win a real war against Israel on their own, he decided that the PA should work to provoke a regional war in which a coalition of Arab armies would defeat, perhaps even destroy, Israel. Saddam Hussein was the key to Arafat's plans. Arafat knew that Saddam was eager and ready to send his armies "to liberate al-Quds." Now Arafat sought to bring his "strategic partnership" and personal alliance with Saddam up to date. He named a confidant, Azzam Azzam al-Ahmad, as his personal envoy to Saddam and as "chief military coordinator" between the Palestinians and Iraq. Azzam led a team to Baghdad to start working with the Iraqi General Staff on contingency plans for Iraqi intervention, the participation of Islamist forces, and—despite the rivalry between Arafat and Assad over who was responsible for Palestine—the revival of the Iran-Iraq-Syria Axis. Azzam also addressed sensitive issues such as the establishment of alternative headquarters for Arafat and his coterie in the Baghdad area, so that, if Gaza fell, they could withdraw and continue the war from afar. Azzam also oversaw the transfer of hundreds of millions of dollars from Palestinian accounts to Iraqi intelligence accounts to fund weapon acquisition and training in Iraq for a Palestinian army that would march with the Iraqi army to liberate al-Quds.

On the local level, Arafat launched a new phase in the militarization of the PA Police Force. Starting in the fall of 1999, the PA police in Gaza had been organized into two brigades as the core of a 12,000-man light infantry division. Numerous police officers from Gaza who had been attending battalion-commander courses throughout the Arab world were brought back and integrated into the PA police. In the spring of 2000, the Gaza officers began running military exercises to transform their forces into an army. The PA also opened an expanded training facility in Jericho to begin a similar transformation of the West Bank police forces. By early April, the Palestinians had a sizable military establishment, including military academies, commando units, and a fledgling navy, air defense force, and air force. Their equipment included armored cars equipped to be used as light tanks and a myriad of anti-tank rockets and missiles, anti-aircraft guns, and light artillery.

In April, Arafat secretly instructed his closest lieutenants to begin preparations for the resumption of anti-Israeli terrorism. Arafat established two centers for these preparations, with their leaders chosen on the basis of complete personal loyalty, proven track records of anti-Israeli violence, and close relations with Islamist terrorist forces. In Gaza, the preparations were entrusted to Muhammad Dahlan, the commander of the Preventive Security Service in the Gaza Strip. In the West Bank, the commander was Marwan Barghouti, the leader of Fatah's Tanzim forces. Almost immediately, select teams from both centers began conducting exploratory terrorist activities. The success of these activities, as well as the enthusiasm both of senior commanders and of rank-and-file members of the PA security organizations, persuaded Arafat in mid-April to order active preparations for a major confrontation with Israel that fall—the Palestinians' war of independence.

JERUSALEM AND WASHINGTON continued to push ahead with the peace process as if there were no change in the PA's approach. Formally, the United States announced the resumption of talks at the expert level at Bolling Air Force Base near Washington, D.C. On April 10, Barak left Jerusalem for consultations in Cairo and Washington. Significantly, Mubarak knew by then about Arafat's contacts with Saddam but did not reveal this crucial fact to Barak. Meeting with Clinton on April 12, Barak reiterated his commitment to far-reaching concessions. A senior White House official reported that "the President was encouraged by the sense of energy from the Prime Minister regarding the Palestinian track," stressing that Barak had "brought new ideas to the table." One of these ideas was for the Clinton administration to expand its role in all aspects of the negotiations. A senior official in Barak's office announced that a U.S. representative would immediately join the talks at Bolling AFB, which seemed to have stalled. Furthermore, Ross would shortly return to the Middle East in order to help formulate the new idea that Clinton and Barak agreed to discuss the following month. In a cabinet meeting convened right after Barak's return to Jerusalem, he announced his intent "to expedite the West Bank withdrawal planned for June as a confidence-building measure to the Palestinians." Barak added that the future Palestinian entity "would be contiguous and its citizens would have the right of free movement." However, he did say he would insist on the demilitarization of a future Palestinian state.

The final-status framework talks between Israel and the PA—which had broken down in March—resumed in Eilat in late April, just as the IDF was starting its pullout from southern Lebanon. Although the Palestinian delegates would not comment on the withdrawal, they markedly hardened their positions and increased their demands. Barak instructed chief negotiator Oded Eran to "show flexibility" in order to reach an agreement quickly, but the Palestinians did not reciprocate. Israel proposed the creation of a Palestinian state covering more than 66 percent of the West Bank and made up of three "cantons" linked by a series of roads and tunnels. While Israel did not commit to the destruction of Jewish settlements, several dozen of these communities were located in areas that would be well within the proposed Palestinian state. Moreover, Barak's secret emissary, Yossi Ginossar, briefed Arafat that Israel was willing to withdraw from Arab villages adjacent to Jerusalem, including Abu-Dis, Azzariya, and Suwahara al-Sharqia. Saeb Erekat replied in Arafat's name, "We will not agree to accept advance payments such as Abu-Dis until the entire third withdrawal is agreed upon." Erekat added that the Palestinians would not agree to anything less than a Palestinian state "with the June 4, 1967, borders, [and] with East Jerusalem as its capital," as well as the right of return.

Prodded by the Clinton administration, Barak met Arafat in Ramallah on the night of May 7–8 to personally assure him of the forthcoming withdrawal and to ask for the resumption of the talks on the third withdrawal and the final-status arrangements. Aware of American pressure, Arafat did not refuse. However, he gave his real reply the next afternoon when thousands of Palestinian rioters attacked IDF positions at both the Tomb of Rachel in Bethlehem and the Ayosh junction near Ramallah. The rioters demanded the release of Palestinian prisoners—an issue not then being discussed. In both locations, Arafat's security forces observed the clashes and intervened only when Israeli soldiers were about to start shooting. The ability of the Palestinian security forces to disperse the crowds at that point suggested that they had been in control of the rioters from the very beginning.

Frustrated with the lack of progress on the permanent-status agreement, the administration had implored Israel to open parallel secret talks in Stockholm, and Barak had agreed. However, by the time the May 8 riots broke out, these talks also had stalled, and Ross rushed to Stockholm to try to prevent their collapse. At this point, however, the primary negotiations fell apart completely when senior PA negotiator Yasser Abed Rabbo learned about the Stockholm talks and resigned in protest. Alarmed by these setbacks, the White House implored Barak to make a dramatic gesture; he obliged by announcing his intention of transferring Abu-Dis and other Jerusalem-area villages to the PA.

———

BY NOW, Damascus and Tehran were afraid that Arafat might not be able to resist the lure of the compromises offered by Washington and Jerusalem. Hence, Damascus leaked through Palestinian sources the idea that Arafat and his top aides were being targeted for assassination by Syrian-backed Palestinians. Reinforcing these leaks, the PFLP-GC's Ahmad Jibril delivered a fiery speech in Lebanon denouncing Arafat on the grounds that his negotiations were preventing a HizbAllah-style military campaign to force an Israeli withdrawal from the West Bank and Gaza. Amin al-Hindi, the chief of General Intelligence in Gaza, told Arafat he had learned from an unnamed European intelligence agency that there was a Syrian plot to liquidate him and the rest of the PA leadership; Arafat did not appear surprised. However, he took more seriously a warning from Jibril Rajub, chief of the Preventive Security Service in the West Bank, who told him of the possibility that he would be attacked from inside Fatah, primarily over his coterie's preference for getting rich rather than fighting for the liberation of Palestine. Consequently, Arafat resumed wearing a bulletproof vest and carrying a pistol in his jacket pocket.

Apprehensive that he would not be able to withstand American pressure and determined to prove Fatah, Damascus, and Tehran wrong, Arafat resolved to effect a breakout. He chose May 15—Nakba Day, the anniversary of Israel's independence on the Western calendar. A few hours after a conciliatory announcement by Barak, Palestinian security forces opened fire on Israeli positions throughout the West Bank and Gaza. Palestinian mobs gathered in the routine spots of contention, like the Ayosh junction, and began throwing rocks at the Israeli positions. When, a few hours later, Israeli troops prepared to respond, Palestinian "policemen" opened automatic fire on the IDF positions, wounding two; two Palestinians were killed in the ensuing exchanges. A cease-fire was negotiated through the joint security committee, but the Palestinians broke it within minutes. The fighting at the Ayosh junction ceased only after Brigadier General Shlomo Oren warned the local PA commander that the IDF would bomb Arafat's Ramallah headquarters unless he promptly ordered a cease-fire.

By this time, however, fighting had spread throughout the territories. In the Jenin area, PA security personnel attacked the local IDF Liaison Unit, wounding its commander. In the Hebron area, mobs stoned Israeli cars, and the local PA troops aimed their guns at the IDF's positions in an attempt to prevent the dispersal of the rioting mob. In Netzarim, in the Gaza Strip, hundreds of Palestinian rioters threw rocks and Molotov cocktails at IDF positions. PA officials claimed that some 10 to 15 of their people were killed, and over 300 wounded, in the several hours before a cease-fire went into effect. Fourteen Israelis were wounded, five of them by gunshots. "The PLO executive committee is very proud of this strong popular uprising which has spread throughout all the camps in the homeland and in exile," the PA's media were reporting by the day's end.

As Arafat had anticipated, the Clinton administration swiftly reacted to the spreading violence while ignoring the stalled talks. In Washington, Albright urged restraint on both sides and the return to a "proper atmosphere" for the peace process. Ross rushed to Rome from Stockholm in order to organize a series of meetings with Barak and Arafat. The next day, violence resumed at a greater number of spots, albeit at a lower level of intensity. The PA's official newspaper *Al-Hayah al-Jadidah* carried a front-page call for escalation: "The fury of the masses must erupt like a volcano in the face of the Israelis, and the land should explode under their feet."

That night, GSS Chief Avi Dichter met Arafat with guarantees from Barak that Israel would soon come up with "new ideas" concerning the permanent status. Arafat then agreed to reduce the violence in at least some of the hot spots. However, on the third day, fighting spread to Jerusalem and other locations, with the emphasis shifting to firefights instead of the ostensibly spontaneous rock throwing and firebomb hurling. The sole exception was the complete absence of Palestinians from the Netzarim junction—a demonstration of Arafat's ability to control his security forces if he had the incentive. On May 17, less than a day after he had met with Dichter, Arafat chaired a meeting of Fatah in Bethlehem. He complained that the demonstrations were too small and orderly; he demanded that women be brought out to demonstrate and that they be "hot." Brigadier General Hajj Ismail, the PA's West Bank police commander, relayed the Israelis' complaints that Tanzim and PA security forces were firing on the IDF. "Get lost," Arafat told Ismail in front of the Fatah militants. After this outburst, Arafat left the room. At about the same time, the PA's Faisal Husseini was explaining to another audience that the strategic objective of the riots was to prepare for the declaration of independence—by now scheduled for September 13—"on all our lands." At that time, columns of refugees would march on the settlements in order to reclaim Palestinian lands at all costs. "The Palestinians will be prepared for a confrontation," Husseini declared. "If the Israelis intercept the marches or cut the roads, the Palestinians will cut the roads connecting Israel to the Jewish settlements in the Palestinian areas, no matter what happens."

As the Stockholm talks dragged on, so did Palestinian violence. On May 18, numerous organizations called for a general mobilization for two "days of rage" to begin the next day. Significantly, Fatah's own Tanzim forces called for "days of rage for the exacerbation of violence and increased activity against Israel and the settlers."

Finally, on May 26—just after the completion of Israel's withdrawal from southern Lebanon—Arafat ordered Fatah and the Palestinian police to gradually end the violent protests.

Although the May mini-Intifadah was short and the losses few, it revealed the extensive upgrading of the Palestinian forces as well as the reassertion of the Tanzim's central role in organized violence and the importance of its leader, Marwan Barghouti. In a May 16 interview with Roni Shaqed of *Yediot Aharonot*, Barghouti claimed that the Tanzim fighters were the dominant force in the confrontations with the IDF: "Only six Palestinian policemen opened fire. All the firing was done by Tanzim activists. We fired lots of bullets from dozens of weapons—Kalashnikovs, M-16 rifles, pistols. This wasn't designed to kill or injure, but to raise morale. We had no intention of harming Israelis. If anyone wants to kill Israelis, there are other ways."

Barghouti told Shaqed that the mini-Intifadah should be considered the precursor of a new strategic dynamics molding the future Palestinian state. "This clash is a signal, a prelude to what will happen on 13 September if we have to declare independence unilaterally. Thousands of youngsters are active in the Tanzim, all of them residents of the West Bank and Gaza Strip, and many are graduates of the Intifadah and Israeli jails," Barghouti explained. "If Arafat declares independence and Israel opposes it, Palestinian security forces will go to the borders of the Green Line and East Jerusalem, and the Tanzim will help our soldiers." He added, "We don't like to make sacrifices, we don't like injuries, but we know that Israel is leaving Lebanon under HizbAllah pressure, so why shouldn't that happen here?"

Both the Islamists and the official Palestinian media emphasized the same theme. "Strength of will and determination can overcome military power," said the Gaza pro-Islamist newspaper *Al-Risalah*. "The jeep defeated the tank, the gun defeated the aircraft, and the explosive charges defeated the laser-guided bombs [in Lebanon]." HAMAS communiqués urged Arafat to break the negotiation process that had made him "submissive and paralyzed" and stop "pursuing holy fighters and sending his people out to thwart the masses who want to stand face to face with the soldiers of the occupation." The Arafat-controlled *Al-Hayah al-Jadidah* stressed "the message Israel delivers to the Palestinians by its withdrawal: We will not give you your rights unless you follow this model." The paper's editor, Hafiz al-Barghouti, drew the primary Palestinian lesson from the events in southern Lebanon: "If blood does not bring victory, it at least bequeaths it to future generations. For the first time, Israeli invaders flee from an Arab land—humiliated, all they want is to stay alive, having tasted death. They did not pee on the negotiation table in order to force their terms, but rather peed in their pants."

However, Arafat realized the need for a major military buildup before the PA could replicate HizbAllah's tactics. Consequently, the PA launched another cycle of militarization and modernization of forces, particularly in the Gaza Strip. By late May, there were 22,000 troops in Gaza alone, distributed among intelligence, preventive security, and police, military, and naval forces. They were equipped with armored personnel carriers and other vehicles, mounted with illegal machine guns and mortars. Furthermore, the Palestinian police and other security forces were completely ignoring such nonmilitary duties as community service and combatting crime. The PA's official announcement that a Palestinian policeman who had shot and seriously wounded an Israeli soldier in Gaza during the latest round of violence had "acted within the framework of his duty" did not bode well for Israel.

Meanwhile, Arafat openly identified HizbAllah as a model for the Palestinian armed struggle. He was stating the obvious, as demonstrated by a poll taken by the London-based Islam-on-Line Internet network, which indicated that 96.7 percent of Muslims worldwide "hoped that the Palestinians would use HizbAllah as a model to fight Israel." Hence, shortly after the Israeli withdrawal, Arafat asked Munir Makdah, the Palestinian Islamist commander, to serve as a go-between with HizbAllah and inquire about the possibility of getting training and weapon shipments from them. When HizbAllah responded affirmatively, Arafat named Lieutenant Colonel Massud Iyad of Force 17 as his personal emissary to the HizbAllah. Iyad left immediately for Lebanon and was promptly presented to Naim Qassim and the HizbAllah high command. Iyad brought them a special message from Arafat inviting HizbAllah to participate in the forthcoming Palestinian war of independence. Qassim accepted the invitation and promised help. Iyad stayed in Lebanon throughout the summer to work out modalities for training Palestinians recruited in Lebanon, to oversee weapon deliveries, and to oversee the establishment of HizbAllah cells and networks throughout the Gaza Strip and West Bank. The character of the work Arafat asked Iyad, Qassim, and Makdah to undertake left no doubt that he was irreversibly committed to war.

―――――

DESPITE THE BRIEF surge of violence, Eran and Erekat met again in Jericho to discuss the third withdrawal and the release of Palestinian prisoners, and the PA also agreed to resume the talks in Stockholm. Buoyed by these developments, Barak traveled to Lisbon on June 1 for a meeting with Clinton. Barak complained that Arafat was stalling by avoiding the central issues of the framework agreement, and Clinton agreed to Barak's request that Albright go to the Middle East to accelerate the negotiations. Barak returned from Lisbon convinced that he had Clinton's unyielding support. He told the cabinet he had received "exceptional compliments from U.S. President Bill Clinton regarding the decision to withdraw the IDF from Lebanon," and he claimed that Clinton shared his apprehensions about the "Palestinian foot-dragging."

However, the extent of the unilateral concessions Barak was willing to make, particularly regarding Jerusalem, had finally provoked a grassroots backlash that the politicians could not ignore. On June 7, the Knesset approved by a 61–48 margin a preliminary reading of a bill to dissolve and head for new elections. Knesset leaders stressed that they considered the new elections to be a de facto referendum on Barak's "peace policy." A defiant Barak declared that he would not hesitate to make the "important decisions" and then seek public support. Politically, he sought to fight the dissolving of the Knesset by offering the SHAS (Sephardic Torah Guardians) party outrageous financial and political incentives. When this failed, he tried to elicit from the Palestinians some gesture indicating a genuine commitment to the peace process.

What he got was a policy communiqué from Fatah that described the peace process as but one element of a comprehensive strategy against Israel. "Negotiations are an important option, but not the only one, for deciding both interim and final status issues," the communiqué explained. "The areas which have been liberated and which are now controlled by the PNA are the areas in which it makes most sense to demonstrate Palestinian sovereignty. Therefore, in those areas, it is legitimate to confront settlers and the Israeli army with all possible means, including the use of arms." The PA media went further, openly challenging not only Israel's right to exist but also the Jewish legacy in the region. For example, columnist Kheiri Mansur wrote in the June 9 *Al-Hayah al-Jadidah* that Israel was faking history and archaeology to "falsely establish its right to the Land of Israel": "Jewish authors and poets," he declared, "wrote about Haifa, Jaffa, Acre, and even Jerusalem, but it was all ideological imagination—no more, no less."

Nevertheless, the Israeli-Palestinian negotiations resumed at Bolling AFB on June 13. On Albright's advice, Israel made a major concession by agreeing to discuss the third withdrawal at the beginning of the session. Even so, the opening round failed to deliver a productive dynamics, and U.S. negotiators were called in to play an intensified role. One of the first things the Americans did was divide the negotiators into two teams, one addressing final status and the other addressing interim issues—exactly the opposite of Barak's frequently reiterated preference. The U.S. team also warned both delegations that "Clinton is taking an active role in negotiations" and suggested that the president must not be disappointed.

Meanwhile, Israeli Military Intelligence briefed Barak on information acquired from numerous sources confirming that Arafat was preparing for "an armed conflict" to be launched "within a few weeks." Among the warning signs were Arafat's support for Tanzim chief Barghouti in the upcoming Fatah internal elections and Arafat's strengthening of military units throughout the West Bank. Barak, however, refused to alter his negotiating strategy on the basis of these warnings. Instead, he spoke with Clinton and Mubarak in an effort to persuade them to convey to Arafat "the importance of reaching a framework agreement and the dangers of not making a real effort to reach such an agreement."

Having been briefed by Mubarak about Barak's state of mind, Arafat ordered his delegation to implement their brinkmanship strategy. On June 15, Erekat broke off negotiations over the third withdrawal and the release of prisoners. The Israeli delegation was surprised by the "crisis," given the goodwill gestures made in the previous sessions. "We don't want goodwill gestures from the Israelis," Erekat said in a public statement. "All we want from Israel is to implement the agreements." The next day, Albright and Ross announced their plan to travel to Israel to persuade Barak and Arafat to agree on the agenda for a White House summit.

———

BILL CLINTON was running out of time. Congress was increasingly skeptical of the administration's peace plans, which involved huge appropriations and a myriad of vague commitments to countries of dubious repute. Therefore, if the legacy was to be achieved, a peace agreement would have to originate from the Middle Eastern antagonists, with Clinton's people serving merely as mediators and facilitators. Such a deal would be possible, Clinton knew, only if Israel committed to unprecedented concessions—a once-in-a-lifetime offer the Palestinians would not be able to refuse. However, because the vast majority of Israelis were dead set against such concessions, it was crucial to get Barak to overrule his countrymen and commit Israel irreversibly to implementing Clinton's plan.

Thus, late June 2000 became a critical time in Barak's political life. Clinton, Albright, and Indyk were continually telling him that only he could deliver a historic end to the conflict with the Palestinians by rising above the mediocrity of the professional bureaucracy—that is, the very civil service and military elite he hailed from—and his fellow politicians. During the summer, there was an endless series of phone calls between Jerusalem and Washington. "Clinton probably spoke on the phone with Barak more than any other leader in the world," Ross recalled. "Barak liked doing business this way. Whatever was important to him usually led to a phone call to the President, and Clinton made it clear that he was available any time to talk." Clinton's primary aim, in which he succeeded, was to convince Barak that he was being made uniquely privy to highly sensitive information upon which he could rely in making decisions. Because his countrymen, Clinton told him, had no access to this kind of information, their opinion was useless in making fateful decisions for Israel.

On June 19, Barak informed the Security Cabinet that "We are reaching the end of the diplomatic corridor that began with the Oslo accords. Israel is committed to an agreement and is willing to take difficult decisions to reach it, one that will safeguard its vital interests. But," he conceded, "we cannot force decisions on the other side." Although Barak did not inform the cabinet about any concrete moves, "senior sources close to the Prime Minister" leaked that he had agreed to a ten-day trilateral summit at Camp David starting July 6. When the Israeli public reacted with dismay, Indyk quickly said conditions were "still not ripe for a summit," while Barak's office lamely noted that "it hasn't yet been agreed that the summit will take place, but if there is agreement, this is a reasonable date."

The following week, first Ross and then Albright arrived to put added pressure on Barak. Albright informed him that because Clinton was adamant on avoiding an embarrassing diplomatic failure, he would not commit to hosting the summit until it had been ascertained that an agreement could be reached. Consequently, Israel provided the United States with a "non-paper"— an unofficial draft for an agreement based on a plan worked out in 1996 by Beilin and Abu-Mazen. This plan called for Israel to withdraw from more than 90 percent of the West Bank, dividing Jerusalem, keeping only 130 of the existing 200 or so settlements under Israeli control, and permitting the return of a certain number of "refugees" into pre-1967 Israel. These steps—exceeding by far the Israeli consensus—were considered by the White House as Israel's starting point, from which additional concessions could be extracted.

On June 28, Arafat met with Albright and told her he was "unimpressed" with Barak's ideas. He stressed that there could be no compromise on 100 percent withdrawal to the 1967 lines, the total return of all Palestinian refugees to their homes in Israel, and the complete eradication of all settlements "just as was done in the Sinai Desert." Indyk and Ross warned Albright that the gaps between the PA and Israel were too large to ensure the success of a summit in the near future. Informed about the American doubts, Barak insisted that a permanent agreement *must* be discussed at a summit and promised to do everything to ensure its success. Returning to Washington, Albright briefed Clinton and opined that Barak would deliver.

———

REALIZING HOW CRUCIAL the summit was for both Clinton and Barak, Arafat assumed that Israel would not strike against, or even complain about, overtly militarized PA forces even if they violated past agreements. Therefore, in late July, he ordered the PA security services to deploy and test the assault elements of their forces. These units increased the pace of their training, concentrating on urban warfare exercises and drills preparing them to conquer Jewish settlements. A foreign observer of these exercises concluded, "It is an army, not a police force. A significant number of the Palestinian battalions conducted exercises in military style. These exercises included the operation of armored vehicles and machine guns, and special emphasis was placed on training snipers."

On Arafat's instruction, the PA also began hoarding food and other necessary supplies. For example, the manager of a Gaza flour mill reported that five large aluminum storage containers had been ordered, each able to hold enough flour to supply the entire population of Gaza for two months. In summer camps run by Fatah associates, children were indoctrinated into terrorism: encouraged to participate in violent demonstrations and taught how to throw Molotov cocktails and stones at IDF positions. PA hospitals started hoarding medicine—at times, at the expense of existing patients—and conducted simulations of receiving hundreds of casualties from the battlefield. Subsequently, large supplies of bandages, infusions, and burn treatments were ordered, and blood drives were launched. Dahlan purchased two generators, one for his home and one for his command headquarters. In western Gaza, tunnels were dug at an unprecedented pace in order to smuggle additional military supplies from Egypt.

On the night of July 3–4, the PLO's Central Committee decided "to declare a Palestinian state on September 13," irrespective of where negotiations stood. The resolution did *not* stipulate that the future Palestinian state would be confined to the West Bank and Gaza; on the contrary, the communiqué stressed the PLO's resolve to establish the state in "all of Palestine" with all of Jerusalem as its capital. Imad Falouji, the PA's communications minister, predicted that war would erupt after Arafat's declaration of statehood—a decisive war, following which "no settler will be able to return to his home." Falouji publicly urged the Islamic Jihad and HAMAS "to join forces with the PA" in anticipation of "the final battle with Israel."

In early July, with attendance at the Camp David summit virtually impossible to avoid, Arafat called for contingency plans for a wave of violent demonstrations—without shooting, however—spanning two weeks, should the need arise to increase pressure on the Clinton administration. Israeli Military Intelligence learned about these instructions almost immediately and warned Barak. When he ignored the warnings and refused to permit active preparations by the IDF, Chief of Staff Mofaz informed the Knesset—a move that resulted in a leak to the Israeli media. Mofaz also ordered the IDF to prepare for escalation. An IDF sector commander remarked, "I'm taking into account a situation in which in September I will have to wage a small war here." Still, Barak would not let any of this interfere with his dealings with Clinton, who, on July 5, announced that he would convene the Middle East peace summit at Camp David on the 11th. "I am leaving for Camp David with a heavy feeling of responsibility for the future of the State of Israel and its people," Barak said. "We will strive for an agreement which will bring separation, good neighborliness, and strengthen Israel's security."

On the eve of the summit, the Israeli government crumbled, as additional parties withdrew their support in the face of overwhelming public opposition to Barak's peace policy. By July 9, Barak represented a government that had the overt support of only 32 Members of the Knesset (out of 120), plus the tacit support of all 10 anti-Zionist Arab MKs. Reflecting Clinton's coaching, Barak was undaunted. He declared that he would persevere "even if I have the support of . . . only a quarter of the Knesset." Israeli diplomatic sources claimed that Barak and Arafat were "already close to a final agreement" involving "far-reaching Israeli concessions." Albright noted that any such agreement would have to include the division of Jerusalem. "It is impossible to totally ignore the yearnings of a billion Arabs for Jerusalem," she explained.

BARAK ARRIVED at Camp David convinced that in an environment of American informality and excellent accommodations and isolated from the Palestinian street and the militants in his own coterie, Arafat would finally see the light. At Camp David, however, Clinton and Barak were also isolated from the realities of the Middle East. They were blind to the fact that Arafat could not, without losing the Palestinian constituency that had been with him since the early 1960s, accept an agreement that would appear to make Palestinian statehood a gift of the Israeli government; statehood could not be won without the cleansing struggle. As well, there was no way Arafat could accept any agreement that did not open the door to the ultimate destruction of Israel—via right of return and the high Arab birth rate or via a regional war.

Palestinian officials have pointed out that this should not have come as a surprise, if only because the Palestinians had repeatedly told the Americans about Arafat's constraints. The White House, however, simply did not believe the Palestinians when they said there could be no compromise over their negotiated positions. Akram Haniyah, a Palestinian journalist known as one of Arafat's close confidants, addressed this point in his "Camp David Papers," published in the Ramallah newspaper *Al-Ayyam* during late July and early August 2000. "The Palestinians used to say to U.S. officials: You would be making a grave mistake if you believed Yassir Arafat would agree to sign an agreement that fails to fulfill the minimum level of Palestinian national rights. The answer used to be a mixture of doubting and suspicious looks and smiles claiming confidence, knowledge, and the ability to make accomplishments. The Palestinians would say to them: The army of the contemporary Palestinian revolution that Fatah launched came from the refugee camps outside Palestine, and any agreement that does not include a just solution to the refugee problem would be an invitation for a more violent revolution from the refugee camps. The answer used to be silence and refusal to listen to anything that contradicts the things on which they based their logic. It is because of all of this that Clinton went to the summit and, based on the recommendations of his advisers, he was confident of his ability to achieve an historical accomplishment with which to end his political career." Reality would confront him very soon.

Internal Security Minister Shlomo Ben-Ami kept a diary during the summit; his July 15 entry, as reported in the April 6, 2001, issue of *Maariv*, is especially revealing. He describes a working meeting between the Israeli and Palestinian delegations attended by Clinton. "I [Ben-Ami] presented our positions, maps etc., then Abu Alaa presented the Palestinian position. He talked in absolute terms: the 1967 borders, international legitimacy, etc. Clinton sat in front of me. I could see how this redhead was fuming. Next thing I knew, Clinton lashed out at Abu Alaa in a very degrading style. He yelled at him: 'Sir, this is not the Security Council, this is not the General Assembly. You can give your lectures there, but don't waste my time. I have a lot at stake here as well.' . . . Clinton blamed the Palestinians for not fulfilling the promise he received from Arafat (to come up with practical proposals). 'A summit's purpose,' Clinton said, 'is to have discussions that are based on sincere intentions and you, the Palestinians, did not come to this summit with sincere intentions.' Then he got up and left the room."

Palestinian officials confirmed the incident, although they attributed Clinton's outburst to an American-Israeli conspiracy. In the Palestinians' eyes, as Haniyah would write, "The Israelis came to consolidate the gains of their war in 1967, and not to make peace that removes the traces of this war. They came to reorganize and legitimize the occupation, instead of searching for a language for dialogue on living and coexisting with neighbors and partners."

This conviction was especially strong concerning Jerusalem and the suggestion, as Ross put it, of "deferring Jerusalem and agreeing on everything else." Arafat's reaction, Haniyah recalled, was to remind the Palestinian delegation over and over that "Jerusalem is not only a Palestinian city; it is an Arab, Islamic, and Christian city." Thus the Palestinians would not negotiate over Jerusalem even when the Israelis made previously unthinkable concessions regarding Israel's control over, and even presence in, the Holy Sites, and particularly the Temple Mount. At one point, in a conversation with Clinton in Barak's presence, Arafat stated that the Israeli preoccupation with the Temple Mount was only a negotiating trick because there had never been a Jewish Temple in Jerusalem.

In his entry for July 24–25—the last night of the Camp David summit—an exasperated Ben-Ami recalled the failure of the Americans to get Arafat to yield even symbolically. Significantly, Ben-Ami grasped what Arafat's position amounted to but could not believe that was what Arafat intended, for his priorities were so alien to the conceptions of the Israeli peace camp. In principle, the Israelis offered to make the Temple Mount an international sacred site with Muslim custodianship on behalf of all religions. Ben-Ami raised this idea with Clinton, and "the President reacted with much enthusiasm: 'not only the Jews worldwide but the Christians support this notion as well.'" However, Arafat and the Palestinians would have none of it—they demanded complete and comprehensive Muslim control over the area. According to Ben-Ami, "[I] told Saib Erekat: 'You are barely 4 million Muslim Palestinians and pretend to represent one billion Muslims regarding the Temple Mount. Clinton's proposals are historic and you are about to miss another opportunity.' I added that Arafat placed the Muslim agenda before the national Palestinian agenda. 'Your national agenda is held hostage in the hands of the Muslim agenda and you will pay a heavy price for this.'"

In fact, Arafat had never had a "national agenda" in Western terms. His sacred objective throughout was the destruction of Israel and the establishment of a Muslim state in its stead. Furthermore, Ben-Ami evidently did not know, perhaps did not care to know, how intense the grassroots Islamist feelings were concerning Jerusalem. On July 21, the Imam of al-Aqsa had given the Islamist perspective on Camp David. His sermon elucidated the irreconcilable contradiction between what Clinton and Barak were expecting Arafat to do and what the Muslim law governing his life and that of his constituency dictated.

To the imam, the entire negotiation process was quintessentially un-Islamic. "The case is not over borders," he said:

> The case should be the illegitimate existence of the Jewish state on Muslim land. . . . In Islam there is no difference between the land that was occupied in 1967 and the land that was occupied in 1948—both are Islamic land that is occupied by Jews and should be liberated. This is how Muslims used to perceive Palestine. That is why it was liberated from the Crusaders after 92 years, during which al-Aqsa Mosque was used as a stable for the Crusaders' horses. We should remember that during the Crusaders' occupation the Muslims wouldn't dare to compromise with the Crusaders over the "East-

ern part of the city," they wouldn't dare to give up any part of Palestine to the Crusaders. This is because Palestine was always being perceived as a precious part of the Muslim land.

The great treason that we face today occurred only when Palestine was separated from the Islamic Creed: It happened when the Arab nationalists took their part in solving what they called then "the Palestinian problem" and handed it over to the secular PLO. . . . It should be clear that Palestine is not owned by the Palestinians. It . . . belongs to all the Muslims. . . .

All these agreements that the traitorous rulers are committing are void and do not bind Muslims to them. . . . Any permanent agreement with the disbelievers is void automatically. The permanent agreement means the canceling of jihad, which can never happen. . . . What a great treason is going on in Camp David!

This sermon was broadcast throughout the Muslim world, even to Muslim communities in the West. Three days later, as the summit was nearing its end, Ikrama Sabri, the mufti of al-Quds and the Whole of Palestine—who had been handpicked by Arafat—issued a series of fatwas undercutting Arafat's ability to reach a compromise even if he wanted to. Sabri rejected the option of "religious sovereignty" over Jerusalem, as proposed by the United States and Israel. "We don't separate between the religious and the political in Islam," he declared. "Hence Muslims can't accept a situation whereby we enjoy religious sovereignty whereas Israel retains political sovereignty." He then proceeded to foreclose any compromise over the "right of return" by issuing a fatwa "forbidding Palestinian refugees to receive compensation in exchange for their land in Occupied Palestine." He decreed that "Palestine in its entirety is a *waqf*—land that belongs to the Muslim Ummah," and therefore it could not be traded by individuals. This fatwa, Sabri explained, was based on a similar decree by Islamic authorities in the 1930s. "Because all of Palestine is Holy Land, any acceptance of compensation would be regarded as selling the land and against Islam. Those who do not want to return have no right to compensation, whatever their reasons." Once again, there was no way Arafat could disregard these fatwas and have any resulting agreement be considered legal, legitimate, and enforceable.

And so, after two weeks of intense negotiations, with extremely high political stakes for both Clinton and Barak, the Camp David summit failed. For Arafat, getting the summit to fail was a major achievement: In Nabil Shaath's words, Arafat "rode home on a white horse" because he had proved that he "still cared about Jerusalem and the refugees" in the face of incredible pressure from the Americans and the Israelis. For Ben-Ami, the primary lesson of Camp David was the impossibility of reaching peace with Arafat.

He stressed this point in an interview published in *Maariv* on April 13, 2001: "At Camp David I wrote to myself: 'We witness here a battle of the Palestinian generations. The older generation is disconnected—it knew what it wanted, but it also realized it was not getting there. The young Palestinian generation at Camp David tried to be pragmatic but it did not have enough legitimacy. The tension between the two generations was obvious.'" Unfortunately, Ben-Ami and the rest of the Barak government would soon forget their own observations under the pressure of short-term political expediency.

———

ARAFAT RETURNED to the Middle East more convinced than ever that the war of independence was the sole viable solution to the Palestinian problem. Therefore, he asked for, and received the same day, the appropriate fatwa from the League of Ulema of Palestine. This was an institutional fatwa and therefore even stronger and more authoritative than Imam Sabri's. It clearly demonstrates the Palestinian elite's irreconcilable hostility to Israel:

> With the Palestinian cause and its gem, Al-Quds al-Sharif [Sacred Jerusalem], . . . at a crossroads, and against the background of the goings-on and the talks at Camp David, we in the League of the Ulema of Palestine would like to emphasize the following:
>
> First, Palestine and its gem, Jerusalem, from the Mediterranean Sea to the Jordan River is Arab and Islamic land and an Islamic trust. It belongs to our people and our Ummah of Arabs and Muslims; it has always been that way for past generations and it is a trust held by all of the Arabs and Muslims and so it is unbelievable that it or any part thereof be surrendered.
>
> Second: Jerusalem is the place where our Prophet Muhammad stopped off on his journey to Heaven; the city is home to Al-Aqsa Mosque; it is the first of the two *qiblas* and is third in rank to the two holy mosques; it is an Arab/Muslim city and has pride of place in the hearts of Muslims throughout the world; the city was occupied by Israel in 1948 and in 1967. Its liberation is a religious, national, and Arab duty that must be executed by all Arabs and Muslims.
>
> Third, the Palestinian refugees and evacuees were wrongly and unjustly made to leave their homeland under the force of Zionist terror and gruesome massacres; they were forced to leave their country and were displaced against their free will. They were made to leave their country by Jewish gangs, and so their return to their cities and villages and homes and properties is a legitimate and historic right that shall not be surrendered no matter how long they have to wait; Zionists must take legal and moral responsibility for that. Therefore, the *sharia*-based ruling is that any arrangement call-

ing for the refugees to be compensated for their right to return or their re-
settlement outside their homeland is, from the point of view of the *sharia,*
null and void. Whoever will choose compensation over the right to return
shall be deemed to have sold his homeland; that compensation shall be unacceptable from the point of view of the *sharia* as judged by the men of religious learning in Palestine and outside of it in the distant and recent past.

Fourth, any treaty that would provide for the relinquishment of Palestine or any part of it, above all Jerusalem, or the right of the Palestinian
refugees to be repatriated to their homeland shall be null and void from the
point of view of the *sharia* and shall not be binding on our people or
Ummah. This is because Palestine is not the property of any single individual or organization of state. Nor is Palestine the property of any single
generation in particular; it is the property of the Arabs and the Muslims
and they have to reject and negate any such relinquishment.

Fifth, the liberation of Palestine and its gem, Jerusalem, and Al-Aqsa
Mosque and the repatriation of the refugees in their millions can hardly
come about at the negotiating table; it can only happen in the jihad, the
route taken by the companions of the Prophet Muhammad and Salah al-
Din al-Ayyubi. Jihad is an ongoing process that shall continue till the Day
of Judgment; it can be halted neither by the injustice of the wrongdoers
nor by the justice of the just.

Moreover, PA officials—even those associated with the peace camp and
the Oslo process—embarked on a campaign of virulent incitement aimed at
reinforcing the inevitability of the jihad. Abu-Alaa, for example, told *Al-
Ayyam* that Israeli negotiators at Camp David had "signaled a desire to demolish the al-Aqsa Mosque." He elaborated this point: "Barak proposed
during the talks at Camp David to give Palestinians 'custodianship' over the
Mosque while Israel would retain sovereignty over the mosque's underneath." This, said Abu-Alaa, was "the most dangerous" proposal he had
"ever heard" because "it was clear that by insisting on controlling what is beneath the mosque, they signaled their intention to destroy the mosque at a
later date."

Polls taken at this time clearly showed that it was not only the Palestinian elites who were ready for war. In late July, the Palestinian Center for Policy and Survey Research asked 1,259 Palestinians from Gaza, the West Bank,
and East Jerusalem what Arafat should do next. The results were all too
clear: 60 percent favored armed clashes with Israel if a peace deal was not
reached by September 13; 67 percent supported Arafat's refusal to compromise at Camp David; 63 percent thought "Palestinians should emulate
the Iranian-backed HizbAllah" and "wage a guerrilla war against Israeli

troops"; and 52 percent supported "armed attacks against Israeli targets"—specifically citing HAMAS's "spate of bombings against Israeli targets that killed scores of people" as the kind of "armed attacks" they would like to see revived.

Upon his return from Camp David, Arafat convened his coterie and announced his decision to launch the war of independence. He ordered his lieutenants to expedite preparations. However, to throw Washington off the scent, Arafat also ordered that rumors be spread that he was considering postponing the declaration of statehood in order to further the chances of the peace process.

Speaking in early March 2001 in the Ein Hilweh refugee camp in southern Lebanon, Imad Falouji, the PA's communications minister and Arafat's special emissary to HAMAS and other Islamist organizations, recalled Arafat's decision to launch the Intifadah. "It had been planned since Chairman Arafat's return from Camp David, when he turned the tables in the face of the former U.S. president and rejected the American conditions," Falouji said. Arafat ordered that the PLO should revive its "military action" groups in order to escalate the fighting using quasi-deniable fronts. As Falouji put it, "the PLO is going back to the '60s, '70s, and '80s. The Fatah Hawks, the Kassam Brigades, the Red Eagle, and all the military action groups are returning to work!" And so they were.

16

The March Toward War (2000)

Clinton Attempts to Grasp His Legacy;
Arafat and the Islamists Jockey for Position

THE BREAKDOWN of Camp David and Arafat's preparations for war took place in an environment shaped by the death of Hafez al-Assad. Although it had been known for three years that Assad's days were numbered, there was no immediate warning of impending death—he suddenly collapsed on June 10 while talking on the phone to Beirut. However, in the weeks preceding his death, the succession struggle had heated up, most notably with the death of former premier Mahmud Zubi in late May. Officially, Zubi committed suicide by shooting two bullets into his head so that he would avoid trial for corruption, but Damascus was rife with rumors that he was assassinated because he had expressed support for the return of Rifaat al-Assad as a more suitable successor than the immature Bashar. Then, on June 5, came the flight of Hikmat Shihabi, the former chief of staff who had been downgraded following the Clinton administration's betrayal of the July 1999 coup plans. Officially, Shihabi fled after reports emerged about his "involvement in corruption cases," although Syrian military sources suggested that Hafez al-Assad considered Shihabi an obstacle to the rise of Assif Shawkat, his son-in-law and Bashar's guardian in the military. However, because of Shihabi's close ties to the United States, he was permitted to escape rather than be eliminated, and he made his way to Los Angeles, where his son lives.

One indication of the degree to which Hafez al-Assad's death came as a surprise is that it took Damascus several hours to amend the Syrian Constitution, changing the minimum age for eligibility to serve as president from forty to thirty-four—Bashar's age. Hafez al-Assad's original plan had been to wait until after Bashar's thirty-fifth birthday to make the constitutional amendment so that the age change would be less conspicuous.

Assuming power, Bashar surrounded himself with a militant young Allawite elite. His primary support lay with Shawkat and a few other younger military and security officers. They convinced Bashar that in the unstable situation prevailing in Syria and in the Middle East as a whole, he would consolidate his power only through a regional war. In such a war, they pointed out, he could gather around himself a group of officers who would form the foundation of a power elite, just as his father did during the Six-Day War in 1967. By that precedent, Syria would not even have to win the war for the leadership to consolidate its power.

Toward this end, Bashar immediately started reviving old connections and forming new ones, making deals with Iran and HizbAllah, Osama bin Laden and the Islamists, and his friends Uday and Qusay, the sons of Saddam Hussein. He agreed to expand Syria's support for jihadist causes in return for security and economic support for his own regime. By late July, this process was in full swing, with the most significant developments taking place in Lebanon.

———

IN THE EARLY SUMMER of 2000, the Iranian and Syrian governments, as well as Osama bin Laden, were working to consolidate a new terrorist infrastructure in Lebanon and the areas controlled by the Palestinian Authority. The terrorist buildup was launched once Tehran and the Arab Islamist leadership allied with it became convinced that the peace process was doomed and the region was actually sliding toward a major crisis. Buoyed by HizbAllah's success in southern Lebanon, the Islamists saw the chance to take control of the jihad against Israel. Moreover, Ayatollah Khamenei and his confidants believed that the spirit of militant jihad would enable them to further consolidate their hold over Tehran at the expense of President Khatami and his reformist colleagues.

The key development in this plan took place soon after Assad's death. Apprehensive that the West, through economic support, would supplant the Iranians as the major foreign influence in Damascus, Tehran moved to deliver what nobody else could: a rapprochement between the Syrian government and the Syrian Muslim Brotherhood (the Ikhwan). Syrian intelligence had had violent clashes with the Syrian Ikhwan and Osama bin Laden's people in northern Lebanon that very spring; by late June, they were all cooperating under Tehran's aegis.

The Iranian achievement was indeed dramatic. Tehran had done nothing less than arrange for the Syrian Muslim Brotherhood to move its offices and center of subversive activities from Jordan to the United Kingdom. Even the Ikhwan's controller general, Sheikh Ali Sadr-al-Din al-Bayanuni, moved to London. To be sure, the Ikhwan leaders in Europe were not all convinced that the new Syrian regime was serious about a rapprochement with them; some pointed out that President Bashar al-Assad's directives ordering the release of dozens of Ikhwan political prisoners were never implemented. Nevertheless, al-Bayanuni instructed the movement's leadership to maintain a positive approach toward the government, and the Ikhwan accordingly issued several statements saying they were "highly optimistic" about their relationship with Bashar al-Assad. In other words, for as long as the Ikhwan were participating in Iran's new strategy against Israel, they could be counted on not to revolt against official Damascus.

At the same time, Iranian intelligence had started organizing the ranks of the Palestinian Islamic Jihad movement, settling differences among the key leaders and building a unified control and supply system. Tehran was determined to consolidate all the Palestine-related movements into a single Secret Islamic Revolutionary Army dominated by Iran's allies. Imad Mughniyah—the veteran Iranian-controlled HizbAllah commander, who has excellent relations with both the radical Islamist movement and Arafat's inner circle—was named the commander of this army.

In mid-July, with the Syrian Ikhwan largely pacified, Tehran delivered an ultimatum to Bashar al-Assad. The occasion was a visit to Damascus and Beirut by Ali Akbar Velayati, the former foreign minister, who had become Khamenei's adviser and troubleshooter; Hojat-ol-Islam Hassan Akhtari, a former ambassador to Damascus; and Hojat-ol-Islam Hussein Sheikh ol-Islam, the current ambassador, in charge of coordinating Iran's control over the Lebanese HizbAllah. Before Velayati's arrival, Syrian officials had hinted that Bashar was more interested in internal reforms than in resuming an armed struggle; after Bashar met with the forceful Velayati, Damascus agreed to the Iranian "suggestions," such as increasing the flow of weapons to Palestinian terrorist organizations. Velayati also met with key Palestinian terrorist leaders—Ahmad Jibril of the PFLP-GC, Colonel Abu Musa of the anti-Arafat branch of the PLO, and three HAMAS leaders who were being sheltered in Damsascus. Velayati informed them of his agreement with Bashar and gave them a total of $3 million to take the initial steps toward fulfilling the new jihad plans.

In late July, HizbAllah began supplying expertise and aid to the Palestinian branches of HAMAS and the Islamic Jihad within the framework of the Secret Islamic Revolutionary Army. According to the plan, once a period of training was completed, Tehran would provide the Palestinian terrorists, via HizbAllah, with long-range rockets and missiles and high-tech terrorist gear (particularly sophisticated detonation devices and high explosives) of types so far provided only to HizbAllah itself.

Iran recognized that Damascus continued to mistrust the Palestinian Islamists—both the Ikhwan-affiliated Palestinian/Syrian "Afghans" and "Bosniaks" (Arabs who had served as mujahideen in Afghanistan and Bosnia) and the Palestinian Liberation Army under Colonel Munir Makdah. The Palestinian Liberation Army, based in the Ein Hilweh refugee camp near Sidon, was, and at this writing is, the most potent Palestinian force in Lebanon. It and the "Afghan" and "Bosniak" forces are all crucial building blocks of the Secret Islamic Revolutionary Army. Therefore, Tehran brought in Osama bin Laden and his Islamist elite to bridge the gap of mistrust between them and Damascus by guaranteeing that Iranian military support would not be used to conspire against Bashar's regime.

In mid-July, the Iranians arranged a meeting in Afghanistan between bin Laden's new "Lebanon team," led by a senior Pakistani aide called Ammar Assadullah, and a Palestinian delegation led by Makdah's emissary, known as Abu-Haykal. The two sides resolved that bin Laden would channel his support via three centers in Lebanon: Ein Hilweh; Nahr al-Bard, a refugee camp and Islamist stronghold near Tripoli, in northern Lebanon; and some Hizb-Allah-controlled areas in the central Bekaa. Soon afterward, Jamal Shihadah Ibrahim, a Syrian Islamist and one of bin Laden's lieutenants, arrived in Ein Hilweh to coordinate the cooperation of all the regional Islamist forces.

In late July, several of bin Laden's terrorists arrived in Ein Hilweh for acclimatization courses on the peculiarities of the Lebanese and Palestinian theaters. The courses were organized by Muhammad Badri al-Isa, also known as Abu-Badr. The courses trained bin Laden's people in HizbAllah tactics of pursuit, the use of Iranian-provided heavy weapons, the laying of ambushes, bomb construction and defusing techniques, local booby-trapping techniques, and clandestine communications. In this context, Abu-Badr also instructed a trusted lieutenant and master forger—a Palestinian known as Hassan Hakim—to work closely with bin Laden's people on preparing local documents for the terrorists expected to arrive soon from Afghanistan, Pakistan, and Western Europe.

Concurrently, bin Laden clandestinely dispatched dozens of highly trained terrorists—most of them Arabs—to the Arafat-controlled parts of the West Bank and Gaza Strip. Their mission was to work with HAMAS, Islamic Jihad, and other local terrorist cadres to prepare for the coming escalation. Bin Laden's emissaries also made contact with Arafat's inner circle and gave them bin Laden's guarantee that the Islamist movements would not challenge Arafat's leadership so long as he declared independence and statehood, committed to the liberation of al-Quds, and launched a jihad against Israel.

Bin Laden's message fell on fertile ground. Arafat had hesitated in declaring independence only because he and his coterie were afraid that any new Intifadah would lead to their overthrow at the hands of a militant Islamist leadership. Therefore, bin Laden's guarantees of Islamist support and legitimization tilted the balance within Arafat's inner circle in favor of going ahead with their plans for September 13.

In late August, Imad Mughniyah arrived in Lebanon and assumed his position as commander of the Secret Islamic Revolutionary Army. Iran also set up two joint operations rooms—one in Beirut to monitor developments in the territories and the other in Ein Hilweh to monitor developments in southern Lebanon. With that, the die was cast for the eruption of the new Palestinian jihad.

———

JERUSALEM WAS AWARE of the buildup of Osama bin Laden's resources in and around Israel. On August 21, Israeli security authorities announced the arrest of a twenty-three-member terrorist network affiliated with bin Laden. The composition of this network revealed much about what the Islamists and Arabs were planning for the region. They were based in the Gaza Strip, but four of its members were Israeli Arabs from the north of the country. Its commander, the twenty-seven-year-old Nabil Okal, was a native of the Jabalya refugee camp in Gaza. As a HAMAS activist in the mid-1990s, Okal was identified as a promising candidate for higher positions, recruited, and sent to Pakistan. After a brief period of tempering with the mujahideen in Afghanistan, he received sophisticated training in both Afghanistan and Pakistan in such subjects as organizing and running terrorist networks and recruiting and dispatching suicide bombers. He also mastered such techniques as the activation of explosive charges by remote control and by telephone (including mobile phones and pagers), the use of anti-tank missiles, and the use of anesthetics to kidnap Israeli soldiers. Returning to Gaza, Okal made contact with the HAMAS leader Sheikh Ahmad Yassin, who helped him recruit HAMAS members in Gaza, Israel, and various Arab countries.

Okal embarked on an ambitious program for a sustained campaign of terrorism. His network prepared to detonate bombs, send suicide bombers to Israeli cities, attack Israeli military patrols in Gaza, and launch missiles at Jewish settlements. Okal was instructed by bin Laden's senior commanders to concentrate on long-term network building. He was to give a high priority to recruiting Israeli Arabs to gather intelligence and obtain weapons and matériel and to identifying promising new recruits for training in Afghanistan and Pakistan. Okal's network was supposed to be supplied through bin Laden's networks in Jordan; however, the ongoing suppression of Islamist networks by the Jordanian security services made this impossible. By the time Okal's network collapsed, one of its members had established contacts with Ahmad Jibril's PFLP-GC in Syria.

The Israelis had started investigating the Okal network in April 2000, as a result of intelligence information recovered from a house in Taibeh where the IDF had clashed with a HAMAS cell. A subsequent operation led to the arrest of four Israeli Arab members who were preparing to move explosives and weapons from a cache in the Negev to one in Tulkarm, in the West Bank. Okal himself was arrested on June 1 as he was returning from Egypt, where he had held discussions with his superiors. Israeli security authorities should have been alarmed, but were not, by the realization that Jibril Rajub's Preventive Security Service had uncovered some of the activities of the bin Laden networks in Nablus back in April but had not disclosed anything to either the Israelis or the CIA, with whom Rajub maintained close relations. Such information could have assisted in rolling back bin Laden networks all over the region, from the Persian Gulf to Yemen.

———

BY THE TIME Arafat returned from Camp David in late July, the whole Palestinian population was engaged in a flurry of activities aimed at mobilizing for the challenges ahead. Israeli intelligence was aware of the bulk of these activities but, on orders from the Barak government, tolerated them because Jerusalem feared that disrupting them, or even taking notice of them, would break the tenuous peace process.

An editorial in the Islamic Jihad's highly popular Gaza newspaper *Al-Istiqlal* captured the mood of the entire Palestinian political spectrum. "What is the next step?" the editorial opened. "This is a frequently asked question these days following the Camp David summit, the infuriated debate on the nature of the negotiations, and the extent to which Arab and Palestinian concessions would reach." The editorial argued that the latest round of negotiations had confirmed what was widely known all along: that neither the United States nor Israel would accept the minimal demands of the Palestinians, namely, control over Jerusalem and the right of return. There was no chance this dynamics would change, given "the traditional U.S. stands, which are hostile to our people and nation and always supportive of Israel, its aggression, and terrorism." Therefore, the question the Palestinian national leadership had to address was, "What will we do if the Zionists refuse to allow the comeback of the five million refugees, return Jerusalem and its Mosque to us, evacuate settlements, and abandon crossings and borders?" The editorial answers, "Our people have only one option, the original option that marked the march of our people and nation. It is the option of jihad, resistance, and wide support for confronting 'Israel' and anybody that backs it. Otherwise, we have nothing left but to accept a humiliating life and become an ethnic minority that waits for further effacement and extermination."

In early August, the HAMAS leadership informed Arafat that the movement "is not opposed to being part of the PLO provided it is restructured on democratic foundations based on elections that would include all the sons of the Palestinian people inside and outside the territories." Arafat was informed authoritatively that HAMAS would compromise on most issues and ignore past abuses as long as the PLO led the people in a jihad. Concurrently, Sheikh Nafidh Azzam of the Islamic Jihad notified Arafat that the movement would "welcome any effort exerted to consolidate the power of the Palestinians" provided it was "based on resistance against the policies of the occupation and on repulsion of the ongoing aggression."

Arafat responded positively. He named Salim al-Zaanun—the speaker of the Palestine National Council, who had negotiated the previous agreements with HAMAS and other Islamist organizations in the mid-1990s—as his special representative in the new cycle of negotiations. Zaanun's prompt reply to HAMAS and Islamic Jihad stressed the importance of dialogue "in light of the current and extremely grave circumstances." He also informed the Islamists that two major rejectionist organizations—the PFLP and the DFLP—had already committed to "the return of their members to the PLO institutions and establishments." Zaanun held lengthy meetings with Sheikh Yassin and the HAMAS leadership and with Sheikh Azzam and the Islamic Jihad leadership. They all agreed that, in the words of Sheikh Azzam, "the Palestinian house should be put back in order on the basis of confrontation with Israel and activation of the people's resources."

A milestone on the road to war took place in mid-August, when Arafat summoned a few senior ministers and security officials for a "sensitive briefing on a possible violent confrontation with Israel." Senior PA commanders surveyed the Palestinian military preparations, the types of weapons in their arsenals, and the Israeli military posture. The briefing outlined the PA's contingency plans and scenarios for the first rounds of fighting. Arafat then met with the seniormost officials to discuss his plans for the anticipated collapse of the diplomatic process. He expected widespread grassroots endorsement of the anticipated fighting. Arafat noted that Azzam Azzam al-Ahmad had just met with Saddam Hussein and senior Iraqi officials, as well as leaders of Palestinian terrorist organizations based in Iraq, and obtained their commitment for comprehensive support for the PA once negotiations collapsed and violence ensued.

Subsequently, on August 18, Colonel Jibril Rajub met with his senior Preventive Security staff at their new headquarters in Bitaniyah. "I know everyone is worried about what might happen if the negotiations collapse," he told his staff. "Many people speak of the possibility of a flare-up of violence, bloodshed, and casualties. I think this fear is dialectical and has its justifications. . . . I would not say matters would proceed peacefully if the negotiations collapse. . . . I do not think the Palestinian people would confront this situation by raising the white flag and declaring their surrender to the fait accompli."

———

WITH JIHADIST SENTIMENTS abounding throughout the population, the PA leadership turned an important part of its attention to the mobilization of Palestinian youth. Arafat ordered the entire teenage population sent to military-style summer camps in the Gaza Strip and the West Bank. There, both boys and girls were subjected to intense anti-Israeli propaganda and training in a wide variety of military and terrorist disciplines. This obligatory summer activity was so outrageous that even the pro-peace process *New York Times* could not ignore it. "It is summer camp time for 25,000 Palestinian teenagers, and strikingly unusual camps they are, too," wrote John F. Burns in the August 8 issue. "As run by the men who handle psychological warfare for Yasir Arafat, the Palestinian leader, they allow no horsing around in the dorm, no fun-in-the-sun by a cool clear lake, no rousing sing-alongs beside a roaring campfire. Instead, there is the chance to stage a mock kidnapping of an Israeli leader by masked Palestinian commandos, ending with the Israeli's bodyguards sprawled dead on the ground. Next, there is the mock attack on an Israeli military post, ending with a sentry being grabbed by the neck and fatally stabbed. Finally, there is the opportunity to excel in stripping and reassembling a real Kalashnikov rifle."

Burns noted that those running the camps incited the youth to a high level of commitment to the liberation of the entire Palestine—that is, the destruction of Israel—a commitment that contradicted the declared objectives of the peace process. Burns recounted a conversation he had with one of the attendees. "Suleiman Nubaim, 16, said the Camp David talks had given new relevance to what he and his friends had been taught about the exploits of the freedom fighters, or 'fedayeen,' the name taken by Palestinian guerrillas of the pre-Oslo period. Like many youths, he said he wanted to join the Palestinian forces. 'I want my country to be free,' he said. 'It's been my dream since I was a small boy.' Asked how he defined Palestinian freedom, he said it included having Jerusalem, and then the rest of Israel. 'As long as Israel occupies any part of our land, in Tel Aviv or Jaffa or Haifa,' he said, 'we have not liberated our homeland.'" The effectiveness of these camps would become clear in the fall, when their graduates were in the forefront of Yassir Arafat's new Intifadah.

Preparations were going forward on other fronts as well. In mid-August, the PA Ministry of Health conducted a training exercise on how to cope with an emergency situation involving many casualties. Palestinian military units expanded their training both for open clashes with the IDF and for attacks on Israeli civilians in roadside ambushes; exercises conducted by the PA police base in Jericho included the hijacking of civilian cars and buses by commando teams. The PA also engaged in a massive weapon-acquisition program. One source was the Russian Mafiya, which was, in the words of a PA security official, "smuggling an enormous number of rifles and other small arms into Palestinian-controlled areas," primarily via Israel. Other sources were the intelligence services of Egypt and Iraq, which sent their contributions across the Sinai and through Jordan, respectively.

Also revealing was the PA's handling of Islamist prisoners during the month leading up to the Intifadah. The PA granted extended vacation leaves to dozens of HAMAS and Islamic Jihad terrorists jailed at the insistence of Israel and the United States. Among the newly freed terrorists were the leading bomb-makers and martyr-recruiters of both organizations, the men who were in command of the Islamist terrorism waves of 1995–96. One of the few who was not released was HAMAS's leading terrorist, Muhammad Dief, who was being held in the Security Services building in Gaza. Actually, Dief was being kept in protective detention by his best friend, Muhammad Dahlan, because of Israel's repeated attempts to assassinate him.

———

BY LATE AUGUST, the Islamist high command was very satisfied with the pace of preparations for the coming jihad. For them, the confrontation with Israel was but one component of a far more ambitious jihad aimed at wresting control over the entire Middle East from the United States and its allies Israel and Saudi Arabia. One of the primary forces preparing for this jihad was the Jamiat-i-Tulaba al-Arabiya, an umbrella organization of various units of Saudi and other Gulf Arab Islamist terrorists based in Pakistan, Kashmir, Afghanistan, and Chechnya. By August, this organization was activating terrorist groups in Afghanistan and Pakistan for major operations designed to gain control over Islam's Holy Shrines in Mecca, Medina, and Jerusalem.

Hence, it was high time to formally declare that a major threshold on the way to confrontation had been crossed. The only person capable of authoritatively delivering such a message was Osama bin Laden, and he did just that despite the constraints imposed on him by the Taliban leadership. On Friday, September 1, bin Laden's people convened a series of meetings of Arab, Pakistani, Afghan, and other terrorists in which they announced the revival of a global jihad to be waged by the entire Muslim Ummah against the *Yahood-u-Nasaara* (Jews and Christians) in order to liberate Islam's Holy Shrines.

The meeting convened in Peshawar, Pakistan, was the most important. Participants included the commanders and key members of the Jamiat-i-Tulaba al-Arabiya and the senior commanders of the various Pakistani, Kashmiri, and Afghan jihadist organizations in whose camps the fighters were being trained. The meeting opened with the reading of a special message from Osama bin Laden. "Waging jihad against *Yahood-u-Nasaara*," bin Laden said, "has become the religious obligation of the Muslims throughout the globe, and if they displayed lethargy in the fulfillment of this obligation they would be held accountable and would have to face the anguish of Almighty on the day of Judgment." Bin Laden argued that the continued occupation of Saudi Arabia by the Americans and of Palestine by the Jews was the key element in the Christian-Jewish design "to impose their hegemony throughout the world" and destroy the Muslim Ummah. Bin Laden emphasized that the three Holy Shrines constitute "the heart in the body of the Muslim Ummah" and warned that "once this heart is captured, God forbid, the body automatically surrenders. And once this heart is forced to stop working, God forbid, the body automatically dies." Bin Laden argued that this was exactly what was happening to the Muslim Ummah. Therefore, "all Muslims should immediately put aside everything and sacrifice to safeguard the heart."

The second part of bin Laden's message was directed to the commanders and men of the Jamiat-i-Tulaba al-Arabiya. He praised their commitment to Islam and declared that their mobilization "would soon prove a renaissance of the Muslim Ummah." Given the character of the jihad they had already committed to waging, this assembly would one day be recognized as "the turning point of the history of the Muslim Ummah."

After bin Laden's message was read, several of the senior commanders present stood up and vowed their commitment to his jihad. They announced their determination to strike out soon and hard. No one doubted that the Jamiat-i-Tulaba al-Arabiya and its supporters and sponsors were very serious.

―――

ALL THIS TIME, President Clinton kept pushing the peace process on every front; the administration even attempted to revive the Syrian track via the exiled Shihabi. Back in late June, when Bashar al-Assad had just taken power, the administration—particularly Sandy Berger—believed that Bashar would be more flexible than his father in return for lavish foreign aid and political support. Actually, Bashar's approach was exactly the opposite: He had already decided he must prove his mettle to the Syrian elite by being more "patriotic" than his father. On Berger's advice, however, the administration invited Shihabi to come to Washington, D.C., from Los Angeles for a series of consultations at a CIA safe house with senior officials from the State Department and the CIA. The Americans wanted to know whether Bashar was really in control and what his relations were with the military and security elites. Shihabi opined that Hafez al-Assad's most enduring legacy was building a cadre loyal to Bashar. The main impediment Bashar would face, Shihabi believed, was Syria's disastrous economy.

Shihabi returned to his son's home in Los Angeles; about a week later George Tenet contacted him and said that he would be getting an important message from Washington by special courier. The whole process was contrived to impress Shihabi with the gravity of the matter. When the message arrived, it said the Clinton administration had decided to support Bashar's reign and expected Shihabi to maintain his contacts with Damascus so that he could contribute to this effort. Shihabi was asked to ascertain just how serious Bashar was about following U.S. policy—that is, the peace process. Shihabi told the courier he was ready to help the administration, and soon afterward he was contacted again and asked to travel to Damascus with a message to Bashar. Essentially, the message informed Bashar that the administration would promise to protect him from his enemies and help him modernize the Syrian economy if he rejoined the peace process.

Syrian security officials were baffled by the American approach and especially by the choice of emissary, given the reason Shihabi had gone into exile. However, fearing the sort of retribution the United States had dealt Iraq, Bashar listened to Clinton's message, permitted Shihabi to stay in Damascus for a week or so, and sent him back with a noncommittal reply. The administration took this reply as "maybe yes," while the Arabs knew it to be a veiled "no."

In early August, Bashar announced in a speech that Syria was intent on achieving a comprehensive and just peace with Israel and the United States. For the White House, this speech, coming shortly after Shihabi's safe return, constituted sufficient reason to elicit public concessions from Barak in order to demonstrate to Bashar just how serious Clinton was about the peace process. Clinton contacted Barak and urged him to reciprocate. A few days later, Barak commented favorably on Bashar's remarks, saying they indicated that Syria's strategic choice was peace. Barak added that Bashar was firmly in control in Damascus and that there was a possibility of renewing negotiations with Syria on the basis of these developments.

Except for a few perfunctory media utterances, Bashar basically ignored the stream of messages. To demonstrate his true intentions, Syria revived extensive military assistance to HizbAllah and the Palestinian rejectionist organizations. Emboldened, HizbAllah conducted a series of provocations along the Israeli-Lebanese border, which, at Clinton's insistence, Israel absorbed without reaction or retaliation. The administration was sufficiently alarmed, however, to dispatch Saudi mediators to try to figure out what was on Bashar's mind. The Saudi officials returned with a mixed message, offering a vague hope for a long-term commitment to peace along with a firm statement that peace was not a viable option in the immediate future. Consequently, Clinton once again turned away from the Syrian track.

———

BACK ON THE Palestinian track, Clinton had resumed pressuring both sides to reach an agreement while he was still in office. In an August 14 interview with *Al-Hayah,* Clinton said, "I greatly hope that the Israeli and Palestinian parties will have reached solutions by [the end of the year], and, with our help, an agreement on Jerusalem that satisfies their demands. I will then be able to open a U.S. embassy in the Palestinian state's capital. I strongly believe that the Jerusalem issue can be solved in a way that achieves the two parties' national aspirations." The *New York Times* quoted "a senior administration official" as stating that the effective deadline for an Israeli-Palestinian permanent settlement was the end of September. The official explained that the Jewish holidays would take up most of October and that the Barak government was not likely to survive very long once the Knesset reconvened in late October.

That report gave Arafat the mistaken notion that if the PA could hold on until late September, the agony of negotiations would be over. Arafat hardened his negotiating position accordingly. The report also gave Fatah an occasion to raise doubts about the United States' ability to mediate an end to the Palestinian-Israeli dispute, especially on sensitive issues such as Jerusalem. "Jerusalem," a Fatah communiqué said, "is occupied territory, and the Israelis must withdraw from it, and especially from the holy places. Palestinians are to have sovereignty over the city, without Israeli interference. Meanwhile, the U.S. continues to pressure Palestinians, threatening to move its embassy from Tel Aviv to Jerusalem. With these actions, the U.S. forfeits its role as an impartial mediator."

Senior Palestinian officials went further, arguing that the United States appeared to believe that "The Palestinians are not a nation with holy sites, constants, and a public opinion. They are merely a group of people with a leader. The problem will be solved when this leader agrees to do what he is asked—intimidation or temptations are sufficient to make him reach such an outcome." The Americans, the Palestinian officials continued, had repeatedly said to Arafat "we are giving you a state"—expecting him to show his gratitude by reneging on his commitment to the liberation of the whole of Palestine. "In other words," the officials explained, "they were behaving as if they were drawing a personal solution for Arafat and not for the Palestinian people." Again, the Temple Mount and the right of return were identified as the issues that would cause the future eruption.

Meanwhile, Jerusalem refused to face reality. The post–Camp David assessment that the IDF's Intelligence branch submitted to the Cabinet noted the PA's military preparations but did not predict an imminent eruption. According to a senior IDF official, Arafat viewed street violence "as a strategic option," not a matter of "irresistible impulse." The official added that "the territories are very quiet, apart from local land disputes." Therefore, the IDF decided that "Arafat is giving priority to concluding negotiations with Israel instead of resorting to violence."

Accordingly, senior Israeli ministers were dispatched to Europe and the United States in an effort to expedite the Palestinian track, and Ben-Ami told the political committee of the Labor Party that a trilateral summit could still take place in September, as long as there was a prior agreement clarifying the parties' positions on the contentious issues. "If we go to another summit, it will have to be on the basis of better, perhaps certain prospects of success," Ben-Ami said. He acknowledged that no agreement was possible without "a solution of the Jerusalem question," but he boasted that because of an intense Israeli diplomatic campaign, "Arafat had failed in his efforts to change the issue of Jerusalem from a national issue into a Muslim issue in his recent travels abroad." He urged Arafat to "accept the fact" that "the process is final and that in the end no one gets his dream."

Senior Israeli negotiators resumed meeting with their Palestinian counterparts under the aegis of Albright and Berger, and at Israel's request, Ross returned to the Middle East on August 17 to explore ideas for new compromises. He floated the idea of having Barak and Arafat meet with Clinton during the U.N.'s special Millennium Summit in New York the following month. Having listened to Ross's ideas, Ben-Ami opined that another summit would be possible only if the PA became notably more flexible. Subsequently, Clinton and Albright talked to Barak at great length about their reading of Arafat and the prospects for peace.

The impact of these conversations was apparent from an address Barak gave at the National Security College. Without any explanation, he said that "now is the time to achieve a permanent agreement with the Palestinians and to renew talks with Syria." He warned Arafat not to declare Palestinian statehood unilaterally, because such a move "would hurt, first and foremost, the Palestinians themselves and could cause damage to Israel's relations with Jordan, Egypt, and other Arab countries." Instead, Barak said, he was offering the Palestinians "an independent state contingent on their readiness to confront the challenges of setting up a state and solving the hardships of its people," as well as "ending the conflict with Israel." Moving on to the Syrian track, Barak stated as fact that Bashar was considering peace with Israel as "a strategic choice that will strengthen Syria's interests and honor." He added that "the door for peace will remain open as long as Syria also acknowledges Israel's honor and interests."

———

BY LATE AUGUST, Ross had failed to achieve a breakthrough, and even the talks on interim-agreement issues—principally the release of prisoners and additional Israeli withdrawals—were suspended. Albright warned Barak that Clinton would decide whether to convene a new summit based on whether anything promising emerged from the bilateral meetings in New York.

In hopes of breaking the deadlock, Ben-Ami traveled to Egypt to hear from Mubarak and Foreign Minister Amr Moussa the "interesting ideas" they supposedly had for bridging the gap on the Jerusalem issue. The "ideas" turned out to be a complete Israeli withdrawal from Jerusalem. Moussa told Ben-Ami that "the idea of partial or shared sovereignty in Jerusalem is a departure from international law, and Egypt cannot agree to that." Egypt, Moussa added, "is not negotiating with the Israelis over the Palestinians, but trying to deal with the Israeli position and bring it back to international law." The Egyptians also opined that Barak was exaggerating his political woes in order to extract unwarranted concessions from Arafat and Clinton.

Following this meeting, Mubarak raised the alarm with the Clinton administration, warning that the Israelis' intransigent and unrealistic position was bound to push the region into crisis. Consequently, Clinton, who was then touring sub-Saharan Africa, announced that on his way back to Washington he would stop in Cairo for urgent consultations with Mubarak. However, when Barak expressed his willingness to travel to Cairo for even a brief meeting, Clinton pointedly replied that he would not have time. Barak had to settle for a briefing from Ross, who told him that, on the basis of Clinton's conversation with Mubarak, "it was possible for the Israelis and Palestinians to reach an agreement." Ross added that the Clinton-Mubarak meeting had paved the way for an Egyptian attempt to persuade Arafat to adopt a more realistic stance on Jerusalem. Arafat himself, however, declared publicly in Morocco that the deliberations over the fate of Jerusalem had already reached a point where there were no viable negotiated alternatives. Therefore the fate of Jerusalem "will be decided by either peace or war."

At this apparent impasse, the Barak government made a startling suggestion. "We must be realistic," a "senior government source" told *Maariv* on August 31. "Muslims control the [Temple] Mount in any event, such that if the question of sovereignty will make or break the agreement, Israel will not cause a problem over this." However, even this trial balloon failed to satisfy the PA. Nabil Shaath insisted that the PA still demanded "total sovereignty over Jerusalem" because the city was sacred only to Muslims and Christians and not to Jews. "Any compromise proposal," he added, "must take this minimalist demand into account."

Both Arafat and Barak traveled to New York in early September for the U.N.'s Millennium Summit, where Barak was subjected to intense pressure from U.S. senior officials and world leaders to give Arafat an honorable way out of the corner he had painted himself into—"an achievement" he could point to when postponing the unilateral declaration of independence scheduled for September 13. Clinton himself was all charm, agreeing to see Barak first. However, he echoed the plea to Barak to be realistic and mature in reciprocating for the forthcoming "breakthrough" in Arafat's position. Barak committed Israel to following Clinton's advice, but in fact there was no breakthrough. On the contrary, Arafat hardened his position on Jerusalem to such an extent that the White House ruled out any prospects for a Barak-Clinton-Arafat summit in the foreseeable future. Ben-Ami sounded a somber note: "In the end, I am confident that an agreement will be reached, but it may come only after another round of fighting."

In the face of all this, Barak's reaction was to say that "The door for peace in the Middle East is still open" and that he hoped "we will find it very soon." Despite the dead end reached in New York, Barak dispatched Ben-Ami and Sher to conduct "relatively low-level talks" with Dahlan and Erekat. The talks' agenda would no longer be "a final-status, end-of-conflict agreement" but rather a limited agreement avoiding the Jerusalem issue. The PA reciprocated on September 10 by convening the PLO Central Council to vote on postponing the declaration of a Palestinian state. Arafat declared that "another chance should be given for peace with Israel," and the Council duly voted the postponement. In fact, Arafat was not doing the Israelis any favor—the declaration of statehood had to wait until he could claim some sort of victory in the Palestinian war of independence.

U.S. officials, not grasping this, reacted to the postponement by opining that "the chances for a final-status agreement between Israel and the Palestinians have slightly increased over the past day." The talks quickly foundered again, however, when Barak explained that he could not consider transferring sovereignty over the Temple Mount to a Muslim body—he had been thinking of some form of international control. The PA rejected this idea outright and announced their desire to reopen issues considered closed, such as the settlements. Arafat himself took up the right of return, stating, "I say to all the refugees that there will be neither peace nor security if you do not return to your homeland. Return is a sacred right. People are fooling themselves if they think it can be traded for a handful of dollars." Ben-Ami reacted harshly in a speech to the United Nations: "It is ridiculous to think that it is possible to establish a state in order to return refugees to a neighboring state."

Politically besieged, Barak announced a "time-out for internal consultations," canceling scheduled meetings. When the Clinton administration expressed displeasure, Barak quickly added that Israeli negotiators would continue meeting U.S. officials. Four hours later, Barak—following his characteristic zig-zag policy line—bowed to Clinton's request and reinstated the talks with the Palestinians. At this point, however, Arafat announced that *he* would not renew the talks until he got a clarification from Barak as to why he had stopped them. The next day, Israel and the PA resumed contacts while waiting for American bridging proposals to be presented, but it was clear to all that the prospects were dim.

———

AS THE Israeli-Palestinian talks limped along, bin Laden's followers in the West proceeded to prepare for the coming eruption of violence. The Islamist leaders had some apprehensions about Western governments' willingness to tolerate incitement related to the Palestinian-Israeli peace process, given the Clinton administration's commitment to it. Therefore, they resolved to take as their "cause" the U.S.-UK treatment of Iraq. Back in early 1998, bin Laden had been very successful in exploiting the U.S. bombing of Iraq to build widespread support. He and his aides had every reason to believe they could do even better this time.

Their approach was elucidated in a set of talking points for the September 15 Friday sermon sent from Pakistan to the Islamist leaders in Western Europe. The key argument of the talking points was that the U.S.-led West was using the confrontation with Iraq as the starting point for a deliberate campaign to destroy the Muslim world. "O Muslims, cooperate to extinguish the fire of America and Britain in Iraq; otherwise the fire may reach all of us," the document read. It deplored "the daily barrage of carnage and destruction which Britain and its big brother the U.S. are meting out as punishment to Muslims, attempting to wipe out any Muslim resistance to their occupation of our lands and usurpation of our resources. Well, enough is enough!!!"

Saddam Hussein, the document stressed, was merely the West's "excuse to have military presence on our soil and to ensure thereby that the Islamic giant Al-Khilafah [the caliphate, or Islamic State] never rises. By keeping bases in Saudi Arabia, Turkey, Israel, Kuwait, etc., not only can the fascist U.S. and British ensure that . . . Western hegemony continues in Muslim countries by the rule of their paid dictators and monarchies, but at the same time they can cripple our economies by stealing our resources and by enforcing embargoes on us and pumping cheap oil as a result." The only way to stop the onslaught on Iraq, and on the Muslim world as a whole, was to deprive the West of its allies in the Middle East, by destabilizing or overthrowing their governments or both. "O Muslims," the document concluded, "support the Islamic movements against the British and American establishment and forces wherever they may be. Support the jihad against the U.S. and Britain, speak up against the evil, put fear into the hearts of the enemy, and work to establish the Khilafah."

The sermons to be based on these talking points would be delivered in Western Europe, where Islamist leaders had been repeatedly warned to speak carefully and not give the governments of the countries where they were located an excuse to crack down on them. Given these special circumstances, that concluding sentence—"Support the jihad against the U.S. and Britain, speak up against the evil, put fear into the hearts of the enemy, and work to establish the Khilafah"—should be considered a call to arms.

At the same time, the Arab states, led by Egypt, were maneuvering to prevent the confrontation between Baghdad and Washington from escalating. In a flurry of secret negotiations, Cairo argued that any U.S. military strike would strengthen the Russian influence in Baghdad. Meanwhile, Cairo guaranteed that Baghdad would immediately stop issuing aggressive statements against Saudi Arabia, the United Arab Emirates, and Kuwait. At Egypt's behest, Iraq kept its military activities below the American "red lines," thus depriving the Clinton administration—in the weeks before yet another presidential election—of any excuse to strike out. In return, the Egyptians assured Saddam that they would help him break the international sanctions and would also assist him in any future military confrontation with Israel and the United States, though not with the Persian Gulf states.

Soon afterward, the so-called humanitarian airlift to Baghdad started. Significantly, the aircraft flying into Baghdad were not just from major powers long opposed to the United States' Iraq policy, such as Russia and France; in fact, they were mainly from Arab countries considered U.S. allies, such as Jordan, Egypt, Morocco, Tunisia, and Yemen.

These flights amounted to the collapse of the United States' "containment" policy, which had prevailed for a decade, and over which the Clinton administration had steadfastly fought the rest of the world. While claiming to be committed to women, children, and the elderly, to the point of unilaterally using massive force on their behalf in the Balkans, the administration had withstood a barrage of recriminations over endemic food shortages, spreading diseases, and rising child mortality in Iraq. President Clinton and Secretary Albright had insisted—most recently, at the Millennium Summit a few weeks earlier—on the importance and effectiveness of the sanctions.

Thus, in carrying out their airlifts, the local powers clearly demonstrated that they no longer feared the vindictive Clinton administration and that they considered their inter-Arab interests more important than following U.S. directives. Indeed, President Mubarak would personally invite Saddam Hussein to participate in the Arab Summit scheduled for late October, in effect rehabilitating Saddam and his regime. Thus, even though public attention would shift to the brewing Palestinian-Israeli clashes, the Iraqi factor would remain high on the Arab agenda as an instrument for confrontation with the United States.

———

THE ISLAMISTS' APPREHENSIONS about the peace process appeared to be proving correct. Arafat had already postponed the declaration of independence. Now, he and his coterie were hinting broadly that they were also postponing the war of independence in order to give the White House a final chance to deliver "peace"—that is, crippling Israeli concessions.

At the very same time, however, Arafat was going out of his way to assure the Islamists that these seemingly major retreats were actually temporary steps of expediency, and that his resolve to carry out the jihad for the destruction of Israel was as strong and genuine as ever. Toward that end, Arafat himself engaged in hectic clandestine discussions with Islamist leaders both in Gaza and elsewhere in the Middle East. In addition, he instructed his key lieutenants to continue discussing practical coordination of operations with the Islamist leaders in Gaza. Some of these contacts were conducted via bin Laden's representatives in the territories and in Lebanon in order to keep them involved on Arafat's side. Arafat also made peace with his estranged friend Munir Makdah, thus unifying the Palestinian forces in southern Lebanon under a militant Islamist leadership. Meanwhile, Arafat's coterie used their old Fatah connections to revive contacts with the Iranians and the Syrians.

Although the Islamist leaders were pleased with the shift toward confrontation and the imminent death of the peace process, there was no way they were going to permit Arafat to emerge as the leader of the new militant trend. It was imperative to let the whole Muslim world—not just the Arab world—know who was the driving force of the new dynamics. First came a manifesto, symbolically dated September 13, from Rifai Ahmad Taha of the Egyptian Islamic Group. Taha's statement was issued by the London Islamic

Observation Center led by Yassir Tawfiq al-Sirri, an Egyptian Islamist and a confidant of bin Laden. The second manifesto, also issued in London, came from another bin Laden confidant, Sheikh Omar Bakri Muhammad. Both messages were crucial to the formulation of the jihadist doctrine.

Taha started by accusing Arafat of selling out to the Americans, like Sadat before him, and thereby betraying sacred Palestine to the Jews. No Muslim could accept this, Taha proclaimed. Hence the Islamic Group "calls on all the Islamic and Arab forces to unite under an Islamic banner to liberate Palestine, first and foremost Jerusalem." Furthermore, he said, "Launching painful strikes on the Jews and the Americans should be the most important religious duty and the main preoccupation of every Muslim capable of doing that. We have to convince these infidel forces that the regiments of faith are capable of reaching them in their bedrooms and that their citadels will not protect them."

Before the Arabs could attempt their onslaught on Israel, however, the United States had to be evicted from the region because only the United States could both restrain Arab regimes from joining the jihad and protect the hated Jews. The first step was for the Islamists to overthrow pro-U.S. regimes and liberate the Holy Shrines in Arabia. "The United States," Taha declared, "must realize first of all that the fate of Palestine as a whole, and not just Jerusalem, depends on the determination of our entire Muslim peoples. It must realize secondly that the idolatrous, puppet regimes in the region will not be able to protect themselves from our people's anger, so how can they protect U.S. interests? It must realize thirdly that its interests are dependent on its consideration for the Islamic peoples' interests. It must realize fourthly that no one will be able to protect its interests in the region as long as it continues to pursue a double standard policy. The United States must watch out for the Muslims' anger because they are capable, God willing, of eradicating the roots of unbelief and infidels."

The fact that the Islamists needed first to clean up their own house in Arabia, Taha emphasized, should not alleviate Israel's fears: "We warn the state of monkeys and swine against persisting with its errors, tyranny, and arrogance. Let it know that our people will never relinquish what has been taken from them by repression, terrorism, trickery, slyness, and treachery whatever the cost." To inspire his listeners, Taha memorialized those who had participated in mass killings of Jews in the past—leaving no doubt that the Islamist jihad would be ruthless and bloody.

The September 22 statement of Sheikh Omar Bakri Muhammad provided the legal-religious Koranic substantiation of Taha's call to arms. According to Sheikh Bakri, both Islamic law and justice forbade any kind of compromise that would leave a Jewish state of any size on Palestinian land.

"There can be no peace," Sheikh Bakri declared, "until all of the stolen area is returned back to the rightful owners. It is inconceivable for any Muslim to agree to take back the garden shed of his illegally occupied house, with the illegal occupant keeping the rest. Not only is it against logic, and all laws known to a civilized world, but more importantly, it is not permitted from the Legislator, Allah." Sheikh Bakri then reminded Arafat—himself a closet Muslim Brother—of his own stellar record in opposing Jewish machinations until he succumbed to the lure of the peace process.

There was only one viable path open to Muslims, Sheikh Bakri decreed, and that was the path of jihad. "O Muslims, take heed of this warning! Do not violate Allah's *deen*. We must reject this peace accord with Israel!! The only way peace would be possible is by removing the existence of Israel, which has seen nothing but violence in that region of the world since its inception, and the war will continue until the Muslims are victorious." Like Taha, Bakri identified the pro-Western Arab governments—both those that had signed agreements with Israel and those that provided bases for an American military presence—as the greatest impediments to the Islamist triumph: "O Muslims, remember that the rulers in the Muslim countries are nothing more than the puppets of the West. They are stumbling over themselves to conclude peace with Israel. . . . These rulers must be removed and replaced with the Islamic ruler, the Khaleefah."

Sheikh Bakri stressed that once united and in control of their own resources, the Muslims would be able to successfully confront both Israel and its U.S.-dominated Western patrons. "O Muslims, look at the power that the Muslim world holds. By raising the price of fuel, one unified body of Muslims would bring the western world to its knees. We have the power, we just need the will." Bakri warned that the mere toleration by certain Arab governments of a peace process legitimizing the right of a Jewish state to exist testified to the dire state of the entire Muslim world. It was therefore imperative for Muslims to rise up before it was too late. "The *only* solution is jihad and we must support it physically, financially, and verbally."

———

THE PARAMOUNT SIGNIFICANCE of these manifestos became clear just as Sheikh Bakri issued his statement. Between September 21 and 23, the Qatar-based al-Jazeera TV, the Arab world's preeminent satellite news network, broadcast repeatedly a brief videotape showing Osama bin Laden, Ayman al-Zawahiri, and Rifai Ahmad Taha meeting in Afghanistan with Sheikh Asadallah, the son of Sheikh Omar Abd-al-Rahman. The three leaders were ostensibly meeting to express their commitment to working for the liberation of Sheikh Omar and his comrades, who have been held in American jails ever since their conviction for terrorist activities, including the 1993 World Trade Center bombing. However, the three used this unprecedented exposure to the entire Arab world to reiterate their call for uncompromising jihad. In addition, by sitting with Taha, bin Laden and Zawahiri confirmed the importance of his manifesto.

Bin Laden was the first to speak on the al-Jazeera tape. He reiterated his loyalty to his comrades languishing in American and Saudi jails and then used that loyalty as the basis for a general statement on the objectives of the jihad: "On this blessed night, we pledge to God Almighty to do all we can to support our religion, to establish the *sharia* of Islam in the land of Islam, to expel the Jews and the Christians from the sacred places, and to endeavor to release our ulema from the United States, from Egypt, from Riyadh, and from all Muslim lands. We pledge this to God Almighty. We beseech God Almighty to grant us His support to fulfill these tasks. He is our Lord and supporter. May God have mercy and grant his blessings to Muhammad and his family."

Taha spoke next, stating his own support for the jailed Sheikh Omar and declaring that "we all have a duty toward that man." He stressed that "we fear that God Almighty shall punish us if we do not perform our duty in freeing him from the prisons of infidelity and tyranny. By God, freeing him is easy for those to whom Allah has given strength."

Zawahiri, like bin Laden, quickly moved from declaring his solidarity with Sheikh Omar to advocating a relentless jihad. "Dear brothers," he said, "I am not trying to play on your emotions or ask you for your sympathy; rather, we are now talking business, we are talking jihad. The situation now is not that of glittering statements. . . . Paganism has grouped itself against Islam and the mujahideen. It is attacking them, imprisoning them, killing them, and targeting them." Zawahiri then admonished the Islamists for not having yet unleashed the jihad against the United States and its allies: "These heathens have spread their forces in Egypt, Yemen, and the Gulf, killing our children, persecuting our scholars, soiling our holy shrines, and stealing our wealth. Dear brothers, let's start working and stop playing. Brothers, we have spoken much and done little. We ask God Almighty to enable us to work for a life of dignity and jihad."

This brief videotape, particularly given bin Laden's personal appearance, brought the Islamist call to jihad to the forefront of the Arab world's attention. In retrospect, it served to mobilize the eruption of violence that was soon to come.

OBLIVIOUS TO these developments, the Clinton administration concentrated on coming up with positions to keep the Israeli-Palestinian negotiations afloat in the second half of September. The Americans worked on wresting additional concessions from Barak, primarily on the fate of Jerusalem, while withholding from him relevant information they had acquired. Most importantly, they had been told by friendly Arab leaders—but did not tell Barak—that Arafat was "determined to unfurl the flag of Palestine on the Temple Mount when he declares Palestinian statehood." Therefore, the administration was informed, "Arafat is currently inclined to reject proposals recommending that solutions to the Jerusalem issue be deferred to some later date." But this was exactly what Clinton asked Barak to agree to. Meanwhile, the administration refused to accept Barak's insistence that any agreement with the PA must contain a clause declaring the "end of the conflict." Clinton thus sought to cancel the only "achievement" Barak could have presented in return for the overwhelming concessions he had already made. Even Barak could not accept such a political posture.

Neither, however, would he give up on the peace process. Goaded by Clinton, he decided that the sought-after breakthrough could be achieved through his personal involvement, and so on September 25, he invited Arafat to his home in Kokhav Yair. According to Barak's office, the prime minister was hoping "to reinforce trust, voice appraisals of the situation, and exchange opinions, but not to conduct point-specific negotiations on subjects that are on the agenda." In a theatrical gesture, Clinton phoned Barak's home during the meeting and urged both leaders to persevere. They told him that they were "determined to make every effort and take advantage of every opportunity to reach agreement." After Clinton hung up, Barak raised various ideas concerning future agreements on Jerusalem. Arafat flatly rejected all of them, warning that if he were to sign an agreement without resolving the Jerusalem question and securing the refugees' right of return, "the Palestinian street [would] erupt." The only thing Barak and Arafat agreed on was dispatching Sher and Erekat for three days of discussions in Washington. State Department officials admitted they were "not very optimistic about the talks."

———

THE KEY to regional conflagration still lay in Lebanon and Syria. Even after the purges in the military, Bashar al-Assad was still being manipulated by the Syrian national security elite. His key military supporter, his brother-in-law General Shawkat, believed that only a major jihad would enable him to prove that he was a strong leader. Despite the dire state of the Syrian armed forces, Bashar's Damascus was increasingly inclined to play the role of catalyst in a regional war, especially because the eruption would originate from either the territories or Lebanon, and therefore Arafat or Iran would be blamed. At the same time, such a jihad, irrespective of its ultimate outcome, would consolidate popular support for Bashar's regime.

Therefore, Bashar ordered his army to signal the Palestinians, and the rest of the region, that Syria was capable of providing a strategic umbrella and of launching a deep first strike to set off the conflagration. On the morning of September 23, in the context of a military exercise, Syria test-launched an NK-SCUD-D ballistic missile. The missile—fired toward northeastern Syria, away from Israel—covered its full theoretical range of approximately 375 miles.

The message was not lost on the key Arab leaders, who determined it was time to break the deadlock. On September 27, Mubarak essentially instructed Arafat to abandon the peace process until further notice. "Clinton is a dead horse," Mubarak told Arafat. "You have no reason to rush to sign an agreement. Better wait for the next President." Mubarak also advised Arafat that Israel was militarily and politically weak and was vulnerable to violence, especially mounting casualties. Thus, by late September, Arafat was desperate to seize the initiative and emerge as the hero of the war soon to erupt.

17

The Outbreak of the Intifadah (2000)

Sharon's Visit to the Temple Mount; Arafat's Cautious Steps Toward War

ARIEL SHARON'S famous visit to the Temple Mount on September 28, 2000, was not the beginning of the Intifadah al-Aqsa, notwithstanding all the political recriminations and media assertions to the contrary. Although Sharon's visit (discussed in detail below) was indeed a milestone event from a political point of view, by the time he set foot on the Temple Mount, the fighting had already been going on for almost a week. Furthermore, the Intifadah al-Aqsa (the al-Aqsa Uprising), as it was initially called, or subsequently the Intifadah al-Istiqlal (the Uprising for Independence), was but one component of the strategic dynamics throughout the Muslim/Arab world. In the summer and fall of 2000, Arafat saw a golden opportunity to instigate the regional war everybody was yearning for but afraid to launch—the war that would allow the Arab world not only to destroy Israel but also to rid itself of the stifling U.S.-led Westernization drive.

Despite the return to Islamic glory they foresaw emerging from that cataclysmic breakout, Arafat, Mubarak (at that time a close confidant of Arafat), and other Arab leaders approached the confrontation with great trepidation. They were determined not to instigate a massive backlash—particularly a U.S. military intervention—through hasty gambits like Saddam Hussein's invasion of Kuwait back in August 1990. The United States' massive bombing of Yugoslavia in the spring of 1999 also loomed large in Arab political awareness. Therefore, Mubarak urged Arafat to start with small cautious moves that, if successful, could serve as a springboard for subsequent escalation. Having witnessed firsthand the close personal relations between Clinton and Barak, Arafat was inclined to follow Mubarak's advice.

As a result, Arafat set a limited objective for the first phase of the war—just to break off the peace process, without severing the Palestinians' contacts with the United States. That way, the Clinton Administration could be manipulated into pressuring Israel to restrain its military reaction, as well as to start negotiations anew, if that seemed expedient, from a position closer to that of the Palestinians. Mubarak, meanwhile, had his own personal reasons for wanting to create a crisis. He was convinced that, in return for "delivering Arafat," saving the peace process, and averting the escalation of the Intifadah into a regional war, he would be able to extract from the Clinton administration massive political and financial support to secure the succession of his son Gamal.

Arafat and Mubarak were also aware of growing strain within the Israeli defense establishment, particularly in the relationship between Barak and the IDF's high command. For Mubarak, Arafat, and Saddam—all of whom studied this matter closely—this tension augmented what the Arab elite interpreted as the weakness demonstrated by the IDF and Israeli society as a whole in the withdrawal from southern Lebanon. These Arab leaders were now convinced that Israel—government, society, and the military—would not be able to stomach the mounting losses from a new eruption of violence.

In Cairo, experts consulted by Mubarak's office predicted that as soon as hostilities erupted, Washington would exert pressure on Barak to demonstrate restraint—thus depriving Israel of a swift victory. Consequently, the attrition element would take hold, eroding the Israeli population's will to survive. These experts added that given economic conditions in the West, the mere threat—and if need be, the imposition—of an oil embargo on the United States and Western Europe would have a dramatic impact on their willingness to assist Israel at its time of dire need.

The experts' working assumptions made sense. The Israeli defense establishment was indeed going through a major crisis because of the confluence of several factors. First was the sharp reduction in the defense budget—ostensibly because of the forthcoming peace; in reality, because the Barak government sought to reduce public opposition to its peace policies by embarking on a domestic spending spree. The budgetary reorientation reached the point where the Air Force commander, Major General Dan Halutz, raised the subject in public. "As chief of the Air Force," he told one interviewer, "I have already reached the conclusion that with the current budget there is almost no chance of the Air Force living up to the expectations attributed to it." He added that he had told this to Barak, only to be rebuffed. "If we do things properly, the next war will last no more than a few days or weeks," Halutz explained. "But for that I need a minimal amount of various types of aircraft that are immediately operational. With the current budget, I doubt that in the next war I will have the necessary number of planes or even enough pilots with an adequate amount of flight hours and sufficient training to carry out the missions with the required quality."

The second factor was the lingering sharp disagreement over the withdrawal from Lebanon and the rules of engagement along the international border. The IDF was most worried about the "lessons learned" by the Palestinians and the implications of their having become so emboldened. Barak refused to address these issues in any way.

Finally, and in retrospect most important, was the crisis of trust on a personal level. To the IDF's high command, the dishonesty Barak and his coterie had displayed in the withdrawal from southern Lebanon was intolerable. The loss of trust was the more painful because Barak had been a chief of staff, and he personally knew and had worked with most of the officers whom he had deceived. In mid-September, the mistrust issue erupted publicly during the ceremony in which Major General Moshe Yaalon formally became deputy chief of staff, replacing Major General Uzi Dayan, whom Barak had chosen to be the chief of Israel's National Security Council. During the ceremony, the chief of staff, General Mofaz, publicly accused Dayan of "untrustworthy behavior." It was clear to all that Mofaz's unprecedented criticism was aimed more at Barak than at Dayan.

People had "acted behind his back," Mofaz said, in determining profound issues of defense policy—a clear reference to the IDF's being misled about the withdrawal from Lebanon. Alluding to Dayan's role as Barak's liaison with the high command, Mofaz summed up his relationship with his former deputy: "There was no trust between us and we reached a point where we could not work together." Mofaz's outburst, unprecedented for the IDF high command, expressed the defense leadership's anguish at what they perceived to be the Barak government's refusal to face reality and its consequent reckless endangerment of the state of Israel.

Before the ceremony ended, Barak approached Mofaz and sharply criticized him. Two days later, addressing the General Staff in Tel Aviv, Barak again scored Mofaz's public criticism of the Dayan appointment and of the cuts in the defense budget. He defended these immensely unpopular moves by stressing his authority as prime minister rather than by explaining the reasons for them. "The General Staff is not a classroom and the Prime Minister is not a teacher," Barak said. "I hope everyone internalizes these things and acts in accordance."

To the Egyptians and Palestinians, Halutz's interviews and Mofaz's outburst served as the final proofs that Israel was weak, indecisive, and uniquely vulnerable. It was in this context that Barak's office made a formal request of the Palestinian leadership to facilitate a visit by Ariel Sharon to the Temple Mount in two weeks' time. Thus Arafat suddenly had the formal justification he needed for the first phase of his war of independence. Within days of receiving Barak's request, Arafat had ordered his troops to gradually commence hostilities. The still-undeclared Intifadah was on.

———

THE PALESTINIANS began with small intrusions into restricted territory that seemed to dare the Israeli security forces to react. For example, Palestinian paramilitary and police patrols that were formally restricted to Area A began penetrating Area B and even Area C. When Israeli security forces merely escorted the Palestinians back to Area A, the PA patrols became more audacious. It soon became clear that their objective was "to show the flag" in Area B and, in the words of a local IDF commander, "get Israel used to the idea" of their presence. These violations continued for more than a week before Israel raised the issue with the PA at the political level. Senior Palestinian officials, including Abu-Alaa, refused to address the complaints, observing that "they no longer recognized the Oslo-mandated division of the territory." Israel complained to the Clinton administration and was advised to demonstrate restraint and understanding.

At the same time, the Palestinians began selective escalations of violence. In the West Bank, the first focus was the Gush Etzion area—the biggest settlement block Israel was seeking to annex in a permanent agreement. Starting in mid-September, the frequency and seriousness of ambushes on the roads and shooting attacks on the kibbutzim increased. The perpetrators were no longer amateur local cells with short supplies of ammunition but disciplined, trained, and well-equipped members of the PA security forces. The attacks were designed not to cause casualties or significant damage but rather to demonstrate the attackers' freedom of movement and unnerve the local residents. In that, the Palestinians were quite successful.

In Gaza, the primary flash point at this early stage was the Netzarim junction in Gush Katif. Starting again in mid-September, rock throwing became "a popular sport among Palestinian youth," according to a local Israeli commander. Every day hundreds of boys of all ages were brought to the junction from nearby refugee camps, along with stockpiles of rocks. As they set to work, Palestinian policemen stationed outside Netzarim did nothing to stop them. After an IDF soldier was hit in the head on September 17, the IDF patrols were permitted to respond with tear gas and rubber bullets. At that point, Palestinian soldiers appeared on the scene and trained their guns on the IDF soldiers; a tense standoff developed. This scenario repeated itself every day. Significantly, the man in charge of the Netzarim clashes was Jihad Amarin, a senior PA security official who had founded in the 1980s, and still commanded, the Companies of the Islamic Jihad, a Fatah-affiliated Islamist terrorist group. Earlier complaints by Israel about Amarin's involvement in anti-Israeli attacks had been largely ignored.

The Netzarim junction clashes steadily escalated until on the night of September 27, a small bomb exploded on the edge of the PA-controlled area while a convoy of cars was returning to the local Jewish settlements. When an IDF patrol arrived to investigate, a much bigger bomb exploded in their faces, wounding several soldiers, one mortally. The rest of the patrol opened fire on some terrorists seen running into the PA-controlled area. When the IDF attempted hot pursuit, the PA troops interfered, enabling the terrorists to escape. Subsequent investigation determined that the bomb was set and activated by a HAMAS cell with the help of the local PA police unit. When Israel's Gaza commander, Brigadier General Yair Naveh, warned that "the Arabs are turning Gaza into another Lebanon," the government rebuked him.

The next major incident took place in Kalkilyeh on the morning of September 28. As an Israeli-PA paramilitary joint patrol was getting ready to start its morning route, a Palestinian policeman walked up to an Israeli jeep. Screaming "Allah hu Akbar!" he shot into the jeep, killing Chief Inspector Yossi Tabaja of the Israeli Border Police and wounding another soldier. The rest of the PA patrol cheered and made no effort to restrain the shooter. The location of this event was significant: "It cannot be chance," said Border Police Commander Major General Yitzhak Dadon, "that the incident occurred in Kalkilyeh, a town in which cooperation with the Palestinians on security issues is extremely high." Indeed, subsequent investigation demonstrated that the incident had been orchestrated by Arafat's inner circle. As the PA expected, the IDF suspended joint patrols—thus creating more favorable conditions for the smuggling of terrorists and weapons.

For Arafat, the Kalkilyeh attack was merely the beginning of a major offensive that would redefine Palestinian-Israeli relations. That morning, he convened a high-level meeting with his closest aides. Mamduh Nofal, the former DFLP military chief, who was present at that meeting, later wrote a book on the basis of his diary. On the morning of September 28, Nofal writes, "Arafat said that it is easy to recruit the street and to draw them into a campaign for Jerusalem. . . . The masses will act even if the [Palestinian] Authority doesn't budge. The campaign has started and it will be long." Nofal describes how Arafat oversaw the preparations for instigating violence. "Arafat gave instructions to the security apparatus to defend the areas of the Palestinian Authority with all means. The protestors were permitted to come up to the IDF barriers and express their rage as they wished. Arafat personally spoke with the commanders and gave them detailed instructions." No less important was Arafat's coordination of operations with the Islamist terrorist organizations. "The heads of HAMAS and [Islamic] Jihad were invited to meetings to prepare the strike and processions of rage. The public was called to come to Al-Aqsa, the number of guards were increased, and a night shift was implemented," Nofal writes.

Still, neither the Clinton administration nor the Barak government was willing to face reality. They refused to recognize that the PA was going out of its way to demonstrate that the security cooperation mechanism—the key to future coexistence—was crumbling. The administration saw the simultaneous outbreaks of violence throughout the territories, including the clear cooperation between HAMAS and the PA security authorities, as merely coincidental outflows of grassroots frustration at the slow progress of the peace process. Barak himself, in his public reaction to the escalating violence, refused to consider a possible breakdown in the peace process and instead called for closer cooperation between Israel and the PA. "We demand and expect the PA to combat terrorism much more effectively," he declared. "We will continue to fight terrorism with all our might."

AT THIS POINT, Barak needed a dramatic breakout—a miracle—to convince the Israeli public that his peace plan was leading somewhere. By mid-September, the main sticking point in the peace process concerned the Holy Sites in Jerusalem. Clinton's proposal that the sovereign of the Temple Mount be an international body, with the day-to-day custodianship in Muslim hands, included explicit guarantees that Jews would have the right to visit and pray in and around the Temple Mount (beyond the Wailing Wall— the holiest site of Judaism). However, Barak had to convince a skeptical Israeli public that such guarantees would be honored. The 1948 cease-fire agreement between Israel and Jordan also included explicit promises of Jewish access to the Wailing Wall and other sites in the Old City, as well as the ancient cemetery of the Mount of Olives. Not only were none of those promises kept while Jordan ruled the Old City, but all thirty-one synagogues, some of them more than a thousand years old, were destroyed; the cemetery was desecrated; and ancient tombstones were used for lavatories. This situation prevailed until Israel returned to East Jerusalem in June 1967. Little wonder that virtually all the Jews of Israel anxiously questioned the new guarantees.

Enter Ariel Sharon. Although his positions and opinions are objectionable to some, he is also an Israeli Jew and, as such, entitled to the full scope of rights to be guaranteed by Arafat and his negotiators. In mid-September, Sharon sought to put the proposed system to a test. In Barak's eyes, Sharon's initiative was a godsend—the miracle he was looking for. Once Sharon was convinced that Jews had free access to the Temple Mount, there would be little the Israeli religious and nationalist Right could do to stall the peace process.

Therefore, when Sharon expressed interest in visiting the Temple Mount, Barak ordered GSS Chief Ami Ayalon to approach Jibril Rajub with a special request to facilitate a smooth and friendly visit. At the time, Rajub had about fifty "security personnel" on the Temple Mount—in gross violation of Israeli-Palestinian agreements but tacitly tolerated by Israel because Rajub was a protégé of the CIA and considered a supporter of peace. Ayalon explained the importance of the Sharon visit, and Rajub promised it would be smooth as long as Sharon refrained from entering any of the mosques or praying publicly. Ayalon agreed that Sharon's visit would be limited to a walk across the paved area of the Temple Mount from the Wailing Wall gate to the King Solomon Stables corner—where personnel of the Waqf were excavating—and back. Just to be on the safe side, Barak personally approached Arafat and once again got assurances that Sharon's visit would be smooth as long as he did not attempt to enter the Holy Mosques.

In fact, Rajub's people and Sheikh Ikrama Sabri's young mob, the Shabab, were preparing for Sharon's visit by collecting large quantities of stones, bottles, and metal rods. Israeli security authorities noted some of these preparations. Therefore, on September 27, the day before Sharon's planned visit, the local Israeli police commander, Yair Yitzhaki, met with the head of the Waqf and requested that he try to prevent outbreaks of violence. The head of the Waqf was noncommittal and warned about the incitement the visit would constitute.

Meanwhile, the date Israel and the PA had agreed on for the Sharon visit was the day before the beginning of the Jewish New Year holidays, when Israel effectively closes down for three days.

By the time Sharon and his escort walked onto the Temple Mount, hundreds of excited Shabab were waiting for him. A group of Palestinian dignitaries came to protest the visit, as did three Arab Knesset Members. With the dignitaries watching from a safe distance, the Shabab threw stones and attempted to get past the Israeli security personnel and reach Sharon and his entourage. Scuffles broke out in which dozens of Palestinians were wounded and twenty-five border policemen were lightly injured. Still, Sharon's deportment was quiet and dignified. He did not pray, did not make any statement, or do anything else that might be interpreted as offensive to the sensitivities of Muslims. Even after he came back near the Wailing Wall under a hail of stones, he remained calm. "I came here as one who believes in coexistence between Jews and Arabs," Sharon told the waiting reporters. "I believe that we can build and develop together. This was a peaceful visit. Is it an instigation for Israeli Jews to come to the Jewish people's holiest site? The provocations came, unfortunately, from the other side, to a large degree in answer to incitement by Arab Knesset Members."

By now, the Shabab had started throwing rocks and stones over the Wailing Wall onto the large pre-holiday throng of Jewish worshipers below. In East Jerusalem, particularly on Saladin Street, rioters stoned traffic. At the Ayosh junction near Ramallah, hundreds of Palestinians rioted for several hours, stoning Israeli cars and IDF positions. When the mob would not disperse, the IDF fired rubber bullets, wounding fifteen rioters.

Violence continued the next day, at the Wailing Wall, at Rachel's Tomb in Bethlehem, in northern Jerusalem, and in Hebron. When Israel still did not attack the PA-controlled areas but instead tried to arrange a series of cease-fires, Arafat ordered the Tanzim into action. By October 2, clashes had spread throughout the West Bank. Around the cities, IDF positions were attacked by small-arms fire and hails of stones. Along the roads, Shabab, led by PA officials, ambushed traffic; they hurled rocks and burning tires as Israeli troops fired rubber bullets in return. In Gaza, Shabab hurled stones at soldiers near the settlements of Kfar Darom and Neve Dekalim. In response, IDF attack helicopters fired anti-tank missiles at PA buildings used as firing posts by the Palestinian security forces. Violent riots also took place in Arab cities throughout Israel, with the fiercest clashes taking place in the Islamist-dominated city of Umm El Fahm.

Strategically most significant was the Palestinian siege of the Joseph's Tomb seminary near Nablus. An Israeli border policeman was wounded in the Tanzim-led attack. Rather than order the IDF to dispatch a large armored unit to relieve the siege and evacuate the trapped students and border policemen, Barak opted for negotiating with Rajub for a local cease-fire and evacuation plan. By the time this plan was implemented, the wounded Israeli had died from loss of blood. After the evacuation was finally completed, Tanzim fighters, Shabab, and PA security personnel destroyed the Jewish religious materials and turned the building into a mosque. The Israeli defense establishment, meanwhile, was in shock over Barak's willingness to sacrifice the life of a wounded officer—an unprecedented deviation from the sacred norms of the IDF's commitment to its personnel. That night, at Rajub's invitation, the Unified Leadership of the Intifadah met defiantly at the Orient House in Jerusalem. They compared that day's "Israeli escape from Nablus" with the earlier "escape from Lebanon" and declared that these constituted the first links in a chain of events that would lead to the establishment of an independent Palestine.

The next morning, Barak agreed to a general cease-fire under conditions dictated by the PA—including unilateral withdrawal of the IDF from forward positions captured in order to contain Palestinian attacks on Israeli civilians. However, in both the Gaza Strip and the West Bank, Israeli border policemen and IDF troops came under gunfire and firebomb attack the moment the withdrawal had been completed. Deputy Chief of Staff Yaalon bitterly complained about the outcome of Barak's gambit. "We totally withdrew our forces from the area," he briefed security officials, "so that it could not be claimed that we were causing provocations—but it didn't work, and the Palestinians resumed the violence. . . . We have identified an initiated process controlled by the PA that can be stopped by the Chairman's order to the Tanzim. So far the Tanzim has not received such an order."

In Washington, Clinton and Albright led a choir condemning Israel, joining the Arabs in describing the outbreak of hostilities as a spontaneous reaction to Sharon's visit. The White House's accusations continued unabated even after Israel supplied documentary evidence that the visit had been coordinated in advance with Arafat and Rajub. A deeply hurt Barak complained to Clinton and Albright but did not break off his participation in the peace process. Instead, through U.S. mediation, he embarked on what Israeli officials described as "intense diplomatic contact" with Arafat. Both Arafat and Barak spoke with Clinton, who urged Barak to demonstrate utmost restraint and promised to convene a trilateral summit once the fighting subsided. "With all sadness, we know that the violence erupted because of the Palestinian Authority," Barak protested publicly. "Soldiers and commanders have been directed to use all means to protect the lives of the soldiers. We will use what is required." The Palestinians would hear nothing about an end to the Intifadah. "We're prepared for all possibilities under the circumstances," Arafat told the Saudi newspaper *Ukaz*. "The Palestinian people have many options at their disposal." Other senior Palestinian officials spoke about the escalation ahead. "The situation continues to deteriorate," Rajub declared. "We are at war!"

————

CRUCIALLY SIGNIFICANT to understanding the Intifadah and its implications are the overall circumstances when the hostilities broke out. As of late September, Yassir Arafat was negotiating with Israel the last modalities of the permanent-status agreement. He was finally to get his Palestinian state, worldwide recognition, and immense financial aid with little or no oversight. Moreover, Clinton was pressing Barak very hard on the Jerusalem issue.

Under such circumstances, it was in Arafat's interest—or so logic would dictate—to demonstrate that the Palestinians were indeed willing and able to guarantee freedom of religious practice for Jews. Hence, even if some Palestinians did find Sharon's visit offensive and spontaneous riots did break out, the PA's myriad of police and security forces should have contained them swiftly in order to demonstrate Arafat's commitment to the peace process.

Not only did Arafat not contain the initial reaction to Sharon's visit, but he also unleashed his own Tanzim forces to initiate, and soon afterward markedly expand, armed clashes throughout the territories. Arafat even activated his networks among the Israeli Arabs and sent them to clash with the Israeli police. These Israeli-Arab networks had been of tremendous political value to Arafat through their influence on the Israeli body politic. Now, having been implicated in the rioting, they became politically useless. If Arafat were not aware of the implications of activating the Israeli Arabs, Knesset Member Ahmad Tibi, one of his closest confidants, was there to advise him. Thus, Arafat deliberately turned what could have been extremely strong proof that peace under the Palestinians' conditions was still possible into the trigger for uncompromising war.

ON OCTOBER 3, Arafat stormed out of a meeting with Secretary of State Madeleine Albright in the U.S. Embassy in Paris. Albright literally ran after him, shouting to the Marine guards, "Shut the gates!" Effectively detained in the U.S. Embassy compound, Arafat returned to the room but refused to discuss substance, let alone change his position, despite Albright's subtle and not-so-subtle threats. Furthermore, the first thing Arafat did once released from captivity was to rush to the Paris office of a confidant, call his headquarters in Gaza, and order a marked escalation in the fighting. He undoubtedly knew U.S. intelligence would intercept his phone call and thus be aware of his order.

Until the fall of 2000, such behavior would have been unthinkable. No leader in the post–Cold War world would have dared to stand up to the American secretary of state in that way. Leaders negotiated and cajoled, bargained and pleaded, over policies they were convinced would be harmful to their countries—but they did not brazenly defy strongly held positions of the U.S. government. Arafat's behavior was therefore a milestone, particularly given his dependence on the United States for foreign aid and pressure on Israel. Moreover, Arafat—the quintessential survivor—was fully aware that both Albright and Clinton tended toward personal vindictiveness. The significance of his dramatic defiance lay not in his commitment to his negotiating position—for his outburst was actually over a nonsense point—but in his demonstration that he no longer feared the Clinton administration.

At the same time, although overshadowed in Western eyes by the Israeli-Palestinian violence, the "humanitarian airlift" to Baghdad was continuing and expanding. On the surface the airlift and Arafat's storming out were not connected. In reality, both events were expressions of the same development: the collapse of U.S. influence in the Arab Middle East at the very time a cursory examination would have suggested that U.S. influence was at its strongest. Essentially, the Arab leaders were telling the United States they had had it with the Clinton administration's imposed solutions for the Middle East and disregard of their own sensitivities. They would not wait for President Clinton to leave office or even for the imminent U.S. elections to formally make him a lame duck.

Not all the Arab leaders involved in these dynamics were rash or reckless. On the contrary, some of them were responsible and mature leaders, prudent survivors and inherently conservative. Hence, Washington should have recognized that their decision to defy the Clinton administration was an expression of a sense of extreme urgency. And these leaders were correct in fearing an imminent crisis. Their people were increasingly dominated by Islamists who refused to accept the U.S.-imposed world order—not just in politics and economics, but primarily in the Westernization of society. While grassroots hostility toward U.S.-driven Westernization had been building up since the early 1990s, only recently had conditions in the Arab world become conducive for confronting America. Catalyzing this change was the succession process in the Arab world during the last years of the twentieth century. Until then, the White House could have its policies implemented by veteran Arab leaders, rewarding them, in turn, with military and other assistance. By the fall of 2000, these veteran leaders—such as Mubarak, King Fahd, and Hafez al-Assad—were either dead or weakened by age, and they or their successors were neither able nor willing to coerce their ruling elites and security forces into accepting the Clinton regional order.

With the immensely popular Islamist upsurge spreading like wildfire, Arab regimes feared their own people's outrage if they stayed out of the airlift to Baghdad more than they feared the Clinton administration's retaliation if they joined it. Arafat, too, was more afraid of his own Islamists than of Clinton. Furthermore, Arafat was convinced he could bolster his power position by instigating a major war—that is, by drawing the armies of Arab countries into a wider conflict. For example, on October 6 he declared in Tunis, "Just as Palestinian and Tunisian blood mixed at Hamam al-Shat, so will Palestinian blood mix with Arab blood in defense of the legitimate rights of our people—at the head of which is the establishment of a Palestinian state with Jerusalem as its capital! Whether some like it or not." Over the next few days, other Palestinian leaders echoed this sentiment. "The continuation of the Palestinian bloodshed might push part of the Arab military to carry out military operations against Israel," declared the head of the PA's National Guidance Directorate, Mazen Izz al-Din. "Also, Palestinian bloodshed will push parts of the Arab countries to launch missiles against Israel as the President of Iraq did in 1991 when he launched thirty-nine missiles against Tel Aviv." Arafat was convinced that if the Arab armies joined the war, their leaders would in effect be recognizing his supreme leadership.

———

IN LATE SEPTEMBER, on the eve of the outbreak of the Intifadah, Iraq's Deputy Prime Minister Tariq Aziz visited Damascus. During his four days there, he met with the entire Syrian leadership, including Bashar al-Assad, in order to discuss Syria's facilitation of the collapse of the embargo on Iraq. Among the steps they agreed on were opening their mutual border to unrestricted commercial activity, reactivating the northern railroad between Mosul in Iraq and al-Qamishli in Syria, and refurbishing oil pipelines between Iraq and Mediterranean ports before the end of 2000. When completed, these steps would provide for the economic recovery of Iraq.

Aziz also laid the foundations for a new comprehensive strategic-military relationship, which was consolidated in the first days of October during a secret visit to Damascus by Qusay Saddam Hussein—by now Saddam's de facto successor. Qusay had an all-night session with his personal friend Bashar, during which he delivered an oral message from his father urging the establishment of unity between Iraq and Syria "at any time and based on any formula which Syrian officials want." Qusay stressed that all of Saddam's earlier proposals to Hafez al-Assad—starting with the Bashar-Uday conversations in the summer of 1996—were still in effect. Qusay also declared that the Intifadah should serve as the catalyst for all-Arab unity and the fateful confrontation with Israel. On behalf of his father, he "placed all of Iraq's resources at Syria's disposal to strengthen the internal situation and to protect Syria's legitimate rights," even without the formal implementation of any step toward unity.

Qusay also reiterated Saddam's resolve to fully support the "three-way axis that includes Baghdad, Damascus, and Tehran" and asked Bashar "to expedite reconciliation efforts and normalization of relations between Iran and Iraq to revive a strategic axis capable of confronting the U.S. aggression against these three countries." In the meantime, Bashar and Qusay agreed, Syria and Iraq would accelerate the operational coordination of their security systems to be ready for a joint effort against Israel in the immediate future. Indeed, delegations of senior military and intelligence officers were exchanged between the two capitals within a few days.

———

WHILE THE INITIAL dynamics of the changes in the Arab world destroyed President Clinton's determined efforts to impose a new regional order, they failed to further an alternative regional order or even to suggest the nature of the future Middle East the Arab leaders would like to see and live in. The radicalization of the Arab street reflected a grassroots movement attempting to cope with modernity, economic decay, and frustration; the Arab-Israeli issue was ever present, but it was far from being the dominant factor in determining the moods of the Arab street. Hence, the urgent imperative was to come up with a new regional order—neither Western nor militant Islamist—and seek regional solutions based on the Arab world's own interests as elucidated by the more farsighted Arab leaders. The key to the future must come from Arab leaders acceptable to the Arab street rather than from a U.S. administration obsessed with the president's "legacy."

This imperative was, or should have been, of great interest not only to the Arabs themselves but also to the Clinton administration, for the mounting crisis in and around Israel did not alter the importance of the Arab Middle East to the strategic and economic interests of the United States and the West as a whole. By the fall of 2000, while the West's attention was focused on the Intifadah al-Aqsa, the Islamist agitation elsewhere in the Arab world was locally oriented. The Arab street listened to the Islamist leadership not because of their commitment to the liberation of al-Quds, but because the Islamists addressed the people's own local and immediate concerns. By failing to notice this, the Clinton administration turned the United States into an irrelevant factor in Arab sociopolitics, as Arab leaders were left to cope by themselves with the crises left behind by Clinton's reckless follies.

———

TEHRAN, MEANWHILE, was preparing to demonstrate that it could fill the void left by the collapse of the U.S. peace process. Over the first weekend of the Intifadah, once it became clear that the hostilities were not a transient phenomenon, Tehran began to activate its own contingency plans for a regional crisis.

To set Tehran's forthcoming actions in the context of Arafat's Intifadah, Mohammad Sadr, Iran's deputy foreign minister for Arab and African affairs, provided an authoritative policy formulation in an October 3 interview with *Al-Hayah*—the most important Arabic-language newspaper. Tehran was going to be a team player in this crisis, Sadr assured the interviewer, and would take "any practical measure that the Islamic countries agree on" against the "Israeli massacres of the Palestinian people." Iran believed that the Arab and Muslim world had reached a historic turning point over the situation in Palestine. "Israeli crimes against the Palestinians," Sadr declared, "are making all the Muslims in the world angry." He stressed that Tehran's ultimate objective was to ensure that Israel "[would] disappear one day" and "all of Palestine [would] return to the Palestinian people." Toward that end, he urged the Islamist forces (HAMAS, the Islamic Jihad Movement, and HizbAllah) to establish "serious cooperation" under Tehran's sponsorship.

The moment Arafat notified the Islamists that he was committed to the resumption of violence, Iranian and Syrian intelligence started organizing a series of high-level consultations with the leadership of HizbAllah and the various Palestinian rejectionist groups led by the PFLP-GC in Beirut, Damascus, and Tehran. At the meeting in Tehran, Khamenei personally assured the delegations of Iran's unyielding support for the anti-Israeli jihad. By the first weekend of October, Iranian intelligence officials had reported to Tehran that "cooperation and coordination among these groups has made important progress in all areas." Most significant was the activation of a "central operations room" for the Islamist and rejectionist organizations. On the instructions of Tehran and Damascus, these groups began preparing for "an increase in tension in the [Israel-Lebanon] border areas, especially by escalating popular moves near the Fataimah Gate and al-Abbad post." Meanwhile, Iran and its allies began preparing the centerpiece of this effort, a series of spectacular and audacious terrorist strikes. These would be planned and implemented through the special headquarters established by Imad Mughniyah and Osama bin Laden in Beirut during the summer but would be claimed by a myriad of "organizations" and "causes."

On October 5, after Arafat's defiance of Albright in Paris, Tehran and Damascus instructed their key Islamist and radical protégés to commit to supporting the Palestinian Intifadah. This commitment was momentous: From now on Arafat would not be able to extricate the Intifadah from the radicals' total jihad for the destruction of Israel even if he wanted to. Although Arafat's own Tanzim militias had launched the Intifadah, the Palestinian forces were actually controlled by the Intifadah Unified Committee, which was dominated by Islamists and radicals. On October 9, representatives of HAMAS and the Islamic Jihad participated as equal partners in a PA cabinet meeting. The cabinet unanimously adopted the Islamists' demand to escalate the fighting into a HizbAllah-style "popular war" irrespective of the status of the U.S.-sponsored negotiations.

In one of their first operational measures, the Iranians and their allies markedly extended Iranian-sponsored broadcasts from Lebanon, which made HizbAllah's al-Manar satellite TV channel "the most preferred media channel in the Palestinian territories." Now Iran organized a Beirut rally in solidarity with the Intifadah and broadcast it to the entire region via al-Manar TV. The presence of Ghazi Sayf-al-Din, regional secretary of the Ba'ath Party was proof of Syria's endorsement. Sayf-al-Din delivered the opening speech, expressing the party's total support for "the popular Intifadah in Palestine." Ramadan Abdallah Shallah, secretary-general of the Islamic Jihad Movement, surveyed the development of the Intifadah and vowed that "resistance and jihad will continue until Palestine is liberated." In an especially important address, HizbAllah Secretary-General Hassan Nasrallah urged the Palestinians to turn the Intifadah into an "armed [Islamic] Revolution" modeled on HizbAllah's struggle for southern Lebanon. Nasrallah then outlined the Iranian-Islamist strategy for the jihad for Palestine. "What is required," he explained, "is to issue a fatwa on jihad, because this would fill the hearts of Jews with fear. The population of the settlements in northern Palestine left their settlements because of the existence of HizbAllah's flag, without the existence of weapons. So how would the situation develop if jihad was declared?"

He then addressed the Palestinians, whom he knew would be watching on al-Manar TV:

> Do not wager on anyone. Do not wait for anyone. You must pursue a clear, specific strategy by benefitting from the experience of the resistance in Lebanon through concentrating on killing the Israeli Jews, because they are afraid of death and you love martyrdom. What is required is to deprive the Israelis of security. By doing this, the march of victory will begin. Afterward, we can say that the march to remove this entity [Israel] has become realistic. You should turn this Intifadah into an armed revolution. Save the bullets, which are being fired at Israeli centers, and direct them toward the chests of the Israelis. If a person does not have bullets, then let him acquire a knife. Let the equation be: An Israeli must be killed in exchange for every Palestinian martyr. Let every Palestinian stab an Israeli. Then, the situation will be reversed. They cannot use nuclear weapons. The liberation of Palestine does not need armies, since the liberation of the south did not require armies, but was liberated from inside the country. We will not talk about what we will do. We in Lebanon, in HizbAllah, and in the Islamic Resistance will be with you. We will not leave you. We will not abandon you. We will stand by you. You can count on us in hard times.

Because virtually all Palestinians are Sunni, the Syrians and Iranians also organized on October 5 a meeting of all the leading Lebanese and Palestinian Sunni imams so that they could issue the fatwa that Nasrallah called for. This meeting, at Fatwa House in Beirut, was chaired by Lebanon's mufti, Sheikh Muhammad Rashid Qabbani. After the meeting, Sheikh Qabbani read a statement that essentially was a fatwa addressed to the Islamic nations, defining the Intifadah as an all-Islamic jihad:

World Zionism has come out in this age of ours with all its evil and aggres-
siveness to occupy our Arab lands in Palestine, to usurp our rights, displace
our people, and spill the blood of our innocent citizens. However, our Nation has refused to acquiesce and our peoples have refused to capitulate.
They have offered enormous sacrifices and depended on God, praise be to
Him, for help. They were not intimidated by international pressure or the
Israeli acts of aggression. They were not cheated into relinquishing their
rights. They have not believed the claims about reconciliation and the illusions of peace.

Israel's oppression has gone to the extreme of insisting on the occupation of the city of Jerusalem. Israel is also seeking to impose its sovereignty
on the holy Al-Haram al-Sharif and the blessed Al-Aqsa Mosque, the First
of the Two Qiblas and the Third Holiest Mosque. It is the mosque that is
cherished by Muslims because it is the site from which their prophet as-
cended to heaven. It is also the graveyard of famous Muslim clergymen and
heroes. On several occasions, oppressive Israel has threatened the existence
of Al-Aqsa Mosque. It has ignited fires inside the mosque, and opened tunnels beneath it; thereby, weakening its structure. It has stormed the
mosque's compound, opened fire at the worshippers in the mosque, and
sought to instill despair in the hearts of the believers. Israel has done all
this so as to demolish Al-Aqsa Mosque and to build the alleged Temple on
the debris of the Mosque so as to turn Jerusalem into the eternal capital of
the Zionists, the killers of Prophets and Messengers.

Today our Palestinian Arab people in Jerusalem and in the heart of Arab
Palestine have rebelled against the premeditated Israeli onslaught whose aim
is to force the Palestinians to concede Jerusalem and to spread the Israeli sovereignty on the Al-Aqsa Mosque and on the Haram Al-Sharif. Israel also
seeks to deal a final blow to the Arab and Islamic will, without having any regard to the Muslims and Christians, who are together facing the same fate.
Oppressive Israel and the unjust new world order bear responsibility for the
collective massacres and crimes which have been committed. The acts of
heroism and sacrifices that are made by the Palestinian Arab people have
drawn the admiration of the world and have restored the self-confidence of
the Arab nation. They have made it possible to launch the jihad and regener-
ated the pride and vigor that is inherent in the Arab Nation. These acts of
heroism and sacrifice have confirmed the capability of the entire Arab Nation
and asserted its rejection of living in humiliation, its love for martyrdom, and
its determination to continue on the path of steadfastness and liberation.

In view of all this, we would like to address our appeal first to the
Palestinian Arab people to attest to the greatness of their stand, to their

dignified attitude, their generous sacrifices, and their great courage. We would like to call on the Palestinian Arab people to continue their steadfastness, all the more so because they represent the honor of the Arab nation at the present time, the title of its dignity and the pointer to its future.

Secondly, we would like to address our appeal to the Arab Nation to hold a summit conference as soon as possible so as to unify Arab ranks, to draft a plan for the liberation of Jerusalem and all of Palestine, to mobilize Arab resources for the fateful battle, to break off the relations which some people have established with Israel, and to establish relations with the major powers on the basis of their position toward the alien Israeli entity which is occupying Palestine. The Arab summit should also end intra-Arab differences, implement the joint Arab defense agreements, form the battalions of the jihad, and enhance the steadfastness of the Palestinians on every level.

Thirdly, we would like to address our appeal to the Islamic World to perform its role in defending its Islamic holy shrines and to adopt a unified position toward the countries which sponsor Israel and provide it with funds, weapons and power that Israel uses to kill our brethren and sons in Palestine.

Finally, we would like to address our appeal to the big powers and the world public. They should know that all the claims about the defense of human rights are illusions unless these states shoulder their responsibilities in defending the vanquished and deterring the oppressor. We would like also to address our appeal to the international organizations to free themselves from the grip of international trusteeship to declare their commitment to their resolutions, and to adopt the international measures that are needed to uproot the Israeli evil and to confiscate the Israeli nuclear weapons.

Essentially, this fatwa outlined the political-military principles of the jihad that the Islamists and their allies and sponsors have been pursuing ever since.

––––––

BY NOW, the Iranians and HizbAllah were ready to unleash the series of spectacular operations they had long been preparing for—on the Israeli-Lebanese border, in the greater Middle East, and overseas. Orchestrated through the Mughniyah–bin Laden headquarters, these operations would establish Iran and the Islamist forces it was sponsoring as the strategically dominant element in the Intifadah irrespective of anything Arafat did.

The first operation took place on October 7 in the disputed sector of the Israeli-Lebanese border known as Har Dov or Shebaa Farms. A HizbAllah Special Operations squad—under the command of Mughniyah and controlled by Pasdaran Intelligence—had gained free access to the border zone by working on and bribing personnel from the Indian UNIFIL battalion, who gave them some UNIFIL uniforms and genuine blue berets. The operation began when the HizbAllah squad detonated a roadside bomb near an Israeli patrol vehicle. The three Israeli soldiers in the vehicle emerged dazed but otherwise unharmed. As they were struggling to get their bearings, they saw a group of UNIFIL soldiers—actually, the dressed-up HizbAllah squad—waving to them and offering help. When the three IDF soldiers started walking in their direction, the HizbAllah squad blew up a Claymore mine, severely wounding the three Israelis, as well as a HizbAllah commander who stood too close. At this point, several HizbAllah SUVs, at least one of them painted like a U.N. vehicle, arrived on the scene and took the Israelis away. That was the last time they were seen. UNIFIL personnel watched the event unfolding, took video footage, but did nothing to help the wounded Israelis. Ayatollah Khamenei had personally approved the operation from start to finish, and Bashar al-Assad was briefed in advance.

Barak rushed to the Lebanese border the next day and promised to achieve the return of the soldiers. He warned Damascus that he considered Syria responsible for their well-being—as if Syria could have any influence on Tehran. Meanwhile, the IDF attacked several targets in southern Lebanon that were commonly associated with HizbAllah but that had nothing to do with Tehran's audacious gambit.

The Iranians' next strike took place the following week in Yemen. On October 12, a Zodiac inflatable motorboat approached the destroyer USS *Cole,* which was on a four-hour refueling stop in the Port of Aden. The Zodiac slammed into the destroyer, causing an explosion that left seventeen crew members dead and thirty-six wounded. Had the Zodiac struck a few dozen feet closer to the center of the *Cole,* the explosion would have sunk the destroyer.

The entire operation indicated exceptionally good advance intelligence—most likely not only in Aden, where Iraqi military intelligence is dominant, but also in Egypt and the Persian Gulf states, where details about the destroyer's schedule could have been obtained. In the months preceding the operation, local supporters had acquired a safe house overlooking the port, to be used for intelligence gathering and as the bomb-making facility. The Zodiac was identical to the ones used by the refueling crews and therefore raised no suspicions. At the core of the bomb was an expertly constructed shaped charge like those the Pasdaran taught trainees to construct in their naval-sabotage school at Bandar Abbas. By the fall of 2000, several graduates of the Bandar Abbas school were in southern Lebanon, answerable to the Mughniyah–bin Laden headquarters. The Sunni martyr-bombers came from the ranks of bin Laden's Saudi "Afghans"—most likely from the Jamiat-i-Tulaba al-Arabiya.

Following the attack on the *Cole,* there came a series of narrowly averted threats to U.S. diplomatic and military facilities throughout the Persian Gulf states, prompting their closure. Then, on October 15, HizbAllah announced the kidnapping of Israeli Colonel (Res.) Elhanan Tenenbaum. Tenenbaum was entrapped while in Europe, having been persuaded to travel to a Middle East country using a false passport and then captured upon arrival. There are indications that this was a long-term operation in which Tenenbaum's desperate efforts to revive his failing business were exploited by his abductors in order to entrap him. There are also indications that the HizbAllah and the Iranians might have confused Tenenbaum with Hannan Tenenbaum, the cover name of a Mossad agent who tried to install a listening device at a HizbAllah operative's apartment in Switzerland. In any case, Israel acquired evidence that this kidnapping was also a Mughniyah operation, although Nasrallah emerged as the spokesman for the kidnappers.

These spectacular operations in Har Dov, the Port of Aden, and Western Europe were perfectly timed and professionally executed. They were urgent undertakings aimed at forestalling the incoming American administration and the new Congress so that they could neither formulate policy nor set priorities. The overall goal was to bring certain issues to the forefront of America's political attention—among them the stability of the Persian Gulf, the need to fight Islamist terrorism, the situation along the Israeli-Lebanese border, and the Syrian factor. Although these issues were seemingly unrelated, their common denominator was Tehran's dominant role; none could be resolved through any agreement between Israel and the Palestinians. Therefore, to truly stabilize the region and protect American vital interests—such as Persian Gulf oil—the United States would have to deal with Tehran rather than Gaza. Significantly, these attacks fit the Iranian penchant for making bold strokes when an American presidential election was underway.

Obsessed with securing Clinton's "legacy" on the Israeli-Palestinian track, the administration completely missed this whole strategic gambit, and the United States would pay dearly for this failure.

———

BY MID-OCTOBER, the fighting in Israel had developed a kind of routine. Palestinian attacks on Israeli settlements and civilian traffic occurred daily. Over time, as the Palestinians' confidence increased, the attacks on Jerusalem neighborhoods, especially Gilo, also increased. This initial phase of the Intifadah was supposed to be a grassroots populist uprising; hence children and youth—the graduates of the PA's summer camps—made regular appearances in "popular" events against the well-armed Israeli soldiers. With foreign TV cameras all around, the Palestinians pitted their young Shabab against IDF positions, throwing stones and firebombs, while PA security personnel fired their assault rifles from behind to provoke IDF retaliation. Palestinian ambulances rushed in ammunition and buckets of rocks to the front line while evacuating the mounting casualties. As the PA had anticipated, the casualties among the children made this a public-relations disaster for Israel.

Because previous attempts at regulating such clashes through negotiations with the Palestinian security authorities had had disastrous outcomes, the IDF continued to react with force. These earlier negotiations had been mediated and supervised by the CIA, and their progress was accompanied by intense pressure on Israel from the Clinton administration to ensure their "success." This process peaked in early October, with the White House promising that if the IDF permitted the security personnel of Jibril Rajub and Tawfiq Tirawi—the chief of general intelligence in the West Bank—to essentially control the Temple Mount and parts of East Jerusalem, the CIA liaison officers with them would ensure a quick end to the fighting. Over the stern objections of the Israeli security forces, Barak ordered the IDF to comply. As East Jerusalem was handed over, the shooting on Gilo and at the Ayosh junction only intensified. The CIA failed miserably, if indeed it tried, to contain the violence. Nevertheless, Clinton sent George Tenet to Israel to revive the security cooperation and the political negotiations, meant to culminate in an international summit in Sharm el-Sheikh.

At the same time, the White House was warning Jerusalem that given the "gut-wrenching images" on the evening news, the administration would find it difficult to "defend Israel" unless it could demonstrate "flexibility" on the political front. Hence, Barak and Ben-Ami, under ferocious pressure from Clinton and Albright, gave the PA forty-eight hours to demonstrate whether Arafat was using violence in order to gain diplomatic concessions or in order to avoid reaching an agreement with Israel at any cost.

At the end of this trial period, and following the horrendous lynching of two Israeli reservists in Ramallah and a brief series of Israeli retaliatory strikes, Arafat formally declared war on Israel. He issued edicts that activated his emergency command bunker and permitted his security forces and the Tanzim to escalate the fighting. He also formally ordered that all future operations be conducted in close cooperation with the Islamists. Significantly, he instructed Dahlan and Amin al-Hindi—CIA friends who were expected in Sharm el-Sheikh for the summit—to stay put and manage for him the escalation in Gaza and the West Bank, respectively. Even though the

Israeli defense establishment was urging the government to contain the Intifadah before it led to a grassroots Islamist upsurge, Barak decided to continue the unilateral restraint.

The schism between Barak and his security elite peaked on the eve of the summit, when the GSS—by far the most "pro-peace" of Israel's security-related institutions—handed Barak a top secret document titled "Arafat—Asset or Liability." This document stated that Arafat was a dangerous man, pushing the theater to the verge of a major war and thus imperiling Israel's strategic achievements in sustaining peace with Jordan and Egypt. By legitimizing terrorism and subversion, the document said, Arafat was endangering the stability of all the region's regimes. Through his uncompromising negotiating positions, he was striving to legitimize the destruction of Israel. The GSS suggested that Israel would be better able to cope with any coalition of power groups that might rise in the aftermath of Arafat's disappearance. "Arafat the man," the document concluded, "constitutes a severe threat to the security of the state. The harm in his disappearance is smaller [than] the harm of his enduring presence."

Barak elected to disregard this scathing assessment of his policy. Instead, he resolved not only to continue to regard Arafat as his negotiating partner but also to accede to Albright's demand that Israel "respect the ceasefire"— as if one existed. Essentially, by following the administration's scenario, Israel relinquished its ability to contain the expansion and popularization of the Intifadah through swift and forceful suppression at the initial phase. Barak knowingly repeated the error that Rabin had unknowingly made in 1987 and that the British Mandate authorities made when the first Intifadah erupted back in 1936.

————

BY NOW, ISRAEL was accumulating intelligence that on October 13 Iraqi military convoys had begun moving toward the Jordanian border. In these convoys were vehicles capable of concealing ballistic missiles tipped with chemical weapons. (Fortunately, this intelligence was also acquired and verified by the United States' own national technical means so that American decision makers could not dismiss it as "Zionist propaganda" or "Israeli hysteria," as they tend to do with intelligence warnings they do not want to act upon.) At the core of the Iraqi force was a 3,000-man brigade of the Hammurabi Division of the Republican Guard. Within days, it was expanded into a 5,000-man force that maneuvered perilously close to the Iraqi-Jordanian border. Eventually, it became clear that this was a demonstrative force, proving Baghdad's resolve to quickly implement the Bashar-Qusay agreement and serving as a test run of Iraq's ability to skirt the Israeli "red lines" and get away with it. The sole reason the Israelis did let them get away with it was a privately delivered warning from the White House against complicating the drive for peace with Arafat. Similarly, the administration refused to address the Iranian-sponsored acts of terrorism along the Israeli-Lebanese border. The White House also insisted that the bombing of the USS *Cole* was a bin Laden operation that had nothing to do with either Iran or Iraq or the whole Arab-Israeli dynamics.

Arab leaders, however, were not oblivious to these developments. Indeed, Mubarak raised the Iraqi factor in his discussions with Clinton and Barak on the eve of the Sharm el-Sheikh summit. Completely ignoring the latest movements of the Iraqi forces, Mubarak apprised Clinton and Barak only of the overwhelming grassroots popularity of the Saddam-Arafat policies. Mubarak then warned that unless Israel accepted, with U.S. guarantees, the Arabs' position, which included Israel's forgoing the use of tanks, helicopters, and other means of "excessive force," he himself would lead the Arab world into supporting the Iraqi strategy against Israel and "its supporters"—a veiled reference to the United States.

In making these threats, Mubarak was facing the regional reality head on. Taken together, the actions of Iran, Iraq, and Syria had demonstrated that Arafat had *no* monopoly on—and no real control over—the escalatory dynamics in the region. Arafat also comprehended these signals, and both he and Mubarak realized that the Intifadah must now be played out within the context of the radical powers' strategic objectives. Therefore, these two sets of events—the just-completed Iranian strategic surge and the just-beginning Iraqi military surge—had far more influence on Arafat, and thus on the ultimate outcome of the Sharm el-Sheikh summit, than all of the promises, threats, and innuendoes that would be made there.

———

WHEN THE INTIFADAH BEGAN, Clinton had promised to hold a trilateral summit once the fighting subsided. This idea had evolved into an international summit, under conditions adversarial to Israel. The key attendees, in addition to Arafat, Barak, and Clinton, would be Mubarak, King Abdallah II of Jordan, and Kofi Annan.

The Sharm el-Sheikh summit, convened on October 16, was dominated by Clinton's desperate quest to clinch an agreement on the eve of the elections. Clinton was by then a wounded president and not really functioning, as demonstrated by his muted reaction to the attack on the USS *Cole*. For his own political reasons—to redeem himself after the successive failures of past Israeli-Palestinian agreements—he cared solely about the narrow Israeli-PA issue even though it had become irrelevant from a strategic point of view. In spite of Mubarak's warning about the importance of regional strategic issues, Clinton and his team were obsessed with Sharon's visit to the Temple Mount and whether the IDF's periodic use of tanks and helicopters did or did not constitute "excessive use of force." Barak continued to faithfully follow Clinton's priorities, unilaterally yielding on the long list of specific security-related steps Arafat was supposed to have implemented as a precondition to any Israeli agreement to renew negotiations.

Arafat himself was largely passive throughout the summit. He knew he had already lost the strategic leadership in the region to Baghdad and Tehran, but he remained determined to retain his tactical prominence. The escalation of violence still offered him a chance at instigating a regional war in which he would become if not the new Saladin, then at least the Saladin-maker. Clinton and Barak missed this point completely.

By the end of the summit, and despite Clinton's staying for an extra day, the parties had proved unable to reach an agreed-upon resolution. Instead, they agreed on a message to be read by Clinton. The key decision was the establishment of the Mitchell Commission, headed by former Senate majority leader George Mitchell, to investigate the causes of the Intifadah and produce a road map for solving the crisis. (The prospects for this "road map" were slim from the outset. Its model, the Mitchell Peace Plan for Northern Ireland, was already collapsing, despite massive unilateral concessions by the British government, which ignored systematic violations by the IRA, particularly regarding disarmament and cessation of violence.) The rest of Clinton's message called for the cessation of hostilities and the establishment of mechanisms—all CIA-supervised—for monitoring the yet-to-be defined cease-fire and revived security cooperation. The only clear-cut components of this process were the withdrawal of Israeli tanks and forces from positions captured during the past few weeks, the lifting of Israeli sieges of Arab cities, and other unilateral "confidence-building measures."

Clinton rejected Israel's demands that the PA re-arrest known terrorists, confiscate illegal weapons, and stop shooting attacks on Israeli civilians—particularly by Fatah's Tanzim and Arafat's own Force 17. In a conversation with Barak, Clinton insisted that pushing these demands would cause the summit to collapse, which would be much worse for Israel than having an unfavorable resolution of the conflict. Barak and Ben-Ami accepted Clinton's assurances. In a post-summit briefing, Danny Yatom echoed Clinton's line: Yes, there were problems with "HAMAS-to-Tanzim" violence, he acknowledged, but Arafat was still the legitimate controlling entity with whom negotiations must continue. Therefore, Arafat must be given the opportunity to prove he was a real partner for peace.

Immediately after the Sharm el-Sheikh summit, in compliance with Clinton's demands, the IDF began to withdraw its tanks. As expected, the Tanzim and the PA security forces exploited these withdrawals to launch massive attacks on Israeli positions throughout the Gaza Strip and the West Bank, including the Gilo neighborhood. Concurrently, PA officials stalled on meetings with the CIA representatives and their Israeli counterparts; Arafat even denied the existence of a five-point secret agreement, reached in Sharm el-Sheikh, between Tenet and his protégé Rajub, specifying agreed-upon practical steps to calm down the territories and suppress Islamist terrorism. However, the PA kept insisting that Israel stick to the original timetable for confidence-building steps; Israel was to ignore the escalation in attacks by the Tanzim and the PA security forces, because they were not controlled by Arafat—and the Clinton declaration referred only to Arafat-related activities. The White House would not comment on these Palestinian interpretations, refused to address "secret agreements"—thus tacitly endorsing Arafat's refusal to abide by the just-reached Tenet-Rajub agreement—and merely implored "both sides" to demonstrate restraint and goodwill. Little wonder that Palestinian leaders—including Yassin and Barghouti—announced that they did not consider the Sharm el-Sheikh agreement binding.

By late October, Arafat, in collaboration with Barghouti and other leaders, had reduced the "popular" element of the Intifadah—such as the use of children to confront the IDF—and instead placed growing reliance on controllable and disciplined forces such as the Tanzim and elements of the PA security forces. This shift was clearly demonstrated during the October 19 "field trip" incident. A group of settlers hiking in Area C made a wrong turn and emerged on a cliff overlooking Nablus. Tanzim and PA security forces attacked them with automatic fire, causing numerous casualties, including fatalities. Despite Israeli coordination with Rajub on the evacuation of the wounded, the PA security forces continued to fire on the med-evac helicopters, as well as on the IDF troops that attempted to evacuate the other hikers. When the White House was informed of the clash, Tenet called Arafat and "demanded" that PA security forces be immediately dispatched to stop the fighting and assist in the evacuation. Arafat replied ambiguously, and intense fighting continued for five hours. Israeli intelligence obtained irrefutable proof that "the highest authorities in the PLO/PA"—a euphemism for Arafat—had ordered the continuation of the fighting.

For Israel, the "field trip" incident was a gross violation not only of the cease-fire but also of all existing security coordination arrangements, including "understandings" reached during and after the Joseph's Tomb crisis only a couple of weeks earlier. For the Palestinians, the absence of massive IDF retaliation constituted a license to escalate their fighting. Arafat tacitly encouraged the escalation. He even joked that he would be talking, in English, about peace during the forthcoming escalation.

The Clinton administration could no longer ignore the travesty of the Palestinian approach to implementing the Sharm el-Sheikh agreement. However, Clinton and Albright reacted by privately pushing Arab leaders to persuade Arafat to reduce hostilities until after the U.S. elections in order to assist Al Gore and Hillary Clinton. Clinton and Albright promised to pay Arafat back with Israeli concessions not only in the interim period but also in the intense final-status negotiations the White House planned for soon after the elections. Albright also asked Crown Prince Abdallah of Saudi Arabia to help persuade Bashar al-Assad—who was invited to Riyadh for the purpose—to reduce Syria's level of support for HizbAllah. This initiative failed miserably, despite the strong efforts of Crown Prince Abdallah and promises of lavish foreign aid to Syria from Saudi Arabia and the Gulf States. Albright's reckless move only convinced official Riyadh that the Clinton administration did not care about the Saudis or about the Arabs as a whole. This conviction was intensified by the administration's failure, while formulating its own policy toward Baghdad, to take account of the mounting Iraqi threat to Saudi Arabia.

18

"The Price of Legacy" (2000)

Riyadh's Dilemma; Enter the "Chechens"

IN LATE OCTOBER, while Clinton was still talking Israeli-Palestinian peace, Saddam and Arafat were doing their best to push the Middle East toward war. But other Arab leaders were not yet ready for the escalation Arafat and Saddam sought. "War is not a game," Mubarak stated on October 19, on the eve of an Arab League summit meeting that he was hosting. "Whoever speaks of war does not know of its cost. If there are people who want us to fight down to the last Egyptian soldier, we are not prepared for that." However, not to be left out of any eruption, Mubarak ordered his military to intensify their preparations.

The Arab Summit held in Cairo on October 21–22 proved to be extraordinarily acrimonious. That the conservative Arab leaders' anxieties were well founded was confirmed when, in a closed meeting, Arafat threatened a flare-up of the entire region if the other leaders did not support his demands. He claimed that Israel was "slaughtering" the Palestinians, but insisted he would not compromise on the key issues of independence, Jerusalem, and the right of return. Not to be accused of abandoning the Palestinians, the Arab leaders committed to donating over $1 billion—in two tightly controlled funds, however, so that Arafat would not see a penny for almost a year.

Their honest opinion did not come out until Crown Prince Abdallah had the opportunity to discuss matters privately with his fellow Gulf State leaders. They were all aware that, from the very beginning of the PLO, Arafat had wanted to create a set of circumstances in which Arab armies would destroy Israel and liberate Palestine for him. The twist in the current situation, the conservative leaders noted, was that Saddam Hussein was getting closer

373

to realizing Arafat's hopes, while Mubarak was convinced that any such eruption would further his own quest for the leadership of the Arab world.

Meanwhile, a bellicose Arafat, returning to Gaza from the Cairo summit, got out of his Mercedes, grabbed a Kalashnikov assault rifle from one of his guards, and brandished it while surveying his honor guard. "The Palestinian people is persevering on its way to Jerusalem—our future capital," Arafat told the jubilant crowd. "And if Barak does not like it—let him go to hell!"

———

BY LATE OCTOBER, Saddam and Arafat, with help from Mubarak, were implementing a two-phase plan: (1) escalating the Intifadah al-Quds to the point where the ensuing upsurge of the Arab street would provide the justification for all other Arab leaders to join the jihad, and (2) provoking a regional conflagration that would implicate both the United States and Saudi Arabia in such a way as to force all other Arab leaders to join the jihad. And that jihad would be for the liberation of *all* the Holy Shrines—not only Jerusalem but Mecca and Medina as well.

Therefore, although the Israeli-Palestinian clashes subsided in the last week of October, the reduction in Palestinian strikes was misleading. A temporary shortage of ammunition caused the lull, but ammunition would be available again after modification of the clandestine supply lines from Iraq via Jordan and from Egypt across the Sinai Peninsula. These supply lines were temporarily shut down to adapt them to handle larger quantities of ammunition as well as heavy weapons (mortars, small-caliber artillery, heavy machine-guns, anti-aircraft weapons, and the like).

Saddam and Arafat personally coordinated the plans for escalating the Intifadah al-Quds, including the related destabilization of Jordan, using direct channels of communication, outside the normal Iraqi-PLO channels. On a day-to-day basis, these contacts were handled by Saddam's son Uday and Arafat's loyal confidant Muhammad Zaidan Abbas—Abu-al-Abbas, of *Achille Lauro* fame.

Their first priority was destabilization of King Abdallah II to condition Jordan for the Iraqi surge westward. Toward this end, Iraqi and Palestinian intelligence operatives—in close cooperation with HAMAS and the Jordanian Ikhwan—organized a myriad of "grassroots" activities, particularly widespread solidarity demonstrations. On October 24, the Iraqi-Palestinian effort passed a major milestone with the launch of the first popular march on Israel. The organizers were able to mobilize from 15,000 to 20,000 marchers—only two-thirds of them Palestinians—to start walking from the Amman area toward the border crossing with Israel. It took the entire Jordanian Special Forces and riot police to finally block the marchers near

Karame—some two and a half miles from the Jordan River. On October 27, the Friday sermons were especially fiery throughout Jordan, and the incited mobs poured into the streets clearly expressing their support for the jihad. The Islamists actively recruited volunteers to join the Palestinian jihad from throughout Jordan, and Amman was warned not to dare block their travel across the Jordan River. King Abdallah got the message, and Jordanian security forces did not interfere with the sizable flow of arms, ammunition, and volunteers to the West Bank.

By late October, the Iraqi forces were ready to surge forward. The Hammurabi Division of the elite Republican Guard was already deployed around the H-3 military compound, roughly fifteen miles from the Jordanian border. The Hammurabi Division was the forward element of al-Quds Corps, which included five heavy divisions as well as dedicated units of heavy artillery and tactical missiles capable of carrying weapons of mass destruction. Now, one of these divisions started to advance toward Syria on a road leading to the Golan front. As agreed by Bashar and Qusay in their secret meeting in early October, the Syrians would provide an anti-aircraft umbrella against possible Israeli air strikes.

A novel aspect of this Iraqi deployment was its preparations for adding a human shield. The Iraqi authorities deployed buses and trucks to all the cities and townships between the western suburbs of Baghdad and the Jordanian border. Mobilization orders were issued to an estimated 500,000 to 650,000 women and children to "volunteer" to accompany al-Quds Corps on its road to "the jihad front." Baghdad was convinced that the mere presence of such a large number of innocent civilians would complicate any Israeli decision to bomb the Iraqi army column; if Israel did bomb, then the images of civilian casualties would turn the world's public opinion against Israel.

Concurrently, another, smaller force, led by a brigade of the Nebuchadnezzar Division of the Republican Guard, was poised to cross the Saudi border between the neutral zone and Rafha. This force was also to be accompanied by human-shield "volunteers."

Neither of these Iraqi expeditionary forces was capable of deciding a war, and both were vulnerable to air strikes by Israel and the United States. However, the issue was not the military capabilities of these expeditionary forces but the political and strategic implications of their mere existence. Baghdad was fully aware of the relevant "red lines"—namely, that the United States would immediately bomb any Iraqi force skirting the Saudi or Kuwaiti border and that Israel would do the same to any Iraqi force getting too close to the Jordanian border. Both Jerusalem and Washington had recently reiterated to Baghdad—via Cairo and Paris—the validity of these "red lines" despite reports about the human shield.

The implications for Riyadh were horrendous. If U.S. warplanes, operating out of bases on Saudi territory, attacked the Iraqi expeditionary forces, Arab propaganda would be able to portray Saudi Arabia as siding with Israel and the United States against the rest of the Arab Nation. Such incitement was bound to motivate the Saudi Islamists and radical Arabists to rebel against the House of al-Saud. Alternatively, if the United States did *not* bomb the Iraqi forces and they crossed into Saudi Arabia, their mere presence was bound to instigate anti-Riyadh riots and rebellions.

Throughout these maneuverings, Saddam and Clinton were playing with fire and into each other's hands. Washington had long been seeking excuses to confront Iraq, only to be prevented at the last minute—for example, by Mubarak's intervention back in mid-September. Now the Clinton administration had plausible reasons to revisit the deal with Egypt. There were Iraqi "fingerprints," as well as Iranian, all over the strike against the USS *Cole*. Beyond that, the White House took seriously Saddam's recent threats to stop the "smuggling" of Iraqi oil to the West and even to sabotage Kuwaiti oil facilities because the continued climb in oil prices was adversely affecting Gore's candidacy. On top of everything else, Clinton considered the predominantly Arab airlift to Baghdad to be a personal insult. Hence, Clinton had numerous personal and political incentives to strike hard against Iraq. However, he also knew that an American strike would bring about the very explosion Saddam was yearning for.

————

ON OCTOBER 26, the Intifadah resumed with a suicide bombing by a boy riding a bicycle near Gush Katif. The bomb caused no damage and no casualties—except for the boy himself—but it heralded the Islamists' return to the armed struggle. Concurrently, there was an increase in ambushes aimed at civilian transportation and roadside bombs aimed at Israeli patrols. Late October also saw the beginning of systematic arson at factories and other businesses in Area A and in free-trade border zones in the Gaza Strip, where both Americans and Israelis had invested money to assist the Palestinian population's economic recovery. Arafat's security personnel undertook a campaign of vandalism to break down the last bit of grassroots Israeli-Palestinian cooperation benefiting the average Palestinian. Consequently, more Palestinians, out of work and embittered, joined the mob violence, if only to get the meager subsidies provided to the Shabab.

By now, Israeli intelligence had evidence—which the United States concurred was irrefutable—that Arafat's closest aides were directly in charge of the escalation. Faced with this evidence, Barak sent his confidant Yossi Ginossar to meet secretly with Arafat and Dahlan in Gaza to discuss resuming negotiations. Ginossar's initiative was rebuffed, as was one by General Amnon Shahak. Palestinian senior officials got the impression that Arafat was deliberately humiliating Barak and attempting to bring down his government.

In fact, Arafat and his coterie were preoccupied with securing their own position against yet another challenge, this one from militant Fatah senior commanders. According to Palestinian sources, many of these commanders now "regard[ed] Arafat as an aging and feeble leader who must be replaced with the establishment of a Palestinian state." Arafat was fully aware of the dynamics within the Palestinian armed movement. He knew that he could retain control only by escalating the armed struggle. However, he was in a bind because of delays in the arrival of the expected weapon convoys from Sudan and Egypt to Gaza and from Iraq via Jordan to the West Bank. And so he needed to pursue two contradictory policies simultaneously. To retain the respect of the Palestinians and their militant leaders, he had to demonstrate defiance by unleashing spectacular terrorist acts in Israel. At the same time, he had to prevent Israel from implementing its retaliatory plans before his own preparations were complete. Toward that end, Arafat maneuvered to generate greater pressure on Barak through the Clinton administration.

First, he personally ordered a series of spectacular terrorist strikes in the main Israeli cities. The key perpetrators were to be members of his own teams—drawn from the Fatah's Tanzim units under Marwan Barghouti, the Preventive Security Service in Gaza under Muhammad Dahlan, and the Preventive Security Service in the West Bank under Jibril Rajub. Only Arafat himself could have ordered such close cooperation among these security bodies and their chieftains. Arafat also authorized cooperation with the Islamic Jihad and HAMAS networks so that they could claim a role in the forthcoming wave of terrorism. This was a very pragmatic decision because only the Islamists were capable of quickly delivering the martyr-terrorists that some of the operations would require.

The first strike took place on October 30. Two men emerged from the PA's compound near Orient House in East Jerusalem, walked casually to the East Jerusalem branch of the Israeli Social Security on Saladin Street, and shot the two security guards at close range, killing one outright and fatally wounding the other. The two hit men escaped into the PA compound. Subsequent investigation identified them as members of Barghouti's Tanzim special units from the Kalandia and al-Umari refugee camps, located between Jerusalem and Ramallah. Rajub's security agents, operating in the Orient House compound, facilitated the operation.

Arafat was alarmed by the fury this operation aroused in Israel and by the killing of three IDF personnel in other clashes with Tanzim forces. Hence, he quickly arranged a nocturnal meeting with Shimon Peres. In that meeting, Peres warned Arafat of the grave consequences of continuing the escalation. Peres also essentially told Arafat that the Israeli government had just voted to instruct the IDF to enter the key West Bank cities and evict Arafat's people. Arafat persuaded Peres to arrange the postponement of the IDF strikes by promising to issue a joint public announcement with Barak the next morning in which both leaders would call for the cessation of hostilities. That night, Peres's confidants leaked the essence of his agreement with Arafat, and Barak—fearful of tarnishing his image as a peacemaker—agreed to go along, against the explicit warnings of Israeli intelligence that Arafat was buying time while preparing to launch the next round of violence.

––––––––

WITH ISRAELI and Arab media highlighting his agreement with Peres, Arafat had to quickly correct his image in the eyes of the militants. Therefore, on the morning of November 2, while Barak was waiting for him to call and partake in their joint announcement, Arafat was busy talking on the phone to his lieutenants.

At 10:30 A.M., sitting in his office in Gaza, Arafat made his first call to Barghouti, who was in a police station in Ramallah. Barghouti was overjoyed to hear the chairman's voice, because Arafat had repeatedly refused to talk to him in the last few days. Now, Arafat was praising him and the Tanzim, and reassuring him that the overall "war situation" was furthering the Palestinians' interests. When Arafat demanded that he expand the Tanzim operations, however, Barghouti complained that the Tanzim had run out of funds. Arafat replied that the shortage of funds made it imperative to escalate the fighting—in order to generate more funds. "The Americans, the Israelis, and the Europeans have stopped sending money," Arafat explained. "The only place left to raise cash is from the Arabs. To get money out of them we have to show what we can do, so it's up to you to put as much pressure as you can on the Jews." Arafat did not mention any cessation of fighting, let alone the cease-fire agreement he had just reached with Peres.

Then, between 12 noon and 1 P.M., Arafat made another call, this one to someone in Dahlan's office in Gaza, and ordered the implementation of a terrorist operation in Jerusalem that had been planned but put on hold. Soon afterward, Gaza called Jerusalem with the coded authorization to strike; and soon after that, a car bomb exploded in the Mahne Yehuda market, killing two and wounding a dozen. The Israeli investigation determined that the car bomb had been constructed and hidden in the Wadi Juzz neighborhood of Jerusalem. The perpetrators were highly trained Tanzim operatives from the Kalandia and al-Umari refugee camps, supported by Rajub's agents in East Jerusalem. In retrospect, it was clear why, for the past few days, cars belonging to Rajub's people had been seen racing through the streets surrounding Mahne Yehuda in the predawn hours: The getaway teams were conducting training exercises. On November 2, once Arafat's authorization was transmitted from Gaza, Rajub's team drove the terrorists to Wadi Juzz and then discreetly escorted them as they drove the car bomb to a narrow street near the Mahne Yehuda market and parked it. The terrorists then loitered in the area, visiting various stores while waiting for a call on their cell phone. Around 3 P.M., they received the authorization, exploded the bomb by remote control, and vanished in one of Rajub's cars.

The car bomb caused so few casualties because Israeli police, knowing that Arafat had ordered a new round of terrorist operations, had forbidden automobile access to the market itself. One of the police sources was Nihad Ahmad Ibrahim, a twenty-five-year-old policeman from Arafat's own compound in Gaza. In late October, he volunteered for an important mission and was accepted because of his "Jewish looks," which included an elegantly trimmed beard and a gold earring in his right ear. On October 30, Nihad was dispatched from Gaza to Nazareth carrying a powerful anti-personnel bomb in a briefcase. He was to hand the bomb to an Israeli Arab who in turn was to blow it up in either Tel Aviv or Haifa on November 2. Nihad was captured by the Israeli security services on the night of November 1–2 with the bomb in his hand.

Meanwhile, to reduce the pressure on Arafat, and on the basis of a prior agreement with Fatah, Islamic Jihad claimed responsibility for the Jerusalem bombing. This trick didn't mollify Barak, who was still waiting for Arafat to call so that they could jointly renounce violence and reiterate their commitment to the peace process. However, the next day, having realized the extent of the information Israel had obtained from the captured Nihad, Arafat announced that he was going to Washington. It was the only way he could induce Clinton to pressure Barak not to do anything that might threaten the resumption of the peace process.

By now, the delayed weapon convoys were finally reaching the PA-held areas and southern Lebanon. A ship carrying ammunition, explosives, and weapons, including Katyusha rockets, arrived in the Sinai from Sudan. From there, Egyptian Military Intelligence helped the Palestinians smuggle the matériel into the Gaza Strip via underground tunnels. With a range exceeding 20 miles, the Katyusha rockets could hit the Israeli ports and electricity-generating plants in Ashkelon and Ashdod. Meanwhile, an Iraqi convoy carrying comparable weapons, as well as shoulder-fired anti-aircraft missiles, raced across Jordan to the Jericho area. According to Palestinian sources, these weapons were intended, among other things, to shut down Israel's main airport, the Ben Gurion Airport near Tel Aviv. In addition, hundreds of

Iranian-made Katyushas with ranges exceeding 35 miles arrived in southern Lebanon via Damascus. These rockets could hit Haifa—a major port city and industrial center—and most of northern Israel.

On November 5, Abdallah al-Shami, the number two official in the Palestinian Islamic Jihad, confirmed that his organization now enjoyed "greater freedom of action" due to support from the PA security forces. He added that the entire Palestinian leadership and resistance movement—including Arafat's people—were determined that "in the territory of historic Palestine there will never be two states. There will be a single state—a Palestinian State—and if the Jews want to live with us, they are welcome to live in the Palestinian state, provided they abide by and respect its laws and regulations."

———

IN VIEW OF Arafat's stonewalling on issuing the joint statement with Barak, and given the increase in his military capabilities, the IDF General Staff produced a new assessment of the preferable strategy for coping with him. The key to the containment and ultimate defeat of the Palestinian forces, the high command now believed, was in evicting Arafat and his coterie from the territories. Barak sent these recommendations back, declaring that any Israeli strategy must be formulated in the context of the peace process. In response to American pressure, he did not even permit the IDF to strike at any of the weapon resupply efforts, despite advance knowledge. And so Barak once again proved that he would rather ignore the mounting threat to Israel than disappoint the lame-duck president of the United States.

Yet, despite his faithful cooperation, Barak could not get the White House to publicly support him. Albright stated repeatedly that the situation was a "great tragedy" and urged both sides to return to the negotiating table. "Senior administration and White House officials"—as described by their Israeli counterparts—even cautiously raised the possibility of Jerusalem's accepting Arafat's demand for international observers in the territories. Barak said he would consider it if Clinton publicly admitted that the Palestinians were responsible for the outbreak of hostilities. Clinton refused. Throughout, senior U.S. officials maintained a careful symmetry, as if both sides were equally to blame. With the political crisis in Israel mounting, Barak insisted that he felt "obliged" to accept Clinton's request to strive for "an agreement." His approval ratings plummeted.

The U.S. elections took place on November 7, followed by the bitter and protracted crisis over the Florida vote count. This drama captured the attention of most Americans, and certainly of the U.S. media. Out of the limelight for the first time in more than eight years, Clinton concentrated on coercing and cajoling Israel into delivering his legacy, even if at the last minute.

———

IT WAS ALSO on November 7 that Egypt and Iraq formally renewed their diplomatic relations, with their respective interest offices becoming embassies. The Iraqi ambassador to Cairo delivered a special message from Saddam to Mubarak urging all-out mobilization to confront the growing regional threat.

Not long afterward, a major threshold was crossed when Saudi Arabia agreed to open its border with Iraq and begin the process of normalizing relations. This change resulted from the movements of the Iraqi armed forces in October, which had threatened to place Saudi Arabia in a de facto alliance with Israel and the United States against the rest of the Arab world. The only way for Riyadh to get out of this untenable position was through a rapprochement with Saddam. And Cairo's resumption of full diplomatic relations with Baghdad in the name of Arab unity had tipped the balance for Riyadh. Thus boxed in, Saudi Arabia took sides in a dangerous conflict the House of al-Saud had been desperate to avoid. Consequently, two major elements in the Arab preparations for war fell into place: (1) there would be no U.S. military intervention from bases in the Arabian Peninsula, and (2) there would be an effective oil embargo against the West in case of a regional eruption.

The Israeli national-security elite—including the high commands of the IDF, Mossad, and the Shin-Beth—responded to these developments by taking the unprecedented step of establishing, with the tacit support of Israel's political leaders across the board, a de facto unified wartime high command. Under this unique arrangement, Chief of Staff Mofaz was the de facto supreme commander, charged with pulling together all the military and security preparations for meeting both a major escalation of the Intifadah and the anticipated regional war dominated by Syria, Iraq, Iran, and Egypt.

This move had started as an off-the-record initiative in response to the Barak government's reluctance to confront the real security challenges facing Israel. As part of Barak's "peace policy," for example, he had imposed deep budget cuts on the IDF, leading to emaciated wartime supplies. Several senior officers were convinced that Israel would require a massive American airlift in order to fight a lengthy war. Therefore, the de facto unified high command invited their American counterparts for an informal "pow-wow" in Eilat the weekend of November 3–5. At this session—chaired by the director-general of the Israeli Defense Ministry, Amos Yaron, and the U.S. assistant secretary of state, Eric Newsom—intelligence officials and military commanders reviewed and compared their regional threat assessments. The consensus that emerged saw imminent danger coming from both the long-range threats posed by Iran and Iraq and the threat of a regional war involving all of Israel's neighbors, irrespective of signed peace agreements. "It was one of the most dramatic changes in the strategic map," declared an Israeli participant.

In a cabinet meeting on November 5, the now emboldened de facto high command made a joint presentation challenging the government's reading of the situation and particularly the likelihood of reviving the peace process. Led by the chief of Military Intelligence, Major General Amos Malka, and the chief of the IDF Intelligence Research Division, Brigadier General Amos Gilad, the briefers did not try to conceal their coordination. On the contrary, they presented their appearance before the Cabinet as the first outward manifestation of the de facto unified high command.

The cabinet tacitly accepted this development for reasons of expediency. By doing so, Barak could continue pursuing his peace policy and avoid any formal alliance with Sharon while Israel's national-security elite proceeded with preparations for war. Indeed, for all subsequent key political-military moves, the de facto high command asked for the approval of the Knesset— thus establishing a wide national consensus—rather than of the narrow and effectively paralyzed Barak government. For example, on November 7, Chief of Staff Mofaz led a group of senior intelligence officers to the Knesset Foreign Affairs and Defense Committee to warn of the Arabs' war preparations and ask for emergency budget approval. In his introductory comments, Mofaz stated that "the likelihood of a full-scale regional conflict is now greater than it has been at any time in the past several years." The intelligence officers who followed noted that "Syria is willing to go to war with Israel if its interests in Lebanon are damaged, and is convinced that it could win such a war" and that "Iran is working behind the scenes to bring about a regional escalation." The briefers also warned that the Palestinians and their allies were pushing for "regime changes"—namely, the overthrow of moderate governments and rulers they perceived to be hostile, starting with Jordan's King Abdallah II.

The new Israeli intelligence assessment concentrated on the realization that all the key militant players in the Middle East had their own reasons for wanting to escalate the Intifadah al-Aqsa into a regional war. Saddam envisioned a Ba'athist empire encompassing Syria and Lebanon and parts of Jordan. Arafat was dreaming of a Greater Palestine that included parts of Israel (delivered to him by an uprising of the Israeli Arabs), Jordan, Lebanon (dominated by radical Muslims and the Palestinians), and the Sinai. The Iranians and the Syrians saw the current conflict as a rare opportunity to change the balance of power in their favor.

And Egypt, because of its powerful, U.S.-equipped armed forces, played an especially significant role. In the first place, given the militancy of the Egyptian population—to a degree not seen since the populist hysteria on the eve of the Six-Day War in 1967—Egypt would have to participate in any jihad or risk a popular/military uprising. Mubarak also wanted to use the crisis atmosphere to get the Egyptian military establishment to back his son Gamal as Egypt's next President. If war did break out, Mubarak hoped to gain his long-sought on-land access to the Mashriq. As well, he was convinced that neither Saddam nor Arafat would be accepted as an all-Arab leader; consequently, he would be able to step in as the leader capable of rehabilitating the postwar Arab world and rebuilding bridges to the West, including arranging for financial and military aid.

The de facto high command was in tune with the Israeli public. Most Israelis had definitely given up on the peace process; they wanted to return to the policy of security-through-deterrence that had worked so well for Israel for most of its existence. However, the majority of Israelis were convinced that only a major war—with its inevitable casualties and destruction of property—could at this point deliver such a posture. Israel had resigned itself to the prospect of immense pain on the road to national recovery. If such a war did not erupt before the next Israeli elections, the voters would surely install as prime minister the leader perceived as best suited to lead the nation through war and back to the proven security-through-deterrence policy. Barak was not on anybody's list of viable candidates except his own.

———

AGAINST THIS BACKGROUND, Clinton, Barak, and Arafat—aided by the soon-to-retire but indefatigable Dennis Ross, who was once again shuttling around the Middle East—were jockeying for a last-ditch summit in Washington in which each planned to squeeze out a dramatic gain.

Clinton wanted to have a summit at the White House that would produce, at the least, "an agreement on principles." He knew that the first priority of the next president of the United States—whether it proved to be Gore or Bush—would be to soothe the bitterness and frustration engendered by the Florida vote-count fiasco. The brand-new president would not have time to deal with a Middle East on the verge of eruption. Clinton was essentially setting up the circumstances for him to be called upon as a super-emissary on behalf of that president (something akin to Jimmy Carter's role in North

Korea and Bosnia). And therein lay the prospect for Clinton's gaining his legacy after all—perhaps even the elusive Nobel Peace Price.

Barak wanted the Clinton administration to bless the principles for an interim agreement with the Palestinians that would enable him to restrain the IDF's inclination to contain the Palestinian escalation by force. Barak (whose approval ratings were approaching single digits) believed he could then use the American endorsement of his policy as the foundation of his "Peace Platform" in the upcoming elections. Under Barak's plan the United States would persuade Arafat to accept the IDF's temporary presence in its current positions in the Gaza Strip in exchange for a unilateral Israeli withdrawal to defensive positions in the West Bank that would leave about 40 percent of the territory in Israeli hands and transform the remaining 60 percent into a de facto Area A—that is, full PA control. By legal definition, these would be "interim lines of separation," to hold until the permanent agreement on borders, the fate of Jerusalem, and the right of return were negotiated at an undetermined future time.

Arafat, the most pragmatic of the three, wanted to improve the opening conditions for the eruption to come. Specifically, he wanted Clinton and the United Nations to force Israel to treat the Palestinian cities in Area A as Bosnia-style sanctuary zones protected by international observers. Like the Bosnian Muslims, the Palestinians would then be able to strike out from these zones with impunity, as the international observers prevented Israel from retaliating. This idea was at the core of Arafat's offer of a unilateral cease-fire in Area A. The lure of a White House agreement, Arafat was convinced, would make Clinton swallow this idea—which, after all, he had supported in Bosnia. If, to attain this, Arafat had to see Clinton and Barak one more time in Washington, so be it.

———

BY THE FALL of 2000, Islamist movements all over the world were putting the struggle for the liberation of al-Aqsa ahead of their own jihads. Notable among these were the Chechen mujahideen.

The Chechens' awareness of the Palestinian jihad stemmed from an emerging trend in Chechen Islamist incitement. In the early summer of 2000, after near defeat by the Russian forces, the Chechen leadership resorted to a classic among Islamist terrorist movements—invoking the "international Jewish conspiracy," an always-available means for an Islamist movement to justify a major setback in its divine jihad.

At this point, the harshest anti-Jewish sentiments were expressed by "Abu-Omar"—the nom-de-guerre of a Chechen commander close to Khattab, then the senior Arab mujahideen commander in Chechnya. However, anti-Jewish incitement was common among Chechen commanders. For example, early in the summer, one of these commanders, Arby Barayev, had stated on television: "The Jews are our enemies, and we will kill them, kidnap and rob them everywhere we meet them." Indeed, a number of Jews, including Israeli citizens, were kidnapped and tortured in Chechnya. Some, including young children and the elderly, were cruelly maimed in order to extract higher ransoms.

On October 8, the Chechen leadership committed itself to supporting the Palestinian jihad when Shamil Basayev, amir of the Supreme Military Majlis ul-Shura of the Mujahideen of the Caucasus chaired an extraordinary session of that body. As reported by Chechen Web sites, "The Supreme Military Majlis ul-Shura expressed its concern over the situation in Al-Quds (Jerusalem) and sharply condemned Israel for the mass killings of Muslims, calling the Israeli leadership the main ringleader of the new wave of violence on Palestinian land." The Majlis then decided the time had come to dispatch a detachment of 153 Chechen mujahideen "to al-Quds to help the Palestinian Muslims." Basayev noted that this detachment "is fully equipped with everything necessary and is capable of acting absolutely autonomously for a sufficiently long time." According to Basayev, this would be only the first Chechen contribution to the Palestinian jihad: "Chechnya is ready to supply 1,500 mujahideen to help the Muslims of Palestine." The Chechens were ready to make this sacrifice despite the escalation of their own war. "No matter what difficulties we experience," Basayev declared, "the main problem for all Muslims is the liberation of Al-Quds. Fighting in Chechnya does not relieve us of responsibility for this holy town."

This seemingly outlandish offer had to be taken seriously. Basayev was sincere in his commitment of 153 mujahideen, although not completely accurate as to where they would be coming from. They would be taken not from Chechnya itself but from training camps in Jordan, Turkey, and Pakistan/Afghanistan. Furthermore, many of them were not of Chechen nationality but were foreign volunteers. Even so, Basayev's diversion of these mujahideen to Israel was a genuine sacrifice, given the manpower shortages the Chechens were experiencing. His gesture manifested yet again the integration of the Chechen revolt into Osama bin Laden's movement, with its universal Islamist priorities taking precedence over the Chechens' own national interest.

A few days later, on October 16, the Chechen leadership issued a long and detailed document headed "URGENT LETTER TO OUR BROTHERS IN PALESTINE." "From the hills of Chechnya," this document began, ". . . we forward this urgent letter to our brothers in Palestine. Even if our homes are thousands of miles apart, our hearts could not be closer to you. We continue to grieve because our beloved Aqsa is in the hands of lawless occupiers, the Jews. Without doubt, they are the worst of all nations Allah has created." The document stressed that given the disparity in military capabilities between the Palestinians and the Israelis, the Intifadah—just like the Chechens' own jihad against the Russians—might take generations before triumph could be attained. "It is true that your weapons are nothing but mere stones. But in your land and in your hands, there is a difference. With you, every stone throws horror in the hearts of the Jews. With you, your stones become like weapons of mass destruction." The Chechens urged the Palestinians to follow their example of enduring losses and sacrifices. "Our nation is a ship, but unlike other ships it only floats in the blood of its sons. The less blood that is sacrificed for the sake of Allah, the lower our ship sinks. And should the blood run dry, then the ship will be destroyed." The document concluded with a specific commitment. "Finally, we promise you that soon, insha-Allah, you will hear of what we do with the brothers of the Jews, the Russians, in retaliation for Al-Aqsa and for you. Wait for a forthcoming operation which we have named 'Operation Al-Aqsa.' That is all that we can do to comfort you and heal your wounds."

There are reasons to suspect that the mid-November hijacking of a Russian Tu-154 aircraft from Makhachkala, Dagestan, was part of Operation Al-Aqsa. While supervising a refueling in Baku, a hijacker mentioned al-Aqsa in the context of his destination, which was Israel. The hijackers had demanded that they be flown to Israel's Ben Gurion airport; however, a pair of Israeli fighter jets forced the Tu-154 to land at the remote Negev airbase of Ovda. Once the airliner was on the ground, a lone, seemingly unbalanced individual claimed to have hijacked it in order "to warn the white race against the rise of the yellow peril." However, numerous questions still remain unanswered. For example, five people with false passports were on board, and both the Russian captain and the Azeri refueling team spoke about several hijackers. One possibility is that the hijackers planned on connecting with on-the-ground accomplices at Ben Gurion but, when forced to land at Ovda, called off the operation so that all but one of them could return to Russia as innocent passengers.

In any case, the "Chechens"—that is, Chechen mujahideen and Arab veterans of the war in Chechnya—started assuming prominent roles in the fighting against Israel, both in the ranks of Arafat's forces in the territories and with HizbAllah in Lebanon.

On November 16, a detachment crossed the Israeli-Lebanese border in the central zone—overlooking the upper Galilee—and traveled unhindered along a civilian road into the northern part of the Golan Heights. The detachment planted a large bomb alongside the Israeli patrol road and safely withdrew into southern Lebanon. The bomb, activated by remote control, went off slightly ahead of time and therefore caused damage but no Israeli casualties.

Subsequent investigation indicated that the remote-control mechanism used was new to the theater and therefore not covered by the myriad of electronic countermeasures used by the IDF. The main charge was concealed in a new fashion—in tree branches, not the "rocks" used by HizbAllah and its Iranian instructors—and therefore was not noticed by the IDF troops. The remote-control fuse, the overall bomb structure, and the form of camouflage were all typical of bombs used against the Russian forces in Chechnya. Moreover, after the operation was completed, a report was sent to the headquarters of the Secret Islamic Revolutionary Army—the Mughniyah–bin Laden operation in Lebanon.

The "Chechens" sent to the West Bank were predominantly Jordanian Circassians—many of them veterans of elite units of the Jordanian special forces and the royal security guard who had served in Chechnya and returned home—as well as Chechen volunteers, including war wounded who had received medical treatment in Jordan, Saudi Arabia, or the Gulf States. In Gaza, the "Chechens" were primarily Arabs—mostly Palestinians, Egyptians, and Saudi Arabians—who had fought with the mujahideen in Chechnya and had then been sent for advanced training to Afghanistan/Pakistan, from where they were diverted to Palestine. Again, there were numerous actual Chechens with them, most of whom had also been sent to the Afghan/Pakistani training programs. The "Chechens" reached Gaza via Egypt with the assistance of Egyptian Military Intelligence, through underground tunnels in the Rafah area or by sea in small fishing boats.

Most of the actual Chechens operating in the territories were experts in urban warfare and fortifications, brought in to teach the Palestinians the lessons of their bitter fighting in Grozny and other cities, where lightly armed Chechen forces engaged Russian heavy armored columns, causing extensive casualties to the Russians. The Palestinians knew that in case of a major escalation, the IDF was planning to use the same type of tactical approach the Russians had used. The Chechens were therefore devising tactics, training Palestinian commanders, and directing the building of fortifications in most Arab towns.

The other group of "Chechen" mujahideen were mostly Arabs with extensive operational experience, mainly as snipers and bomb-makers. They worked with Arafat's elite units and not only imparted their knowledge but also actually participated in operations. For example, the sniper who, on November 24, killed Israeli Major Sharon Arma while he was walking inside an Israeli divisional headquarters in the Gaza Strip was one of these Arab mujahideen.

Ultimately, the "Chechens" had a profound impact on the overall character of the Intifadah. Although they operated in the ranks of Arafat's own forces, they were fierce Islamists. Most of them had been handled via bin Laden's establishment—commonly known as al-Qaeda, meaning "the base" or "foundation"—and were committed to his message of uncompromising global jihad. Ideologically, they were also very close to HAMAS; a few of them had been members of the HAMAS Izz al-Din al-Qassim Brigades before leaving Gaza and Nablus for advanced training in Afghanistan/Pakistan. Thus, the prominent role of these "Chechens" in Arafat's special operations was bound to draw HAMAS into closer cooperation with his Fatah organization and thus further Islamicize the Intifadah.

IN THE SECOND HALF of November, Arafat crossed a major threshold with a series of terrorist bombings. In aggregate, these bombings sent the message that Arafat was no longer interested in any contact, clandestine or overt, with either the Clinton administration or the Barak government. In launching these strikes, Arafat's closest lieutenants—Muhammad Dahlan, Jibril Rajub, and Marwan Barghouti—implemented the chairman's instructions to completely disrupt all lines of communication between the Palestinian Authority and both Israel and the United States, at both the working level and the senior-official level (leaving only the emergency direct telephone channel Arafat maintained with the Clinton administration through the good offices of Mubarak and Prince Bandar bin Sultan).

The move was impelled by Arafat's and Barak's visits to Washington and New York earlier in the month. President Clinton had put strong pressure on Arafat to agree to a last-hurrah summit in Washington in late December or early January, just before Clinton left office. Clinton had also demanded that Arafat commit in advance that at the end of that summit he would sign, with Barak, some form of interim agreement on nonbelligerency and a commitment to peace between Israel and an ultimately independent Palestine.

Barak was willing to go along with Clinton's ideas even though the Israeli de facto high command bitterly opposed any additional Israeli concessions. On November 16, Barak publicly retracted a long-held Israeli "red line"—namely, that hostilities would have to end before Israel would agree to resume negotiations. "We will not check each and every [violent] event," Barak declared. "If over there, in some spot at the edge of the desert, somebody opens fire, this will not prevent us from attending the summit."

As for Arafat, he had no intention of signing any such agreement as Clinton demanded. However, since the cost of saying "no" to Clinton would be high, he decided that he could avoid the need to reply directly by bringing about the collapse of all communications. Although he might once have been willing to accept a mini-state in the 1967 boundaries—and some Palestinian leaders still were—this was no longer a viable option. Arafat's own Fatah and Tanzim forces, and even more so HAMAS and the Islamic Jihad, had conditioned their support for his leadership on his declaring an independent Palestine stretching "from the Sea to the River" (essentially, the entire British Mandate area and not just the West Bank and Gaza Strip, or even the area covered by the original 1947 Partition Plan) and inviting all refugees "to implement their right of return." According to Palestinian officials, the most likely date for the declaration of independence was December 31, 2000—the thirty-fifth anniversary of Fatah's first terrorist operation against Israel. Putting the declaration in the context of this anniversary would symbolize the Palestinians' resolve to continue with their struggle until their original objective was achieved: the destruction of Israel. Needless to say, not even the Israeli doves, nor most of the international community, could accept this objective. Such a declaration of independence would not be compatible with a return to the peace process.

———

AS OF MID-NOVEMBER, Arafat's coterie were convinced they had ample time to prepare the region for their declaration of independence and the regional war they expected to follow. Then their timetables were disrupted by Barak's eagerness to please Clinton virtually at all costs.

On the night of November 17, Barak secretly sent Amnon Shahak to offer Arafat and Dahlan new concessions and "confidence-building measures" suggested by Clinton. During this meeting, Arafat grasped how desperate Barak was to end the violence. Arafat and Dahlan first insisted they had nothing to do with the spread of terrorism. Shahak responded by presenting Israeli intelligence connecting Dahlan directly both to the wholesale release of Islamist terrorists from Palestinian jails and to major attacks on Israeli settlements and clashes with the IDF. Arafat immediately demanded a guarantee from Israel that Dahlan would not be assassinated. To their amazement, Shahak called Barak on the spot, and Barak agreed. Deprived of any legitimate excuse for breaking off negotiations, Arafat and Dahlan decided that the disruption of contacts must be expedited and made drastic and irreversible. They made this decision just as a buoyant Shahak was reporting to Barak the "successful and promising outcome" of his secret talks.

The Palestinians' first move came in the early morning of November 18—that is, just a few hours after Shahak's visit. A lone Palestinian entered a forward Israeli position manned by three Golani Brigade soldiers near Kfar Darom in the Gaza Strip. The Palestinian fired his Kalashnikov from close range (4–5 yards), killing one soldier and mortally wounding another before the third soldier in the position, himself also slightly wounded, gunned the assailant down.

With this incident, Arafat sent a direct and clear message that the Palestinians were no longer interested in the communications regime established back in 1996 and resuscitated by President Clinton following the Sharm el-Sheikh summit. Significantly, this system of communications was personally run by CIA Director George Tenet—perhaps Arafat's most loyal supporter in the Clinton administration. Tenet had originally established it when the CIA was supposed to be the supervisor, facilitator, and arbiter of Israeli-Palestinian cooperation in fighting Islamist terrorism. As relations between Israel and the Palestinian Authority deteriorated, Tenet had the CIA step in and become the mediator, and ultimately sole venue of communications, between the Israeli and Palestinian security services. In order to ensure the Palestinians' cooperation, the CIA lavished training, sophisticated equipment, and operational funds on their security and intelligence services. Throughout, Tenet insisted on hands-on involvement, developing in the process strong personal bonds with Arafat and Dahlan. Indeed, the U.S. government had recently requested Israel to take Dahlan's nephew, who had been severely wounded in a clash with the IDF, for emergency treatment at a Tel Aviv hospital (where he eventually died).

At the core of Tenet's communications channels were a few "safe corridors" across the Israeli lines that enabled Palestinian senior officials and their emissaries to go clandestinely to meetings with CIA officials arriving from the Agency's station in Tel Aviv. Despite its misgivings about foreign intelligence activities on its soil, the Barak government had succumbed to the insistence of Clinton, Albright, and Tenet that such direct personal contacts with Arafat's inner circle were crucial to sustaining the peace process.

Physically, the primary communications channel with Gaza was a corridor leading from Israel near Kfar Darom, through a greenhouse area, then along the edge of a camp for both foreign workers from the Far East and Palestinian workers, and then into a PA-controlled zone. The routine presence of so many diverse people enabled emissaries to blend in when approaching the corridor from either end. Moreover, large segments of the passageway were intentionally hidden from the view of the Israeli observation positions. IDF troops were instructed not to challenge Palestinians rushing through the corridor in the middle of the night.

Early in the morning of Saturday, November 18, Bahaa Adi Said, a twenty-nine-year-old major in Dahlan's Preventive Security Service, entered the corridor. He proceeded unchallenged across the Israeli lines, but then suddenly slipped under a loose barbed-wire fence, entered the IDF's forward observation post, and opened fire on its startled occupants. At the PLO's request, his body was immediately returned to the Palestinian Authority. At the funeral, it became clear that Bahaa Adi Said was no ordinary security officer. He was a veteran member of Arafat's own Fatah Hawks—the well-armed clandestine strike force that had carried out Arafat's dirty work (such as the assassination of rivals and enforcement of cooperation) during the first Intifadah (1987–1993). "Bahaa had gone into the [Kfar Darom] settlement several times during the first Intifadah," one of his friends said at the Gaza gravesite, "sometimes to attack, sometimes to seize weapons or supplies, but this time he won martyrdom after killing Israelis. It is a new phase inaugurated by the blood of Bahaa, and we swear to avenge his holy blood."

On the Palestinian side, three people knew the exact location of the corridor and the modalities for safe passage: Arafat, Dahlan, and Dahlan's personal assistant (who did not know everything). In other words, only Arafat or Dahlan could have briefed Bahaa Adi Said about the specifics of using the safe corridor so that he could appear to be an emissary. Dahlan would not have done such a thing without, at the very least, Arafat's explicit approval. Furthermore, Bahaa Adi Said was a loyal veteran of Arafat's operation and would not have carried out such an attack without being sure it was on Arafat's own orders.

————

IF INDEED Arafat and Dahlan arranged this attack to signal Washington and Jerusalem that there was no point in further communications, it did not work. On November 19, Barak called Arafat to work on the phrasing of Arafat's promise—made only to European media—to order the cessation of fire on Israeli targets from Area A. Barak noted "with pleasure" the recent drop in violence, which he attributed to Arafat's efforts.

Because the first message didn't get through to the Barak government, Arafat needed to shock the Israelis into massive retaliation, including actions that Jerusalem would consider punitive but that would actually be serving Arafat's ultimate objective. Dahlan was entrusted with finding an appropriate target, and he chose the school bus serving the Kfar Darom community. It would be a low-risk operation, for the clearly marked bus traveled every day on a road jointly controlled by the IDF and the PA police. Just how important the school bus operation was could be deduced from the fact that Dahlan's second-in-command, Rashid Abu-Shabak, personally supervised the preparation of the bomb. This was a special explosive device in which a small HE (High Explosives) charge shot a 120-mm mortar shell with immense momentum through the bus's armor plate so that the shell exploded inside the bus, showering the occupants with shrapnel. A senior member of

Fatah led the attack. Wearing his official police uniform, he stood by the roadside and signaled the firing team to activate the charge when the bus passed by him. Two teachers were killed and a dozen children were wounded, many losing limbs.

As expected, Israel reacted harshly to this clearly intentional attack. The Israeli Air Force and Navy shelled some fifteen headquarters of PA security forces throughout the Gaza Strip. Since the Palestinians had anticipated these retaliatory strikes, however, they had moved key people and equipment out of these buildings—the most important of them to shelters in the el-Arish area provided by Egyptian Military Intelligence. Meanwhile, Barak sent word to Arafat that his commitment to preserve Dahlan's life would be honored. A defiant Dahlan immediately addressed the public in Gaza. "The [Israeli] attack will not subdue our struggle for independence," he declared.

In Washington, Albright took the unusual step of talking to the media about the Middle East before informing the local leaders what she was about to say. She started out with a perfunctory condemnation of the "heinous attack" on the school bus and called on the Palestinian Authority to join her in condemning the incident. However, she did not suggest who was responsible for the attack, even though Washington already had all the relevant intelligence about Arafat's and Dahlan's responsibility. Instead, she urged both sides to show restraint. She then launched into what the *New York Times* termed "the most severe warning to Israel by the Clinton administration since the fighting broke out seven weeks ago." She blamed the Israelis for the mounting tension, declaring, "The Israelis also need to understand that the excessive use of force is not the right way to go." A State Department spokesman reiterated that the Israeli government must know by now that "violence cannot solve the problem in the Middle East." National Security spokesman P. J. Crowley said that while the United States condemned the "act of terrorism against schoolchildren and their teachers," Washington was primarily "concerned about the excessive use of force in response."

This time, Arafat's plan almost worked. By now, the Israeli General Staff had an idea of the intensity of the clandestine contacts between Barak and Arafat. The General Staff was most perturbed by Barak's failure to inform it about these contacts —reminiscent of his concealment of the negotiations for the withdrawal from southern Lebanon. Now the General Staff realized that Arafat's recent statement about restraining the violence had been coordinated with Barak's office and that Arafat's demands for unilateral restraint by the IDF had been agreed to by Barak. In addition, there was growing bitterness among senior IDF officers who had been ordered to attend what they considered "humiliating" security coordination meetings with PA senior officials and CIA "supervisors," where Israel was constantly abused and nothing tangible was ever resolved. After the attack on the school bus, the General Staff formally expressed its opposition to further meetings with Palestinian officers until the latter demonstrated effective measures to contain the violence.

For Barak, the detailed intelligence about Arafat's and Dahlan's responsibility for the school bus attack, and particularly their awareness of the repercussions the attack would have on Israeli politics, constituted a personal blow. Before this, Barak had been convinced from his own contacts with the Palestinian leadership, as well as from input by Ross, Albright, and Clinton, that Arafat knew the Palestinians would not get a better deal from any other Israeli leader and therefore would not escalate the confrontation to the point where Barak's minority government would be toppled. Now Barak was forced to conclude that Arafat no longer cared about his, Barak's, survival in power.

———

CONFRONTED WITH REALITY, Barak was reluctantly prepared to go along with the long-standing position of Israel's military and intelligence leadership. However, a phone call from Albright gave him the excuse he needed to return to the peace process, as the only way to remedy the negative impact of the Israelis' "excessive use of force." Barak overruled his security chiefs and immediately resumed contacts with an increasingly frustrated Arafat.

And so Arafat ordered yet another escalation. On the morning of November 21—the day after the Israeli strikes and just before Albright launched her attack on Israel—the PLO began advertising its next move. Hassan Asfur, a member of the Palestinian leadership and a close confidant of Arafat, issued the first response. "We will avenge," he declared. "Tel Aviv and Jerusalem are not far away." Marwan Barghouti echoed Asfur's sentiments, stressing that "the situation will now deteriorate."

Barghouti knew what he was talking about: At that very time, Tanzim teams from the Jenin and Nablus networks were already working with Nablus-based teams of Rajub's Preventive Security Service on the next strike—this time at the heart of Israel. On November 22, a car bomb exploded next to a full commuter bus in the coastal town of Hadera, killing two and wounding over sixty civilians. The initial forensic investigation identified the bomb as having the same type of remote-control fuse as the one used in the recent bombing in the Mahne Yehuda market. Now Arafat had no doubt that Israel would *have* to retaliate.

But this was not to be. Albright immediately called Arafat in Cairo. Soon afterward, she called Ben-Ami and informed him that Arafat had told her he wanted to revive the stalled negotiations. "If this is serious," Ben-Ami later told Israeli Radio, "it could be a sign of distress or a desire to exit this cycle of violence. It is our duty to at least permit the Americans to check that matter." Soon afterward, the Israeli cabinet formally decided not to retaliate for the Hadera bombing. The Palestinians, however, quickly dismissed the idea of an imminent resumption of negotiations. "There can be no return soon to the negotiations before Israel implements the Sharm el-Sheikh understandings," said Palestinian official Abu-Rudeineh. Pressed by the Clinton administration, Barak bowed to this demand as well, sending Deputy Defense Minister Ephraim Sneh and General Yaakov Orr to the Erez checkpoint on the night of November 23 to discuss implementation with the PA's Secretary-General Tayeb Abdel Rahim and Minister of Justice Jamil al-Tarifi. Afterward, Sneh acknowledged that "no operative agreements" were reached. Nevertheless, he announced, there would be "a continuation to this dialogue."

More than any previous event, this meeting at the Erez checkpoint symbolizes the futility of the whole desperate effort to revive negotiations with Arafat. Israel had committed to the meeting late in the morning of November 23, and Sneh and Orr kept the appointment that night. However, around noontime Dahlan's forces shelled the Israeli part of the District Coordination and Cooperation Office in Neve Dekalim as Israeli and Palestinian officers, along with a CIA liaison officer, were about to meet, at the request of the Palestinians, to come up with new initiatives to defuse the tension in the Gaza Strip. One Israeli officer was killed and several were wounded. The event was a milestone in more than one respect. There was no doubt that Dahlan's officers had intentionally entrapped the Israeli officers—the very same people with whom they were meeting every day in a supposed effort to contain the violence. The office was shelled with a 120-mm mortar—a weapon the Palestinians were forbidden by several agreements to have. The system of District Coordination and Cooperation Offices was the last surviving venue for ongoing direct communication between Israeli and Palestinian officers; through its services, numerous local problems were still being resolved without the use of force. Following the perfidious shelling, Israel closed all the offices and ordered the Palestinians off the premises. The American officials were recalled to Tel Aviv.

And still Barak refused to shut the door on the resumption of negotiations. On November 24, he took a call from Arafat, who was visiting President Vladimir Putin in the Kremlin. On the phone, Barak announced a major unilateral gesture: Israel would lift its closure of the key Palestinian cities by the start of the Holy Month of Ramadan (on November 26 or 27), provided that "violence stops from the Palestinian side." Barak and Arafat also agreed "to resume operations" of the District Coordination and Cooperation Offices, which Israel had just closed. In return, Arafat pledged "to do

everything in [his] power" to end the violence. However, he made no commitment to return to the peace process.

On the night of November 25, Barak convened his key advisers at his official residence in Jerusalem to discuss ideas for calming the situation and reviving communication with the Palestinians. During this meeting, Barak
called Arafat several times to get his opinion on various Israeli suggestions.
Barak got the impression that Arafat was leaning toward accepting practical
arrangements for a cease-fire, and so he immediately sent Shahak and former
GSS chief Ami Ayalon to meet with Arafat. Barak chose Ayalon because he
seemed to have established good relationships with both Arafat and Dahlan.
In the meeting, however, Arafat was hostile and insulting, conveying the clear
message that he would not accept any Israeli-originated proposal under any
circumstances. Nevertheless, to Barak and other senior Israeli officials, as
long as Arafat was willing to meet with Israelis, there was the slim possibility
that he would see reason and commit to returning to the peace process.

By late November, there had emerged a distinct pattern of behavior on
the part of Barak and his Security Cabinet. Essentially, every Israeli military
action was measured not by its effectiveness but by the impact it might have
on Arafat's willingness "to stay in touch." According to Barak's aides, "he
either speaks to Arafat or sends envoys to him nearly every day." In the same
vein, Barak took it upon himself to adopt Albright's latest plan for "reducing
the volume of violence"; his government learned about it from CNN. Barak
completely ignored exceptionally reliable intelligence to the effect that Arafat
was committed to further escalation unless Israel succeeded in launching debilitating strikes against his forces. Barak also ignored repeated warnings
that any delay in acting would lead to unnecessary casualties among both
soldiers and civilians. The result was a crisis of trust that some senior officers
described as the most profound rift between the military and the government
in the history of Israel.

In despair, Chief of Staff Mofaz publicly disclosed that the inner cabinet
had already rejected "dozens of plans" calling for serious strikes: "We present plans for the inner cabinet's approval, but the inner cabinet rejects them."
Other senior officers also vented their frustration publicly. For example, the
Air Force chief of staff, Brigadier General Amos Yadlin, stated in a lecture
that the "pinprick strikes" intended as "messages to Arafat" had proved useless. "It is not working," Yadlin said. "The only way is to hit with all your
might. Otherwise, the other side becomes immune to the attacks." Yadlin did
not challenge the government's mantra that "the Israeli-Palestinian conflict
cannot be resolved with pure military might." However, he insisted that there
were viable military means to force Arafat to end the mini-war against Israel.

"Because we can't achieve victory does not mean that we have no military solution," Yadlin said. "There's a huge area in between."

———

WHILE BARAK and his cabinet kept ignoring their military and intelligence chiefs, Arafat and his coterie were paying very close attention. They knew that the Israeli security elite was correct in its reading of the situation and that its counsel for action, if adopted by the government, would lead to the suppression of the Intifadah. With the Clinton administration winding down, Arafat believed, it was only a question of time before the Israeli government would come to its senses, to the detriment of the Palestinians' cause. In preparation for the possibility of being driven into exile, Arafat and his coterie had recently activated several of the emergency headquarters they had been preparing in areas surrounding Israel, the most important being in Larnaca (Cyprus), el-Arish (Sinai), and Ein Hilweh (Lebanon).

Arafat meanwhile was facing renewed grassroots criticism of his coterie—the "Tunis gang." As the plight of the Palestinian population worsened, so did complaints about "symbols of corruption" in their midst. On November 21, Arafat's own newspaper, Al-Hayah al-Jadidah, published an article by a senior Fatah official, Kamal al-Astal, urging an "institutional uprising" to remove corrupt officials before the public accused Fatah of "wasting the blood of the martyrs." Al-Astal warned Arafat—whom he did not blame—of the consequences of not confronting the corruption issue squarely. "We have lost our credibility in the eyes of the Arabs. I think a majority of Palestinians in the occupied territories and many in the Arab world feel that they should not give money to the Palestinian Authority because we lack transparency."

Therefore, Arafat set off on a new tack, openly rebuffing the United States as the regional mediator and floating instead the idea of creating an Arab-dominated international force to give the Palestinians a Kosovo-style independent state. In meetings with world leaders during the fall and winter, Arafat repeatedly noted the Kosovo Liberation Army's success in instigating NATO's entry into Kosovo. "Arafat is operating on the Kosovo model," an Israeli security official remarked, "and has the feeling that little by little it is working."

Arafat knew that Israel would adamantly refuse to allow foreign forces on its soil—particularly the Arab-dominated force Arafat was advocating. But the mere suggestion of such an international formula—particularly given the Russian and French desire to undercut U.S. influence in the Middle East—would generate pressure on Israel not to escalate to the point of deciding the conflict militarily, thus buying time for Arafat's allies to complete their preparations for the regional war. The Iraqi high command wanted to fight in the spring of 2001, and so Arafat had to find ways to keep the Intifadah escalating until then without provoking a decisive Israeli retaliation.

———

ARAFAT'S EVOLVING STRATEGY—and statements such as Sheikh Yassin's vow to unleash "a Ramadan of blood"—did not go unnoticed in the more conservative Arab capitals. A recent bombing in Riyadh made the point even more sharply. Responsible Arab leaders were becoming painfully aware that the only way to avoid grassroots Islamist uprisings in their own countries was to adopt harsh positions vis-à-vis both Israel and the United States.

In a speech delivered on November 23, the clear-sighted Saudi Crown Prince Abdallah bin Abdul Aziz offered a bleak assessment of the situation in the Middle East, and specifically of the American call for returning to the peace process. "People say there is hope of a détente, but I doubt it," Prince Abdallah said. "The Arab people are shocked by the current behavior of Israel." For the entire Arab world, the crisis amounted to the collapse of the effort at reconciliation launched with the Madrid Conference in 1991. The Arabs had tried "to eradicate the feelings of hatred" toward Israel, only to be rebuffed. "We have wanted to cohabit with them, but while making sure their hegemony is not imposed on us," Prince Abdallah lamented. "They humiliate us, and humiliation is difficult, very difficult [to accept]."

However, the brunt of Prince Abdallah's criticism was aimed at the United States and Western Europe for launching and sustaining the Arab-Israeli political process that had brought the entire region to the verge of eruption. The Israeli use of "tanks and aircraft . . . against children resisting with stones" had been made possible by other powers, Prince Abdallah explained. "We know who is helping them [Israel] and who is giving them support in the United States and Europe. Everybody is helping them. But such help will not last forever even if it goes on for ten, twenty, fifty years, or even a century. The Arabs surround them [Israel] from all sides, and thanks to God they [the Arabs] are growing stronger." Meanwhile, the Arab-Israeli confrontation had already been transformed into a struggle for the future of all Muslims and Arabs. "Al-Quds is the most important issue for us. Even if we have to sacrifice our children . . . we will never surrender, never." Al-Quds is "firstly a matter of Muslim dignity," Prince Abdallah declared, "then of the Arabs and finally of the other religions, except that of the looting Jews." The Jews "should be ashamed because they have no intention to make concessions." Instead, "they lack humanism, morals and principles. Their aim is to humiliate the Arab-Islamic world, including Muslims and Christians. But, by the grace of God, they will be defeated."

Two days later, in a major address to his cabinet, Saddam Hussein underscored the need for conservative Arab leaders to look to the stability of their own regimes. "The Arab masses," Saddam declared, "are called upon to attack all U.S. and Zionist interests and to track down those defending such interests [in the Arab world]. Regimes which do not believe in the national struggle must change [their stand] or vanish. Those who do not change must be overthrown." What would cause the West to change its policy vis-à-vis the Arab-Israeli conflict, Saddam said, was a credible threat to the vital interests of the West, such as oil. "The Arabs must convince the United States and Britain that all their interests are threatened so long as Zionism continues to exist." In the meantime, all Arabs had to work toward a lasting and just solution to the Palestine problem—namely, eradication of the Jewish presence in the region. "Every Jewish immigrant should leave Palestine for good and return to his country of origin," Saddam explained. "So long as Jewish immigrants remain on Palestinian soil, there will never be stability in the region."

19

A Winter of Fire (2000–2001)

Clinton's Last Hurrah;
Enter Bush, Exit Barak

DURING THE last week of November 2000—even as Israeli officials were talking of a "last-chance window of opportunity" to reach an agreement with Arafat—the Barak government took a series of steps suggesting it finally understood that Israel was facing a serious threat. Over the weekend of November 24–26, Barak quietly yielded to the long-time urging of his high command and ordered Chief of Staff Mofaz to begin active preparations for a general regional war. By the end of the month, the Knesset had approved all necessary emergency procedures.

Regardless of how such a war began—that is, regardless of who struck first—the IDF anticipated a two-phase war. In the first phase, the Israelis would be fighting the Palestinian forces, including the host of foreigners operating in their ranks. The IDF would strive to quickly restore the freedom of secure movement within Israel so that its major force groupings could be switched rapidly from one front to another. In the second phase, the Israelis would strike decisively at participating Arab countries, at both the strategic-military and the national-infrastructure levels. Israel was fully aware that the various Arab armed forces—most notably the Egyptian—had markedly improved during the 1990s, with their acquisition of the latest U.S. weaponry. Given the inevitable high level of Israeli casualties and rear-area destruction, Jerusalem resolved that it needed to achieve an overwhelming military decision quickly, rendering its opponents incapable of returning to war within a short time, while giving them incentives to enter the diplomatic process, where a triumphant Israel would be magnanimous.

———

THE IDF ENVISIONED the first phase of the war as an escalation of the current mini-war: Preventive operations would reduce the threat to Jewish settlements and the suburbs of Jerusalem. A series of brief offensive surges by small tank and elite infantry units would create buffer zones around the key points of contention. In the second stage, the IDF intended to send heavy columns of tanks and armored personnel carriers, with extensive support from helicopters and fighter-bombers, into the centers of all Palestinian-Arab cities in order to destroy all vestiges of PA security activities. The IDF intended to physically destroy all police stations, garrisons, and intelligence headquarters and to seize as many security and intelligence officers as possible and throw them across the border. The only matter still being debated was whether to revive direct Israeli control over Palestinian population centers or to encourage legitimate indigenous individuals and institutions to assume power in place of Arafat's PA.

The IDF was determined to avoid letting these operations drag on into protracted urban warfare. Therefore, elite tank and infantry units, including veterans of the former Lebanese security zone, were pulled out of routine activities and sent for intensive training in the Negev Desert. At a military base there, the IDF constructed models of the various areas marked for reoccupation. The training stressed urban warfare in heavily populated areas, with the aim of reducing civilian casualties and collateral damage as much as possible.

The chances that the IDF would have to launch this phase of the war increased markedly in early December because of the Palestinians' own preparations for initiating escalation. The Palestinian war plans called for the creation of three contiguous blocks of land as well as secure corridors to both Egypt and Jordan. In Gaza, the Palestinians would focus on overrunning two isolated Jewish settlements and establishing a military presence on the Mediterranean shore and along the Egyptian border in order to ensure the flow of weapons, oil, and reinforcements. In the center of the West Bank—the area surrounding Jerusalem—the Palestinians would concentrate on unifying the four blocks—Ramallah, Beit-El-Ofra, Bethlehem-Hebron, and Jericho (including access to Jordan)—into a single fighting front. In the northern part of the West Bank, they would strive to unify the two blocks—Nablus and Kalkilyeh/Tulkarm/Jenin—into a single front and to establish a secure corridor to Jericho for the flow of weapons, oil, and reinforcements from Iraq via Jordan. Starting in late November, new mobile strike teams—known as the "Shadow Forces" and organized from among the intelligence and security forces and the Tanzim—began moving to strategic locations.

As for the second phase of the war—the regional phase—Israel was most anxious about scenarios where the pace and sequence of events would be dominated by the Arabs. Jerusalem's apprehensions were not about Israel's ultimate victory but about the probable extent of Israeli losses. In particular, the overhanging threat of SSMs launched from Syria, Iraq, Iran, or Egypt against civilian targets in the coastal plains, even if only with conventional warheads, served as a strong incentive for Israel to launch a regionwide preemptive strike. Nevertheless, the Barak government was most preoccupied with two scenarios based on the Arabs firing the first shot.

The IDF's first scenario assumed an Iraqi-Palestinian catalyst. In this scenario, the excuse for war would be provided by Arafat's unilateral declaration of independence and an ensuing cry for help against a real or imaginary Israeli threat. Another variant had Arafat provoking the war through an especially lethal terrorist strike at the heart of Israel that would elicit massive retaliation. Either way, the previously coordinated Iraqi military surge through Jordan to help Arafat's forces would follow. Syria and Iran might well join Iraq, forming a mighty Eastern Front. Egypt would not be able to stay out of such a coalition once the shooting began.

The second scenario assumed a Lebanon-based catalyst. In this scenario, Israel would be hit by a terrorist provocation perpetrated by some combination of HizbAllah, HAMAS, Islamic Jihad, and the bin Laden–affiliated networks. With Syrian units intentionally deployed among the HizbAllah forward positions, any Israeli retaliatory strike would surely hit Syrian forces. Bashar al-Assad and his brother-in-law General Shawkat were only too eager to strike back. The Iraqis and Iranians would then have their excuse to intervene in the name of Muslim solidarity. "The Iraqis would love to participate in either conflict," a senior Israeli source told Steve Rodan of MENL (the Middle East News Line). "Hafiz Assad was not interested in cooperating with Iraq. Bashar is interested and wants to cooperate." The Iraqi military units near the Syrian border had already completed their command, control, and communications arrangements with the local Syrian command so that their advance to the Golan front could start instantaneously. Again, the immense outcry of the Arab street would drag Egypt and Jordan into the fray.

Politically, Israeli officials concluded, the Lebanese option was the more tempting for the Arabs because it would enable them to launch a retaliatory war. On the other hand, this option gave Bashar and his Iranian patrons a prominent role in the conflagration. Because Arafat and Saddam were determined to be the preeminent leaders of the jihad against Israel, they might be reluctant to take this route. The problem was, the Israeli officials acknowledged, that once Arafat and Saddam committed to launching a war, Tehran and Damascus might seize the initiative and instigate the terrorist provocation from Lebanon on their own.

The IDF would have preferred to make its own preemptive strike against the neighboring states and their armies. Furthermore, it would have loved to preemptively destroy at least some of the ballistic missiles arrayed against Israel. However, while Jerusalem might be able to come up with an internationally acceptable reason for strikes against Syria, Iraq, and Iran, it could not take on Egypt without dire geopolitical consequences.

The Egyptian factor was especially problematical because, although peace still officially existed, Mubarak had already defined Egypt's *casus belli* back in the spring of 1997 and committed to an all-Arab war strategy during his brief visit to Damascus that July. By late 2000, Egypt was providing extensive military assistance to the Palestinian forces in Gaza; and, in violation of the Israeli-Egyptian peace accord, Egyptian armed forces were clearly preparing for war. Still, given the close Egyptian-U.S. relations and the formal Israeli-Egyptian peace, the IDF could not strike out preemptively, exposing Israel to an Egyptian retaliatory missile strike even if the initial Israeli strikes against the well-defended SSM sites of Syria, Iraq, and Iran were highly successful. The marked expansion of the Egyptian–North Korean missile development program added to Israel's anxiety, as did the just-confirmed operational status of Libya's first Nodong-1 SSMs which had been acquired for Egyptian use, even though those missiles were then targeted on southern Europe.

Ultimately, given the national trauma of the 1973 Yom Kippur War, any Israeli government—whether led by hawks, doves, or a combination—would be hard pressed to avoid a preemptive move once it had been presented with irrefutable evidence of an irreversible Arab commitment to war. Furthermore, virtually the entire population of Israel felt deeply betrayed by the Arab world because of the failure of the peace process—that is, the inability of Arabs and Israelis to come to terms of nonviolent coexistence. This sentiment would be a critical factor in Israel's willingness to inflict devastation on its foes. Moreover, the entire IDF—from generals to privates—had experienced tremendous frustration over Barak's policy of self-restraint. Now, with his peace policy about to collapse, Barak was telling his high command that if war broke out, the government would follow its recommendations and not impose any restraints.

———

BY NOW, there were worrisome signs all over the Middle East. On Friday, December 1, the Islamist leadership decreed that the fateful confrontation with Israel would take place during the month of Ramadan, which had started on November 27. The Islamists issued an especially explicit fatwa: "In light of the increased and continuing atrocities being committed by the fascist State of Israel, the Islamic Scholars around the world have declared this Ramadan a month of Intifadah, and it is a divine obligation upon the Muslims world-wide to respond to this call from the scholars of Islam verbally, financially, physically, and militarily!" The fatwa clearly defined the ultimate objective of this effort: "to liberate all our land under occupation," or, in other words, the destruction of Israel.

On the political front, Arafat was resolutely snubbing Mubarak so that he could give Mubarak a fig leaf of deniability in case of war: Mubarak, ostensibly the voice of moderation, would be able to claim that he had not had the chance to advise Arafat against instigating war. At the same time, the Egyptian Army had activated its emergency storage sites—just as a precaution, of course.

On the military front, Iraqi forces continued to linger near the Jordanian and Syrian borders. "The situation is very sensitive," a senior Israeli security source noted in early December, because "Iraqi-Syrian relations have never been better." Meanwhile, the Syrians had started redeploying their armed forces in Lebanon to wartime positions—significantly deploying their air-defense assets against anticipated Israeli air strikes. These movements took place a few days after Israel warned for the first time since the mid-1980s that it would strike Syrian objectives in case of a major terrorist strike from Lebanon. "If the deterioration in the north continues," National Security Adviser Uzi Dayan announced, "it will be inevitable that Syrian and Lebanese power centers will be struck." Damascus replied swiftly. "Syria and its allies are determined to confront all the Israeli threats," a senior Syrian defense official declared, "and will not waver from their resolute commitment to supporting the Palestinian Intifadah until its final triumph."

The following week, the Syrians started redeploying their 30,000 troops in Lebanon in new wartime dispositions—ready to absorb a preemptive strike and then go on a counteroffensive toward the Israeli border. In addition, the Syrian-Iraqi secret agreement for military cooperation was formally activated, with new understandings that Syrian and Iraqi air force, missile, and air-defense units would be permitted to operate out of each other's bases in case of war with Israel. This arrangement would permit the Iraqis to quickly deploy and reinforce the Syrians, and the Syrians to withdraw to safe bases in Iraq. The five Iraqi divisions near the Jordanian and Syrian borders were put on heightened alert, and there was an increase in the flow of supplies and ammunition to their logistical bases.

The die seemed to have been cast.

———

EHUD BARAK was fast approaching a political dead end. In late November, he began floating trial balloons about resigning and calling for new elections, in hopes that the Israeli Left would rally around him. But they did not. At the same time, he seemed to have realized that denying the Intifadah had harmed his credibility. His statement in the December 3 cabinet meeting reflected this realization. "The current Palestinian violence is not the consequence of our approach [at Camp David], but stems from a conscious choice by the other side, which wants to appear to have attained independence through bloodshed and confrontation. This cannot surprise us and, in the end, stems from the substantial differences between the two sides' interests," he said, and quickly leaked his statement to the Israeli media.

In early December, the Clinton administration's "spin doctors," seriously worried about Barak's ability to survive an election campaign, leaked that high-level Israeli and Palestinian officials were meeting secretly under U.S. sponsorship, with the aim of holding Clinton's last-hurrah summit and concluding an Israeli-Palestinian agreement. They also leaked a warning that the deadline for such an agreement was December 20; after that, there would be nothing Clinton could do.

The CIA also played the leak game. "High-level U.S. intelligence sources" indicated that Arafat was losing control over the territories and that only continued Israeli concessions—irrespective of the intensity of the fighting—would prevent his collapse and the rise of HAMAS. Official Washington perceived these leaks as less a matter of professional intelligence analysis than a desire to protect George Tenet's image, given his direct involvement in the Israeli-Palestinian negotiations and his all-out support for Arafat.

Meanwhile, Terje Larsen was in Tel Aviv, holding a marathon of informal discussions with the veterans of Oslo and Oslo B in an effort to reach the core of an "Oslo C" that would restart the peace process. Barak clung to this slender thread, repeatedly sending Yossi Ginossar on secret missions to Arafat with ideas for further Israeli concessions in return for a cease-fire. Arafat ignored Barak's overtures and instructed Tanzim and Shadow teams to escalate their fire against Jerusalem and main arteries of transportation.

At the same time, a Fatah communiqué urged violent demonstrations in honor of the thirteenth anniversary of the original Intifadah. Fatah and the Islamist movements agreed that the protests should begin at the Temple Mount, to be followed by "days of rage" throughout the territories. What made these days of rage particularly significant was the context in which they were conducted: In a December 7 interview with *Al-Hayah al-Jadidah*, the Fatah Central Committee's Sakhr Habash offered one of the clearest elucidations yet of the true objectives of the new Intifadah: "After the Camp David summit it became clear to the Fatah movement, as brother Abu-Ammar [Arafat] had warned, that the next phase requires us to prepare for conflict, because Barak is not a partner capable of complying with our people's aspirations." The Intifadah, Habash went on, was designed to put an end to the political process and start the next phase—the Palestinian war of independence. Violence "did not break out in order to improve our bargaining ability in the negotiations, nor as a reaction to Sharon's provocative visit to Al-Haram Al-Sharif: this was only the spark," Habash elaborated. "The Intifadah endorsed the PLO's national plan that reflects the aspirations of our people: the establishment of an independent state with Jerusalem as its capital in the borders of June 4, 1967, and ensuring the Right of Return and compensation for Palestinian refugees." The attainment of a Palestinian state in the territories would be an instrument for the ultimate destruction of Israel: "When we declare the establishment of a state and independence, we will have the right to liberate the rest of the occupied land."

Habash emphasized the Camp David disappointment as a turning point in the Palestinian national struggle. The Palestinians "thought that President Clinton would be able to put pressure on the Israeli government before leaving the White House so that Barak would agree to a political solution acceptable to us." But this did not happen, and, therefore, there was no substitute for uncompromising armed struggle. "The Intifadah must continue. When the Zionist society has suffered heavy losses," Habash explained, "it will demand that its government achieve a peace based on international legitimacy. Any damage we cause to the Zionist society and to American interests will bring us closer to our goal."

The December 8 protests erupted according to plan, even though the Israelis had taken various precautions. For example, only residents of East Jerusalem were permitted to attend the Friday prayers on the Temple Mount; however, some 125,000 attended. After listening to the virulent sermons, they began rioting. When the Shabab started leaving the Temple Mount compound, they were joined by organized groups of Tanzim fighters from refugee camps north of Jerusalem. Together, they rampaged through the Arab Quarter of the Old City, along the Via Dolorosa, and in areas near the Damascus Gate, finally setting fire to the Israeli police station near the Lions Gate. The police tried to disperse the Shabab with rubber-coated bullets, but the rioting mob overwhelmed them; twenty-one policemen were wounded by rocks, and some ten Palestinians were wounded by bullets and/or rocks. Rather than render first aid, the rioters covered their hands and faces with the blood of their wounded friends and stormed the bewildered security forces. Others wrote jihadist slogans and made handprints with blood on nearby walls. The orgy of hatred startled even the most experienced observers. No one could imagine that these frenzy-driven Tanzim fighters would soon go back to coexisting with Jews.

During the two "days of rage" that followed the Jerusalem riots, PA-affiliated forces fired on Jerusalem neighborhoods and conducted roadside ambushes. Notable in these operations was the increased professionalism of the key teams. Their fire was more disciplined and accurate than before, meaning they wasted far less ammunition. On Sunday, December 10, the PA formally endorsed the days of rage. PA papers carried a special four-page insert giving the day-by-day schedule for the coming week's violence and stressing specific events organized by both Fatah and HAMAS. The next Friday was declared "general escalation day," and the leadership expected "expanded resistance activity and confrontation in the villages, and breaking the siege on Al-Aqsa and the Holy City."

Also on December 10, a GSS security detachment captured Amin al-Hindi, along with a few bodyguards, taking pictures of the houses of senior IDF officers in two neighborhoods near Tel Aviv. Hindi had used his VIP certificate—provided by Israel—to travel to these neighborhoods. A search of the car netted several loaded handguns, professional cameras (originally provided to PA officials by the CIA to assist them in their anti-terrorism operations), cellular phones, and detailed notes. When police arrived to arrest him, Hindi presented his VIP card and claimed the equivalent of diplomatic immunity. He explained that his driver had got lost on the way from Gaza to Ramallah. Hindi's excuses were so preposterous, and the evidence so airtight, that he was arrested. However, two hours later Barak's office ordered his release and the suppression of the case, even though the notes found in Hindi's car proved that he was preparing not only for attacks on the houses of senior Israeli officials and officers, but also for attacks on Ben Gurion Airport and for the disruption of all Jewish traffic to Jerusalem.

THAT SAME DAY, Barak resigned and called for elections on February 6, 2001. Not only a prime minister with barely 25 percent of the Knesset behind him but now also officially a lame duck, Barak saw in this situation a license to relentlessly pursue an agreement with Arafat. He was now immune to any sanctions from the Knesset, and he believed the voters would go with him if he delivered peace.

As fighting continued to escalate throughout the territories, with fire attacks and ambushes becoming routine, Barak forbade deterrence through retaliation. He didn't modify his instructions even when Israeli Military Intelligence confronted him with evidence of Arafat's instructions to prepare an escalating terrorism campaign designed to topple Barak's government. Arafat was operating on the basis of a pragmatic logic: If Barak won, it would constitute a mandate for peace, and the United States was bound to demand cessation of hostilities and a return to the negotiating table. If Barak lost, however, it would surely be to a right-wing politician, with whom Arafat could claim he was unable to deal. But rather than face the reality of what Arafat was doing, Barak continued to go along with the White House's ceaseless quest for compromise.

By now, even the Clinton administration was no longer sure Arafat was genuinely interested in the peace process. On December 13, Ross met with Arafat in Morocco to clarify the point but got only an inconclusive response. Jerusalem leaped on the ambiguity, however—"Arafat says he wants an agreement," Israeli sources gloated—and, with time running out, the White House decided to go forward. Toward that end, Clinton's team offered its own outline for an Israeli-Palestinian solution—"the Clinton proposal"—and announced that Albright would travel to the Middle East over the next two weeks and lead a final effort to consolidate an agreement. The White House also suggested getting high-level teams back to Bolling AFB to study the Clinton proposal as the basis for a permanent agreement. Barak embraced the idea enthusiastically, but Arafat demurred. Arafat did not budge even when Clinton phoned him and, in an hour-long conversation, personally promised him full control over East Jerusalem and sovereignty over the Temple Mount.

On the night of December 15, Arafat called his coterie together. He complained he could no longer withstand the American and West European pressure to resume the peace process. Hence, he told them, he would accept Clinton's invitation and send a delegation to Washington. Furthermore, he would insist that the Clinton proposal be the only document on the table—an irresistible option for Clinton. The real mandate of the Palestinian delegation, however, would be to stall for time and ensure that the Israelis would be blamed for the eventual collapse of the talks. Given Clinton's commitment, Arafat was sure the Israelis would not dare take any military initiative while the talks were going on. Meanwhile, the Palestinians and their allies would expedite their preparations for the internationalization of the Intifadah.

The next night, Dahlan, Erekat, and Abed Rabbo met with Ben-Ami and Sher to discuss the upcoming Washington negotiations. Dahlan delivered Arafat's veiled threat: Yes, there was still the possibility of making peace with Israel despite its "use of excessive force"; however, the Israeli tanks would not scare the Palestinians and deter them from persevering in their struggle for national salvation. The Israelis completely ignored Dahlan's real message. All Ben-Ami and Sher cared to hear was Arafat's agreement to send a delegation to Washington. Jerusalem's euphoria persisted even as Abed Rabbo told PA Radio the next morning that the PA did not object to the talks' resumption, but "the Intifadah will continue at the same time."

And so between December 19 and 23, Israeli and Palestinian delegations met at Bolling AFB and argued over the intricacies of the Clinton proposal. The American team, led by the indefatigable Ross, brought up a series of "floating ideas" to bridge each new point of contention the Palestinians provided. By now, the Israeli delegation had agreed to withdraw to the June 4, 1967, border with minute changes and to demonstrate "flexibility" over the fate of the settlements—which amounted to agreeing to dismantle them. The Israelis further agreed that 5 percent of Mubarak's triangle and 3 percent of the Negev in the Halutza area, adjacent to the Egyptian border, would be given to the PA in territorial exchanges and that Israel would absorb tens of thousands of refugees through family reunions and for "humanitarian considerations." But the Palestinians kept devising new demands, leading some of the American officials to suggest the Palestinians were dragging their feet until the arrival of the new Bush administration, which the Arab world perceived as more pro-Arab.

On the 21st, Barak instructed Sher and Ben-Ami to go to any lengths to get the Palestinians to sign "anything that would look like an agreement." Barak wanted something he could present in the election campaign as the outline for a "framework agreement." The Palestinians rejected the idea with disdain. Finally, in despair that all his concessions had come to nothing, and angered by a lethal roadside ambush near Jerusalem, on December 22 Barak instructed Sher and Ben-Ami to withdraw all Israeli offers concerning Jerusalem. The Palestinians were stunned; reportedly, Erekat even tried to assault Ben-Ami. And so the talks at Bolling AFB ended. The next day, Clinton called the delegations to a concluding session at the White House. Formally, he announced that he had given his proposal to the two sides for further study. The Israelis immediately agreed. The Palestinians, following Arafat's instructions, remained noncommittal.

————

BY NOW, Washington and the rest of the Western world were sliding into the Christmas and New Year holiday season—too preoccupied with celebrations to deal with the Middle East. Thus the Arab leaders were free to decide their next moves on their own, without Western pressure. In retrospect, a turning point took place on December 24, when Arafat met with Mubarak in Cairo. Mubarak told Arafat he had to make a decision. If he wanted to sign anything, Mubarak said, he should do it now, as time was fast running out on Clinton's presidency. Then again, Mubarak warned, there was no guarantee that President Bush would even try to enforce his predecessor's commitments. Perhaps, Mubarak suggested, Arafat would do better to prepare for an alternative policy—namely, escalating the level of confrontation.

Mubarak, as before, was not a disinterested advisor. If Barak, sensing that an agreement was close, revived his concessions on the Jerusalem issue, the resulting agreement would make Arafat and his ally Saddam Hussein the liberators of Jerusalem, and especially al-Aqsa. That would end Mubarak's aspirations to return Cairo to the leadership of the Arab world. On the other hand, in the aftermath of a regional war, Egypt's—that is, Mubarak's—role as the negotiator with the United States on a cease-fire and ultimately a long-term settlement would be crucial. And that role, Mubarak concluded, would empower him as the leader of the Arab world. Hence, on December 25, Mubarak refused to see Barak despite repeated pleas. He also instructed the Egyptian military to expedite preparations for the coming escalation—thus sending a clear signal to Iraq, Syria, and the Palestinians.

Barak and his inner circle, meanwhile, had decided that Arafat was not committing to a peace agreement because he was afraid of hard-liners among the Palestinians. Therefore, Barak resolved to "save Arafat" by offering him additional concessions that even most of the hard-liners would not be able to reject out of hand—particularly regarding sovereignty over the Temple Mount and the right of return, as well as transforming the few settlement blocks Israel insisted on retaining into Palestinian territory under long-term lease to Israel. President Clinton, with whom Barak consulted in great detail before making his offer, was enthusiastic and encouraged Barak to go all the way. He had guarantees, Clinton assured Barak in lengthy phone conversations, that Arafat would not resist Clinton's pressure so long as he was given something he could present to his people as a tangible achievement—that is, additional concessions from Barak.

———

SENIOR IDF OFFICERS who participated in the Bolling AFB negotiations had returned to Israel "shocked" by the concessions offered by Ben-Ami and Sher, who would not listen to objections raised by the IDF representatives. Then came Barak's new concessions, going beyond even the Clinton proposal. In a cabinet meeting on December 27, Mofaz confronted Barak. From a military point of view, Mofaz declared, implementation of the Clinton proposal would leave Israel exposed to a point where its very existence would be threatened. "Clinton's proposal does not provide for the prerequisites to defending Israel's strategic rear," Mofaz warned. "The Israeli deterrence posture will be harmed to an unacceptable degree, and the Israeli retaliatory capacity will be severely constrained." Later, Dichter also warned Barak that given the relationship between Arafat and various power centers in the PA, a Palestinian state resulting from the current negotiations would be "a terrorism-sponsoring state," with Arafat unwilling, and perhaps unable, to contain anti-Israeli terrorism.

Rather than answer his critics, Barak suggested a trilateral summit—himself, Arafat, and Mubarak—in Sharm el-Sheikh on the 28th, at which he promised to make the additional concessions. Mubarak would then persuade Arafat to return to Washington and sign some sort of agreement. However, despite pressure from the White House to "help Barak," Arafat was adamant in his refusal. He would not go to Washington and would not sign anything. According to a senior Israeli official, while Clinton and Barak remained convinced that Arafat was "playing one of his brinkmanship games," Dahlan delivered Arafat's response. On the morning of December 28, a couple of small bombs exploded ten minutes apart on a bus in Tel Aviv. The bombs were small, causing virtually no injuries, and so no retaliation was warranted. However, that same morning, a large bomb exploded at a Gaza checkpoint, killing two Israeli officers and wounding two soldiers. Both the Tel Aviv and the Gaza bombs were activated by the telltale cellular phone fuse, leaving little doubt that Dahlan's operatives were responsible—and, in turn, that Arafat had given the order. Meanwhile, Arafat told Mubarak and official Riyadh that he'd "rather wait ten or even fifteen years" than accept Clinton's plan. Mubarak assured Arafat that he would help him scuttle the Clinton proposal with as little damage to the PA as humanly possible.

To a great extent, Mubarak's position reinforced Arafat's inclinations. Both leaders had suddenly had second thoughts about the Arabs' ability to confront Israel. Egyptian strategists argued that the Arabs could not afford a miscalculation: If pushed into a corner, Israel might surge as it had in the Six-Day War. "From here stems the danger of war," Muhammad Sid-Ahmad argued in the official *Al-Ahram,* "and it is up to the Arabs to avert the danger by coming up with a third way that is neither the peace process in its traditional form nor an inevitable slide into a war situation."

The Arab world was also apprehensive about the incoming Bush administration despite its purported pro-Arab tilt. In mid-December, as the president-elect was beginning to shape his administration, Arab leaders pondered his known interest in the oil politics of the Persian Gulf. George W. Bush, like his father, had close personal relations with Prince Bandar bin Sultan—widely perceived as a major factor in the incoming administration's position on several Middle East issues. Also of great importance was the policy Bush would adopt toward Saddam Hussein—"the unfinished task of his father's Presidency," in the words of a senior Arab official.

Saddam preempted the Bush administration's inevitable interest in Iraq by announcing the formation of "the Special Iraqi Force for the Liberation of Jerusalem"—spearheaded by the six divisions and support units already deployed near the Jordanian and Syrian borders. He also assigned to that force a unit of martyr-commandos—unimportant from a military point of view but of crucial significance from a political-strategic point of view, given the need to placate the Islamists. By emphasizing Baghdad's commitment to the sacred Palestinian Intifadah, Saddam in essence forestalled Bush's expected attempt to rebuild his father's anti-Iraq coalition.

Fully aware of the grave consequences of an overt alliance with Saddam Hussein, Bashar al-Assad determined to thoroughly confirm Baghdad's sincerity before he committed Syria to going to war. Therefore, he sent his brother Mahir on a secret two-day visit to Baghdad to confer with his friend Qusay Saddam Hussein and a host of intelligence, Republican Guard, and military senior officers. Satisfied with Mahir's report, Bashar established a special high-level committee to oversee the political and military coordination between Syria and Iraq. This was no empty gesture. Syrian and Iraqi armored units, including elements of the Hammurabi Division, quickly began joint exercises in western Iraq near the Syrian border. The exercises were designed to smooth and perfect the coordination of operational-level headquarters, communication systems, and support elements of the two armies. Both Damascus and Baghdad were extremely pleased with the results.

Concurrently, Baghdad expanded its cooperation with Tehran. Under the guise of confronting the Kurds, sizable Iraqi forces deployed to the northern parts of the country. However, rather than being concentrated against centers of Kurdish insurgency, the new Iraqi deployment spread out along the railroad line and the main highway that stretched from northern Syria through Iraqi Kurdistan and on to Iran. Such lines of transportation would be crucial to the shipping of Iranian reinforcements. Moreover, Baghdad permitted the Iranians to fly weapons for HizbAllah, the Palestinian rejectionists, and the Syrians through Iraqi air space. "Since the route over Turkey is not suitable for these flights," Iranian Transportation Minister Mahmoud Hojjati explained, "and wanting to develop relations with Iraq, particularly in transportation, Iran believes these flights should go over Iraq." Meanwhile, the IRGC Commander, Brigadier General Rahim Safavi, publicly threatened to launch intermediate-range missiles toward Israel and American assets in the region. "The strong missiles of Iran are capable of imposing a very harsh blow that will be impossible to bear," Safavi told a radio interviewer.

Arafat played an active role in these dynamics. In mid-December, he started making weekly visits to Amman—not to meet with Jordanian officials but rather to hold lengthy private consultations with Azzam Azzam al-Ahmad, his emissary to Baghdad. On December 27, Arafat sent Jibril Rajub to Amman to coordinate the flow of Iraqi aid to the West Bank, as well as to assure Baghdad that Arafat had no intention of going along with the Clinton proposal.

Saddam Hussein himself elucidated Iraq's Palestine policy in his Christmas Greeting speech, read on Iraqi TV. Saddam stressed that "the escalation of the Intifadah of our mujahid and patient people in Palestine against the

Zionist invaders, who desecrate the holy places of the Muslims and Christians in Palestine, and its jewel: Holy Jerusalem," necessitated urgent action. He urged all Arabs irrespective of their religion to "support our kinfolk in Palestine in the face of the Zionists' conspiracy, which aims to Judaize Jerusalem and other Palestinian territories, and annihilate the Palestinian people—both Muslims and Christians—with support from the United States." The Arabs' determination to reverse this trend, Saddam emphasized, "means [that] we should follow, in our confrontation against the enemies of God and humanity . . . the path of jihad, without which we cannot achieve what we strive to achieve in order to realize rights, promote justice and peace, and rescue humanity from the evils of the criminal, aggressive murderers." Saddam committed Iraq "to joining in the honor of liberating Palestine and regaining it, free and glorious, from the River to the Sea." Over the next few days, Saddam's message was broadcast throughout the Arab world and was repeated and analyzed in the Iraqi media, sending a clear signal: Iraq was ready for war.

With all eyes focused on Baghdad, on the first of the year, Saddam oversaw the two largest military parades since the Gulf War. The first was a popular parade of battalions of mujahideen and volunteers to liberate Palestine. Baghdad claimed that over six million fighters had already volunteered "to sacrifice themselves for Jerusalem." The second parade was a show of conventional military might. Well over a thousand tanks and several hundred armored fighting vehicles and artillery pieces, along with an assortment of ballistic and anti-aircraft missiles, rumbled through Baghdad's Grand Festivities Square for more than four hours. Throughout, jet fighters flew and helicopter gunships hovered over central Baghdad. Formations of white-hooded figures with only their eyes showing—martyr-mujahideen—stood ready to confront Israel. A huge poster showed Iraqi horses trampling an Israeli flag in front of the Dome of the Rock, with Saddam looking on, godlike, from the sky. Saddam himself, in a dark blue three-piece suit, fired a hunting rifle into the air to salute the passing troops. The parade was billed as a festive sendoff for the Iraqi forces going to liberate Palestine.

The day after the parade, Saddam vanished. A couple of days later, Egyptian security sources spread rumors that he had had a serious stroke during or soon after the parade and had been taken to a military hospital in such bad condition that he might already have died. Iraqi TV added to the hype, and even knowledgeable Arab officials and journalists were reporting that Saddam was at a Baghdad hospital having suffered severe chest pains. In reality, Saddam was not dead or even sick. He had left Baghdad for an emergency bunker in the depths of the northwestern desert, where he hid for about a week, fearing an Israeli preemptive strike. He and his generals spent much of the time discussing operational plans and military capabilities for the forthcoming jihad. However, he was also accompanied by his new bride (his third wife), a twenty-seven-year-old beauty he had just met while visiting Iraq's center for strategic studies.

———

WITH SADDAM declaring his readiness to go to war, the time was ripe for Arafat to order an escalation that would prompt Israeli retaliation but without the risk of U.S. intervention on Israel's behalf. Arafat chose to provoke the Israeli settlers into rampages and riots. Because Clinton had already deemed the settlements "illegal" and "obstacles to peace," Arafat reasoned, Washington could not easily condemn the Palestinians for reacting with violence against the settlers. Hence, the eventual Israeli intervention to save them would give Arafat his excuse to break off all contacts with Israel, because the intervention would prove that Israel had no intention of dismantling the settlements.

The campaign was to be launched on December 31, the thirty-fifth anniversary of the establishment of Fatah. First came an ultimatum delivered by a senior Tanzim official in a conversation he knew would be reported to Israelis. He said the Fatah leadership had decided to make the settlers' life hell because the American and Israeli negotiating positions were not serious. Imad Falouji, the PA's communications minister, echoed these sentiments, stating that "the Palestinians have the right to eliminate the settlers" and that "if the settlers did not leave immediately, they would leave in coffins."

The same day, the Tanzim attacked Benjamin Zeev Kahane and his family, killing Kahane and his wife, Taliya, and wounding their five young daughters. The son of the late Meir Kahane—himself assassinated in New York by an Islamist terrorist in 1990—Benjamin Zeev Kahane led what was widely considered an extremist segment of the settlers' movement. In assassinating him, the PA anticipated a flare-up of revenge strikes by his followers. The investigation by Israeli security forces confirmed that the assassination was a well-planned operation. It was preceded by a lengthy collection of intelligence on Kahane's movements and the selection of an ambush position accessible to an escape vehicle—not normally used in the routine ambushes of random targets. A highly trained attack team delivered the swift and lethal strike against a moving vehicle. During the ambush, the team was in radio contact with Tanzim headquarters in Ramallah. Ultimately, however, the Kahane assassination failed from a strategic point of view because, although Kahane's followers rioted during the funeral in West Jerusalem, they did not attack Arabs.

The next day, January 1, saw a major flare-up of Palestinian ambushes all over the territories and in adjacent areas within Israel proper. In addition, a car bomb exploded in Netanya. The following day, a senior Military Intelligence officer briefed the Knesset. "Arafat gave the green light for strikes and terrorist operations, and the perpetrators are his senior personnel, but they carry out the operations in a way that prevents directly blaming them," the officer reported. Arafat's people were coordinating future terrorist operations with HAMAS and Islamic Jihad, and HizbAllah assets in southern Lebanon were being activated. "We ain't seen nothing yet," the officer concluded.

Concurrently, Military Intelligence briefed the Israeli inner cabinet about highly sensitive data, obtained from Arab sources, on the contingency plans that Arafat was coordinating with other Arab leaders. Arafat still anticipated a major retaliation for the Kahane assassination, which would permit him to emerge as the defender of the Temple Mount, urging the Arab world to come help him save al-Aqsa. Saddam had already committed to firing three or four ballistic missiles at Tel Aviv and Haifa, the cabinet was told, and HizbAllah was planning to launch missiles and rockets at Haifa and northern Israel. Soon afterward, Iraqi forces would start moving into Jordan while Palestinian forces in Lebanon would begin a "march of return." At that point, Syria would join the war in the name of Arab solidarity. This scenario, the briefer stressed, was known to be fact by an impeccable source.

The number of routine ambushes and roadside bombs kept escalating over the next few days, and Fatah units, with assistance from HizbAllah, launched mortar shells into Har Dov and nearby Israeli communities. The IDF returned fire but did not cross the Lebanese border. When the fighting in the Gaza Strip escalated, IDF tanks penetrated PA-held territory and blocked key arteries of transportation—dividing the PA-held area into three pockets for a few days. Meanwhile, Israeli armored units deployed to the Jordan Valley in preparation for an Iraqi offensive.

In mid-January, Arafat's security personnel kidnapped an Israeli settler and took him to Han Yunis, in the Gaza Strip, for interrogation. The IDF approached the PA security forces through the CIA-sponsored security coordination mechanism and provided detailed information on the settler's whereabouts. Israel and the United States asked for the PA's help in obtaining his release. The Palestinian officials procrastinated. A Golani Brigade force deployed to enter Han Yunis and attempt to rescue the settler, but Barak stopped them in order to give Arafat another chance to resolve the matter peacefully. The PA security forces warned the kidnappers, giving them time to kill the settler and dump his body near the greenhouses of a nearby settlement.

———

BY NOW, Iraqi force movements were so menacing that even the Clinton administration could no longer ignore them. On the contrary, there were indications that Clinton's people were looking for ways to exploit these move-

ments for their own last-minute political benefit. Senior White House officials intimated that a confrontation with the hated Saddam Hussein would
bolster the President's image as a decisive leader as he was leaving office. As
well, such a confrontation would also provide an excuse for the collapse of
the peace process—a kind of "Saddam did it" public impression. Hence, the
readiness status of U.S. forces throughout the Middle East gradually increased. On January 11, two Patriot missile batteries deployed to Israel—ostensibly for a joint exercise, but with a full missile allocation. Three
additional batteries deployed to Saudi Arabia and one to Kuwait.

At this point, several senior IDF officers again spoke out publicly. General Halutz, the Air Force commander, noted that in case of a war unleashed
against Israel, the Air Force would be able to buy time for the mobilization of
reserves—but very little beyond that. He added that because of the growing
tension in the region, the entire Air Force was being kept in the air every day,
at a high cost in spare parts and fuel, as well as the crews' accumulating fa-
tigue. Deputy Chief of Staff Yaalon's assessment was even starker. He maintained that the current Intifadah was as crucial for the very existence of
Israel as the War of Independence of the late 1940s. He observed that the
Palestinian forces were yet to use some of the heavy weapons and other "special equipment" known to be in their possession. Although the Palestinian
leadership expected Israeli society to collapse within a short time, the mere
endurance of Israeli society, Yaalon argued, would not make the Palestinians
and their Arab partners give up on this fateful confrontation. On the contrary, he warned, the effect of the attrition element was as yet unknown,
given Israel's penchant for quick decisions.

On January 14 and 15, the movements of Iraqi armored units close to
the Jordanian border intensified. The fact that this was the tenth anniversary
of the outbreak of Desert Storm was not lost on the Iraqis or their neighbors. Several Arab officials suggested that Saddam might be preparing a surprise for Bush on his inauguration day. Mubarak, apprehensive about the
possibility of a last-minute reaction from Clinton, made an effort to cool
Saddam down, but it proved fruitless.

Indeed, Saddam was now immersed in the Palestinian issue. To discuss
the practical aspects of the forthcoming war, he received a high-level Palestinian delegation led by Arafat's "foreign minister," Faruk Kaddoumi, and
including Azzam Azzam al-Ahmad, Arafat's point man in Baghdad. In a
closed meeting, Saddam impressed the delegation with his vision for the region. "Palestine is Iraq's extension," he told them, "and Iraq is Palestine's extension. Both people are in the same foxhole on the fateful front-line against
Zionism." In other words, there was no Jordan between Iraq and Palestine,
and there would be no separate agreements with or about Israel. The essence

of this meeting was more pragmatic, though, focusing on coordinating emergency procedures, including escape routes for Arafat and his coterie in case they had to flee the territories.

After the closed meeting, Saddam and the Palestinian delegation staged a public meeting, which was broadcast on Iraqi TV and radio on January 16. Saddam set the tone by stating that "there can never be stability, security, or peace in the region so long as there are immigrant Jews usurping the land of Palestine." Therefore, "the solution is the emigration of the Jews from Palestine." Since the Jews would not leave on their own, they would have to be evicted by force. "When artillery guns begin to fire their shells" at Israel, he declared, the immigrant-settlers will "pack up and leave." Israel, Saddam assured the Palestinians, "cannot stand in the face of continuous artillery shelling for six months." In contrast, Saddam claimed, on the basis of Iraq's twenty years of combat experience, that even if Iraq were struck by "U.S. planes," it could still "hold on for a year."

Most revealing, however, was the discussion of the negotiated process, for Kaddoumi rose to Saddam's challenges. At first, Saddam repeatedly cut off his Palestinian guests with curt comments to the effect that he was aware they could not say much "for political reasons." Kaddoumi responded by reminding Saddam that the PLO had accepted the "Three Nos" of the Khartoum Summit of September 1, 1967—no negotiations with Israel, no recognition of Israel, no peace with Israel—and still did. The Palestinians "rejected Resolution 242" when it was introduced in 1967, and "we still do." Kaddoumi reiterated the Palestinians' enduring gratitude for anti-American terrorism: Although those who attacked the USS *Cole* were not Palestinians, the attack was in support of the Intifadah. The Palestinians, Kaddoumi assured Saddam, would "remain strugglers until doomsday."

The next day, General Yassin Tahah Muhammad, the commander of Iraq's Artillery and Missile Forces, declared that his forces were ready and eager to receive Saddam's order to start bombarding Israel with "heavy artillery"—that is, ballistic missiles. The same day, Uday reiterated that Kuwait was an integral part of Greater Iraq.

———

ON JANUARY 1, a despondent Barak met with his peace-process coterie—a few loyalists and the senior IDF officers and intelligence officials supporting them—and told them he realized the peace process was over and a regional war was inevitable, most likely within the next week. He therefore instructed the IDF to begin preparations for a host of contingencies ranging from a regionwide preemptive strike to absorbing an Arab first strike.

Significantly, what had brought Barak to that point of despair was not concrete intelligence about the dynamics in key Arab capitals, but rather a secret letter from Israel's attorney general, Elyakim Rubinshtein, advising him that he should desist from the peace process during the election campaign. Barak had no "moral authority," Rubinshtein argued, to determine the fate of the nation when his own political fate hung in the balance. "While there is no legal limitation on a government during an election period, the legal consideration is not the central one. The instructions of the law are designed only to prevent the creation of a vacuum in authority—and not for the setting of dramatic, fateful, all-encompassing changes such as an agreement with the Palestinians." Rubinshtein warned Barak that any "election-eve agreement" with the Palestinians "should be such that it does not raise even the suspicion that it was subject to time-related considerations—namely, election considerations." Barak's efforts, Rubinshtein added, might already be futile, because any agreement he reached would ultimately have to be ratified by a post-election Knesset.

However, Clinton kept pushing. During a series of meetings with Arafat at the White House, Clinton unilaterally agreed to a reduction in Israeli security requirements, including halving the length of time for an Israeli presence in the Jordan Valley from twelve to six years and drastically reducing the forces Israel would be permitted to hold there. Clinton completely disregarded Arafat's responsibility for the recent bombings in Tel Aviv and Netanya, although U.S. intelligence recognized it.

During these sessions, Clinton called Barak a few times trying to elicit concessions that would answer Arafat's latest demands. When Barak hesitated, Clinton became impatient, even angry. Some of Clinton's close aides now made contact with Arab officials concerning the peace process without informing Israel, let alone asking whether Israel could live with the new ideas being floated. Clinton had returned to the behavior shown vis-à-vis Netanyahu, but it was a bitter first for Barak.

Even so, all that Arafat would give was "a qualified yes" followed by a long list of profound reservations. Since he could not refuse Clinton's offers outright, Arafat conditioned his final acceptance on the endorsement of the Arab League—an endorsement he knew would not come. Meeting in Cairo, the foreign ministers of the Arab League unanimously supported Arafat's "reservations" and announced that the Arab right of return to Israel was "sacred" and "could never be abandoned." Still, Clinton was now publicly expounding his position that it was no longer possible to prevent the establishment of an independent Palestinian state with its capital in Jerusalem.

By January 4, Barak had had it. Arafat was returning from the Arab League meeting in Cairo, where all Barak's hopes were dashed. Out of the blue, Barak instructed the Air Force commander to prevent Arafat's plane from landing at Gaza Airport. "Let him circle a little bit in the air," Barak told those around him. "Maybe this way he'll understand that one day we might get tired of him and he'll have nowhere to return to." And so as Arafat's plane neared Gaza Airport, the IDF's flight control notified the crew that the airport was closed and that if they proceeded they would be intercepted by Israeli fighters. Having been informed of these instructions, Arafat rushed to the cockpit, grabbed a microphone and started cursing anybody who might be listening. (Barak was kept constantly informed of the "progress.") According to Israeli officials, the spectacle lasted about an hour and a half, until Arafat called Mubarak, who interceded with Barak, and Arafat was finally allowed to land. Predictably, the incident served only to make Arafat even angrier at Barak for the humiliation.

On January 8, as the PA resumed firing into Jerusalem, Tenet organized a meeting in Cairo of Israeli and PA senior security delegations. Tenet's objective was to wrest from the Israeli security officials additional concessions that the White House had failed to elicit from the politicians. However, when Tenet demanded greater Israeli cooperation with the Palestinians, the Israelis, led by GSS chief Dichter, confronted him with detailed intelligence about the direct responsibility of his protégés Dahlan and Hindi for terrorism, including Hindi's direct supervision of the ambushes on the roads leading to Jerusalem. Dichter's case was airtight, and Tenet was caught off balance. Acrimonious exchanges erupted all around, and the meeting collapsed.

That night, more than a quarter of a million Israelis rallied in Jerusalem against additional concessions. It was either the largest or the second largest demonstration in Israel's history (the other being the anti-Sharon rally back in the summer of 1982, over Israel's alleged complicity in the massacre at two refugee camps near Beirut). It was a clear expression that the public rejected Barak's desperate efforts to reach some sort of agreement with Arafat. Furthermore, Clinton, in a bitter speech in New York, had announced the end of his own efforts. Yet instead of sinking deeper into despondency, Barak suddenly recovered and ordered a small and fiercely loyal coterie to accelerate their efforts to get an agreement at all costs.

The next day, Mofaz testified to the Knesset's Defense and Foreign Affairs Committee and repeated his warning that the Clinton plan was detrimental to Israel's ability to cope with a major crisis, but this did not slow Barak down. On January 10, he sent Shahak, Dichter, and two IDF generals for a meeting in Gaza with Erekat and Tirawi. Barak was now willing to discuss "a statement of principles" rather than insist on a signed agreement, the

Israelis explained, and would accept a U.S.-dominated supervisory mechanism, which amounted de facto to the international presence long demanded by Arafat and resisted by Barak. As an act of good faith, Shahak reported the unilateral removal of a few Israeli tank units from strategic locations. The Palestinians listened and then said that the offers were in the right direction but not enough to warrant reducing the level of violence, let alone signing anything. The Palestinians did not rule out the possibility of a follow-up meeting, however. Although Barak and Shahak considered the meeting a great success, the Israeli security leadership was apoplectic over the danger to front-line troops posed by the unilateral withdrawal.

To remind Jerusalem of the alternative to accepting Arafat's demands, PA operatives left a powerful bomb with the customary cell-phone fuse in a religious neighborhood in Jerusalem. By sheer miracle, a passerby noticed the phone and, without thinking twice, pulled out the wires connected to it. According to the subsequent GSS investigation, Dahlan's aides produced the bomb on Arafat's instructions and then passed it along to an elite team answering to Tirawi, who placed it in Jerusalem. Barak did not see in this incident any reason to slow down the quest for peace.

Over the next few days, against a background of continuing violence, there was a whirlwind of meetings involving Peres and Arafat, Larsen (who had returned to Tel Aviv, eager to help Barak and Peres) and Barghouti, and Ben-Ami, Mubarak, and Arafat. These meetings culminated in the marathon negotiations held ceaselessly between January 21 and 27 in the Taba resort in the Sinai, in an effort to reach a framework agreement before the Israeli elections. This audacious and desperate gamble by Barak stood in stark contradiction to the formal warning issued by the attorney general only three weeks before. However, Barak was now being threatened not only by Sharon, the Likud candidate, but also by a drive to replace him with Peres as the peace camp's candidate. To survive this challenge, Barak had to outperform Peres on the peace front; hence, his gamble on Taba.

The PA's Abed Rabbo stated on the eve of the negotiations that "there's no more room for neutrality": The Palestinians must do everything they can to help the Israeli peace camp win the elections. Behind the soothing words, however, Taba was an all-out effort by the Palestinian negotiators to exhaust the Israelis and extort previously inconceivable concessions. To ensure that Arafat was fully aware of the extent of the concessions the Israelis were willing to make, Barak opened a secret channel to him behind the backs of his own negotiators. Through what was called the "business channel," these communications were conducted by Yossi Ginossar and Halid Salaam—officially Arafat's "financial adviser" and in reality one of the top managers of his hidden fortune. All key issues were addressed and agreed upon in the business channel before they reached the negotiating table in Taba. While Barak was convinced he was having meaningful negotiations through this back channel, Arafat and his coterie were referring to him by the code name "Abu-Limon," the father of lemon—that is, the one who can be squeezed.

Meanwhile, thinking of their own post-Barak careers in the Labor Party, Shahak, Beilin, and Ben-Ami were running their own separate negotiations with the Palestinians and making promises in total disregard of the instructions they received from Barak. Barak, who was constantly briefed on these activities through the business channel, sent his confidant Sher to enforce discipline in Taba, but to no avail. Instead, the three now started coordinating their positions with Peres. Abu-Alaa, who was fully aware of these dynamics, openly suggested that Arafat sign "some piece of paper" in order to help Peres replace Barak.

Throughout these official and unofficial talks, the violence continued. A particularly chilling incident involved a young Palestinian woman who had been chatting on the Internet with a sixteen-year-old Israeli boy about peace and reconciliation. On January 15, she suggested that they meet. He trusted her, took a bus to a Jerusalem neighborhood, and was met by a hit team answering to Barghouti. They robbed and brutally killed him, dumping his body in northern Jerusalem.

On January 23, two masked terrorists burst into a restaurant in Tulkarm frequented by a few Israelis who were still doing business with Palestinians. The terrorists grabbed two young Israelis and executed them on the spot, shooting them in the head. HAMAS claimed the victims were GSS agents, although they were known as restaurateurs from Tel Aviv and ardent supporters of the peace camp. The GSS gave Barak detailed intelligence implicating Arafat's senior officials in ordering the grisly killing. Rather than retaliate militarily, however, Barak responded by formally suspending the Taba talks while keeping the business channel open.

The next day, another Israeli civilian was killed, this time in northern Jerusalem. The polls were devastating. With the elections two weeks away, Sharon was leading Barak by 20 percent. Even more significant was the public's mood: 78 percent were seriously worried about the future of the State of Israel, and 68 percent lived in fear for their personal safety on a daily basis. A vast majority attributed the current conditions to Barak and his policies.

Nevertheless, Barak "consented" to a cabinet decision to resume the Taba talks before it was too late. Now Arafat publicly humiliated Barak. On January 25, Palestinian officials leaked that Muhammad Rashid—another of Arafat's "financial advisers"—had met in Vienna with a small Israeli delegation that included Ariel Sharon's son and confidant, Omri Sharon. Arafat's message was clear. Rather than attempting to save Barak or empower Peres, he would open communications with the man almost certain to become the next prime minister. The next day, the Taba conference finally collapsed, despite last-minute efforts by Shahak, Beilin, and Ben-Ami to come up with "constructive ideas" for "creative phrasing" of a resolution document. "It all ended in a *harta-barta* [that is, like 'shit']," gloated Dahlan in front of Israeli journalists.

Still, the indefatigable Peres remained intent on personally squeezing an agreement from Arafat. The following day, at the World Economic Forum in Davos, the two were sitting together on a panel, along with Amr Moussa. Peres spoke about his optimism that the understandings reached in Taba would eventually mature into a permanent agreement. In response, Arafat launched into a virulent attack on Israel, accusing it of conducting "cruel and barbaric war in the fascist traditions" and calling on the international community to penalize Israel and save the Palestinians.

―――――

THE DAY BEFORE the Taba talks began, George W. Bush was sworn in as the forty-third president of the United States. Even before then, his team had begun to test the Middle East waters. One recommendation—made by James Baker, who had just saved Bush's victory in the Florida vote-count crisis—was to revive the Syrian track in order to draw Damascus back into an anti-Iraq alliance dominated by Riyadh. Colin Powell, soon to be secretary of state, concurred. He recommended that Bush revive his father's grand anti-Saddam alliance as the cornerstone of his Middle East policy rather than attempt to outdo Clinton on the Arab-Israeli scene. Baker's confidant Edward Djerejian was dispatched to Damascus to raise these issues with Bashar al-Assad. Although Bashar received Djerejian amicably, he ordered the Syrian defense establishment to send a series of signals clearly expressing Syria's true priorities.

On January 20, the Syrian armed forces went on the highest level of wartime readiness. They then began forward-deploying a myriad of air-defense systems, including mobile SAM batteries. This was followed by a test launch of the recently acquired NK-SCUD-D. This missile, with a range of 450 miles, is capable of covering the whole of Israel from protected bases inside Syria and is therefore an ideal weapon for a surprise attack. The overall message Bashar was attempting to convey to friends and foes alike was that Damascus was determined to be the preeminent strategic force in the Arab world.

There followed a demonstration of the increasing Syrian-Iraqi military cooperation, including joint exercises near the border between the two countries. The exercises were planned to improve coordination between various headquarters, air-defense units, and communications elements—all generating electronic emissions that Damascus and Baghdad knew would be monitored, collected, and analyzed by both Israel and the United States. Once again, the

message was clear: the Syrian-Iraqi military alliance was being strengthened irrespective of Washington's inducements and threats.

Meanwhile, the United States and Israel learned that Ukraine and Yugoslavia had sold Iraq a new generation of SAMs—derivatives of the Soviet-
era SA-6s. By late January, a virtual airlift of sophisticated weapons and
equipment moved from Ukraine to Iraq. According to some estimates, the
Iraqis had deployed as many as thirty-six new batteries with fiber-optic lines
of communication and a new generation of radar and electronic warfare systems. The Iraqi Air Defense forces began training for ambushes of American
and British aircraft enforcing the no-fly zone.

On January 24, Bashar al-Assad traveled to Tehran—his first foreign
visit as president—to assure the Iranians that the increased Syrian-Iraqi military cooperation was not coming at the expense of the Syrian-Iranian strategic alliance and to consolidate the Iran-Iraq-Syria axis for the forthcoming
war. The talks addressed such specific issues as cooperation in the development and production of ballistic missiles and weapons of mass destruction.
In their public speeches, Bashar, Khamenei, and Khatami all noted that Israel
was at its weakest point in recent years because of the Palestinian Intifadah,
the reverberations of HizbAllah's victory in Lebanon, and the change in administration in Washington. Bashar explicitly declared that "Israel and the
United States are in a position of weakness and on the defensive, and, despite
all the pressures that weigh on the Palestinian people, the uprising continues.
Now the Palestinians, instead of throwing stones, are taking arms." The
Syrian-Iranian strategic alliance "must be aimed at protecting the interests of
all Arab and Islamic countries in the region," Bashar continued. "The whole
world has recognized that Israel has never desired peace and will never desire
peace. Nine years of fruitless discussions confirm that." Responding,
Khatami alluded to the primacy of the military option. "A stable peace cannot be reached without the realization of the Palestinian people's rights," he
said. "Our two countries are moving toward the realization of the just rights
of all Muslim nations with the cooperation of Arab and Islamic countries.

———

JERUSALEM AND WASHINGTON agreed that the recent Iraqi troop
movements indicated the distinct possibility of an Iraqi strike against Israel.
Their apprehension increased when Iraqi military intelligence officers
showed up in Amman, for the first time since the Gulf crisis a decade before.
These officers held clandestine meetings with Palestinian supporters and
agents and surveyed Jordan's key roads, working out new supply routes for
the PA as well as an emergency escape route for Arafat. Meanwhile, seeking
to give Amman an added incentive to tolerate these activities, Saddam invited

a delegation of 170 Jordanian senior officials and businessmen to Baghdad to negotiate a free trade zone under conditions most favorable to the Jordanians. Given the mounting economic crisis in Jordan, King Abdallah was reluctant to scuttle the prospect of job-creating ventures.

By now, Israel had completed a major emergency acquisition of spare parts, ammunition, and other military equipment. The IDF upgraded the operational status of all weapon systems and conducted emergency mobilization exercises, with emphasis on its ability to react swiftly to a surprise attack where ballistic missiles would hit Israel's urban centers. The IDF also constructed control points and fortified positions overlooking the key axes of transportation leading from the Jordan Valley to Jerusalem and other key cities. On January 25, the United States deployed additional Patriot-related personnel and assets to both Israel and the Persian Gulf allies. The deployment to Israel involved about 400 members of the 69th Air Defense Artillery Brigade based near Frankfurt, Germany, ostensibly for the Juniper Cobra exercise scheduled to begin on February 8. The readiness level of the U.S. armed forces was raised, and several air-defense and medical corps were flown from the United States to the Middle East. Pentagon sources acknowledged that U.S. forces in Germany and Italy were placed on higher alert status.

The U.S. deployment was completed on February 5, as tension was peaking. There were sizable troop movements in Israel, western Iraq, and southern Lebanon, including the deployment of long-range rockets with their Iranian and HizbAllah crews to the vicinity of the Israeli border. The Bush administration advised the Syrians not to cooperate with the Iraqis' regional designs. Rebuffed by Damascus, Washington turned to Jerusalem, urging the Barak government to demonstrate extreme restraint vis-à-vis the Palestinians in order to reduce the likelihood of provocation.

On February 6, Israel went to the polls. Sharon's victory over Barak—62.5 percent to 37.4 percent—was the largest margin since the victory of David Ben Gurion, the country's founding father, in the first election in Israel's history. Both Sharon and Barak knew that the election amounted above all to the sound defeat of Barak's "peace policy." Furthermore, escalation in the Intifadah was virtually inevitable, increasing the likelihood of a regional war. Hence, Sharon immediately sought to establish the widest possible government of national unity, stressing that with Israel in the midst of potentially the most fateful crisis in its history, it was imperative to have a national consensus on the challenges and solutions.

———

A SINGLE MORTAR SHELL launched at the Netzarim settlement in Gaza on January 30 symbolized the start of a new phase in the Intifadah. It heralded an era where the Palestinians would openly use heavy weapons forbidden by the various Palestinian-Israeli agreements. Furthermore, the shooting team belonged to HizbAllah. The deployment of such teams to the Gaza Strip to help the Palestinians with long-range weapons was part of the comprehensive agreement obtained the previous summer by Lieutenant Colonel Massud Iyad of Force 17, acting as Arafat's personal emissary to HizbAllah.

Concurrently, HizbAllah forces in southern Lebanon were reinforced, deploying an array of long-range Katyusha rockets and Fajr missiles to forward positions near the border. A couple of days after the Israeli elections, Nasrallah urged the Arabs not to fear Sharon and promised that HizbAllah would continue to spearhead the decisive confrontation with Israel. "Those who forced Israel to withdraw from Lebanon can also defeat Israel," he declared. "If the Arabs acquire Faith, Will, the Spirit of Jihad, and Readiness for Martyrdom, they will be able to confront all threats."

During the previous fall, Israel had started intercepting weapons smuggled from Lebanon in a clandestine underwater war. Back in September, Colonel Iyad had established a supply line for a wide variety of matériel, including ammunition, high explosives, rocket-propelled grenades, Katyusha rockets, SAGGER ATGMs, and even Stinger SAMs. The weapons were packed in water-resistant packages, which were then put into heavy drums, which were in turn sealed by welding and then covered with thick layers of tar. These barrels were loaded onto small transport ships sailing from Lebanon to Port Said and other Egyptian ports. As the ships passed near Gaza, usually at night, the crew would dump the barrels into the sea. Palestinian frogmen, waiting on civilian fishing boats, would jump into the water and attach towlines to the barrels so that the boats could drag them to shore.

After Israel discovered this method of smuggling, Israeli patrol boats started forcing the transport ships leaving Lebanon to sail farther away from the coast, significantly complicating the weapon drops. Consequently, with the tacit agreement of Egyptian military intelligence, the weapon ships started sailing straight to Egypt and then returning along routes closer to the shore, safely dropping the barrels. It took Israel some time to become aware of the Egyptians' complicity.

By December, Israeli intelligence had established a fairly good monitoring system in Lebanon for identifying weapon-carrying boats. However, the Barak government ruled out sinking them in international waters, and searching too frequently would have alerted HizbAllah and the Palestinians to the Israelis' advance knowledge, as well as embarrassing the Egyptian government. Therefore, Israel embarked on a clandestine nocturnal war against the Palestinian frogmen. Underwater ambushes by Israel's Naval Commando teams (the equivalent of the American SEALs) proved successful, and a growing number of barrels ended up on Israeli-controlled beaches. In mid-January, HizbAllah notified Iran about the problems it was encountering. Consequently, a senior team of Pasdaran SEAL-equivalents was deployed to Tyre and the Beirut area, where they established an underwater-warfare training program for HizbAllah. In late January, HizbAllah teams, along with their Iranian instructors, started escorting the weapon-dumping ships, protecting the barrels until the Palestinian frogmen arrived. The Israelis expanded their clandestine war to include these teams as well. On one occasion, the IDF seized 40 weapon barrels containing 50 RPG launchers, 1,000 rockets, and scores of 60-mm mortar rounds.

By early January, the Palestinians who had been recruited in the camps in southern Lebanon and trained as special forces by the Iranians and HizbAllah were ready for deployment to Gaza. The Pasdaran experts recommended that a few senior instructors—all Iranians—should accompany the graduates to advise them as they went into action against Israel. Arafat consented, and the Iranians arrived in Gaza, followed by several HizbAllah teams. Israel could not ignore this threat. On Arafat's instructions, Iyad had been named the senior liaison officer with the Iranians and HizbAllah. On February 13, two Israeli gunships hit Iyad's car, killing him on the spot. Soon afterward, Israeli special forces arrested his son. It took the PA-HizbAllah-Iranian cooperation program months to recover from this setback.

———

IN EARLY FEBRUARY, even before Sharon took office, the IDF high command concluded that the new government would introduce a heightened pace of operations against the PA. At the core of the new military policy would be covert operations by a host of special forces, as well as deep and swift raids by small and highly flexible armored "fists," along with combat and assault helicopters. Barak would not implement any of these plans, fearing Clinton's negative reaction, but Sharon was eager to put them into action.

Concurrently, the fighting again escalated in the territories—with shellings of settlements in Gaza, ambushes on roads in the West Bank, and shootings in Jerusalem neighborhoods, especially Gilo. Israeli civilian casualties were mounting, and Israeli intelligence provided the Barak government with conclusive evidence that the perpetrators were members of elite teams answering directly to the uppermost leaders of the PA's security and intelligence organs. Dichter briefed the cabinet that "Arafat is the only one who is capable of acting against all the groups to bring about a drop in the violence," and he had shown no inclination to do so. Faced with this evidence, and given its abysmal showing in the elections, the Barak government was finally ready to tacitly acknowledge the failure of its peace policy. A week after the elections, the government formally voted that neither Clinton's bridging proposals nor the proposals put forth at Camp David or at Taba were binding on Sharon's incoming government.

A further escalation took place within a couple of days. A bus rammed into a group of Israeli soldiers and civilians waiting for transportation at an Ashkelon road junction, killing eight and wounding more than twenty-five. The thirty-year-old driver, who was captured after a chase, did not fit the profile of a terrorist. He had been employed by the Egged bus company for five years, transporting Arab workers to and from the Gaza Strip; he had family, and he had no known connection with any political or religious group. Yet he readily admitted that his action was premeditated, although he would state no motive other than emotional anguish.

Meanwhile, IDF units and PA strike forces clashed regularly throughout the Gaza Strip. As a rule, the Palestinian teams would emerge from, and withdraw into, densely populated refugee camps so that the Israelis' retaliatory fire invariably hit houses and inflicted civilian casualties. Ultimately, these rounds of attacks and counterattacks contributed to the further radicalization of the Palestinian population.

ON FEBRUARY 16, in retaliation for Iraq's growing audacity and effectiveness in challenging the enforcement of the no-fly zone, U.S. and U.K. aircraft bombed six Iraqi radar posts, command posts, and fiber-optics communications sites relatively close to Baghdad. The next day, Saddam ordered his armed forces to assume wartime readiness. The first units to react were the six divisions in western Iraq, which now moved farther westward toward the Jordanian and Syrian borders. At the same time, intense activities that could be interpreted as preparations for launching ballistic missiles were detected in bases throughout western and southern Iraq. U.S. and Israeli intelligence agreed that the Iraqis were preparing for ballistic-missile strikes against Israel, Saudi Arabia, and Kuwait, with the inclination to use any retaliation as the excuse for launching an all-out war against Israel. With Riyadh reluctant to permit the American use of Saudi bases in connection with hostilities involving Israel, the IDF, with some help from U.S. forces in Turkey, would have to bear the brunt of the anticipated confrontation. Consequently, Israeli air-defense units, along with the U.S. Patriot units still in training, were deployed to emergency positions. The *Aegis*-class cruiser USS *Porter* sailed off the southern coast of Israel, covering the theater with its radar.

By February 22, Iraqi SSM units were deployed and on the move throughout the western desert—capable of launching their first missiles in less than twenty-four hours. Concurrently, HizbAllah forces in southern

Lebanon went on alert following instructions from Damascus. The intense communications between Arafat, Saddam, and Bashar—detected by Israeli and U.S. intelligence—added to the growing apprehension.

That evening, analysts in both Washington and Jerusalem concluded that all was ready for a regional war—short of the final "Go" from Saddam Hussein. Intelligence services and governments in Western Europe must have shared this impression. Just as the high-level officials in Washington and Jerusalem were reaching agreement about the situation in Iraq and the appropriate response, the French government, and reportedly also the British, warned Saddam's inner circle through clandestine emergency channels of communication that they *knew for a fact* that Israel was about to use neutron weapons against the Iraqi expeditionary forces and the suspected missile sites if the movement toward war was not stopped.

With Washington unaware of the European warnings, two U.S. strike formations took off—one from the Incirlik base in Turkey, the other from a Sixth Fleet carrier—and headed toward western Iraq. Large formations of the Israeli Air Force were also in the air off the Syrian coast—ready to head toward Iraq should Iraqi missiles fall on Israel. The first American formations were engaged in the Mosul area by Iraqi air-defense units, which launched some thirty-five SAMs and heavy anti-aircraft barrages. The U.S. aircraft counterattacked with missiles and bombs—causing negligible damage because of the quality of the Iraqi camouflage and concealment.

By now, however, the Iraqi forces throughout the area were visibly standing down, in a way that was noticed by all possible intelligence collection systems. It seemed that Saddam had decided not to ignore the French warning and risk an Israeli nuclear strike.

But Baghdad had not given up its commitment to war. Within a month, the Chinese began delivering replacement equipment for the damaged fiber optics, as well as strategic technologies needed by Iraq's resurgent military industries. The Iraqis had also tried to establish a weapon acquisition center in Moscow under the command of Brigadier General Saadi Muhammad Subhi. However, Moscow would not tolerate such a flagrant presence, and so Subhi and his twenty-officer team moved to the open arms of Minsk, where they activated a new weapon acquisition center and established modalities for airlifting the systems acquired. The Iraqis also began a recruitment drive throughout the former Soviet Union for officers, scientists, and technicians to expedite the upgrading of the country's defense industrial infrastructure and the modernization of its electronic warfare and force deployment. By the end of February, dozens of such experts had been hired and sent to Baghdad. In addition, large quantities of radar and missile equipment were being smuggled into Iraq via Iran. On February 27, Saddam told a conference of Iraq's senior air-defense officers (now responsible for Iraq's ballistic missiles, in order to circumvent U.N. sanctions) and officials of the Atomic Energy Commission that Iraq was prepared to intervene militarily on behalf of the Palestinians or other Arab states. "We will deliver terrible strikes on the United States and cause the enemy to pay a heavy price, if it dares to continue attacking Iraq. Iraq will not permit the enemy to harm any other part of the Arab Nation," the Iraqi media quoted Saddam as saying.

Meanwhile, Arafat had unleashed his forces in anticipation of the eruption that never came. While Jerusalem was focused on events in western Iraq, Palestinian and HizbAllah teams launched several mortar shells at Israeli targets near the Gaza Strip. The firing position used by the PA teams could also be used for longer-range attacks on Israeli coastal cities, seaports, and power stations. Therefore, Barak ordered stern measures in retaliation, including cutting the Gaza Strip into several pockets by blocking key transportation arteries.

For General Mofaz, the situation was simple and straightforward. "The PA has become a terrorist entity," he said. "Arafat and the PA seniors encourage and dispatch Fatah, Tanzim, and HAMAS personnel to carry out operations." This escalation would be Sharon's first major challenge, even before he was formally sworn in as prime minister. And the new Bush administration's first direct exposure to the region—the visit of Secretary of State Colin Powell—would take place in the context of the escalation.

20

Sharon Strikes Back (2001)

Egypt and Saudi Arabia Declining, Iraq and Iran Surging

AS SHARON WORKED to put together his new government, the Bush administration saw no reason to change the priorities suggested by Jim Baker back in January. The main priority would be to shift the local powers' attention away from the Israeli-Palestinian quagmire and toward confronting Saddam Hussein. Colin Powell, spearheading the administration's effort, charmed his way through the Middle East on his first comprehensive visit to the region—exchanging jokes with Mubarak, driving King Abdallah's new Mercedes. But this was all show. Arab leaders were extremely reluctant to form a new coalition against Iraq. Damascus would hear nothing about breaking the expanding Syrian-Iraqi strategic alliance; after much pressure and cajoling, it agreed only to cosmetic supervision of the flow of Iraqi oil through Syrian pipelines. The Middle East was marching to its own drum, local leaders impressed upon Powell, and to be effective, the United States would have to adjust its pace accordingly. Bush's preoccupation with Iraq was out of sync, they stressed. It would take the Bush administration some time to comprehend this message.

The military activities in Egypt were especially worrisome to those watching the warning signs throughout the region. By early March, Egypt had called up reservists and started an intense training program to prepare them for a possible war with Israel. Egyptian senior officers, in their traditional Muslim holiday greetings to Mubarak, emphasized the readiness of the armed forces to confront "any possible threat." Concurrently, the Egyptian media harshly criticized Sharon's new "war government." Repeated efforts by both Jerusalem and Washington to convince Cairo that Sharon was committed to preserving the peace with Egypt had no visible impact on either the Egyptian military or the government-controlled media. Hence the IDF started calling up its own reservists in anticipation.

Meanwhile, Israeli officials had been appalled by Powell's insistence that "opposition to Arafat"—rather than the chairman himself—was behind the continued violence and that therefore Israel should help Arafat rather than fight his forces. Instead, the Israeli security elite urged Sharon to commit to contingency plans for an offensive against both the PA and HizbAllah. Deputy Chief of Staff Yaalon, heading a delegation of senior officers to brief Sharon, argued that "such an offensive is required to prove to the Palestinians, Arab states, and Iran that Israel is capable of defeating any military coalition." Specifically, the officers advocated the resumption of preemptive raids in both Area A and southern Lebanon. They also urged Sharon to approve swift, massive strikes in retaliation for future terrorist strikes.

The IDF's recommendations were also reflected in public statements. "It is not practical to reach a full agreement with the Palestinians at this time, even if the violence stops," National Security Council Chairman Dayan noted in a lecture. "We must respond to their call for war, while leaving an opening for a staged agreement." Dayan added that the PA must be made to understand that "they cannot fight in the present while talking about the future." In another lecture, Chief of Staff Mofaz reported on the increased flow of weapons into the PA-controlled areas and the ensuing escalation in the fighting. "This escalation is due to the fact that more and more Palestinian policemen and more and more people from the security agencies from the Palestinian side are taking part in the terror activity and in the violence," Mofaz said. In early March, General Malka, chief of Military Intelligence, told the Knesset's Foreign Affairs and Defense Committee that Arafat had given his "blessing for all organizations to carry out terror." The most important recent development, Malka stated, was that "the violence is premeditated by official PA security organizations and is no longer a popular uprising."

ISRAEL'S NEW NATIONAL-UNITY government was sworn in on March 7, 2001, with Sharon as prime minister, his old adversary Shimon Peres as foreign minister, the irrepressible Uzi Landau of the Likud in the thankless position of minister of domestic security, and Benjamin Ben-Eliezer as defense minister.

Although a member of the Labor Party, Ben-Eliezer is a retired brigadier general who had served directly under Sharon for many years and enjoyed close relations with him. The new government's primary concern was the growing threat of a general war, including the use of ballistic missiles and weapons of mass destruction. However, within a few days of the government's swearing in, Ben-Eliezer came face to face with the urgent need to intensify the fight against the Palestinians. During his first visit to the IDF's positions in Gaza, a Palestinian sniper fired two bullets at him as he observed the Palestinian dispositions from a rooftop. The heavyset Ben-Eliezer is easily recognizable, and the sniper must have known whom he was shooting at.

Yaalon took an early opportunity to brief the Sharon government on the cooperation between the PA and the Islamist and rejectionist groups. "I place the responsibility for the violence from the start on the PA," he said. The PA security forces, he reported, were deliberately releasing HAMAS and Islamic Jihad terrorists from jail and sending them to attack Israeli objectives. In many of these attacks, the perpetrators were wearing PA uniforms. "PA Chairman Yasser Arafat is using violence as a strategic weapon," a senior Israeli defense official explained. "He gives a green light to terrorism by releasing prisoners and by incitement."

The PA had also just finished setting up a solid new command-and-control structure in the territories. This structure was based on five regional centers—Ramallah, Nablus, Hebron, Gaza, and Han Yunis—and was optimized for withstanding the retaliatory onslaught Arafat was clearly anticipating. Arafat continued to use any available means to prepare for a new escalation. For example, during Powell's visit, less than an hour after the secretary of state left Arafat's Ramallah headquarters to return to Jerusalem, Arafat called a secret meeting of his security elite from the entire West Bank. He was confident Israel would not strike with Powell in the area. Arafat told the gathered officials to ignore his forthcoming political maneuvers, particularly in relation to peace-process initiatives, and instead to intensify the terrorist strikes. These strikes, he intimated, were aimed at provoking a massive Israeli retaliation in order to give Saddam an excuse to intervene. Arafat specifically instructed his commanders to give high priority to strikes at the heart of Israel, using deniable Islamist assets. On cue, HAMAS issued a communiqué announcing that it intended to resume terrorist attacks against Israelis "as soon as the Sharon government takes office" and boasting of having "ten suicide attackers" ready to strike out.

Arafat's lieutenants started implementing his instructions the very next day. That morning, a suicide bomber mingled with a civilian crowd in Netanya and exploded the bomb he was carrying on his person, leaving three dead and over seventy injured. The explosion took place opposite the city's central bus station; presumably the terrorist had planned to board a bus but, having seen the police inspecting IDs and packages, detonated his bomb ahead of time. As expected, HAMAS claimed responsibility for the attack, identifying the perpetrator as a resident of the refugee camp Nur Shams near Tulkarm—a Tanzim stronghold.

The Netanya bombing, along with a spate of shooting attacks and ambushes throughout the territories, alarmed the Bush administration, and the CIA immediately pressured Jerusalem to resume security coordination with Barghouti, giving him "an achievement" as an incentive to calm Arafat down. The CIA arranged a meeting between Barghouti and his aides and Dichter and senior GSS officials. The Palestinians were hostile, accusing Israel of provoking the new cycle of violence. The Israelis confronted Barghouti with evidence that on explicit instructions from Arafat, he had been directly responsible for recent operations in the Jerusalem area—operations such as the assassinations at the Social Security office in October, the car bomb near the Mahne Yehuda market in November, and the assassination of the Kahanes in December. Israel had an airtight case, demonstrating that Mahmud Damra, the local Force 17 commander, was directly in charge of these operations on behalf of, and closely coordinating with, Barghouti. The CIA representatives concurred with the Israeli data and warned Barghouti that such activities were not conducive to the peace process. Barghouti shrugged and would not commit to stopping the Intifadah. Back at his headquarters, he concluded that, given his refusal to bend, it was inevitable that the United States would pressure Arafat to contain him. Hence, he determined to increase his cooperation with Iraq, to provide Arafat with deniability, and to reduce his own dependence on Arafat.

When Israeli intelligence learned about Barghouti's contacts with the Iraqis, the IDF intensified its countermeasures—sending both armored columns and special forces into Area A to destroy PA facilities and other installations that supported the terrorist strikes in Israel. As well, the IDF stepped up its work of digging deep trenches around key sectors—Arab towns and townships and key roads—in order to hinder would-be car-bombers. By the time these efforts were completed, the West Bank was effectively divided into six major pockets, each surrounded by IDF forces.

———

SADDAM CAME THROUGH with the assistance Barghouti requested, permitting Barghouti to announce that the Tanzim would continue to fight irrespective of Arafat's instructions. Saddam also increased his influence in the territories by sending Iraqi intelligence officers to advise and train the various PA forces.

With the IDF tightening the enclosure of the key Palestinian cities, Barghouti and his allies arranged the first major confrontation over the enclosures, a large-scale demonstration at the Bir Zeit university campus. Significantly, Azzam Azzam al-Ahmad, Arafat's emissary to Baghdad, marched at the head of the column, clearly signaling Saddam's approval. This campaign peaked on March 14, when rioters led by Tanzim operatives stormed an IDF position. The Israeli soldiers abandoned their post rather than fire into the mob, but they returned later and took it back, using rubber-coated bullets to minimize Palestinian casualties. Barghouti, who observed the clash from afar, gloated over the achievement.

Arafat, meanwhile, was seeking to enhance his own posture in the Arab world by threatening not to come to the next Arab League summit, scheduled for late March in Amman, unless he was accompanied by a rehabilitated Saddam Hussein. Arafat played the summit game in a way that constituted a veiled threat to Saudi Arabia and the other Gulf States, which had started demanding that he account for the aid money they had sent the Palestinians. Arafat promised widespread solidarity riots throughout the Arab world if the conservative leaders failed to support the Palestinian jihad and its protector, Saddam Hussein.

As for Saddam, the key challenge he faced in his effort to consolidate a unified war front was the difficulty of forging a truly intimate trilateral relationship among Iraq, Syria, and the PA. While Saddam and his sons had extremely close relations with both Bashar al-Assad and Yassir Arafat, the schism that had existed between Arafat and Hafez al-Assad had continued with Bashar. Saddam decided to capitalize on the Amman Summit to arrange a meeting between the two.

THE BUSH ADMINISTRATION was still recovering from Powell's visit to the Middle East while preparing for Sharon's first visit to Washington as prime minister. The White House was aware of the enthusiastic support for Sharon on Capitol Hill, as well as the hostility there toward Arafat—a principled stance sharpened by frustration over the CIA's failure to achieve a tangible reduction in the violence. Therefore, Powell suggested downplaying the Palestinian track and, instead, pushing for resumption of the Syrian track. This initiative was warmly supported by Baker and hence by Bush Sr., and the White House decided to go ahead with it, completely ignoring Bashar's disdain for Powell during their recent meeting and his refusal to break off relations with Iraq or to crack down on HizbAllah. Bush called Bashar on the eve of Sharon's arrival to elicit some promise of cooperation. Because Bashar did not hang up on Bush, Powell and the State Department took his answer as "a qualified yes." To make sure that nobody in the region suspected him of being a peacemaker, however, Bashar attended Syrian military maneuvers and delivered a fiery speech proclaiming that there was no difference between one Israeli leader and another—they were all warmongers and aggressors.

The Bush administration was now pressuring Israel for an "achievement" in the peace process that could be associated with Sharon's visit. Given Bashar's less-than-enthusiastic response, the State Department resolved not to give up on the Palestinian track. Hence, on March 17, Sharon permitted GSS Chief Dichter to meet with Amin al-Hindi, Arafat's chief of general intelligence in Gaza and a protégé of Tenet, who arranged the meeting. Nothing came of it. The PA would not cooperate with the Sharon government on security issues, Hindi stated. Just to make sure Sharon understood Arafat's position, two hours later PA security forces made their first use of an anti-tank missile near Neve Dekalim in the Gaza Strip. Although neither damage nor casualties resulted, Arafat's message got through.

By then, however, Sharon was on his way to Washington for what would prove to be a highly successful visit. Sharon's personal relations with Bush—going back to Bush's visit to Israel in the late 1980s, remained close. The two men decided to go on calling each other by their first names, as they had done for more than a decade. In the Oval Office, Sharon outlined Israel's security concerns, as well as his general policies and intentions. Bush was most receptive, and his senior team maintained the same attitude in subsequent discussions. These turned to grand strategy, including common approaches to Iraq and Iran, as well as the problem of global terrorism. Sharon raised ideas about Israel's confronting the PLO/PA and Iraq in case of a major escalation, and Bush endorsed his ideas—especially because Sharon requested that the United States stay out of the conflict in order to avoid causing difficulties for the Saudis. Sharon was warned not to provoke hostilities, but the White House understood that Israeli retaliatory strikes would be painful and far-reaching.

Sharon also received enthusiastic support from Congress. Moreover, his meetings with the congressional leadership rejuvenated the American Jewish political elite's support for Israel and furthered their understanding of Israel's security problems. This was publicly demonstrated at the AIPAC conference in Washington, which coincided with Sharon's visit.

The only sour notes, from Sharon's point of view, were the coolness of senior State Department officials and the CIA's continued involvement in the peace process. Having explained at great length the extent of Arafat's duplicity and his direct involvement in terrorism, Sharon got Bush to agree to curtail the CIA's activities in Israel. However, because of domestic political considerations, Bush ultimately reversed that decision, and Tenet was allowed to keep the CIA actively involved in efforts to revive Israeli-Palestinian contacts.

———

WHILE SHARON was in Washington, Arafat ordered an all-out escalation of violence in the territories, showing that he clearly understood the pressure on Sharon not to do anything that might embarrass his hosts. Consequently, precedents were set for the "acceptability" of previously unthinkable acts by the PA security forces. There were more mortar shells, more ambushes, and more riots every day, with the IDF remaining largely passive. Arafat's dares peaked on March 21 when a large car bomb—a Dahlan-style bomb with the characteristic cellular-phone fuse—was placed in an ultra-Orthodox neighborhood of West Jerusalem. A passerby saw the phone and the wires and called the police; sappers neutralized the bomb with literally minutes to spare.

Concurrently, numerous moves were made to strengthen the northern front. Bashar al-Assad told a Jordanian journalist that Sharon had sent an emissary for secret talks, but that he, Bashar, had refused to meet with him. There was no point in any bilateral talks, he added, because Palestine's liberation should precede the Golan's. Meanwhile, Iran's foreign minister, Kamal Kharrazi, traveled to Beirut to coordinate a war-instigating provocation with HizbAllah and the Palestinian terrorist organizations. He also met with Bashar in Damascus to refine the coordination of the Iranian/Syrian and Iraqi operations in a future war.

Arafat made every effort to demonstrate that the PA was an integral part of these preparations. Significantly, Faisal Husseini was in Beirut at the same time as Kharrazi—ostensibly to deliver lectures about Jerusalem. On the eve of the Amman Summit, Husseini visited Ein Hilweh and publicly met with Munir Makdah, Arafat's erstwhile protégé turned Islamist challenger. Husseini delivered a fiery speech, calling for the destruction of Israel and reiterating Arafat's commitment to the uncompromising interpretation of the right of return.

On the morning of March 26, just before leaving for the Amman Summit, Arafat met with his senior commanders in Ramallah and told them to prepare for a "100-day campaign"—an all-out confrontation with Israel, which, if the PA prevailed, would lead the international community to pressure Israel to accept a Palestinian state. Arafat specifically discussed outrageous terrorist operations that would provoke Israel to react with "excessive" force during the Arab Summit—thus inflaming spirits in Amman. Arafat also activated a new senior team—made up of Tirawi, al-Hindi, and Arafat's brother Musa—in charge of the escalation. Islamist terrorists loosely affiliated with HAMAS and Islamic Jihad were assigned to this command team.

Implementation of Arafat's instructions started almost immediately. First came a dramatic operation the PA had been preparing for some ten days. PA combat engineers had dug an underground tunnel from Gaza to the main agricultural water reservoir near Nahal Oz, inside pre-1967 Israel, and planted a powerful bomb there. Shortly after Arafat's meeting with his commanders, the engineers set off the bomb, causing massive flooding in the suburbs of Gaza City. During the Amman Summit, Arafat would insist that Israel had attempted to destroy the Gaza Strip with this flood. Later that day, IDF soldiers at an observation post in Hebron watched helplessly as a Tanzim sniper, using a U.S.-made rifle and scope provided by the CIA, shot in cold blood a ten-month-old baby girl lying in her crib. The sniper first shot the baby's father in the leg; then, when everyone turned to help him, leaving the crib exposed, the sniper fired a single shot into the baby's head. As expected, this horrendous murder incited both riots by the enraged settlers and an IDF retaliation against the neighborhood from which the sniper had fired. In Amman, Arafat used these events to demonstrate the dangers faced by the Palestinians.

————

THE ARAB LEAGUE SUMMIT was, as usual, preceded by meetings at the ministerial level, as well as meetings of chiefs of intelligence and security forces, providing an opportunity for exchanges of opinion without the public postures national leaders had to adopt. The senior officials in attendance were all apprehensive about the consequences of a regional war. Their sole disagreement was over when this war would break out. Those who were close to the PA maintained that Israel could not tolerate Arafat's provocations for long. They warned that having gained Bush's personal approval, Sharon would most likely unleash the IDF within the next ten days. Other officials expected the war to erupt in late May or early June—the optimal time for the Israelis to use their superior air power. Saudi and other Gulf State officials expressed their displeasure with the slide to war but seemed resigned to the idea that the Palestinians and their allies were adamant on dragging the entire region into a catastrophe and that there was nothing the other Arab leaders could do to stop them.

These discussions exposed how much political power Egypt and Saudi Arabia had lost. Mubarak's inability to bring economic progress to Egypt and to cope with the population explosion had left the country spiraling down into near collapse. He had diverted vast financial resources, in the form of lavish foreign aid from the United States, to feed the growing corruption among his cronies and the military. In Amman, Mubarak allowed himself to be dragged into conspiracies and war preparations just to remain relevant in a whirlwind he could not control or even influence. Similarly, the Saudi leadership was consumed by a revived succession crisis—as various of Crown Prince Abdallah's half brothers and nephews maneuvered either to supplant him as successor to the ailing King Fahd or to succeed him as Crown Prince if he did become King—and was unable to deal with the Islamist fervor stirred up by the Intifadah. Riyadh feared the economic repercussions of a war and an oil embargo and feared even more the implications of a regional war for Saudi Arabia's domestic stability and the very survival of the House of al-Saud. Yet Saudi senior officials could not elucidate a reason for their country's staying out of a regional war for the liberation of al-Aqsa/al-Quds. They simply went along with the PA-generated rhetoric of militancy.

Bashar al-Assad set the tone for the formal summit with a virulently anti-Jewish speech. "There is one persistent thing in the Middle East—the extremism and racism of the Israeli people," Bashar declared. "The Israeli public is more racist than the Nazis." Bashar explained that the Israeli public "assassinated Rabin" and "overthrew" Peres, Netanyahu, and Barak, simply because they had attempted to further the peace process. Then the Israelis elected the "notorious criminal" Sharon in order to destroy any chance for peace. The Arab Nation, however, was determined to reclaim the stolen Arab lands: "The moment the Arab leaders adopt the brave decision [to confront Israel], the 300 million Arabs will support them." The current policies had "failed to restore the Arabs' rights," Bashar reminded his audience. Therefore, it was imperative to capitalize on the ongoing Intifadah and escalate the confrontation with Israel. "The Palestinian Question is the central challenge of Syria. We are with them until we force the Israeli withdrawal to the June 1967 lines, till the establishment of an independent state with Jerusalem as its capital, and until the return of all refugees to their homes. We are united with them in supporting the Intifadah," Bashar concluded. As expected, all the other Arab leaders publicly followed the same line.

The reconciliation of Bashar and Arafat, as well as transaction of other highly important business, took place in private meetings among key leaders. In one series of meetings Arafat discussed with Bashar and Iraqi Vice President Izzat Ibrahim al-Duri, as well as senior officials from both countries, the political and strategic aspects of launching a regional war. They all agreed that it was imperative to act before the new Bush administration became intimately involved in the Middle East. Through emissaries in Amman, Tehran committed to funding the bulk of this undertaking. Israeli intelligence acquired full transcripts of these meetings, and Sharon instructed that a copy of the entire text be given directly to President Bush.

On March 28, the Arab leaders ended their brief summit by taking up a host of regional issues. They welcomed the resolution of a border dispute between Saudi Arabia and Qatar and reiterated their pro forma support for the United Arab Emirates' claim to three islands held by Iran; however, their pleas to Tehran and expressions of regret over its policies were low key. On the Palestinian issue, the leaders agreed to increase their financial support to the PA, although the conditionality of payments did little to meet Arafat's complaints that only a small fraction of the $1 billion already committed had actually been transferred to his coffers. Most significant was the fact that the Arab League bowed to Palestinian pressure and adjourned without agreement on a resolution regarding the U.N. sanctions on Iraq, despite all-out efforts by Saudi Arabia and Kuwait—another manifestation of those countries' declining influence.

Just as the Arab Summit was wrapping up, Israel launched a major offensive against key Palestinian infrastructure and military objectives in five cities throughout the West Bank and the Gaza Strip. These attacks—with tanks and helicopter gunships—were directed principally against the facilities of Arafat's own Force 17, including a garrison less than 100 yards from Arafat's house. An Israeli military spokesman explained that "Force 17 is responsible for the escalation in violence. This is our signal that we won't tolerate any more attacks from this body." Addressing the role of Islamist martyr-bombers in the recent escalation, Israeli senior officials told MENL's Steve Rodan that Israel had adopted "a new policy that holds the Palestinian Authority as responsible for attacks against the Jewish state." They explained that "the policy is meant to strike the interests of PA Chairman Yasser Arafat while limiting restrictions on the Palestinian population" and that "the policy will be directed at terrorist elements." At the same time, Jerusalem rushed to assure friends and foes alike that the new offensive did not signal the end of the peace process. A senior official noted that "our policy is aimed at preventing the Palestinians from winning political gains through violence. . . . We will not leave the initiative in the hands of the terrorists." The PA remained defiant. "Our retaliation will be the most painful Israel has ever experienced," announced a senior Tanzim official.

The alarmed Bush administration urged Arafat to stop the escalation before it got out of control. "The signal I'm sending to the Palestinians is stop the violence," Bush himself told reporters. "I can't make it any more clear." While Bush's comments were largely neutral, subsequent public diplomacy pointed the finger at Israel and showed complete obliviousness to what was going on elsewhere in the Middle East. For example, testifying before Congress, Assistant Secretary of State for Near East Affairs Edward Walker (who had briefly been Ambassador to Israel in 1999 but was recalled for being too anti-Israel) said the United States was "perplexed" by Arafat's behavior and opined that Arafat had launched the Intifadah in order to gain concessions after the failed Camp David summit. The administration rushed to mitigate the impression left by Walker's testimony; however, it also called on Israel to "exercise restraint in its military response" and stated that Israel "should take steps to restore normalcy to the lives of the Palestinian people by easing closures and removing checkpoints." Having provided the Bush administration with detailed intelligence about the PA-Iraqi-Syrian war designs—which were the reason for the swift Israeli crackdown on the latest cycle of Palestinian violence—Sharon's security "kitchenette" (the few Cabinet ministers he trusted most) was both surprised by and furious at Washington's public reaction.

On Friday, March 30—Land Day, as observed by the Israeli Arabs—the main event was in the Israeli-Arab village of Sakhnin, where a nonviolent procession challenged Israel's right to exist. The marchers carried the flags of the PLO, HizbAllah, Syria, and Iraq, as well as portraits of Gamal Abd-al-Nasser—the symbol of commitment to pan-Arabism and the destruction of Israel. The demonstrators burned the flags of Israel and the United States. Meanwhile, the PA unleashed both mobs and armed strike teams against the IDF throughout the territories. In retaliation, IDF tanks shelled several buildings that served as PA firing positions in the Ramallah area, killing two. In Jerusalem, police evacuated the Western Wall plaza for approximately one hour as Israeli Arabs threw rocks and blocked paths in the Old City.

The next day, violence continued throughout the territories and in Israel proper, with retaliation by Israeli gunships and heavy mortars. Over the weekend, the PA conducted a major military exercise in preparation for a possible Israeli invasion of the West Bank and the Gaza Strip. The exercise included defense of major roads as well as "a response by commandos"—in other words, terrorist attacks on IDF positions and civilian communities. Significantly, the PA security forces and the Tanzim forces jointly took part in the exercise, operating in a fully integrated mode.

Alarmed by the possibility of a spiraling escalation, Sharon dispatched his son Omri, along with his adviser Yossi Ginossar, for a secret meeting with Arafat in Ramallah on the night of April 1–2. However, the message Sharon sent was confusing. While Israel would not negotiate under fire, Omri told Arafat, Israel also had no intention of markedly escalating the conflict by invading PA-held areas. To a great extent, Sharon's message served as an incentive for Arafat to sustain the status quo of a tolerable level of anti-Israeli violence. On April 4, Israel's message to the PA was further blurred when Peres met with Nabil Shaath, Yasser Abed Rabbo, and Saeb Erekat at a conference in Athens. One of Peres's confidants described the meeting as "one step toward resumption of negotiations," although Peres himself insisted that "no peace negotiations" took place but rather "talks aimed at stopping the violence."

On the night of April 4–5, Colin Powell arranged for a high-level security meeting in Tel Aviv chaired by a senior CIA official—a clear reversal of Bush's recent promise to Sharon. Emboldened by the Athens meeting, the Palestinians were abrasive and only raised demands for Israeli concessions, including the unconditional withdrawal of all IDF forces from around PA cities and an end to the enclosure of the PA areas. The Palestinians flatly refused to discuss Israel's demand that they re-arrest HAMAS and Islamic Jihad terrorists released from PA jails—a demand endorsed by the CIA representative. The meeting ended on a tense and hostile note.

AS THE PA DELEGATION was returning to Gaza from the Tel Aviv meeting, Dahlan pulled a masterstroke that shifted the outside world's attention away from the PA's refusal to abide by its promises and toward Israel's alleged aggression. Soon after the Palestinian VIP convoy of three SUVs passed the Israeli checkpoint, automatic fire came from the back window of the lead SUV—Dahlan's own vehicle. This meant that none other than Dahlan's bodyguards had fired at the IDF troops. The Israelis returned their fire, damaging one of the cars and slightly wounding two of Dahlan's bodyguards. The three SUVs sped toward a PA building, and, once shielded by the building, the occupants resumed fire.

While the shooting was still going on, Dahlan used his cell phone to call Prince Bandar bin Sultan, the Saudi Ambassador to Washington. Dahlan theatrically told Bandar that the IDF had just attempted to assassinate the entire Palestinian delegation because they would not succumb to the Israeli-American pressure. Dahlan described their dramatic escape and let Prince Bandar listen to the sounds of battle over the phone. Bandar immediately called Powell and then Tenet, threatening a major crisis if the United States did not intervene. Tenet added his voice to Bandar's, warning Powell of the dire implications if even the semblance of an Israeli assassination attempt went without a swift and stern reaction from Washington.

Powell quickly called Sharon and scolded him about the "unacceptable" incident. Powell would hear nothing about the unprovoked attack on the Israeli checkpoint from Dahlan's car. Despite Sharon's repeated offers, the CIA refused to have its own officers visit the scene to look at the bullet holes and collect forensic evidence. Instead, Powell coerced Sharon into sending him a letter describing the shooting incident as "regrettable" and leaving open the possibility that the shots fired at the Israeli checkpoint might have come from near the Dahlan convoy and not from the convoy itself. This vague description contradicted the results of the forensic investigation conducted by the IDF and the Israeli police—which concluded that the source of fire was a point covered by the tracks of Dahlan's car.

The next day fighting broke out in the Gaza Strip—a preplanned outburst of "spontaneous rage" over the alleged attempt on Dahlan's life. The first round of mortar shells aimed at Israeli villages was fired by Force 17 teams under the command of Dahlan's deputy, Colonel Rashid Abu-Shabak, though it was publicly attributed to HAMAS. The IDF retaliated during the night, firing on buildings belonging to the PA General Intelligence Service and Force 17. Helicopter gunships also attacked PA military installations all over the Gaza Strip. Once again, the cycle of fighting continued for several days. On April 10, an IDF senior officer conceded that Israel had "failed to deter" and could "no longer scare" the PA through such retaliatory exchanges. Consequently, on the 11th, Israel launched "a limited ground war" against the PA. IDF armored units entered some 300 yards into the Khan Yunis area and destroyed a dozen PA military posts used for shelling Gush Katif settlements. The PA acknowledged two fatalities and over twenty wounded and claimed that numerous civilian houses were destroyed. Palestinian sources stressed that "this was the first time Israeli military forces operated openly in territory controlled by the PA."

This escalation heightened the long-standing Palestinian fears of a decisive Israeli onslaught. Furthermore, when Arafat called Powell and asked for a U.S.-imposed cease-fire, Powell would only promise to get the Israelis to renew the security negotiations. Arafat interpreted this as a tacit American green light for Jerusalem to attack the PA. Believing that Sharon would soon order his assassination, Arafat changed his helicopter to an official Jordanian helicopter, which he believed Israel would not dare shoot down. He also sent emissaries to Mubarak to secure asylum in Egypt should the need arise and to ask Mubarak to ask Washington to coerce Israel into a unilateral ceasefire. When Cairo failed to deliver a quick cessation of hostilities, Arafat turned to Riyadh, asking the royal family to put pressure on the Bush administration—so that it would order Israel not to assassinate him.

Prince Bandar did raise Arafat's fears with the White House, which arranged a special meeting of Israeli and Palestinian security officials at Ambassador Indyk's private residence near Tel Aviv. The meeting was contentious, with the Palestinians demanding a series of unilateral concessions—most of which were endorsed by Ambassador Indyk, who also confirmed the Israeli guarantee not to assassinate Arafat.

A few days later, when Arafat expressed doubts about that guarantee, Sharon sent Omri along with Dichter to meet him in Ramallah and renew the pledge that Israel would not attempt to kill him. Omri and Dichter also raised the issue of mortar fire. A senior Israeli official later reported that it was a "difficult" conversation. Dichter presented Arafat with detailed intelligence proving that the Palestinian mortar fire was being conducted under the protection of Arafat's senior aides. Dichter warned that Israel would have to retaliate unless the mortar fire stopped. With great theatrics, Arafat lifted the phone receiver, called one of his senior officers, and berated him for not carrying out his, Arafat's, order to stop the mortar fire. Then Arafat turned triumphantly to Omri and promised that from then on there would be fewer incidents. He did not promise that there would be no incidents. It was "one big show," the senior Israeli official remarked.

The moment Arafat felt secure again, he ordered renewed escalation, starting with mortar shelling and fire attacks throughout the Gaza Strip— eliciting the now routine IDF raids into Area A. After a couple days of such exchanges, Arafat was confident that Jerusalem would not implement Dichter's threats. Hence, on April 16, the PA fired a few mortar shells into the city of Sderot—not far from Sharon's farm. Israel reacted with a large-scale attack on the Gaza Strip. "In light of the intolerable shooting actions against Israeli towns," said the IDF's communiqué, "the order [was given] to the IDF to take action within the Gaza Strip in order to clarify to the Palestinians that the State of Israel will not accept this type of incident." At the same time, Jerusalem announced that Israel had no intention of permanently holding Area A territory and that the IDF would withdraw once the Palestinians "act[ed] against terrorism from within their territory." Israel did acknowledge that the IDF's mission could last a long time. "We will remain [in Gaza] for days, weeks, or months, as long as it takes," Brigadier General Yair Naveh told reporters.

That was not to be. Powell called immediately and berated both Sharon and Peres. State Department spokesman Richard Boucher quoted Powell as saying that Israel's reaction was "excessive and disproportionate." At the CIA's request, Dichter flew to Cairo, where Arafat and Rajub were already meeting with Mubarak, and raised the possibility of a cease-fire and withdrawal. Instead, Arafat ordered all available PA forces to attack the IDF incursion relentlessly. Israeli intelligence promptly informed Sharon, who decided to avoid unnecessary casualties and minimize the political damage by ordering the IDF to withdraw. The PA immediately resumed firing mortar shells into the Sderot area and planting roadside bombs. The next morning, a smaller IDF force returned to Area A, destroying the PA positions from which the mortars had been fired. The Israeli security cabinet met and decided to continue the retaliatory measures if the shelling continued.

———

HAVING RETURNED from Amman, where he was clearly the most aggressive leader present, Bashar al-Assad resolved to demonstrate that he was serious about the policies he had advocated to the rest of the Arab world. As before, HizbAllah would be Damascus's willing instrument.

The first public indication that an escalation was afoot came on April 3, when Sheikh Nasrallah delivered an address at a Shiite conference in

Lebanon. He reiterated that the Islamists' ultimate objective was the destruction of Israel and emphasized that the Israeli threat extended to the entire region: "In the future the Jews will confront the Arabs over their rights also in the Nile and the Euphrates. . . . The very existence of Israel is the gravest and most dangerous disease threatening the Lebanese, Palestinians, Arabs, and Muslims. The region will know no peace for as long as Israel exists." Significantly, Nasrallah connected his own assertions with the positions taken by Bashar. "The President of Syria said the right things during the Arab Summit when he described Israeli society as the most racist society in existence," Nasrallah declared. "We have to continue and struggle against this disease as we have succeeded in doing in recent years." HizbAllah would soon answer his call to arms.

Concurrently, Israeli military sources told Steve Rodan that "the Syrian military appears to be building positions to launch an attack on Israeli defenses in the Golan." What especially worried Israel was that Syria was building structures in abandoned and partially destroyed villages from which the Army could launch commando raids against the Israeli forward positions. The Israeli high command briefed the government that the Syrian Army's efforts would give Damascus the option of preempting in case an eruption in southern Lebanon escalated out of control and all-out war seemed inevitable.

Meanwhile, HizbAllah continued to increase the tension so that it could provoke Israel without a direct attack. It conducted an intense campaign against the families of former SLA troops and other Christian Lebanese who had remained in southern Lebanon after the Israeli withdrawal. In the first days of April there was a sudden spate of activity: shops bombed, agricultural equipment and homes destroyed, and leading figures in the villages threatened with assassination. HizbAllah made sure everyone knew who was behind this campaign. As HizbAllah expected, Jerusalem felt considerable pressure to save Israel's abandoned allies.

On April 11, the 30,000-strong Syrian forces in Lebanon were put on high alert. Officially, the alert was instituted in order to protect the more than 1 million Syrian laborers in Lebanon from attacks by Lebanese opposition forces. In fact, although there were numerous such attacks in the spring of 2001, these actions did not threaten the Syrian presence, and the Syrians knew it. Rather, their forces remained deployed in dispositions optimized for withstanding a major Israeli attack. On April 12, Beirut sent Syrian-controlled security forces to the village of Shebaa, on the Lebanese-Israeli border, to investigate reported attacks on Syrian laborers by former members of the SLA. The commotion created by their activities masked HizbAllah's last-minute preparations for a new escalation.

The next day, HizbAllah launched a major attack on an Israeli outpost on Har Dov (Shebaa Farms). IDF artillery and gunships responded by attacking HizbAllah positions and Lebanese villages sheltering HizbAllah forces, leading to protracted exchanges of fire throughout the entire region. These were the heaviest clashes in several months.

Israeli intelligence confirmed that Damascus had given the orders for the operation, which had strategic as well as tactical objectives. On the tactical level, Syria wanted HizbAllah to provoke Israeli retaliation that would, in turn, lead Beirut to ask Damascus for protection. On the strategic level, Bashar had to prove to the Syrian elite, and to the rest of the Arab world, that he was capable of acting on his brave words at the Amman Summit. Furthermore, Damascus sought to seize the initiative from Baghdad by demonstrating that Syria was in control of the escalation potential in the region.

Acting on this detailed intelligence material, Sharon decided to strike at Syrian strategic objectives to demonstrate Jerusalem's awareness of Damascus's responsibility for the Har Dov attack. On the night of April 15–16, four Israeli F-16s attacked Syrian military installations in Dahr al-Baydar, some 12 miles east of Beirut, north of the Beirut-Damascus road. The planes fired six missiles, destroying three Syrian targets—a communications center, an anti-aircraft battery, and an early-warning radar station. The Dahr al-Baydar station was considered the most strategically important Syrian radar site in Lebanon, located at a key position overlooking most of southern and eastern Lebanon. Three Syrian soldiers were killed and another six were injured in the Israeli strike. Syrian air-defense fire was sporadic and ineffective. At daybreak, Israeli aircraft resumed patrolling the skies of Lebanon. Subsequently, Syrian officials vowed unspecified retaliation, while, at the same time, Damascus delivered messages to Jerusalem via Paris that it did not want a wider war with Israel.

There was some truth in the Syrian messages. By early April, the Syrian high command had completed a major study assessing Syria's prospects in a near-term regional war. The study's conclusions were mixed. It found that the buildup and modernization of the Syrian Army had progressed to a point where there was no reason for Syria not to go to war, provided it did not have to fight on two fronts—that is, provided Turkey was not a participant. For Damascus this was a major concern because Israel continued to deploy air force and other military assets in Turkey. Hence, in mid-April Syria invited a high-level Turkish military delegation to Damascus, where senior officials pressured them to curtail their cooperation with Israel. The mere fact that a senior Turkish delegation was willing to go to Damascus and listen to the Syrian demands was an indication of the decline of Israel's deterrence posture. Damascus's confidence was also enhanced by the arrival of an Egyptian emissary bearing Mubarak's pledge to help Syria in any war against Israel.

The Syrians did refuse Tehran's offer to launch a ballistic-missile strike against Israel, citing their reluctance to go to war before all preparations were completed. By now, however, the Iranians were adamant on demonstrating their own strategic preeminence in the region. Therefore, on April 18, they launched a barrage of between 56 and 72 SSMs—a mix of NK-SCUD-Cs and the locally produced Shehab-2s—against the Mujahedin ul-Khalq, an Iranian opposition terrorist group based in eastern Iraq. According to U.S. estimates, the Iranians fired about 20 percent of their arsenal in a single day. All the preparations, the deployment of over fifty launch vehicles to two forward bases, and the actual firing of a massive first barrage and a smaller follow-up barrage were conducted in complete radio silence and perfect camouflage. The operation caught the United States and Israel entirely by surprise—a serious wake-up call as to the regional threats facing Israel. Subsequently, Iran sent a delegation to Damascus led by the senior commanders of the attack on the Mujahedin ul-Khalq. They brought with them aerial pictures and videotapes of the SSM barrage. The Iranians once again urged the Syrians to permit a surprise ballistic-missile attack on Israel. This time, the Syrians were more receptive.

———

HIZBALLAH'S APRIL 13 provocation, including the overt Syrian support, had been precisely timed to enhance the position of both HizbAllah and Damascus at a major terrorism conference to be convened in Tehran on April 20. The Syrians wanted to ensure that when Sheikh Nasrallah and the HizbAllah's supreme leadership were discussing their next move, they did not overlook the centrality of Syria's sponsorship. HizbAllah, for its part, was determined to secure its center-stage position among HAMAS, Islamic Jihad, and a host of radical Palestinian groups all vying for Tehran's financial and intelligence support.

The HizbAllah delegation, led by Nasrallah, arrived in Tehran ahead of the other delegations and received a warm welcome from the entire Iranian leadership. Khamenei urged Nasrallah to continue the strikes against Israel while expanding HizbAllah's cooperation with other radical Palestinian and Lebanese groups. "The HizbAllah should be vigilant and take the initiative in fighting against the Zionist regime," Khamenei told Nasrallah. Senior Iranian officials promised Nasrallah that shipments of weapons—particularly long-range rockets and anti-tank missiles—would be accelerated, and Tehran formulated new modalities of cooperation between Iranian intelligence and Arafat's Force 17 under the aegis of HizbAllah. On the Iranian side, this new cooperation in support of spectacular terrorist operations against Israel would be under the personal command of Imad Mughniyah, who had fought in the ranks of Force 17 during the early 1980s and had maintained communications with Arafat. On the Palestinian side, Arafat's emissaries would be shielded by Munir Makdah in Ein Hilweh.

The formal conference opened on April 23, with delegations from some thirty-five Muslim states attending. The declared objective was to coordinate additional support for the Palestinian Intifadah. PLO Central Committee Chairman Salim al-Zaanun—Arafat's point man in dealing with HAMAS and other Islamist groups—represented the PA. Until the last minute, Arafat himself was expected in Tehran, but he canceled because of intense pressure from Washington.

Khamenei set the tone of the conference by clearly stating the objective of all those present: the imminent destruction of Israel. Citing the lessons learned from the withdrawal from southern Lebanon, Khamenei maintained that Israel could soon be eliminated. "I assure you," he said, "that the Israeli regime is decayed from within, and the present generation is by no means prepared to make any sacrifices for its preservation." In a bellicose speech, Nasrallah committed HizbAllah to sustained operations against Israel, both on its own and in cooperation with various Palestinian organizations. "The fully armed Zionist military should wait for surprise attacks by Palestinian resistance groups," Nasrallah warned. "Victory belongs to us." HAMAS leader Khalid Mashal concurred: "Our people categorically reject any return to the negotiating table. We want suicide attacks and mortar attacks."

Most significant was Zaanun's speech. "The Oslo Agreements were an illusion, and the Israeli-Palestinian peace process is at a dead end. Oslo was a castle of sand," Zaanun proclaimed, speaking as Arafat's representative.

———

TEHRAN'S GROWING INVOLVEMENT was taking place just as the Bush administration—prompted by pressure from Prince Bandar on the United States to contain the spiraling escalation—was reversing its hands-off policy and attempting to revive the Middle East peace process. In mid-April, Bush and Powell called Sharon and several Arab leaders to inform them of Washington's new approach. Concurrently, Assistant Secretary of State Walker went to the region to try "to restore calm," as he explained during his first stop, in Amman. "We are actively engaged with the parties," he added, "and eventually we will be more engaged in the future." However, he could gain no cooperation from Damascus or any other Arab capital in containing the growing tension. Hence, he recommended that the United States focus on allaying the Arab world's concerns by reducing the pressure on Iraq and by eliciting more concessions from Jerusalem on the Palestinian track.

Arafat realized he would have to appear to be complying with the new U.S. initiative. Moreover, Mubarak assured him that he, Arafat, could finally be invited to the Bush White House if the United States were able to point to "sincere efforts" by the PA to contain violence. As usual, Arafat decided to play both sides. While notifying Mubarak of his intent to cooperate with the Americans, he convened in Ramallah on April 20–21 a secret meeting of the West Bank Tanzim leadership. "In the coming days you will hear a lot of talk about diplomatic contacts, reduction of violence, and peace," Arafat told the Tanzim commanders. "You will hear a lot of talk about my support for one thing or another. I ask you, my brethren in arms and struggle, don't pay any attention to this talk and don't let them confuse you. Yours is a single sacred obligation—to persevere and escalate the armed struggle against the Zionist enemy." Arafat acknowledged that he might have to pretend to cooperate with the peace process. However, he assured his commanders, "You and no-body else know what my real position is. You and only you know that I will never withdraw even a single millimeter from this position. And God be with you and your actions." Israeli intelligence promptly reported this meeting to the Sharon government.

Nonetheless, Jerusalem complied with Washington's demands. The United States organized meetings between representatives of Sharon and Arafat on the renewal of the diplomatic process. On April 20, the IDF opened the main roads throughout the Gaza Strip to uninterrupted Palestinian traffic, even though Arafat refused to cooperate with the CIA and the GSS in stopping mortar fire into Israel. In addition, the Israeli cabinet adopted a policy of "small signature" operations rather than larger sweeps in order to reduce points of contention with the Bush administration.

If anything, Israel's demonstration of "flexibility" only projected a sense of weakness and self-doubt. For the first time, the Arab world had tangible proof that Sharon—whose wrath they had feared so much—could, like his predecessors, be manipulated and pressured by the United States. The Arab response was swift and assertive. Mubarak openly suggested that war was the Arab world's preferable course of action. "If the talks really turned to war, the Americans would get involved and prevent an all-out war from happening," Mubarak said, as quoted by his state-owned media. "Yet as bad as war is, at least you know what you are dealing with. Worse than open war is this terror, which can strike anywhere and at any time." Mubarak stressed that it was his own experience dealing with Sharon that drove him to advocate the war option. "When he came to power, everyone told me that no real peace was to be made with Sharon. I defended him and said, 'Wait, give him time,'" the Cairo media quoted Mubarak as saying. "Now I have the impression he is only interested in violence." Concurrently, King Abdallah and senior Jordanian officials warned that the Middle East could no longer stand the building tension.

Arafat picked up the signal, and the next day saw a marked escalation in the fighting—right after yet another U.S.-supervised security coordination meeting. First came the resumption of mortar fire from the Gaza Strip into Israel proper. Then a car bomb exploded in Or Yehuda, a township on the road to Ben Gurion Airport; the bomb had all the signs of a PA operation. A few hours later, Arafat's own forces opened automatic fire on Gilo. Several roadside bombs were exploded and small-arms ambushes were carried out throughout the territories. On the cabinet's instructions, the IDF exercised "utmost restraint"—in many cases not even returning fire.

In ordering this escalation, Arafat was following the wishes not only of his fellow Arab leaders but also of his own public. A poll conducted by a PA research institute found, for example, that 54.4 percent "very much" supported martyrdom bombing against Israel, while 19.3 percent supported it "to some extent," 10.1 percent objected "to some extent," and only 5.8 percent objected "vehemently" to such bombing.

As the violence continued, the CIA's Tel Aviv station arranged yet another round of security talks in Ramallah. The CIA was only a "facilitator," CIA spokesman Mark Mansfield insisted. The CIA "is not to negotiate; it is not to mediate; it is to provide a venue and invite people to come to a meeting." After the Ramallah talks, an exasperated senior Israeli official gave a rather different account. As in previous cycles of negotiations, he related, "we repeated our position that the Palestinians have to stop the violence, and discussed ways to improve the situation for the Palestinian population," whereupon the CIA asked Israel to do "something" in order "to ease the Palestinians' lives" and thus improve Arafat's standing. Under such circumstances, the Israeli official wondered, where was the incentive for Arafat to cease fire?

Nevertheless, in late April, Sharon succumbed to pressure from both his son Omri and Peres to give Arafat another chance. The Bush administration encouraged this approach, citing Arafat's not visiting Tehran as a concession worthy of an Israeli reward. On the night of April 24–25, Omri telephoned Arafat and talked with him at length, and Peres warmly endorsed his efforts. Consequently, Sharon agreed to the formation of an Israeli-Palestinian security committee. He also agreed to send Peres to Cairo and Amman in order to discuss modalities for loosening the Israeli enclosure of Palestinian cities, as well as the release of PA funds frozen in Israeli banks, in return for a Palestinian cease-fire or, at the very least, a tangible reduction in the intensity of violence.

Instead, Palestinian terrorism increased markedly. Arafat ordered this outbreak of violence against the recommendation of his most militant commanders, who noted the dwindling stockpiles of supplies, including AK-47 bullets. Nevertheless, Arafat ordered the escalation to increase the pressure on Israel as Peres was getting ready to travel to Cairo. Furthermore, for the first time, Arafat's own Fatah claimed responsibility for a mortar shelling. "Mortar shells are not our only weapon, and Ashkelon is not far away," the Fatah communiqué concluded.

In retrospect, the explosion of a martyr-driven car bomb near a school bus on the road to Netanya was especially significant. The driver was heading toward Netanya when, just in front of an IDF checkpoint, a Prison Service van approached him from behind. The martyr-bomber must have feared that he was about to be caught, and so he got as close as he could to the school bus and blew himself up. The armored bus absorbed the blast, and none of the children were injured. As it turned out, this operation was the first conducted by a special HAMAS network that would not be captured until September 30. By that time, it would be responsible for several more bombs that killed eight Israelis and wounded over a hundred. This network was directly controlled by the HAMAS headquarters in Damascus. Most of its members were Palestinian students recruited during their studies in Syria, Yemen, Sudan, and other Arab countries. They were sent to Damascus, where they were trained by Syrian and Iranian intelligence officers in sophisticated bombing, guerrilla warfare, the kidnapping of soldiers, and other clandestine craft. By the time they were sent back to their homes in Samaria, they were highly skilled terrorists.

This and other elite Islamist networks had been kept as sleeper resources, to be activated only for major operations. Activation of this network was one of the first acts taken by a refined Intifadah high command, formed to give prominence to the Islamists and thus to their sponsors, Tehran and Damascus. At the core of the new high command was a council made up of Arafat, Dahlan, Dahlan's deputy Rashid Abu-Shabak, and Sakhr Habash, formally the head of the National-Islamic Committee for the Furthering of the Intifadah; Amin al-Hindi and Musa Arafat were also invited to attend some of the council meetings. Habash, Arafat's boyhood friend and long-time confidant, now became his trusted emissary to the Islamist terrorists. After council meetings in which Arafat nodded approval of the overall need to carry out a terrorist operation, Habash alone would get specific instructions from Arafat. He then collected operational details and, when needed, the wherewithal—sophisticated fuses, cell-phone detonators, martyrs' bomb-webs, mortars, ammunition—from Dahlan's people and delivered the instructions and equipment to the operational chief of either HAMAS or Islamic Jihad. Arafat's need for a gap of deniability required that the Islamists decide the final details on their own. At the same time, these arrangements ensured that the overall strategy was tightly controlled by Arafat himself.

———

ON SHARON'S ORDERS, the IDF restrained its responses to the heightened wave of terrorism so that it wouldn't complicate Peres's efforts to revive negotiations. Sharon's decision was reinforced by positive feedback from the ongoing talks between Omri and Abu-Alaa. Using this venue, senior Palestinian officials assured the Israelis that the PA would agree to a protracted cease-fire—perhaps as long as four months—provided this would lead to the resumption of U.S.-led negotiations and Arafat's reception at the White House. Peres quietly checked with the State Department and got Powell's warm endorsement. Washington also informed Cairo of its support for the Peres initiative.

On April 29, Peres seemed to have been vindicated. Coming out of a meeting with Peres, Mubarak dramatically announced that the Palestinians had agreed to a four-week cease-fire, which would lead to the resumption of diplomatic negotiations. Egyptian Foreign Minister Amr Moussa assured skeptical diplomats that Israel and the Palestinians were indeed conducting "direct talks on the subject of a cease-fire agreement, and also regarding the renewal of negotiations."

Palestinian officials were quick to ridicule Mubarak's announcement. Senior PA officials leaked that Omri's proposal was so outrageous that Abu-Alaa had not even bothered to inform Arafat about it before rejecting it out of hand. Arafat would never order the cessation of the Intifadah after he had assured everybody it would continue until the attainment of full independence, another senior PA official maintained. On the night of April 29–30, Arafat, escorted by Abu-Shabak, met once again with Barghouti and senior Tanzim commanders in Ramallah. In a dramatic address, Arafat pledged to lead the Intifadah until victory.

Mubarak insisted that Peres had shown him "a secret agreement" stipulating the cease-fire. "Had I not seen this document with my own eyes, I would not have talked about a cease-fire," Mubarak told senior Egyptian officials. By this time, the Israeli security kitchenette had concluded that Jerusalem and Washington had been victims of a Palestinian disinformation campaign aimed at clearing Arafat's visit to the White House without his having to rein in the terrorists. Jerusalem resolved to fight back. "The situation on the ground is intolerable and, except for words, the Palestinian Authority is not doing anything serious," Sharon said in a message to King Abdallah of Jordan. "If the Palestinian Authority does not act to halt the violence, Israel will be obliged to do so." Over the next forty-eight hours, several HAMAS and Fatah terrorists were killed in a series of mysterious explosions in buildings and cars throughout the territories. Israeli officials denied any involvement in the bombings, attributing them to "work-related accidents" among the terrorists themselves.

The Sharon government waited until May 2 and the expected disappointing conclusion of Peres's latest round of discussions in Cairo, Amman, and Washington before it formally announced the new tougher strategy against the PA. "If Arafat won't deal with terror, we will deal with terror, and this will be done while preventing escalation," Sharon said at the end of a condolence visit to a bereaved family. In a briefing to defense officials the next day, he announced that Israel would apply new tactics, including deniable undertakings, in confronting the Intifadah. "We haven't exploited all of the means to stop terrorism," Sharon said. "There will be things that we say and things that we won't say, things that we will keep secret forever and those that we will deny." On May 7, Ben-Eliezer stated that the IDF had been given a free hand to conduct operations in PA-controlled areas. "In principle, I have approved any entry into Area A if that is necessary for our security," he said. "You don't expect me to stop a commander from entering Area A during a pursuit until he obtains my approval."

RELEASE OF THE Mitchell Commission Report found the key regional players engaged in strategic posturing. The Mitchell Commission was the real legacy of the Clinton administration. Having been appointed by President Clinton back on October 17, 2000, to investigate the reasons for the Intifadah and outline modalities for solving the Israeli-Palestinian conflict, it now, on May 6, 2001, delivered its report. As expected, the report echoed the Clinton policy and dodged the crucial question of responsibility for the outbreak of hostilities. The report did call for an unconditional cessation of violence but coupled this with an immediate halt to all Israeli settlement activity and the prompt implementation of all existing agreements. The report considered these actions to be necessary precursors to the resumption of permanent-status negotiations from the point they had reached when they collapsed—somewhere between Camp David, Taba, and the Clinton proposal. In short, the Middle East envisioned by the Mitchell Commission Report was definitely *not* the Middle East envisioned by the current government of Israel. Pressure from Washington and Western Europe to adopt the report only led to growing tension in the region.

Meanwhile, Pope John Paul II's visit to the Middle East prompted Arab political leaders and senior Muslim clergy to lay out for Western consumption the attitude toward Jews and Israel that they had heretofore confined mostly to sermons and speeches intended for their own people. These leaders implored the pope to revive what some of them termed "the historic alliance" of Muslims and Christians against the Jews. In a diatribe given as he greeted the pope in Damascus on May 5, Bashar al-Assad explicitly depicted the Jewish threat. Bashar attributed Israel's policies to the Jewish religion. He argued that "our brethren in Palestine are being murdered and tortured, justice is being violated, and as a result territories in Lebanon, the Golan, and Palestine have been occupied by those who even killed the principle of equality when they claimed that God created a people distinguished above all other peoples. We notice them aggressing against Muslim and Christian Holy Sites in Palestine, violating the sanctity of the Holy Mosque [of Al-Aqsa], of the Church of [the Holy] Sepulcher in Jerusalem, and of the Church of the Nativity in Bethlehem. They try to kill all the principles of divine faiths with the same mentality of betraying Jesus Christ and torturing him, and in the same way that they tried to commit treachery against Prophet Muhammad (peace be upon him)." The fact that the pope stuck to his prepared written comments instead of extemporaneously rebutting this anti-Semitic argumentation was perceived by the Arab world as a tacit endorsement. However, the virulence of these anti-Jewish sentiments was not lost on the Christian world. "If this is what President Assad really thinks about the Jews," French Cardinal Jean-Marie Lustiger subsequently noted, "then all I have to say to all those seeking peace in the Middle East is: 'Don't waste your time. Go back to your countries and find something else to do.'"

———

ON THURSDAY, May 3, Arafat ordered a new cycle of intense violence. That day, Tirawi and other senior General Intelligence officers suddenly vacated their Ramallah offices and moved to an undisclosed location. Most senior PA security and intelligence officers stopped answering their phones and turned off their cell phones. They were clearly anticipating serious Israeli retribution.

The next day, in the wake of a virulent sermon, Muslim worshipers on the Temple Mount began hurling stones at Jewish worshipers at the Wailing Wall below them. When the Waqf personnel—including some fifty security personnel answering to Jibril Rajub—refused to stop the violence, Israeli police broke into the Temple Mount plaza and forced the rioters out. No shots were fired, and only a few light injuries were sustained in the scuffles. As expected, however, the Israelis' entry into the Temple Mount was enough to spark a new wave of violence—much of it preplanned by the PA security organs. Several mortar shells were fired from Gaza into Israel proper and into nearby settlements. Protracted exchanges of gunfire took place throughout the West Bank, with the IDF closing some key arteries to civilian traffic because of repeated ambushes. When attacks on Gilo did not subside, an IDF armored column entered Beit Jallah and engaged the PA forces there—the largest incursion into Area A in the West Bank to date.

Mortar shelling and fire attacks intensified over the next few days. A bomb exploded in a Tel Aviv suburb, injuring five civilians—the first action acknowledged by HizbAllah-Palestine, now operating with PA approval in the Gaza Strip, as arranged at the terrorism conference in Tehran. With PA operations intensifying in the Judean mountains south of Jerusalem, an IDF tank force destroyed the headquarters of Tirawi's General Intelligence Service. The strike came shortly after Israeli intelligence provided the government with proof that Tirawi was directly responsible for the Palestinian attacks in the area. Arafat reacted with fury, claiming that "Israel threatens the entire Palestinian people."

On the night of May 10–11, as Palestinian attacks continued to escalate, IDF gunships destroyed three military facilities in the Gaza Strip: Dahlan's Gaza intelligence headquarters; the Saraya building in Gaza City, which housed PA security installations; and a PA factory that produced mortars and rocket-propelled grenades. Some twenty PA security personnel were injured in the strikes. The IDF also "cleaned" a section of the Egyptian border in the Rafah area, destroying smuggling tunnels and PA positions protecting them. As fighting raged throughout the territories, the Fatah movement called for "a state of alert" and announced plans to "restructure the popular resistance committees" in order to better "direct the war against Israel."

Throughout this escalation, Jerusalem made sure both Arafat and the Bush administration were cognizant of its strategic objectives. Even at the height of the IDF attacks, messages were sent to Arafat stressing that breaking his hold on power was not the objective. This position was also stated publicly. "The instructions of the political echelons to the IDF," General Mofaz declared after a cabinet meeting, "are to limit the PA's freedom of action—to signal to the [Palestinian] Authority but not to cause its collapse." The Bush administration, meanwhile, rushed to save Arafat from the consequences of the escalation he himself had unleashed. On May 12, Tenet met with Dahlan, and they agreed that the PA would re-arrest the recently released HAMAS and Islamic Jihad terrorists whose arrests had been demanded by the CIA (rather than Israel). In return, the Bush administration would publicly recognize Arafat's contribution to the peace process, invite him to Washington, and pressure Israel to stop the military escalation. Dahlan assured Tenet that Arafat had agreed to these arrangements and that Washington would see tangible results the very next day.

What in fact happened the next morning is that Arafat personally ordered the prompt release of Abdul Aziz Rantisi—the vitriolic HAMAS leader who was at that time the sole Islamist prisoner in the PA's jails. Rantisi's release was immediately implemented with great fanfare. Arafat's signal was crystal clear.

On the night of May 14, the IDF launched a new offensive throughout the territories—one of the fiercest to date. The objective was to seriously harm the forces Arafat was most likely to rely on to defend himself and his regime in time of crisis. In the central Gaza Strip, Navy gunboats shelled a Coast Guard post at Nusseirat, and helicopter gunships attacked several PA installations in Gaza City and at the Jabalya refugee camp, destroying most of the PA's Russian-built armored personnel carriers. Although the PA had been permitted to import these vehicles in riot-control configuration, at the time of the strike they were being refitted as fighting vehicles. In the West Bank, the IDF destroyed PA positions near Tulkarm and Ramallah; five PA officers were killed during a clash with Israeli troops. "The Israel Defense Forces will continue to act firmly against terrorists and their launchers, who hurt both the Israeli population and the Palestinian population, in every way they see fit, and will not accept any harm done to Israeli civilians and IDF soldiers," read the Israeli military statement.

The climax of this cycle of violence was the killing of two fourteen-year-old boys, one of them a U.S. citizen, in a settlement south of Jerusalem. The boys had taken a shortcut some 300 yards from the settlement's farthest-outlying house. They were set upon by a group of local Arabs, dragged into a cave, and murdered slowly and with extreme cruelty; the attackers finished by mutilating the bodies. This incident was the more alarming because it was a chance encounter and not a premeditated attack. Perhaps this outburst of cruelty accurately reflected the extent of the prevailing Palestinian hatred and rage—the outcome of years of virulent incitement in the mosques and PA media.

On May 15, Arafat would formalize and intensify this hatred as he launched a new stage of the Intifadah.

21

Nakba Day (2001)

Arafat's Double-Speak; Jockeying on the Northern Front

ON MAY 15, the Arab world commemorates Nakba Day—*nakba* being the Arabic for catastrophe, calamity, or holocaust. In political Arabic, *Nakba* refers to the establishment of Israel on May 15, 1948.

On May 15, 2001, the PA media carried a major speech by Yassir Arafat. It was an emotional speech, full of Arafat's characteristic double-speak—he used peace-related phraseology for the benefit of Western monitors, while lacing the text with explicit signals of his real intentions so that his home audience could not miss them. Essentially, in this speech, he blurred the distinction between the fighting of 1948 and the current Intifadah, and he sought to delegitimize the Jewish connection to the land of Israel and its history and heritage.

Arafat started by declaring that the Intifadah was as much an uprising against the legacy of the original Nakba—that is, the establishment of the State of Israel—as against what remained of the 1967 occupation of the territories:

> On this day, the day we commemorate the Nakba that befell our people on 15 May 1948, our entire people—men, women, elders, young, cubs and flowers, the people of exceeding strength—rise to announce to the world the word of truth, justice, and history. They will say that our people, the Palestinian people, faced injustice which is unprecedented in history. They will also say that this noble people who were dispersed by the grand conspiracy and whose homeland was usurped with the force of arms and aggression would not accept this black destiny that was concocted by the grand conspiracy against their existence, homeland, their Christian and Islamic holy places, and against their lives, history, and future. Our people

have experienced 53 years of tribulation, pain, and dispersal in and outside the homeland. With their deep-rooted faith, our people remain committed to their principles in the face of the grand conspiracy with an unrelenting willpower. They will not bow their heads or give in. Generation after generation has been offering sacrifices and martyrdom for 53 years in the hope that the world would rise from its long slumber and recognize the brilliant Palestinian reality whose immortal flame is illuminated by the blood of those who are more blessed than all of us: the martyrs for the homeland, freedom, glory, and for rejuvenating the struggle against the fierce conspiracy.

Masses of our steadfast Palestinian people, who are mujahedin in a heroic manner, blind force will not hold for long in the face of justice, truth, and historical authenticity. The attempt to falsify history by missiles, shells, planes, and tanks will not succeed. This is so because we have right to our side and we defend a just cause that cannot be wiped out by tank shells, poisonous gases, internationally prohibited weapons, or guided missiles. These kill defenseless citizens, infants, and strike at peaceful citizens in the Palestinian cities. These cities have been under siege for the eighth consecutive month by the tanks, the guns, and the aircraft, not to mention all the other forms of military escalation, and the economic, financial, and supply siege.

Arafat had no hope, he declared, that Israel would change its behavior on its own because "the executioner is relishing the shedding of Palestinian blood, thanks to the blind military machine and international protection granted to him by influential and hegemonistic powers in the international community [i.e., the United States]. Double standards prevail and the resolutions of international legitimacy are being trampled." It was because of the inequality in power and might rather than historical justice, Arafat explained, that the Palestinians "accepted and recognized these resolutions in order to prevent bloodshed, establish the peace of the brave, secure a homeland and a state for the Palestinian people on their land, and protect the Christian and Islamic holy places." Here Arafat revealed the core of his political double-speak: the distinction between a Palestinian state and the Palestinian homeland. The Arabic word for "state" denotes a transient entity; a state might be established in whatever part of Palestine Israel withdraws from. The Arabic word for "homeland" denotes sacred land; the homeland is the entire Palestine, and no compromise over it is permissible or possible. Arafat's speech was therefore a refined restating of the 1974 Phased Plan.

Arafat mentioned the interests of the "Israeli people" but not the State of Israel as a legitimate and valid entity. In the coming phase of the Intifadah, Arafat stated—the new period of "rage"—the Palestinians, would be fighting as much for the reversal of the original Nakba as they would be for the reversal of the 1967 "occupation." Arafat's Nakba Day address thus openly set out the essential goal of the Intifadah: the destruction of Israel and its replacement with an Arab-Muslim state.

———

EVEN BEFORE ARAFAT gave his speech, the Islamists and PA had been preparing intensely for a military escalation. As agreed at the Tehran conference, several squads of HizbAllah experts—mostly Lebanese and Palestinians, plus a few Israeli-Arabs—were smuggled into the Gaza Strip. None of them had been involved in terrorist and/or nationalist activities in Israel before and thus were most likely unknown to the Israeli security services. Both Arafat and the Iranian leadership were convinced that a major eruption of Islamist violence in relation to al-Aqsa would inflame not only the territories but also the Israeli Arabs—thus confirming in action Arafat's identification of the Intifadah with the resistance to the original Nakba.

Jerusalem correctly understood that the Palestinians' growing audacity stemmed from their sense of Israel's condition after the withdrawal from Lebanon the previous May. "It was perceived in the Arab consciousness as a sign that Israel was becoming weak, and encouraged the Arabs to continue attacking on other fronts," General Yaalon noted. "This conflict is the most significant one since the War of Independence, and it will have ramifications on how the Arab world perceives Israel's staying power. The victor will be the one who has greater ability to withstand." The next day, General Mofaz told the Knesset Foreign Affairs and Defense Committee that the PA had "decided to seek political gains through violent means" and that toward this end the PA was "acting in full cooperation" with the Islamist terrorist organizations. The mounting flow of illegal weapons and ammunition, Mofaz pointed out, also testified to the PA's commitment to escalation.

Meanwhile, a series of well-coordinated "popular" riots throughout the territories answered Arafat's call for "days of rage." Abbas Zaki, a Fatah leader and PNC member, declared the ultimate objective: "War will continue until total victory. The Jews should prepare ships in order to leave our land." Mobs stormed Israeli positions with stones and firebombs while PA security personnel fired from nearby buildings, thus provoking the IDF into using rubber and live bullets. Some 200 Palestinians were injured in the clashes, and the PA later reported that 5 died of their wounds. HAMAS was planning a mortar barrage in Gaza when an IDF tank destroyed the car carrying the crew and a couple of mortars; two of Sheikh Yassin's bodyguards were among those killed. Along the Israeli-Lebanese border, HizbAllah teams fired several ATGMs and RPGs against IDF positions. Small-arms and artillery exchanges erupted soon afterward.

———

ULTIMATELY, JERUSALEM was most apprehensive about the escalation potential along the Lebanese border. Israeli Military Intelligence confirmed that HizbAllah conducted its attack at the behest of Damascus and that Syrian senior officials had delivered both specific instructions and shipments of missiles and rockets to the HizbAllah forces in southern Lebanon. Moreover, Syrian senior officials had openly declared their willingness to fight. "We in Syria are never afraid of war. As military men, this is both our choice and destiny," Defense Minister Tlass stated in mid-May. "We are also happy to step up the conflict if that is what they [the Israelis] want." Tlass emphasized Syria's commitment to the HizbAllah. "Nothing could drive us away from our strategic alliance with HizbAllah," he said. "We will never abandon it . . . regardless of the cost or sacrifices." Hence, Jerusalem decided to warn Bashar al-Assad against continuing with the planned escalation. On May 17, while observing an IDF exercise on the Golan, Ben-Eliezer took the opportunity to deliver the warning publicly: "Israel will not strike at the HizbAllah, who hide behind women and children, but rather at those responsible for what's happening. I say to you, Bashar al-Assad—I'll tell you something—violence won't help, and it's worth it for you to return to the negotiating table."

Bashar was evidently shaken by the threat. The next day, he traveled to Sharm el-Sheikh for previously scheduled talks with Mubarak meant to last for three days. Bashar shifted the focus of the meeting to the current crisis and demanded an all-Arab confrontation with Israel in response to Ben-Eliezer's warning. Mubarak advocated prudence, noting that the Arabs were ill prepared, militarily and politically, to carry out the escalation advocated by Bashar. As Mubarak spoke, Bashar became increasingly angry; at a certain point he implied that he had doubts about Mubarak's enduring commitment to the Arab cause. Mubarak retorted with a comment about the haste and inexperience of young leaders—a comment Bashar interpreted as harsh criticism. He broke off the discussion, stood up and left the room, and immediately returned to Syria—having stayed only five hours in Sharm el-Sheikh. Over the next few days, Syrian media intensified their calls for all-out support for the Intifadah, arguing that any Israeli military success against the PA would be an even greater calamity than the original Nakba.

Cairo revealed its true state of mind in the announcement, at about the same time, of major military exercises aimed at testing Egypt's land-based offensive capabilities. The exercises would take place over an entire year and would be spearheaded by the Third Army and the Second Army—the key forces earmarked for a future war with Israel. As Egyptian senior military officials briefed their counterparts in other Arab countries, the exercises would involve a simulated conflict in which major armored and mechanized units, with extensive air and helicopter support, would attack "enemy" forces as they approached the Egyptian border on the eastern part of the Sinai Peninsula. Left unsaid was that Israel is the only country bordering Egypt on the eastern Sinai. In mid-May, the Third Army began its forward deployment. By May 19, Egypt had a major offensive force deployed close to the Suez Canal.

All these activities drew the attention of the Bush administration. However, instead of addressing the real but complex threat—that Syria might provoke a regional eruption through HizbAllah—Washington opted to pursue the easy, though most likely futile, path of attempting to rejuvenate the Israeli-Palestinian negotiations. Washington's logic was that because the Israeli-Palestinian dispute dominated Arab awareness, furthering its solution along pro-Arab lines would generate greater willingness to cooperate with the United States on other matters. But Washington ignored the reality that virtually all the conflicts in the region were driven by local factors considered crucial by those involved. Whatever the dynamics along the Palestinian-Israeli track, it could not overcome the indigenous root causes of the other regional crises. Nevertheless, on May 18, Bush chaired high-level consultations on new approaches to reviving the peace process, including implementation of the Mitchell Report.

ON MAY 17, the leaders of the key terrorist organizations, both PA-affiliated and Islamist, attended a meeting convened by Arafat in his Gaza office. The time had come, he said, to unify the ranks—to form a cohesive front made up of the Tanzim, Force 17, HAMAS, Islamic Jihad, and other militant groups—in order to seize the initiative from Israel and the United States. Arafat told the gathered commanders that for all intents and purposes there were no longer any limitations on striking out at Israel. However, he asked that, for the time being, operations inside Israel be claimed by the Islamist organizations.

The very next day, a martyr-bomber blew himself up at the entrance to a shopping mall in Netanya, killing six and wounding over seventy. Both the HizbAllah-Palestine and HAMAS's Izz al-Din al-Qassim quickly claimed responsibility. "We, in the Qassim Brigades, reiterate that the Intifadah is the only viable option, and that the martyr-mujahedin deeply shake the Zionist entity," said the martyr in his goodbye video. In Ramallah, PA police escorted a huge "spontaneous" march expressing solidarity with the martyr and calling for the destruction of Israel. The marchers carried PA flags as well as Islamist flags. That same day saw many other incidents, including mortar shelling in the Gaza Strip and ambushes of civilian traffic in the West Bank. In retaliation, for the first time since the Six-Day War, Israel used fighter-bombers against Palestinian targets: Israeli F-16s destroyed the Force 17 headquarters in Ramallah and several PA security installations in Nablus. "When it comes to Israel's security, there will be no compromises," Sharon stated in reply to international criticism. Air attacks continued over the next couple of days, with the PA claiming 15 fatalities and 130 wounded.

When Washington still did not intervene to stop the Israeli retaliatory strikes, Arafat took a desperate step, using Jibril Rajub, a close protégé of both Tenet and Indyk. On the afternoon of May 20, a PA sniper opened fire from a position inside Rajub's home on the outskirts of Ramallah and wounded an Israeli soldier. In response, an Israeli tank shelled the house, damaging the external wall and some luxury cars parked in the yard. Rajub immediately complained to Washington, which reacted harshly. Meeting with Israeli media, Indyk stated: "Those who would stop the violence, Palestinian police or the head of the Palestinian security organization in the West Bank, Jibril Rajub, are being hit, bombed, shelled, killed by the Israeli Defense Forces. Maybe the strategy is to encourage them to act against their own people. But I don't imagine that there is an example in history where such a strategy has succeeded." Powell, Tenet, and other senior officials called Sharon to complain. "At the end of the day negotiations must start again," Powell said in Washington. "But negotiations cannot start in this current situation of intense violence and a total lack of confidence and trust between the two parties." He added that Israel was expected to take the first step.

Thus, as Arafat expected, this single and essentially minor incident, because it involved a protégé of Washington, completely changed the Bush administration's approach to the unfolding crisis. Forgotten were the Palestinian "days of rage" and the terrorist strikes that had elicited the Israeli retaliatory bombing. All that mattered was the swift containment of the Israeli actions before one of the CIA's protégés was seriously hurt—irrespective of the extent of his actual involvement in the fighting. When criticized for ignoring the Palestinian terrorism generally, and specifically the compelling forensic evidence that shots had indeed been fired from Rajub's house, U.S. senior officials attributed the administration's position to pressure from Arab allies. They noted that both Mubarak and Crown Prince Abdallah had urged the administration to stop what they termed "the escalation in Israeli attacks on the Palestinians." The United States had to act accordingly or risk a crisis with its allies, the officials explained.

ON MAY 23, Sharon succumbed to American pressure and announced "a significant cooling-off period." On Sharon's orders, the IDF would cease fighting "except in cases of genuine danger to human life." The Israelis also envisioned "the implementation of confidence-building measures" by both sides, including a de facto freeze on settlement activities by the Israelis and meaningful arrests of terrorists by the Palestinian security forces. Sharon urged the Palestinians to cooperate with his initiative. "Nothing will be gained through violence," he said. "Peace requires painful compromises on both sides, but it can only be attained at the negotiating table." Israeli officials intimated that Shimon Peres and Omri Sharon, using "a secret channel to Arafat," had obtained the latter's commitment to stop the violence and resume serious negotiations the moment Israel froze settlement construction. Bush phoned Sharon and congratulated him on the cease-fire.

The first Palestinian reaction came from Rajub. "I can't understand this term cease-fire," he said. "We are the victims. We are not in a war between the two of us. There is a unilateral war, unilateral attacks by the Israelis against the Palestinian people." Fatah and HAMAS leaders made the possibility of a cease-fire conditional on the Israelis' unconditional acceptance of all their demands. Theirs was a struggle for the liberation of the entire Palestine, they maintained, and they would not cease violence until they had realized their objective. Several of Arafat's own confidants informed him that they would ignore his explicit orders to cease fire. By the time he met with U.S. diplomats, Arafat had already renounced the cease-fire. Arriving in Paris later that day, he declared: "For as long as Sharon does not accept the Mitchell Plan fully [in other words, as interpreted by the PA], there will not be any cease-fire."

In fact, PA operations escalated quite distinctly right after Sharon's declaration of the cease-fire and the U.S. endorsement of it. It was as if the PA were attempting to test the Israelis' self-restraint. Even Peres acknowledged to his confidants that the IDF had irrefutable intelligence that "not only has Arafat not ordered a cease-fire, he has even instructed his men to intensify their attacks against Israel." Indeed, the last week of May saw a continued escalation in Palestinian terrorism, including a persistent effort to cause heavy civilian casualties.

On May 24, Bush, who had previously refused any direct contact with Arafat, phoned him and urged him to formally call for the end of the Intifadah. Bush was rebuffed. He then called Sharon and urged him to persevere with the unilateral cease-fire despite the ongoing wave of terrorism.

The same day, Tel Aviv's central bus station was evacuated and the whole area cordoned off for several tense hours after intelligence warnings revealed that two terrorists were about to set off a huge bomb. Although both terrorists succeeded in evading the Israeli dragnet, the explosion was averted.

However, while the search for the terrorists was still in progress, Jerusalem notified Cairo that in case of massive carnage, particularly if weapons of mass destruction were utilized, Israel's retaliation would be furious and massive—to the point of destroying the PA—even if that might lead to a regional war. If that was not what Cairo wanted, Jerusalem suggested, it should find ways of restraining Arafat before the region's stability completely crumbled.

An alarmed Mubarak immediately called Riyadh. A couple of days later, he flew to Jeddah for an urgent summit with King Fahd and Crown Prince Abdallah. The defense, foreign, and oil ministers, as well as senior intelligence and military officials, of both countries participated in some of the discussions. In the key session, Mubarak told Abdallah that the moment of truth had come. Both Arafat and Bashar were playing with fire, Mubarak warned. With Syria, Iraq, and Iran all eager for battle, the region could easily go up in flames. Abdallah agreed with Mubarak that given the mood of the Arab street, no government in the region would be able to stay out of such a war. The two leaders also concurred that at the end of the war, Iraq and Syria would be empowered at the expense of Egypt and Saudi Arabia. Because Damascus and Baghdad were beyond control or influence, the key to preventing the crisis was the containment of Israel—something only Washington could deliver. Hence, Mubarak and Abdallah decided to approach Washington with a package deal: Saudi Arabia would see to it that OPEC reduced oil prices in return for American pressure on Israel.

On May 28, Prince Bandar took the Saudi-Egyptian proposal to the White House, which immediately queried Jerusalem about the possibility of Powell's traveling to the region in order to revive negotiations. Jerusalem agreed, and, in the face of mounting pressure on the government to react to the continuing wave of bombings, Sharon ordered the IDF to "sit tight." "Despite the agony and the senseless killings," a senior official in Sharon's office explained, "we are willing to give the Palestinians another chance."

Violence continued throughout Israel and the territories over the next two days, with several Israeli civilians being killed in roadside ambushes. Finally, in Gaza, a joint HizbAllah-Palestine and HAMAS detachment, in cooperation with Fatah, abducted two American correspondents for *Newsweek* and held them for several hours as, in the words of the senior Fatah commander, "a warning to the Bush administration to end its support for Israel." When Dahlan passed along Arafat's order to release the journalists, the abductors ignored him—clearly demonstrating their defiance and strength.

————

THE SUDDEN DEATH, on May 30, of Faisal Husseini was a milestone event for the Palestinian national movement. The scion of a prominent old

Palestinian family and the orphaned son of Abdul Qadir Husseini—a top
Palestinian commander during the War of Independence, who was killed in
combat near Jerusalem—Faisal Husseini was one of the most promising of
the younger Palestinian leaders, as witness his role in the Israeli-Palestinian
talks back in the winter of 1992–93. Arafat was wary of Husseini but had
had to give him the "Jerusalem portfolio" or else risk alienating the Palestinian elite of the Greater Jerusalem area. During 2001, Husseini was raising his
profile in the leadership of the Intifadah, particularly as a troubleshooter capable of mending fences between Arafat and his old enemies. In that capacity, he had rebuilt close cooperation with the Palestinian leadership in
Lebanon and had attended the terrorism conference in Tehran.

Now, in late May, Arafat dispatched Husseini to Kuwait to restore relations with the royal family so that the PLO could raise funds there again despite Arafat's active solidarity with Saddam Hussein. This time, even
Husseini was unable to deliver results for Arafat. Soon after his arrival in
Kuwait, he had a series of sharp and heated debates with senior Kuwaiti officials about Arafat and the future of the Palestinian movement. He suffered a
heart attack during one of these debates and died shortly afterward. But his
impact continued, through his last words and his last journey.

In the days after Husseini's death, several Arab media outlets published
accounts of off-the-record conversations he had recently had with their edi-
tors and correspondents. Husseini was outspoken and frank, and these conversations, published as interviews, constitute a particularly revealing
expression of the aspirations and intentions of the Palestinian elite. Especially revealing was the conversation with Shafiq Ahmad Ali of the Egyptian
Nasserite daily *Al-Arabi*. Husseini had met with Shafiq Ahmad Ali on his
way to Kuwait, and so this may well have been his last conversation with a
journalist.

The published account—as translated and edited by the Middle East
Media Resource Institute (MEMRI)—begins with the interviewer's observa-
tion that the current plight of the Palestinians "is a natural consequence of
Arafat's signing the Oslo Accords." Husseini replied,

> Following the signing of the Oslo Accords . . . I said three things:
>
> First: following a long period of "pregnancy" we brought a child into
> the world [the Oslo Accords] who is smaller, weaker, and uglier than what
> we had hoped for. However, despite it all, this is still our child, and we must
> nurture, strengthen and develop it so that he is able to stand on his own
> two feet.
>
> Second, we are the Jews of the 21st Century. . . . They infiltrated our
> country using various methods, using all kinds of passports, and they suffered

greatly in the process. They even had to face humiliation but they did it all for one goal: to enter our country and root themselves in it prior to our expulsion out of it. We must act in the same way they did. [We must] return [to the land], settle it, and develop new roots in our land from where we were expelled, whatever the price may be.

Third, the [ancient] Greek Army was unable to break into Troy due to [internal] disputes and disagreements. The Greek forces started retreating one after the other, and the Greek king ended up facing the walls of Troy all by himself, and he . . . ended up leading a failed assault on Troy's walls.

[Following these events] the people of Troy climbed on top of the walls of their city and could not find any traces of the Greek army, except for a giant wooden horse. They cheered and celebrated, thinking that the Greek troops were routed and while retreating left a harmless wooden horse as spoils of war. So they opened the gates of the city and brought in the wooden horse. We all know what happened next.

Had the U.S. and Israel not realized, before Oslo, that all that was left of the Palestinian National movement and the Pan-Arab movement was a wooden horse called Arafat or the PLO, they would never have opened their fortified gates and let it inside their walls.

Despite the fact that we entered these walls in order to build, unlike the Greeks who entered them in order to destroy, I now tell you all, all these to whom I spoke in a secret meeting during the days of Oslo: "Climb into the horse and don't question what type of material the horse is made of. Climb into the horse, and we shall transform your climbing into that horse into a beginning of a building era rather than an era of the end of hope."

And indeed, there are those who climbed into the horse and are [now] inside [the PA territory] whether they supported the Oslo Accords or not.

Shafiq Ahmad Ali then steered the conversation to the evolution of the Palestinian Authority in the post-Oslo era. Was the establishment of the PA the Palestinians' coming out of the horse? he asked. No, replied Husseini, during the initial period of the PA's consolidation, Palestinians were still hiding inside their Trojan horse: already inside the walled city—that is, Israel—but still not ready to take on their enemies in the decisive battle. "In my opinion," Husseini elaborated, "the Intifada itself is the coming down out of the horse. Rather than getting into the old arguments . . . this effort [the Intifada] could have been much better, broader, and more significant had we made it clearer to ourselves that the Oslo agreement, or any other agreement, is just a temporary procedure, or just a step toward something bigger." The Intifadah is the true catharsis of the Palestinian national movement, Husseini explained, and hence, regardless of its flaws, "the Intifada is always right."

Because the objective of both the Oslo process and the Intifadah is the establishment of a Palestinian state, Shafiq Ahmad Ali queried further, "What are the borders of the Palestinian state you are referring to, and what kind of 'Jerusalem' would you accept as the capital of your state?" Husseini's reply was lengthy and most illuminating:

With this question you are dragging me into talking about what we refer to as our "strategic" goals and our "political" goals, or the phased goals. The "strategic" goals are the "higher" goals, the "long-term goals," or the "unwavering goals," the goals that are based on solid Pan-Arab historic rights and principles. Whereas the "political" goals are those goals which were set for a temporary time-frame, considering the [constraints of] the existing international system, the balance of power, our own abilities, and other considerations which "vary" from time to time.

When we are asking all the Palestinian forces and factions to look at the Oslo Agreement and at other agreements as "temporary" procedures, or phased goals, this means that we are ambushing the Israelis and cheating them. . . . In 1947, in accordance with [the U.N.] Partition Plan, they [the Israelis] decided to declare statehood on 55% of the land of Palestine, which they later increased to 78% during the War of 1948, and then again [increased] to 100% during the War of 1967. Despite all that, they never attempted to make [a] secret of their long-term goal, which is "Greater Israel" from the Nile to the Euphrates. Similarly, if we agree to declare our state over what is now only 22% of Palestine, meaning the West Bank and Gaza—our ultimate goal is [still] the liberation of all historical Palestine from the [Jordan] River to the [Mediterranean] sea, even if this means that the conflict will last for another thousand years or for many generations.

In short, we are exactly like they are. We distinguish the strategic, long-term goals from the political phased goals, which we are compelled to temporarily accept due to international pressure. If you are asking me as a Pan-Arab nationalist what are the Palestinian borders according to the higher strategy, I will immediately reply: "from the river to the sea." Palestine in its entirety is an Arab land, the land of the Arab nation, a land no one can sell or buy, and it is impossible to remain silent while someone is stealing it, even if this requires time and even [if it means paying] a high price.

If you are asking me, as a man who belongs to the Islamic Faith, my answer is also "from the river to the sea," the entire land is an Islamic Waqf which can not be bought or sold, and it is impossible to remain silent while someone is stealing it. . . .

If you are asking me as an ordinary Palestinian, from the "inside" or from the Diaspora, you will get the same answer and without any hesitations.

However, what I am able to achieve and live on right now, due to [constraints of] the international system, is not, of course, Palestine "from the river to the sea." In order for us to fulfill all of our dreams regarding Palestine, we must, first of all, wake up and realize where we are standing. On the other hand, if we will continue to behave as if we are still dreaming, we will not find a place to put our feet on. . . .

As I once said in the past: our eyes must continue to focus on the higher goal. The real danger is that I might forget [it], and while advancing towards my short-term goal I might turn my back on my long-term goal, which is the liberation of Palestine from the river to the sea.

At Arafat's request, warmly endorsed by the United States and Western Europe, the Israeli government permitted Husseini to be buried near his father, not far from the eastern wall of the Temple Mount. Arafat was not permitted to attend the funeral in Jerusalem, and so the PA held a memorial service in Ramallah, chaired by Arafat, in the course of which extremely militant speeches were delivered. Arafat then escorted the coffin to the edge of Area A, from where a huge procession of cars waving Palestinian flags and anti-Israeli placards drove on into Jerusalem. Wearing a Palestinian military uniform, Sakhr Habash escorted the coffin into Jerusalem and onto the Temple Mount. The religious ceremony at the gravesite was quickly transformed into a reiteration of Arafat's Nakba Day themes. Faisal Husseini's "martyrdom" in the pursuit of the Intifadah was identical to his father's death in combat against the Jews in 1948, the eulogies went, and, in the same way, the ongoing Intifadah is a direct continuation of the Palestinian war of the late 1940s. The common objective is the destruction of Israel and the establishment of a Palestinian-Arab state in its stead, several speakers proclaimed. The excited audience repeatedly screamed: *"Allah Akbar!"* "Slaughter the Jews!" "We won!" and "We are returning to Jerusalem!" "Oh Faisal," his relative Adnan Husseini repeatedly declared over the fresh grave, "Jerusalem was liberated today!"

———

THE ENTIRE ISRAELI DEFENSE posture was put to the test on June 1–2. Late that night, a lone young man mingled in a crowd of teenagers at the door of the Dolphinarium, a Tel Aviv beachfront discotheque popular with emigrants from the former Soviet Union. Surrounded by hundreds of teenagers, he blew himself up, killing more than twenty and wounding close to a hundred. The sight of blood and gore in the heart of the Tel Aviv entertainment district and the plight of the hurt and frightened teenagers shocked a country largely hardened by previous waves of terrorist attacks.

Sharon's kitchenette convened that night for an emergency session. That a martyrdom attack had occurred at this time was no surprise—only the specifics were. IDF Intelligence had warned the government that the highest levels of the PA had endorsed a spectacular strike by the Islamists. The day before the attack, IDF Intelligence had reported that Arafat personally had just ordered three expert bomb-makers freed from PA jails. Now IDF senior officers reported to the kitchenette that the Tel Aviv bombing must be considered the start of a new wave of lethal terrorism. The IDF offered to implement a contingency plan that called for fighter-bomber and attack-helicopter strikes at both PA and Islamist targets throughout the West Bank and the Gaza Strip. "We were about to launch a devastating air strike," a senior security source told Steve Rodan.

At the same time, the Israeli leadership—both military and civilian—had to take into account the regional context. Because of the signs of impending regional war, the IDF's elite units had already been held back from countering the Intifadah. Now the kitchenette weighed the IDF's recommendation for a massive air campaign against accumulating intelligence concerning the regional dynamics. The kitchenette apprehended that the Dolphinarium attack might have been intended to provoke the regional eruption Israel had long sought to avoid. Hence, Sharon and the kitchenette decided not to decide about retaliation. "The air strike," the source told Rodan, "has been suspended until further notice." Instead, the Air Force would carry out extensive exercises in the airspace over Israel and the territories. Fighter-bombers dived and made low-altitude passes—including sonic booms—over Palestinian cities around the clock, providing a reminder of Israel's might. The general exercise also served both as cover for putting the Air Force and related IDF units on high wartime readiness and as a deterrent to Arab/Muslim powers seeking to exploit Jerusalem's preoccupation with the Dolphinarium bombing.

By the time the Israeli cabinet convened again, later on June 2, Arafat had already, in what had by now become a macabre routine, declared a ceasefire, announced his resolve to cooperate with the United States and Israel, and promised to launch a genuine war on Islamist terrorism. But Arafat's colleagues quickly put his announcement into perspective. The Fatah leadership also met for an emergency session on June 2 and urged all Palestinians to "prepare for an Israeli invasion of PA areas." The "Coalition of National and Islamic Groups"—made up of thirteen organizations, including al-Fatah, HAMAS, and the Islamic Jihad—announced that they were reserving their right to continue to "defend themselves" against Israeli occupation. "The Intifadah and the armed resistance will continue for as long as even one settler or one soldier remains in the conquered Palestinian territories," Marwan Barghouti declared. On June 3, the Supreme Coordination Committee of the Local National and Islamic Committees called for the escalation of the Intifadah and announced that as far as it was concerned the cease-fire did not exist. Because the Committee was Arafat's primary instrument for coordinating policies and military strategy with the Islamist and other radical Palestinian bodies, and because its chief was Arafat's close confidant Sakhr Habash, this announcement amounted to a back-door clarification by Arafat that the talk about cease-fire and fighting terrorism was solely for the consumption of foreign leaders so that they would contain Israel's retaliation.

At this point, the Bush administration joined the fray. Appearing on the Sunday morning talk shows, Powell hailed Arafat's "very important statement," though he insisted that implementation was crucial. "My message for Arafat is pretty direct and clear," Powell said. "This is the time to bring the violence under control." Powell added that "the U.S. will be deeply involved. The president and I and all the members of our national security team are involved." Under pressure from Bush, Powell, and German Foreign Minister Joschka Fischer (then in Tel Aviv) and not certain about the advisability of diverting resources from war preparations in order to escalate the fighting against the PA, Sharon procrastinated. In the meantime, he declared his acceptance of a policy of restraint. "Even restraint is part of strength," Sharon told a Tel Aviv press conference.

As THE VIOLENCE continued throughout the territories—from roadside ambushes and bombs to mortar attacks in the Gaza Strip area—Bush, alarmed by the evaporation of the "Arafat cease-fire," dispatched Tenet to the Middle East on a rescue mission. "We believe enough progress has been made on the cease-fire that it is time to send George Tenet to the Middle East to start serious discussions at the security level about how to make sure the cease-fire continues," Bush told reporters. Jerusalem promised full cooperation with Tenet, and Sharon met with him in this spirit. Sharon did urge Tenet to pressure Arafat to arrest Islamist terrorists, end the violence completely, and stop incitement by the PA media. When Tenet expressed doubts about Arafat's ability to meet all these demands, Sharon agreed to reduce the list of wanted Islamists from 120 to 34—with the CIA's concurrence on all. Sharon assured Tenet that if Arafat made tangible progress on these three issues, Israel would be forthcoming. Meeting with Tenet the next day, Arafat would hear nothing of his requests. Arafat's close aides reiterated publicly that he would not arrest anybody. Still, Tenet reported hope and progress.

By now, the Israeli public, the popular media, and a large number of politicians from across the political spectrum were urging the government to abandon its inexplicable self-restraint. At the same time, the Israeli peace camp—small but politically powerful and staunchly supported by the media elite—kept urging that Arafat be given another chance. These disputes reverberated into the cabinet and created tremendous strain within Sharon's increasingly fragile government of national unity. Furthermore, the peace camp relentlessly attempted to force Sharon to resume negotiations by conjuring up private arrangements with Arafat and others in the PA elite. These essentially illegal initiatives were tacitly supported by Peres, who also gave Yossi Beilin the go-ahead to start arranging an Israeli-PA summit with the help of the European Union. In the process, Beilin, with or without Peres's knowledge, committed to a profound change in Israel's cease-fire policy. Instead of the long-standing demand for a complete cessation of hostilities as a precondition for resuming negotiations, Beilin agreed that stopping the fighting in three specified areas—Beit Jallah/Gilo, Netzarim, and Rafah—would suffice. On June 8, Peres met with U.S. special envoy William Burns to discuss modalities for implementing the Mitchell Report as if the resumption of negotiations were a foregone conclusion. Burns stressed that the coming days would be "critical" and urged Israel to do everything possible to ensure the next phase of the political process. "Now there is a chance to thicken the delicate layer of the cease-fire," Peres concurred, "and to pave a road that will lead to peace."

———

AT THE VERY SAME TIME that Burns and Peres were meeting, a more down-to-earth response to the crisis was taking place in Haifa. The security forces and emergency services held a major exercise to ascertain the area's ability to cope with potential rocket or missile attacks on the local chemical plants and oil refineries. The exercise assumed the use of weapons of mass destruction by HizbAllah and its key sponsors—Syria and Iran—and tested the performance and coordination of the military and civilian emergency services. This first such exercise in Israel's history reflected the growing anxiety of official Jerusalem.

In fact, the anxiety was heightened by the discovery that the Islamists had just used biological warfare against Israel. Autopsies on the remnants of the martyr-bombers from Netanya and the Dolphinarium revealed that both were infected with a highly contagious strain of hepatitis B. Presumably, HAMAS hoped to infect those injured in the attack through contact with the bombers' contaminated blood and flesh. In fact, only a few Israelis were infected, and timely treatment prevented fatalities. However, this was a horrific milestone in the use of martyrdom bombing.

George Tenet, meanwhile, had been working on "creative" modalities for breaking the deadlock. On June 10, having failed to reconcile the Israeli and

PA positions, he presented his own plan. As Israeli officials reported it to Steve Rodan, the Tenet plan involved "a cooling-off period of between 3 [and] 4 weeks of cease-fire followed by diplomatic talks between Israel and the PA." And, "meanwhile, the PA would arrest Islamic bombers, end incitement against Israel, collect illegal weapons and renew intelligence exchange and security meetings with Israel. Israel, according to the Tenet plan, would pledge to end attacks on the Palestinians and order the military to withdraw to the lines in the West Bank and Gaza Strip deployed in September [2000]." Jerusalem was most perturbed by the proviso that the PA would "collect"— as opposed to "destroy"—heavy weapons. This amounted to legitimizing the PA's holding of these weapons, the possession of which was deemed illegal by previous Israeli-Palestinian agreements—and the United States was a formal guarantor of these agreements. As well, the PA would be expected to arrest only the thirty-four terrorists on the latest compromise list.

Nevertheless, in order not to antagonize the Bush administration, Jerusalem decided to accept the Tenet plan as it stood. At this point, however, the Palestinians balked. Tenet spent most of the next day with Arafat and his key aides in a desperate effort to prevent the collapse of his mission. Tenet even promised Arafat that the Bush administration would invite him to the White House with all the honors due a head of state the moment he, Tenet, could demonstrate Arafat's genuine commitment to the cease-fire and renewed negotiations. Still, Arafat would not budge. Finally, on June 13, Tenet proposed, and Sharon agreed, that Israel would unilaterally act "as if some agreement has been reached," withdrawing the IDF from forward positions and lifting the closure of Arab towns. Jerusalem stuck to this promise even though Military Intelligence had obtained solid proof that senior PA security officials had notified the Islamist terrorist leadership that they "[would] never be arrested." Tenet left the region later that day, expressing hope and optimism.

———

IN THE FACE OF Tenet's tenacity, it was imperative for Arafat to prove that he was still committed to the Intifadah. On the night of June 12–13, at the very same time Tenet and Arafat were holding their concluding discussions, a detachment of PA security officers from East Jerusalem attacked the first Israeli vehicle they saw. That the victim proved to be a Greek Orthodox monk mattered little to the Palestinians. They had succeeded in shaming the president of the United States by bringing the Intifadah back into Jerusalem just as his CIA director was supposed to be ushering in a new era in U.S.-PA relations.

On June 14, PA General Intelligence used a Palestinian who had been working as an agent of Israel to assassinate a senior Israeli intelligence officer.

That morning, south of Jerusalem, the turned agent came to a meeting with his Israeli handler, Lieutenant Colonel Yehuda Adri. Approaching Adri's car, the agent drew a handgun and shot at close range, killing Adri and wounding an IDF security officer; the officer nonetheless chased and killed the Palestinian agent. The military arm of Fatah formally claimed responsibility for Adri's assassination, attributing it to revenge for Israeli assassinations of key Palestinian commanders. Significantly, Fatah stressed that the decision on the assassination was made at "the highest possible echelons" of the PA's leadership—a euphemism for Arafat. Palestinian sources reported that Arafat had approved (in principle) the idea of assassinating Adri some three months beforehand, but had given the specific order to his chief of General Intelligence, Tirawi, just shortly before the operation—that is, when Tenet was still in the country. Moreover, Tirawi—one of Tenet's protégés—personally oversaw the implementation. These details, eagerly provided by individuals close to Arafat, were meant to emphasize his disdain for Tenet and his plan.

On June 15, as Palestinian ambushes, sniper attacks, roadside bombs, mortar attacks, and the like continued to escalate, the PA also started organizing "spontaneous" demonstrations and riots against the cease-fire and the Tenet plan. The rioters burned pictures of Tenet as well as Israeli and American flags. Nevertheless, the CIA convened yet another high-level security coordination meeting with the expressed agenda of discussing how to "continue" implementing the "cease-fire." Moreover, the CIA elicited an advance Israeli promise for further unilateral relaxation of security measures—including the opening of additional roads to Palestinian traffic and the reopening of the Rafah border crossing—and used this promise to convince Arafat to approve the PA's participation in the meeting. Hence, Israel was deprived of the ability to use these concessions in the actual negotiations. For their part, the PA representatives arrogantly refused to even consider detaining, let alone arresting, Islamist terrorists. Predictably, the meeting ended without any tangible results. Still, that afternoon, Jerusalem ordered the IDF to begin pulling back tanks and dismantling roadblocks in "quiet areas." By June 17 there was, in the words of the IDF, a "certain reduction" in Palestinian violence, but even Indyk acknowledged that "it is still not quiet."

When, a few days later, the kitchenette decided to begin a "re-assessment of the cease-fire" in view of its "unilateral nature, given the continued terrorism and incitement and lack of arrest of terrorists by the PA," Washington immediately urged Jerusalem not to do anything drastic. Washington reinforced the pressure on Jerusalem through a series of public pronouncements equating the behavior of Israel and the PA. "Over the past few days, as we know, we have seen an upsurge in violence and in shootings," State Department spokesman Richard Boucher said on June 20. "We certainly regret the loss of life on both sides over the past few days, and we call on both sides to redouble their efforts to bring down the violence. We are encouraged by the efforts made by both sides. But continued success requires good faith and sustained efforts from both sides to fully implement the work plan." That night, Sharon convened the security cabinet to discuss how to deal with the American pressure. The cabinet decided that "Israel will continue its efforts to implement the Tenet document." Ultimately, Jerusalem went along with Tenet's charade "agreement" and "cease-fire" for the *sole* reason that it was apprehensive, if not downright afraid, of the Bush administration's reaction if it refused. What really mattered to Jerusalem was the extent of U.S. support in any forthcoming regional war.

The previous day, Sharon had told a delegation of American Jewish leaders that "the continued violation of the cease-fire by the Palestinians and murderous attacks create an unbearable situation that will not enable Israel to continue with its present approach over time." Sharon then made an oblique reference to the gathering clouds of war. "War is the last resort, and we currently have other options to try and resolve the security situation. To go to war today, in my opinion, is totally incorrect and inappropriate. This is not something we should do," he said without elaborating further.

———

THE REVIVAL of Iraq's active interest in a regional war was confirmed in late May when Saddam named Qusay—his younger son and intended heir—commander of the al-Quds Army and one of the two deputy military chiefs of the Iraqi Ba'ath Party (where Saddam himself is the military chief). Qusay's appointment made him the next-to-highest authority, second only to his father, in all issues pertaining to both internal and external security. The specific appointment of Qusay as commander of the al-Quds Army strongly suggested that Saddam was indeed committed to a regional war, because he would not have put his intended successor in charge of a lost cause.

Baghdad's reaction to a U.S.-U.K. proposal to overhaul the U.N. sanctions regime only heightened the crisis. Several Iraqi officials presented the U.N. deliberations as proof of the West's determination to confront, rather than compromise with, Baghdad. On June 9, Saddam himself delivered a bellicose address to his cabinet that took the message even further, arguing that the continuation of the sanctions regime would inevitably lead to a military confrontation. "It is necessary to let our people know the details . . . the whole truth," Saddam told the cabinet. "Then when the confrontation occurs, we will be victorious because . . . the battle is a battle of national independence."

In Jordan, there was a sudden increase in Islamist and rejectionist groups' preparations for an uprising aimed at the overthrow of King Abdallah. The flow of military assistance from both the PA and Iraq was unmistakable. The PA was also using HAMAS and HizbAllah cells in Jordan's sprawling refugee camps to reach the radicalized Islamist youth. In early June, King Abdallah instructed his security services to crack down on the subversion before it was too late. Several Palestinians were arrested, and large caches of weapons and explosives were discovered. By the middle of the month, Palestinians under the age of 50, even if they were Jordanian citizens holding valid Jordanian passports, were no longer permitted to return to Jordan having once left. Hundreds of Palestinian Islamists were detained without explanation.

Meanwhile, Syria clearly expressed its growing preoccupation with the possibility of war in its negotiations with Russia over military supplies. Arriving in Moscow in late May, General Tlass requested a major weapons deal with speedy delivery. The key items on Tlass's list were upgrade kits for Syrian tanks, including guided missiles and shells; numerous surface-to-air missiles, including the latest version of the S-300 (Russia's answer to the U.S. Patriot); new fighter-bombers; and huge quantities of ammunition and spare parts for Syria's Soviet-made arsenal. Of paramount significance was the Syrian request for long-range reconnaissance platforms, from spy satellites to MiG-25REs. The price tag on these Syrian "emergency" requests exceeded $1 billion even at Russia's cut-rate prices. Throughout their visit, Tlass and his aides repeatedly attempted to impress upon the Russians the urgency of this weapons deal.

Then on June 3, Syria's Vice President Abdul Halim Haddam collapsed while delivering a speech on live TV in Tripoli, Lebanon. He had suffered a major heart attack and took some time to recuperate. Haddam had been one of Bashar's strongest pillars of support among the older generation; his absence weakened the self-confidence of the younger leaders and decreased Bashar's willingness to embark on military adventures. A few days after Haddam's collapse, Bashar told Crown Prince Abdallah that he would "not provide Sharon with an excuse to deliver a military strike against . . . Syria, because Sharon is looking forward to such a gift." On June 14, Damascus announced the redeployment of Syrian forces in Lebanon away from predominantly Christian areas to more remote sites. It seemed that for the time being, Syria was pulling itself out of the war cycle.

By now, thanks to reports from Russian officials throughout the Arab world, as well as Arab senior officers traveling to Russia, Moscow was beginning to realize the strategic significance of the MiG-25RE reconnaissance aircraft it had offered to Damascus. At the time, Damascus had no usable targeting information on Israel's strategic rear. Until recently, Syria's plan had been to launch a surprise attack with ballistic missiles tipped with chemical and biological weapons. For that, it was enough to hit somewhere near the center of Israel's main cities. Now, however, Damascus was being warned by its allies to adopt a doctrine of a first strike with conventional warheads or else risk Israel's full retaliatory wrath. To use conventional warheads effectively, Syria desperately needed accurate targeting data. The MiG-25RE would supply such data, covering the deep interior of Israel while flying at extremely high speeds just outside Israeli air space—thus giving the Syrians strategic first-strike capabilities against Israel. Once the Kremlin was apprised of these implications by the U.S. Congress and others, it decided to cancel the entire deal. The Russian move was so sudden that a Syrian Air Force delegation was on its way to Moscow when it was informed of the Russian decision. A furious Bashar al-Assad expelled Russian engineers from the oil fields and from some major Syrian-Iraqi transportation projects (roads, railroads, and oil pipelines), but Moscow would not relent.

———

THESE LATEST MANEUVERS shifted attention once again to Iraq, which Washington, Jerusalem, and Ankara were concerned might be willing to do anything to break out of its remaining isolation. Their apprehensions were manifested in an unprecedented trilateral—U.S., Israeli, and Turkish—air force exercise in the second half of June. This exercise, called Anatolian Eagle, spoke volumes about the participants' strategic concerns. Its target was "Pikacho," the cruel dictator ruling "Torusland." The scenario began with Pikacho unleashing his armies against the indigenous population of the "Cymria" region of Torusland. The combination of the military build-up in Torusland and the flow of refugees—victims of ethnic cleansing—from Cymria to the neighboring democratic "Cappodocia" made the situation in Cappodocia intolerable. That Cappodocia and Torusland had a history of enmity long preceding the reign of Pikacho only heightened the anxieties of the Cappodocians, who appealed to their allies in the "Blue Coalition"—the United States, Israel, and Turkey—to send expeditionary forces to counter Pikacho's aggressive designs.

For the two weeks of Anatolian Eagle, the Blue Forces conducted an intense air campaign against the Red Forces of Torusland, including the use of live ordnance. The operations exercised included long-range strategic bombing, air-defense suppression, counter-air operations, deep heliborne raids of various types, and the sustenance of elite forces in the deep rear of the enemy through long-distance paradrops of equipment and supplies. By the time Anatolian Eagle ended, the United States and its principal regional allies had clearly demonstrated for friends and foes alike their ability to launch a well-coordinated joint air campaign. In any new major conflagration, unlike the

Gulf War, the United States would not need to rely on resources in the Arabian Peninsula in order to devastate Iraq—or Syria, for that matter. The strategic ramifications were not lost on the key Arab states. However, they reacted primarily with defiance and despair, feeling that they needed to strike out immediately, before they lost the capability to do so.

Baghdad was under no illusions as to what Torusland really was, and who Pikacho was. On June 17, Saddam told his cabinet that the time was ripe for going to war against the United States and Israel. Over the next few days, Iraqi TV showed Saddam and his two sons engaged in mobilization activities. The streets of Baghdad were full of rumors.

On June 20, while Anatolian Eagle was picking up steam, Iraq capitalized on a routine U.S.-U.K. air strike in the Kurdistan no-fly zone in order to instigate a regional crisis. Iraqi media reported that U.S. and U.K. fighters operating out of the Incirlik air base in Turkey had intentionally bombed a full soccer stadium in the middle of a game, killing twenty-three and wounding eleven more. Because Iraqi TV broadcast the match live, the carnage was seen by the entire region. In fact, the incident was a sophisticated and ruthless provocation. A radar simulator was hidden in the stadium. The American and British fighters detected the radiation and thought the Iraqis were homing air-defense missiles on them. Following standard procedures, the fighters launched missiles against the source of the radiation—missiles that therefore hit the stadium, killing civilians. Immediately, Saddam ordered the Iraqi armed forces on high alert, and Iraqi TV unleashed a preplanned incitement campaign that included showing pieces of the U.S.-made missiles and gruesome pictures of injured civilians.

The Iraqi propaganda was followed by swift and large-scale military movements all over the country and the evacuation of military and security headquarters from Baghdad to emergency locations in the western desert. Once again, Qusay was identified as the overall commander of the military effort, signaling the importance of the Iraqi moves.

––––––

THE SUMMER OF 2001 found the IDF severely strained—forced to deal with the escalating Intifadah while diverting its best units to preparing for the anticipated regional conflagration. Moreover, the Sharon government routinely disrupted the IDF's methods of operation in reaction to pressure from Washington. For example, as a unilateral demonstration of reduction of "excessive force," the IDF was forbidden to use tank fire, which had given it a big advantage after dark because of the tanks' sophisticated electro-optical sensors. Similarly, the government curtailed assertive operations, raids, and preventive measures. The IDF knew, and the kitchenette concurred, that Arafat was exploiting the Israeli goodwill to smuggle in weapons and move heavy mortars and other forbidden weapons to forward positions. Still, Jerusalem did not dare confront Washington with these facts, let alone free the IDF to do what was in the best security interests of Israel.

On the U.S. side, power struggles within the administration influenced the White House more than did the realities in the Middle East. Powell and Tenet, supported by the State Department and the CIA institutionally, as well as by the Senate, were using the Middle East peace process as an instrument for containing the Cheney-Rumsfeld faction and the Department of Defense institutionally. At the core of the power struggle was the president's fixation on Saddam Hussein's Iraq. The Powell-Tenet faction believed that a pro-PLO peace process would undercut the longstanding assumption in the Arab world that the United States was inherently pro-Israeli and anti-Arab and, in so doing, would reduce the fervent Arab opposition to the United States' confronting Iraq. With the Cheney-Rumsfeld faction unable to come up with an alternative solution to the enduring problem of Saddam's longevity, the president was increasingly inclined to go along with Powell and Tenet. This rift came to the fore in the context of Sharon's visit to Washington in late June.

Even before President Bush met with Sharon and had a chance to get his response to various U.S. concerns, Bush made his own statement to the media. He reiterated his determination to send Powell to the Middle East immediately, even though Israel had urged the White House to wait for the region to calm down first. Bush also publicly stated that there was enough progress in cooling down the Intifadah for further steps in implementing the Mitchell Report to be undertaken—a sharp rebuke of Sharon's insistence on a complete cease-fire before any negotiations could resume. Moreover, U.S. officials were quick to leak that Bush's mention of the Mitchell Report was designed to signal to Washington's Arab allies that the United States would not be following Sharon's timetable. "We believe you've got to keep moving forward or the whole situation will fall apart on us," a senior official explained. "We can't stay in the cease-fire-only arena indefinitely."

Once Bush and Sharon were inside the White House together, the tone became more cordial, but the message was still sharp: no war, no escalation, no "complicating" Bush's summer. Bush then demanded more Israeli concessions, including a freeze on settlement activities, in order to give Arafat an incentive to persevere. Bush asked Sharon to be "realistic" in determining what constituted reduction or cessation of Palestinian violence and also demanded that Israel not topple Arafat because, given Tenet's high-profile maneuvers and Powell's forthcoming mission, this would make the administration "look stupid"—a term actually used by a White House official involved in the talks.

The contradictions in Powell's declared positions during his brief Middle East tour reflected the administration's confusion. Regarding the territories, Powell demanded international observers and later talked to Arafat about their presence as a fait accompli. He added that the peace process was "a package" and explained that "we have to end the violence, at least for a number of days, before we open the package"—thus adopting Arafat's refusal to commit to a permanent cessation of hostilities. However, after meeting with Mubarak in Cairo, Powell said: "Nobody is claiming that the level of violence is down where anybody could say it was either realistic or zero. But at the end of the day it is Mr. Sharon who will make that judgment."

Ultimately, Sharon was willing to make additional concessions to Bush way beyond the Israeli "red lines" in order to ensure U.S. support in case the next threat of regional war proved not to be a false alarm.

———

ON HIS WAY to the Middle East, Powell stopped off in Paris, where he reported to Crown Prince Abdallah on the understandings between Bush and Sharon and attempted to gain his support for the new American oil-pricing policy and permission to use bases in Saudi Arabia in case of war with Iraq. Abdallah was noncommittal regarding a U.S. confrontation with Iraq. In due course, Saudi emissaries informed Baghdad of the American demands and Abdallah's position.

This Saudi gesture was the first action in a fledgling dynamics that would change the real power structure in the Middle East. Back in early June, Bashar had assured Abdallah of Tehran's and Baghdad's desire for a reduction of tension with Riyadh and relayed their apprehensions of a U.S.-Zionist conspiracy aimed at drawing the whole region into "a cauldron of fire none of us will survive." This conspiracy, Bashar pointed out, would prove most dangerous for Saudi Arabia and the other Gulf States because they would be implicated as being on the Zionist side if Western forces once again operated from their territory. Now, on the heels of Anatolian Eagle, Powell's briefing of Abdallah confirmed, directly from the mouth of one of the most senior officials of the Bush administration, the plausibility of Riyadh's worst nightmares.

When Abdallah confronted Bashar with the issue of Syrian-Iraqi relations, Bashar stressed the significance of the younger generation's alliance and suggested that if Abdallah truly wanted to ensure that he was succeeded by one of his own sons—rather than by the U.S.-sponsored Prince Bandar—he and his sons should join the alliance. As if on cue, Arafat, personally and via emissaries, started transmitting Saddam Hussein's assurances to Riyadh. Already apprehensive about the lingering U.S. military presence in Saudi Arabia and fearing the CIA (including the possibility of an assassination to clear the way for Bandar's ascent), Abdallah decided to further explore the idea of realignment. He instructed a team of a few close family members to begin quasi-formal discussions with both Baghdad and Tehran on the possibility of establishing a clandestine long-term security posture that would be inherently anti-American and anti-Israeli. Relaying the contents of Powell's personal briefing was Crown Prince Abdallah's first demonstration of goodwill in what would be lengthy and fateful negotiations.

———

BESIDES WASHINGTON and the regional powers themselves, Moscow was also keeping a worried eye on events in the Middle East. In early July, the Russian General Staff completed a major study that concluded: "War in the Middle East has not just become simply a reality. It is almost inevitable and unavoidable."

The study identified the convergence of several factors as the key to the slide to war. The first of these was the inherent instability of Bashar al-Assad's regime. At the root of Bashar's plight, as the Russians saw it, was the deterioration of Syria's overall socioeconomic condition, combined with Bashar's alienation of the very elements of the power structure that would be crucial in suppressing eruptions of popular discontent. "Bashar Assad managed to turn against him the highest echelons of the Syrian generals," the study explained, "[by] vanquishing for many influential generals sources of income and well established business—first and foremost the smuggling of contraband [via Lebanon]. The transfer of officers that have long forgotten the reality of military service to the Bekaa Valley and the anti-Israeli strategic axis made them Bashar's personal enemies." The growing influence of Rifaat al-Assad among the upper echelons of the Syrian security and defense establishment further aggravated this phenomenon, with most veteran leaders considering Rifaat to be the sole viable savior of Syria from Bashar. "In so unstable a situation, war is the only way for Bashar to remain in power," the study noted. "All attention would be glued to the events on the front for the duration of the war. And, after the practically unavoidable defeat, it would be possible to conduct purges in the army and the special services."

The second factor was Iraq's "amassing a large grouping/concentration of forces on the border with Jordan." The study identified two main reasons for the Iraqi build-up. "Either Saddam would try to break through onto the Arab-Israeli front through Jordan, or this is a deceptive maneuver so that in case of aggravation of the internal political situation in Syria he will be able to dispatch the troops there." The study anticipated the concurrent launching of a wave of Islamist terrorism by bin Laden's supporters throughout the

West—a wave of terrorism that would seriously complicate Washington's and London's ability to confront Baghdad.

The third factor was the repercussions of the death of King Hussein back in January of 1999. "The late King Hussein was one of the most influential politicians who could . . . contain the urges of the Palestinians to blow up the peace, always influence Hafiz al-Assad's extremist outbursts, and soften the positions of Saddam Hussein," the study explained. "There is no King Hussein now, so there is no restraining factor."

The fourth factor was what the Russians judged to be the irreversible demise of the U.S.-sponsored Israeli-Palestinian peace process. Arafat's power position was at the core of this factor. "Yassir Arafat is not capable of controlling the activities of such extremist organizations as HAMAS, Tanzim, Fatah, as well as other less known but more radical groupings, and especially the pro-Iranian movement HizbAllah. Moreover, radical peace agreements with Israel which take into consideration Israeli interests constitute a death sentence to Arafat." Therefore, to survive, Arafat had no choice but to facilitate the escalation of the armed struggle. At the same time, the growing Israeli preoccupation with the specter of regional war made it imperative for the IDF to swiftly and decisively defeat the Palestinians. "Currently, Israel is actively preparing for a big war," the study reported. It identified Israel's recent destruction (on July 1) of another Syrian radar station as a major step in these preparations because "Israel's strikes leave the Syrians without 'eyes and ears.'" The Russians were most alarmed about the escalation potential should the Arabs succeed in launching a first strike because "in case the very existence of Israel should be threatened, that country's leadership is quite capable of sanctioning the use of nuclear weapons. In any case, Israeli 'sources' are trying hard to make sure that Damascus and Baghdad should not forget this."

"Thus," the General Staff concluded, "all that now remains is to wait for who will start first." However, they noted, "the most unexpected things take place in the Orient—sometimes at the very last minute."

22

"Kill a Settler Every Day" (2001)

The Lebanonization of the Intifadah;
Bush's Saddam Fixation

ON JULY 2, sitting in his Gaza office, Arafat called Barghouti, who was in
Ramallah, and instructed him to kill a Jew before the end of the day. Arafat
specified that he would prefer an attack inside Israel proper, or at the very least
in Area C. Israeli intelligence intercepted and recorded the call and promptly
gave the kitchenette a transcript. In another early July phone call, Arafat instructed his senior commanders to "kill a settler every day" and to "shoot at
settlers everywhere." "Woe to you," he admonished his commanders, "if you
let them reach their homes in peace or travel in the roads peacefully." What
prompted these orders was the Palestinians' assessment of the overall outcome
of Sharon's visit to Washington and the need to prevent the Bush administration from furthering its understandings with the Sharon government.

In an early July meeting with senior officials in Gaza, Arafat explicitly
stressed the irrelevance of the political process—much more so than in earlier meetings. "Don't pay attention to what I say in the media, the television,
or in public sessions," he warned them. "You should refer only to instructions you receive from me in writing." Concurrently, other Palestinian leaders
once again acknowledged that they were still committed to the Phased Plan
and that their ultimate objective was the destruction of Israel. "The goal of
the current Intifada is a Palestinian state," Barghouti flatly told the *New
Yorker*, "but afterwards, there will be even greater things for which to strive.
There is no room for more than one state between the Jordan River and the
Mediterranean."

However, fully cognizant of the political ramifications of the coming escalation, the Palestinian security chiefs decided on a gradual approach while

encouraging HAMAS and the Islamic Jihad to formally break from the "cease-fire" and declare their commitment to a renewed jihad. Action followed immediately. On July 3, two car bombs exploded near Ben Gurion Airport. There was considerable damage but no fatalities. More important was the PA's own testing of the security procedures near the official residences of the president and prime minister of Israel. A simulated car bomb was left near the corner of Zhabotinsky and Arlozerov Streets, and a bomb bag was left in a nearby bus station, while a team of PA security officials monitored the reaction of the Israeli security forces. The PA also tested the access routes into west and central Jerusalem through the various Israeli security layers; then escape cars entered the center of Jerusalem and safely evacuated the Palestinian teams. Israeli intelligence learned about the PA's activities from its sources rather than by noticing them at the time.

———

TO MANY IN WASHINGTON, Moscow, and Jerusalem, the second week of July was looking more and more like a time of decision in the Arab world—whether to join the Intifadah and escalate it into a regional war or to let Arafat slug it out with an increasingly frustrated Israel. For his part, Arafat remained adamant on escalating the Intifadah irrespective of whether or not he would be provoking a regional eruption. The recent arrival in Gaza of engineers from Bosnia, Egypt, and Bulgaria to assist in building clandestine infrastructure for the production of heavy weapons and ammunition, as well as for their maintenance under siege conditions, testified to Arafat's expectations. As well, a sudden move of some $4 billion from Arafat's secret West European accounts to a new set of accounts in Singapore made it seem as if he feared that the Americans and Europeans would decide to freeze his assets. By now, HAMAS and the Islamic Jihad had endorsed the PA's policies and even expressed their willingness to join a unified national-emergency leadership with Arafat at the helm.

Meanwhile, special IRGC teams had traveled from Tehran to southern Lebanon via Damascus to give the HizbAllah rocket crews technical assistance—and also additional supervision, to ensure that there was no "local initiative," with the weapons now deployed so close to the Israeli border. Furthermore, the Syrians' mid-June "withdrawal" of troops from Beirut had actually permitted reinforcement of the Syrian deployment in the Bekaa—better protecting the approaches to Damascus. Joint Iraqi-Syrian field headquarters were activated, and numerous liaison officers were exchanged between the two armies. Iraq also tested a new long-range surface-to-air missile not far from the Kuwaiti border—a demonstration both of Iraq's increased military capabilities and of the brazenness of Saddam Hussein.

Confronted with all these developments, Mubarak and Crown Prince Abdallah entered into intense consultations by phone and via emissaries. The two leaders concurred that given Arafat's preparations and his combative mood, he risked provoking a massive Israeli reaction. To prevent such a reaction, and the regional eruption that would surely follow, the Saudis pushed the Bush administration to pressure Jerusalem, while Mubarak sent Omar Suleiman, the chief of Egyptian Intelligence, to Israel with an unprecedented harsh letter to Sharon. Mubarak demanded that Israel cease the use of "excessive force" and threatened to reverse the entire peace process—starting with the Camp David accords, which had remained at least nominally in force since 1979—if Israel brought about Arafat's collapse. There was not a single word of criticism of Arafat in either Mubarak's letter or Suleiman's discussions with Israeli senior officials. The Bush administration joined in, dispatching David Satterfield, the newly appointed deputy assistant secretary of state for Near East Affairs, to Jerusalem with instructions to expedite Israel's implementation of the Mitchell and Tenet plans. In a gesture to an anxious Jerusalem, Powell did call Arafat to tell him that the "cooling-off period" leading to resumed negotiations could not begin unless he did more to reduce (not end) the violence.

This growing foreign pressure exasperated even the Israeli peace camp. Peres publicly complained that the PA had yet to fulfill its promise to combat terrorism and violence. Although Arafat and senior aides informed Tenet of specific measures they had undertaken, Peres observed, "unfortunately, to date we do not see any results." Furthermore, despite Mubarak's ostensible role as peacemaker, the smuggling of weapons and ammunition through underground tunnels in Rafah increased markedly. Large weapons shipments were kept in storehouses at the El-Arish Air Base, from which, with the active assistance of Egyptian Military Intelligence, smaller quantities were moved forward to the Egyptian suburbs of Rafah whenever the Egyptians were sure the IDF would not intercept them. The sharp contrast between Cairo's words and deeds infuriated Israel.

———

ON JULY 12, in a lecture in Gush Etzion, General Mofaz reacted to the upsurge of Palestinian violence and terrorism. He stressed that *all* the PA's security organs—Fatah, Force 17, General Intelligence, Naval Intelligence, General Bureau—were involved in terrorism, and "all of them have Jewish blood on their hands." Later that day, IDF Intelligence informed the security cabinet that Arafat had formally given the green light to HAMAS and Islamic Jihad to escalate their strikes in the territories as well to carry out spectacular martyrdom operations in Israel's main cities. Expert HizbAllah teams, the IDF reported, had recently been brought to the territories in order to direct the "Lebanonization" of the Intifadah.

In the face of the PA's escalation, and the mounting U.S. and Egyptian pressure not to react, Sharon sent Omri for a meeting with Arafat in Ramallah on the night of July 12–13. Reading from a page of handwritten instructions from his father, Omri delivered a contradictory message. On the one hand, he stated that despite the ongoing U.S. pressure, the IDF would retaliate if the violence continued. On the other hand, he assured Arafat that Israel had no intention of either killing him or toppling the PA as an entity. Omri also gave Arafat intelligence warnings on Islamist terrorist strikes being planned and requested his assistance in thwarting them. Arafat listened, did not react or comment, and did not commit to anything. By the time Omri left, Arafat understood and so conveyed to his lieutenants that he could get away with murder.

The next few days saw a further escalation throughout the territories. Israeli intelligence intercepted Arafat's own instructions for this escalation and on July 15 issued a warning to the security system and to the public of "lethal" and "horrific" terrorist threats. Significantly, the IDF discovered that instructions had been issued to teams already inside Israel to begin the mass killing of civilians in martyrdom operations and with remote-control car bombs.

Jerusalem expressed its growing exasperation in a series of public statements by Israeli leaders. "We are not in a situation of restraint, as some people call it," Sharon argued on July 18. "We are working according to a policy decided upon by the Cabinet, combining strong strikes against terrorists who are planning and carrying out attacks against us, while preserving Israel's diplomatic interests. True, it is hard, but this is the correct way now." In an interview with BBC radio, Peres noted the mounting frustration with continued Palestinian violence. Israel, he said, "did not have a single day without funerals, without ambulances, without sirens."

––––––––

ON THE NIGHT of July 20, Arafat called in his closest confidants in the Palestinian security apparatus—Dahlan, Abu-Shabak, Habash, and Tirawi—for a highly secret discussion about the prospects of the Intifadah. Arafat complained that the joint operations with HAMAS and the Islamic Jihad were not working because Israel had penetrated these organizations. Israel was assassinating too many senior terrorist commanders, he continued, and given the recent capture of key Islamist terrorists, Israel certainly knew the extent of the PA-Islamist cooperation. Therefore, Arafat decreed, the Tanzim and other PA-affiliated organs must be brought back into the forefront of the

Intifadah and, together with General Intelligence, take over the security mechanism as well as implementation of struggle plans. The Tanzim, Arafat instructed, should return to the front line "with full might." The next day, as usual at times of great escalation, Arafat hit the road—this time to Saudi Arabia and the Persian Gulf sheikhdoms.

During the morning of July 22, Palestinian terrorists planted some fifteen pipe bombs throughout Haifa. They also had a martyr-bomber at the ready: He was to exploit the commotion after the string of explosions, mix in with the crowd, and blow himself up. However, Israeli security forces captured the would-be martyr before he had a chance to activate his charge. He told his interrogators about the pipe bombs, and all fifteen were safely removed and neutralized.

The failure of the Haifa operation heightened the tension between Arafat and his "Tunisians," on the one hand, and, on the other, the combative younger generation who were the foot soldiers of the Intifadah. Arafat's comments about the Islamists during the recent nocturnal meeting found their way into the Palestinian street. The result was a series of armed clashes, including an attack on Musa Arafat. An alarmed Habash called Arafat in Abu-Dhabi and urged him to return to Gaza immediately, before the "Intifadah generation" took over from his coterie. On the morning of July 25, Palestinian Radio dramatically halted its regular broadcast, and the announcer read, in a grim voice, the following message from Arafat: "All the forces that tear apart the unity of the people in this time of a fateful struggle should know that they are taking upon themselves the huge responsibility that will determine the fate of the Palestinian people."

However, with rumors spreading about his mistrust of the Islamists, Arafat felt compelled to demonstrate anew his commitment to the all-Islamic cause. He was given his opportunity by an Israeli fringe group, the Temple Mount Faithful (the same group that had provided the excuse for the Al-Aqsa riots back in 1990). In late July, the group appealed to the Israeli Supreme Court for permission to hold a symbolic cornerstone-laying ceremony for the Third Temple on the Temple Mount. The court rejected their request but did permit them to hold a ceremony near the Old City's Dung Gate. Although the court forbade the Temple Mount Faithful access to the Temple Mount itself, and although they obeyed the court's order, Arafat seized on the mere legal procedure as the catalyst for a new wave of incitement.

On July 27, Ikrama Sabri, the mufti of Jerusalem, delivered a fiery sermon at al-Aqsa, urging all Muslims to "physically defend the Temple Mount from the Zionists." Sheikh Sabri insisted that the Supreme Court decision was actually part of a widespread conspiracy aimed at the destruction of

Islam's holy mosques. The Muslim world must avert this threat at all costs, he proclaimed. The PA-controlled media gave prominence to Sabri's call to arms, and Arafat personally ordered Tirawi to inflame Jerusalem and, specifically, the Temple Mount.

Tirawi selected July 29—for Jews, the day of commemoration of the fall of Jerusalem to foreign invaders and the burning of the Temples—for a series of terrorist strikes throughout Jerusalem. The main event, as Arafat had ordered, was at the Temple Mount, where several hundred "worshipers" up above attacked the Jewish worshipers at the Wailing Wall below with bottles and rocks. Consequently, even on such a special day, Israeli police forced the Jews to stop their lamentation prayers and evacuate the area. Jibril Rajub's security guards on the Temple Mount had not intervened or made any attempt to prevent the attack on the Jews. They finally went into action—against the Israeli police who tried to break up the riot and stop the hurling of stones, rocks, and bottles.

The next day, Arafat, hiding in Tunis, ordered the expansion of the fighting. He specifically instructed his forces to strike out inside Israeli cities, introduce mortars and heavy weapons to additional West Bank "fronts," and lay ambushes inside the Green Line. All of these instructions were carried out promptly.

At this point, the IDF's frustration burst into the open. On July 31, speaking at an IDF induction center, General Mofaz stated: "Over the last few days, there has been a sharp escalation in terror attacks under the direction of the Palestinian Authority. Since September, in my opinion, Arafat has given a 'green light' to mass killings in Israeli cities. This trend is being accelerated. There is now an unprecedented number of assaults against Israeli targets. I said before that at least 57 of the Israelis murdered were victims of terrorist activity perpetrated by the various security arms of the Palestinian Authority and Fatah." Mofaz publicly ridiculed the U.S.-mediated security arrangements with the PA. "The Palestinians arrest wanted terrorists just for show—the 'arrested' terrorists are kept in safe remote houses and depart from there to carry out terrorist attacks." Mofaz saw no viable political solution and urged the government to adopt more stern military measures. "We must erect an 'iron wall' to protect the citizens of the State of Israel and annihilate terrorism," he concluded.

Cornered, Sharon called Powell the next day to warn that Israel had to continue its "policy of counter-terrorism measures . . . Israel reserves the right to defend its citizens, just like the U.S.," Sharon said. He added that Israel would adopt self-restraint the moment Arafat started arresting terrorists, abiding by the cease-fire, or taking other credible steps to prevent terrorist attacks on Israel. Powell listened and, when Sharon had finished, reiterated his urging that Israel not do anything that would either bring down the PA or irreversibly end the peace process.

———

BY THIS TIME, another complication had been added. In mid-July, Mubarak had gone to Germany for emergency medical treatment, raising fears of possible incapacitation and the trauma of a succession struggle. Now, upon his return, he conducted a sudden and thorough purge of the Egyptian military and security elite. Among those ordered to resign were the commander of the Air Defense Forces, the chief of the Northern Command, a senior officer in Military Intelligence, the deputy interior minister responsible for internal security, and a deputy defense minister. Most of these men were transferred to civilian positions amounting to political banishment. There must have been a sense of tremendous urgency because they all were relieved of their duties without successors having been named. The first successor would be announced only a week afterward.

None of the newly appointed senior officers and officials was considered pro-American; hence, they were more likely to actively support the resumption of hostilities. At the same time, Cairo announced the beginning of a major exercise of the Third Army near the Suez Canal that would culminate in a storm-crossing of the Canal as well as the transfer of forces through the eight tunnels underneath.

Iraq's current activities made these developments in Egypt the more worrisome. Between July 10 and 14, some 800 to 1,000 Iraqi special forces penetrated Jordan in small teams. Once inside Jordan, the Iraqi teams linked up with Palestinian cells; some made their way to the West Bank, while others went underground in Palestinian refugee camps in Jordan. The Palestinian teams were assigned to help prepare for upheavals in Jordan in the context of an eventual Iraqi invasion. Meanwhile, the forward deployment of Iraqi troops near the Jordanian border continued unabated.

Jerusalem, Amman, and Washington were particularly alarmed by these maneuvers because of a major speech delivered by Saddam Hussein on July 17. "Say to your enemies," Saddam urged the Arab world, "the enemies of our Arab Nation, who are the foul Jewish usurpers, their covetous allies, and all the colonialists and their abject servants: stop abusing the Arab Nation." Saddam promised that Allah would bestow "glory upon the courageous mujahideen and all free and honest men who fight for the freedom of their [Arab] countries."

The next day, Saddam convened his high command and announced that in the wake of "the great Iraqi triumph" over the U.N. sanctions, the time was ripe to launch the second phase of the war for "the eviction of the Americans from Iraq." The first phase had been Iraq's challenging the no-fly zones. The second phase would be its rallying the Arabs through an Arab-Israeli conflagration in support of the Palestinians. A practical and pragmatic Saddam added that Iraqi involvement in a war for the liberation of Palestine would make it impossible for any Arab regime to support U.S. strikes against Iraq.

In private conversations with European counterparts, Egyptian senior military analysts elaborated on the significance of Saddam's address to the high command. The Egyptians cited intelligence on U.S. regional designs that Washington had supposedly shared with Cairo at the highest levels—implying that Baghdad was in possession of this ultra-sensitive intelligence when Saddam made his address. The Iraqi surge westward, the Egyptians explained, would take place mainly via Jordan in order to thwart the U.S. design for an Israeli-Turkish pincer movement against Iraq. In the U.S. grand design, as related by the Egyptians, an Israeli pincer arm would penetrate central Iraq, having traversed a compliant Jordan, while a Turkish pincer arm would advance via Kurdistan into north-central Iraq. Cairo, the Egyptians told the Europeans, had been asked by Washington to stay out of the war and not exploit the crisis against Israel. The Egyptians implied that Cairo had no intention of complying—that it would put solidarity with the Palestinians above the United States' priorities.

Unfolding military activities in southern Iraq gave added weight to Saddam's address to his high command. Iraq's test-firing of its new-generation surface-to-air missile back on July 2 had delivered a clear message to Kuwait and Saudi Arabia. However, the technical details concerning the SAM and its support system were far more important than the political signal. The SAM was an Iraqi design, consisting of an advanced SA-6b with improved inertial guidance, installed atop a booster stage that was a derivative of one of Iraq's new generation of ballistic missiles. Unlike most SAM systems, this one, in order to avoid vulnerability to Western radar-homing missiles, did not use locally deployed radars. Instead, it relied on a new early-warning radar chain developed by the PRC. At the center of this chain were two Czech-built Tamara radar systems capable of detecting U.S. stealth aircraft. (Iraq had sought to acquire these two radar systems back in 1997–98 and paid in full. At Washington's insistence, Prague canceled the sale; however, an inventory of the Tesla-Pardubice company in late 2000 revealed that the two systems had "disappeared.") The entire chain of radar stations fed several command centers via underground fiber-optic cables; the command centers, in turn, provided data on approaching targets, again via underground fiber-optic cables, to air-defense command centers in southern Iraq. (Back in February, the United States and United Kingdom had tried, and failed, to destroy this underground communications network.) When a hostile aircraft approached, the early-warning radar provided the data for the booster trajectory, bringing the SA-6b close enough to the target plane that its internal homing and guidance system could pick up the target and come in for the kill.

In mid-July, Iraq began putting its new SAM system to operational use. On July 19, a single missile was launched toward a U.S. Navy E-2C Hawkeye surveillance aircraft on patrol over Kuwait. Apparently, the SA-6b's guidance system failed to pick up the slow turbo-prop aircraft, for the missile arced in its general vicinity and crashed harmlessly. Then on the 24th the Iraqis took aim at a U.S. Air Force U-2 reconnaissance aircraft flying at 60,000 feet—theoretically outside the lethal envelope of any known Iraqi weapon. This time the SAM worked very well, homing in on the U-2 and nearly slamming into it. Only the quick reactions of the pilot, coupled with the aircraft's electronic countermeasures (ECM) suite, averted a shootdown. Undaunted, on July 30 the Iraqis fired a barrage of the new SAMs toward a USAF E-3 AWACS loitering deep inside Saudi Arabia. Once again, the missiles failed to hit the plane because of its sophisticated ECM, but some of them came very close. Encouraged, Saddam met with his air defense chief, Shahin Yassin Muhammad, and other senior officers and ordered them to redouble their efforts to bring down American and British aircraft.

————

PRESSURED BY both Amman and Jerusalem to do something about the Iraqi encroachments into Jordan—and upset, to say the least, by the Iraqi attempts to shoot down American aircraft—the Bush White House decided to formulate a regional solution to the "Saddam problem." Washington pressured Amman in turn to lower the profile of its cooperation with Israel and instead to endorse the U.S. effort to rejuvenate the 1990–91 anti-Iraqi coalition, including Saudi Arabia, Egypt, the Gulf States, and even Syria. Bush personally told both King Abdallah of Jordan and Crown Prince Abdallah of Saudi Arabia that the reemergence of such a coalition would surely deter Saddam and make him end his provocations. If this didn't work, Bush promised the Arab leaders, the United States would act promptly and decisively. From these political maneuvers, and from a series of meetings with U.S. defense officials, senior Arab officials concluded that the United States was planning to attack Iraq by the end of August. Throughout these contacts, the Saudis sounded most friendly and cooperative. However, the moment the Americans left, the Saudis sent emissaries to Baghdad and Cairo to assure both regimes that Riyadh was not part of the American game plan.

Emboldened, the Iraqi teams continued to infiltrate into Jordan so that by the end of July they had 1,200 to 1,500 troops there. The Iraqi teams were becoming brazen, openly showing themselves in radical sectors of the sprawling Palestinian refugee camps. Shielded by the Palestinians, they were able to evade the Jordanian security forces and carry out their mission of transferring weapons and ammunition to PLO and HAMAS cells in Jordan and the West Bank. When Amman sent off heliborne hunting parties against them, Iraqi fighter planes appeared near the Jordanian border. The moment the Iraqis flew too close, the Israeli Air Force scrambled fighters and anti-SAM strike aircraft, which darted to meet them. The Iraqi fighters withdrew before contact was made.

Over the next few days, Iraqi fighters continued to patrol—but now at a safe distance from the border—under the watchful eye of Israeli aircraft patrolling just west of the Jordan River. The tense aerial standoff enabled the Jordanians to carry out hot-pursuit raids all over the country; several of these got all the way to the river, where Israeli special forces took up the hunt. By this time, however, U.S. pressure and assurances were affecting Amman's decision making. Hence, as Jordanian elite units were closing in on the Iraqi pockets, ready to assault them, they were ordered by the king to halt and not provoke any escalation.

———

AS THE WHOLE Middle East prepared for a climactic development, the various Palestinian organizations were putting their rivalries aside in order to better face the coming challenges. Around August 7, the PA, HAMAS, and Islamic Jihad reached a formal understanding on the tenets of a "government of national unity." Four principles stood at the core of this understanding: (1) HAMAS recognized the distinct phase of establishing a Palestinian state in the 1967 boundaries with Jerusalem as its capital; (2) the Islamists recognized the validity of UNSC Resolutions 242 and 338; (3) the PA vowed to persevere with the armed Intifadah until the realization of the Palestinians' legitimate aspirations, the establishment of a Palestinian state, and the implementation of all pertinent U.N. resolutions; and (4) the Islamists would receive meaningful portfolios in a new Palestinian cabinet. The careful wording of article 3 was a euphemism for Arafat's renewed commitment to continuing the struggle until Israel had been destroyed.

Behind this maneuver was Arafat's recognition of the need to present a broad consensus when appealing for all-Arab assistance. In announcing the government of national unity, senior PA negotiator Yasser Abed Rabbo stressed that there would be no return to the peace process: "The dream of Oslo died, and those most hit are the Oslo supporters. Therefore, the time has come for those who opposed Oslo to unite with these who supported Oslo in furthering the struggle presently conducted by the Palestinian people. Perhaps this move is belated, but it is imperative." Arafat himself pointed out the profound change in the PA's official policy. "The Palestinian leadership is committed to the peace process," he told his confidants, "but it cannot be expected to limit its role to that of the guardian and protector of the Israeli occupation."

The long-awaited major provocation came at around 2 P.M. on August 9. A martyr-bomber blew himself up inside a Sbarro restaurant in the center of western Jerusalem, killing eighteen, including six infants, and wounding well over a hundred. Most of the victims were women and small children. The bomb contained nails in order to increase the number of casualties. HAMAS was quick to claim responsibility, announcing that a Jenin-area cell had launched the operation in order "to avenge the blood of our children, women, and old people and in defense of Al-Quds and Palestine." The HAMAS communiqué promised more to come: "This retaliation is the first in a series of Qassim strikes that will teach the Zionists an unforgettable lesson as a penalty for their cowardly act of liquidating mujahedin and activists of the Palestinian people."

Barghouti and other PLO-related leaders praised the strike as a "heroic action." The Fatah movement also praised it. The spontaneous expressions of joy throughout the PA-controlled areas clearly told what the street felt: Hundreds of Palestinians danced and sang in the streets, firing guns in the air. Crowd leaders praised HAMAS and the Islamic Jihad for "killing the Jews." Islamists handed out candies and sweet cakes to the crowds—a traditional demonstration of having no sadness at the death of a martyr. "Even the animals in the fields are happy about this attack," declared an Islamic Jihad spokesman. Only when international pressure grew did Arafat condemn the "killing of innocents" and call for an immediate cease-fire by both Israel and the Palestinians. Arafat's message was virtually identical to the one he had issued after the Dolphinarium bombing in June.

The Israeli government pondered an appropriate reaction to the Sbarro carnage, amidst a public outcry not to repeat the "restraint" that had followed the Dolphinarium bombing. Complicating the issue was the fact that the Israeli security services had known about the HAMAS perpetrator and the general outline of the operation. They had asked the PA's security services, via the CIA, to arrest the man and break down the Jenin cell, but the Palestinians had refused. In the end, the Security Cabinet decided on a "measured response." Besides destroying a number of largely empty buildings belonging to the PA security forces throughout the territories, IDF and police teams seized numerous Palestinian buildings in the Jerusalem area, including the Orient House and the "Governor's House" in Abu-Dis—thus depriving the PA of a presence in greater Jerusalem. The Muslim world reacted with fury. Hatem Abdul Qader, a Fatah leader, warned that the Israeli actions "will bring the Intifadah into Jerusalem": "We will not relinquish any means in order to reverse the Israeli decision."

Meanwhile, Arafat rushed to assure the Americans that he, particularly via Tenet's protégé Rajub, was confronting Islamist terrorists. Actually, he was doing exactly the opposite. Between August 9 and 11, he and Yassin met at least twice to finalize the establishment of the national unity government and to coordinate operations. They jointly decided to expedite the massive Israeli retaliation they considered inevitable by launching yet another major attack. Consequently, on August 12, a martyr-bomber blew himself up at a café in the Haifa area. This bombing was less successful than the Sbarro one, however, because of the quick action of the café's owner. The would-be martyr said "goodbye" to a waitress as he walked in. She screamed, and the owner reacted swiftly, throwing a chair at him. Hence the bomb exploded in the doorway, causing only a few casualties. Furthermore, parts of the bomb remained intact, enabling the Israeli security authorities to make a breakthrough in their investigation.

Shortly thereafter, Israeli intelligence reported to the government that they had proof of Arafat's direct responsibility for the latest martyr-bombings even though the martyrs were Islamists. Intelligence officials confirmed that Arafat had specifically instructed Dahlan (in Gaza) and Tirawi (in the West Bank) to organize a sustained campaign of Islamist terrorism at the heart of Israel. To ensure that these martyrdom operations served the PA's strategic objectives, Dahlan and Tirawi themselves were to select the targets and timing. For quality control, PA bomb-makers made the explosive-webs and handed them over to the would-be martyrs, whom the Islamists had prepared and delivered. The cabinet was provided with irrefutable intelligence that this system was responsible for both the Jerusalem and the Haifa bombings.

But Arafat was already one step ahead of Sharon's kitchenette. On the night of August 12–13, he convened two meetings in his Ramallah headquarters. The first session, attended by key Palestinian political leaders usually associated with the "peace camp," addressed a new "Peres initiative"—the idea floated by Peres, and endorsed by Powell, of giving Arafat "one last chance" to suppress terrorism. Arafat ridiculed the whole undertaking, commenting that nobody should take Peres seriously any more. However, Arafat did recognize the practical value of feigning cooperation with the Peres-Powell "lifeline" as the best way to postpone the Israeli strike, and so, with a smirk, he instructed his "diplomats" to continue the peace-process rhetoric for as long as possible. Arafat then threw everybody out of the room except Sakhr Habash and a handful of other close confidants. To them, he stated that the policy of encouraging the Islamist strikes was attaining its objectives and decreed that it should be expanded and escalated, albeit under tighter control. Habash was assigned to closely supervise how both Tirawi and Dahlan were implementing Arafat's instructions on the handling of the Islamists. Arafat stressed the importance of inflicting heavy civilian casualties because it was the only tactic that seemed to have an effect on Sharon and the Israeli public.

By this time, the government had decided on its form of retaliation. That night, a small IDF armored column penetrated into Jenin and destroyed the governor's building as well as several buildings belonging to the security forces. The brief defense effort by a few defiant Palestinians was crushed by the Israeli tanks and gunships. IDF raiding parties also struck at nearby refugee camps, destroying specific facilities and arresting terrorists. The IDF vacated Jenin before first light. Although the PA leadership expressed outrage, it was relieved by the symbolic and restrained character of the Israeli retaliation.

———

A PRIMARY FACTOR influencing Jerusalem toward self-restraint was the mounting threat of war from Cairo. In a conversation with a Scandinavian journalist, a senior Egyptian intelligence officer reinforced Mubarak's warning of early July, flatly stating that Cairo was considering "canceling the 1979 peace treaty with Israel if the latter invades PA territory." A senior security official declared that Israel "had to be deterred" from "destroying" Arafat. These were not empty words, for Egypt had announced that the major military exercise scheduled for September would involve live-fire maneuvers. This meant that Egypt could not only concentrate huge forces near the Suez Canal—the entire Third Army and a host of auxiliary forces—but also push forward large quantities of ammunition and other supplies under the cover of exercise requirements.

This is exactly what had occurred back in the fall of 1973, in preparation for the Egyptian surprise attack on Yom Kippur. Jerusalem now found itself in a quandary: at what point should it attempt to stop the advance of the Third Army into the Sinai? Any such attempt would surely propel the entire region into war. However, because Israel had reduced its forces in the Negev to a symbolic level since its withdrawal from the Sinai in 1982, if Egypt's maneuvers were in fact the first step toward war, a failure by the Israeli Air Force to destroy the Third Army deep inside the Sinai Peninsula would be disastrous for Israel's very existence. Hence the kitchenette opted to exercise self-restraint toward Arafat rather than be compelled to test Cairo's true intentions.

Washington, meanwhile, could no longer ignore movements on the northern front—principally a visit to Baghdad by Ahmad Miro, the Syrian prime minister, leading a major delegation of ministers, senior officials, and businessmen. The official reason for the visit was to expand the Syrian-Iraqi economic and political alliance. In fact, Miro and Taha Yassin Ramadan, Iraq's vice president, also needed to complete and have ratified the myriad of mutual security agreements the two countries had been working on.

On August 15, the United States took action. A lone F-16 took off from the Incirlik base in Turkey and proceeded to fly for some 23 minutes in a straight line through northeastern Syria, crossing into Iraq at the edge of the northern no-fly zone. When the Syrians complained, the United States apologized for "a navigational error." In fact, the F-16 was on a sensitive reconnaissance mission, aimed at provoking the local air-defense and communications networks into working in emergency mode. The Syrians and Iraqis grabbed the bait. The United States intercepted the communications between the Syrian air defense and their Iraqi counterparts in which the Syrians reported the progress of the F-16 and handed over tracking data to the Iraqis in case they wanted to shoot it down. The United States now had airtight evidence from its own sources—as distinct from data provided by Israel, Jordan, and other allies—about the intimate cooperation between the Syrian and Iraqi military systems. The next day, General Tommy Franks, the U.S. Commander in the region, rushed to Jordan to discuss the latest developments with the king and his high command. The Jordanians concluded that the United States was seriously considering preempting Saddam's plans for a regional conflagration by launching a massive bombing of Iraq.

Over the previous few weeks, there had been an undeclared and perhaps even unformulated but nevertheless profound transformation of U.S. policy vis-à-vis Israel and the Palestinians. The Bush White House was convinced that for its coalition building and ultimate strike against Iraq to succeed, the Palestinian-Iraqi provocation had to be prevented. Because Arafat and HAMAS were not likely to comply with U.S. demands, the only way to prevent such an eruption was by pressuring Israel into not reacting to cycles of terrorism and civilian casualties. Obsessed with getting Riyadh to spearhead yet another confrontation with Iraq, or at the very least to permit the use of Saudi bases and facilities, the Bush White House no longer had the slightest interest in the particulars of the Palestinian terrorist strikes in Israel—that is, the reason for Jerusalem's desire to conduct military operations. The "peace process" and "mutual restraint" rhetoric had become simply a fig leaf for the administration's real objectives. Therefore, in insisting that the Americans address the PA's responsibility for acts of terrorism against Israeli civilians, Jerusalem was repeatedly forcing them to confront reality—reminding them of their choices and priorities. Hence, the Bush White House increasingly considered the Sharon government to be a major source of irritation.

The shrewd Crown Prince Abdallah saw through the American maneuvers but interpreted them differently from the way Bush intended. Abdallah genuinely believes the conspiracy theories of how "the Jews are controlling America"—particularly Washington and the media. This was on his mind when he considered the Bush White House's willingness to sacrifice Israel on the altar of a revived anti-Saddam coalition. If the Americans were capable of betraying Israel—America's special and unique Jewish ally—what can an Arab "friend" expect the moment U.S. interests shift elsewhere? It would be far safer, Abdallah reasoned, for Saudi Arabia to follow Tehran's advice and stick together with the region's other Muslim powers against the perfidious Americans. He therefore instructed his confidants to expedite their efforts to consolidate a working alliance with Tehran and Baghdad.

―――――

WITHIN ISRAEL, violence of all sorts continued. The new center of activity was the Gilo neighborhood of Jerusalem, where Palestinian fire had intensified day and night. Finally, Sharon ordered the IDF to move five armored and elite infantry columns toward Beit Jallah and Beit Sakhur in order to clear out the Palestinians' firing positions.

At this point Peres intervened, threatening to leave the government—thus bringing it down—if Sharon refused to give Arafat yet one more "last chance." Sharon succumbed to the pressure and called off the raids. However, Arafat did little in return, and on August 19 Sheikh Yassin issued an open challenge. "Martyrdom operations are the democratic right of the Palestinian people, and they are the only democracy Israel is understanding," he declared. "One can feel the palpable fear in Israel. They are afraid of the hanging question where and when the next strike will take place."

On August 20, Sharon and Ben-Eliezer convened a special meeting of the high command. Yaalon, representing the IDF's position, urged the political echelons to adopt the policy of an "airtight wall" against the PA. The PA should be politically, economically, and militarily isolated, Yaalon argued; Israel should stop all contacts with Arafat—particularly the demeaning "security coordination"—until the PA either collapsed or came to its senses. The high command asked Sharon and Ben-Eliezer for greater freedom of action in initiating preemptive and preventive operations, as well as in launching swift and massive retaliatory strikes. Sharon listened, expressed his appreciation and empathy, but committed to nothing.

The PA expressed *its* appreciation for Israeli self-restraint by blowing up a car bomb in Jerusalem on August 21. The bomb was unusually sophisticated. First, a small charge exploded, attracting the attention of the security forces. But inside the car was a far more powerful charge—some 22 pounds of high explosives, with nails—primed to be blown up, most likely by remote control, when enough people surrounded the car. Sappers managed to neutralize this charge at the last moment. Subsequent investigation confirmed that it was built by Iraqi Military Intelligence and/or by Palestinian experts trained by them. Moreover, police records showed that the car had been parked in the same place for three days. Hence, the bombs must have been installed in full view in the middle of west Jerusalem—quite a professional achievement.

The same day, Arafat gave an explicit order to complete the Lebanonization of the Intifadah. He convened an urgent meeting with Sakhr Habash, Musa Arafat, Tawfiq Tirawi, and Hakam Balawi—a veteran terrorist operative and a new member of the inner circle. "From this moment on," Arafat told them, "I give you the order to bring about the Lebanonization of the war with Israel. You will set the area aflame. You will do everything else. You know what you are supposed to be doing." The escalation would be a team effort—with key roles for the Palestinian Islamists, the Syrian-sponsored radicals, and HizbAllah—but tightly controlled by Arafat and the inner circle. The most important outcome of the meeting was the establishment of the Emergency Committee of the Fatah Movement as a new terrorist organization comparable to the Tanzim. Balawi was named commander of the Emergency Committee, and Ahmad Adiq, the Tanzim commander in Nablus, was named chief of operations. By the end of August, Balawi would eclipse Barghouti in the Intifadah leadership—creating competition among the militant groups of the Fatah to prove their importance to the Intifadah.

Returning from a brief visit to Cairo on August 25, Arafat emerged in public carrying his Kalashnikov. It was a clear message to all: they were seeing Arafat the fighter, the mujahid, not the peace-making diplomat.

———

A CONCURRENT INCIDENT in Damascus shed light on the undercurrents elsewhere in the Arab world. On August 18, Bashar al-Assad traveled to Kuwait for a short visit in order to get financial assistance for Syria's ailing economy, especially in view of the cost of the anti-Israeli buildup. Official Kuwaiti reports about the visit were formal and cold.

Meanwhile, Iraqi Vice President Ramadan had traveled to Yemen for what was to be a lengthy visit covering a host of official and clandestine issues—most notably the growing role of Yemen in breaking the international sanctions on Iraq. However, on the night of August 22, Ramadan suddenly cut short his visit and flew to Syria. Arriving at the Damascus airport at night, he immediately rushed to a meeting with Bashar.

First, Bashar described to Ramadan the hard discussions he had had in Kuwait. The Kuwaitis, Bashar said, had negotiated with him on behalf of Saudi Arabia and other Gulf States as well. The Kuwaitis had threatened that unless Syria immediately broke off all economic and security relations with Iraq, the Kuwaitis and the others would immediately cut their aid to Syria. Bashar assured Ramadan that he had held fast and refused to end the close cooperation between "our sisterly states" against "traitors to the Arab cause."

In this context, Bashar made a most disturbing comment. He pointed out to Ramadan that this was not the first time the Kuwaitis had tried to contain the anti-imperialist and anti-Zionist struggle through economic pressure. He added that his own recent encounter "might prove even more momentous than that of Izzat Ibrahim"—a clear reference to the last-minute effort by Kuwait and Saudi Arabia to prevent Iraq from going to war in late July 1990. Ramadan congratulated Bashar on his steadfast commitment to their common cause, but neither side elaborated further on this comment.

———

ON AUGUST 27, fighting in the territories escalated yet again, with Israeli civilian casualties incurred. Most significant was the renewal of fire on Gilo. When Sharon had halted the IDF's advance two weeks earlier, he promised that the IDF would seize Beit Jallah immediately if shooting resumed. Now, with Palestinian fire escalating, he had to order the IDF into action. After midnight, several columns of IDF armored forces and paratroopers entered Beit Jallah and Beit Sakhur. By 3 A.M., the key strategic sections of both towns were in Israeli hands. The government ordered the IDF to destroy the entire PA infrastructure so that the Palestinians could not resume firing on Jerusalem when the IDF ultimately withdrew. This included destroying weapon and ammunition caches, as well as destroying buildings used as firing positions. The IDF was instructed to make a thorough job of it. Unlike previous incursions into Area A, this time there would be no rush to withdraw.

The evening of August 28 saw further escalation, with the Palestinians firing 60-mm mortars on Gilo as well as 0.5-inch heavy machine guns. Both weapons were fired from Bethlehem proper—a first. Meanwhile, the IDF continued its mop-up sweeps in the area. Although Washington concurred that the continued firing on Gilo was intolerable, the administration changed its tune the moment the IDF actions went beyond a symbolic gesture. Powell pressured Sharon by phone to withdraw immediately and unconditionally, and U.S. diplomats and CIA representatives started to explore with the PA arrangements that would permit a speedy Israeli withdrawal. That Arafat refused to address the *sole* Israeli demand—no more shooting on Gilo and other Jewish neighborhoods—did not diminish Washington's zeal. The IDF stayed a second night in the captured sector.

The next morning, U.S. officials started to tie in the demand for an immediate Israeli withdrawal with the demand for a Palestinian cease-fire.

Arafat responded by openly deploying mortars and other heavy weapons in Nativity Square in Bethlehem—daring Israel to strike out near Christianity's holy sites. Even when provided with aerial photographs of these weapons, the United States refused to intercede with the PA. Mortar and heavy machine-gun fire on Gilo continued all this time, as well as clashes between PA security forces and the IDF's mopping-up forces. Pressured by the United States, Sharon permitted Peres to try to reach some understanding with Arafat, but to no avail.

On the morning of the 29th, as IDF teams began capturing a new set of positions used by the PA security forces, Arafat notified Peres and the Americans that he was ready to order a cease-fire by 2 P.M. provided it would lead to an IDF withdrawal. As a gesture, the IDF stopped its mopping-up operations. When the Palestinian fire did not stop and more mortar shells fell on Gilo, the IDF renewed assertive operations. Arafat now vowed to cease fire by 8 P.M. The government ordered the IDF to stop initiated operations again but also to prepare to spend another night in Beit Jallah and Beit Sakhur. Meanwhile, Powell called Arafat to ask him to help restore quiet to the area—as if quiet had existed before the Israeli incursion and as if Arafat were not responsible for the firing in the first place. Later, Powell leaked to the Washington media elite the content of his talk with Arafat, with the aim of building public pressure on Sharon.

At this point, Arafat called Peres and promised to make an effort to quiet the area if the IDF withdrew by 8 P.M. PA officials added an ultimatum: There would be a marked escalation if the IDF did *not* withdraw by 8. The kitchenette met after 10 P.M. and decided to consider the vague arrangements discussed between Peres and Arafat as a core agreement on a cease-fire. Around midnight, the IDF was ordered to withdraw, and by 5 A.M. it was back in its forward positions in the Gilo area, even though IDF local commanders had requested an additional twenty-four to forty-eight hours to do the thorough job Sharon had initially ordered. Palestinian forces celebrated their great victory over "the Jews," firing in the air and into Gilo.

In deciding to withdraw from Gilo, the kitchenette was influenced by the pressure from the United States and from Peres, but, much more important, it wanted to get Gilo off the agenda so that it could concentrate on a potential war emergency in the north. On the morning of August 30, Sharon and the kitchenette arrived at the headquarters of Israel's Northern Command for emergency consultations and briefings. The visit and the anxiety were prompted by high-quality intelligence, confirmed by aerial photos and SIGINT, concerning active preparations by Iranian teams in southern Lebanon and concurrent movements by the Syrian and Iraqi armed forces. The IDF wanted to know whether to preempt. The kitchenette would not decide.

Israeli intelligence had also learned that Arafat and his coterie had just completed the organization of escape routes to both Egypt and Iraq. Baghdad had already activated Arafat's substitute headquarters so that he could resume commanding the Intifadah the moment he reached Iraq, and Egyptian military intelligence had assisted the Palestinians in refurbishing and stockpiling their emergency bunkers in the eastern Sinai. This spate of activity suggested to Israel that Arafat thought he might need these emergency facilities in the very near future.

By the end of August, the territories were, in the words of a senior Israeli official, "aflame"—just as Arafat had demanded—and the Israeli public was clamoring for security and urging decisive military action.

———

THE RUSSIAN GENERAL STAFF'S analysis back in July of the megatrends in the Middle East was largely corroborated by a study prepared for President Putin by the Moscow-based Institute for Israel and Middle East Studies. The study was completed by the Institute's Director, Yevgeny Satanovsky, one of Russia's—and the world's—leading Middle East experts.

The Satanovsky study identified the inherent instability of the key Arab countries as the primary reason for the growing threat of war. After reviewing the specific situations in Jordan, Syria, and Iraq, Satanovsky predicted that "war will be sparked by the current confrontation between Israel and the Palestinian Authority." However, the duration and intensity of "the regional war . . . will stem from domestic instability within key regimes in the Middle East." Therefore, Satanovsky concluded, to prevent or contain a regional eruption, Moscow must focus on supporting stable and responsible governments throughout the Arab world.

Putin and Sharon discussed these sentiments and ideas during a brief visit the latter paid to Moscow in early September. During an important private breakfast meeting between the two, which lasted two hours, Putin set the tone for the meeting, stating up front that "Russia is a natural ally of Israel."

Using detailed maps and diagrams, Sharon then surveyed the Iranian strategic threat to Israel, with emphasis on the significance of the flow of technology from Russia to Iran. Putin offered to establish a Russian-Israeli committee to study the Iranian issue, but he pointed out the crucial importance of Iran for Russia's geostrategic posture. Russia had no intention of contributing to the threat against Israel, Putin added, but Russia was not going to abandon its growing influence in Iran either. The two leaders shared apprehensions about the danger posed by the tottering regimes in the Arab world, and they agreed on the need to foster stable regimes amenable to close cooperation with Russia and coexistence with Israel. Putin warned Sharon that the ongoing Israeli-Palestinian military confrontation was hastening the slide toward a war that would serve nobody's interests. Putin opined that Israel should not be so sensitive to "world opinion"—his euphemism for the United States—and instead do what it preaches: namely, swiftly crush Palestinian terrorism and then embark upon a solution of the Palestinian problem. Sharon had no convincing reply.

Putin also noted that the Islamist terrorist movements in the Arab world had emboldened Islamist militants at the heart of Asia. Russia was thus seeking closer cooperation with Israel, and also with India, in suppressing the Islamist menace before it got out of hand. Sharon concurred that cooperation against Islamist terrorism and militancy was a necessity. Declaring that "terrorism can be defeated," he committed to expanding bilateral and trilateral cooperation in a wide variety of anti-terrorist measures—a move that would become crucial to global dynamics sooner than either Putin or Sharon could anticipate.

———

THE TENSION in the Persian Gulf ratcheted upward after the Iraqis shot down a U.S. unmanned reconnaissance plane over southern Iraq. When the Americans asked the Saudis and Kuwaitis to conduct intensified patrols along their borders with Iraq to attempt to locate, and if possible retrieve, the missing plane, Iraq decided to capitalize on these activities in order to remind its neighbors of its military capabilities. Hence, Iraqi forces ambushed a Saudi National Guard patrol of about a dozen men that was moving close to the unmarked border in the area of Mahfari Salibhat, killing at least one Saudi soldier. Other Iraqi patrols audaciously maneuvered near both Kuwaiti and Saudi border lines. By Thursday, August 30, with movements of U.S. forces intensifying in the Gulf region and in Europe, Gulf leaders were convinced that the United States would attack Iraq over the coming weekend.

Intense inter-Arab consultations followed. On Saturday, Crown Prince Abdallah invited Arafat to Jeddah. Arriving at the palace, Arafat was confronted by a battery of Abdallah's inner circle, including Foreign Minister Saud al-Faisal and Ambassador Bandar bin Sultan. Abdallah warned Arafat that the PA's anti-American incitement was attracting Washington's attention to inter-Arab politics without achieving anything tangible. Above all, Abdallah cautioned, Arafat must not permit PLO-affiliated terrorist teams to participate in Iraqi-sponsored anti-U.S. terrorism in the Gulf States. Any Palestinian involvement in Iraqi terrorism would pull the rug out from under the Gulf States' desperate effort to avert a war between the United States and Iraq. Arafat promised to comply but demanded clandestine funds for the Palestinian war effort as well as political help in Washington. Crown Prince Abdallah readily promised both.

Also on Saturday, King Abdallah of Jordan traveled to Alexandria for an emergency meeting with Mubarak. The king was certain that the moment the United States attacked Iraq, the Iraqis would unleash an all-out offensive on Israel—via Jordan. In order to expedite their advance, the Palestinians would inflame Jordan to such an extent that the Hashemites would not survive irrespective of the outcome of the war. Moreover, Abdallah opined, Syria had already determined to join the fray because Bashar feared that he would miss a historic opportunity to be a liberator of Palestine. King Abdallah wanted to know whether Egypt also intended to join the onslaught against Israel. Mubarak did not give Abdallah a clear answer about Egypt's own plans, but he strongly agreed that the U.S. attack on Iraq must be prevented at all costs.

On Monday, September 3, Mubarak flew to Damascus for an emergency meeting with Bashar. Mubarak wanted assurances that if the United States did not attack Iraq, Syria would not provoke a regional war by attacking Israel, either directly or via HizbAllah. Mubarak also wanted to confirm Syria's determination to actively assist Iraq in case of a U.S. strike. Having received affirmative answers to both his queries, Mubarak returned to Cairo and warned the Bush White House of the "ominous ramifications" of a major attack on Iraq. The White House got the message. Later that day, the U.S. Air Force launched four strikes against Iraqi air-defense targets in the al-Samawah area some 125 miles south of Baghdad. Ostensibly, the strikes were in response to intensified Iraqi air activities, but the Arabs understood the strikes to be a must-do-something way of bowing out of the planned massive attack on Iraq.

––––––

THE ARAB WORLD saw the Arab leaders' success in forestalling the U.S. attack as a great victory. Emboldened, the Arabs resumed their slide toward war against Israel as the sole viable breakout from the region's stagnation, with Arafat immediately ordering a new cycle of escalation.

Because the Palestinians so hastily implemented his order, the Israeli security forces had some initial success in mitigating the effects of some potentially highly lethal strikes. On September 4, the Israeli security forces closed in on a martyr-bomber as he was trying to get into the middle of a crowd in downtown Jerusalem dressed like an observant Jew, with a skullcap. When two Border Policemen grabbed him, he blew himself up, wounding thirteen; dozens could have been killed had he blown himself up in the right place. On September 8, a large bomb exploded in Nazareth. Investigation determined that it was in transit to a more heavily populated location and exploded ahead of time.

The balance shifted on September 9, a day of carnage that succeeded in shaking up Israel and its government. In the Jordan Valley, Palestinians attacked a school bus transporting teachers to school. The driver and two female teachers were killed, and several other teachers were wounded. Witnesses reported that the attackers had been closely following and watching the mini-bus so that the attackers knew full well that most of the passengers were women. The same morning, a martyr-bomber exploded a car bomb near Netanya, wounding twelve and causing heavy damage. The car-bomb—full of white phosphorus to increase burns and fire damage—was intended for the center of Netanya; however, stopping at a road junction, the martyr saw a Prison Service vehicle stopping behind him and blew himself up rather than be caught. That afternoon, a fifty-five-year-old Israeli Arab blew himself up in the Nahariya train station, killing three and wounding scores. Immediately after the Nahariya strike was reported, HizbAllah and Palestinian sources in Lebanon claimed the operation in the name of a Palestinian from southern Lebanon who, the sources said, was aided by HizbAllah in reaching Nahariya. The obvious purpose of the claim was to provoke an Israeli retaliation against Lebanon and—if Israel were to act on its recent warnings to Damascus—also against Syrian military targets, thus setting off the regional war.

The IDF immediately launched the customary gunship strikes on Ramallah-area security buildings, but everybody on both sides of the divide knew this was a knee-jerk reaction, while Jerusalem deliberated an appropriate response. On the night of September 9–10, Sharon and the kitchenette arrived at the headquarters of the IDF's Central Command for specific discussions with the local senior commanders. The kitchenette needed to ascertain whether the IDF could cope simultaneously with the escalation of Palestinian terrorism and the mounting Iraqi-Syrian threat. The IDF succeeded in convincing the kitchenette that it could cope with both of these threats if it were permitted freedom of action. Perhaps because Sharon was emboldened by Putin's scolding, or perhaps because of the repeated urging of his old friend Rehavam Zeevi, a founding father of Israel's anti-terrorism doctrine, the kitchenette ultimately resolved that "retaliation" for the carnage of September 9 would be effective only if it served as the beginning of a sustained Israeli offensive. The IDF would thus embark on a series of major initiated operations designed to crush the PA's terrorism-sponsoring infrastructure and forces before the terrorists implemented their own plans at great cost to Israeli civilians. Sharon ordered the IDF to take on Jenin as the first operation of the new strategy.

Jenin was selected because Israeli Intelligence confirmed that all the operations of September 9 were controlled and run by Tirawi's Jenin networks in cooperation with the local Islamists—HAMAS, the Islamic Jihad, and

HizbAllah. The indoctrination and training of the Israeli Arab had also taken place in Jenin. Once again, the PA had refused to act on a specific advance warning delivered via the CIA and had not arrested the key Islamists involved in the September 9 operations.

Therefore, the following night, large-scale IDF forces closed in on Jenin as helicopters hovered above. Islamist, Fatah, and Force 17 troops deployed with heavy weapons to resist the Israeli strike, and the imams in Jenin's mosques encouraged the believers to commit martyrdom in order to inflict heavy Israeli casualties. "A cemetery is awaiting the Israelis if they dare to enter the Authority's area. We are waiting for them," boasted a Force 17 commander. "Tens of youth with explosive-webs, gas tanks, and dynamite are awaiting the Israelis. We are ready for the IDF to come in."

The PA leadership anticipated that the IDF's attack on Jenin would be the catalyst for war that Arafat and Saddam had been yearning for. However, by the time the IDF completed its initial deployment, it was midmorning in Washington and New York. The date was September 11, 2001, and the Middle East, like the rest of the world, was another place.

23

New Beginnings (2001–2002)

The War on Terrorism and the War in Israel

THE EVENTS OF SEPTEMBER 11 galvanized the Muslim world in an unprecedented way, not least because the terrorists' message was brought home to the entire world as never before. The September 11 attacks were perfectly suited to the electronic information age. Millions of people remained glued to their TV screens, watching with horror and helplessness—or with glee and defiance—as the airliners slammed into the World Trade Center towers. Via satellite TV, the entire world saw images of the bright explosions and, subsequently, the horrific collapse of the two huge skyscrapers in rolling clouds of smoke and dust. People all over the world watched as terror reverberated throughout the United States. Official Washington was evacuated on live TV, its empty streets guarded by an army of nervous policemen. A cloud of smoke billowing above the Pentagon served as a constant reminder. To TV viewers worldwide, that morning's spectacle was at one and the same time a demonstration of the omnipresence of Western informational technology and an expression of the outrageous challenge posed by Islamist terrorism.

The primary audience for these horrendous attacks was the Muslim world—both the street and the ruling elites. For the vast majority of Muslims—irrespective of their position in society or their view of Islamism—the desperate heroism of the perpetrators, their embrace of martyrdom, brought a sense of pride. The targets of this spectacular strike had been chosen as a symbolic gesture to the Muslim world and particularly to the leaders of pro-U.S. states. The United States' global power and presence is manifested in its financial might and its military might. The terrorists had struck at the center of the U.S. financial empire by bringing down the World Trade Center and, albeit symbolically, at the center of U.S. military might by hitting the Pentagon. The message to the Arab world was clear: You cannot rely on the Americans to protect their friends, for they are incapable of protecting their own cities.

In the Middle East, the September 11 strikes accorded a new urgency to the global Islamist struggle against the United States and its allies. Significantly, the Islamists singled out Jews—rather than Zionists—as crucial allies of the United States. Under these circumstances, the struggle for Palestine—more accurately, the liberation of al-Aqsa and al-Quds—was no longer an end in itself but rather an integral and very important component of the larger jihad. Arafat—ostensibly a former Ikhwani (Muslim Brother) but actually someone who has remained a closet Ikhwani all his life—relished the Islamicization and globalization of the struggle against Israel because the new posture increased the likelihood of outside military intervention on his behalf. At the same time, however, he found himself competing with Osama bin Laden for the attention and admiration of the Arab world.

Indeed, with news of the attacks came an outpouring of support for bin Laden, both as an individual and as the symbol of Islamist militancy. In virtually every Palestinian city, crowds celebrated, firing in the air and distributing candies to passersby. In Nablus, crowds marched in celebration, waving the HAMAS flag and chanting, "Beloved bin Laden, strike Tel Aviv!" Others chanted: "Let the Americans know the meaning of death!" In East Jerusalem, drivers honked their horns in triumph. "The Americans give the Israelis Apache helicopters to bomb our houses," explained a young Palestinian. "They give them diplomatic support and intelligence help on how to kill us." When these celebrations attracted media attention, the PA arrested an AP photographer and threatened to execute him if Western media broadcast the images of Palestinian jubilation.

Public-opinion surveys conducted throughout the Arab world in the next few months confirmed just how severe the challenge was. In an interview with Elaine Sciolino of the *New York Times* in late January 2002, Saudi Arabia's chief of intelligence, Prince Nawwaf bin Abdul Aziz, acknowledged that the vast majority of his country's young adults felt considerable sympathy for bin Laden's cause, even though they rejected the attacks on New York and Washington. According to a Saudi intelligence survey of educated Saudis between the ages of twenty-five and forty-one, taken in mid-October, 95 percent of those surveyed "supported bin Laden's cause." Prince Nawwaf attributed the results to "the feelings of the people against the United States" stemming from the United States' "unflinching support of Israel against the Palestinians."

In their initial reactions, the Palestinian media reflected the complexity of the situation. The Islamists rejoiced in the strike. In Gaza, the Islamist weekly *Al-Risala* published an open letter, "To America," by Atallah Abu al-Subh. "America, oh sword of oppression, arrogance and sin; do you remember how you crushed the humanity of man?" Abu al-Subh asked. "America, have you ever tasted the taste of horror, sorrow, and pain? This is the taste that has been our lot for so long." Abu al-Subh called the strikes an answer to the Arabs' prayers. "We stand in line and beg Allah to give you to drink from the cup of humiliation—and behold, heaven has answered. . . . Allah has answered our prayers; the sword of vengeance has reached America and will strike again and again!" The Islamist attacks, Abu al-Subh argued, were the obvious reaction to U.S. policies worldwide—not just in the Middle East. "America, you planted in the hearts of all men and animals the seedling of hatred of you! You never considered that the day would come when the saplings would grow and put out your eyes, even if those eyes were placed at the top of the World Trade Center, among the clouds." The strikes also generated hope for change among the Arabs. "America, it transpires that you are weaker than the weak, and that you are as wretched as any refugee that you forced to flee with his children, his wife, and the clothes on his back from a village that was once on the coast of Palestine." Abu al-Subh concluded with a harsh warning: "There is no doubt that this is a deed unprecedented in ancient and modern history. You cannot but realize that the perpetrator will strike again and again if you continue with your corruption."

At the same time, however, PLO/PA senior officials worried that the preoccupation of the United States and much of the rest of the world with finding and punishing the perpetrators would create a hostile climate toward all Muslim and Arab causes. At the very least, the media's preoccupation with the strikes diverted public attention from the Palestinian cause. The director-general of the PA's Information Ministry, Hassan al-Kashef, stressed this point in a mid-September article in *Al-Hayah al-Jadidah*. "Why are the Arabs acting like guilty parties? Why do [the Arab media] continue to give us this revolting flow of hypocrisy and obsequiousness toward the U.S.? . . . The Arab and Islamic political and media interest has veered from the daily Israeli tank and helicopter attacks on our soil. . . . The eyes of the Arab media remain riveted on the ruins of three buildings in New York and Washington. The [Arab] media are participating in the media blackout imposed on what is happening to us, on our land." Al-Kashef argued that the Israelis and the Americans were themselves guilty of acts of terrorism greater than the events of September 11. "If the airplanes' blasting into the World Trade Center towers in New York is considered terror carried out by a few individuals, the murder of Arabs by

Israel and by American weapons and all the American killings of Arabs in Iraq, in the Sudan, and in Libya is official terror, and those responsible are the U.S. and Israel. These are war crimes; these are crimes of mass destruction. . . . The Arabs trample their [own] rights and honor with feet trembling with fear of punishment for a crime they did not commit. This is the truth. The Palestinians should exclude themselves from this Arab situation, because they are fighters, not murderers, and because they are the victims of Israeli terror—terror in which the occupier Israel uses American weapons."

―――――

IMMEDIATELY AFTER September 11, Washington asked all its allies, including Israel, to contain local crises and instead divert their intelligence and counterterrorism resources to supporting the U.S.-led "war on terrorism." The Bush administration specifically urged Jerusalem to look the other way as Washington tried to get such countries as Syria and Iran to "join the coalition." Washington also sought to provide a cushion of comfort for a Riyadh petrified by the idea of confronting its own Islamists.

Sharon immediately committed to helping the United States in whatever way he could, starting by winding down the IDF counterattack on Jenin that had begun on September 11. Jerusalem's task was not made easier when Abu-Alaa proclaimed that any international war on terrorism should start with an attack on Israel—the perpetrator of anti-Palestinian terrorism. Nevertheless, the kitchenette was determined to find a way to go along with Washington's request that Jerusalem adopt unilateral measures to reduce the level of violence so that Arab states' resistance to cooperating with the United States would be lowered.

Initially, Jerusalem sought to gain Arafat's concurrence in helping the United States in its hour of need. On September 15, Omri Sharon and Avi Gil, Peres's chief of staff, met with Arafat in Gaza and assured him that if the PA sustained even the semblance of a cease-fire, Israel would reduce IDF operations. Arafat refused to commit. On September 18, the kitchenette decided to reduce the tension unilaterally, and Sharon declared a cease-fire even though he had no Palestinian commitment of reciprocity. He instructed the IDF to stop all initiated operations and exercise "maximal self-restraint" in cases of Palestinian attacks. IDF units also carried out unilateral withdrawals in the Jericho and Jenin areas. Still Palestinian violence continued, albeit at a somewhat lower intensity.

The next day, Arafat rushed to Sharm el-Sheikh for an emergency meeting with Mubarak to find out if Jerusalem and Washington were serious about reducing Israeli operations. Bush reacted by citing "a glimmer of hope" for the cessation of hostilities, and Arafat in turn promised to pressure the Islamists to cooperate with the cease-fire. He quickly arranged a meeting with Sheikh Yassin, in which he explained that Sharon was in a bind because of the American pressure, and therefore a temporary cessation of hostilities could lead to major unilateral concessions. Still the violence continued, and not only on the part of the Islamists—Fatah teams inflicted Israeli civilian casualties in a series of ambushes. By September 22, the fighting had returned to its pre-cease-fire level, and the heavy fire on Gilo had resumed.

Saddam, meanwhile, anticipating an imminent U.S. onslaught on Iraq and determined to make good use of his military resources before they were destroyed, once again put the Iraqi military on wartime readiness. However, he was calmed down by Saudi secret emissaries, who assured him that Riyadh would not give the United States permission to use Saudi bases in the context of the war on terrorism.

Cognizant of this dynamic, Arafat bought time by agreeing to meet with Peres in Gaza on the morning of September 26. The agenda contained familiar topics: the cease-fire, additional Israeli concessions, and the possibility of resuming implementation of the Tenet and Mitchell plans. Peres and Arafat were in the midst of their meeting when the building shook with a massive explosion: PA security forces had blown up a large bomb (more than 200 pounds) in a tunnel under a nearby Israeli stronghold, causing heavy damage. A few days before, as part of the Israeli concessions, Dahlan had been permitted to move a large number of forces to the Rafah area—ostensibly in order to stop the illegal weapon smuggling. Actually, Dahlan took advantage of this situation to transfer combat engineers, who dug a long tunnel into the stronghold and placed the bomb. The Palestinians pointedly exploded it at the very same time Peres was negotiating with Arafat. Heavy fighting erupted immediately afterward, as the PA security forces attempted to prevent Israeli rescue teams from reaching the stronghold. Even Peres realized there was no point in continuing to talk with Arafat.

On the 27th, Arafat gave the order to provoke the territories to an unprecedented degree. And so it was. The following day, Friday, Islamist leaders and imams stressed the Intifadah's ultimate objective: the destruction of Israel. "For as long as there is a single Jew in Jaffa and in Haifa, the Palestinians [will] not put down their arms," Abdul Aziz Rantisi declared in Gaza. After the Friday prayers, in virtually every Palestinian city close to an IDF position, enraged mobs attacked the IDF with stones and firebombs. To ensure that the IDF would fire on the rioters, PA security personnel fired on the IDF over the heads of the mob. The IDF responded as expected and, by the end of the day, had killed at least ten Palestinians and wounded over forty. On the 29th, when the IDF started moving forces to prepare for the resumption of initiated operations, the PA asked the CIA for a security coordination meeting, promising that "today we'll start quieting down the territories." Washington urged Jerusalem to give Arafat another chance, and the IDF unilaterally lifted the closure of Jericho. Israeli officials conceded that these moves were undertaken solely so as "not to refuse the Americans" rather than in accordance with their reading of the situation in the territories.

On October 1, a car bomb exploded in Jerusalem. After Islamic Jihad claimed responsibility, Tirawi announced that the PA would not arrest the Islamists that Israel wanted—and demanded. Still Washington insisted that Jerusalem persevere with the "cease-fire," and the Sharon government ordered the IDF to continue to implement measures that would ease the situation, as if nothing had happened. It took the six simultaneous attacks on October 2—all planned and carried out by Dahlan's people, on Arafat's orders—to get Jerusalem to face reality. Sharon finally unleashed the IDF on the Gaza Strip in a series of retaliatory strikes.

––––––

THE UNITED STATES began bombing al-Qaeda and Taliban positions in Afghanistan on October 7. As the U.S. bombing intensified, bin Laden made his first post–September 11 appearance on al-Jazeera TV. In Gaza, tens of thousands reacted by rioting in support of bin Laden and the Islamist cause. Arafat got the message. He needed to force the world's attention back onto the Palestinian question, even if negatively.

Meanwhile, Iran and Syria had decided to break out of what they saw as a deadlock in regional dynamics by shattering American illusions about possible roles for both of them in the anti-terrorism coalition. Iran markedly intensified the flow of rockets, missiles, anti-aircraft guns, and other weapons to HizbAllah via Syria. When the Islamist forces in southern Lebanon were deemed ready to meet a large-scale Israeli retaliation, Damascus and Tehran ordered the activation of an audacious plan long in preparation. On October 17, a PFLP team assassinated Rehavam Zeevi, Israel's minister of tourism, in his hotel in Jerusalem. Zeevi was a target of unique significance—a retired major general who had been a founding father of Israel's anti-terrorism doctrine, an unrepentant right-wing politician, and, most important, a close friend and brother in arms of Ariel Sharon for some sixty years. Arafat promised to arrest the perpetrators but apprehended only small fry. In fact, the PFLP's senior commanders had consulted with Tirawi about the advisability of the assassination, and Tirawi had notified Arafat before granting permission and arranging to provide support for the strike. In addition, on Arafat's instructions, Tirawi had consulted with Iraqi military intelligence in order to ascertain that an escalation of Israeli retaliation (inevitable in Arafat's eyes) into regional war would also serve Iraq's interests.

In fact, the Israeli cabinet did examine the options of retaliation against the PFLP's chief sponsor, Syria, or its main bases in southern and eastern Lebanon. Jerusalem had no doubt, however, that any such retaliation would indeed ignite the whole region—making any future Arab cooperation with the U.S. war on terrorism impossible. Hence, Jerusalem decided once again to put the American and general Western interest ahead of Israel's specific interest and ruled out attacks on Syria and Lebanon. Instead, Jerusalem issued an ultimatum to Arafat to apprehend the assassins and their commanders. When Peres called Arafat personally and urged him to cooperate lest he lose the opportunity to revive the peace process, Arafat did not completely stifle his giggles.

Over the next few days, the IDF escalated initiated operations in the Ramallah area, from which the assassins had operated. The PA retaliated with a series of lethal ambushes all over the territories. The IDF in turn expanded its initiated operations to the entire West Bank, shutting down seven cities and killing at least twenty PA troops while wounding fifty in a series of clashes. Rather than appreciating Israel's self-sacrifice in not retaliating against Syria and Lebanon, however, Washington kept urging further Israeli restraint. "Israel Defense Forces should be withdrawn immediately from all Palestinian controlled areas and no further such incursions should be made," State Department spokesman Phil Reeker declared on October 22.

Ultimately, Jerusalem succumbed. Preparing for a visit to Washington, Sharon told the Bush administration that he was committed to presenting the Palestinians with a state as part of an interim agreement rather than waiting for completion of permanent-status negotiations. On October 26, the kitchenette ordered the IDF to unilaterally commence a gradual withdrawal from PA-ruled areas. Consequently, the CIA organized a meeting of Israeli and Palestinian military representatives to discuss the PA's effort to capture Zeevi's assassins. The Israeli withdrawal continued even as General Malka, chief of Military Intelligence, informed the cabinet that there were "serious warnings of impending suicide attacks" and that the PA was "doing nothing about arresting the many terrorists walking around freely in its midst." Malka added that the United States had "applauded Arafat too early" and that "the PA translated this to mean that it had received a passing grade, and stopped working to thwart terrorism." Malka was proved right on the 28th, when two terrorists, driving slowly along a busy street in Hadera, opened fire at pedestrians on both sides of the street, killing four and wounding forty-four before Israeli police shot them. The Islamic Jihad claimed responsibility for the shootings, but Tirawi was the real force behind them.

Nobody should have been surprised by this attack. On Friday, October 26, the five key military entities in the territories—HAMAS's Izz al-Din al-Qassim Brigades, Fatah's al-Aqsa Martyrs Brigades, Islamic Jihad's al-Quds

Brigades, the PFLP's Martyr Abu-Ali Mustafa Battalions, and the DFLP's Palestinian National Resistance Battalions—issued a joint flier vowing that the Intifadah would continue despite international plots and pressures. The next day, Arafat convened a secret meeting at his office with the senior commanders of the PA's intelligence arms—Fatah, Tanzim, HAMAS, Islamic Jihad, and the PFLP—and the DFLP to discuss "confronting the challenges" facing the Palestinians. Arafat delivered a lengthy speech devoted mainly to the U.S. war against terrorism and the rising tide of Islamist militancy throughout the Arab world. At the climax of his speech, Arafat repeated the same sentence four times: "The essence of the Palestinian struggle is the foundation [of Islam], and Palestine is the genuine and original foundation [of jihad], and he who does not like this reality can go and drink all the sea-water of Gaza!" The assembled commanders jumped to their feet, shouting: "Palestine is the foundation, and the foundation is Palestine!" The Arabic word for foundation is *al-qaeda*—the name of Osama bin Laden's organization. Thus, Arafat in effect united the Intifadah with the Islamists' war against the U.S.-led West.

These were not empty words. Arafat's point man in Lebanon, Sultan Abdul Ayn, met with HizbAllah chief Nasrallah to discuss the coordinated escalation of fighting against Israel from southern Lebanon and the territories. In addition, Arafat permitted HizbAllah to open "facilities" in his Ein Hilweh stronghold for the recruitment and training of young Palestinian Islamists for joint PLO-HizbAllah operations.

A few days later, Israeli intelligence warned the cabinet of a joint PA-Islamist campaign to assassinate senior Israeli leaders and commanders. Israeli Arabs were active participants in this campaign. A few hours after the warning was leaked to the Israeli media, Fatah's al-Aqsa Brigades issued a communiqué warning that Israeli military commanders would be targets for their attacks. "This is an open war and the blood of our martyrs will not go away and the al-Aqsa Brigades will not go away and will resist," the communiqué said. At the same time, Arafat sent a handwritten message to his key commanders in the territories demanding intensification of spectacular terrorist strikes against Israeli civilians in order to ensure that he and "the Palestinian issue" remained at the top of the world agenda and TV coverage. The first half of November accordingly saw an escalation in the Palestinians' strikes and efforts to conduct martyrdom operations in the heart of Israel. However, by now more than half of Israel was in a constant state of high readiness, and Israeli security services thwarted the potentially most lethal operations.

———

U.S. AND WEST EUROPEAN diplomats had been floating ideas for a diplomatic breakthrough with Arafat. Now they offered a deal according to which the IDF would withdraw unilaterally to its pre-Intifadah positions; all Israelis, both military units and settlements, would be evacuated from Gaza, and Israel would hand over an additional 1 percent of Area C in the West Bank; and Jerusalem would commit to recognizing an independent Palestinian state—all in return for "a meaningful security cooperation." Arafat refused to even address the offer in view of the "American aggression" against "Arab and Muslim brethren"—that is, the war against terrorism. "The hour of freedom and independence to our entire people, land, and holy places is fast approaching," Arafat declared on November 14. "The shed Palestinian blood will not be in vain."

At this point, frustrated with both the lack of progress in the war on terrorism—particularly bin Laden's ability to evade the American dragnet—and the growing instability throughout the Middle East, the Bush administration decided to send retired Marine Corps General Anthony Zinni and Assistant Secretary of State William Burns as mediators in the Palestinian-Israeli dispute. Washington held very low expectations for this initiative in terms of a Palestinian-Israeli settlement. However, it would demonstrate the administration's concern for the Palestinian cause, in hopes of drawing the Arab rulers—particularly the Saudis—into cooperation in the war on terrorism.

By failing to react to the ensuing series of Palestinian statements and actions, the administration clearly revealed its lack of interest in the real situation in the Middle East. In his Friday sermon on November 23, the Arafat-appointed mufti of Jerusalem, Sheikh Ikrama Sabri, reiterated his call for the complete destruction of Israel. "The residents of Jerusalem are temporary; we will get rid of them and conquer all of holy Palestine," Sabri told a cheering crowd at al-Aqsa. In Gaza, Arafat ordered increased shelling of Israeli targets with Qassem-1 rockets and mortars. A few days later, the Israeli Security Services exposed "Iraqi involvement" in PA-affiliated cells in Ramallah and Jenin. These Tirawi-controlled cells were responsible for a host of bombing attacks; when finally caught, they were preparing to shoot down passenger aircraft at Ben Gurion Airport and shell the runways with mortars, as well as to explode bombs in downtown Jerusalem and Tel Aviv. The Security Services also thwarted an attempt by Fatah's al-Aqsa Brigades to assassinate Sharon; in response, the Brigades vowed to continue targeting Sharon and other high officials. Throughout, the now "routine" ambushes and roadside bombings continued.

Zinni and Burns arrived in Israel on November 26, as Sharon was preparing to travel to Washington and so was most vulnerable to U.S. pressure. Jerusalem accordingly made every effort to cooperate with the American team. Arafat, however, had other ideas and so instructed his close lieutenants. On November 29, while Sharon was in the United States, the PA launched a new wave of terrorism in Israel proper. First, two martyr-terrorists opened fire in the center of Afulla, killing two and wounding fifty before they in turn were killed. Then a martyr-bomber blew up a bus near Hadera, killing four and wounding close to a dozen; Fatah and Islamic Jihad claimed "joint responsibility" for this attack. There followed the worst twenty-four hours since the beginning of the Intifadah: 26 Israeli civilians were killed and over 275 wounded in a series of terror attacks throughout the country, including several bombings in Jerusalem, an ambush in northern Gaza, and a martyr-bombing in Haifa. Jerusalem provided Washington with detailed intelligence proving that Arafat was directly responsible for the wave of terrorism. For example, one of the martyrs in Jerusalem belonged not to an Islamist organization but to Tirawi's General Security Services. Zinni's response was to rush to see Arafat in Ramallah and urge him to fight terrorism. Powell called Arafat and told him he must "act resolutely" against the Islamist terrorists. Arafat declared a "state of emergency" but did nothing else.

Rather than return to Israel immediately, Sharon elected to stay in Washington and plead Israel's case to Bush. At the White House, Sharon promised Bush that Israel did not plan to topple Arafat's regime, but he also presented Bush with evidence directly connecting Arafat and the PA security organs to the latest spate of terrorism. Bush's reaction, however, was to stress Arafat's role in the fight against terrorism. "Chairman Arafat and the Palestinian Authority must immediately find and arrest those responsible for the hideous murders," Bush told reporters. "They must also act swiftly and decisively against the organizations that support them." U.S. officials expressed displeasure with the IDF's resumption of the closure of Jenin, Kalkilyeh, Nablus, and Tulkarm and with a helicopter strike on Arafat's headquarters in Gaza in which both of his personal helicopters and several buildings were destroyed. (Arafat was in Ramallah at the time and thus was never in danger.)

Only after his return to Israel on December 2 did Sharon openly contradict Bush. "Arafat is the biggest obstacle to peace and stability in the Middle East," Sharon said in an address to the nation. "Arafat and the PA are directly responsible for the serious situation we now face. It is impossible for the terrorists to do what they do without receiving shelter and aid from Arafat. They are allowed headquarters and training camps next to Arafat's headquarters. He has done nothing to deter them." Sharon, however, would not criticize the United States. "Bush said the U.S. is a true friend and partner of Israel. In peace, and in the war against terrorism, the U.S. and Israel stand together," Sharon declared.

After a contentious five-hour meeting, the government declared the Palestinian Authority a "terrorist supporting entity" and empowered the kitchenette to decide on specific steps to ensure comprehensive pressure on the PA. The kitchenette, however, at Washington's urging, decided to give Arafat one more "last chance." The next day, Peres talked with Arafat twice. "He called me," Peres told reporters, "and said that he can't make arrests because Israel is stopping him from moving his forces. I told him that it's now up to him: 'In the next 12 hours, you can determine our attitude to the Palestinian Authority. You have received a list of 36 names [of the terrorists Israel most wanted]. I strongly recommend that you arrest them.'"

Arafat did make a few perfunctory arrests, whereupon, in response to criticism from the Islamists, his lieutenants announced the end of the campaign. "There is no way the Palestinian Authority can continue the arrests amid the Israeli attacks," Fatah commander Hussein al-Sheik said. "We can't keep them in jail while Israel bombs PA installations." Indeed, most of the Islamist terrorists were promptly released. Ben-Eliezer conceded that the PA arrested "no more than 2 [or] 3 significant terrorists—and even they are being held in hotel-like conditions. . . . The PA stands behind and creates this terrorism, and we are trying to get it to leave that path and to bring it back to the only way there is, and that is the path of diplomacy." Jerusalem expressed its support for Zinni's continued meetings with Arafat. Meanwhile, an editorial issued by the Palestine News Agency (WAFA) called on Palestinians to "cease taking any action that might harm the Palestinians and the Palestinian case and the legitimate struggle, and to stop all actions against civilians that provide the Israeli government with excuses to launch these attacks, and means to gain international sympathy at the expense of the defenseless Palestinian people."

———

IN EARLY DECEMBER, Washington was becoming increasingly apprehensive as the PA media took a distinctly pro–bin Laden and anti-U.S. line, calling Americans "infidels" and "Crusaders" and Bush "the head of world terror." The December 7 sermon at al-Aqsa Mosque, delivered by Mohammed Hassin and broadcast on PA Radio, was typical of this trend. "The [battle] cry 'To help Islam!' continues to echo in the Muslim world. Is anyone responding? Here the Mongolians and Crusaders are raising their heads and enlisting armies to fight the Islamic nations in an oppressive campaign, under the label of 'terrorism,' which the infidels are attaching to the Arabs and Muslims, for the purpose of realizing their imperialist interests, and to spread their control over the Muslim countries and their resources. If terrorism—as viewed by America, the leader of world terror—is the killing of innocent civilians, we have to ask: . . . Is the killing of Afghani civilians and their expulsion as refugees in their country and in neighboring countries considered terrorism? Does the continued siege on Iraq, continued aggression against it in the North and South, and the death of children due to the shortage of food and medicine enter the category of terrorism? Cannot these war crimes, and the rest of the conditions to which Muslims are subjected in Chechnya, Kashmir, and the Philippines, be categorized as terrorism, according to the American perception of terrorism? There is no place for a weak nation [America] among the nations of this world, one which was blinded by the intoxication of power and understands nothing but the language of interests and hegemony." Given the known relationships between the PA and the Palestinian Islamists and between the Palestinian Islamists and their counterparts all over the world, Washington now rightly feared that bin Laden's global jihad would expand into the Palestinian Intifadah.

Washington's anxieties were aggravated by Cairo's repeated warnings that Israeli strikes against the PA could spread into a confrontation with the whole Arab world. Mubarak told Bush, as he had told Sharon in July, that Egypt would not "tolerate" the destruction of Arafat's regime. If Israel toppled Arafat, Mubarak elaborated, "the people's patience will run out and this will force governments to engage in an arms race, with the goal of acquiring weapons of mass destruction. . . . Then the entire region, including Israel, is liable to be annihilated." Senior Egyptian military officials affirmed the willingness of the Egyptian armed forces to participate in such a war. "The recent developments require the Egyptian armed forces to preserve a high level of preparedness and readiness to confront any challenge and threat," Defense Minister Tantawi declared.

Alarmed, the administration instructed Zinni to issue an ultimatum to both Sharon and Arafat: They had forty-eight hours to demonstrate "real progress" toward cessation of hostilities and the return to negotiations. Sharon accepted the ultimatum, although HAMAS, Islamic Jihad, and even Arafat's own Fatah declared that any consideration of a cease-fire was "premature." However, Washington would not be distracted by such declarations and continued the pressure on Jerusalem to pretend that Arafat was complying with the "cease-fire."

On December 10, as Zinni was rushing for a meeting with Arafat, a truck full of explosives and gas tanks blew up at the entrance to Ramallah, just missing his motorcade. Even this attempt on Zinni's life did not make the Bush administration change its mind. However, the next day, Zinni reported that Arafat had flatly refused all his requests for reductions in the Palestinian violence. Zinni conceded that it was impossible to reach an agreement with Arafat even if Israel were to make all the concessions asked for by the United States.

ON THE NIGHT of December 12–13, a Palestinian squad exploded two large bombs near a bus approaching the settlement of Emanuel in Samaria. When the damaged bus tried to speed toward the settlement, three gunmen opened automatic fire at both the wounded passengers and the Israeli security forces rushing to their aid. Ten Israelis were killed and some thirty were wounded. Significantly, the three perpetrators killed by the IDF—all members of Arafat's own al-Aqsa Martyrs Brigades—were among the thirty-three whose names had been submitted by Israel, via the CIA, to the PA a few weeks earlier with a warning that they were actively preparing for a major operation. The PA had refused to take any action. Arafat's foreknowledge of the operation was confirmed when Israel and the United States learned that he had been evacuated from his Ramallah headquarters to a nearby "secret location"—a fortified underground bunker in the Ramallah area—just before the attack on Emanuel.

As a result of these circumstances, the Sharon government ignored Washington's pressure and decided to "freeze all contacts" with Arafat and the PA. The government also ordered the IDF to launch a major offensive aimed at destroying the PA's security and weapons infrastructure. The next day, the IDF was instructed to escalate the offensive "to destroy the authority" of Arafat. Israeli military sources told Steve Rodan that the operation was "meant to whittle away Arafat's rule until the point where he either flees into exile or succumbs to the demands of Israel and the United States to crack down on Islamic insurgents." The sources stressed that Arafat himself was not a target for assassination. "The idea is to remove all pretense of power so he can answer to his people without his weapons, security forces, and prisons," a senior military source explained. Despite U.S. pressure, the IDF offensive continued to escalate for the next couple of days, with the emphasis put on clearing and securing the key axes of transportation the IDF would need in case of a regional war. Throughout the offensive, however, the IDF remained under constraints based on political rather than military considerations.

Besieged, Arafat delivered an address on PA Radio on December 16, calling for an end to attacks on Israel. He explained that in the aftermath of September 11, the Palestinians must not be associated with terrorism. "I again call for the complete and immediate halt in all military activities," he said. "I renew the call for a complete cessation of any activities, particularly suicide attacks which we have condemned and always condemned. We will punish all those who plan and execute [these attacks]." There was, however, nothing conciliatory about Arafat's speech, which expressed hostility toward Israel. Ultimately, he was pleading with the Islamists and with his own forces not to go over the edge into a confrontation the PA would not be able to survive.

IDF studies determined that in the forty-eight hours following Arafat's speech, the level of Palestinian violence—including operations by Arafat's own Fatah and PA Security Forces—remained constant. Nevertheless, Sharon permitted senior security officials to attend a meeting with their Palestinian counterparts organized and chaired by the CIA. The three-hour meeting failed to achieve anything except some additional unilateral Israeli concessions.

Emboldened by having survived the Israeli onslaught, Arafat rushed to placate the Islamists. At a December 18 rally in Ramallah, he called for martyrs for the jihad. "We will sacrifice ourselves for our holy places and we will strengthen our hold over them, and we are willing to give seventy of our martyrs for every one of their martyrs in this campaign, because this is our holy land," Arafat proclaimed to a cheering crowd. "We will defend the holy land with our blood and with our spirit," he screamed. "We do not only wear uniforms; we are all military. We are all martyrs in paradise." The crowd shouted back that millions of martyrs were on their way to liberate al-Quds. In a reference to the Americans' demands that he confront the Islamists, Arafat urged all Palestinians to "hold tight": "Nobody would be able to divide us, to separate us from this holy land of ours."

Nevertheless, Jerusalem did not break off either the PA-Israeli security coordination meetings or the "pre-cease-fire peace talks" going on between Peres and Abu-Alaa. In late December, Abu-Alaa expressed "cautious optimism" about the outcome of the most recent round of talks. He and Peres, he reported, had been "exchanging ideas about the establishment of a Palestinian state in the 1967 borders with Jerusalem as its capital." Peres, according to Abu-Alaa, had agreed that Israel would recognize a Palestinian state within eight weeks of the signing of an interim agreement. This was a sharp deviation from Sharon's position that the talks would not go beyond a possible Palestinian state on 42 percent of the territories—the area already conceded to the PA—which would be established following negotiations that would commence only after six weeks of a total cease-fire and a PA war against terrorism, including the collection of illegal weapons. Peres, however, did not deny Abu-Alaa's assertion and concurred that the talks would resume in the first week of January 2002.

Peres was living on another planet from Lieutenant General Amos Gilad, the senior IDF commander in the territories. On December 26, Gilad provided the IDF's assessment of relations with the Palestinians. "As long as Arafat lives, he will not give up his strategic vision and he would rather leave history as the leader of the entire Palestinian people who did not make concessions on fundamental issues. Therefore, we cannot reach peace with him for he will never give up on the Right of Return," Gilad said. "Arafat is our greatest threat, and many did not understand it for a long time. He is connected to terrorism and is using it as an instrument interlinked with his political activities. I think his vision is based on the belief in the power of Palestinian demography—that ultimately power will transfer to the Palestinians. Throughout the period since Oslo, he is moving along two parallel paths: one is terrorism and the other is the political process that was aimed to soften us, along with the terrorism. For as long as the progress suited him, he went along with us. The moment the interim agreements were completed, and he realized he could not get everything he wanted, particularly the Right of Return, he decided it was time to reactivate the combined process of politics and terrorism. He decided to resume violence."

———

BY THE END of 2001, there had been a dramatic realignment of the regional powers—prompted by the rethinking of the situation in the Middle East, and the Muslim world as a whole, by the Saudi leadership and particularly Crown Prince Abdallah. Throughout the Muslim world, Riyadh observed, both the ruling elites and the people overwhelmingly supported what Osama bin Laden was advocating. Hence, any American attempt to uproot bin Laden's brand of militant Islamism would place the United States on a collision course with the entire Muslim world. Furthermore, Abdallah believed, Iran, Iraq, and Syria, having been "flagged" by Washington, had pressing incentives to preempt the expected U.S. attack on them by initiating military operations against Israel. Under such conditions, there was no way the House of al-Saud could support the West and survive the ensuing Islamist uprising among its own people. Therefore, it was imperative to keep Saudi Arabia from being sucked into the devouring whirlwind the United States was seen as instigating. The first step was to get U.S. forces out of Saudi Arabia and the Gulf States. This decision was motivated not by anti-Americanism but by a pragmatic determination to keep Saudi Arabia from being implicated in the so-called American-Zionist conspiracy against Iraq and the liberation of Palestine.

Indeed, the intensifying succession struggle in Saudi Arabia complicated the dynamics of the region even further. Prince Sultan and his faction, the chief challengers to Crown Prince Abdallah, were maneuvering to have the United States put them in power and suppress the Islamist opposition by force. Despite the pro-U.S. rhetoric of Prince Sultan and his son Prince Bandar, implementation of such a scenario would have been calamitous for the United States' long-term interests in the entire Arab/Muslim world. Abdallah's plan, by contrast, seemed hostile, but would have sustained the U.S. economic presence and influence in the Arabian Peninsula.

However, Washington was jolted by the Saudis' hints about withdrawing U.S. forces and reacted with fury to Riyadh's quiet prodding. There followed the second step in Abdallah's effort to preempt an Islamist eruption—namely, consolidation of the new regional alliance with Iraq and Iran that had started taking shape in August. In early December, secret emissaries shuttled between Riyadh, Baghdad, and Tehran, carrying a series of documents that codified the new strategic relationships; the papers were personally approved by Abdallah, Saddam, and Khamenei. (Syria, a non-signatory because it is not a Persian Gulf state, was considered an active partner.) In Saudi Arabia, the new alliance was especially popular among the tribal and religious elites, partly because it was perceived as anti-American, but more importantly because of the potential it offered for attaining coexistence with the Islamists—thus reducing the bin Laden threat.

For the Saudi intelligence chieftains ordered to implement their leaders' decisions, the challenge was to evict the United States from the region not through direct confrontation over the Persian Gulf but in the aftermath of a strategic defeat, if not the outright destruction, of Israel. Consequently, the key regional powers intensified their assistance to terrorists operating inside and around Israel in order to provoke the desired eruption. Saudi government agencies, for example, provided crucial support for the HAMAS and PA efforts to develop their Qassem rockets. This cooperation was exposed in early January through Israel's capture of a HAMAS messenger bearing the results of research and testing in institutes of the Ministry of Defense and Aviation. Especially significant was the support the Iranians gave the PA by sending weapons to the territories and building up the capabilities of HizbAllah in southern Lebanon.

———

BY LATE DECEMBER, the war in Afghanistan seemed to be winding down, with U.S. achievements falling short of expectations. Osama bin Laden, his closest aides, and the Taliban leadership were missing, as were most of the al-Qaeda and Taliban forces and weapons known to have been deployed throughout Afghanistan. Instead of pursuing them further, however, Washington was diverting attention to Iraq and Iran. Oblivious to the dread among the Arab ruling elites that a U.S. attack on Iraq would ignite the entire Middle East with all-consuming Islamist flames, the Bush administration persisted in seeking Arab, and particularly Saudi Arabian, support for turning the war on terrorism against Iraq and Iran. Once again, it sought to placate Riyadh with Israeli concessions to the Palestinians.

For Arafat, the new regional dynamics was potentially disastrous. He feared the United States would try to impose a solution in order to stop the

Palestinian issue from further complicating the war on terrorism. And because any imposed solution would entail the Palestinians' recognizing Israel, such an option was unacceptable. Therefore, Arafat was committed to escalating the Intifadah to the point where resumption of negotiations with Israel would be impossible. His Arab allies feared Washington's reaction but saw no alternative. As Amr Moussa—now the secretary-general of the Arab League and one of Arafat's staunchest supporters—pointed out, the Palestinian question was at the fringes of historic events. Everybody in the Arab world, not to mention the West, was consumed by more urgent problems—namely, the U.S.-led war against Islamist terrorism.

And so Arafat began telling his confidants that he was preparing the most important statement of his life. The essence of this statement would be that all his efforts to make peace with Israel—from Oslo to Camp David to Taba and Paris and with Clinton and Mitchell and Tenet and Zinni—had irrevocably failed. No peaceful solution or compromise was possible. Hence, he would be declaring an end to the peace process and the beginning of the Palestinian war of independence and liberation. The war would culminate in the conclusive reversal of the Nakba—that is, the destruction of Israel.

Arafat intimated to his confidants that the Palestinians would be well equipped for this undertaking. Thanks to a concentrated effort led by Fuad Shubaki—a close confidant of Arafat and one of his key money managers—who had been shuttling between Gaza, Lebanon, Jordan, and Iraq, the PA had acquired a massive amount of weapons during the winter of 2001–02. The weapons, smuggled in via Egypt and Jordan, included mortars, Katyusha rockets, anti-tank missiles, and shoulder-fired surface-to-air missiles. The PA had also amassed enough small arms and ammunition to arm the entire population in case of a full-scale Israeli invasion of the Gaza Strip.

The capture of the *Karine A* exposed the extent of the PA's efforts to acquire weapons. On the night of January 2–3, Israeli Special Forces intercepted the ship in the Red Sea, some 300 miles off the Israeli coast. It carried approximately 50 tons of weapons—including 122-mm Katyusha rockets and anti-tank missiles—in eighty-three canisters specially constructed for clandestine delivery in the sea. The canisters were built in Iran with sophisticated mechanisms for underwater flotation and collection.

The *Karine A* seizure answered several key points of contention between Jerusalem and Washington. The crew was made up of PA naval personnel, and the captain was a lieutenant colonel in the PA Navy. The crew confirmed that the weapons on board were intended for an escalation of the Intifadah into Israel proper. Documents with Arafat's signature found on board proved that he was directly involved in the weapons' acquisition. Moreover, Muhammad Dahlan—Tenet's favorite and one of Arafat's closest confidants—directly oversaw the operation, which he ran from a safe house in Dubai. Dahlan also personally coordinated cooperation with the Egyptian authorities.

The *Karine A* was part of an Iranian effort to arm terrorist forces all over the region. The ship had been serviced at high-security workshops at the Bandar Abbas Naval Base, and the clandestine loading had been accomplished off Kish Island. The HizbAllah liaison officer captured on board confirmed Iran's involvement. Additionally, the ship's planned passage through the Suez Canal in order to offload the weapons into smaller "fishing boats" just outside the Alexandria Naval Base indicated that Egypt was involved. These "fishing boats" were to sail through Egyptian territorial waters off the northern Sinai, ultimately dropping the weapons off the Gaza coast. Money for the operation came from conservative Islamists in the Arabian Peninsula, collected through Islamic charities in Jeddah and channeled to Iran via official Riyadh.

The intercept of the *Karine A* meant that the uppermost circles of the Bush White House received irrefutable evidence of who was involved. This evidence forced Washington to reconsider some of the most basic tenets of its regional policy—namely, who was friend and who was foe. Jerusalem's efforts to convince Washington were aided by senior PA officials who bragged that the PA's arsenals in the territories "already have heavy weapons of the types captured on the ship *Karine A* and even heavier weapons."

––––––

THE EVOLUTION of the U.S.-led war on terrorism helped transform the Israeli-Palestinian struggle into an integral part of the Islamists' global war against the West. The United States was now concentrating on Syria, Iraq, and Iran as key components of what President Bush would call "the axis of evil." In this global constellation, Arafat once again became the catalyst for the all-Arab/all-Islamic onslaught on Israel for the liberation of al-Quds. To that end, he repeatedly unleashed cycles of terrorism followed by calls for cease-fire to forestall Israeli retaliation until the Arab/Muslim world was ready for war.

By now, as a direct by-product of the U.S. operations in Afghanistan, a growing number of al-Qaeda forces were reaching the Middle East and specifically the Israeli-Palestinian theater. By late fall 2001, these al-Qaeda terrorists and fighters were moving into Lebanon and Syria, having been smuggled out of Afghanistan via Pakistan, Iran, and Iraq. The Islamic Revolutionary Guards Corps organized the clandestine transfer, with the transport costs once again covered with Saudi Arabian money. By early February, a few hundred fighters and terrorists were already in Lebanon—mainly in Ein Hilweh and other Palestinian refugee camps. While most of them were

Arabs, there were also dozens of both Chechens and Kurds, as well as smaller numbers of Central Asians, Kashmiris, and Western Europeans.

From Ein Hilweh, 80 to 100 of the most experienced fighters and terrorists were quickly smuggled into the Gaza Strip in a program personally run by Muhammad Dahlan. Each al-Qaeda member transferred to the territories received a $5,000 bonus in cash—also from Saudi Arabian money. The first wave of al-Qaeda terrorists included experts in the technology of weapons of mass destruction.

Meanwhile, most of the Chechens were sent to HizbAllah bases in the Bekaa, where they absorbed local tactics while sharing their expertise in anti-aircraft attacks, urban guerrilla tactics, and the use of sophisticated explosives. By late February, additional battle-hardened Chechens and Kurds arrived in Lebanon from the Caucasus and northern Iraq, respectively. Their transport was coordinated by the bin Laden–Mughniyah forward headquarters in southern Beirut under the personal command of Muhammad Abu-Zubaidah—the number three commander in al-Qaeda (after bin Laden and Ayman al-Zawahiri). In early 2002, the United States identified Zubaidah as the driving force behind the resurrection of the al-Qaeda networks in the West. He directed this endeavor from numerous headquarters in Lebanon and Syria, in cooperation with Syrian and Iranian intelligence, HizbAllah, and the Palestinians.

———

IN EARLY JANUARY, Arafat ordered the launching of the Palestinian "Tet Offensive"—intentionally named after the Vietcong offensive of early 1968. Although the Americans and South Vietnamese were victorious against the original Tet Offensive, the media coverage caused a profound shift in the attitude toward the war both among ordinary American citizens and at the highest levels of the Johnson administration and thus sowed the seeds for the ultimate U.S.–South Vietnamese defeat. Through the Palestinian "Tet Offensive," Arafat was adamant on proving to the entire Muslim world—no matter what the outcome for the Palestinians themselves, including the level of civilian casualties—that he was the greatest mujahid around, capable of ensnaring the United States in a regional quagmire so that it would be incapable of taking on bin Laden, Iran, and Iraq. In return for this strategic upheaval, Arafat's logic went, the Arab world would help the Palestinians to liberate their land by destroying Israel.

To ensure smooth and prompt execution of his orders, Arafat named two most trusted confidants as the field commanders of the Tet Offensive. In the West Bank, the commander would be Tirawi, operating via the al-Aqsa Martyrs Brigades. In the Gaza Strip, it would be Dahlan, operating via the

Saladin Brigades—the Gaza-based counterpart of the al-Aqsa Martyrs Brigades. These umbrella organizations facilitated the use of all available armed entities—including the Tanzim, Fatah, the PA security forces, Islamic Jihad, HAMAS, the PFLP, the DFLP, HizbAllah, and al-Qaeda. Furthermore, Tirawi's and Dahlan's command cells both included a strong contingent of Iraqi and Iranian intelligence officers as well as HizbAllah and al-Qaeda expert terrorists. Arafat specified that the forthcoming offensive must include operations carried out in close cooperation with, and even with the direct participation of, Iraqi Military Intelligence and Special Forces operatives already in the West Bank. He also dispatched Azzam Azzam al-Ahmad—his point man in Iraq—to Baghdad for the final and detailed coordination of the Iraqis' active role.

On January 9, the Palestinians launched an unprecedented spate of terrorism throughout Israel, starting with an attack on a stronghold inside Israel proper, which caused four Israeli fatalities. The attackers belonged to the PA security forces operating under Dahlan. There followed an intensification of Palestinian ambushes, roadside bombings, and martyrdom-bombings. Apprehensive about the possibility of a regional eruption, Israel reacted with a largely symbolic gesture—committing Arafat to de facto "house arrest" in Ramallah. However, in the face of escalating attacks on Israeli civilians—in which Arafat's own Tanzim "crossed every 'red line,'" in the words of a senior Israeli defense official—the IDF intensified its raids, capturing cities and refugee camps and holding them for limited periods of time. Nonetheless, because Washington had assured Arafat that he and his inner circle were not at risk of assassination by Israel, Arafat saw no reason to contain the escalatory cycle. On the contrary, he ordered further escalation.

Around January 20, Arafat committed to his "last battle." He started telling his confidants, quoting Koranic verses and traditions, of the imperative to rush to martyrdom in order to pave the way for the apocalyptic eruption. The unrepentant, if closeted, Muslim Brother now openly sought to cause the flames of Islamist zeal to spread through the Arab world so that no government would be able to resist the grassroots outcry to join the jihad for the liberation of al-Quds. "For al-Quds and the Palestinian land I am ready to fight and die a martyr," Arafat declared in Ramallah on January 21. He then ordered activation of the PA's 20,000-strong "blue police" as a new assault force.

A new cycle of terrorist attacks in Tel Aviv, Jerusalem, Haifa, and other cities raised the level of Israeli civilian casualties yet again, prompting Jerusalem to undertake major retaliatory raids, in which the IDF held Gaza and other cities for days at a time while completing anti-terrorist mop-up operations. These raids, in turn, incited wider segments of the Palestinian population into active fighting against Israel—the popular escalation Arafat was seeking. "For as long as Sharon is in power there will not be any peace negotiations," Barghouti declared in early February. Arafat raised the ante in a February 6 speech broadcast on PA TV: "Yes, brothers, with our souls and blood we redeem you, O Palestine! This is the decision of the people of exceeding strength. This is a sacred bond. We are up to this duty. You know I am saying this because I know our people. I know what it means that in the midst of this economic (not only military) crisis, yet none of them complained. However, they said: God is Great! Glory to God and His Prophet! Jihad, jihad, jihad, jihad, jihad!"

The PA reached a milestone on February 14. An Israeli vehicle was ambushed in Gaza, prompting, as expected, an Israeli reaction force, led by the latest Merkava Mk.3 tank, to rush to the rescue of the attacked civilians. As the tank approached the scene, a shaped charge inside a pop-up magnetic mine exploded underneath it, destroying it completely and killing three of the four crew members. This feat gave the entire Arab world a huge morale boost. Significantly, the perpetrators employed techniques and specialized equipment used in Afghanistan and Chechnya and brought to the territories by the latest infusion of al-Qaeda volunteers.

As attacks and counterattacks continued over the next several days, Sharon stressed the self-imposed constraints under which his government was operating. "Today, we are at war," he told the kitchenette on February 20. "But this is a war against terrorism. We must not be dragged into a regional war. We must find the way to deal with terrorism without dragging the people into [regional] war. Period."

Of strategic significance was the attempt, on February 27, of a terrorist squad to penetrate from Egypt and hit both Israeli and U.S. military facilities in the central Negev; the squad was destroyed after a lengthy chase. That this attempted attack took place at the very same time Dahlan and al-Hindi were meeting with Dichter and Major General Giora Eiland, the chief of the IDF's Planning Division, and a CIA representative at the house of the U.S. Ambassador near Tel Aviv added to the hilarious unreality of the situation. Subsequently, PA forces resumed small-arms and mortar fire at Gilo. On March 2, a martyr-bomber dressed as a religious Jew blew himself up in Jerusalem, causing heavy loss of life to families coming out of a religious service.

By early March, however, Arafat had already missed his train. His "Tet Offensive" had caused much suffering and damage but had not provoked the greater regional eruption he was seeking. Within the Israeli-Palestinian dynamics, he could not deliver the tangible achievement of a Palestinian state because he could not bring himself to declare the conflict over and recognize Israel's right to exist. All the "plans" and "ideas" that Peres and Abu-Alaa continued to churn out were unable to dent this reality.

24

Facing Reality (2002 and Beyond)

Operation Defensive Shield: Toward "a New Middle East"

IN EARLY 2002, as Arafat was launching his "Tet Offensive," an intimate dialogue was developing between Washington and Jerusalem, with the goal of formulating a common strategy vis-à-vis Islamist terrorists and rogue states such as Syria, Iraq, and Iran. The tenets of this grand strategy for the Middle East—a strategy in which Israel is the United States' primary partner—were consolidated during the unprecedented visit to Washington in early February by Sharon and the entire Israeli national security elite, led by Defense Minister Ben-Eliezer and Internal Security Minister Landau. Integral to this strategy is the ultimate destruction of Arafat's terrorist capabilities so that it will become possible for Washington and Jerusalem to concentrate on the primary challenge—namely, shaping the future of the Middle East. But until Arafat's terrorist threat is eliminated, Israeli-initiated operations are to be directed toward meeting specific terrorist threats and toward clearing and securing the main transportation arteries.

Arafat, Saddam, and most other Arab leaders were frightened, if not outright petrified, by the specter of a wide-ranging U.S. assault on terrorism and its sponsoring states. In response, they ignited the Intifadah. They aimed to inflict casualties among Israeli civilians to the point of provoking major Israeli reprisals, thus impelling the Bush administration to concentrate on containing the Israeli-Palestinian conflict rather than pursuing the war on terrorism.

On March 3, the Israeli cabinet was briefed that "Arafat gave the green light to the Palestinian organizations" to carry out a new terrorism offensive. The intelligence briefer stressed that there was no longer any difference between the various organizations—be they Islamist or PA-controlled—because "all of them adopted the strategy of terrorism with Arafat's approval." The briefer noted that Arafat now oversaw, under a unified command structure, the PA security forces, the Tanzim, and al-Aqsa Martyrs Brigades, comprising over 30,000 troops. The government resolved that there was no alternative to the IDF's taking over the territories and destroying the terrorism infrastructure. Left undetermined were the timing and the justification for such an undertaking.

This intelligence was soon confirmed by the statements of Palestinian terrorist leaders made to both to Israeli interrogators and friendly foreign interviewers. Among these was a late-March 2002 interview with "Nassir"—the Al-Aqsa Martyrs Brigade leader in the Bethlehem area responsible for numerous martyrdom-bombings in the Jerusalem area. "Arafat is the key man. If he tells us 'Go ahead,' we go. If he wants to stop us, we stop. Our military action is linked to political talks," Nassir told Francesco Battistini of *Corriere della Sera*. Asked about Arafat's latest public condemnation of suicide operations, Nassir was emphatic: "He is under pressure from the Israelis. If he does not condemn us, he has problems. What is said on TV, however, has nothing to do with real politics."

The PA ushered in the new cycle of violence on March 3 with a lethal ambush at an IDF roadblock, killing ten and wounding scores. The sniper's M-1 carbine and the tactics used—namely, having a concealed assault group with automatic weapons waiting to ambush the reaction force—were identical to the IRA's long-time modus operandi, prompting Israel to ask the British security authorities to investigate the possibility that IRA trainers and/or operatives were working with the Palestinians.

A couple of days later, a martyr-bombing in Afulla killed five and wounded some sixty-five civilians. The same day, another would-be martyr attacked a restaurant in Tel Aviv, shooting and throwing grenades until he was killed by a policeman. Subsequent interrogation of the terrorist's support cadres confirmed that he was sent by Tirawi, which meant on Arafat's orders. In the Gaza Strip, a joint HAMAS-Fatah team fired three Qassem-2 rockets toward Sderot, wounding a baby.

Torn between the public outcry in Israel and Washington's calls for restraint (not to harm the delicate maneuvers needed to consolidate a coalition against Iraq), Sharon decided to signal his displeasure with Arafat. On the night of March 5–6, Israeli gunships fired several missiles at a building adjacent to Arafat's personal offices in Ramallah as he was meeting with the European Union's representative and having a phone conference with Peres. The Israelis could hear the thuds of the missile hits, the crumbling of parts of the building, and Arafat's hysterical cursing. Senior PA officials threatened to assassinate Israeli leaders if Israel continued to hit objectives in Arafat's vicinity. Predictably, Powell harshly criticized Sharon for escalating the crisis while acknowledging that Arafat "could and should do more" to fight terrorism.

Undaunted, the kitchenette decided to embark on a widespread offensive and maintain it until the PA began operating resolutely against the terrorists in its midst. On Sharon's orders, IDF elite units raided numerous refugee camps, destroying bomb factories, capturing weapons, and arresting hundreds of suspects. On March 8, Israel crossed a new line. Led by special forces and the Golani Brigade, the IDF assaulted the congested urban center known as the Tulkarm refugee camp. In swift and intense fighting, over 50 Palestinians were killed and 200 wounded, and over 600, including 50 senior commanders, were captured by and/or surrendered to the IDF. The Israelis captured or destroyed large quantities of weapons and explosives—including a Qassem-2 factory and an arsenal of ten operational rockets. Huge quantities of documents and intelligence matériel were captured. The IDF suffered a single fatality and a few nonfatal casualties. Over the next few days the IDF launched comparable assaults on other terrorism centers, with similar results. Altogether, more than 200 Palestinians were killed and 1,200 captured—most of them members of Arafat-related forces and organizations.

———

THROUGH ALL OF THIS, the Bush administration was proving that its predecessor had no monopoly on hypocrisy. While Bush and Powell were criticizing the Israeli assault, urging quick withdrawal, and announcing the imminent arrival of General Zinni in an effort to consolidate a new cease-fire, experts from Delta Force, the SEALs, and other elite U.S. units were rushing to Israel to watch the IDF in action, studying its tactics and methods in order to incorporate them in the U.S. war on terrorism in Afghanistan and elsewhere. The Americans also asked Israel to part with some of its indigenously developed weapons and intelligence-collection systems for urban warfare—weapons and systems that were being used in the very operations Bush and Powell were condemning—so that U.S. forces could use them in the escalating fighting in Afghanistan. Israel complied with the vast majority of the Americans' requests.

With Zinni soon to arrive in Israel, the White House urged Jerusalem not to complicate his mission, and Sharon committed to a week of self-restraint. "We are still seeking cease-fire, but we will continue to act forcefully again the Palestinians," Sharon told his Security Cabinet the next day. A senior official in the prime minister's office added: "We will conduct this war with all our might until we get results, even if it takes several weeks. We are in the midst of a difficult war. And in war . . . one inflicts and one suffers [casualties]. There are many difficult moments, but one must persevere and continue forward." In sharp contrast to the offensive raids of the previous week, the IDF resumed the now largely pointless shelling of empty buildings from gunboats and helicopter gunships.

Meanwhile, Israeli intelligence had presented the cabinet with irrefutable evidence that the PA was taking advantage of Jerusalem's self-restraint to prepare a series of strikes within Israel. Sharon authorized the IDF to surge into Ramallah and several sectors of the Gaza Strip in a series of preventive raids. Some fourteen Palestinians were killed and close to a hundred were wounded in the first night of fighting. By the morning of March 11, the IDF controlled all of Ramallah except for Arafat's compound. At the same time, the IDF quietly conducted a series of raids all over the territories to preemptively destroy as much as possible of the terrorism infrastructure, making it more difficult for the Palestinians to disrupt the Zinni mission with spectacular provocation. The Israelis captured several senior HAMAS, Islamic Jihad, and Fatah-affiliated commanders, along with weapons and explosives. Altogether, well over forty Palestinians were killed in this round of fighting.

With the Palestinians under intense pressure, the terrorist coalition in southern Lebanon diverted Jerusalem's attention with an audacious strike in the Upper Galilee. On the morning of March 12, they ambushed civilian traffic deep inside Israel, killing six civilians and wounding many others. This highly professional operation must have been in preparation for several days. The terrorists first clandestinely crossed Israel's sophisticated fence. They were dressed in IDF uniforms, and so Israeli security forces were hesitant to shoot for fear of inflicting friendly-fire casualties. Eventually two of the terrorists were encountered and killed. Fatah's al-Aqsa Martyrs Brigades claimed responsibility for the operation, but Israeli intelligence later learned that the perpetrators were al-Qaeda operatives, with logistical and intelligence support from HizbAllah and the Iranian Pasdaran.

For its own reasons, the government decided not to retaliate for the attack in the Galilee. It also decided to redeploy IDF forces away from contentious points. Within a few days, the IDF's achievements in the territories were allowed to go to waste, as the government ordered it to relax the pressure on Ramallah and the Gaza Strip. When the IDF presented intelligence from numerous sources to the effect that there would be strikes around the beginning of Passover and requested a host of preventive measures on that basis, the kitchenette rejected the request on the grounds that the intelligence warnings were far too vague to act upon. For the first time since Sharon replaced Barak as prime minister, Mofaz went public with his objections, telling reporters that "the political echelon decided to exit Ramallah against my recommendation." In fact, *all* Jerusalem's decisions at this point were made in order to help the White House, as Zinni headed for Israel and Vice President Cheney prepared to visit the region in a desperate effort to convince the Arabs to join the United States against Iraq.

During Cheney's visit to the Middle East the Bush administration finally grasped the extent of Arab hostility to the United States and Arab opposition to the war on terrorism. U.S. officials also learned about the close operational cooperation between Baghdad and Ramallah. There was no longer any doubt that the Palestinians would assist Iraq in thwarting any U.S. threat by opening a second front—through regionwide terrorism and threats of subversion in the key Arab states, particularly Saudi Arabia and the Persian Gulf states. Had Arafat accepted U.S. proposals to move toward implementing the Tenet and Mitchell plans, he would have hampered the PA's ability to assist Saddam at his hour of need, and Arafat would hear nothing of it.

Indeed, Israeli intelligence could find no indication that Arafat had ordered his security forces to fight terrorism, arrest Islamist activists, collect illegal weapons, or even stop terrorist operations in progress. Instead, Arafat responded to U.S. pressure with the suicide bombing of a bus in northern Israel that killed seven and wounded twenty-seven. Nevertheless, Sharon approved Israel's participation that evening in a meeting of the security coordination committee convened and chaired by Zinni. Predictably, nothing came of that meeting.

Meanwhile, Cairo and Riyadh were pressuring Washington and Jerusalem to allow Arafat to attend the upcoming Arab League summit in Beirut. Arafat's presence, Egyptian and Saudi senior officials argued, would be tantamount to his acceptance of the rejuvenated peace process. However, Israel still constrained his movements. To find a fig leaf to allow Sharon to let Arafat leave Ramallah, Cheney, who had just refused to meet Arafat in Ramallah, now agreed to return to the Middle East and meet him in Cairo. Once in Cairo, Arafat would be able to proceed to Beirut with Mubarak. However, to warrant the proposed meeting with Cheney, Arafat had to commit to fighting terrorism—and he would not. So Arafat missed the Beirut summit.

Many other Arab leaders—including Mubarak—also missed the summit, for a different reason: They feared assassination by bin Laden's terrorists in cooperation with HizbAllah and the Palestinian Islamists. Crown Prince Abdallah did attend and presented a new version of the "peace plan" he had first floated in February; this version, as rewritten by Amr Mussa, introduced a series of preconditions and demands on Israel—demands the Arabs knew very well were not acceptable to Washington, let alone Jerusalem. Since Arafat could not attend the summit in person, he had sent a speech via satellite; however, it was so virulent that the Lebanese would not permit it to be transmitted to the summit hall, causing the PLO delegation to storm out. All these activities, however, served as a cover for the real business of the summit: the formal end to the Arab world's rift with Iraq. Iraqi Vice President Izzat Ibrahim al-Duri signed a reconciliation agreement with Kuwait, and Crown Prince Abdallah publicly hugged Izzat, providing a symbol of the new amity of the Arab League. More important, once Izzat signed the reconciliation document, member states were forbidden by the regulations of the Arab League to participate in any U.S. attack on Iraq—now formally returned to the flock of Arab brethren.

That afternoon, March 21, a suicide bomber blew himself up in downtown Jerusalem, causing numerous casualties. Again, Fatah's al-Aqsa Martyrs Brigades claimed the bombing. Marwan Barghouti stated that it was in revenge for the IDF's anti-terrorist operations and Zinni's pro-Israeli policies. "The responsibility [for the bombing] is on the IDF and Zinni," Barghouti said. This bombing was particularly significant because Arafat implicated himself in it, knowingly and intentionally. The martyr-bomber, Muhammad Hashaika, was a Fatah member and a PA policeman in the village of Taluza, near Nablus. In early March, Israel had identified him as a "ticking bomb" (a would-be martyr-bomber ready for action) and, through the CIA, demanded his arrest by the PA. With Cheney expected in the region, Arafat ordered the arrest of Hashaika and a few other terrorists. However, on the night of March 17–18, Arafat specifically asked Zinni to intercede with Israel and obtain permission to transfer Hashaika from the Nablus jail to Ramallah for further interrogation. Israel agreed and permitted a PA van, with an escort of U.S. diplomatic cars, to convey Hashaika to Ramallah, where he was handed over to Tirawi's personal office. It was in Tirawi's office that Hashaika was provided with his sophisticated web-bomb and sent to blow himself up in Jerusalem.

When Fatah's al-Aqsa Martyrs Brigades claimed responsibility for the bombing, Zinni demanded that Arafat crack down on the Brigades. Arafat refused, saying, "If I crack down on the Brigades, HAMAS will get stronger—why should I want to do that?" Meanwhile, Jibril Rajub, one of the PA officials closest to the CIA, hailed al-Aqsa Martyrs Brigades as "the noblest phenomenon in the history of the Fatah, because they restored the movement's honor." He then pledged that "the [Palestinian] Authority will not act against the al-Aqsa Brigades."

Arafat continued to personally coordinate operations with HAMAS, Islamic Jihad, and other terrorist organizations. For example, on the night of March 21–22—right after the Jerusalem bombing—Arafat chaired a strategy session of the "National and Islamic Factions," an unofficial grouping of like-minded terrorists. Among the participants were Sheikh Hassan Yussuf, a leading HAMAS official; Qays al-Samarrai (also called Abu-Layla), a member of the Political Bureau of the DFLP; and senior Fatah and PA military officials. (The Islamic Jihad representative was absent because of Israeli activity near his hiding place.) The participants discussed and decided how to markedly escalate the wave of terrorism on the eve of Passover. The Israeli cabinet was briefed the next morning about the meeting and its decision.

———

ON PASSOVER EVE—the night of March 27–28—a martyr-bomber walked into a hotel in Netanya and blew himself up in the middle of a Seder crowd, killing some thirty and wounding hundreds. Among the victims were relatives of those who died in the Dolphinarium bombing, invited for a communal Seder to help alleviate their pain.

Although HAMAS was quick to take responsibility, substantial accumulated intelligence implicated Arafat. At the very least, he was present at meetings where forthcoming operations were discussed. Israeli intelligence learned that he had specifically instructed that "a wave of martyrdom-seekers" be unleashed on Israel's cities. Jerusalem could not ignore this intelligence any longer. "Israel has demonstrated utmost restraint in the last couple of weeks of severe [terrorist] strikes in order to give the Zinni mission a chance," a senior military official stated. "This policy will have to be re-examined now." With public rage in Israel at an all-time high, there was no way Sharon could take at face value Arafat's promises that this time he was "ready" (note: not "committed") to "fight terrorism" and observe a cease-fire. Having been briefed throughout about Arafat's plans, the Bush administration knew better than to pressure Israel to continue demonstrating restraint. The IDF started calling up reserves, and standing army units were deployed in and around the main Palestinian cities.

On March 28, the IDF launched Operation Defensive Shield, aimed at crushing the Palestinian terrorist infrastructure. The Sharon government was committed to a thorough operation lasting several weeks, which would include seizing, holding, and mopping up wide tracts of PA-held territory. Before Operation Defensive Shield was over, the IDF had activated elements of five divisions, comprising 21 regiments. Altogether, some 30,000 Israeli troops participated in the operation, more than half of them reservists.

Almost immediately after Sharon gave the order, IDF forces began pouring into Ramallah. This time the Israelis did not stop at the edges of Arafat's compound: They had been instructed to besiege and isolate Arafat and his coterie in a corner of their compound.

The PA reacted by unleashing several terrorist operations that were already in the pipeline. On March 29, a sixteen-year-old Palestinian girl blew herself up in a West Jerusalem supermarket, killing an Israeli girl and wounding scores. The Palestinian girl was a Fatah activist—one of dozens provided with bomb belts or webs in preparation for the "wave" of bomb-ings Arafat had ordered. The next day, Israeli Border Police succeeded in in-tercepting a car bomb on the coastal plain. One officer was killed in an exchange of fire with the terrorists; the driver blew himself up as the officers were closing in on him. That night, a martyr-bomber entered a popular café in Tel Aviv and blew himself up, killing one and wounding over thirty. Al-Aqsa Martyrs Brigades claimed responsibility. The next morning, March 31, a bomber blew himself up in a Haifa restaurant owned by an Israeli Arab and popular with the city's Arab population; fifteen were killed and over thirty wounded, many of them Arabs. Both HAMAS and Islamic Jihad claimed responsibility. Another bomber struck at the medical emergency cen-ter in a settlement block south of Jerusalem—the main source of medical services for both Arabs and Jews in the region.

Consequently, Sharon ordered the IDF to accelerate and expand its pre-ventive operations. Teams of intelligence operatives and special forces launched a highly successful campaign of hunting down would-be martyrs on the loose. A leader of al-Aqsa Martyrs Brigades going by the nom de guerre of Abu-Mujahed responded by warning that unless Israel withdrew immediately from Arafat's compound in Ramallah, "unprecedented military actions will be carried out in Tel Aviv, Haifa, Jerusalem, and everywhere else, that will exceed the imagination of everybody in Israel." These actions, Abu-Mujahed advised, were imminent. "Our people have prepared hundreds of would-be martyrs ready to hit every spot in Israel, if the Israeli aggression against our president and our people continues," he said. "The perpetrators of strikes will reduce to rock bottom the security of all Israelis and will shake the [public] order and stability in Israel until its government changes its pol-icy." At about the same time, HAMAS threatened to assassinate Sharon.

As for Arafat, he declared that the Palestinians would "never surrender" and that they would be "making their way to Jerusalem by the millions as martyrs." He himself, he added, would seek martyrdom rather than reach a compromise with Israel. Nevertheless, the kitchenette decided not to recant on Sharon's promise to Bush not to kill Arafat or send him into exile. In-stead, the Israelis would keep Arafat and a small group of associates—including Zeevi's killers—confined to a few underground rooms in the Ramallah compound. After a day of tight siege, the IDF restored water and electricity, at the request of the United States and Western Europe, and per-mitted supplies of fresh food and medications to reach Arafat and his col-leagues. Meanwhile, the IDF explored the compound. Over the next few days it would discover a treasure trove of documents, as well as large stockpiles of small arms, sabotage/terrorism equipment (including bomb-webs for martyr-bombers), and heavy weapons forbidden by Oslo (including anti-tank weapons made in Iraq and Iran). The IDF also discovered large quantities (hundreds of thousands) of counterfeit U.S. dollars and Israeli new shekels, as well as plates for printing these bills.

March 31 was the turning point in the new phase of fighting. The Palestinians' goal was for Arafat to emerge victorious on April 1, having freed himself from the Israeli siege. He would then demand a meeting with a U.S. delegation led by Zinni and a senior CIA official, at which he would argue that there was no military solution to the Palestinian crisis because Israel was incapable of defeating the PA forces. Toward this end, Tirawi organized a complex undertaking. First, the PA brought to Ramallah between twenty and thirty West European "peace activists," among them Palestinian agents. They immediately crossed the Israeli lines in a demonstration of solidarity with Arafat—bringing Tirawi and Arafat details of Israeli dispositions. The European agents then got instructions from Tirawi, which they were to relay to his operatives outside the compound. The Europeans were also asked to escort some twenty Palestinians out of the compound. The IDF detected the ploy and surrounded the group as it emerged from the bunker; however, a few Europeans and a couple of Palestinians exploited the resulting melee to escape, and they then managed to activate Tirawi's contingency plan.

That night, a force drawn from the Tanzim and al-Aqsa Martyrs Brigades tried to fight its way from central Ramallah to Arafat's compound. However, IDF special forces were waiting for them. In the intense battle that ensued—six hours of fighting in a built-up area—Palestinian martyr-bombers repeatedly tried to assault Israeli positions in order to open passageways for their comrades. In the end, six Palestinians were killed, two of them martyr-bombers, and some twenty wounded, four of them fatally; at least one bomber was shot by the IDF before he could detonate his bomb. In contrast, there were no Israeli casualties. By the end of the day, Arafat's hopes of at least symbolically breaking the Israeli siege had been dashed. Instead, Arafat had to accept Zinni's arrival under the Israelis' conditions, which included Zinni being taken on a tour of the compound and its arsenal.

———

BASED ON THE initial discovery of weapon stockpiles and the progress in hunting down terrorist leaders, the IDF high command asked the cabinet on March 31 to approve operations of several months' duration. While Sharon and his kitchenette were studying the request, the IDF and the security forces escalated their operations. In a series of daring raids, special units arrested senior terrorist commanders of various Fatah factions (including Tanzim and al-Aqsa Martyrs Brigades), HAMAS, Islamic Jihad, and a score of other groups. When PA security personnel opened fire on Gilo, local IDF forces quickly captured Beit Jallah, Beit Sakhur, and the approaches to Bethlehem. On April 1, the IDF launched a series of offensive raids, seizing Tulkarm and Kalkilyeh.

Over the next few days, Israel continued to expand Operation Defensive Shield, with the IDF consolidating its hold over key Palestinian cities and entering new ones. The primary objectives were now the centers (the *kasbahs*) of the old cities such as Nablus, Jenin, and Bethlehem, as well as the congested refugee camps around them with their narrow alleys and overlapping buildings. In order to minimize civilian casualties, the IDF used tanks and helicopters sparingly, sending infantry units in first despite the risk of higher Israeli casualties. The IDF infantrymen engaged in intense house-to-house fighting, facing booby traps and suicide bombers as well as the cynical use of civilians as human shields. Despite the intense fighting, IDF losses remained low because of sophisticated tactics and specialized equipment. In the course of these operations, the IDF captured hundreds of wanted terrorists and a wide variety of weapons and other military equipment.

Although Israel had launched Operation Defensive Shield with the knowledge and tacit support of the Bush administration, Washington was shocked by the eruption of anti-Jewish feeling throughout Western Europe—the most intense wave since the late 1930s, on the eve of the Second World War and the Holocaust. The administration was even more worried by the virulence of anti-American and anti-Jewish sentiment throughout the Muslim world, which it feared would impair its ability to gain support for its war on terrorism. That this outbreak of hatred had occurred in the context of Israel's war on Islamist terrorism did not seem to mean anything to Washington. Hence, in early April, Bush started taking a harsh position toward Israel, publicly demanding cessation of hostilities and withdrawal from the Palestinian cities. He offered to send Powell and a host of other senior officials to discuss a "cease-fire." A close examination of Bush's statements would have revealed their vagueness, especially the absence of explicit demands upon Sharon or support for Arafat—the Europeans' darling. Nevertheless, Jerusalem felt compelled to bow to Bush's statements because they had political impact. On April 5, Zinni met with Arafat, breaking his isolation. Zinni returned, relaying Arafat's unrealistic demands and his refusal to make any compromises. Still, Jerusalem was preparing to wind up Operation Defensive Shield earlier than it had planned in response to the Bush administration's admonitions.

On April 6, Tony Blair traveled to Bush's ranch in Crawford, Texas, for a previously scheduled summit meeting. Stressing the vital and growing British contribution to the war on terrorism, Blair told Bush that London would find it increasingly difficult to sustain support for Washington without a shift in the administration's policy toward the Palestinians. Moreover, Blair argued, taking on Iraq would be inconceivable without support from the conservative Arabs, particularly the Saudis.

The Western Europeans also demanded that Arafat be saved and indeed assisted. Regarding Palestinian terrorism, Western European officials said they "understood" the despair of the Palestinians, leading to suicide operations, and they insisted that the White House take this factor into consideration in formulating its Middle East policy. As a result of this pressure, Bush demanded an immediate Israeli withdrawal from the Palestinian cities, while senior administration officials hardened their criticism of Israel on the Sunday talk shows. Essentially, the administration adopted the position of the State Department, the European Union, and the Arab states—absolving Arafat and the PA of responsibility for terrorism and blaming it instead on despair resulting from the "Israeli occupation."

Jerusalem was particularly annoyed by the continued criticism from the White House because it had been permitting American officers and senior NCOs, mainly from various specialized anti-terrorist units, to closely observe the IDF's operations and to share battlefield experiences and captured intelligence (including prisoners) for use in the U.S. war on terrorism. In addition, Jerusalem had amended its approach to the mounting Syrian threat in order not to undermine Washington's priorities vis-à-vis Iraq.

———

THE CLIMAX OF Operation Defensive Shield began with the IDF's approach in the early morning hours of April 2 to the main refugee camp near Jenin—called Qandahar Camp by the Palestinians. By April 8, the fighting was essentially limited to the center of an intensely built-up area of about 600 by 800 yards, and particularly a few complexes of some 70 by 70 yards each. The defenders had prepared well for the IDF's arrival. Sheikh Jamal Abu al-Hija, the local commander of the HAMAS Izz al-Din al-Qassim Brigades, told al-Jazeera TV that his men had placed "explosive devices on the roads and in the houses" the IDF was likely to utilize. Thabet Mardawi, the senior Islamic Jihad commander in Jenin (who would eventually surrender to the IDF), told CNN that his men had planted numerous crudely made bombs and booby traps—"big ones" for tanks and "others the size of a water bottle" for the infantry. He estimated that anywhere from 1,000 to 2,000 bombs and booby traps were spread through the camp. "Omar," an Islamic Jihad bomb-maker, told *Al-Ahram Weekly* that "We had more than 50 houses booby-trapped around the camp." The Palestinians had evidently received expert assistance in their preparations, for some of the bombs found by the IDF in Jenin were identical to booby traps and mines used by the IRA against the British security forces.

Nevertheless, in order to minimize civilian casualties, the IDF elected to send infantry units—reservists as well as elite special forces—rather than tanks into the refugee camp. Mardawi was incredulous about the IDF's decision. "It was like hunting . . . like being given a prize. I couldn't believe it when I saw the soldiers," he told CNN. "The Israelis knew that any soldier who went into the camp like that was going to get killed." Mardawi acknowledged that there was intense fighting but no massacre. "It was a very hard fight. We fought at close quarters," he explained, "sometimes just a matter of a few meters between us, sometimes even in the same house." "Omar" bragged about how Islamic Jihad exploited the Israelis' reluctance to hurt innocent civilians. "We all stopped shooting and the women went out to tell the soldiers that we had run out of bullets and were leaving," he said. The women then led the soldiers to what turned out to be a booby-trapped area covered by a joint force of Islamic Jihad and Fatah al-Aqsa Martyrs Brigades. Four IDF soldiers were killed in this incident because the IDF ceased fire to enable the women to vacate the area.

The turning point in the Jenin fighting took place on April 9, when thirteen Israeli reservists were killed and another seven wounded in a single incident. The key to understanding this event was provided by Sheikh Jamal Abu al-Hija. On the eve of this climactic clash, he recounted, the HAMAS fighters were joined by youths who "filled their school bags with explosive devices" to prepare to become martyr-bombers. The local Islamic Jihad commander, Abu Jandal, told al-Jazeera that "there are children stationed in the houses with explosive belts at their sides." As the event unfolded, the IDF reservists were advancing down a narrow alley, when a ten-year-old—a boy who could have been their own child—came running toward them with his school bag. The Israelis called to him to clear the way and get out of the fire zone. Instead, the boy kept running toward them, and when he got close, he activated trip wires and blew himself up. Subsequent explosions brought the surrounding buildings down on the IDF soldiers. The besieged reservist force, with all its casualties, then came under intense fire from snipers waiting on nearby rooftops in anticipation of the child blowing himself up. The IDF force was ultimately relieved by a SEAL-equivalent force that broke through the Palestinian lines in fierce close-range combat.

After that incident, the IDF brought in heavy engineering equipment, tanks, and armored personnel carriers, as well as air cover from helicopter gunships. The IDF now opened a few wide lanes for the safe movement of its armored forces, flattening certain areas within the center of the 600- by 800-yard fighting zone. The battle ended soon afterward, with the remaining 200 or so Palestinians, led by Mardawi, surrendering to the IDF rather than letting themselves be crushed by the Israelis' superior firepower.

According to IDF data, twenty-three Israelis and forty-six Palestinians—two of whom were civilians—were killed in the nine days of the Jenin fighting. This substantially agrees with the PA's internal figures. On April 30, Kadoura Mousa Kadoura, the director of Fatah for the northern West Bank, reported to Arafat that only fifty-six Palestinians had been killed. Among the fatalities included in Kadoura's calculations were several victims of booby traps activated after the IDF's withdrawal.

The facts, however, could not catch up with the story of the Jenin "massacre," which was being widely circulated and believed. "Jenin has turned into Jeningrad," Arafat told CNN. In speaking to Western journalists and diplomats, Nabil Shaath insisted there were some 3,000 fatalities—most of them civilians killed in cold blood. The Western European media, particularly the British, repeated and embellished the message without any independent confirmation. It did not help either that the IDF, fearing casualties due to booby traps, did not permit the media into the camp. By late April, the Arab media were hysterical with horror stories about Israeli atrocities in Jenin.

However, by this time, Israel had already agreed to cooperate with Washington's call for an extra effort to strive for a cease-fire. Back on April 8, bowing to U.S. pressure, the IDF had begun withdrawing from cities where its operations had been mostly completed— Kalkilyeh and Tulkarm being the first.

The moment the IDF completed its withdrawal from the first Arab cities, Arafat went to work. On the morning of April 11—the day Powell was due to return to the Middle East—a suicide bomber blew himself up on a bus from Haifa, killing eight and wounding twenty. The explosion lifted the bus more than a yard in the air and turned the front of the bus into a skeleton of charred metal. Passing cars hit by the blast were hurled from the highway, wounding some of their occupants. The HAMAS martyr-bomber had come from the recently reopened Tulkarm; however, the operation relied on an in-place support system involving Israeli Arabs.

———

ARAFAT, WHO WAS determined to make negotiations impossible, now committed to yet another audacious undertaking—an attempt on Powell's life. This was a premeditated and well-thought-out operation. Back on April

5, during his meeting with Zinni, Arafat had made a special request—a personal favor. A police officer from a very important family in Gaza, a pillar of Arafat's power structure, had just been killed at Arafat's compound. It was imperative to get the body to Gaza for proper burial, Arafat pleaded. Zinni requested Jerusalem to make an exception to the siege, noting that the dead man was a member of Rajub's forces and that Rajub is close to the CIA. Jerusalem consented on April 7–8, and Islam demands prompt burial of the dead. However, the PA was not ready to dispatch the body until the evening of April 11—at about the same time Powell was due to arrive at Ben Gurion Airport.

Unbeknownst to the Palestinians, Israeli security forces were following the ambulance bearing the officer's body as it left the Ramallah area. Their suspicions deepened when the ambulance made a "wrong turn" and headed toward Highway 1—connecting Ben Gurion Airport and Jerusalem—instead of taking the road to Gaza. As the ambulance was about to enter Highway 1, it was ambushed and stopped by an Israeli anti-terrorist unit. A quick search netted a huge bomb installed under the policeman's body and a martyr's bomb-web under the seat next to the driver. The two supposed Red Crescent medics told their interrogators that their plan was to park the ambulance near a bend in the road where Powell's convoy was bound to slow down. They would open the vehicle's hood as if they had an engine problem. Once the limousine got close to the ambulance, the driver was to blow it up, in the expectation that the convoy would stop and the security personnel would rush to investigate the explosion. Exploiting the confusion, the other "medic" was to run to the limousine, try to get in, and blow himself up either inside the limousine or pressed against its exterior. The Palestinians were convinced that even if he was outside the limousine, his bomb was sufficiently strong to at the very least injure Powell, Peres, and the other dignitaries inside. Although Arafat was certainly involved in the plot, given his insistence on transporting the dead policeman to Gaza, the Bush administration decided to proceed with Powell's mission as if nothing had happened. To save the United States embarrassment, Israel agreed to suppress reporting of the incident.

Undaunted, Arafat ordered another audacious operation. This time, a suicide bomber blew herself up in the Mahne Yehuda market in Jerusalem, killing six and injuring more than sixty; al-Aqsa Martyrs Brigades immediately claimed the operation. The explosion occurred just as Powell was heading to an Air Force helicopter a few hundred yards away. He and his entourage could hear the explosion and see the smoke rising, and a few minutes later their helicopter overflew the explosion site. Seeing the carnage below at first hand, Powell was shocked. Still, he remained adamant on resurrecting the negotiations.

Powell started a series of meetings with Sharon, Arafat, and senior officials on both sides. On April 14, he thought he was getting close to a breakthrough. Sharon had agreed to additional Israeli concessions if Powell could
demonstrate "progress." Jerusalem even reversed its long-standing opposition to a regional peace conference (instead of bilateral negotiations). Ultimately, however, Powell's effort proved to be yet another exercise in futility,
as the Palestinians kept raising the ante. Arafat made any agreement contingent on unconditional Israeli withdrawal to the September 2000 lines and a
commitment by Israel to withdraw to the June 4, 1967, lines and to implement an unrestricted right of return. Having failed to gain any meaningful
cooperation from Arafat, Powell traveled to Beirut and Damascus to see if
he could somehow reduce tension along the Israeli-Lebanese border. Back in
Israel, Powell held another round of meetings with Arafat and Sharon in an
effort to produce a joint statement as a starting point for resuming negotiations. Arafat flatly refused. Instead, the Palestinians escalated their terrorist
operations, including repeated attempts—thwarted by Israeli security
forces—to penetrate and strike at western Jerusalem. The Israeli commitment to withdraw from both Nablus and Jenin within hours—which was
made solely in order to boost Powell's standing—had no impact on the
Palestinians. On April 17, soon after the failure of Powell's latest meeting
with Arafat, Mubarak capped the Arab world's insult to Powell and the
United States by flatly refusing to meet with Powell in Cairo on his way back
to the United States. Mubarak said there was no point in such a meeting
given the overall situation in the Middle East, particularly the renewed
threat of a regional war.

———

IN FACT, the threat of regional war formed the backdrop for the entire Israeli-Palestinian military and political dynamic. Back in late March, as Israeli-Palestinian tension mounted, numerous strategic activities commenced
on Israel's northern front. At Damascus's initiative, Syria, Iraq, and Iran activated and checked key provisions in their strategic cooperation. Some of
the communications exchanged among the three capitals were clearly intended to be intercepted by Israel and the United States—thus delivering a
message of deterrence. At the same time, the Iranians started a massive airlift
to Damascus from both Tehran and Bandar Abbas, overflying Iraq. Hundreds of IRGC officers and senior NCOs arrived with the airlift and deployed to southern Lebanon to assist HizbAllah in its planned encounters
with the IDF. The Iranians provided highly specialized skills not otherwise
available to HizbAllah, and they delivered huge quantities of weapons and
ammunition. Tehran also deposited millions of U.S. dollars in Syrian and

Lebanese banks to be used as operational funds. Cooperation and coordination between Syrian intelligence and Palestinian radical groups increased and included the transfer of al-Qaeda terrorists to the Palestinians' camps. Cadres of Islamist terrorist organizations from Saudi Arabia and the Gulf States arrived in Damascus for refresher courses and operational briefings, provided by Syrians and Iranians. The Syrians and Iranians also started to organize new Sunni Islamist fighting units under the banner of HizbAllah and the Secret Islamic Revolutionary Army; these units were made up of al-Qaeda fighters and newly recruited Palestinians. All these activities were conducted in close coordination with Arafat, whose representatives in Lebanon were kept up to date via Munir Makdah.

The moment Israel launched Operation Defensive Shield, fighting spread to the Israeli-Lebanese border. On March 30, HizbAllah launched massive shelling throughout the eastern sector of the border, well beyond the Shebaa Farms zone. The IDF ordered vacationers to evacuate the Mount Hermon ski resort as Israeli gunships and fighter-bombers attacked targets throughout southern Lebanon. The next day, HizbAllah expanded the fire exchanges to the western sector—for the first time since the Israeli withdrawal from southern Lebanon. By this time, large-scale weapon convoys were arriving in southern Lebanon from Syrian-controlled stockpiles, indicating Damascus's support for a protracted conflict. Over the next few days, HizbAllah escalated the cross-border shelling, along with sporadic Katyusha firing, while Israel continued to exercise maximum restraint in order to avoid opening a second front—one, moreover, that carried the risk of full-scale war with Syria. However, Israel asked the United States, France, and other powers that had good relations with Damascus to convey a warning that unless HizbAllah was restrained by closing off its supply of weapons and ammunition—that is, unless Syria stopped providing these—Israeli retaliation would no longer be limited to HizbAllah positions near the border. Still, HizbAllah continued to dare Israel, and Jerusalem elected to continue its self-restraint.

Damascus perceived the contrast between Israeli warnings and the IDF's self-restraint as a sign of weakness, which Syria was determined to exploit. Consequently, on April 3, the first HizbAllah detachments crossed the Lebanese border, under a heavy barrage of missile, rocket, and artillery fire. Israel retaliated with fire from artillery and helicopter gunships. The same day, the Syrian armed forces in Lebanon began defensive redeployment to the eastern Bekaa, where they consolidated their defense of the western approaches to Damascus. Additional units deployed from northern and eastern Syria, beefing up the dispositions between the Lebanese border and Damascus. All these deployments suggested that Syria was anticipating an Israeli offensive aimed at Damascus. The sense of foreboding was heightened when

Iraqi Vice President Taha Yassin Ramadan arrived in Damascus for emergency talks with Bashar al-Assad. HizbAllah chief Nasrallah also went to Damascus for talks with Bashar and visiting Iranian officials. On April 5, the IDF called up a limited number of reservists for a possible war in the north. Nevertheless, HizbAllah expanded its launches of Katyusha rockets and mortar barrages throughout northeastern Israel and the Golan Heights.

On April 8, Israeli Military Intelligence reported to the cabinet that "HizbAllah made the decision to drag us into a second front." The cabinet instructed the IDF to avoid stepping into that trap. The cabinet did, however, authorize the IDF to resume special operations in southern Lebanon, which it did, capturing or destroying recently replenished weapon stockpiles.

Also on April 8, Nasrallah publicly renewed his vow of solidarity with the Palestinians' Intifadah and threatened to expand the clashes to the entire Israeli-Lebanese border. As shelling and fire exchanges escalated, the IDF increased its deployment of combat units—including tanks and artillery—to the Lebanese and Syrian borders. "A military confrontation in the area is virtually inevitable," opined a senior officer in the region. The Israeli Air Force was put on wartime alert in anticipation of a Syrian attempt to launch a surprise barrage of ballistic missiles.

By April 11, HizbAllah had fired more than 1,000 rockets and mortar shells at Israeli targets, and HizbAllah detachments made repeated efforts to storm isolated IDF strongholds. Bashar pointedly ignored Israeli and American warnings and instead ordered a marked escalation. Tehran, however, worried that the Syrian provocations were getting out of hand. On April 12, Iranian Foreign Minister Kamal Kharrazi arrived in Beirut and urged prudence in view of the Israeli buildup in the north and the IDF's progress against the Palestinians. "Under these circumstances, we must examine things soberly and demonstrate self-control, in order not to give Israel any excuse to expand its theater of war in order to make up for its ineptitude in Palestine," Kharrazi warned.

Still, both Jerusalem and Washington remained apprehensive. That same day, the day Powell's helicopter flew over the Mahne Yehuda market, the secretary of state visited the headquarters of Israel's Northern Command, where he received a detailed briefing about the activities of HizbAllah, al-Qaeda, the Syrians, and the Iranians. Later, Powell told aides the briefing was "an unsettling eye-opener."

———

A PRIMARY INFLUENCE on the Bush administration's policy formulation at this point was the emergence of a new terrorism threat to the United States—one that involved the PA. In late March and early April, a body made up of Arafat loyalists, Palestinian Islamists, and followers of Osama bin Laden started preparing to resume international terrorism. The new terrorism campaign was explicitly modeled on Arafat's Black September Organization of the 1970s. Muhammad Dahlan and his HAMAS friend Muhammad Deif emerged as the driving force behind this initiative. Starting in the last week of March, the Gaza-based pair appealed to Libya, Iran, and Syria (via HizbAllah), as well as to Osama bin Laden and his sponsors in Pakistan, for help in establishing a terrorist organization for operations against Israel, pro-Western Arab countries, and the U.S.-led West.

According to Libyan and Egyptian sources, the new Palestinian group would "carry out martyrdom operations" against Israel and would make plans "to assassinate Arab leaders and officials colluding with the United States and Israel in the crimes against the Palestinian people." The Palestinian emissaries who approached Libya specified that their group would be based on "the Black September Organization and the groups that were led by Wadi Haddad," both of which were supported by Qadhafi in the 1970s and early 1980s. Egyptian security officials were convinced that the new group did not lack either the resources or the determination to act and that it was capable of launching operations "immediately."

The prospect of a new Black September Organization was first explicitly mentioned on March 29, when the chief of Fatah forces in Lebanon, Brigadier General Sultan Abu-al-Aynayn, hosted Palestinian officials from Beirut at his headquarters at the Al-Rashidiyah refugee camp near Tyre. The primary purpose of the meeting was to inform the officials that, on Arafat's instructions, "there were no longer any red lines constraining the Palestinians," and therefore the Fatah fighters would soon "launch attacks across the Lebanon-Israel border." However, Abu-al-Aynayn devoted most of his time to discussing Fatah's reaction to the escalating fighting in the territories, the siege of Arafat's compound, and the possibility that Arafat might be harmed by Israel. The only viable way to put an end to these activities, Abu-al-Aynayn suggested, was by forcing the United States into coercing Israel to desist. Hence, the Palestinian diaspora should be mobilized to launch attacks against "Zionist and U.S. interests" all over the world. "Our reach is long, and with this continuous struggle we have the right to respond," Abu-al-Aynayn argued. He added that if Washington failed to intervene and save Arafat and the PA, the Palestinians would resort to the tactics of Black September. "The world forced us once before to create an organization called Black September," he said. "We hope the world won't force us to use the tactics of Black September once again."

The fact that the Palestinians sought help from Osama bin Laden and his Pakistani patrons offers insight into the ideological framework of this initiative.

In late March, a high-level delegation of Palestinian Islamists (based in Lebanon and Syria) arrived in Pakistan, bringing a handwritten appeal from Sheikh Ahmad Yassin. The Palestinians, Yassin wrote, were currently "the victims of the most hideous campaign of annihilation in the contemporary history of Palestine." But the Islamists did not intend to accept this situation. "We affirm that in spite of the grisly campaign our people will not kneel down and will bravely confront the attackers with the help of Allah. Moreover, our resistance factions will chase that malicious enemy in all areas of Palestine," Yassin vowed. "And it is a jihad until either victory or martyrdom!" He then appealed to the Muslim world for any possible help. The Palestinian delegation that delivered Yassin's message held extensive discussions with their Pakistani hosts as to how this help might be provided.

The initial response of the bin Laden camp came on April 2, stressing the central role of Arafat's Fatah forces. A group calling itself the bin Laden Brigades-Palestine issued a statement formally integrating the Islamist and Fatah wave of anti-Israeli terrorism into bin Laden's global jihad. The bin Laden Brigades announced that their forces were now at the disposal of "Al-Aqsa Martyrs Brigades and fighter commander Marwan al-Barghouti" to fight "alongside the Brigades' fighters and the Islamic factions." The statement emphasized that numerous Palestinian factions, specifically including al-Aqsa Martyrs Brigades, "[had] become part of the International Front for Fighting Jews and Christians, led by Osama bin Laden." They now "[had] found the path of Islam and adopted the line of genuine resistance of the jihad movement and Islamic resistance, that is the path of jihad and martyrdom for the sake of God, and discarded forever the lies of the alleged peace and the myths of negotiations."

The general thrust of this communiqué was confirmed in Gaza by the Unified Leadership of the Intifadah—the umbrella organization covering Fatah's Tanzim, Fatah's al-Aqsa Martyrs Brigades, HAMAS, Islamic Jihad, the PFLP, and the DFLP. On April 2, the Unified Leadership issued a communiqué calling for anti-U.S. terrorist operations all over the world. "The United States is backing the Israeli assault on the Palestinians," the communiqué said. "Therefore, U.S. facilities, targets, and interests throughout the world should be harmed."

Operationally, the Palestinian components of the new organization derived from Makdah's Palestinian Liberation Army—itself a crucial building block of the Secret Islamic Revolutionary Army under Mughniyah's command. Back in February, Muhammad Abu-Zubaidah—the number three man in al-Qaeda—had traveled to Beirut to upgrade and revitalize the bin Laden–Mughniyah forward headquarters in preparation for the next wave of international terrorism. Now, Arafat was striving to integrate the PA into this framework.

Meanwhile, in late March, the IDF had discovered several Zodiac motorboats buried in the sand along the coastline near Netanya, Tel Aviv, and Ashdod. In some cases, tracks leading away from the beaches indicated that men had carried a weight estimated by the trackers to be 80 to 150 pounds. The Israeli security forces launched a clandestine but intense pursuit. Subsequently, Israeli intelligence confirmed from interrogation and other sources that the operation involving the Zodiacs was jointly planned and organized by commanders answering to bin Laden, Makdah, Mughniyah, and Syrian intelligence (via Jihad Jibril of the PFLP-GC). Arafat's intelligence and security entities provided intelligence and on-site support. The objective was an unprecedented attack on Israel. Plans called for terrorists to hit seven population centers on the coastline simultaneously in order to break the deadlock and demonstrate the Palestinians' ability to evade the closure imposed by the Israelis.

Additional evidence confirming the relationship between Arafat's Fatah and the Islamist terrorist movement accumulated during Operation Defensive Shield. For example, bin Laden's April 2 communiqué had identified Barghouti as commander of al-Aqsa Martyrs Brigades—a title he had not used publicly. On April 15, after the Israelis had captured and arrested Barghouti, al-Aqsa Martyrs Brigades issued a communiqué acknowledging that he was indeed their leader: "The recent days proved that the al-Aqsa Brigades, under the leadership of our brother, the fighter Marwan al-Barghouti, are facing the enemy virtually on their own and thus demonstrating to the entire world the courage and bravery of Marwan al-Barghouti." Meanwhile, two senior Fatah leaders captured in Jenin, Nassir Awis and Jemal Ahwil, told their Israeli interrogators about their cooperation with Makdah in preparing Fatah attacks against Israel. According to Awis and Ahwil, Makdah's forces in Lebanon had transferred large sums of money, specialized equipment, and personnel to Fatah cells in Nablus and Jenin. Makdah was kept apprised of the attacks being planned, Awis and Ahwil recounted, and he personally intervened in directing terrorist activities inside Israel from bases in the West Bank.

BY MID-APRIL, on the eve of Crown Prince Abdallah's visit to President Bush's ranch in Texas, regional dynamics took precedence over the Israeli-Palestinian conflict. Most Arab leaders and senior military officers were deeply worried about the Bush administration's continuing fixation on Saddam Hussein. They were convinced that the key to any future U.S. invasion of Iraq was access via Israel and Jordan. Given Arafat's enduring alliance with Saddam, the Arab leaders concluded, securing this access route would necessitate toppling the PA, most likely in a joint operation by Israel and Jordan. Adoption of this military strategy would also mean that the United States would no longer feel the need for "Arab support" in the war on terrorism, resulting in a marked decrease in the Arab world's importance in Washington. Moreover, reliance on Jordan would mean support for the Hashemites, who have a strong legal claim to control over the Hijaz and Islam's Holy Shrines, and thus are the greatest threat to the House of al-Saud's custodianship of the Holy Shrines.

Hence, Saudi Arabia embarked on desperate efforts to prevent the United States from taking on Iraq. In mid-April, Crown Prince Abdallah sought and received special guarantees from Saddam that Iraq would not invade Saudi Arabia and would not harm its oil fields for as long as Riyadh did not permit the United States to operate out of its bases. Soon afterward, Riyadh ordered the dismantling of the "Saudi"—actually U.S.—central command and control base at the Prince Sultan Air Base. Sophisticated equipment worth an estimated $5.6 billion was thrown out in the sand and sun, where it was irreparably damaged. Saudi Foreign Minister Saud al-Faisal then rushed to Moscow to meet with Putin and the Kremlin elite. Prince Saud told the Russians that by insisting that Riyadh participate, or even take sides, in the war on terrorism, the United States was pushing Saudi Arabia to the brink of collapse. To survive, Riyadh must disengage itself from America's strategic influence and must therefore find a new partner-protector. If Moscow did not become Riyadh's new patron, Prince Saud warned an incredulous Putin, Riyadh would have no alternative but to further consolidate its "alliance" with Tehran and Baghdad. (Riyadh had also asked Pakistan and various Arab friends to test the waters in Beijing.) In rebuffing Prince Saud's initiative, Putin drew the contrast between Russia's alliance with the United States against Islamist terrorism and the Saudis' enormous and crucial support for anti-Russian Islamist terrorism and insurgency from Chechnya to Central Asia.

Riyadh soon made its strategic shift abundantly clear. Officially claiming it to be a "routine exercise"—while quietly warning about an Israeli threat to Jordan—Riyadh established a nine-brigade force near Tabuk, in the northwestern part of the country, by redeploying forces from the Iraqi-Kuwaiti-Saudi border zone, and put the new force on wartime alert. Riyadh also deployed air force and air-defense units to the Tabuk region. According to senior Saudi defense officials, "instructions have been issued to the Saudi Air Force and Air Defense to intercept, but not engage, the Israeli warplanes."

Over the previous couple of weeks, Iraqi troops had also been moving; in particular, three or four armored divisions of the Republican Guard had joined the al-Quds Force close to the Jordanian border (though Riyadh still justified its troop movements by insisting that the threat to the kingdom necessitated a buildup against Israel and Jordan, including the redeployment of units formerly earmarked for meeting threats from Iraq). At the same time, Syrian troops in Lebanon and southern Syria were placed on heightened readiness. Even Cairo joined the war campaign: On April 26, Prime Minister Atef Obeid stated in an interview with *Al-Itihad* of Abu-Dhabi that if the other Arab countries covered the estimated costs of $100 billion, Egypt would go to war against Israel. Meanwhile, Palestinian and Iraqi efforts to destabilize Jordan had intensified to the point where King Abdallah moved his family to his palace in Aqaba and started coordinating emergency evacuation plans with Israel and Egypt.

By this time, Arab officials were warning of an imminent Israeli attack on Lebanon and Syria. Jordanian political analyst Sultan al-Hattab explained that "Sharon has put the whole region under fire and bloodshed by his brutal and disastrous aggression against the Palestinians, which has paralyzed the Arab regimes and crippled them from taking any actions that would stop him." Sharon, Arab officials claimed, was now planning to exploit the Arab weakness in order to "ignite the situation at the borders with Syria, Lebanon and even Egypt in order to begin the implementation of his plans of mass transfer of Palestinians to Lebanon, Jordan and Gaza." The ongoing Israeli military operations, al-Hattab warned, were the precursor to this grand design. Hence, he stressed, "if Sharon continues with his aggression against the Palestinians, the fragile situation in the Arab world will explode in the forthcoming summer." Syrian and Lebanese officials echoed this theme, arguing that it was imperative for the United States to contain Sharon before he set off a regional conflagration.

Crown Prince Abdallah arrived in Crawford, Texas, on April 26 with the primary objective of making the president understand just how fragile the stability of the Arab world was. Overwhelming grassroots support for bin Laden and the Islamist cause, the Crown Prince argued, as well as widespread hostility to the United States, had created a situation where a small spark—be it Palestine-related or Iraq-related—would cause an explosion whose fire would consume all the region's pro-Western regimes, starting with the House of al-Saud. Abdallah insisted that negotiated settlements with both Arafat and Saddam Hussein were necessary. He suggested a Saudi role in these efforts and offered to travel to Baghdad himself to jump-start negotiations with Saddam. Despite the excellent rapport between Bush and Abdallah, the talks ended inconclusively, with Bush emphasizing that the United States would not permit anybody to "crush" Israel.

The two men did come to a general understanding, however, on the distribution of responsibility between the United States and Saudi Arabia for calming the Israeli-Palestinian front. In essence, the Saudis would lead an Arab effort to contain the PA and Arafat, as well as to persuade HAMAS, Islamic Jihad, and other Islamists to stop the suicide bombings, in return for Israel's lifting the siege on Arafat's compound. In Crawford, Abdallah claimed that Arafat had given him his word that if Israel withdrew, he would end the activities of the suicide bombers. In this context, on April 28 Jerusalem accepted Bush's "ideas" about resolving the siege question, including the incarceration of Zeevi's assassins in Jericho under U.S.-British supervision. Sharon defined the compromise as a "least of evils" given the regional and global strategic dynamics. On the basis of assurances by Riyadh and Cairo, Bush promised Jerusalem that Arafat would denounce terrorism in no uncertain way within seventy-two hours.

Of course, he did not. On the contrary, fighting desperately for his own survival at the helm, Arafat sought a rejuvenation of terrorism. He knew the Bush administration was studying the idea of having Israel and Jordan jointly control the West Bank—empowering the local leading families as the first step toward a wide autonomy in connection with Jordan. Because such a program would alleviate the socioeconomic suffering of the local population, it would be immensely popular. Under this plan, Arafat's reign would be limited to the Gaza Strip, where he would be under strong Egyptian influence and supervision.

Equally worrying, from Arafat's point of view, was the brewing struggle between Dahlan and Rajub. In the aftermath of Operation Defensive Shield, Rajub was on the decline, having lost his "Pentagon" in the course of the fighting and having earned the ire of the Islamists by approving the surrender of some of his staff. Rajub now blamed Prince Bandar and the Bush administration for permitting Israel to destroy his power base—making him an unlikely partner in any future peace process. In contrast, Dahlan had kept Gaza quiet and thus positioned himself for future prominence regardless of his involvement in terrorism. In fact, Dahlan provided a highly important demonstration of the true balance of power within the PA and the extent to which terrorist strikes—from spectacular martyrdom-bombings to low-level roadside ambushes—could be controlled. Dahlan reached an agreement with Dief and Sheikh Yassin to prevent an Israeli onslaught on the Gaza Strip by containing the local cells and networks of both the Islamists and the PA security forces. It worked, for there was nearly complete silence in and around the Gaza Strip—suggesting that, had Arafat really wanted to, he could have arranged for at least a short-term cease-fire all along.

Dahlan emerged from Operation Defensive Shield as a "clean" but vindictive leader. He sought to maintain his legitimacy in the eyes of an increasingly militant street through a harsh political posture. There could not, he stated publicly, be any political process unless and until Israeli achievements since September 2000 were irrevocably and unconditionally reversed. "The Palestinian people is thinking about revenge—not a peace process," Dahlan declared on April 23. In early May, when he sensed that his popularity was not increasing fast enough, terrorist operations out of Gaza started up again. Initially, these were cautious and low-key undertakings—enough to boost Dahlan's popularity without either warranting an Israeli onslaught or tarnishing Dahlan in Tenet's eyes.

Arafat, the quintessential survivor, was far from oblivious to these dynamics. In late April, in the face of the U.S.-Saudi ideas, he ordered a new cycle of terrorism—most spectacularly, the narrowly averted attempt to use a truck bomb to bring down a skyscraper in Tel Aviv. As expected, the renewed strikes within Israel provoked increasingly fierce retaliatory and preventive raids by the IDF. The Israeli escalation focused world attention on Arafat—thus achieving his objective of remaining the sole recognized leader.

In early May, Sharon came to Washington for the first time since Operation Defensive Shield. Jerusalem feared that the Bush administration had not given up on the seemingly impossible task of gaining Arab support for a confrontation with Iraq and that Israel would be called upon to make additional concessions in order to clear the way. Hence, Sharon brought detailed intelligence reports about the PA's and Arafat's responsibility for terrorism, about their embezzlement of foreign-aid money, and about the overall plight of the Palestinian Arab population. Sharon argued that for any tangible solution, let alone peace, to be possible, Arafat would have to go. The White House generally agreed with the Israeli analysis except for the Saddam factor. The administration opposed "dumping" Arafat for precisely the reason Sharon had foreseen.

On May 7, with Sharon still in Washington, Arafat demonstrated his continuing "centrality." In a southern suburb of Tel Aviv, a martyr-bomber walked into a pool hall and gambling club frequented by rich Arabs from Ramallah and blew himself up. He was aided by an Israeli-based mixed couple (Arab husband, Ukrainian wife) connected to PA intelligence. Seventeen people were killed and over forty wounded. Although HAMAS claimed responsibility, Israeli intelligence demonstrated that it was a Tirawi operation perpetrated via the Tanzim and al-Aqsa Martyrs Brigades—which meant that it was launched on Arafat's explicit order. Sharon cut short his visit to Washington and rushed home after his meeting with Bush. As Arafat must have expected, the focus of the Bush-Sharon meeting shifted from discussion of a PA-*sans*-Arafat to working with the PA-*avec*-Arafat to reduce the terrorism menace.

Meanwhile, PA security sources affiliated with Rajub leaked information that the perpetrator had come from Gaza. At first, this information prompted

Israel to prepare for a "Defensive Shield 2" against the Gaza Strip that would have destroyed Rajub's archrival, Dahlan. However, the United States persuaded Jerusalem to postpone the operation, and once Israeli intelligence ascertained Tirawi's responsibility, Jerusalem's attention shifted back to Arafat. In fact, Dahlan *was* preparing for a major escalation. The IDF located and ultimately sank a Palestinian weapons ship that had left Lebanon for the Gaza coast; the cargo to be unloaded was larger than that of the *Karine A*.

WITH THE ARAB WORLD increasingly nervous about the Bush administration's next moves, Mubarak called an emergency summit with Crown Prince Abdallah and Bashar al-Assad in Sharm el-Sheikh. Arafat sent Dahlan and Shaath to the summit to represent the PA's interests. Officially, the primary result of this meeting was the participants' endorsement of the suggestions Abdallah had made to Bush at Crawford—particularly the suggestion that the Arabs should pressure the Islamist organizations to stop acts of suicide terrorism before they provoked an Israeli retaliation that Arafat and the PA could not survive. (Rantisi and other Islamist leaders later denied that any such Arab pressure had been applied.) Mubarak, Bashar, and Abdallah also, for Dahlan and Shaath's benefit, warned Israel not to invade the Gaza Strip.

The real objective of the Sharm el-Sheikh summit, however, was to formulate a common strategy for dealing with the rising importance of Jordan as the key to a U.S. surge into Iraq. Abdallah considered this option intolerable, for it would shatter the tenuous status quo in the Middle East. Therefore, the Saudis would continue to build up their forces on their northern border with Jordan. The Saudis also asked Egypt and Syria to cooperate in increasing their influence over the PA in order to forestall the emergence of a U.S.-Israeli-Jordanian solution. Toward that end, Abdallah and Mubarak also met privately with Dahlan. They promised him all-out support—financial, political (vis-à-vis Washington), and military—if he rebuilt the PA security organs in a way that would deprive Israel of any excuse for invading the territories. Whether Arafat would be part of the "new PA" was left up to Dahlan, although Abdallah expressed his opinion that Arafat should stay as a symbol that the Americans could not dislodge, thus buying time for Dahlan to realize their common plans. Dahlan agreed wholeheartedly with this scheme.

On May 15, Arafat returned to center stage, delivering a televised Nakba Day speech. The original text in Arabic differed significantly from the Palestinian News Authority's "official translation," which the West used in assessing Arafat's policies. In fact, this was the most militant speech Arafat had given in a long time, even though he did call for major reforms in the PA.

The roots of the conflict and the current plight of the Palestinian people, Arafat declared, should be traced to the original Nakba—the establishment of Israel. Arafat recounted his efforts to achieve the "peace of the brave" with Israel and told how he was repeatedly rebuffed by Israel and the United States, even at Camp David and Taba. Finally, he said, Israel had realized that it could no longer deny the justice of the Palestinians' demands, and so, in order to put an end to negotiations, the government had Sharon ignite the Intifadah by violating the sanctity of the Temple Mount. Since then, "our people in every town, village, and [refugee] camp remained steadfast in facing the occupation, closures, massacres, and aggression. . . . No city, camp, village, town, house, or even a hut [has] been spared from the Israeli military attacks with tanks, aircraft, and suffocating siege." Arafat dwelled on the latest round of fighting, accusing Israel of unwarranted aggression. He assumed responsibility for the various diplomatic compromises, particularly in Ramallah and in the Church of the Nativity in Bethlehem, insisting there was no other way, and then promised to correct any mistakes made during these negotiations. "At this time, we badly need to reassess our plans, policies, and correct . . . and amend our march toward national independence with complete honesty, sincerity, faith, and firmness." He promised more struggle, sacrifices, and hard times ahead, and he elucidated the character of the peace he was ready to negotiate. "Let us remember the Treaty of Hudaibiya," he said. "I say this based on concern for the national and pan-Arab interest of our people and nation, and out of our keenness to strengthen world solidarity with your people and cause." He obliquely addressed the enduring need for terrorism by endorsing "all" forms of struggle: "All forms of our national struggle must be strengthened and must focus on the need to achieve our people's dream to establish the independent Palestinian state with Holy Jerusalem as its capital on our land that was occupied in 1967. This was decided by our PNC when it declared independence and the independent state in Algiers in 1988." Significantly, the 1988 document bases its legitimacy on the 1974 "Phases Program/ Phased Plan." Toward the end of the speech, Arafat made a thinly veiled reference to the Palestinians' claim to the entire Palestine. "This holy land is a trust [*waqf*] in our care," he reminded his audience.

A new spate of martyrdom-bombings in Israel's main cities immediately followed Arafat's Nakba Day speech. Fatah's al-Aqsa Martyrs Brigades, the Islamic Jihad, and even the PFLP claimed responsibility; in reality, all were carried out under the auspices of the National and Islamic Committee for the

Furthering of the Intifadah, closely supervised by Sakhr Habash on behalf of Arafat. Although the IDF and Israeli Security Services had an impressive rate of preventive capture and/or killing of would-be martyr-terrorists, thus forestalling a huge number of fatalities, some terrorists still got through. Most notable was a martyr-bomber who blew himself up in an ice cream parlor near Tel Aviv, killing a fifty-six-year-old woman and her eighteen-month-old granddaughter. Ten of the thirty wounded were young children or babies.

———

IN LATE MAY, Arafat decided that martyrdom operations against Israeli civilians were no longer sufficient to serving Palestinian interests. Instead, the Palestinian leadership resolved to instigate a major clash through a whole new type of spectacular strike. First came the May 23 attempt to blow up the Pi-Glilot fuel and gas distribution center near Tel Aviv. A sophisticated incendiary and blast charge, with the classic cell-phone fuse, was concealed under a tanker truck that was to load up at the distribution center. The bomb was detonated on time by an observer who could see the truck reaching one of the main pumps. Fortunately, it was a heating-oil pump, and the fuel was not explosive; the fire spread slowly and was put out by the center's automated fire-control system. Had the truck been loading regular fuel or natural gas, a huge explosion would have taken place. That night, an attempt to steal a crop duster parked at an isolated airstrip was foiled by guards, but the terrorist escaped. Also that night, a security guard near a nightclub in southern Tel Aviv killed the driver of a car bomb as he was about to ram the club; the car exploded at a safe distance. Initial evidence accumulated by Israeli intelligence suggested that the perpetrators of at least Pi-Glilot and the crop duster attempt were expert terrorists supported from the renewed bin Laden–Mughniyah center in Lebanon.

Jerusalem found itself in a profound quandary. On the one hand, Palestinian leaders left no doubt that terrorism would continue to escalate. HAMAS's Sheikh Yassin set the tone on May 24, vowing to continue terrorist operations until Israel had been destroyed. "A people that does not have helicopters and tanks requires martyr-mujahideen," he declared. On the 27th, Khalid Mashal, also of HAMAS, vowed to continue martyrdom strikes until Israel's demise. "These sacred operations are the most effective weapon in the arsenal of the Palestinian resistance movement," he said. The same day, Hussein al-Sheik, a senior Tanzim leader, also vowed to continue terrorist strikes inside Israel and described al-Aqsa Martyrs Brigades as "a blessed phenomenon that the Fatah is proud of." These were not empty words. The Israeli high command pointed to accumulating intelligence about concrete preparations for a myriad of highly lethal strikes.

On the other hand, although the Bush administration remained ambivalent about Arafat's ability or willingness to deliver reforms, it kept putting pressure on Jerusalem not to do anything drastic against the PA's leadership. "The Americans are watching the situation," a senior Arab foreign policy adviser told Patrick Tyler of the *New York Times*. "The most important thing going on right now is the dialogue among the Palestinians themselves. Arafat is admitting mistakes and he is reassessing how to be a better Arafat if he wants to stay."

Meanwhile, Tenet was studying ideas for profound reforms of the PA's security apparatus based on Dahlan's ascent but with an emaciated Arafat as the titular leader in Gaza. However, senior PA security officials in Gaza reported that Dahlan had decided to "resign from his post" and stated that he "does not wish to occupy any security post in the coming stage." Instead, they noted, "his ambition [is] to occupy a political position." Crown Prince Abdallah had been told of Dahlan's decision, they added. In other words, Dahlan elected to move away from challenging Arafat's hold on power—thus bringing down the U.S. plan.

As for Arafat, his coterie left no doubt about where he saw himself. For example, on May 28, Brigadier General Mazen Izz al-Din, the chief of political indoctrination of the Palestine National Security Forces, told a rally in Gaza that Arafat was and would remain the undisputed leader of the Palestinian struggle. "We have to be truthful and honest and spell it out. One day history will expose the fact that the whole Intifadah and its instructions came from Brother Commander Yassir Arafat," the general said. "Arafat is [still] in the front line of the first trench of the Intifadah."

Throughout, Israeli intelligence and the high command remained convinced, on the basis of excellent intelligence and aggregate experience, that Arafat would never tolerate the curtailment of his powers and that he would never recognize Israel's right to exist or give up the right of return. He would rather inflame the region in alliance with Iraq and the radicals. Speaking as "a senior Israeli military official," a frustrated Yaalon told Michael Gordon of the *New York Times* that "there was no point in America's undertaking a diplomatic mission to rebuild the Palestinian security force while Yasser Arafat was in charge." In internal forums, the leaders of Israeli intelligence and the high command insisted that Israel must undertake drastic preventive measures, going so far as to seize the territories and hold them until the Area A segments could be handed over to legitimate Palestinian leaders. The debate became so heated that Sharon was moved to admonish both Mofaz and Dichter in the middle of the May 29 cabinet meeting.

By now, Tehran and Damascus rushed to seize the initiative—organizing a terrorists' summit to reiterate the justification and encouragement of martyrdom operations. The summit convened in Tehran on June 1 under the cover of a conference expressing solidarity with the Palestinian Intifadah and commemorating the thirteenth anniversary of the death of Imam Khomeini. The participants included most Iranian leaders, Hojatoleslam Ali-Akbar Mohtashemi-Pur (the Iranian founder of the HizbAllah), senior Pasdaran commanders from Lebanon, senior Syrian intelligence officials, the chiefs of the PFLP-GC, HizbAllah, Islamic Jihad, HAMAS, and a few smaller groups, as well as Imad Mughniyah and a key bin Laden commander from the Persian Gulf. Senior Iranian officials stressed the conference aimed to send a message that Tehran was still capable of playing "the card of exporting revolution and terrorism." They noted that in their deliberations, the various terrorist chiefs "underscored [their] commitment to armed jihad and martyrdom operations as the only and successful weapons in a disproportionate battle." Tehran allocated a special budget of $50 million for these operations. Tehran also promised speedy delivery of a host of weapons—from long-range rockets to shoulder-fired surface-to-air missiles—as well as providing training for additional terrorists in using ultra-light and micro-light aircraft.

The Tehran resolutions were acted upon on June 5, when a car bomb driven by an Islamic Jihad martyr slammed into a bus near the Megiddo junction in northern Israel, killing seventeen and wounding scores. Iranian officials stressed "the precision of the planning and implementation, so that the designers, by choosing an appropriate time and place, were able to impose the highest number of casualties on the Israelis. The place where the bombs were detonated was near the Megiddo prison, where Palestinian prisoners are kept, and it had been carefully chosen so that the prisoners could hear the sound of the explosion and see the explosion scene." The Iranian officials emphasized the long-term strategic impact of the new wave of martyrdom-bombing. Faced with the Islamists' resolve, they explained, "the prospects are dark for the Zionists. The continuation of martyrdom-seeking operations will make the regime sink into more horror and nightmare in the future, and it seems impossible to get rid of this nightmare."

With Tenet in the region to help the reforms in the PA's security services, Israel's reaction to the Megiddo bombing was mute. Arafat, however, was cognizant of the significance of the Iranian initiative. "The situation in Palestine is at the edge of explosion," read a June 8 WAFA statement. Unless the international community swiftly delivered on the Palestinians' demands, "the whole region will witness a disastrous explosion that will impact not only the region but the stability of the whole world." Concurrently, not to be outshined by the Iran-sponsored Islamists and fearing U.S. pressure to embark on reforms, stop terrorism, and revive the negotiation process, Arafat ordered Tirawi to launch an outburst of violence so as to focus both the world and

Palestinian attention on him. Tirawi activated networks controlled by the PA's General Intelligence, using members of HAMAS as martyr-bombers. On June 18, a Palestinian blew himself up on a city bus in southern Jerusalem, killing nineteen and wounding many others. The next day, another Palestinian blew himself up at a crowded bus stop in northern Jerusalem, killing five—including yet another grandmother and the infant granddaughter she was holding in her arms—and injuring at least twenty-five.

This time, Jerusalem followed the recommendation of the high command, launching a major offensive—Operation Resolute Way. Essentially, Israel transformed Area A in the West Bank, except for Jericho, into Area B. The IDF established routine military presence in all the cities, with the special forces conducting preemptive and preventive raids, while the Palestinians were permitted to run their daily affairs. The IDF also laid siege to and occupied all of the major cities and refugee camps. Arafat was kept bottled up in his Ramallah compound. Jerusalem declared that Operation Resolute Way signaled a protracted undertaking by the IDF with no end in sight. In early July, IDF operations gradually expanded to include the Gaza Strip as well.

Throughout this operation, Israel provided the White House with specific intelligence proving that Arafat had given the order for the Jerusalem bombing. Jerusalem also shared intelligence with the United States on Arafat's preparations for a future terrorist campaign. This latest intelligence came on top of the wealth of PA documents found by Israel in Ramallah and elsewhere that was also shared with the United States and now authenticated by the U.S. intelligence community. For President Bush, this intelligence confirmed Arafat's direct involvement in, and responsibility for, the escalating terrorism.

This realization led to a most profound change in U.S. policy toward Arafat and the Palestinian Authority to be elucidated in President Bush's June 24 speech. The White House finally concluded that it cannot expect Arab support for the war on terrorism, particularly against Saddam's Iraq. The United States would now work with a small group of close allies rather than strive for wider coalitions and tacit endorsement. In this context, Arafat would now be treated by the United States on the basis of his actions and words rather than the impact such moves might have on the Arab world's posture. Hence, Bush articulated in his speech what experts had long concluded—that Arafat was an implacable impediment to peace. Bush endorsed the current Israeli policy, observing that under present conditions "Israeli citizens will continue to be victimized by terrorists, and so Israel will continue to defend herself." To break the deadlock of violence, Bush urged the Palestinians to replace Arafat with a leader "not compromised by terror." With such a "new and different Palestinian leadership," the Palestinians could attain peace and an independent state within three years. "When the Palestinians have new leaders, institutions and security arrangements, the U.S. will support the creation of a Palestinian state," Bush said. "If Palestinians embrace democracy, confront corruption, and firmly reject terror, they can count on America's support for creation of a provisional state of Palestine." Bush demanded that Arab states take specific actions in order to demonstrate their commitment to peace and siding with the United States. "Every nation actually committed to peace will stop the flow of money, equipment and recruits to terrorist groups seeking the destruction of Israel, including Hamas, Islamic Jihad and Hezbollah. Every nation actually committed to peace must block the shipment of Iranian supplies to these groups and oppose regimes that promote terror, like Iraq. And Syria must choose the right side in the war on terror by closing terrorist camps and expelling terrorist organizations."

Arab reaction was virulent. The United States encountered widespread Arab hostility, particularly from Egypt and Saudi Arabia, over the issue of Washington's right to urge the replacement of Arab leaders—even if they were terrorists like Arafat—because this would create a precedent that threatened their own regimes. On July 2, the leading editorial in the official Egyptian paper *Al-Akhbar* urged all Arab ruling elites "to draw attention to the fact that this U.S. desire to change an elected leadership poses a threat to Arab interests and to the future of the entire Arab system. It will be any [other] Arab regime's turn if it differs in the future with the United States." With most Arab capitals consumed by bitter succession crises, the looming specter of Washington's effecting future leadership by empowering legitimate and democratic-oriented ruling elites is indeed a major threat to all existing Arab leaders and their chosen heirs.

Arafat quickly comprehended the severity of the new American policy as elucidated in Bush's speech and resolved to prepare for a fateful war with Israel and the United States while buying time through rhetoric about his commitment to democratic reforms. As is the case with all delicate circumstances, Arafat's real intentions were broadcast as a Fatah communiqué. On July 1st, the Fatah issued a warning that it was about to resume terrorist operations of the type conducted by Black September in the 1970s. The Fatah communiqué, issued in the name of "all military groups affiliated with the Fatah Movement," urged "all [Palestinian] fighters from the national and Islamic forces to strike Zionist and American targets/interests everywhere." The communiqué also declared that "the Fatah Organization and the Al-Aqsa Martyrs Brigades warn U.S. President George Bush that they will revert to the terrorist activities of the 1970s if the campaign against Yassir Arafat does not stop." To demonstrate the new era of cooperation, the PA security forces facilitated Sheikh Yassin's attendance at a public rally in Gaza—a stark contradiction to Arafat's promise to place the HAMAS leader under house arrest.

These were not empty words, for Arafat organized in early July a special emergency command and control group comprised of his new inner-circle in order to escalate the war and resist pressures emanating from Bush's initiative. The members of Arafat's new inner-circle are Tawfiq Tirawi (Arafat's closest aide, chief of General Intelligence, and the effective commander of all the Fatah's fighting arms—Tanzim, al-Aqsa Martyrs Brigades, etc.—as well as the coordinator of cooperation with Iraqi intelligence); Rashid Abu-Shabak (although formally Dahlan's deputy and replacement, actually Tirawi's man in the Gaza Strip); Sakhr Habash (formally the head of the National and Islamic Committee for the Furthering of the Intifadah and effectively Arafat's chief emissary to all terrorist organizations, organizing cooperation and ensuring deniability); Faysal Abu-Sharah (the commander of Force 17—Arafat's praetorian guards); Mahmud Damarah (the commander of the Force 17 units at Arafat's compound in Ramallah, thus actually responsible for Arafat's personal security); Salim al-Zaanun (in charge of Arafat's ties with HAMAS and the Islamists); Maher Ghanim (Zaanun's deputy in Damascus, where he coordinates activities with Syrian intelligence and the rejectionist organizations); and Tayeb Abdel Rahim (Zaanun's man in the Gaza Strip, where he coordinates activities with the local HAMAS and Islamist leaders).

Arafat's anticipated war is a debilitating clash with Israel provoked by spectacular terrorism in conjunction with the anticipated U.S.-led war against Iraq. This war will be waged in cooperation with the HizbAllah, HAMAS, and other groups sponsored by Iran, Syria, and Iraq. The ultimate objective is to flare up the entire Middle East in case of a mounting American threat to Iraq. Arafat is cognizant that any such encounter will dearly cost the Palestinian population—from heavy civilian casualties and unprecedented damage to the complete reversal of whatever political achievements they might have gained in the last decade. Hence, Arafat feared that local leaders—those who grew as part of the "interior"—might actively oppose his embarking on such contingencies because of the horrendous price the average Palestinian would have to pay. Hence, to secure his new inner-circle group and the war they would be waging, Arafat embarked on a thorough purge of all other components of his security machine. His first priority was to ensure that the PA security organs did not challenge the new power elite. Indeed, Arafat purged chiefs with grassroots followings, family relations in the territories, or connections to the Islamists, and instead elevated veteran "Tunisians" and pro-Iraqis that are fiercely loyal to him but weak and powerless in their own right.

The extent of Arafat's desperation is reflected in the identity of the officials purged and elevated, as in the unprecedented resistance to these moves. The key chiefs Arafat tried to remove are Jibril Rajub (who rose in the territories and whose brother is a HAMAS chief in the Hebron area), Mahmud Abu-Marzuq (who rose in Gaza and whose brother is one of the leaders of HAMAS based in Damascus), and Ghazi Jabali (the popular commander of the Police who was neutralized by a kick upwards to a meaningless advisory position). In an unprecedented move, Rajub's officers rebelled against his purge and warned Arafat they would not obey the nominated successor. Meanwhile, having been stripped of power and privilege, Muhammad Dahlan resigned and sought refuge in London along with Muhammad Rashid, who had just lost his signature rights to Arafat's bank accounts. From London, Dahlan and Rashid communicate with George Tenet, Omar Suleiman (Chief of Egyptian Intelligence), and Omri Sharon in anticipation for leading roles in the post-Arafat leadership. On July 10, Arafat nominated Dahlan as his National Security Advisor in order to wean him away from dealing with the United States and Israel, but Dahlan declined, refusing to return to Ramallah and meet with Arafat.

The key officials elevated by Arafat are Razek al-Yahya (the new pro-Iraq Minister of the Interior and a veteran Arafat loyalist who lives in Amman and thus lacks grassroots power base); Zuheir Manasrah (Rajub's intended replacement, a former aide of Abu-Jihad who, although the Governor of Jenin, spent the entire Operation Defensive Shield hiding in Amman ostensibly due to ill health); and Omar Ashur (Abu-Marzuq's replacement, another former aide to Abu-Jihad who lacks a grassroots power base). All these nominations are parts of Arafat's desperate struggle to remain relevant and avoid the emergence of challenges from other leaders—particularly the looming deals between the West and would-be successors.

By now, Arafat was convinced that the only way to survive at the helm was through a cataclysmic regional eruption aimed to destroy Israel as well confront the United States. Such an eruption would be an integral component of Baghdad's plans to preempt the U.S. assault on Iraq. Saddam Hussein encouraged Arafat to persevere in both public and private. On July 2, Saddam delivered a major address that defined his uncompromising Palestinian policy. "In the [Arab] Nation's fateful issues, we do not discuss secondary points, but base our views on main principles, including the fact that Palestine is Arab and Palestinian and that the Jews who immigrated to it are foreigners." Saddam argued that the Arabs should reverse the current situation "through [armed] struggle and jihad. The Palestinians have begun struggle, jihad, and generous sacrifices. Therefore, duty requires that we support them." Alluding to Bush's speech, Saddam declared that "we take pride in

Mr. Yasser Arafat as a Palestinian struggler and mujahid first before his post as a president of a republic." Ultimately, however, there is no substitute to the destruction of Israel and the establishment of an Arab-Palestinian state in its stead. "We demand the liberation of all of Palestine," Saddam stressed. "We believe that this responds to logic, right, and fairness. The Jews who came from countries that exist on the map should return to these countries. As for the Jews, Christians, and Muslims who had been in Palestine before 1948, they should remain in Palestine and be governed by a free and direct choice of those who lead them and take care of their affairs."

Starting in late June, in the aftermath of Bush's speech on the Middle East, Saddam grew worried about an impending confrontation with the United States. He convened an unprecedented meeting with his most senior aides in which he elucidated the gravity of the situation in terms of strategic commitments as opposed to actual military threat—while ridiculing U.S. performance in northern Iraq and Afghanistan. "Now the criminal Bush has ignored all the red lines and violated all political internal morals, all that is forbidden, and all norms and conventions, and has left Iraq no room to be tolerant in this issue," Saddam told his aides. He stressed he did not fear for his own life given his faith in God to whose will he (Saddam) attributed the repeated failures of the CIA to assassinate him. Saddam feared for the destiny of the Arab World. "What pains me is that the United States is using all its dominion and tyranny not just to humiliate Iraq, but to humiliate every Arab in the land of Arabs and every Muslim in the land of Islam, as well as every Arab and Muslim outside the land of Islam. Bush tells all of these people that he is the decision maker, and just as he rejected Yasser Arafat, he will reject Saddam Hussein, and tomorrow will reject Bashar al-Assad, and after that another Arab leader until U.S. domination reaches the rights, wealth, and destiny of the Arab [world]," Saddam concluded.

Baghdad's apprehension about the United States's grand designs were further elucidated in an early July editorial in *Babil* attributed to Uday Saddam Hussein. The preeminent looming threat was Washington's commitment for redrafting the Middle East borders in order to consolidate its hegemony over the region. "The Saudis were first to realize that the Americans seek to divide their kingdom," *Babil* explained, and adapted their relationship with Iraq accordingly. Hence, "Iraq will be willing to come to the rescue of Saudi [Arabia] if it is asked." The Palestinians were the first objective of the American grand design, the *Babil* editorial argued, for Jordan had already been designated "an alternative homeland for the Palestinians" in order to free Sharon's hands. "The implementation of the partition plan," *Babil* warned, "is linked to eliminating the Palestinian Intifadah, and in order to achieve that goal they have to attack Iraq."

Baghdad was determined to confront the American threat. In the above meeting with Saddam, his son Qusay, who had since been nominated both Minister of Defense and Deputy Commander-in-Chief of the Armed Forces in anticipation for the great war, defined the nature of the Iraqi response. He argued that so far Iraq had dealt "cautiously, conservatively, rationally, and responsibly" with the U.S. aggression, as well as used "only limited defensive means" in support of the Palestinians. This was about to change drastically. "I am confident that our entire Nation will be set aflame and they [the Americans] must know that the entire region will turn into rubble with Israel at the forefront. If Bin Laden truly did carry out the September attacks as they claim, then as God is my witness, we will prove to them that what happened in September is a picnic compared to the wrath of Saddam Hussein," Qusay assured his father and his aides.

Qusay's were not empty threats. According to senior Arab security officials who visited Baghdad in early July, Saddam already "put the final touches to a plan for a counterattack that involves the use of biological and chemical weapons. The plan calls for launching attacks in the whole of the Middle East." The Iraqi air force intensified its training, particularly long-range strikes with aerial refueling hardly attempted for a decade. Special Unit 223—Iraq's preeminent ballistic missiles force—was put on high alert with experts conditioning its chemical and biological warheads for imminent use. Also mobilized was "Saddam's Martyrs" force—a 35,000-strong praetorian guard comprised solely of Saddam's own Takrit tribe under Uday's command that serves the regimes last resort defenses as well as the primary instrument of ruthlessly purging the ranks of the defense establishment of traitors. The Martyrs' activation signaled Saddam's resolve to forestall any possible cooperation between elements of the Iraqi army and the U.S.-sponsored Iraqi opposition.

Meanwhile, hundreds of non-Iraqis—mainly PLO-affiliated Palestinians and al-Qaeda-affiliated Islamists—were trained by Unit 999 of Iraqi intelligence for suicide operations with the use of weapons of mass destruction. According to the senior Arab security officials, some of these graduates already "succeeded in infiltrating several Arab countries. They are provided with instructions, secret codes, and advanced weapons." On July 12, the Baghdad-based Congress of Arab Popular Forces—Iraq's umbrella organization for sponsoring terrorism—issued a communiqué about the forthcoming terrorism campaign. "Political parties, parliaments, trade unions and all nationalist, Islamist and leftist [organizations] across the Arab world and among Arabs in exile should . . . prepare to resist any aggression against Iraq," the communiqué read. "They should consider U.S. interests and presence, as well as the allies and agents who assist [Washington], a target in responding firmly to the forces of evil and strike them with all available means."

Damascus also reacted with fury to Bush's speech, with Bashar reasserting his staunch support for the HizbAllah and the Palestinians in defiance of Bush's warning. Instead, Bashar ordered the acceleration of the terrorist buildup in southern Lebanon in accordance with the resolutions of the Tehran conference, including Mughniyah's nomination as the local supreme commander. By mid July, Mughniyah's command included some 12,000 trained Shiite fighters and an arsenal of heavy weapons, including over 10,000 missiles and rockets, as well as some 10,000 Palestinian fighters and between 100 and 130 al-Qaeda veterans who arrived recently via Pakistan and Iran. Mughniyah's forces were deployed in a series of fortifications covering a 10- to 15-mile-wide sector north of the Israeli-Lebanese border, with a central headquarters built in an underground bunker complex under a hill in an eastern neighborhood of Sidon overlooking the Mediterranean. The new command enjoyed lavish logistical, intelligence, and financial support from Iran and Syria, including an expanded and dedicated training infrastructure in Lebanon, Syria, and Iran. Indeed, some officials considered this buildup a more urgent threat to the United States than Saddam's. On July 7, Chairman of the Senate's Select Committee on Intelligence, Senator Bob Graham, stated that "there are some things that we need to do that are more urgent [than attacking Iraq]. One of those is to deal with these training camps that have developed particularly in Syria and Lebanon where the next generation of terrorists are being prepared."

Starting late June, Arab leaders, particularly Crown Prince Abdallah, concluded from their contacts with the White House that there would be no reprieve for Arafat. These leaders informed Arafat that neither the U.S. nor Israel would agree to deal with him again and that he would have to be replaced if the Palestinian issue was to be kept alive. Arafat ignored all pleas and rejected several offers to go into exile. Still, starting early July, Amman was rife with rumors that Arafat would step down before the end of 2002. In response, Arafat's coterie tacitly informed Arab leaders that unless the United States delivered Israel, he would attempt a last-minute crisis, instigating a regional war along the lines of Saddam Hussein. Riyadh took these hints of a regional eruption most seriously, a senior Saudi official acknowledged. "The least that can happen is that the Arab region will explode in a way unmatched throughout history but only after US interests and embassies outside and even inside America are attacked in an unprecedented manner. Everything indicates that after today, what will happen between Bush Jr. and

Saddam is greater and more dangerous than what happened between Saddam and Bush Sr.," he warned.

In mid-July, bin Laden's friend and confidant Abd-al-Barri Atwan warned of a major war breaking out as much because of domestic political considerations in the United States as Washington's desperation to avoid collapse of pro-Western regimes in the region. Writing in *Al-Quds al-Arabi,* of which he is the chief editor, Atwan anticipated Washington's "launching preemptive attacks on countries that could threaten U.S. interests and before they actually reach this stage of threat. Iraq occupies first place as a definite target in this scheme." Baghdad was the victim of a major conspiracy, he explained. "The decision to strike Iraq is primarily an Israeli and not an American one. Israel's officials and leaders of the Jewish lobby who support them are the ones leading the gang of the advocates of overthrowing the Iraqi regime and installing in its place a pro-Western one that negates Iraq's Arab and Islamic role and mortgages its oil resources for the next dozens of years." If the U.S.-Israeli campaign was allowed to prevail, Atwan warned, it would usher in a calamity of historical significance because the West would once again be able to dictate the power structure of the Arab world. "We are witnessing a stage similar to the one that followed Turkey's defeat and the partitioning of the region after the First World War. In the same way that Hashemite kings were installed then in Syria, Iraq, and Jordan, the same scenario is now being played in Iraq, at least for the first stage, and will be played in the Hijaz in the second stage," Atwan explained. Only a widespread grassroots resistance throughout the Arab world could still reverse this calamity. "They conspired against the Intifadah and are now conspiring against Iraq and its noble and good people," Atwan warned. "We pray to God Almighty to repel their deceit and let the [Arab] awakening be on the way."

Meanwhile, Israel remained in a state of readiness for spectacular terrorist operations. Several car-bombs and would-be martyr-bombers were caught before they could do damage—the direct result of the IDF's presence in the territories. However, both Jerusalem and Ramallah knew that sooner or later they would have to deal with the aftermath of "the one that got through." And both Arafat and the Islamists were doing their utmost to launch a devastating terrorist operation. However, by mid-July, Jerusalem was less apprehensive about its ability to react properly because since late June, in the aftermath of Bush's speech, a close, even intimate, understanding developed between Bush and Sharon on the next phase of the remaking of a post-war Middle East. Both leaders shared a mutual conviction that the rise of a new generation of Arab leaders—committed to the betterment of their peoples' fate and the democratization of their countries—was the key to the long-term stabilization of the Middle East. However, with most current Arab leaders hunkering down, refusing to leave, and using the sponsorship of terrorism as their first line of defense against the United States and its allies, escalation was seemingly inevitable.

Given Arafat's pivotal role in both preventing the solution of the Palestinian question and supporting Saddam's preemptive surge, his removal from leadership and active politics became imperative for both solving the Israeli-Palestinian crisis and reducing the probability of a regional eruption. The Bush administration had finally concurred with the Israeli reading of the regional dynamics. The White House was now intimating support for the continued Israeli hold over the territories until meaningful negotiations with a post-Arafat leadership commenced. For example, in a July 8 White House briefing, the president was asked, with "security in its current state," was he—the president—"perfectly comfortable to have the Israelis where they are?" Bush's answer was explicit: "I would hope that everybody got the message that we all have responsibilities to fight off terrorist attacks, yeah." Nor was the Bush administration shy about its hopes for the removal of Arafat and his coterie. In late June, a very senior member of the Bush White House privately told a senior Israeli minister that the administration "would not shed a tear if you [Israel] get rid of Arafat." And on July 11, National Security Adviser Condoleezza Rice told Israel's Channel 2 TV News that the Bush administration resolved that the entire PA leadership should be replaced, and not just Arafat, before a meaningful quest for peace could start. "It's not just a question of one man," Rice said, "it's an entire political regime that needs to be changed, so that one man does not control the lives of the entire population."

By mid-July, both Arafat and Saddam escalated their defiance of the United States, convinced that the fateful violent eruption was imminent. Arafat announced his determination to run for reelection in the 2003 presidential elections and openly ridiculed the U.S. calls for his removal. In a major speech commemorating the 1968 Ba'ath Revolution, Saddam discussed Iraq's forthcoming war with the United States. He warned "all evil tyrants and oppressors of the world: You will never defeat me this time. Never! Even if you come together from all over the world, and invite all the devils as well, to stand by you." Iraq's revolutionary steadfastness is "armed with swords, bow and spear, carrying its shield or gun and cannon," he declared. Saddam prepared the Iraqis to endure sacrifices and sufferings in the coming war but assured them of an ultimate victory just like that of the Palestinian Intifadah. "The Palestinian people is victorious thanks to the stance of every Palestinian man and woman and their generous sacrifices and their readiness to give more," he explained.

The significance of Saddam's speech was underscored by the immense attention paid throughout the Arab world, in the media, among the ruling elites, and in Islamist circles. Most revealing was Atwan's analysis in an interview with al-Jazeera TV. Atwan noted that Saddam "had great self-assurance; he was confident of victory." Saddam's speech was most effective in gaining Arab support because he used Islamist terminology made immensely popular by bin Laden and the Palestinian Islamists in order to inspire confidence in Iraq's ultimate triumph. Atwan stressed that "the Iraqi president spoke with the spirit of martyrdom, exactly like the Palestinian martyrs before they carry out their attacks against Israeli targets, just like the martyr who appears on a videotape, whether he is from HizbAllah, al-Aqsa [Martyrs] Brigades, or Izz al-Din al-Qassim Brigades." Atwan singled out the language and metaphors used by Saddam. "In addition to the tone of self-confidence and defiance, the Iraqi president was speaking like Sheikh Saddam Hussein or Mujahid Sheikh Saddam Hussein and not like the Iraqi Ba'ath Party leader," Atwan emphasized. "In fact he was just like Sheikh Osama bin Laden, the same Koranic verses, the same prayers, the same confidence in victory. This demonstrates a new phase in the Iraqi president's strategy."

And so, by mid-July 2002, the Middle East was baking in an unprecedented heat wave, waiting anxiously for the escalating violence and terrorism to transform into the seemingly inevitable eruption of the old-new regional war.

Conclusion

BY SUMMER 2002, the Bush administration freed the United States from the shackles of the "Peace Process" myth, faced reality, and concentrated on furthering the U.S. national interest throughout the Middle East. Israel remained on high alert, with its security services working feverishly to stop would-be martyr-bombers and thus prevent additional cycles of carnage. Should a major attack take place, however, Israel would have no alternative but to retaliate while taking yet stronger measures to prevent future cycles of lethal terrorism from being inflicted upon its citizenry.

Such dynamics would effectively divert attention from the gathering clouds around Saddam Hussein's Iraq—as intended by Arafat, Saddam, and most Arab leaders. At the very least, the escalation of terrorism would continue to derail the repeated U.S. efforts at rejuvenating negotiations—still in the hope that the Saudis, the Egyptians, or both would support a U.S. attack on Iraq.

They will not, for two profound reasons: (1) The Arab world will not be influenced by any concessions the United States might be able to wrest from Israel, and (2) the Arab world knows Arafat would never genuinely embrace any agreement acceptable to either the United States or Israel.

In an opinion piece in the *Wall Street Journal* in early April 2002, Fouad Ajami succinctly elucidated Washington's quandary: "We can't impose a 'settlement' of the Israeli-Palestinian struggle: That would be hubris. And we can't fall for the myth that Palestine is what ails Egypt, for example, or Iraq, and that al-Qaeda's adherents are driven also by the passions of Palestine. We can't hold our own war hostage to Arafat's campaign of terror. That world is what it is, and we shall not be given a warrant for a strike against Iraq, or a reprieve from anti-Americanism, by accommodating Arafat or the al-Aqsa Martyrs' Brigade." Instead, the Bush administration should remember Crown Prince Abdallah's warnings of a Middle East exploding because of the overwhelming popularity of the Islamist message. The Arab street was preoccupied with immediate domestic problems, Abdallah had made clear; its anger was only aggravated—not created—by solidarity with the Palestinian jihad for the destruction of Israel.

Most perplexing in this dynamic was Washington's unrelenting quest for a negotiated settlement with Arafat because the Palestinian elite had never concealed its ultimate objectives. Already in early 2000, Kamal al-Astal, a senior "foreign ministry" official, analyzed the then-intense negotiations with Israel in an article in *Al-Siyasah al-Filastiniyah*. The "political agreement" negotiated with Israel was "a manifestation of a temporary Hudna [cease-fire]" and not a permanent solution. There could be no termination of the conflict because "the Arab-Zionist conflict is a civilizational conflict that will prevail even if a peace agreement is signed," al-Astal explained. Even if a peace agreement was signed, "the region [would] continue to live in the shadow of the axiom—imperfect peace and interminable war." Al-Astal stressed that "the [current] reconciliation [was] not historic" and that "the struggle [would] continue in all the trenches" irrespective of the negotiated process. The PA was on the road to "a political arrangement not a historical reconciliation," al-Astal concluded. Writing in *Al-Hayah al-Jadidah* on January 30, 2001, Sakhr Habash was even more explicit about the PA's ultimate objectives: "Experience has proven that peace could not be attained without the establishment of the Palestinian state on all the land. We are undergoing a phase in the struggle in which we can push the Zionist society into abandoning Zionism, for there could be no co-existence between Zionism and the Palestinian national movement. The Jews . . . should become citizens of the state of the future—the Democratic State of Palestine."

If there were any doubt about Arafat's own real objectives, a secret message he sent to his key followers among the Israeli Arabs on September 30, 2001, should have set the record straight. The IDF discovered a copy of this message in Arafat's compound during Operation Defensive Shield and has since shared it with the Bush White House. The message was addressed to all Palestinians, who, "[for] more than half a century, [have been] fighting the conqueror who plunders our land and homeland." Even when living under the Israeli yoke, Arafat stresses, Israel's Arabs must not forget that "you are its [Palestine's] original and lawful owners, and you are its heirs until the day you are resurrected." The Israeli Arabs are an integral part of "the blessed al-Aqsa Intifadah which our people is waging in the liberated territories and occupied territories, and abroad around the world," Arafat writes. "Indeed, the people, with all its sects and groups, started the Intifadah everywhere it could. They have interlaced the ties that connect the sons of Jerusalem and the West Bank with those of the Gaza Strip and those of the cities occupied since 1948—who have always been and will forever be the natural depth and fortified wall of our Palestinian people and its just cause." Through the Intifadah, "we will draw up with blood the map of the one single homeland and the one single people."

Arafat has no use for any pragmatic peace plan that other Arab leaders might support or sponsor. "Today, we expect absolutely nothing of the rulers of the [Arab] Nation, which is overcome with sleepiness and bound by silence and overwhelmed by cowardice. We are expectant and we follow with dreamy nationalist eyes our families and great people in the towns and villages of the steadfast resistance of 1948. For they share the cause and the fate, share the one single national dream. The Intifadah of al-Aqsa and Independence already fulfilled the unity and national alliance of all the sons of the determined Palestinian people, despite the blocks created by the occupation, despite all the acts of massacre committed by the Zionist gangs since the Nakba of 1948." The struggle "will continue to be the Intifadah of the one single people and the one single outburst of blood . . . a prolonged Intifadah of rage . . . a prolonged Intifadah of independence." Arafat assures his followers that they are "the lawful owners of the land . . . of the independent homeland and independent state," and he will lead their common struggle until "we will establish our independent Palestinian state" and thus reverse the legacy of the Nakba.

It is this sacred quest for the maximalist solution—for an Islamist state stretching "from the Sea to the River"—that fuels the Intifadah and leads a multitude of Palestinian youth to become martyr-bombers and terrorists. And there is nothing the modern world can offer these youth—the disciples of both Yassir Arafat and Osama bin Laden—to convince them to stop their wrathful jihad. Herein lies the quintessence of Israel's enduring plight.

THE CURRENT CRISIS has profoundly transformed Israeli society—particularly the so-called peace camp. This transformation reveals the most consequential error made by Yassir Arafat, Hosni Mubarak, and the Arab political establishment as a whole. Just as many of the Americans and Israelis who have been involved in negotiations over the years remained woefully ignorant of the Arabs' circumstances, so these Arab leaders simply did not have a clue—perhaps did not care at all—about the true aspirations and motives of their Israeli interlocutors.

Going to Oslo in the early 1990s, the Israeli peace camp—which later expanded to include wide segments of the Israeli population—wanted one thing: for Israel to be accepted, recognized, and legitimized by the Arab world. For that, Israel was willing to pay an extremely heavy price: in the withdrawal from strategically important territories, in economic burdens (ranging from added security costs to lavish aid to the Palestinians and various Arab states), in everyday security (it was clear that Islamist terrorism would continue, while Israel's ability to react would be limited), in the surrender of Jewish historical and holy sites to Arab control, and in social trauma (the bitter rift among Israel's nationalist, peace, religious, and post-Zionist camps). Nevertheless, the majority of Israelis were willing to take these risks, to pay all or most of this heavy price, for "peace." Even the bulk of the nationalist camp was willing to pay such a price for genuine peace. Their objection to the "peace process"—which has since been proved right—was based on their assessment that Arafat and his coterie were not interested in peace. The Israeli nationalists did *not* challenge the assertion that Israel will ultimately have to pay a high price for genuine peace.

By mid-2000, after seven years of unilateral concessions and withdrawals, the most dovish government in Israel's history was willing to move beyond the national consensus and surrender the holiest sites of Judaism to foreign sovereignty in order to reach a permanent agreement with the Palestinian Authority. Instead of being embraced by the Palestinians, the Barak government was insulted and rebuffed. Arafat made it clear that he still refused to recognize the right of a Jewish Israel to exist—first by insisting on the unconditional right of return of Palestinian refugees to pre-1967 Israel, with the ensuing transformation of the country into a Muslim-majority "Democratic State," and later by inciting the Israeli Arabs to revolt. Arafat also clearly demonstrated in a most insulting manner that he did not care about the sacrifices the Barak government was willing to make in order to achieve peace. During the Camp David summit in July 2000, after telling Clinton—in Barak's presence—that there had never been a Jewish Temple in Jerusalem, Arafat then asserted that all the haggling over Jerusalem was merely a Jewish conspiracy aimed at depriving him (Arafat) of his rights as a Muslim Arab.

Eruption of the Intifadah in the fall of 2000 caused a profound backlash in the entire Israeli population, including the most dovish wing of the peace camp. Israeli society has been united once again by the realization that there is an existential threat to the state of Israel. Virtually all Israelis once again perceive themselves as "a few Jews besieged by an ocean of hostile Arabs." For those in the peace camp, these sentiments are intensified by the humiliation and pain of Arafat's betrayal and the collapse of their dreams and aspirations. The majority of Israelis have reluctantly adopted the conviction of the nationalist camp that there is nothing to talk about and nobody to talk with.

Instead, a national consensus has emerged: The Arabs must be taught a lesson. As the IDF's operations in the spring of 2002 demonstrate, as a matter of national security, Israel has once again turned to preemptive strikes, heavy strategic punishment of all involved in a threat to Israel, and the expansion of security buffers by pushing Israel's borders outward. At the same time, democratic Israel remains extremely sensitive to the loss of life and limb among its military personnel and civilian population. Hence, there has emerged a very peculiar consensus: to wait until the last minute before unleashing the IDF, but once it has been unleashed, to have it deliver the most devastating and painful punishment possible upon *all* of Israel's foes.

———

AT THE DAWN of a new century and a new millennium, the Arab/Muslim Middle East is driven once again by its genuine indigenous dynamics. In stark contrast to the impression created by the Clinton administration's imposition of the peace process, the militarization and radicalization of the Arab world have broken through to the surface. The grassroots outbursts of hatred and violence accurately reflect the interactions among the region's leaders, including clandestine preparations for war and sponsorship of terrorism. That certain operations were almost launched and then canceled at the last moment was an aberration—a reaction to U.S. threats, not a demonstration that the Arab world had undergone a change of heart and become resigned to coexistence with Israel. Not only is the real Middle East in the early 21st century still the most volatile and dangerous region in the world, but, in addition, the enduring legacy of the Clinton administration's "humanitarian aggression" (as European officials call it) has been to make the Arab world even more virulently radicalized and uncompromisingly hostile to the U.S.-led West.

The unfolding crisis in the Middle East could still evolve into the widely anticipated major regional war as a cataclysmic breakout from the stifling constraints of the peace process. What the Clinton administration accomplished with its Middle East policy was to create in Muslim eyes the image of a weak and subservient Israel, vulnerable to political pressure from the United States and military onslaught by its neighbors, while at the same time arousing frustration and wrath toward the United States because of its failure to "deliver" Israel. The dramatic achievement of bin Laden's terrorist strikes of September 11, 2001, convinced the Muslim world of both the inherent weakness and the implacable hostility of the United States. In early 2002, the growing specter of a U.S.-led assault on Iraq provided the Arab world with an added incentive to launch a decisive jihad against Israel before the United States could attack.

Recently, Arab propaganda has begun referring to current events in Israel as the Intifadah al-Istiqlal (roughly, the struggle of independence), which will ultimately establish a Palestinian Islamic State stretching "from the Sea to the River"—that is, where Israel once was. This message is extremely popular at the grassroots level throughout the Arab and Muslim world. All Arab leaders know that no "peace process" can deliver this outcome and that the incited Arab street will not accept anything less. Hence, the key to the survival of the current Arab leaders, and of their chosen heirs and successors, lies in the waging of jihad—the next Arab-Israeli War.

In mid-May, Israel came close to launching a series of deep strikes against Syria in response to the Syrian-sponsored HizbAllah operations—fully cognizant that such a retaliatory strike would unleash a regional war. Israeli forces were already forward deployed when Washington, fearing the regional eruption Crown Prince Abdallah warned about, interceded with Jerusalem and Sharon agreed to postpone the strike. Nevertheless, in early June 2002 intelligence efforts were accumulating indicators of an imminent escalation. Appearing before the Knesset's Foreign Affairs and Defense Committee on June 4, Israel's new chief of Military Intelligence, Major General Aharon Zeevi-Farkash, warned that HizbAllah is planning to launch a "unique" attack along the Lebanese border in conjunction with "mega-attacks" by Fatah and the Palestinian Islamists. Consequently, with the buildup in both southern Lebanon and Syria expanding, the Israeli cabinet approved on June 20 the military's request for emergency call-up of large reserve units to bolster the forces arrayed along the borders with Lebanon and Syria.

The threat of regional war is particularly alarming because of the Arabs' growing confidence in their ability to restrain Israeli retaliation. Most horrifying is the increasingly coherent nuclear element in the Iranian-Syrian strategic threat. Tehran defined the importance of the nuclear factor back in the fall of 2001. Delivering the al-Quds Day Sermon in mid-December, Hashemi-Rafsanjani predicted "the elimination of the Israel problem with the use of one nuclear bomb" as the core of the Iranian doctrine. "If one day the Muslim world will be equipped with the weapons that Israel has now," he stated, "that day will bring the world's arrogance to a dead end, since the use of one nuclear bomb against Israel will leave nothing on the face of the earth, whereas to the Islamic world it will only inflict damage."

In the spring of 2002, Iran crossed a major operational threshold with the successful test-firing of the Shihab-3 ballistic missile. Launched from the Semnan region on May 1, the Shihab-3 achieved a range of more than 600 miles and struck its intended target—a major first. Any lingering doubts about the actuality of the Iranian nuclear threat were dispelled on May 24, during the Bush-Putin summit in Moscow, in a briefing by the Russian Deputy Chief of the General Staff, General Yuri Baluyevsky. Addressing the significance of the Iranian ballistic-missile program as a regional and global threat, Baluyevsky was most explicit: "Iran does have nuclear weapons. Of course, these are nonstrategic nuclear weapons. I mean these are not ICBMs with a range of more than 5,500 kilometers and more." While Iran may not be able to hit Moscow or Washington with its nuclear-tipped missiles, it can certainly strike Israel.

Thus, the early summer of 2002 finds Jerusalem contemplating if and when to strike out at its neighbors. The mere cessation of hostilities with the Palestinians will no longer suffice to placate the Israeli public. And in democratic countries, governments are most sensitive to popular rage. Hence, the only way to avoid a regional war is to convince the Israeli public that the Arab world is changing in such a way that the overall threat to Israel's existence is subsiding. This can be achieved only by the swift consolidation of "a new Middle East" in which the key Arab governments will redirect their energies toward domestic economic development and will make a meaningful commitment to peaceful coexistence with everybody—including Israel. Only the beginning of such a transformation—which will also reduce the vulnerability of the Arab governments and societies themselves to the rise of militant Islamism and internal subversion—will alleviate Israel's mistrust and fear. The Arabs should be aware that the current trauma in Israel is so great that it might take a generation for the Jewish wounds to heal. In the meantime, it is in everybody's best interests to calm down the Middle East and make it an environment conducive to peaceful coexistence.

Appendix A:
Partial Cast of Characters

Madeleine Albright U.S. Secretary of State (1997–2001).

Yassir Arafat Leader of PLO (1969–) and Chairman of Palestinian Authority (1996–). Also cofounder and leader of Fatah.

Bashar al-Assad Hafez al-Assad's son and president of Syria (2000–).

Hafez al-Assad President of Syria (1971–2000).

Ehud Barak Israeli Prime Minister and Minister of Defense (1999–2001).

George Bush, Sr. President of the United States (1989–1993).

George W. Bush President of the United States (2001–).

Warren Christopher U.S. Secretary of State (1993–1997).

Bill Clinton President of the United States (1993–2001).

King Fahd King of Saudi Arabia (1982–).

Ali Akbar Hashemi-Rafsanjani President of Iran (1989–1997) and Chief of the powerful Expediency Council (1998–).

King Hussein King of Jordan (1953–1999).

Saddam Hussein President of Iraq (1979–).

Ayatolla Ali Khameni Leader of the Islamic Revolution and supreme religious leader of Iran (1989–).

Shaul Mofaz Chief of the General Staff of the IDF (1998–2002).

Husni Mubarak President of Egypt (1981–).

Binyamin Netanyahu Israeli Prime Minister (1996–1999).

Shimon Peres Israeli Foreign Minister (1992–1995) and Prime Minister (1995–1996).

Colin Powell U.S. Secretary of State (2001–).

Yitzhak Rabin Israeli Prime Minister (1992–1995).

Ariel Sharon Israeli Foreign Minister (1998–1999) and Prime Minister (2001–).

George Tenet Director of the Central Intelligence Agency (CIA) (1997–).

Moshe Yaalon Chief of the General Staff of the IDF (2002–).

Appendix B:
Chronology of Events

Circa 633	Beginning of Muslim rule of Middle East
1099–1187	Reign of Christian Crusaders in Middle East
1187	Saladin violates his cease-fire agreement with the Crusaders and launches a surprise attack that allows him to capture Jerusalem
1798	Napoleon arrives in Egypt—beginning of modern Western subjugation of the Muslim world
November 2, 1917	The Balfour Declaration in which the United Kingdom commits to the establishment of a Jewish homeland in Palestine
Circa 1917	End of Ottoman rule of Middle East
1918	End of World War I
1920	British Mandate established for takeover of Palestine
1928	Founding of Muslim Brotherhood
1929	Arab mobs slaughter Jewish community in Hebron, and the British force survivors to evacuate
1936–39	First Intifadah
1947–48	Israeli War of Independence
November 29, 1947	UN decision on the Partition of Palestine into Jewish and Arab states
May 15, 1948	Establishment of Israel
October 1956	Sinai War
1964	Establishment of the Palestine Liberation Organization (PLO)
1964	Adoption of original Palestinian Covenant
June 1967	Six-Day War
September 1, 1967	Khartoum Summit, at which the "Three Nos" are accepted by the PLO: no negotiations with Israel, no recognition of Israel, no peace with Israel
November 22, 1967	Passage of U.N. Resolution 242
1968	Adoption of new Palestinian Covenant

September 1972	Arafat's Black September Organization murders 11 Israeli athletes at Olympic Games in Munich
April 1973	Arafat's closest aides in Black September are assassinated
October 1973	Yom Kippur War
November 13, 1974	Yassir Arafat addresses United Nations
February 1, 1979	Ayatollah Khomeini returns to Iran
November 4, 1979	Invasion of U.S. embassy in Tehran by Islamic militants
1979	Egypt and Israel sign peace treaty at Camp David
September 23, 1980	Iraq goes to war with Iran
1982–85	War in Lebanon between IDF, who invaded in early June 1982, and Palestinian and Shiite units under command of Syrian special forces and Iranian intelligence
1983	Formation of HizbAllah
December 1987–1993	First Intifadah in the Israeli-held territories launched by Islamists
July 20, 1988	War between Iran and Iraq ends
August 18, 1988	HAMAS adopts HAMAS Covenant, claiming leadership over Palestinian struggle as part of Muslim Brotherhood's global jihad
November 1988	Arafat declares Palestinian independence
February 1989	Debut of Arab Co-operational Council (ACC)
March 1990	Baghdad establishes the Front of the Islamic Army for the Liberation of Palestine (FIALP); Palestinian and Iraqi officials transform the PLO's forces into the Palestinian Liberation Army (PLA)
August 2, 1990	Iraq invades Kuwait
October 8, 1990	Palestinians gather at Al-Aqsa Mosque, assault Jewish worshipers at the Wailing Wall, and burn local police station
November 7, 1990	President Bush dispatches additional American troops to the Persian Gulf
January 17–February 28, 1991	The Gulf War
September 1991	Official demise of the Soviet Union and end of the Cold War
September 13, 1993	Peres and Mahmoud Abbas sign formal Declaration of Principles on South Lawn of the White House (Oslo Accords)

September 28, 1995	Peres and Arafat sign final Oslo B agreement in White House
September– October 1995	PLO and HAMAS talks in Cairo
November 5, 1995	Rabin assassinated
November 22, 1995	Peres becomes prime minister of Israel
December 1995	Trilateral negotiations begin at Wye River Plantation between U.S., Israel, and Syria; talks continue through 1996; "60 points of normalization" are outlined
January 20, 1998	Trilateral summit between Clinton, Netanyahu, and Arafat in Washington
January 22, 1998	*Washington Post* publishes story of Monica Lewinsky and Clinton's affair
October 19, 1998	First day of Wye summit between Israel and the Palestinian Authority in Maryland.
October 23, 1998	Netanyahu, Arafat, and Clinton sign the Wye accords.
May 17, 1999	Ehud Barak wins the election in Israel
November 1999	U.S.- Israeli- Palestinian trilateral summit in Oslo
January 2000	Syrian-Israeli talks begin in Shepherdstown, WV; Clinton drafts "Shepherdstown Document"
January 2000	Barak reopens negotiations with the Palestinian Authority that had stalled in early December. Israel agrees to a withdrawal from 5.1 percent of the West Bank and to release 22 Palestinian prisoners; however, Arafat changes demands for January 20 final withdrawal
April 2000	Arafat orders active preparations for the Palestinians' war of independence
May 15, 2000	(Nakba Day) Palestinian security forces open fire on Israeli positions throughout the West Bank and Gaza; Palestinian mobs begin throwing rocks at Israeli positions; Palestinian "policemen" open automatic fire on the IDF positions. Fighting spreads to Jenin, Hebron, and Netzarim
July 11, 2000	U.S.-Israeli-Palestinian Authority trilateral summit at Camp David; summit fails after two weeks of intense negotiations
September 28, 2000	Outbreak of the Second Intifadah as planned and prepared by Arafat's PA

October 3, 2000	Arafat storms out of meeting with Albright in U.S. embassy in Paris; later, he phones in order to escalate the fighting
October 12, 2000	Islamist terrorists ram the USS *Cole* in Yemen
January 8, 2001	PA resumes firing into Jerusalem; George Tenet organizes a meeting in Cairo of Israeli and PA senior security delegations to wrest Israeli concessions, but the meeting collapses. More than a quarter of a million Israelis rally in Jerusalem against additional concessions
January 20, 2001	George W. Bush is sworn in as president of the United States
February 6, 2001	Sharon is elected prime minister of Israel
March 26, 2001	Arafat meets with his senior commanders in Ramallah and tells them to prepare for a "100-day campaign"
March 30, 2001	Land Day, a nonviolent procession in Sakhnin, challenges Israel's right to exist
April 11, 2001	Israel launches a "limited ground war" against the PA; Syrian forces in Lebanon are put on high alert
April 20, 2001	IDF opens the main roads throughout the Gaza Strip to uninterrupted Palestinian traffic
April 23, 2001	Major terrorism conference is held in Tehran to coordinate additional support for the Palestinian Intifadah
April 29, 2001	Following meeting with Peres, Mubarak announces that the Palestinians have agreed to a four-week cease-fire, which would lead to a resumption of diplomatic relations; however, later that night Arafat pledges to lead the Intifadah until victory during a meeting in Ramallah
May 15, 2001	Nakba Day. PA media carries Arafat's speech in which he blurs the distinction between the fighting of 1948 and the current Intifadah, as well addresses the goal of the Intifadah: the destruction of Israel and its replacement with an Arab-Muslim state. Following his speech a series of riots breaks out throughout the territories, thereby answering Arafat's call for "days of rage." HizbAllah fires ATGMs and RPGs against IDF positions
July 30, 2001	Arafat orders expansion of the fighting, instructing forces to strike inside Israeli cities, to introduce mor-

	tars and heavy weapons to additional sites in the West Bank, and to lay ambushes inside the Green Line. Iraq fires a barrage of new SAMs toward a U.S. Air Force E-3 AWACS loitering inside Saudi Arabia
September 10–11, 2001	Large-scale IDF forces attack Jenin
September 11, 2001	Hijacked planes strike World Trade Center towers in New York; hijacked plane crashes into Pentagon in Washington, D.C.; another hijacked plane crashes in Pennsylvania. Sharon winds down IDF counterattack on Jenin
September 18, 2001	Israel decides to reduce tension unilaterally and Sharon declares a cease-fire, although fighting returns to precease-fire level by September 22
September 26, 2001	Arafat meets with Peres in Gaza to discuss the cease-fire, additional Israeli concessions, and the possibility of resuming implementation of the Tenet and Mitchell plans. PA security forces explode a bomb in a tunnel under a nearby Israeli stronghold
October 2, 2001	Arafat's people launch six simultaneous attacks; Sharon orders the IDF to respond with retaliatory strikes
October 7, 2001	U.S. begins bombing al-Qaeda and Taliban positions in Afghanistan
October 17, 2001	A PFLP team assassinates Rehavam Zeevi, Israel's minister of tourism, in his hotel in Jerusalem
October 26, 2001	Jerusalem orders the IDF to unilaterally commence a gradual withdrawal from PA-ruled areas
November 26, 2001	Retired Marine Corps General Anthony Zinni and Assistant Secretary of State William Burns arrive in Israel as mediators in the Palestinian-Israeli dispute; Sharon prepares to leave for the U.S.
December 16, 2001	Arafat delivers an address on PA Radio calling for an end to attacks on Israel; however, fighting during the 48 hours following the speech remains constant
December 18, 2001	Arafat calls for martyrs for the jihad at a rally in Ramallah
Early January, 2002	Arafat orders the launching of the Palestinian "Tet Offensive"
January 20, 2002	Arafat commits to his "last battle"
March 21, 2002	Crown Prince Abdallah presents new version of the "peace plan;" Iraq signs a reconciliation agreement

with Kuwait, thus forbidding member states of the Arab League from participating in any U.S. attack on Iraq, according to Arab League regulations. A suicide bomber blows himself up in downtown Jerusalem; Fatah's Martyrs-Brigades claim responsibility

March 21–22, 2002 — Arafat chairs a strategy session of the "National and Islamic Factions," at which the participants discuss how to markedly escalate the wave of terrorism on the eve of Passover.

March 27–28, 2002 (Passover Eve) — A martyr-bomber blows himself up in the middle of a Seder crowd in a hotel in Netanya; HAMAS claims responsibility

March 28, 2002 — The IDF launches Operation Defensive Shield, aimed at crushing the Palestinian terrorist infrastructure; the IDF besieges and isolates Arafat and his coterie

April 26, 2002 — In an interview, Prime Minister Atef Obeid states that if the other Arab countries cover the estimated costs of $100 billion, Egypt will go to war with Israel. Crown Prince Abdallah arrives in Crawford, Texas, to meet with President Bush; they agree that the Saudis will lead an Arab effort to contain the PA and Arafat, as well as persuade HAMAS, Islamic Jihad, and other Islamists to stop the suicide bombings in return for Israel's lifting the siege on Arafat's compound

April 28, 2002 — Jerusalem accepts Bush's "ideas" about resolving the siege, including the incarceration of Zeevi's assassins in Jericho under U.S.-British supervision; Bush promises that Arafat will denounce terrorism in no uncertain way within seventy-two hours. However, Arafat orders a new cycle of terrorism, including an attempt to use a truck bomb to bring down a skyscraper in Tel Aviv; Israel responds with retaliatory and preventive raids by the IDF

Early May 2002 — Sharon comes to Washington and argues that in order for there to be peace Arafat must go; Washington disagrees

May 15, 2002 — Arafat delivers televised Nakba Day speech, which is followed by a spate of martyrdom-bombings in Israel's main cities, including one in an ice cream parlor near Tel Aviv

June 1, 2002	Terrorist summit is held in Tehran under the cover of a conference expressing solidarity with the Palestinian Intifadah and commemorating the 13th anniversary of the death of Imam Khomeini. Iran allocates $50 million to martyrdom operations and promises a weapons delivery
June 19, 2002	A martyr-bomber blows himself up at a crowded bus stop in northern Jerusalem. Jerusalem responds by launching Operation Resolute Way
June 24, 2002	In a speech, Bush concludes that the United States can no longer work with Arafat. He urges the Palestinians to elect a new democratically-inclined leadership "not tainted by terrorism" as a precondition for the establishment of a Palestinian State
July 1, 2002	The Fatah issues a warning that it is about to resume terrorist operations of the type conducted by Black September in the 1970s
July 2, 2002	Saddam delivers a major address that defines his Palestinian policy, demanding the liberation of Palestine
July 10, 2002	Arafat nominates Dahlan as his National Security Advisor in order to wean him from dealing with the United States and Israel, but Dahlan declines, refusing to return to Ramallah and meet with Arafat

Glossary

4 June 1967 line The actual lines held by the Israeli and Arab armies at the outbreak of the Six-Day War. These lines were different from the formal cease-fire lines that defined Israel's recognized borders on the basis of the bilateral cease-fire agreements signed by Israel and its Arab neighbors in 1948–49, in the aftermath of Israel's War of Independence. Most of the changes between the June 4 line and the cease-fire line were the result of encroachments by force by Arab armies (mainly the Syrians) during the 1950s that Israel failed to dislodge because of military and political reasons. The U.S. does not recognize the 4 June 1967 lines on the principle that any legitimization of seizure and annexing of territory by force of arms could serve as a precedent for others to do likewise.

ACC The Arab Co-operation Council (ACC) was declared in Baghdad in February 1989 as an alliance of Iraq, Egypt, Jordan, and Yemen, as well as the PLO as an unofficial member. Ostensibly aimed to further economic co-operation between the four Arab allies, the ACC was to be Saddam Hussein's primary instrument in mobilizing an Arab military alliance for the next war with Israel. The ACC vanished in the fall of 1990, following Iraq's invasion of Kuwait and the U.S. commitment to Kuwait's liberation.

"Afghans" The term used to describe the foreign, predominantly Arab, fighters who fought in Afghanistan against the Soviets and their allies during the 1980s, as well as the various Islamists who have received military/terrorist training in Afghanistan/Pakistan since the 1990s and have participated in the local fratricidal skirmishes there. The "Afghans" constitute the core of the Islamist terrorist movement worldwide because of their expertise, zeal, and brotherhood.

Allawite A small sect of Shiite Islam that emerged as a distinct community in the ninth century along Syria's Mediterranean coastline. The Allawites trace their roots to a regiment from the Medina area that fought with the Prophet's forces until its remaining members settled in western Syria. They are organized in tightly bonded clans and tribes with mutual commitment to each other. In the twentieth century, the Allawites sought advancement in society by joining the military and security forces, and espousing all-Arab "progressive" ideologies such as Ba'athism. At the same time, the Allawites sustained their strong communal structure, ensuring mutual defense against the surrounding and overwhelming militant Sunni Islam, and often making alliances with the region's other non-Muslim minorities.

Allah The word for *God* in Arabic and all other languages used by Muslims.

al-Qaeda Commonly translated as "the base" or "the foundation." Al-Qaeda is the loose, all encompassing entity established by Osama bin Laden in the 1980s and presently embraces all like-minded Islamists—both individuals and organizations. Al-Qaeda serves as a cover for the sustenance of numerous distinct terrorist cells and networks that are routinely referred to as "al-Qaeda" cells or members.

Arabism The ideology stressing the centrality and supremacy of everything Arab in the entire Muslim world. The ideological justification for Arabism is that Islam hailed from Arabia and its Prophet Muhammad was an Arab. In the modern era, Arabism also transformed into a militant nationalist ideology urging the unification of all Arabs—Muslims and non-Muslims, conservative and westernized—as the basis for the Arabs' wresting control over the Middle East and triumphing over their foreign foes (Israel, Iran, the United States, the West, etc.).

Ba'athism "Renaissance" in Arabic. The popular name for the Arab Socialist Renaissance Party that presently rules in both Syria and Iraq. A nationalist secularist ideology that emerged in the 1930s urging the use of modernization as a primary instrument for reviving Arab glory, independence, and might in the modern world. Because of its non-Muslim character (one of the Ba'ath founders was Christian) and its nationalist/chauvinist fervor, the Ba'ath became prevalent among the region military and security elites. Ba'athism became the official ideology in Syria and Iraq in the aftermath of numerous military coups by Ba'athist officers.

Bayan A doctrinal manifesto or policy statement.

DFLP The Democratic Front for the Liberation of Palestine. An original member organization of the Palestinian Liberation Organization (PLO). Established by Naif Hawatima (a Christian-Arab from Jordan) on February 22, 1969, with a distinct leftist-revolutionary, almost Leninist, ideology. Operationally, the DFLP maintained close relations with the KGB, enjoying Soviet operational support and training, while carrying out "favors" for the USSR.

Druze A people of Arab origin dwelling in Syria, Lebanon, and Israel. Organized into tight families and clans, the Druze secretive religion is a blend of early Islam and mythical traditions of the pre-Islamic era. Loyalty to one's own people and community are most important. Inherently open to modernization and progress, the Druze emerged as leading security, military, and government officials in the countries where they live.

Fatah (al-Fatah) Arabic for "occupation" and "triumph." Also, the acronyms for the Palestinian National Liberation Movement. Yasser Arafat's own organization and as such the core of the PLO. Established in October 1959 as a revolutionary organization of militant Palestinians in the Diaspora, it was aimed at coercing the Arab world into destroying Israel by force and establishing an independent Palestinian state. Starting the mid 1960s, the Fatah adopted the revolutionary armed struggle as its key activity and established diverse assault forces that use terrorism as their primary form of struggle against Israel.

Fatwa The legal opinion of a Muslim court or a learned religious leader (Imam) in response to a specific query, usually on a contemporary issue. The Fatwa provides guidance for, and creates precedents about, key issues affecting the Muslim world.

FIALP The Front of the Islamic Army for the Liberation of Palestine (FIALP) established by Iraq in early March 1990 under the command of Hassan al-Hassan as a new Islamist organization that would be Baghdad's own instrument in the coming terrorist war. The FIALP "vanished" in the aftermath of the Gulf War.

Force 17 Arafat's own force of bodyguards and internal security, that is also used for carrying out specialized "operations" for Arafat. Established in 1970 in Lebanon, Force 17 has since provided the cover for a host of terrorist operations all over the world under such cover names as the Black September Organization (in the 1970s) and the Leadership's Security (1980s).

HAMAS Arabic for "fighting spirit, bravery." The acronym in Arabic for the Islamic Resistance Movement. Established in mid-1988 as the Sunni Islamist terrorist movement of the Muslim Brotherhood. HAMAS is operating in Israel, the Israeli-held territories, and the areas controlled by Yassir Arafat's Palestinian Authority.

HizbAllah In Arabic the "Party of God." Originally the name of the Lebanon-based, Iran-sponsored Shiite terrorist organization established in the early 1980s. Currently the name HizbAllah is used to signal strong sponsorship and control by Iran for any terrorist organization whether it is local, such as HizbAllah of the (Persian) Gulf and HizbAllah Palestine, or international, such as HizbAllah International.

IDF Acronym for the Israel Defense Forces. The armed forces of the State of Israel.

Intifadah In Arabic, the term means literally "shaking off" (the flu, bugs, etc.). In the late 1980s the term was adopted into the Islamist and later all-Muslim lexicon as a definition for a grassroots popular uprising such as the one then occurring in the Israeli-administered territories.

Islamic Jihad The generic name for the elite strike forces of several Islamist terrorist organizations—both Sunni and Shiite—used to convey messages and claim responsibility for terrorist operations without implicating the organizations and sponsoring states actually responsible. The Palestinian Islamic Jihad Movement is a series of localized cells operating in Israel and the territories with extensive support from, and under operational control of, both Syria and Iran.

Islamism/Islamist Islamism is a radical political ideology using the tenets of Islam as a justification for its quest for power and for the carrying out of indiscriminate violence and terrorism. The term Islamist does not refer either to someone who might be labeled "Muslim" because of inherited religious beliefs and culture or to aspects of Islam, such as Islamic belief or the Islamic state. The term Islamist denotes the overwhelming prevalence of the political aspect—particularly radicalism, extremism, and militancy—as pursued and perpetrated under the banner of Islam as interpreted by the practitioners. While commonly used in professional literature, the term Islamist is not often used by American journalists and other writers, who prefer such terms as Islamic intellectual, Islamic fundamentalist, or Islamic militant. Such usage, however, blurs the distinction between the majority of Muslims and a minority comprised of extremist terrorists.

Jihad A politically and religiously loaded term that means literally "striving." Jihad is used by Muslims to describe holy war and related support activities (funding, weapons acquisition, etc.). Although in modern and moderate Arabic and Persian, jihad is now used to define major undertakings ("construction jihad" to rebuild war-devastated Iran, for example), the militant Islamists still cling to the original and narrow definition of jihad—"holy war against the enemies of Islam"—as the sole meaning of the word.

Knesset The Parliament of the State of Israel.

Majlis The Parliament of the Islamic Republic of Iran.

Maronites A Christian-Lebanese people who trace their roots to the Phoenicians of the Biblical era. They are composed of tight and mutually protective communities that survived close to 1,500 years of Arab-Muslim onslaught and occupation, only to launch a revival in the second half of the 20th century. The very existence of the Maronites in Lebanon is presently threatened by the Syrian occupation of Lebanon and the Iran-sponsored Islamicization campaigns.

Mossad Literally, the "Institute." Officially, the Institute for Special Tasks, the Mossad is the foreign intelligence arm of the State of Israel (like the CIA or the United Kingdom's SIS/Mi-6).

Mufti Religious/political title of notables adopted into Arabic from the days of the Ottoman Empire.

Mujahideen Those who wage the jihad; Islam's holy warriors.

Muslim An individual who practices Islam.

Muslim Brotherhood An extremist religious organization with political connotations established by al-Bana in Egypt in 1928 in order to fight the British colonial authorities under the banner of Islam. The Muslim Brotherhood has since become a worldwide conservative Islamist organization dedicated to propagating the "true" and "fundamental" teaching of Islam in the religious field, the social field (by providing social services, education, etc.), and the political field (by establishing Islamic regimes).

Nakba Arabic for "disaster," "calamity," or "holocaust." Politically, the Nakba is used to denote the establishment of the State of Israel on May 15, 1948.

Oslo Accords The set of agreements signed by a succession of Israeli governments and Yassir Arafat. Named after the first set of agreements initialed in Oslo, Norway, in late August 1993.

PA (Palestinian Authority) The Palestinian self-governing arm established in 1994 by Israel and Yassir Arafat in order to provide the Palestinians with an interim self-governing authority for the areas to be evacuated by Israel in advance of the then-anticipated Israeli-Palestinian peace agreement and the ensuing establishment of an independent Palestinian state.

PLO (Palestinian Liberation Organization) Yassir Arafat's umbrella organization of numerous Palestinian revolutionary and terrorist organizations. The PLO was established in May 1964; at that time, it was committed to the destruction of Israel and disassociating itself from any claim to the West Bank and the Gaza Strip (then under Jordanian and Egyptian control, respectively). The PLO is presently used by Arafat as a vehicle for activities and pronouncements too extremist for the PA.

Pasdaran Persian for the Islamic Revolutionary Guard Corps, Iran's Islamist fiercely loyal military force that is also active in sponsorship of terrorism and subversion worldwide.

PFLP The Popular Front for the Liberation of Palestine. The second most important component of the PLO, the PFLP was established in December 1967 by George Habash (an Arab-Christian) with extensive support from Syria. Since then, the PFLP has been one of the most active and effective Palestinian terrorist organizations.

PFLP-GC The Popular Front for the Liberation of Palestine–General Command. A radicalized offshoot of the PFLP established in April 1968 by Ahmad Jibril (a Syrian officer of Palestinian origin) with extensive support from Syrian intelligence. Since then, the PFLP-GC has been one of the most active and effective Palestinian terrorist organization, closely cooperating with Syria, Iran, and numerous Islamist organizations.

SAVAMA The internal intelligence and security organization of the Islamic Republic of Iran.

Shin-Beth Hebrew acronym of the General Security Service. The internal security arm of the State of Israel (like the United Kingdom's MI-5 or only the counterespionage and counterterrorism arms of the FBI).

Shiite Muslim The second largest branch of Islam, named after the followers or partisans of Imam Ali (*Shiite* means "partisans" or "followers"). The Shiites consider the divinely guided Imam Ali and his descendants as the only legitimate successors of the prophet Muhammad. The Shiites formed as a distinct religious-political community in the second half of the seventh century in the aftermath of an extremely violent struggle for power over the Islamic world. Consequently the Shiites include the practice of jihad and the sanctification of martyrdom as Pillars of Faith in addition to the commonly accepted Five Pillars of Faith. Although political power is assigned to Ali's descendants, supreme authority is in the hands of the ulema, with the spiritual leader considered the ultimate authority of the state and the community. Iran is the only distinctly Shiite state. Significant Shiite communities with distinct sociopolitical character are found in Lebanon, Iraq, Afghanistan, Pakistan, and India.

Six-Day War (1967) The war waged by Israel from June 4 to June 10, 1967, against the armed forces of Egypt, Jordan, Syria, and Iraq, as well as volunteer and auxiliary units from virtually all the other Arab countries. The war's origins include the mid-May entrance of Egyptian forces into the Sinai Peninsula (demilitarized since Israel's first withdrawal in 1957), the Egyptian blocking of the Straits of Tiran (Israel's gateway to the Red Sea and the Far East), and a Syrian military build-up on the Golan Heights. In the aftermath of this war, Israel was in control of the Sinai Peninsula, the West Bank, and the Golan Heights.

SLA The South Lebanon Army. Initially, an amalgamation of local militias—Christian, Druze, and Shiite—established by the villagers of south Lebanon during the early 1970s in order to resist the influx of Palestinian terrorists into their midst. By the late 1970s, and more so the early 1980s, the SLA enjoyed extensive Israeli support, and was the de-facto ruler of the Israeli security belt. The SLA and the IDF held the line until Israel's unilateral withdrawal from south Lebanon in May 2000.

Sunni Muslim The majority of Muslims are Sunnis. In defining its character, Sunni Islam puts the main emphasis on following the Koran, Islam's holy book, and the Sunnah, which can be translated as "message," "legacy," "way," or "example" of the Prophet Muhammad and adhering to tradition as precedent setting. Sunnis obey the Sharia—the code of laws that regulates daily behavior and social relations as well as issues of property and commerce. They accept the Five Pillars of Faith as tenets of their belief. The Sunnis believe that since the death of Prophet Muhammad, no man has served as a divine intermediary between Allah and humankind (and so they reject the distinction of Imam Ali, which is part of Shiite belief). They also believe in the participation of the community of Muslims in choosing their leaders, starting with the popular selection of Abu Bakr as the Prophet's successor. At present the main differences between Sunni and Shiite Islam lie in the principles of judicial decision and jurisprudence (including civil law issues), the character of the holidays, the essence of their relationship with infidels, and details of the practice of prayer and other aspects of the rituals.

Tanzim The special forces of the Fatah Movement, established in the late 1990s as a deniable arm ostensibly made out of volunteers (in reality well-paid Fatah operatives). Their role was to spearhead clashes with Israel without implicating the PA's security authorities. The Tanzim is one of the most active forces during the current Intifadah.

ulema The senior religious authorities of a community (state) who together constitute the supreme authority as far as guidance, jurisprudence, and legislation are concerned. In countries with Islamic governments (Saudi Arabia, Iran) the ulema constitutes a supreme authority whose approval the government seeks for major political moves and whom the government rarely crosses.

Ummah The Nation. The term used to denote all Muslims wherever they are, and who are committed to each other's assistance and fate.

VEVAK The external intelligence arm of the Islamic Republic of Iran. Subsequently became the Ministry of Intelligence and absorbed the SAVAMA.

Wahhabi Islam The Saudi branch of Islam. Established by Sheikh Muhammad ibn Abd al-Wahab (1703/4-1797/8) in the Najd. Wahhabism stresses the purification of Islam through self-example and/or the propagation and proselytizing of "the right Islam." At the core of Wahhabism is Abd al-Wahab's decree that in addition to the known Five Pillars of Islam, there is a Sixth Hidden Pillar—fighting the jihad to spread Islam and defeat its enemies. The belief in the Sixth Pillar is at the core of bin Laden's doctrine.

Waqf The land that belongs to the Muslim Ummah and therefore cannot be ceded to non-Muslims.

Wye River Accords The agreements reached by Clinton, Netanyahu, and Arafat in October 1998, which were to serve as the framework and roadmap for subsequent negotiations, the permanent status agreement, and the establishment of a Palestinian state.

Yom Kippur War (1973) Israel's war against Syria and Egypt during October 1973. The war started with an Arab surprise attack in which the Egyptian force crossed the Suez Canal and the Syrians occupied large portion of the Golan Heights. At the end of the war—brought about by a cease-fire imposed by the United States, the USSR, and the UN—Israel had reversed most of the Arabs' initial achievements as well as seized large territories in Egypt and Syria. The post-war political maneuvers served as the launch-pad for the Israeli-Egyptian peace process.

Zionism The national liberation and self-determination movement of the Jewish people. The modernist, liberal, and nationalist-oriented branch of Zionism emerged in Europe in the second half of the 19th century—a result of the influence of Europe's enlightenment and the emancipation of the Jews. The main achievement of the Zionist movement is the establishment and sustenance of the State of Israel as a Jewish democratic state.

A Note on Sources and Methods

THE DAILY NEWS about Palestinian suicide bombers emerging from cities controlled by Arafat's Palestinian Authority to prey on and kill innocent women and children at the heart of Israel's urban centers attests to the failure of the so-called "peace process." For many years, the quest for Arab-Israeli peace has been the cornerstone of Washington's Middle East policy. During the 1990s, while the United States basked in the glory of the "peace process," the Arab World was elucidating—with a growing frustration wrought by the West's ignoring their situation—their implacable hostility to any dynamics that would fail to deliver the Islamists' maximalist demands. In a poem published in October 1995, Nizar Qabbani called the Oslo Accords "the peace of the cowards" and "the peace of selling [out] in installments."

Fouad Ajami's excellent translation, published in his book *The Dream Palace of the Arabs,* captures Qabbani's—and the Arab world's—frustration and anguish: "In our hands they left / a sardine can called Gaza / and a dry bone called Jericho. / . . . / After this secret romance in Oslo / we came out barren. / They gave us a homeland / smaller than a single grain of wheat / a homeland to swallow without water / like aspirin pills. / Oh, we dreamed of a green peace / and a white crescent / and a blue sea. / Now we find ourselves / on a dung-heap." Ajami stressed that having been published in *Al-Hayah*—the most important Arabic newspaper—Qabbani's poem, "The Hurried Ones," became an "overnight sensation" in the Arab world. Nevertheless, some seven years after the poem was published in Arabic and some four years after Ajami's excellent translation into English, senior officials in Washington are still mesmerized by the specter of the Israeli-Palestinian "peace process" and by the prospects of rejuvenating it once the right formula—the "diplomatic horizon" in Peres's phraseology—is found. The inseparably intertwined Palestinian terrorism campaign and Israeli-American quest for a diplomatic solution continue to spiral at the time of writing.

Writing a book on such still-unfolding events is therefore quite a challenge—all the more so when the pace of events kept accelerating at the time of writing. Furthermore, this is a book about high politics, the events they inspired and the activities they caused—the ramifications of actions both taken and not taken. The ultimate outcome of the dynamics addressed in such a book thus reveals how much is at stake for all the leaders—political, military and terrorist—involved in these events. This reality has direct bearing on the commonly available public record. Leaders use the media in order to manipulate unfolding political dynamics through leaks and releases, influence the record of their actions, and ensure their legacy in history. Quite frequently, the truth and objective historical record are sacrificed on the altar of both short-term political expediency and long-term "legacy." And, of course, there are still unknown dynamics—clandestine contacts, covert operations, political arm twisting and handshakes—accomplished in the dark.

The Middle East, and particularly the Arab-Israeli peace process, has always been both a uniquely emotional issue and a politically driven one. Many careers have risen and fallen over these dynamics. Presently, numerous senior officials—particularly Israeli and American—involved in many of these events use their public articulations to justify their past actions and opinions, particularly given their horrendous outcomes. Moreover, key newspapers and periodicals in the West, most notably the U.S. and Israel, adopted strong positions in support of peace policies during the 1990s which tainted their reporting. They have yet to deliver a fair assessment of the ramifications of these positions and their impact on the body-politic in the vibrant and public-opinion conscious democracies in both Washington and Jerusalem. Throughout, a few individuals have emerged as the standard bearers of the "peace process" policy drive. Presently, "facts" and their overall context are easy victims to their quest for a "record" in history.

All of this has to be taken into consideration by any would-be author. Not that there is a lack of material to work with. The Middle East, particularly the Arab-Israeli conflict, is one of the most intensely covered, yet least-known and comprehended, subjects. While there is a huge volume of news media, academic studies, and personal memoirs, most Western literature has largely provided a superficial commentary of the subjects at hand. Irrespective of the opinions expressed and positions taken, most of the literature available in English relates to a Western frame of reference and values.

In the United States, there is an institutional commitment, as well as an academic bias, among the media elite, academia, and foreign policy makers. The movement of people between these institutions has generated a symbiotic relationship and mutual dependence that keeps dominating both the academic publications and the institutional policy formulation process. At the root of this vicious cycle is the academic world—the place of schooling for the would-be practitioners and reporters, as well as the primary source of the professional literature. In his recent book *Ivory Towers on Sand: The Failure of Middle Eastern Studies in America*, Martin Kramer elucidated the crisis among the academic experts of Middle East studies: "For more than twenty years they have interpreted and predicted Middle Eastern politics with a supreme confidence in their own powers. . . . It is no exaggeration to say that America's academics have failed to predict or explain the major evolutions of Middle Eastern politics and society over the two decades. Time and again, academics have been taken by surprise by their subjects; time and again, their paradigms have been swept away by events."

The failure of the U.S. academic Middle East studies has direct bearing on Washington's body politic because the leading officials in both the State Department and the Central Intelligence Agency (CIA) dealing with the Middle East—the Arabists—are products of this educational system. Kramer observed in his *Arab Awakening and Islamic Revival* that the Arabists, "despite the best intentions and close familiarity with the Arabs, showed a marked tendency to be fatally wrong. As serving diplomats, they sometimes imperiled not only themselves but the interests of the United States." Despite the diversity of their career patterns and fields of expertise, noted Robert Kaplan in his book *The Arabists,* a dominant common denominator among them was the hostility toward Israel and uncritically taking the Arabs' side in the Arab-Israeli conflict. The civility of the diplomatic service and academia should not mislead. "In the long list of historical adversaries of the Jews," Kaplan noted, "the Arabists could easily claim to be the least noxious. The best enemies, in other words."

These biases are not an abstract issue for they constitute the basis for the policy formulation process of several U.S. administrations. Recent practitioners noted the relevance of these sentiments in key segments of official Washington. Reuel Marc Gerecht, a former CIA officer and Middle East expert, stressed the point in an early June 2002 article in the *Weekly Standard:* "To wit, America's support of Israel—not America's position as the preeminent Western power—is the root cause of American-Muslim tension in the Arab world. The Near East Bureau at the State Department has been stubbornly blind to the concurrence of Israel's victories over its Arab foes and the extraordinary increase of American influence throughout the region. . . . And the CIA, which usually mirrors the State Department's analysis and mood in the Middle East, is perhaps even more hostile to any interpretation of the region that doesn't cast Israel as the overwhelming cause of anti-American sentiment in the Muslim world. The Directorate of Operations, which has usually set the tone for the CIA and certainly does under Tenet, has a particularly difficult time escaping the prism of the Israeli-Palestinian confrontation."

These institutional biases dominate both the still unfolding politics and their public recording by both the mass media and the academic literature. Powell's State Department and Tenet's CIA are still actively engaged in the resurrection and reinventing of the Palestinian security forces just after having seen their Palestinian protégés and their CIA-trained and funded "security men" immersed in anti-Israeli terrorism with Islamist zeal and motivation. It took President Bush's speech on June 24, 2002, to begin unraveling the institutional commitment to Arafat and his "Tunisian" elite as the key to a resurrected "peace process"—a commitment deriving its legitimacy and quintessence from the failed Oslo process. In official Washington's cruel and unforgiving environment, it is inconceivable that the architects and proponents of these policies and practices would come clean honestly—admitting that their policies had been fundamentally wrong as well as accurately and objectively articulating the facts or events they had obviously missed and/or disregarded—if only because the mere suggestion of failure or error would be tantamount to a self-inflicted career-ending verdict. Instead, officials and institutions strive to prolong policies beyond their obvious demise—justifying their practice through supportive media.

Moreover, the U.S. and Western European media elite is directly affected by this institutional bias, primarily because the State Department and the CIA are the principal sources of leaks, briefing, and background material to the American media elite. Hence, it is only natural that the institutions' biases and tendency to skew data would find their way into the media's reporting and opinion-setting editorializing. The media elite relies on the expertise of the "chic academia" as their professional yardstick while, at the very same time, the media serves as a primary source of raw information for the academic work. Ultimately, all these trends keep reinforcing each other to the point of a total commitment to specific postures. And like their official counterparts, the American media elite is reluctant to admit errors or manipulations. Consequently, many of the American books, scholarly and journalistic articles about, as well as routine media coverage of, the Arab-Israeli conflict are products of this posture.

Furthermore, most of the readily available material covers only a fraction of the relevant activities. The media mainly addresses the political exchanges, public declarations of leaders, and the most flagrant acts of violence and terrorism and their impact on the political process—that is, the subjects that interest and affect the Arabists in and out of government. However, there are other aspects to the story, primarily those involving and directly affecting the Arabs and the Israelis. After all, nothing—from "mega-trends" to "conspiracies"—happens in a vacuum. Large and small events are implemented by human beings, and strategic interests are fought over with weapons at hand by soldiers, intelligence operatives, mujahideen, and terrorists. Alexandre Count de Marenches, the late Chief of French Intelligence, stressed the centrality of the hidden history:

As one of the longest-standing leaders of Western intelligence, I have learned that there are two sorts of history. There is the history we see and hear, the official history; and there is the secret history—the things that happen behind the scenes, in the dark, that go bump in the night. When one has a true world view, both become comprehensible. Both are essential. As a player in the first and a manipulator in the second, I have attempted to bring to my work the kind of understanding of both aspects of history that is vital if we are to be able to function in a world increasingly dominated by pernicious forces seeking to undermine our most fundamental values and basic institutions.

Historians John Loftus and Mark Aarons consider the "hidden" history to be the element crucial in comprehending historical trends and world events. "Known history is like . . . a series of harsh, twisted, seemingly un-connected branches. The hidden parts of history, the covert sides, are more orderly and rational, but can be seen and understood only if you are told where to look. The holes in history are what make sense of the thing. The hidden motives, secret agendas, classified purposes: All these tell the why of human events."

Missing as well from the conventional literature is the emotional as-pect—so domineering in Middle Eastern politics. The complexities of Arab society and power structure are glossed over through the use of Western-like frames of reference. However, there is far more to the political process in the Middle East than meets the eye. There are currents and relationships that dominate the life and functioning of society. On the one hand, there is the friendship and hospitality of individuals, the pragmatic and often self-con-tradictory relationships grassroots leaders develop in order to sustain the in-terests of their extended families, clans, and tribes. On the other hand, there is the passion of radicalism and extremism, the vulnerability of wide seg-ments of the downtrodden to the seduction of incitement, and the depth of the virulence and hatred expressed by all-too-many. The mere awareness of all these aspects constitute an introduction to the "street" politics of the Arab world—the complex, multilayered, and vibrant relationship between the oppressed and their authoritarian leaders. No less important is the ease of the leaders' ability to manipulate, indoctrinate, and drive segments of so-ciety to extremes, which is the central role of Islam in these regimes—both the traditional framework of Islam and the politicized and radicalized Is-lamism. All of these undercurrents strongly influence the Arab position in the Arab-Israeli conflict, and ultimately affect the leaders' positions.

Hence, in writing *The High Cost of Peace,* I relied as much as possible on contemporary indigenous sources, that is, material collected from, as well as engagements and communications with, senior officials and professional staff—both Israeli and Arab—directly involved in the events described. However, the human memory is far from being perfect, and, with time, details and fine points may become obscure. Moreover, with so much in the balance—from the fate of peoples to the careers and legacies of leaders—individuals' memories tend to tilt in their own favor. Hence, whenever possible, I relied on minutes and written reports, as well as contemporary documents and "non-papers," prepared by the officials and staff. As well, I relied heavily both on the region's vibrant media—broadcast, electronic (Internet), and printed—as well as a huge number of personal contacts on all sides of the divide. The list of the periodicals consulted can be found below.

In recent years, specialized electronic news-services and on-line periodicals have become an indispensable source of timely reporting. Officials and experts alike use these elite outlets as both sources of their own knowledge and as the primary vehicle for disseminating their own take on events. As such, these newsletters and periodicals constitute a contemporary record of events against which the more private communications can be checked. Of the large quantity of news-services, two merit singling out for their unequaled quality: the Middle East News Line (MENL) with its chief editor Steve Rodan is an indispensable resource for news and analysis on regional security matters. Comprehensive news and insightful analysis of global security developments is provided by the Global Information System (GIS) with its chief editor Gregory R. Copley. (I have to stress that the GIS is objectively an excellent resource even though I have written several stories for it.) Also of significance is Yigal Carmon's Middle East Media Research Institute (MEMRI)—a most valuable source of annotated translations and analysis of media from the entire Middle East. Boaz Ganor's Institute for Counter-Terrorism (ICT) publishes excellent studies and maintains one of the finest archives on international terrorism with an emphasis on the Middle East. Giora Shamis's DEBKAfile is also noteworthy because of the unique scoops and intriguing analysis of Middle Eastern affairs they repeatedly publish.

Thus, *The High Cost of Peace* is largely based on extensive indigenous source material from the Middle East—Israel, the various Arab States, and the Palestinian organizations involved— obtained and acquired by the author. Additional primary original source material comes from numerous Western European countries, Russia, southwest Asia, and other parts of the Muslim world. Moreover, I have had extensive interviews and communications with numerous government officials, diplomats, "spooks" of many shades, senior security and defense officials, as well as terrorists, militia commanders, émigrés, and other involved individuals from all sides of the Middle East's tangled web of loyalties and associations. These unique sources supplement the large quantities of open sources—primarily regional media—that by themselves provide a wealth of data and documentation. This open source material includes wire-service reports by local and international news agencies; numerous articles from local newspapers, periodicals, and newsletters; numerous articles from newspapers, periodicals, and newsletters of the Arab émigré community in Western Europe; numerous articles from newspapers, periodicals, newsletters, and academic journals in the U.S., Europe, Russia, etc.; transcripts of broadcasts by the local electronic media (mostly translated by the U.S. Government's excellent Foreign Broadcast Information Service, or FBIS); huge quantities of original source material retrieved through the Internet. For background information, a unique collection of primary sources—plus original publications, documents, and reports—developed over more than a quarter of a century of intensive research was also consulted. This wide range of sources constitutes a unique database for expert analysis regarding the subjects in question.

This dry definition of sources does not do justice to the human element involved. Over a quarter of a century, numerous people have made tremendous contributions to my knowledge and understanding in two major ways.

1. All the many hundreds, if not thousands, of people from all over the world who talked to me, communicated in other ways, sent stuff from obscure places and at times at a risk to life and liberty. Special thanks to those who patiently told me things as well as answered what must have been countless dumb and overly detailed questions. Thanks to those who sought, acquired, and delivered piles of documents and other material in "funny" languages and illegible scripts. Many of these individuals live and operate "on the other side." They have communicated and provided material at great risk to themselves and their families. They have done so because they really care about their own countries and peoples. Others, usually members of "the other camp," have communicated because they want to make sure we understand what they stand for and believe in. Theirs was not an easy task either.

2. It is not enough to have the wide variety of periodicals, newspapers, bulletins, newsletters, communiques, and other written material pour in from the region. Quality varies from the absurd to the excellent, and so do reliability and pertinence. But they are all important for in their wide diversity and variety they constitute an accurate reflection of the colorful and vibrant civilization. But these nuances are not easy to detect and comprehend. Thus, thanks to those "native speakers" who patiently translated and explained the multiple layers of meanings and innuendoes in these flowery, rich, and fascinating languages of the Muslim East. Thanks to all the translators and readers who worked with me over the years, teaching me how to "read" the stuff even when I thought I knew the language. Well, I knew the alphabet.

Despite the diversity and multitude of the sources used, and despite the frequent use of published material, the precise noting of sources is inadvisable in this kind of writing. The safety and survival of the human sources is the reason. As a rule, the moment a critical work is published, hostile counterintelligence and security organs launch relentless efforts to discover and silence the human sources still in their midst. Whenever such an individual is exposed, that individual along with his/her family are punished most severely—usually by torture and death—in order to deter others. Using "anonymous sources" or "officials" as specific entries in an otherwise academic-style source-noting is not sufficient to protect most human sources—particularly those providing access to most sensitive inside information. The distinction, via detailed source notes, of what material was acquired from human sources expedites the ability of the hostile counterintelligence and security organs to narrow down the scope of search, better identify the institutions from where the leaks came, and ultimately hunt down the human sources. It has been my experience, both as the Director of the Congressional Task Force on Terrorism and Unconventional Warfare and as a published author, that when confronted with a monolithic text in which the specific sources have been blurred, the hostile counterintelligence and security organs find it virtually impossible to narrow down their searches and thus stifle the human sources.

We owe it to these brave individuals who, at great risk to themselves and their loved ones, provide crucial and distinct information. Every conceivable effort must be made to shield and protect them. The omission of precise source notes is the least one can do.

FINALLY, a word about books. I'm an avid reader of books. Good books, serious books, are unique in that they enable their author(s) to reflect on the subject in breadth and depth, gather their thoughts, analyze the material as well as report facts, and, ultimately, draw clear conclusions and express opinions. Hence, despite the shortcomings of American Middle East scholarship as described above, books still provide not only a wealth of factual data but provoke the reader into reflecting and contemplating on the authors' approach to, and analysis of, the books' subjects, irrespective of whether one ends up in agreement or disagreement with any of these books and their authors. Among the thousands of books about the Middle East that I've read over the years and consulted while writing *The High Cost of Peace,* those that follow stand out because of the wealth of material and/or the coherence of argument—again, irrespective of whether I agree or disagree with the individual authors' analyses and conclusions. The list includes the books in English, Hebrew, French, and Russian that I've found of most interest and value.

Of note are books by Arab authors—published in the West and mostly in English—that provide sophisticated depiction and analysis of their "side" of the story. These are quality works the like of which cannot be found in Arabic. The literature about the Arab-Israeli conflict, and Middle East affairs in general, published in Israel in Hebrew is excellent—vibrant and multi-faceted, reflecting a multitude of opinions and approaches often conflicting and constantly debating each other through more books and monographs. Unfortunately, the translation of Israeli scholarship into English, particularly in the United States, is selective and largely tainted in support of the "peace process." There are a few exceptions such as Netanyahu's books. The situation is far better in the United Kingdom where a few small publishers have published works by Israeli experts on the basis of their academic quality rather than political correctness. Among the books listed below are also memoirs of key participants, mostly Israeli, in the drama covered in this book. Unfortunately, but not surprisingly, these works are self-serving and extremely optimistic about the forthcoming prospects of the peace process. In retrospect, these memoirs reflect their authors' false hope and further highlight the error in their reading of the Middle East megatrends. The key American officials involved in the peace process have not published their memoirs at the time of writing.

Two series of books provide crucial factual information about the region's security, political, and military affairs. The Middle East Military Balance series, published almost annually since 1983 by the Jaffe Center of Strategic Studies of the Tel-Aviv University, thoroughly covers a rather narrow subject. While these books have been repeatedly accused, and not without reason, of taking a "Dovish" approach in their analysis and coverage of the region's political and security dynamics, the Middle East Military Balance series remains the most important source of the pertinent military data and balance of forces—that is, of the numbers and figures. The Washington-based Defense and Foreign Affairs Handbook series (consisting of both books and CD-ROMs), to which I've contributed over the years, also includes detailed coverage of the armed forces and their arsenals. However, the Handbooks go far beyond that, providing comprehensive background material and analysis of the countries, their overall political systems, and defense postures. Furthermore, the D&FA Handbooks are more global and strictly objective in their analysis.

And then, there are the main books and monographs used for writing *The High Cost of Peace*. As described above, I selected the titles whose contributions I consider to be the most valuable. They are organized alphabetically by subject matter.

Selected Bibliography

BOOKS AND MONOGRAPHS

Key: H: Hebrew   F: French   R: Russian   A: Arabic

The following are the main books and monographs used for writing *The High Cost of Peace.*

Arab and Middle Eastern Politics
——. *Negotiations in the Middle East: The Lessons of Fifty Years.* Tel-Aviv: Dayan Center, 1993. [H]

Aburish, Said K. *A Brutal Friendship.* London: Victor Gollancz, 1997.

Ahrari, M.E. (ed). *Change and Continuity in the Middle East: Conflict Resolution and Prospects for Peace.* New York, NY: St. Martin's, 1996.

Ajami, Fouad. *The Arab Predicament: Arab Political Thought and Practice Since 1967.* Cambridge, MA: Cambridge University Press, 1981.

Ajami, Fouad. *The Dream Palace of the Arabs.* New York, NY: Pantheon, 1998.

Atkeson, Edward B. The *Powder Keg: An Intelligence Officer's Guide to Military Forces in the Middle East 1996–2000.* Falls Church, VA: Nova, 1996.

Ayalon, Ami. *A History of the Arab Press.* Tel-Aviv: Ma'arachot, 2000. [H]

Ayubi, Nazih N. *Political Islam: Religion and Politics in the Arab World.* London: Routledge, 1991.

Ayubi, Nazih N. *Over-Stating the Arab State: Politics and Society in the Middle East.* London: I.B.Tauris, 1995.

Bausin, Lev. *Don't Recruit the Sphinx.* Moscow: Gcya, 1998. [R]

Binder, Leonard (ed). *Ethnic Conflict and International Politics in the Middle East.* Gainesville, FL: University Press of Florida, 1999.

Bodansky, Yossef. *Islamic Anti-Semitism as a Political Instrument.* Shaarei Tikva: ACPR, 1999.

Butt, Gerald. *A Rock and a Hard Place: Origins of Arab-Western Conflict in the Middle East.* London: HarperCollins, 1994.

Choueiri, Youssef M. *Arab Nationalism: A History*. Oxford: Blackwell, 2000.

Cooley, John K. *Payback: America's Long War in the Middle East*. Washington, D.C.: Brassey's (U.S.), 1991.

Cordesman, Anthony H. *Perilous Prospects: The Peace Process and the Arab-Israeli Military Balance*. Boulder, CO: Westview Press, 1996.

Cordesman, Anthony H. *Iran's Military Forces in Transition*. Westport, CT: Praeger, 1999.

Cordesman, Anthony H. *Peace and War: The Arab-Israeli Military Balance Enters the 21st Century*. Westport, CT: Praeger, 2002.

Evron, Yair. *Conflict and Security Building Measures in the Israel-Arab Context*. Tel-Aviv: Tami Steinmetz Center, 1995. [H]

Feiler, Gil. *Funding Islamic Terrorism: HAMAS, Islamic Jihad, and HizbAllah*. Herzeliya: ICT, 1999. [H]

Feldman, Shai and Abdullah Toukan. *Bridging the Gap: A Future Security Architecture for the Middle East*. Lanham, MD: Rowman & Littlefield, 1997.

Field, Michael. *Inside the Arab World*. Cambridge, MA: Harvard University Press, 1995.

Fuller, Graham and Rend Rahim Francke. *The Arab Shi'a: The Forgotten Muslims*. New York, NY: St. Martin's, 1999.

Gerges, Fawaz A. *America and Political Islam: Clash of Cultures or Clash of Interests?* Cambridge, MA: Cambridge University Press, 1999.

Haseeb, Khair el-Din (ed). *The Future of the Arab Nation: Challenges and Options*. Beirut: Centre for Arab Unity Studies, 1991.

Haseeb, Khair el-Din (ed). *Arab-Iranian Relations*. Beirut: Centre for Arab Unity Studies, 1998.

Haselkorn, Avigdor. *The Continuing Storm: Iraq, Poisonous Weapons, and Deterrence*. New Haven, CT: Yale University Press, 1999.

Heikal, Mohammed. *Secret Channels*. London: HarperCollins, 1996.

Hinnebusch, Raymond and Anoushiravan Ehteshami (eds). *The Foreign Policies of Middle East States*. Boulder, CO: Lynne Reinner, 2002.

Hoveyda, Fereydoun. *The Brocken Crescent*. Westport, CT: Praeger, 1998.

Humphreys, R. Stephen. *Between Memory and Desire: The Middle East in a Troubled Age*. Berkeley, CA: University of California Press, 1999.

Jansen, Johannes J.G. *The Dual Nature of Islamic Fundamentalism*. Ithaca, NY: Cornell University Press, 1997.

Kedourie, Elie. *Politics in the Middle East*. Oxford: Oxford University Press, 1992.

Kienle, Eberhard. *Ba'th vs. Ba'th: The Conflict Between Syria and Iraq 1968–1989*. London: I.B. Tauris, 1990.

Kirpichenko, Vadim. *Intelligence Service: Faces and Personalities*. Moscow: Geya, 1998. [R]

Kohn, Hans. *Nationalism and Imperialism in the Hither East*. New York, NY: Howard Fertig, 1969 (reprint of the 1932 edition).

Korany, Bahgat, Paul Noble, and Rex Brynen (eds). *The Many Faces of National Security in the Arab World*. New York, NY: St. Martin's Press, 1993.

Krakhmalov, Sergei. *Notes of a Military Attache*. Moscow: Russkaya Razvedka, 2000. [R]

Kramer, Martin. *Arab Awakening and Islamic Revival*. New Brunswick, NJ: Transaction Publishers, 1996.

Landau, Jacob M. *The Politics of Pan-Islam: Ideology and Organization*. Oxford: Clarendon Press, 1990.

Lewis, Bernard. *The Middle East: A Brief History of the Last 2,000 Years*. New York, NY: Scribner, 1995.

Lewis, Bernard. *The Multiple Identities of the Middle East*. New York, NY: Schocken Books, 1998.

Litvak, Meir (ed). *Islam and Democracy in the Arab World*. Tel-Aviv: HaKibbutz haMeuhad, 1997. [H]

Luciani, Giacomo (ed). *The Arab State*. Berkeley, CA: University of California Press, 1990.

Maddy-Weitzman, Bruce and Efraim Inbar (eds). *Religious Radicalism in the Greater Middle East*. London: Frank Cass, 1997.

Miller, Judith. *God Has Ninety-Nine Names: Reporting From a Militant Middle East*. New York, NY: Simon & Schuster, 1996.

Mlechin, Leonid M. *Yevgeny Primakov: The History of One Career*. Moscow: Tsentrpoligraf, 1999. [R]

Moten, Abdul Rashid. *Political Science: An Islamic Perspective*. New York, NY: St. Martin's Press, 1996.

Moussalli, Ahmad S. (ed). *Islamic Fundamentalism: Myths and Realities*. Reading: Ithaca, 1998.

Mufti, Malik. *Sovereign Creations: Pan-Arabism and Political Order in Syria and Iraq*. Ithaca, NY: Cornell University Press, 1996.

Murden, Simon W. *Islam, the Middle East, and the New Global Hegemony*. Boulder, CO: Lynne Rienner, 2002.

Pipes, Daniel. *The Hidden Hand: Middle East Fears of Conspiracy*. New York, NY: St. Martin's Press, 1996.

Primakov, Yevgeny M. *Years in Big-Time Politics*. Moscow: Sovershenno Sekretno, 1999. [R]

Primakov, Yevgeny M. *Eight Months Plus. . .* Moscow: Mysl', 2001. [R]

Pryce-Jones, David. *The Closed Circle: An Interpretation of the Arabs*. New York, NY: Harper & Row, 1989.

Pyrlin, Ye.D. *Middle Eastern Labyrinth*. Moscow: Gruppa Gross, 1996. [R]

Quandt, William B. *Peace Process: American Diplomacy and the Arab-Israeli Conflict Since 1967*. Washington, D.C.: The Brookings Institution, 1993.

Rejwan, Nissim. *Arabs Face the Modern World: Religious, Cultural and Political Responses to the West*. Gainesville, FL: University Press of Florida, 1998.

Salem, Paul. *Bitter Legacy, Ideology and Politics in the Arab World*. Syracuse, NY: Syracuse University Press, 1994.

Salvatore, Armando. *Islam and the Political Discourse of Modernity*. Reading: Ithaca Press, 1997.

Shadid, Anthony. *Legacy of the Prophet: Despots, Democrats and the New Politics of Islam*. Boulder, CO: Westview, 2001.

Shay, Shaul. *Terror in the Name of the Imam: Twenty Years of Shiite Terrorism 1979–1999*. Herzeliya: ICT, 2001. [H]

Shohamy, Elana and Smadar Donitsa-Schmidt. *Jews Vs. Arabs: Language Attitudes and Stereotypes*. Tel-Aviv: Tami Steinmetz Center, 1998.

Sidahmed, Abdel Salam & Anoushiravan Ehteshami. *Islamic Fundamentalism*. Boulder, CO: Westview, 1996.

Sonn, Tamara. *Between Qur'an and Crown: The Challenge of Political Legitimacy in the Arab World*. Boulder, CO: Westview, 1990.

Taheri, Amir. *The Cauldron: The Middle East Behind the Headlines*. London: Huchinson, 1988.

Tal, Nachman. *Islamic Fundamentalism: The Case of Egypt and Jordan*. Tel-Aviv: Papirus, 1999. [H]

Tibi, Bassam. *Arab Nationalism*. New York, NY: St. Martin's Press, 1981 (1971).

Vatikiotis, P.J. *Islam and the State*. London: Croom Helm 1987.

Viorst, Milton. *Sandcastles: The Arabs in Search of the Modern World*. New York, NY: Alfred A. Knopf, 1994.

Viorst, Milton. *In the Shadow of the Prophet: The Struggle for the Soul of Islam*. New York, NY: Anchor Books, 1998.

Wolfsfeld, Gadi. *Constructing News About Peace*. Tel-Aviv: Tami Steinmetz Center, 1997.

Zubaida, Sami. *Islam, the People and the State*. London: I.B. Tauris, 1993.

Egypt

Abdo, Geneive. *No God But God: Egypt and the Triumph of Islam*. Oxford: Oxford University Press, 2000.

Aftandilian, Gregory L. *Egypt's Bid for Arab Leadership: Implications for U.S. Policy*. New York, NY: Council on Foreign Relations, 1993.

Asya, Ilan. *The Dayan Syndrom: Four Wars and One Peace—The Concealed Factor.* Tel-Aviv: Yediot Ahronot, 1995.

Asya, Ilan. *Arab Territorial Continuity: a Core or a Cause for the Arab-Israeli Conflict.* Ariel: ACPR, 1998.

el-Awaisi, Adb al-Fattah Muhammad. *The Muslim Brothers and the Palestine Question 1928–1947.* London: Tauris Academic Studies, 1998.

Dowek, Ephraim. *Israeli-Egyptians Relations 1980–2000.* London: Frank Cass, 2001.

Gaffney, Patrick. *The Prophet's Pulpit: Islamic Preaching in Contemporary Egypt.* Berkeley, CA: University of California Press, 1994.

Hatina, Meir. *Islam in Modern Egypt.* Tel-Aviv: HaKibbutz heMeuhad, 2000. [H]

Lorenz, Joseph P. *Egypt and the Arabs: Foreign Policy and the Search for National Identity.* Boulder, CO: Westview, 1990.

al-Mahdi, Amin. *The Other Opinion.* Tel-Aviv: HaKibbutz haMeuhad, 2001. [H]

Marr, Phebe (ed). *Egypt at the Crossroads: Domestic Stability and Regional Role.* Washington, DC: NDU Press, 1999.

Pine, Shawn. *The Egyptian Threat and the Prospects for War in the Middle East.* shaarei Tikva: ACPR, 2000.

Talhami, Ghada Hashem. *Palestine and Egyptian National Identity.* Westport, CT: Praeger, 1992.

Weaver, Mary Anne. *A Portrait of Egypt: A Journey Through the World of Militant Islam.* New York, NY: Farrar, Strauss and Giroux, 1999.

Iraq and the Gulf Wars

Aburish, Said K. *Saddam Hussein: The Politics of Revenge.* New York, NY: Bloomsbury, 2000.

Ahrari, M.E. (ed). *The Gulf and International Security: The 1980s and Beyond.* New York, NY: St. Martin's Press, 1989.

Algosaibi, Ghazi A., *The Gulf Crisis: An Attempt to Understand.* London: KPI, 1991.

Ali, Omar. *Crisis in the Arabian Gulf: An Independent Iraqi View.* Westport, CT: Praeger, 1993.

Amos, Deborah. *Lines in the Sand: Desert Storm and the Remaking of the Arab World.* New York, NY: Simon and Schuster, 1992.

Anderson, Ewan W. and Khalil H Rashidian. *Iraq and the Continuing Middle East Crisis.* New York, NY: St. Martin's Press, 1991.

Baram, Amatzia. *Culture, History & Ideology in the Formation of Ba'athist Iraq, 1968–89.* New York, NY: St. Martin's Press, 1991.

Baram, Amatzia and Barry Rubin (eds). *Iraq's Road to War.* New York, NY: St. Martin's Press, 1993.

Baram, Amatzia. *Building Toward Crisis: Saddam Husayn's Strategy for Survival.* Washington, D.C.: Washington Institute for Near East Policy, 1998.

Belonogov, Aleksandr M. *The Ministry of Foreign Affairs, the Kremlin, the Kuwait Crisis.* Moscow: Olma-Press, 2001. [R]

Bengio, Ofra (ed). *Saddam Speaks on the Gulf Crisis: A Collection of Documents.* Tel-Aviv: Dayan Center, 1992.

Bengio, Ofra. *Saddam's Iraq: Political Discourse and the Language of Power.* Tel-Aviv: HaKibbutz haMeuhad, 1996. [H]

Bin, Alberto, Richard Hill, and Archer Jones. *Desert Storm: A Forgotten War.* Westport, CT: Praeger, 1998.

Bulloch, John and Harvey Morris. *Saddam's War: The Origins of the Kuwait Conflict and the International Response.* London: Faber and Faber, 1991.

Clawson, Patrick L. (ed). *Iraq Strategy Review.* Washington, D.C.: Washington Institute for Near East Policy, 1998.

Cockburn, Andrew and Patrick Cockburn. *Out of the Ashes: The Resurrection of Saddam Hussein.* New York, NY: HarperCollins, 1999.

Cordesman, Anthony H., *After the Storm: The Changing Military Balance in the Middle East.* Boulder, CO: Westview, 1993.

Cordesman, Anthony H., *Iran and Iraq: The Threat From the Northern Gulf.* Boulder, CO: Westview, 1994.

Cordesman, Anthony H., *Iraq and the War of Sanctions.* Westport, CT: Praeger, 1999.

Danchev, Alex and Dan Keohane (eds). *International perspectives on the Gulf Conflict 1990–91.* London: MacMillan, 1994.

Darwish, Adel & Gregory Alexander. *Unholy Babylon: The Secret History of Saddam's War.* New York, NY: St. Martin's Press, 1991.

Davies, Charles (ed). *After the War: Iraq, Iran and the Arab Gulf.* Chichester: Carden Publications, 1990.

Faour, Muhammad. *The Arab World After Desert Storm.* Washington, D.C.: U.S. Institute of Peace Press, 1993.

Francona, Rick. *Ally to Adversary: An Eyewitness Account of Iraq's Fall From Grace.* Annapolis, MD: Naval Institute Press, 1999.

Freedman, Lawrence and Efraim Karsh. *The Gulf War 1990–1991: Diplomacy and War in the New World Order.* Princeton, NJ: Princeton University Press, 1993.

Hamza, Khidhir. *Saddam's Bombmaker.* New York, NY: Scribner, 2000.

Hazelton, Fran. *Iraq Since the Gulf War: Prospects for Democracy.* London: Zed Books, 1994.

Heikal, Mohamed. *Illusions of Triumph: An Arab View of the Gulf War.* London: HarperCollins, 1992.

Henderson, Simon. *Instant Empire: Saddam Hussein's Ambition for Iraq.* San Francisco, CA: Mercury House, 1991.

Hiro, Dilip. *Desert Shield to Desert Storm: The Second Gulf War.* London: Paladin, 1992.

Hiro, Dilip. *Neighbors, Not Friends: Iraq and Iran After the Gulf Wars.* London: Routledge, 2001.

Ibrahim, Ibrahim (ed). *The Gulf Crisis: Background and Consequences.* Washington, D.C.: Center for Contemporary Arab Studies, 1992.

Ismael, Tareq Y. and Jacqueline S. Ismael (eds). *The Gulf War and the New World Order: International Relations of the Middle East.* Gainesville, FL: University Press of Florida, 1994.

Jacquard, Roland. *The Secret Cards of the Gulf War.* Paris: Edition-1, 1991.

Jentleson, Bruce W. *With Friends Like These: Reagan, Bush, and Saddam 1982–1990.* New York, NY: W.W.Norton, 1994.

Karsh, Efraim and Inari Rautsi. *Saddam Hussein: A Political Biography.* New York, NY: Free Press, 1991.

Khadduri, Majid and Edmund Ghareeb. *War in the Gulf 1990–91: The Iraq-Kuwait Conflict and Its Implications.* Oxford: Oxford University Press, 1997.

Khaled bin Sultan with Patrick Seale. *Desert Warrior: A Personal View of the Gulf War by the Joint Forces Commander.* London: HarperCollins, 1995.

Khalidi, Walid. *The Gulf Crisis: Origins and Consequences.* Washington, D.C.: Institute for Palestinian Studies, 1991.

al-Khalil, Samir (pseud). *Republic of Fear: The Politics of Modern Iraq.* Berkeley, CA: University of California Press, 1989.

Levran, Aharon. *The Storm's Interpretation: Strategic Implications of the Second Gulf War.* Ramat-Gan: BESA, 1993. [H]

Mohamedou, Mohammad-Mahmoud. *Iraq and the Second Gulf War: State Building and Regional Security.* San Francisco, CA: Austin & Winfield, 1998.

Mottale, Morris M. *The Origins of the Gulf Wars.* Lanham, MD: UPA, 2001.

Munro, Alan. *An Embassy at War: Politics and Diplomacy Behind the Gulf War.* Washington, D.C.: Brassey's, 1996.

Palmer, Michael A. *Guardians of the Gulf.* New York, NY: Free Press, 1992.

Pelletiere, Stephen C., Douglas V. Johnson II, and Leif R. Rosenberge. *Iraqi Power and U.S. Security in the Middle East.* Carlisle Barracks, PA: U.S. Army War College, 1990.

Pelletiere, Stephen C., and Douglas V. Johnson II. *Lessons Learned: The Iran-Iraq War*. Carlisle Barracks, PA: U.S. Army War College, 1991.

Piscatori, James (ed). *Islamic Fundamentalisms and the Gulf Crisis*. Chicago, IL: American Academy of Arts and Sciences, 1991.

Primakov, Evgueni. *Mission to Baghdad: History of Secret Negotiations*. Paris: Editions du Seuil, 1991. [F]

Rahman, H. The *Making of the Gulf War: Origins of Kuwait's Long-Standing Territorial Dispute with Iraq*. Reading: Ithaca Press, 1997.

Ramadan, Michael. *In the Shadow of Saddam*. Auckland: Greenzone, 1999.

Rashid, Nasser Ibrahim and Esber Ibrahim Shaheen. *Saudi Arabia and the Gulf War*. Joplin, MO: International Institute of Technology, 1992.

Ritter, Scott. *Endgame: Solving the Iraq Problem Once and For All*. New York, NY: Simon & Schuster, 1999.

Rubin, Barry. *Cauldron of Turmoil: America in the Middle East*. New York, NY: Harcourt Brace Jovanovich, 1992.

Salinger, Pierre and Eric Laurent. *The Gulf War: The Secret Dossier*. Paris: Olivier Orban, 1991. [F]

Salinger, Pierre and Eric Laurent. *Secret Dossier: The Hidden Agenda Behind the Gulf War*. New York, NY: Penguin, 1991.

Sciolino, Elaine. *The Outlaw State: Saddam Hussein's Quest for Power and the Gulf Crisis*. New York, NY: John Wiley & Sons, 1991.

Sumaida, Hussein with Carole Jerome. *Circle of Fear: A Renegade's Journey From the Mossad to the Iraqi Secret Service*. Toronto: Stoddart, 1991.

Teicher, Howard and Gayle Radley Teicher. *Twin Pillars to Desert Storm: America's Flawed Vision in the Middle East From Nixon to Bush*. New York, NY: William Morrow, 1993.

Trevan, Tim. *Saddam's Secrets: The Hunt for Iraq's Hidden Weapons*. London: HarperCollins, 1999.

Wurmser, David. *Tyranny's Ally: America's Failure to Defeat Saddam Hussein*. Washington, D.C.: AEI Press, 1999.

Yahia, Latif and Karl Wendl. *I Was Saddam's Son*. New York, NY: Arcade, 1997.

Yariv, Aharon (ed). *War in the Gulf: Implications for Israel*. Tel-Aviv: JCSS, 1992.

Israel

Arens, Moshe. *Broken Covenant: American Foreign Policy and the Crisis Between the U.S. and Israel*. New York, NY: Simon & Schuster, 1995.

Bar-Joseph, Uri (ed). *Israel's National Security Towards the 21st Century*. London: Frank Cass, 2001.

Barder, Christopher. *Oslo's Gift of "Peace": The Destruction of Israel's Security*. Shaarei Tikva: ACPR, 2001.

Begin, Ze'ev Binyamin. *A Sad Story*. Tel-Aviv: Yediot Ahronot, 2000.

Beilin, Yossi. *Touching the Peace*. Tel-Aviv: Yediot Ahronot, 1997. [H]

Beilin, Yossi. *Touching Peace: From the Oslo Accord to a Final Agreement*. New York, NY: Weinfeld and Nicholson, 1999.

Ben-Ami, Shlomo. *A Place for Everybody: Eli Bar-Navi Talks With Shlomo Ben-Ami*. Tel-Aviv: HaKibbutz haMeuhad, 1998. [H]

Bentsur, Eytan. *Making Peace: A First-Hand Account of the Arab-Israeli Peace Process*. Westport, CT: Praeger, 2001.

Bergman, Ahron. *Israel's Wars: 1947–93*. London: Routledge, 2000.

Bovin, Aleksandr Ye. *Five Years Among Jews and Foreign Service Personnel*. Moscow: Zakharov, 2000. [R]

Carmel, Hezi (ed.). *Intelligence for Peace*. Tel-Aviv: Yediot Ahronot, 1998. [H]

Cohen, Eliot A., Michael J. Eisenstadt, and Andrew J. Bacevich. *Knives, Tanks and Missiles: Israel's Security Revolution*. Washington, D.C.: The Washington Institute for Near East Policy, 1998.

Doriel, Joseph. *Out of Running-Mad Systems*. Herzeliya: Atheret, 1996. [H]

Dror, Yehezkel. *Grand-Strategic Thinking for Israel*. Ariel: ACPR, 1998.

Einhorn, Talia. *The Arab-Israeli Peace Mirage: Legal Perspectives*. Shaarei Tikva: ACPR, 2002.

Gilbert, Martin. *Israel: A History*. New York, NY: William Morrow, 1998.

Gillon, Carmi. *Shin-Beth Between the Schisms*. Tel-Aviv: Yediot Ahronot, 2000. [H]

Golan, Haggai (ed). *Israel's Security Web: Core Issues of Israel's National Security in Its Sixth Decade*. Tel-Aviv: Ma'arachot, 2001. [H]

Kanovsky, Eliyahu. *Arab-Israel Peace Agreements Since Camp David: A Look Backward and a Look Ahead*. Ariel: ACPR, 1997.

Katz, Samuel. *Battleground: Fact & Fantasy in Palestine*. New York, NY: Steimatzky/Shapolsky, 1985.

Katz, Samuel M. *The Hunt for the Engineer: How Israeli Agents Tracked the Hamas Master Bomber*. New York, NY: Fromm International, 1999.

Kimche, David. *The Last Option: After Nasser, Arafat & Saddam Hussein*. New York, NY: Charles Scribner's Sons, 1991.

LaGuardia, Anton. *Holy Land Unholy War*. London: John Murray, 2001.

Levran, Aharon. *Israeli Strategy After Desert Storm: Lessons of the Second Gulf War*. London: Frank Cass, 1997.

Levran, Aharon. *The Decline of Israeli Deterrence*. Shaarei Tikva: ACPR, 2001.

Levran, Aharon. *Decisive Power*. Shaarei Tikva: ACPR, 2002. [H]

Misgav, Haim. *Talks with Yitzhak Shamir*. Tel Aviv: Sifriyat Poalim, 1997. [H]

Naveh, Dan. *Executive Secrets*. Tel-Aviv: Yediot Ahronot, 1999. [H]

Netanyahu, Benjamin. *A Place Among the Nations: Israel and the World*. New York, NY: Bantam, 1993.

Peres, Shimon. *The New Middle East*. New York, NY: Henry Holt, 1993.

Peres, Shimon. *Battling for Peace*. New York, NY: Random House, 1995.

Peres, Shimon and Robert Littell. *For the Future of Israel*. Baltimore, MD: Johns Hopkins University Press, 1998.

Perry, Yaakov. *Strike First*. Tel-Aviv: Keshet, 1999. [H]

Rabin, Yitzhak. *The Rabin Memoirs*. Berkeley, CA: University of California Press, 1996.

Rabinovich, Itamar. *Waging Peace: Israel and the Arabs at the End of the Century*. New York, NY: Farrar, Straus and Giroux, 1999.

Rejwan, Nissim. *Israel's Place in the Middle East: A Pluralist Perspective*. Gainesville, FL: University Press of Florida, 1999.

Sagie, Uri. *Lights Within the Fog*. Tel-Aviv: Yediot Ahronot, 1998. [H]

Savir, Uri. *The Process: 1,100 Days That Changed the Middle East*. New York, NY: Random House, 1998.

Shamir, Yitzhak. *Summing-Up*. Tel-Aviv: Edanim, 1994. [H]

Sherman, Martin. *Paradigms of Peace for the Middle East*. Ariel: ACPR, 1998.

Shoham, Dany. *Chemical and Biological Weapons in the Arab Countries and Iran An Existential Threat to Israel?* Shaarei Tikva: ACPR, 2001.

Sohar, Ezrah. *A Concubine in the Middle East: American Israeli Relations*. Jerusalem: Gefen, 1999.

Stav, Arieh (ed). *Israel at the Crossroads*. Ariel: ACPR, 1997.

Stav, Arieh (ed). *Political Strategy in the Era of Systemic Breakdown*. Tel-Aviv: Modan, 1997. [H]

Stav, Arieh. *Yitzhak Rabin: "... Palestine Will Rise Upon the Ruins of the State of Israel."* Shaarei Tikva: ACPR, 2000.

Sutton, Rafi. *Lost Opportunities*. Tel-Aviv: Ma'ariv, 1994. [H]

Tal, Israel. *National Security: The Few Against the Many*. Tel-Aviv: Dvir, 1996. [H]

Tira, Ron. *Forming an Israeli Policy Toward Syria*. Tel-Aviv: Yediot Ahronot, 2000. [H]

Tsiddon-Chatto, Yoash. *After Oslo: The Quest for Political Stability*. Ariel: ACPR, 1998.

Tsiddon-Chatto, Yoash. *Israel-Arabia: Eye to Eye With the Future*. Shaarei Tikva: ACPR, 2001.

Tsiddon-Chatto, Yoash. *Non-Classified Realities Affecting Israel's Air Force 2005–2010*. Shaarei Tikva: ACPR, 2002.

Yaniv, Avner. *Politics and Strategy in Israel*. Tel-Aviv: Sifriat Poalim, 1994. [H]

Jordan

Bligh, Alexsander. *Jordanian-Israeli Strategic Partnership in Historical Perspective.* Ariel: ACPR, 1998.

Dallas, Roland. *King Hussein: A Life on the Edge.* London: Profile, 1999.

Israeli, Raphael. *The Israel-Jordan Agreement: A Missed Opportunity.* Ariel: ACPR, 1998.

Segev, Samuel. *Crossing the Jordan: Israel's Hard Road to Peace.* New York, NY: St. Martin's, 1998.

Zak, Moshe. *Hussein Makes Peace.* Ramat Gan: BESA, 1996. [H]

Lebanon

Amir, Ahron (ed). *The Black Book: South Lebanon, a Story of Flight, Betrayal and Disgrace.* Jerusalem: Carmel, 2001. [H]

Hagopian, Elaine C. *Amal and the Palestinians: Understanding the Battle of the Camps.* Belmont, MA: Association of Arab-American University Graduates, 1985.

Hatem, Robert M. ("Cobra"). *From Israel to Damascus: The Painful Road of Blood, Betrayal, and Deception.* Pride International Publications, 1999.

Jaber, Hala. *Hezbollah: Born With a Vengeance.* New York, NY: Columbia University Press, 1997.

Kramer, Martin. *Fadlallah: The Compass of Hizbullah.* Tel-Aviv: Dayan Center, 1998. [H]

Ranstorp, Magnus. *The Hizb'Allah in Lebanon.* New York, NY: St. Martin's, 1997

Saad-Ghorayeb, Amal. *Hizbu'llah: Politics and Religion.* London: Pluto, 2002.

Shapira, Shimon. *Hizbullah: Between Iran and Lebanon.* Tel-Aviv: HaKibbutz haMeuhad, 2000. [H]

Soueid, Mahmoud. *Israel in Lebanon.* Beirut: Revue d'etudes Palestiniennes, 2000. [F]

Palestinian Issues

Abbas, Mahmoud (Abu-Mazen). *Through Secret Channels.* London: Garnet Publishing, 1995.

Abboushi, W.F. *The Unmaking of Palestine.* Brattleboro, VT: Amana, 1990.

Abu-Amr, Ziad. *Islamic Fundamentalism in the West Bank and Gaza.* Bloomington, IN: Indiana University Press, 1994.

Abu-Iyad [Salah Khalaf] & Eric Rouleau. *Without a Motherland.* Jerusalem: Mifras, 1979. [H]

Abu-Odeh, Adnan. *Jordanians, Palestinians & The Hashemite Kingdom in the Middle East Peace Process.* Washington, D.C.: United States Institute of Peace Press,1999.

Aburish, Said K. *Cry Palestine.* Boulder, CO: Westview Press, 1993.

Aburish, Said K. *Arafat: From Defender to Dictator.* New York, NY: Bloomsbury, 1998.

Alestin, F. *Palestine in the Zionist Noose.* Moscow: Yuridicheskya Literatura, 1988. [R]

Alexander, Yonah & Sinai Joshua. *Terrorism: The PLO Connection.* New York, NY: Crane Russak, 1989.

Arnon-Ohanna, Yuval & Aryeh Y. Yodfat. *PLO: Portrait of an Organization.* Tel-Aviv: Sifriyat Maariv, 1985. [H]

Aruri, Nasser H. *The Obstruction of Peace.* Monroe, MN: Common Courage Press, 1995.

Bechor, Guy. *Lexicon of the PLO* (updated edition). Tel-Aviv: Ma'arachot, 1995. [H]

Becker, Jillian. *The PLO.* New York, NY: St. Martin's Press, 1984.

Berger, Marshall J. and Thomas A. Indinopulos. *Jerusalem's Holy Places & the Peace Process.* Washington, D.C.: The Washington Institute for Near East Policy, 1998.

Bodansky, Yossef. *Arafat's "Peace Process."* Ariel: ACPR, 1997.

Brynen, Rex. *Sanctuary and Survival: The PLO in Lebanon.* Boulder, CO: Westview Press, 1990.

Brynen, Rex (ed.). *Echoes of the Intifadah.* Boulder, CO: Westview Press, 1991.

Cattan, Henry. *The Palestine Question.* London: Croom Helm, 1988.

Cubert, Harold M. *The PFLP's Changing Role in the Middle East.* London: Frank Cass, 1997.

Dmitriyev, Ye. *The Palestinian Tragedy.* Moscow: International Relations, 1986. [R]

Ehrenfeld, Rachel. *Arafat: the World's "Blind Spot."* Ariel: ICPR, 1997.

Farsoun, Samih K. & Christina E. Zacharia. *The Palestinians: A Stateless Nation.* Boulder, CO: Westview Press, 1997.

Fedoseyev P.N. (ed.). *The Palestine Problem: Aggression, Resistance, Ways of Settlement.* Moscow: USSR Academy of Science, 1984.

Frangi, Abdallah. *The PLO and Palestine.* London: Zed Books, 1983.

Giacaman, G. & D.J. Lonning (eds). *After Oslo: New Realities, Old Problems.* London: Pluto Press, 1998.

Gilber, Gad G. & Asher Susser (eds.). *At the Core of the Conflict: The Intifadah.* Tel-Aviv: HaKibutz haMeuhad, 1992. [H]

Gowers, Andrew & Tony Walker. *Behind the Myth: Yasser Arafat and the Palestinian Revolution.* New York, NY: Olive Branch Press, 1992.

Gresh, Alain. *The PLO: The Struggle Within* (2nd Edition). London: Zed Books, 1988.

Gresh, Alain & Vidal Dominique. *The Middle East: War Without End?* London: Lawrence and Wishart, 1988.

al-Hamad, Jawad and Eyad al-Bargothi (eds). *A Study in the Political Ideology of the Islamic Resistance Movement (HAMAS) 1987–1996.* Amman: Dar el-Bashir, 1997. [E & A]

Harkabi, Yehoshafat. *The Palestinian Covenant and its Meaning.* Jerusalem: 1974. [H]

Hart, Alan. *Arafat: Terrorist or Peacemaker?* London: Sidgwick & Jackson, 1984.

Hatina, Meir. *Palestinian Radicalism: The Islamic Jihad Movement.* Tel-Aviv: Dayan Center, 1994. [H]

Hatina, Meir. *Islam and Salvation in Palestine: The Islamic Jihad Movement.* Tel-Aviv: Dayan Center, 2001.

Havakook, Ya'acov and Saleh Shakib. *Islamic Terrorism: Profile of the HAMAS Movement.* Tel-Aviv: Ma'arachot, 1999. [H]

Hess, Amirah. *To Drink the Water From the Sea in Gaza.* Tel-Aviv: Am Oved, 1997. [H]

Hiro, Dilip. *Sharing the Promised Land: An Interwoven Tale of Israelis and Palestinians.* London: Hodder & Stoughton, 1999.

Hirschfeld, Yair. *Oslo: The Formula for Peace.* Tel-Aviv: Am Oved, 2000. [H]

Hroub, Khaled. *Hamas: Political Thought and Practice.* Washington, D.C.: Institute for Palestinian Studies, 2000.

Hudson, Michael C. (ed.). *The Palestinians: New Directions.* Washington, D.C.: Center for Contemporary Arab Studies, 1990.

Hunter, F. Robert. *The Palestinian Uprising.* Berkeley, CA: University of California Press, 1991.

Hussein, Mehmood. *The Palestine Liberation Organization.* Delhi: University Publishers (India), 1974.

Inbari, Pinhas. *The Palestinian Option.* Jerusalem: Karmel Pres, 1989. [H]

Inbari, Pinhas. *Triangle on the Jordan.* Jerusalem: Cana, 1982. [H]

Inbari, Pinhas. *With Broken Swords.* Tel-Aviv: Ma'arahot, 1994. [H]

Israeli, Raphael. *Fundamentalist Islam and Israel.* Lanham, MD: UPA, 1993.

Israeli, Raphael. *Muslim Fundamentalism in Israel.* London: Brassey's (UK), 1993.

Israeli, Raphael (ed.). *PLO in Lebanon.* New York, NY: St. Martin's, 1983.

Israeli, Raphael and Shlomo Sharan. *Education, Identity State Building and the Peace Process*. Shaarei Tikva: ACPR, 1999.

Kass, Ilana and Brad O'Neill. *The Deadly Embrace*. Lanham, MD: University Press of America, 1997.

Khalidi, Rashid. *Under Siege: PLO Decision Making During the 1982 War*. New York, NY: Columbia University Press, 1986.

Khalidi, Rashid. *At a Critical Juncture*. Washington, D.C.: The Center for Contemporary Arab Studies, 1989.

Khalidi, Rashid. *Palestinian Identity: The Construction of a Modern National Consciousness*. New York, NY: Columbia University Press, 1997.

Kimchi, Shaul; Shmuel Even, and Gerald Post. *Yasser Arafat: Psychological Profile and Strategic Analysis*. Herzeliya: ICT, 2001. [H]

Klein, Menachem. *The PLO and the Intifadah: Between Euphoria and Despair*. Tel-Aviv: The Dayan Center, 1991. [H]

Klein, Menachem. *Shattering a Taboo: The Contacts Toward a Permanent Status Agreement in Jerusalem 1994–2001*. Jerusalem: The Jerusalem Institute for Israel Studies, 2001. [H]

Klein, Yitzhak. *Israel's War with the Palestinians: Sources, Political Objectives, and Operational Means*. Shaarei Tikva: ACPR, 2001.

Kozodoy, Neal (ed). *The Mideast Peace Process: An Autopsy*. San Francisco, CA: Encounter Books, 2002.

Kudryavtsev, A.V. *The Muslim World and the Palestinian Problem*. Moscow: Nauka, 1990. [R]

Kurz, Anat (ed.). *Islamic Terrorism and Israel*. Tel-Aviv: The Jaffe Center, 1993. [H]

Laffin, John. *The PLO Connection*. London: Corgi Books, 1982.

Layish, Aharon (ed.). *The Arabs in Israel: Between Religious Revival and National Awakening*. Jerusalem: HaMizrah heHadash, Magnus, 1989. [H]

Livingstone, Neil C. & David Halevy. *Inside the PLO*. New York, NY: Morrow, 1990.

Luft, Gal. *The Palestinian Security Forces: Capabilities and Effects on the Arab-Israeli Military Balance*. Shaarei Tikva: ACPR, 2001.

Makovsky, David. *Making Peace With the PLO*. Boulder, CO: Westview Press, 1996.

Maoz, Moshe. *Palestinian Leadership on the West Bank*. London: Frank Cass, 1984.

Maoz, Moshe & Kedar B"Z (eds.). *The Palestinian National Movement: From Confrontation to Reconciliation?* Tel-Aviv: Ma'arahot, 1996. [H]

Maslaha, Nur. *Imperial Israel and the Palestinians*. London: Pluto Press, 2000.

Merari, Ariel & Shlomi Elad. *The International Dimension of Palestinian Terrorism*. Tel-Aviv: HaKibutz haMeuhad, 1986. [H]

Milton-Edwards, Beverly. *Islamic Politics in Palestine*. London: Tauris, 1996.

Mishal, Shaul. *The PLO under Arafat: Between Gun and Olive Branch*. New Haven, CT: Yale University Press, 1986.

Mishal, Shaul & Reuben Aharoni. *Stones Are Not Everything: The Intifadah and the Flyers as Weapons*. Tel-Aviv: HaKibutz haMeuhad, 1989. [H]

Mishal, Shaul & Avraham Sela. *HAMAS: A Behavioral Profile*. Tel-Aviv: Tami Steinmetz Center, 1997.

Mishal, Shaul & Avraham Sela. *The HAMAS Wind: Violence and Coexistence*. Tel-Aviv: Yediot Ahronot, 1999. [H]

Mussalam, Dr. Sami. *The Palestine Liberation Organization*. Brattleboro, VT: Amana, 1990.

Nasr, Kameel B. *Arab and Israeli Terrorism*. Jefferson, NC: McFarland, 1997.

Nassar, Jamal R. *The Palestine Liberation Organization*. New York, NY: Praeger, 1991.

Norton, Augustus Richard & Martin H. Greenberg (eds.). *The International Relations of the Palestine Liberation Organization*. 1989.

Nusse, Andrea. *Muslim Palestine: The Ideology of HAMAS*. Amsterdam: Harwood Academic Publishers, 1998.

Paolucci, Henry. *Zionism, the Superpowers, and the PLO*. New York, NY: Griffon House, 1982.

Pavlowsky, Agnes. *HAMAS or The Mirror of Palestinian Frustrations*. Paris: L'Harmattan, 2000. [F]

Paz, Reuven. *Suicide and Jihad in Palestinian Radical Islam*. Tel-Aviv: Dayan Center, 1998. [H]

Paz, Reuven. *"Sleeping With the Enemy": A Reconciliation Process as Part of Counter-Terrorism: Is Hamas Capable of "Hudna"?* Herzeliya: ICT, 1998.

Peters, Joan. *From Time Immemorial: The Origins of the Arab-Jewish conflict Over Palestine*. New York, NY: Harper & Row, 1984.

Pyrlin, Yevgeny D. *Hundred Years of Fighting (1897–1997): Genesis, Evolution, Current Condition and Perspectives for the Resolution of the Palestinian Problem*. Moscow: Rosspen, 2001. [R]

Rabie, Mohamed. *U.S.-PLO Dialogue: Secret Diplomacy and Conflict Resolution*. Gainesville, FL: University Press of Florida, 1995.

Rekhess, Elie. *The Arabs in Israeli Politics: Dilemmas of Identity*. Tel-Aviv: Dayan Center, 1998. [H]

Rekhess, Elie & Tamar Yegnes, (eds.). *Arab Politics in Israel at a Crossroad.* Tel-Aviv: Dayan Center, 1995. [H]

Rigby, Andrew. *Living the Intifadah.* London: Zed, 1991.

Robinson, Glenn E. *Building a Palestinian State: The Incomplete Revolution.* Bloomington, IN: Indiana University Press, 1997.

Rubin, Barry. *The PLO's New Policy: Evolution Until Victory?* Washington, D.C.: The Washington Institute for Near East Policy, 1989.

Rubin, Barry. *Revolution Until Victory?* Cambridge, MA: Harvard University Press, 1994.

Rubin, Barry. *The Transformation of Palestinian Politics.* Cambridge, MA: Harvard University Press, 1999.

Rubinstein, Danny. *The Fig Tree Embrace: The "Right of Return" of the Palestinians.* Jerusalem: Keter, 1990. [H]

Rubinstein, Danny. *The Mystery of Arafat.* South Royalton, VT: Steerforth Press, 1995.

Rubinstein, Danny. *Arafat: A Portrait.* Tel Aviv: Zmora-Bitan, 2001.

Sahilyeh, Emile F. *The PLO After the Lebanon War.* Boulder, CO: Westview Press, 1986.

Sahilyeh, Emile F. *In Search of Leadership.* Washington, D.C.: The Brookings Institution, 1988.

Sayigh, Yezid. *Armed Struggle and the Search for Peace: The Palestinian National Movement, 1949–1993.* Oxford: Clarendon Press, 1997.

Shabath, Yehezkel. *HAMAS and the Peace Process.* Shaarei Tikva: ACPR, 2001.

Schiff, Ze'ev & Ehud Ya'ari. *Intifadah.* Jerusalem: Schocken, 1990. [H]

Schoenberg, Harris O. *A Mandate for Terror.* New York, NY: Shapolsky Books, 1989.

Sela, Michal (ed. & tr.). *Palestinian Society Facing the Intermediary Phase.* Tel-Aviv: Tami Steinmetz Center, 1995. [H]

Shadid, Mohammed K. *The United States and the Palestinians.* New York, NY: St. Martin's Press, 1981.

Shaked, Ronni & Aviva Shabi. *HAMAS.* Jerusalem: Keter, 1994. [H]

Shalev, Aryeh. *The Intifadah: Causes and Effects.* Tel-Aviv: The Jaffe Center for Strategic Studies, 1991.

Shemesh, Moshe. *The Palestinian Entity 1959–1974: Arab Politics and the PLO.* London: Frank Cass, 1996.

Sher, Gilead. *Just Beyond Reach: The Israeli-Palestinian Peace Negotiations 1999–2001.* Tel-Aviv: Yediot Ahronot, 2001. [H]

Shilo, Gideon. *Israeli Arabs in the Eyes of the Arab States and the PLO.* Jerusalem: Magnes Press, 1982. [H]

Stav, Arieh (ed). *Israel and a Palestinian State: Zero Sum Game?* Tel-Aviv: Zmora-Bitan, 2001.

Susser, Asher. *The PLO After the War in Lebanon.* Tel Aviv: Kibutz Meukhad, 1985. [H]

Swirski, Shlomo & Ilan Pappe (eds.). *The Intifadah: An Inside View.* Tel-Aviv: Mifras, 1992. [H]

Touma, Emile. *The Palestinian National Movement and the Arab World.* Tel-Aviv: Mifras Books, 1990. [H]

Wallach, John & Janet Wallach. *Arafat: In the Eyes of the Beholder* (2nd. Ed.). New York, NY: Birch Lane Press, 1997.

Wallach, John & Janet Wallach. *The New Palestinians.* Rocklin, CA: Prima, 1992.

White, Patrick. *Let Us Be Free.* Clifton, NJ: Kingston Press, 1989.

Yodfat, Aryeh Y. & Yuval Arnon-Ohanna. *PLO: Strategy and Tactics.* New York, NY: St. Martin's Press, 1981.

Saudi Arabia and the Gulf States

Abir, Mordechai. *Saudi Arabia in the Oil Era: Regime and Elites; Conflict and Collaboration.* Boulder, CO: Westview Press, 1988.

Abir, Mordechai. *Saudi Arabia: Government, Society and the Gulf Crisis.* London: Routledge, 1993.

Aburish, Said K. *The Rise, Corruption and Coming Fall of the House of Saud.* New York, NY: St. Martin's Press, 1994.

Aleksandrov, Igor A. *The Monarchies of the Persian Gulf: The Modernization Stage.* Moscow: Delo I Servis, 2000. [R]

Brown, Anthony Cave. *Oil, God and Gold.* Boston, MA: Houghton Mifflin, 1999.

Ehsanullah, Ehsan. *Siyasa Shariyya: The Anthropology of Injustice, The Case of Saudi Kingdom.* Surrey: The Hajra Sanaullah Trust, 1994.

Fandy, Mamoun. *Saudi Arabia and the Politics of Dissent.* New York, NY: St. Martin's Press, 1999.

Foulquier, Jean-Michel. *Saudi Arabia: The Protege Dictatorship.* Paris: Albin Michel, 1995. [F]

Grraz, Liesl. *The Turbulent Gulf: People, Politics, and Power.* London: I.B.Tauris, 1992.

Herb, Michael. *All in the Family.* Albany, NY: State University of New York, 1999.

Kechichian, Joseph A. *Succession in Saudi Arabia.* New York, NY: Palgrave, 2001.

Kemp, Geoffrey and Janice Gross Stein (eds). *Powder Keg in the Middle East: The Struggle for Gulf Security.* Lanham, MD: Rowman & Littlefield, 1995.

Long, David E. *The Kingdom of Saudi Arabia.* Gainesville, FL: University of Florida Press, 1997.

Rashid, Nasser Ibrahim and Esber Ibrahim Shaheen. *King Fahd and Saudi Arabia's Great Evolution.* Joplin, MO: International Institute of Technology, 1987.

Vassilev, Alexei. *The History of Saudi Arabia.* London: Saqi Books, 1999.

Wilson, Peter W. and Douglas F. Graham. *Saudi Arabia: The Coming Storm.* Armonk, NY: M.E.Sharpe, 1994.

Syria

————. *Syria: Handbook.* Moscow: Nauka, 1992. [R]

Bacevich, Andrew, Michael Eisenstadt, and Carl Ford. *Supporting Peace: America's Role in an Israel-Syria Peace Agreement.* Washington, D.C.: The Washington Institute for Near East Policy, 1994.

Batatu, Hanna. *Syria's Peasantry, the Descendants of Its Lesser Rural Notables, and Their Politics.* Princeton, NJ: Princeton University Press, 1999.

Cobban, Helena. *The Israeli-Syrian Peace Talks: 1991–96 and Beyond.* Washington, D.C.: United States Institute of Peace Press, 1999.

Ehteshami, Anoushiravan and Raymond A. Hinnebusch. *Syria and Iran: Middle Powers in a Penetrated Regional System.* London: Routledge, 1997.

Ettinger, Yoram. *The Golan Heights and the Facts.* Shaarei Tikva: ACPR, 2000.

Hofman, Ronen and Boaz Ganor. *Syria and Terrorism: Terrorism as an Instrument for Realizing Syrian Interests.* Herzeliya: ICT, 1997. [H]

Lawson, Fred H. *Why Syria Goes to War: Thirty Years of Confrontation.* Ithaca, NY: Cornell University Press, 1996.

Levran, Aharon. *Israel-Syria: A Senseless Peace at an Unbearable Price.* Shaarei Tikva: ACPR, 2000.

Pine, Shawn. *Myopic Vision: Israel Withdrawal from the Golan Heights and the Prospects of War With Syria.* Shaarei Tikva: ACPR, 1998.

Quilliam, Neil. *Syria and the New World Order.* Reading: Ithaca Press, 1999.

Rabinovich, Itamar. *The Brink of Peace: The Israeli-Syrian Negotiations.* Princeton, NJ: Princeton University Press, 1998.

Seale, Patrick. *Asad: The Struggle for the Middle East.* Berkeley, CA: University of California Press, 1990 (1988).

Shalev, Aryeh. *Israel and Syria: Peace and Security on the Golan.* Tel-Aviv: Papirus, 1993. [H]

Shalev, Aryeh. *Israel and Syria: Peace and Security on the Golan.* Tel-Aviv: JCSS, 1994.

Talhami, Ghada Hashem. *Syria and the Palestinians: The Clash of Nationalisms*. Gainesville, FL: University Press of Florida, 2001.

Tsiddon-Chatto, Yoash et.al. *Peace With Syria: No Margin For Error*. Shaarei Tikva: ACPR, 2000.

Van Dam, Nikolaos. *The Struggle for Power in Syria*. London: I.B.Tauris, 1996.

Wedeen, Lisa. *Ambiguities of Domination: Politics, Rhetoric, and Symbols in Contemporary Syria*. Chicago: University of Chicago Press, 1999.

Zisser, Eyal. *Assad's Syria at a Crossroads*. Tel-Aviv: HaKibbutz haMeuchad, 1999. [H]

Zisser, Eyal. *Assad's Legacy: Syria in Transition*. Washington Square, NY: New York University Press, 2001.

U.S. Politics

Baker, James A. III with Thomas M. DeFrank. *The Politics of Diplomacy: Revolution, War and Peace, 1989–1992*. New York, NY: Putnam, 1995.

Bush, George and Brent Scowcroft. *A World Transformed*. New York, NY: Alfred A. Knopf, 1998.

Christopher, Warren. *Chances of a Lifetime*. New York, NY: 2001.

Kaplan, Robert D. *The Arabists: The Romance of an American Elite*. New York, NY: Free Press, 1993.

Kramer, Martin. *Ivory Towers on Sand: The Failure of Middle Eastern Studies in America*. Washington, D.C.: The Washington Institute for Near East Policy, 2001.

Lippman, Thomas W. *Madeleine Albright and the New American Diplomacy*. Boulder, CO: Westview Press, 2000.

NEWS AGENCIES AND PERIODICALS

These are the main news agencies and periodicals used for writing *The High Cost of Peace*:

News Agencies

AFP (France)
ANATOLIA (Turkey)
ANSA (Italy)
AP (U.S.)
EFE (Spain)
FNS (Russia)
HINA (Croatia)
INA (Iraq)
INTERFAX (Russia)

IPS (France-based Iranian Opposition)
IRNA (Iran)
ITAR-TASS (Russia)
KYODO (Japan)
Lebanon News Wire (Lebanon)
MENA (Egypt)
PANA (Pan-African)
Petra (Jordan)

REUTERS (U.S./U.K.)
RIA-Novosti (Russia)
SANA (Syria)
SDA (Switzerland)
SPA (Saudi Arabia)
SUNA (Sudan)

TANJUG (Yugoslavia)
TASS (U.S.S.R.)
UPI (U.S./U.K.)
WAFA (Palestinian Authority)
XINHUA (People's Republic of China)

Main Periodicals and Newspapers (Both Paper and Electronic Editions)

26 September (Yemen)
Abd-Rabouh (Jordan)
Addis Tribune (Ethiopia)
Akhbar (Pakistan)
Al-Ahd (Lebanon)
Al-Ahram (Egypt)
Al-Ahram al-Masai (Egypt)
Al-Akhbar (Egypt)
Al-Alam (U.K.-based Arab)
Al-Anwar (Lebanon)
Al-Ayam (Bahrain)
Al-Ayyam (Palestinian Authority)
Al-Ayyam (Yemen)
Al-Baath (Syria)
Al-Bayan (U.A.E.)
Al-Dustour (Jordan)
Al-Gumhuria (Egypt)
Al-Hadath (Jordan)
Al-Hayah (U.K.-based Arab)
Al-Hayah Al-Jadidah (P.A.)
Al-Islah (U.K.-based Arab)
Al-Istiqlal (P.A.)
Al-Itidal (Saudi Arabia)
Al-Ittihad (U.A.E.)
Al-Jazirah (Saudi Arabia)
Al-Khaleej (U.A.E.)
Al-Madinah (Saudi Arabia)
Al-Majalla (U.K.-based Arab)
Al-Massaiah (Saudi Arabia)
Al-Messa (Egypt)
Al-Mizan (U.K.-based Arab)
Al-Mussawar (Egypt)
Al-Nahar (Lebanon)

Al-Qabas (Kuwait)
Al-Quds (P.A.)
Al-Quds al-Arabi (U.K.-based Arab)
Al-Rai (Jordan)
Al-Raya (Qatar)
Al-Sabeel (Jordan)
Al-Safir (Lebanon)
Al-Shaab (Egypt)
Al-Sharq al-Awsat (U.K.-based Arab)
Al-Shira (Lebanon)
Al-Thawarah (Syria)
Al-Vefagh (Iran)
Al-Wafd (Egypt)
Al-Watan (Kuweit)
Al-Watan (Oman)
Al-Watan (Qatar)
Al-Watan al-Arabi (Europe-based Arab)
Al-Wasat (U.K.-based Arab)
Arab News (Saudi Arabia)
Asian Age (India\U.K.)
Ausaf (Pakistan)
Avazov Focus (Sarajevo)
Bahrain Tribune (Bahrain)
BiH Eksklusiv (Croatia, Bosnian Croats)
Bild (Germany)
Borba (Yugoslavia)
Bota Sot (Switzerland-based Kosovo Albanian nationalist opposition)

Bulvar (Turkey)
Corriere Della Sera (Italy)
The Crescent International
    (U.K./Canada)
Daily Excelsior (India)
Daily Hot News (Pakistan)
Daily Jang (Pakistan)
Daily Jasarat (Pakistan)
Daily News (Pakistan)
Daily News (Tanzania)
The Daily Star (Lebanon)
Daily Telegraph (U.K.)
Danas (Croatia)
Dawn (Pakistan)
Deccan Herald (India)
Defence Journal (Pakistan)
Defense & Foreign Affairs: Strategic
    Policy (U.K./U.S.)
Delo (Slovenia)
Der Spiegel (Germany)
Die Welt (Germany)
Dnevni Avaz (Sarajevo)
Dnevni Telegraf (Yugoslavia)
Dnevnik (Slovenia)
Duga (Yugoslavia)
The East-African (Kenya)
Economist (U.K.)
Egyptian Gazette (Egypt)
Ekonomska Politika (Yugoslavia)
Ettela'at (Iran)
European (U.K.)
Express (Tanzania)
Far Eastern Economic Review
    (Hong Kong)
Financial Times (U.K.)
Flaka e Vellazarimit (Macedonia)
Focus (Germany)
Focus (Sarajevo)
Foreign Affairs (U.S.)
Foreign Policy (U.S.)
Foreign Report (U.K.)

Frankfurter Allgemeine Zeitung
    (Germany)
Friday Times (Pakistan)
The Frontier Post (Pakistan)
Glas Slavonije (Croatia, Slavonia)
Glas Srpski (Republika Srpska)
Glasnik (Croatia)
Globe and Mail (Canada)
Globus (Croatia)
Guardian (U.K.)
Gulf Daily News (Bahrain)
Gulf News (U.A.E.)
Gulf Times (Qatar)
Ha'Aretz (Israel)
Ham-Shahri (Iran)
The Hindu (India)
Hindustan Times (India)
Home News (Sudan)
Hong Kong Standard (Hong Kong)
Hrvatska Rijec (Sarajevo)
Hrvatski Obzor (Croatia)
Hrvatski Vojnik (Croatia)
Hurmat (Pakistan)
Hurriyet (Turkey)
Independent (U.K.)
India Defence Review (India)
India Today (India)
The Indian Express (India)
Indus News (Pakistan)
Intelligence Newsletter (France)
Intervju (Yugoslavia)
Iran Daily (Iran)
Iran News (Iran)
Iran Shahr (Iran)
Israeli & Global News (U.S.)
Izvestiya (Russia)
JANE's Defence Weekly (U.K.)
JANE's Intelligence Review (for-
    merly JANE's Soviet Intelli-
    gence Review) (U.K.)
Jang (Pakistan)

Jasarat (Pakistan)
Javnost (Republic of Srpska)
Jerusalem Post (Israel)
Jerusalem Times (P.A.)
Jeune Afrique (France)
Jomhuri-ye Islami (Iran)
Jordan Times (Jordan)
The Kashmir Times (India)
The Kashmir Monitor (India)
Keyhan (U.K.-based Iranian
    opposition)
Keyhan (Iran)
Khabrain (Pakistan)
Khaleej Times (U.A.E.)
Kosova Daily Report (Pristina)
Krasnaya Zvezda (Russia)
Kuwait Times (Kuwait)
L'Evenement du Jeudi (France)
L'Express (France)
Le Figaro (France)
Le Monde (France)
Le Nouvel Observateur (France)
Le Point (France)
Ljiljan (Sarajevo)
Los Angeles Times (U.S.)
Ma'ariv (Israel)
Magyar Szo (Yugoslavia,
    Vojvodina)
Mashriq (Pakistan)
Middle East Times (Egypt)
Milliyet (Turkey)
Mirror (U.K.)
Mladina (Slovenia)
The Monitor (Uganda)
Monitor (Yugoslavia, Montenegro)
The Muslim (Pakistan)
Muslim News (U.K.)
Nasa Borba (Yugoslavia)
The Nation (Kenya)
The Nation (Pakistan)
Nawa-i-Waqt (Pakistan)

Nedeljni Telegraf (Yugoslavia)
Nedjeljna Dalmacija (Croatia,
    Dalmatia)
New Vision (Uganda)
New York Times (U.S.)
The News (Pakistan)
The News International (Pakistan)
News India-Times (India)
Newsweek (U.S.)
Nezavisimaya Gazeta (Russia)
Nida-e-Khilfat (Pakistan)
Nida-ul-Islam (Australia)
Nimrooz (U.K.-based Iranian
    opposition)
Nin (Yugoslavia)
Nova Bosna (Germany)
Nova Makedonija (Macedonia)
Novi List (Croatia)
Observer (U.K.)
October (Egypt)
Odbrana (Macedonia)
Oman Daily (Oman)
Oman Daily Observer (Oman)
L'Orient-Le Jour (Lebanon)
Oslobodjenje (Sarajevo and
    international edition in
    Slovenia)
Oslobodjenje (Republika Srpska)
Pakistan (Pakistan)
The Pakistan Observer (Pakistan)
The Pakistan Times (Pakistan)
Pobjeda (Yugoslavia, Montenegro)
Politika (Yugoslavia)
Politika Ekspress (Yugoslavia)
Puls (Macedonia)
La Revue du Liban (Lebanon)
Rose al-Youssuf (Egypt)
SAPRA Review (India)
Segodnya (Russia)
Shihan (Jordan)
Slobodna Bosna (Sarajevo)

Slobodna Dalmacija (Croatia, Dalmatia)
Slovenec (Slovenia)
South China Morning Post (Hong Kong)
Srpska Rec (Yugoslavia)
The Star (Jordan)
The Statesman (India)
The Straits Times (Singapore)
The Sunday Telegraph (U.K.)
The Sunday Times (U.K.)
Svijet (Yugoslavia)
Syria Daily (Syria)
Takbeer (Pakistan)
Tehran Times (Iran)
Telegraf (Yugoslavia)
The Telegraph (India)
The Telegraph (U.K.)
The Times (U.K.)
The Times (U.S. & European editions)
The Times of India (India)
Tishrin (Syria)
Turkish Daily News (Turkey)

Syria Times (Syria)
Ukaz (Saudi Arabia)
U.S. News & World Report (U.S.)
Vecer (Macedonia)
Vecernje Novine (Sarajevo)
Vecernje Novosti (Yugoslavia)
Vecernji List (Croatia)
Vesti (Germany)
Vjestnik (Croatia)
Vojska (Yugoslavia)
Voyenno Istoricheskiy Zhurnal (Russia)
Vreme (Yugoslavia)
WarReport (U.K.)
Washington Post (U.S.)
Washington Times (U.S.)
Weekly Review (Kenya)
Y-net (Israel)
Yediot Aharonot (Israel)
Yemen Times (Yemen)
Zarubezhnoye Voyennye Obozreniye (Russia)
Zindagi (Pakistan)

INDEX